1-20

BY ELIZABETH HARDWICK

The Ghostly Lover (1945)

The Simple Truth (1955)

The Selected Letters of William James (editor) (1961)

A View of My Own (1962)

Seduction and Betrayal (1974)

Sleepless Nights (1979)

Bartleby in Manhattan (1983)

Sight-Readings (1998)

The New York Stories of Elizabeth Hardwick (2010)

The Collected Essays of Elizabeth Hardwick (2017)

BY ROBERT LOWELL

Land of Unlikeness (1944)

Lord Weary's Castle (1946)

The Mills of the Kavanaughs (1951)

Life Studies (1959)

Phaedra (translation) (1961)

Imitations (1961)

For the Union Dead (1964)

The Old Glory (plays) (1965)

Near the Ocean (1967)

Prometheus Bound (translation) (1967)

The Voyage and Other Versions of Poems by Baudelaire (1968)

Notebook 1967–68 (1969; *Notebook*, revised and expanded edition, 1970)

History (1973)

For Lizzie and Harriet (1973)

The Dolphin (1973)

Selected Poems (1976; revised edition, 1977)

Day by Day (1977)

The Oresteia of Aeschylus (translation) (1978)

Collected Prose (1987)

Collected Poems (2003)

The Letters of Robert Lowell (2005)

Selected Poems: Expanded Edition (2007)

Words in Air: The Complete Correspondence Between Elizabeth Bishop and Robert Lowell (2008)

New Selected Poems (2017)

The Dolphin: Two Versions, 1972–1973 (2019)

The
Dolphin Letters,
1970–1979

The Dolphin Letters, 1970–1979

ELIZABETH HARDWICK,

ROBERT LOWELL,

and Their Circle

Edited by Saskia Hamilton

Farrar, Straus and Giroux

New York

Farrar, Straus and Giroux
120 Broadway, New York 10271

Grateful acknowledgment is made to the Harry Ransom Center at the University
of Texas at Austin for permission to reprint scans of the letters found throughout.

Library of Congress Cataloging-in-Publication Data
Names: Hamilton, Saskia, 1967– editor. | Hardwick, Elizabeth. Correspondence.
 Selections. | Lowell, Robert, 1917–1977. Correspondence. Selections.
Title: The dolphin letters, 1970–1979 : Elizabeth Hardwick, Robert Lowell and
 their circle / edited by Saskia Hamilton.
Description: First edition. | New York : Farrar, Straus and Giroux, 2019. | Includes
 bibliographical references and index.
Identifiers: LCCN 2019016287 | ISBN 9780374141264 (hardcover)
Subjects: LCSH: Hardwick, Elizabeth—Correspondence. | Lowell, Robert,
 1917–1977—Correspondence.
Classification: LCC PS3515.A5672 Z48 2019 | DDC 811/.52—dc23
LC record available at https://lccn.loc.gov/2019016287

Designed by Jonathan D. Lippincott

Our books may be purchased in bulk for promotional, educational, or business use. Please
contact your local bookseller or the Macmillan Corporate and Premium Sales Department at
1-800-221-7945, extension 5442, or by e-mail at MacmillanSpecialMarkets@macmillan.com.

www.fsgbooks.com
www.twitter.com/fsgbooks • www.facebook.com/fsgbooks

1 3 5 7 9 10 8 6 4 2

CONTENTS

INTRODUCTION

Should revelation be sealed like private letters,
till all the beneficiaries are dead,
and our proper names become improper Lives?
—Robert Lowell, "Draw" [Doubt 1], The Dolphin

Was that written for the archives? Who is speaking?
—Elizabeth Hardwick, Sleepless Nights

Until the end of her life, Elizabeth Hardwick wondered what had happened to the letters she wrote to Robert Lowell during the 1970s. They "are lost or gone," she said to Lowell's biographer and, referring to the use Lowell had made of her letters in his book *The Dolphin*, she added, "I suppose he was so busy *cutting them up!*" (*laughter*).[1]

The Dolphin Letters collects the correspondence between Hardwick and Lowell during the last seven years of Lowell's life—Hardwick's side of which surfaced only after her death more than thirty years later—and offers a portrait of two writers at a time of intense personal crisis and creative innovation. Both relied on intelligent and telegraphic communications with each other while going through their

---

1. Elizabeth Hardwick, interview with Ian Hamilton, October 26, 1979, Ian Hamilton Papers, British Library. Robert Lowell, *The Dolphin* (1973).

separation and divorce; and afterward, through the years during which Lowell published four books of poetry, including *The Dolphin*, Hardwick wrote *Seduction and Betrayal: Women and Literature* and *Sleepless Nights*, and their daughter, Harriet, grew from thirteen to twenty years old. A written record cannot but be incomplete— "your whole self and your writing self are different," as Hardwick once remarked[1]—and this portrait is necessarily partial, framed as it is by a period of distress that alters the proportions of the lives represented. Lowell's romance with and marriage to Caroline Blackwood happen offstage, as does the family life they made with their son, Sheridan, Blackwood's three daughters, and Harriet. Hardwick's romantic involvements during this period are not mentioned. Nevertheless, the correspondence gives us their written character and temperament both within and outside of the marriage during this period (included in the book are significant exchanges with friends in their circle), in their distinct qualities of mind and sentence.

The book opens with Hardwick's return to New York with Harriet after a family trip to Italy in the spring of 1970. Lowell and Hardwick were both fifty-three years old and had been married since 1949. Harriet was due back at school to finish the seventh grade, and Hardwick to finish the semester's teaching at Barnard College. Lowell, who was on his way to take up an eight-week fellowship at All Souls College, Oxford, extended his travels from Rome to Amsterdam to visit old friends, and then on to England. He was at the time considering a separate teaching offer from the University of Essex, which would have involved moving the family to England for two years, not least to seek respite from the stresses of his recent American life. These included his commitments to teaching (he commuted every week from New York to Harvard) and to activism—a "dedication," as Hardwick called it,[2] that both she and Lowell observed their entire adult lives. The claims of political engagement on both writers during the years of anti-war protests and the civil rights movement were serious, and yet the "scene" by 1970, during the first Nixon administration, struck Hardwick as "an utter, odd shambles, a nothing," she wrote to Mary McCarthy before

1. Elizabeth Hardwick, interview with David Farrell, October 9, 1977, Louie B. Nunn Center for Oral History, University of Kentucky Libraries.
2. Hardwick to Lowell, April 19, 1971.

the family trip. "The phone rings all day with meetings one could attend, plays one is urged to go to in the freezing night, an occasional unwanted invitation, malignant growths of mail, bills [. . .] And the depressing quiet in the midst of so much rush and anxiousness. You feel as if you'd been in a play running for years and then it closed and you went uptown and no one called."[1] "Almost everyone understands how one would want to leave America temporarily," Lowell wrote to Hardwick that April.[2]

Lowell arrived at All Souls on April 24. Six days later, he attended a party in his honor given by his British publisher, Faber & Faber. Caroline Blackwood, whom he had met some years previously, was there, and they were reintroduced.[3] Blackwood was thirty-eight years old. She later recalled that "after the Faber party, he moved into Redcliffe Square [Blackwood's London house]—I mean instantly, that night."[4] Traveling from All Souls to London and back over the next six weeks, Lowell returned often in his thoughts to Matthew Arnold's Scholar-Gipsy,[5] a man of "pregnant parts and quick inventive brain" who tires of modern life and seeks shelter in the pastoral of Oxford. Though Lowell was far from idle during this period—his work included preparing *Notebook* for publication, adding new poems, revising old ones, engaging Blackwood as critic and scribe[6]—he writes to Hardwick that "this is almost the first time since lithium"[7] that he had not been ceaselessly working. But a longing for rest had been a sign of impending turmoil in his past.[8] "Take leisure to be wise," he writes in the last of the letters to

---

1. Hardwick to Mary McCarthy, February 9, 1970.
2. Lowell to Hardwick, April 27, 1970.
3. Robert Silvers, whom Blackwood was dating, had written to Lowell in advance of his trip to put him in touch with her: "Would you like to see Caroline in London. I know she'd be very glad to see you" (Silvers to Lowell [March 1970?]).
4. Ian Hamilton, *Robert Lowell: A Biography* (1983), p. 398.
5. Of whom Lowell had written in an earlier poem "Soft Wood," set in Castine, Maine: "Sometimes I have supposed seals | must live as long as the Scholar Gypsy" (Lowell's spelling of Arnold's "Gipsy"; "Soft Wood" 1–2, *For the Union Dead*).
6. See corrections to *Notebook* proofs in Blackwood's hand; Farrar, Straus and Giroux, Inc., Manuscripts and Archives Division, New York Public Library.
7. Lowell to Hardwick, June 14, 1970. Lowell was prescribed lithium in 1967, relatively early in its introduction in the United States, and before its approval by the Food and Drug Administration.
8. See, for example, his manic letters in 1954 in *The Letters of Robert Lowell*, ed. Saskia Hamilton (2005), pp. 212, 214–16, 221, 229–30, and 234–37.

Hardwick that float on the fiction of all being well[1]—just six days before announcing by telegram that "PERSONAL DIFFICULTIES MAKE TRIP TO NEW YORK IMPOSSIBLE RIGHT AWAY."[2]

During Lowell and Hardwick's previous twenty-one years together, Lowell had suffered at least ten major manic episodes and at least fifteen hospitalizations, and was administered the therapies available at the time (seclusion and shock treatment in 1949; chlorpromazine, hydrotherapy, and psychoanalysis from the 1950s until the mid-1960s; lithium, newly available in the United States, in his fiftieth year). Manic-depressive illness is an episodic but also a progressive disease; and by 1961 Lowell's cycle of acute mania, hospitalization, and depression began to recur yearly.[3] Part of the tremendous activity and spectacle of the manic phases—"people loved to take part in them," Hardwick wrote; "they were very like *The Idiot*,[4] not at all like a mad killer"—involved falling in love, often implausibly. Hardwick said that during his breakdowns she was "deeply distressed, frantic, and all the rest" when "faced with these humiliating, recurring situations." They were humiliating for him, too, later, after he "'came to,'" when he was "sad, worried, always ashamed and fearful," she wrote. "And when he was well, it seemed so miraculous that the old gifts of person and art were still there, as if they had been stored in some serene, safe box somewhere." At home again after the hospital, "he returned to his days, which were regular," reading, writing, studying. "And yet there he was, this unique soul for whom one felt great pity. His fate was like a strange, almost mythical two-engined machine, one running to doom and the other to salvation."[5]

"Fortunately, Cal[6] was 'well' much more of his life than he was

---

1. Lowell to Hardwick, June 14, 1970. Arnold: "What leisure to grow wise" ("Stanzas in Memory of the Author of 'Obermann' " 69–76); see also footnote 1 on page 37 (Lowell to Hardwick, May 17, 1970).

2. Lowell to Hardwick, June 20, 1970.

3. Before 1961, Lowell's major manic episodes had occurred every two to three years—in 1949, 1952, 1954, 1957, and 1959.

4. By Dostoevsky (1869).

5. "Cal Working, etc.," excerpt of a letter from Elizabeth Hardwick to Ian Hamilton [1981 or 1982]; see pages 473–75. Cf. John Milton: "But that two-handed engine at the door | Stands ready to smite once, and smite no more" ("Lycidas" 130–31).

6. Lowell's nickname: "I'm called Cal, but I won't explain why. None of the prototypes are flattering: Calvin, Caligula, Caliban, Calvin Coolidge, Calligraphy—with merciless irony" (to Eliza

not," Hardwick added. "Otherwise his large and difficult, for him, production would not exist."[1] A. L. Rowse described him as "*most sympathetic.* [. . .] He was sane, sensitive, perceptive and responsive, full of original thoughts, rather a dear, and obviously a man of genius."[2] Derek Walcott wondered "what biographer could catch the heartbreaking smile, his wit, his solicitude, his shyness? [. . .] Clouds covered him, but when they went, he was extraordinarily gentle."[3]

When Lowell was first prescribed lithium, it granted him release from both the yearly attacks and his anxiety about when the next would strike. One should not "understate how powerful it might have been for him to be freed of such a severe and painful illness," Harriet Lowell writes. "If a salt could stop the attacks, that meant the illness was not caused by some terrible character flaw."[4] On lithium, Lowell wrote to Elizabeth Bishop, "even my well life is much changed, as tho I'd once been in danger of falling with every step I took."[5] He began to write a "notebook" of sonnet-like poems (fourteen lines, rhyming internally but to no set scheme), notations of "fleeting feelings, insights, perceptions, marginal half-thoughts and how these bear down on one's life," as Frank Bidart described them.[6]

But to some old friends there seemed another, subtle change, as if the difference in his character and temperament when well and when sick was a little less distinct, even if his gentleness and intelligence were undiminished. From 1967 to 1970 Lowell worked on the "unstopping composition" of the *Notebook* poems (numbering 377 by the publication of the third edition), which was connected, Lowell wrote to Hardwick in apology, to the "stirring and blurring" of drinking. "I've been hard going the last couple of years, though when haven't I been?"[7] Harriet Lowell remembers her mother saying that he was

beth Bishop [August 21, 1947], *Words in Air*, ed. Thomas Travisano with Saskia Hamilton [2008], p. 7).

1. Elizabeth Hardwick to Ian Hamilton [1981 or 1982].

2. *The Diaries of A. L. Rowse*, ed. Richard Ollard (2003), p. 336.

3. Walcott, "On Robert Lowell," *New York Review of Books*, March 1, 1984.

4. Harriet Lowell, email message to editor, January 28, 2017.

5. Lowell to Bishop, January 12, 1968, in *Words in Air*, p. 639; quoted also in Kay Redfield Jamison, *Robert Lowell: Setting the River on Fire; A Study of Genius, Mania, and Character* (2017), p. 179.

6. Quoted in Ian Hamilton, *Robert Lowell: A Biography*, p. 420.

7. Lowell to Hardwick, January 9, 1969, in *The Letters of Robert Lowell*, pp. 509–10. Harriet remembers that during those years there was a "subtle" change in him, something a little "blunt"

"simmering" during those years. As Kay Redfield Jamison writes, "Although Lowell fit the clinical profile of someone likely to respond to lithium [. . .] he was put on lithium late in his illness, and stability is harder to achieve after repeated episodes of mania. Lowell also drank heavily at times, most notably when he was manic, which almost certainly affected his response" to the drug. "It is possible that the lithium capped his mania well enough to allow him to write with some of the productive advantage of mild mania."[1] Esther Brooks recalled that during the years of lithium treatment, "the well person and the unwell person seemed to rub together in a strange kind of muted euphoria. One no longer feared that he would go mad but one kept waiting for the delicate and exquisite side of his mind to assert itself once again."[2]

In May 1970, Hardwick sensed very quickly from Lowell's silences and evasions that he was again in love, and that he was "not at all well." By mid-May, her letters appear to be keeping up a pretense of daily conversation—about Harriet and the household, plans for moving to England, the social scene, the extraordinary political events unfolding, the U.S. bombing of Cambodia, the New Haven Black Panther trials, the killings of students at Kent State and Jackson State—because she knew something was wrong but couldn't ask. "PERSONAL DIFFICUL-TIES": as she feared, his affair (with whom, she had yet to learn) and his weeks at All Souls were prelude to a severe manic episode—his first since his lithium treatment had begun three years earlier. During the summer of 1970, it was not clear to anyone, Lowell included, whether his feelings for Blackwood were symptomatic of his illness. After nearly two months, when Hardwick finally learned with whom

---

about his feelings sometimes, that "he smoked a little more, drank a little more—not alcoholic drinking, but—a little edgier, more irritable," "perhaps out of an occasional excess of energy" ("On Robert Lowell," Oral History Project, Harvard University [September 29, 2016]; interview with the editor, January 28, 2017). See also Elizabeth Bishop to Anny Baumann, November 14 and 15, 1967, in which Bishop shares a concern with Hardwick about the effect on Lowell of the "constant excitement, marches, demonstrations, drinking, and so on." One evening Lowell, having just returned from a "very strenuous" trip, was "off to 'Poets for Peace' or something about VIETNAM & stayed up till 5 a.m., etc.—confessed to a hangover, had lunch with me down here & caught the plane to Harvard for three days of hard work, more & more people, parties & so on." She adds that "he has so much better things to give the world (as his wife said) than hasty reactions to all the pressures here in N.Y." See *One Art: Letters*, ed. Robert Giroux (1994), pp. 480–81.

1. Jamison, *Robert Lowell: Setting the River on Fire*, pp. 180, 182.

2. Esther Brooks, "Remembering Cal," in *Robert Lowell: A Tribute*, ed. Rolando Anzilotti (1979), pp. 42–43; quoted in Jamison, *Robert Lowell: Setting the River on Fire*, p. 181.

Lowell had taken up, she was doubtful about Blackwood as a part-ner for him. Part of her distress was not knowing whether Blackwood could "cope with his mental illness if it returned full force," Harriet Lowell writes.[1]

Though none of Lowell's previous affairs had lasted, this alliance proved different. "I am not mad and hold to you with reason," he later wrote in a poem to Blackwood.[2] Thanks to the efficacy of the lithium treatment, from his recovery in the fall of 1970 until 1975,[3] the passionate and productive years he spent with Blackwood and their family marked the longest period his mania was stabilized since the first serious occur-rence of the disease.[4] And once Hardwick was relieved of her fears for his safety and sanity, and for Harriet's well-being, the "certain euphoria (60%)"[5] she felt at being on her own led to a richly generative time spent on her own writing. In some ways, "my mother was never freer or more lively" than during the period that followed, Harriet recalls.[6]

Lowell and Hardwick's separation was conducted mostly through let-ters in the summer and fall of 1970. A practical reason for writing in-stead of telephoning was the expense of transatlantic calls and the uneven quality of reception (crossed lines, echoes) impeding the flow of conversation. "I am sorry I was so mute on the phone. At the start two others seemed competing with you," Lowell writes after one such call.[7] But they were also lifelong writers of letters, and were critically and artistically interested in the form.[8] Contrary to a reader's expec-tations that we might find in letters the writer "at his nap, slumped,

---

1. Email message to editor, January 28, 2017.

2. "Knowing" [*Marriage* 5] 11, *The Dolphin*.

3. In 1975, his lithium levels became unstable, and he once again began to experience manic episodes.

4. Ivana Lowell writes of her memories of Lowell when he was well that he "was the gentlest, coziest man possible. A tall teddy-bearish presence, he instantly nicknamed me Mischief because I teased him so much" (*Why Not Say What Happened?* [2010], p. 27).

5. According to Mary McCarthy (Blair Clark notes from a conversation with McCarthy, July 23, 1970, Blair Clark Papers, HRC).

6. Email message to editor, April 4, 2019.

7. Lowell to Hardwick [postmarked 30 April 1970 but written on April 29], 1970.

8. See, for example, *The Selected Letters of William James*, edited and with an introduction by Elizabeth Hardwick (1961).

open-mouthed, profoundly himself without thought for appearances,"
Hardwick wrote about literary correspondence in 1953, "letters are
above all useful as a means of expressing the ideal self; and no other
method of communication is quite so good for this purpose. In con-
versation, those uneasy eyes upon you, those lips ready with an emen-
dation before you have begun to speak, are a powerful deterrent to
unreality, even to hope."[1] She would later write, in an essay about fic-
tional correspondence in Richardson's *Clarissa*, that a letter is partly
"one's own evidence, [. . .] the writer holds all the cards, controls every-
thing about himself and about those assertions he wishes to make con-
cerning events or the worth of others."[2] A letter is also of the moment,
and quickly posted. Harder to control in a genuine correspondence
(not one written for the art of fiction) is the vacillation of feeling from
one letter to the next.

Letters both real and fictional are a formal device in Lowell's po-
etry of the late 1960s and early 1970s, and in Hardwick's prose. Exper-
imenting with autobiography and immediacy in the *Notebook* poems,
Lowell had versed a letter from Allen Tate into a poem for the 1969 first
edition. In the spring of 1970, he did the same with a letter from Eliza-
beth Bishop for the third edition. That autumn, as he began to write in
his adapted sonnet form about a "suffering hero?"[3] being drawn into
what precipitates the end of a long marriage, he turned to Hardwick's
letters to help tell the tale of "one man, two women, the common novel
plot."[4] In *The Dolphin*, the wife and daughter left behind are given
voice in Lowell's "cut" and "doctored" versions of Hardwick's letters.
From Lowell's point of view, they are thereby made real "beyond my
invention."[5]

1. Hardwick, *A View of My Own* (1962), p. 3.

2. Hardwick, "Seduction and Betrayal" II, *New York Review of Books* (June 14, 1970); written
and published before Hardwick had read *The Dolphin*. Reprinted in *Seduction and Betrayal* (1974),
p. 195.

3. As Lowell described his speaker in "The Poet Robert Lowell—Seen by Christopher Ricks,"
Listener (June 21, 1973), p. 831.

4. Lowell, *Exorcism* [2] 10–11, *The Dolphin*. Compare lines from George Meredith's 1862 sonnet
sequence, *Modern Love*: "Let us see. | The actors are, it seems, the usual three: | Husband, and
wife, and lover." Lowell thought of *Modern Love*, a collection of adapted sonnets (sixteen lines
long) about marital unhappiness, as a model for *The Dolphin*. See "The Poet Robert Lowell—
Seen by Christopher Ricks," p. 832.

5. Lowell to Elizabeth Bishop, March 28, 1972.

During those years, Hardwick was immersed in letters from their past as she ordered Lowell's papers for their eventual sale to archives. ("About the 'papers,'—'Aspern'—which I have not looked at since I first and last went through them. Have I the strength?" Hardwick wrote to Lowell after their separation. "I hate them and hate to let them go; the damned things are my life also."[1]) *Sleepless Nights*, which took shape following the publication of *The Dolphin*, is not a "short-wave autobiography," as her narrator first had in mind to write, but a novel that "fades in and out, local voices mixing with the mysterious static of the cadences of strangers" thousands of miles apart.[2] Although Hardwick's sources were many, what she had learned in her years of absorption in literary correspondence, in poems, and in the prose of poets ("one of my passions"[3]), shows in the novel's lyric brevity and pacing. Its narrator, whose name is Elizabeth, writes to a "Dearest M.," and is "always waking up to address myself to B. and D. and C.—those whom I dare not ring up until morning and yet must talk to throughout the night."[4] These interlocutors may share initials with Mary (McCarthy), Barbara (Epstein), Devie (Meade), and Cal (Lowell), though they are not they exactly, either.

Central to Lowell and Hardwick's exchange of letters in the 1970s, and to the work they made during this period, is a debate about the limits of art—what occasions a work of art; what moral and artistic license artists have to make use of their lives as material; what formal innovations such debates give rise to. "The whole question of the rights and duties, the decencies and discretions of the insurmountable desire to *know*," as Henry James calls it,[5] is given form in the decisions Lowell and Hardwick made in *The Dolphin* and *Sleepless Nights*. The illustrations and annotations in the present edition point especially to

---

1. Hardwick to Lowell, June 28, 1971; Hardwick refers to Henry James's tale *The Aspern Papers* (1888, revised 1908).
2. Hardwick, "Writing a Novel," *New York Review of Books*, October 18, 1973. Cf. Boris Pasternak: "I am not writing my autobiography. [. . .] Together with its principal character I think that only heroes deserve a real biography, but that the history of a poet is not to be presented in such a form. One would have to collect such a biography from unessentials, which would bear witness to concessions for compassion and constraint" (*Safe Conduct*, trans. Babette Deutsch [1958], p. 26).
3. Elizabeth Hardwick, "The Art of Fiction No. 87," interview by Darryl Pinckney, *Paris Review*, no. 96 (Summer 1985).
4. Hardwick, *Sleepless Nights* (1979), p. 151.
5. In an 1893 review of Gustave Flaubert's letters in *Literary Criticism*, vol. 2 (1984), p. 297.

those works, and to significant earlier drafts, since both were much revised before final publication. Included herein are illustrations of individual poems from "The Dolphin" manuscript that draw from letters Lowell received and wrote. (The complete draft of Lowell's manuscript that was circulated to friends in 1972 is now published in *The Dolphin: Two Versions, 1972–1973*.) Also included is "Writing a Novel," Hardwick's story as published in *The New York Review of Books*, which she transformed into *Sleepless Nights*.

Hardwick carefully saved Lowell's letters, many of which were subsequently published in *The Letters of Robert Lowell*. But as for Hardwick's side of the correspondence, "they're all gone," as she repeated to Ian Hamilton. Lowell had written to Hardwick in 1976, "I regret the Letters in Dolphin."[1] Still, he was unwilling to return them to her. "This is real *Aspern Papers*," she told Hamilton:

> At one time I said to him, "Well *I* would like, for history, to *see* those letters you say are mine. And that you put in my voice. Because I can't remember and just want to see how they went." I said "you've got to bring those to me." Well, very sheepishly [. . .] he gave me, well, it was three worthless little letters,[2] and I said [*reproachful*] "Oh, Cal." He said "I can't find them," and without making a big issue out of it I said, "I really want to see them." It was of interest to me.[3]

Lowell died without resolving this with Hardwick, and for the subsequent thirty years she was given no opportunity to reread the letters she had written to him—never able (to borrow from T. S. Eliot) to "unravel the web of memory and invention and discover how far and in what ways" her letters had been transformed.[4] Lowell feared that Hardwick might destroy them (though "zeroxes"[5] could have been

---

1. Lowell to Hardwick, July 2, 1976.

2. Hardwick told Ian Hamilton that she put the three returned letters in an envelope and subsequently lost it.

3. Elizabeth Hardwick, interview with Ian Hamilton, October 26, 1979, Ian Hamilton Papers, British Library.

4. As T. S. Eliot writes about James Joyce in the preface to Stanislaus Joyce's *My Brother's Keeper* (1958); quoted in Philip Horne, "Revealers and Concealers," *Essays in Criticism* 43, no. 4 (October 1993): p. 278.

5. As Lowell spelled "xeroxes."

made).[1] It is more likely that Hardwick would have preserved them, however regretfully,[2] if they had been returned to her. "I know that she believed in archives," Harriet Lowell recalls, "and had great qualms about any meddling with them. I don't know of her ever wavering on this point."[3]

Caroline Blackwood did not return the letters to Hardwick after Lowell's death in 1977. Nor were they included in the estate's 1982 sale of his papers. Hardwick reported that Frank Bidart had "found only a few perfunctory letters"[4] from her to Lowell when Bidart organized the papers for the estate, and had told her "there is nothing there for you." Hardwick thought that Blackwood "tore them up, there's no other explanation."[5]

What actually happened was that in April 1978, seven months after Lowell's death, Blackwood had put 102 letters and postcards written by Hardwick in a large envelope and mailed them to Bidart for safekeeping. "There was nothing passive about Caroline," her daughter Evgenia Citkowitz remembers. "The fact that she did send them to Frank, [Lowell's] editor and friend, is noteworthy, otherwise they would have surely disappeared or have been left to be uncovered some other way. [. . .] In the end, despite the bitterness, Caroline understood how important these letters were; how they documented the period for them all."[6] By agreeing to receive the envelope, Bidart believed himself to be acting not only as Blackwood wished but as Lowell did, too. He put the envelope under his bed, and later transferred it to the Houghton Library at Harvard University, with a cover note stating

---

1. Lowell prevaricated with Hardwick, but Frank Bidart says Lowell told him he did not want to return the letters to Hardwick because he believed she might destroy them. Bidart says that Lowell cared about the survival of Hardwick's letters. He wanted the evidence of what he had done to them, his "aesthetic act of transformation," to be preserved (interview with editor, January 29, 2017).

2. Hardwick, referring to the time she found out about Lowell's affair with Caroline Blackwood: "I wrote some terrible letters about Caroline, ten pages long, horrible worthless schizophrenia" (Elizabeth Hardwick, interview with Ian Hamilton, October 26, 1979, Ian Hamilton Papers, British Library).

3. Email message to editor, April 4, 2019.

4. The twelve letters that were included by the Lowell Estate in the sale of his papers to the HRC in 1982.

5. Elizabeth Hardwick, interview with Ian Hamilton, October 26, 1979, Ian Hamilton Papers, British Library.

6. Email message to editor, December 31, 2016.

that "This packet of letters belongs to the Estate of Robert Lowell, *not to me*," and that "they are to be kept here at the Houghton Library until the death of Elizabeth Hardwick."[1]

Elizabeth Hardwick died on December 2, 2007. Bidart informed Evgenia Citkowitz about the envelope in May 2010, and she suggested that he and I catalogue its contents for the Lowell estate. When we did, it appeared to be an incomplete but substantial gathering, covering the time between April 1970, when Lowell and Hardwick parted in Europe, to Lowell's final year. There is a significant gap in the fall of 1970, a period that Lowell dramatizes in *The Dolphin*. In *The Dolphin*, fifteen poems contain lines spoken or written by the "Lizzie" and "Harriet" characters. At least six of these invite us to think that Lowell drew on letters, but there is no source for them in the envelope.[2] If letters are missing, it is unknown whether Lowell misplaced them during the composing of the poems or if they were later set aside, lost, or destroyed.

Of the letters that did survive, what to do with them—whether to publish and what to publish—raises "the quarrel beside which all others are mild and arrangeable, the eternal dispute between the public and the private, between curiosity and delicacy."[3] The decision was left to Harriet Lowell as legatee of her mother's estate, and to Harriet and Sheridan Lowell as heirs of their father. Harriet regrets not being given a chance to ask Hardwick about her wishes for these letters. But despite Harriet's personal misgivings,[4] she recognized

---

1. Frank Bidart, July 1, 1988, cover letter to MS Storage 244, Houghton Library.

2. Including, from *The Dolphin*, "Voices" and "Letter" [*Hospital* 1 and 2]; "Records"; "Communication"; "Foxfur"; and, from "The Dolphin" manuscript, "*The Messiah*" [*Flight to New York* 2] (which was removed from the published book, but three lines of which were incorporated into "In the Mail").

3. Henry James, "She and He: Recent Documents" (1897), reprinted as "George Sand," in *Literary Criticism*, vol. 2 (1984), p. 740.

4. Harriet has expressed regret that her mother's "remarkable recovery is not more visible in these letters," to give a truer and more balanced picture of her parents' lives, of their civility and lack of bitterness toward one another. "Most of these letters were written at the height of my mother's distress and it seems unfair that the record is so distorting—this is not my mother." Once it was clear the marriage was over, Hardwick "got back to the business of writing and rebuilding her life in New York" (email message to editor, April 4, 2019). Evgenia Citkowitz, who was the first person in the family to learn of the survival of Hardwick's letters, also supported their publication, despite her own apprehensions about characterizations of Caroline Blackwood to be found in them.

that her mother's letters "were preserved to be placed in an archive." However, leaving the letters open to quotation, paraphrase, or sensation without context concerned her. As the literary executor to both estates, she judged it best to publish the correspondence, despite the exposure of their parents' lives and their own childhoods that publication represents. The estates were reluctant to ask the same of some others, still living, whose family and private lives are taken up intimately in the correspondence. Hence the omission in this edition of some brief passages.[1]

∼

The Dolphin, Hardwick wrote, "hurt me as much as anything in my life." She objected to what she saw as the distortions in Lowell's portrait of her, the distortions of chronology ("I have found in the book letters from the very early period of my distress, attached to a sestet written long after"[2]), and especially the attribution to her of words that were not hers ("of course I *mind* the lines *seeming* to have issued from me"[3]). "In general, she did not object to him writing about his life (which meant her)," Harriet Lowell recalls. "This was different. [. . .] She felt he misrepresented her. [. . .] It wasn't so much that it was revealing and embarrassing, but it was ungenerous."[4] "I have since the publication been analyzed under my own name in print, given some good marks as a wife and person by some readings, general disparagement and rebuke by other readings," Hardwick wrote to Lowell's publishers. "The facts are not in the nature of facts because of the disguise as poetry and so cannot be answered."[5]

Nor did Hardwick think the poems themselves were very good, as she told Elizabeth Bishop: "It seemed so sad that the work was, certainly in that part that relies upon me and Harriet, so inane, empty, unnecessary. I cannot understand how three years of work could have left so many fatuities, indiscretions, bad lines still there on the page."[6] She never changed her opinion of the poems, and their publication affected

---

1. Detailed on page xxxvii.
2. Hardwick to Robert Giroux, July 5, 1973.
3. Hardwick to Lowell, June 20, 1976.
4. Quoted in Jamison, *Robert Lowell: Setting the River on Fire*, p. 348.
5. Hardwick to Robert Giroux, July 5, 1973.
6. Hardwick to Elizabeth Bishop, July 27, 1973.

the candor with which she wrote subsequent letters. After *The Dolphin* was published, one has the sense that Hardwick is looking right back at one while writing to her correspondent; knowing whatever she writes may be overheard, become part of someone's record; knowing how inexorably she would be drawn into the surf of literary history. "It is one of the most peculiar and terrifying sensations to have yourself or someone you have really loved and deeply known suddenly lighted up in a way that seems so far from the real, the true," Hardwick wrote to Bishop.[1]

Elizabeth Bishop's objections to Lowell's use of Hardwick's letters in "The Dolphin" manuscript—*"art just isn't worth that much"*[2]—are often cited, the terms of her objection less so. Clive James wrote in *The Times Literary Supplement* in May 2014, for instance: "Lowell wanted [Bishop's] endorsement for his bizarre temerity in stealing his wife Elizabeth Hardwick's letters to use unchanged in his poetry."[3] Rather than "use unchanged," it was the "mixture of fact & fiction" to which Bishop particularly objected. She quoted Thomas Hardy, that "if any statements in the dress of fiction are covertly hinted to be fact, all must be fact, and nothing else but fact" because "the power of getting lies believed about people [. . .] by stirring in a few truths, is a horror to contemplate."[4] Bishop wrote, "you have *changed* her letters":

> One can use one's life as material—one does, anyway—but these letters—aren't you violating a trust? IF you were given permission—IF you hadn't changed them . . . etc. But *art just isn't worth that much* [. . .] The letters, as you have used them, present fearful problems: what's true, what isn't; how one can bear to witness such suffering and yet not know how much of it one *needn't* suffer with, how much has been "made up," and so on.[5]

---

1. Hardwick to Elizabeth Bishop, October 18, 1973.
2. Elizabeth Bishop to Lowell, March 21, 1972.
3. Clive James, "Love in a Life: Lessons in the 'Shutting up' of Poetry," *Times Literary Supplement*, May 16, 2014, p. 14.
4. Thomas Hardy to James Douglas, November 10, 1912; quoted in Florence Emily Hardy, *The Life of Thomas Hardy, 1840–1928* (1962), pp. 358–59.
5. Elizabeth Bishop to Lowell, March 21, 1972.

In defense of his practice, Lowell saw the changes he made to the letters and conversations he used as mild, even protective, in "the dress of fiction":

> Let me \re/phrase for myself your moral objections. It's the revelation (with documents?) of a wife wanting her husband not to leave her, and who \does/ leave her. That's the trouble, not the mixture of truth and fiction. Fiction—no one would object if \I/ said Lizzie was wearing a purple and red dress, when it was yellow. Actually my versions of her letters are true enough, only softer and drastically cut. The original is heartbreaking, but interminable.[1]

He adds that the poems in "Lizzie's" voice "are made up of a mixture of quotes, improvisation, paraphrase."[2]

Readers can now compare lines in "The Dolphin" manuscript and *The Dolphin* with some of the original letters to see the kinds of artistic choice, formal and semantic, that Lowell made. The springtime poem "Green Sore" awakens to an ache of new life, new beginnings; the Caroline character is pregnant, "the new spring fields extend like a green sore." He quotes from a letter in "the morning mail" that "brings the familiar voice to Kent"[3]: "not that I wish you entirely well, far from it." The words Hardwick actually wrote were, "I don't entirely wish you well, far from it, of course."[4] Lowell plucks from Hardwick's letter not what she writes of her own conflicting and simultaneous feelings and wishes ("*I* don't *entirely* wish you well"), but what her words mean to him internally ("not that I wish you *entirely well*"). Musically, Lowell undoes Hardwick's cadence for a rearrangement more fitting to the sense of jarred, anxious waking he wants for his poem. The rearrangement forecloses on her meanings, and makes possible a picture of a Lizzie character who, it is implied, does not wish him "entirely

---

1. Lowell to Elizabeth Bishop, Easter Tuesday, [April 4], 1972.
2. Hardwick's (and Blackwood's) were not the only letters that Lowell drew upon for *The Dolphin* in this way. Letters to and from friends that are included in the present edition also inspired lines—letters from William Alfred, Frank Bidart, Blair Clark, and Adrienne Rich in particular (though these sources and figures are not named in the poems as Hardwick and Blackwood are).
3. "Green Sore" [*Burden* 5] 4–6, with line 6 cancelled, the "Dolphin" manuscript.
4. Hardwick to Lowell, March 21, 1971.

well," or entirely healed. They become "words of a moment's menace" that "stay for life," he writes in the published version.[1] Lowell's rewriting of Hardwick's words does not affect the "common novel plot" but captures a variation in his own feeling that he judged to be true to his experience, or true to the characters he was writing for his "half fiction."[2] And so his words are "true enough" for his poem, his source transformed in accordance with an artistic practice Lowell observed (with his own words and the words of others) throughout his life.[3]

But Bishop wasn't convinced by Lowell's rephrasing of her objections in terms of the disclosures of his plot. Changing Hardwick's written words and changing the color of her dress are not quite apposite. Bishop wrote again to say: "I quoted Hardy exactly, & the point was that one *can't* mix fact & fiction."[4] The documentary or collage element in American modernist writing had long been a point of interest and disagreement between Bishop and Lowell. William Carlos Williams's use of Marcia Nardi's letters for the "Cress" character in *Paterson* came up early in their friendship, in terms very similar to their discussion twenty-four years later. Lowell's artistic interest in the practice and Bishop's unease with its encroachments on trust had shadowed their exchange in the early 1960s about Lowell's poem "The Scream," based on Bishop's short story "In the Village,"[5] and Bishop's silence upon Lowell's apology for "versing one of your letters into my poems" in 1970.[6]

---

1. "Green Sore" [*Marriage* 7] 3, *The Dolphin*.

2. Lowell: "to ask compassion . . . this book, half fiction" ("Dolphin" 13, *The Dolphin*).

3. Lowell: "'You didn't write, you *rewrote*. . . .'" (*Randall Jarrell* [3]13, *History* [1973]).

4. Elizabeth Bishop to Lowell, April 10 (Monday?) [1972].

5. Elizabeth Bishop to Lowell: "I still felt he shouldn't have used the letters from that woman—to me it seems mean, & they're much too overpowering emotionally for the rest of it so that the whole poem suffers [. . .] I think Williams has always had a streak of insensitivity" (June 30 [1948]). Lowell to Elizabeth Bishop, on the Nardi letters: "1) so terrifyingly and typically real, and yet I don't think I'd want to read many of them straight—too monotonous, pathological. Yet in the poem they are placed and not pathological, the agony is absorbed. 2) Aren't they really hardest on Williams himself (Paterson), a damning of his insensitivity. She's mad, but he, like Aeneas[,] can't handle her and shows up badly. I think that's their purpose in the poem" (July 2 [1948]). See *Words in Air*, pp. 38–40. See also Lowell's poem "Publication Day" [*May* 18], *Notebook70*, and "Publication Day," *History*, based on a letter from Marcia Nardi; and David Kalstone's analysis of Bishop and Lowell's exchanges through the years about collage in *Becoming a Poet: Elizabeth Bishop with Marianne Moore and Robert Lowell* (1989), pp. 137–38, 199–202, and 234–43.

6. "Letter with Poems for a Letter with Poems" [*For Elizabeth Bishop* 3], *Notebook70*, which he wrote after receiving Bishop's letter of February 27, 1970. See *Words in Air*, pp. 663–67.

Hardwick's own reflections on these issues, formal and moral, can be found in *Sleepless Nights*. Darryl Pinckney suggests that when Hardwick returned after many years to first-person fiction, her "lack of interest in herself" was a "formal problem and her determination not to write about Robert Lowell a principle. She wrote instead about what a life with him had allowed her to think about: beautiful writing and great literature and human weirdness."[1] Hardwick's misgivings and demurrals about personal exposure, her tonal brilliance, her feeling for interiority and the interplay between what's recalled and what's archived, came together in a novel that behaves like a work of memory and a work of invention at once, driven not by narrative but by what Henry James first called "the life of the mind." Her glance turns to Lowell at several moments in *Sleepless Nights*, such as when the speaker considers changing the hair color of "the Mister":

> How is the Mister this morning? Josette would say. The Mister? Shall I turn his devastated brown hair to red, which few have? Appalling disarray of trouser and jacket and feet stuffed into stretched socks. Kindly smile, showing short teeth like his mother's.[2]

But "shall I?" marks a distance, perhaps measured of "compassion and constraint,"[3] between her fiction and Lowell's. ("Why not say what happened?"—the interrogative permission given to Lowell by Hardwick herself when he was writing the *Life Studies* poems[4]—is a line from his late poem "Epilogue."[5]) However much *Sleepless Nights*

---

1. Darryl Pinckney, "The Ethics of Admiration: Arendt, McCarthy, Hardwick, Sontag," *Three-penny Review* 135 (Fall 2013). Hardwick: "My interest falls upon the routinely outcast, the safely unwanted, the self-destructive, the self-deluding and, especially, the irregular" ("Scene from an Autobiography," *Prose* 4 [Spring 1972], p. 51).

2. Hardwick, *Sleepless Nights*, p. 121. For "the Mister?" compare "the Master" (Henry James).

3. Boris Pasternak, *Safe Conduct*, p. 26.

4. About the writing of *Life Studies* (1959), Lowell said in an interview, "I started one of these poems in Marvell's four-foot couplet and showed it to my wife. And she said, 'Why not say what really happened?' (It wasn't the one about her.) The metre just seemed to prevent any honesty on the subject" (A. Alvarez, "Robert Lowell in Conversation," *Observer*, July 21, 1963, p. 19; reprinted in Jeffrey Meyers, ed., *Robert Lowell: Interviews and Memoirs* (1988), p. 75; quoted in *Collected Poems* [2003], p. 1149).

5. Robert Lowell, "Epilogue" 15, *Day by Day* (1977).

employs real addresses (239 Marlborough Street, 67th Street) and apparently real addressees (M., B., D., and C.), it is not documentary art but invention.[1] Mary McCarthy returns to the question in her 1979 letter to Hardwick about *Sleepless Nights*:

> I wonder what Cal would think. He'd be put out somewhat in his vanity to find himself figuring mainly as an absence and absence that the reader doesn't miss. Even during the years when he was evidently on the scene, e.g. in Amsterdam. I like your idea of wondering whether you might not change his hair color to red—very funny, and it demonstrates how little his thisness (*haecceitas*), rather than \mere/ thatness, matters.[2]

⁓

What do a writer's letters tell us that is different from biography or the plot of a life? It is a search for something elusive, the genesis of a work of art, "that internal history," T. S. Eliot writes, "which may have much or may have little relation to the external facts, that internal crisis over which our imagination is tempted to brood too long."[3] Working with the same raw materials as poetry and fiction—noticings, moments of attention and inattention, formal concerns—letters process their material differently, and may store it in anticipation of poems or fictions for years. The habits of mind, association, and phrasemaking are as much prospective as retrospective. Conversely, the poem-as-letter trades on the intimacy and immediacy of a letter but is not looking forward (to a conversation or a meeting). It is looking back, as literature does. And it assumes a different formal and essential nature when it takes its

---

1. Hazel Rowley observes that the letters in *Sleepless Nights* "are *from* the author, not *to* the author; there is no breach of copyright involved, no breach of ethics; they are fictional and do not need to be in quotation marks" ("Poetic Justice: Elizabeth Hardwick's *Sleepless Nights*," *Texas Studies in Literature and Language* 39, no. 4 [Winter 1997], p. 412).

2. Mary McCarthy to Hardwick, June 4, 1979. Cf. Hannah Arendt, writing of Duns Scotus: "Contemplation of the *summum bonum*, of the 'highest thing,' ergo, God, would be the ideal of the intellect, which is always grounded in intuition, the grasping of a thing in its 'thisness,' *haecceitas*, which in this life is imperfect not only because here the highest remains unknown but also because intuition of thisness is imperfect" (*The Life of the Mind*, ed. Mary McCarthy [1978], p. 144).

3. "Shakespeare and Montaigne," *Times Literary Supplement*, December 24, 1925, p. 895; unsigned, following the practice of the *TLS* at the time.

place not in an envelope, nor in a volume issued for private circulation among friends, but in that public thing offered for sale, a book.

In July 1970, Lowell was hospitalized for mania at London's Greenways Nursing Home, where he was alone and stranded, Blackwood having departed. Hardwick flew to London in early August for a brief visit[1]—she found him "in awful shape physically," only able to "go about for an hour at the most & then just collapses"—and then returned to their summer house in Castine, Maine. Although he was still in the hospital, Lowell had recovered enough by August 11th to write his thanks. He had not yet decided what to do, whether to return to his family in America or make a new life with Blackwood.

> Dearest Lizzie:
> There's cold in the the air, enough to make me rub my feet for warmth. And th\en/ a colder, perhaps truer air in Maine. Illusions, surely! The true Maine is always at [a] distance. You are there. And this morning I can reach to you. O I hope I have reached Harriet Lowell, To whom I have sent many postcards, terrible things like the horseguards which you were so gracious as to buy, stamp and leave me.
> Goodbye, My Love,
> Cal[2]

Lowell rewrote his letter as a poem for *The Farther Shore* sequence in "The Dolphin" manuscript, entitled "Notes for an unwritten Letter":

> Ice ~~of first autumn~~ \in the air/, enough to make me hold
> my ~~feet~~ \socks/ for warmth. A purer cold in Maine—
> all things are truer there, truth~~'s~~ \is a/ foreign language.
> The terrible postcards you bought and stamped for me
> ~~are mailed~~ \have gone/ to Harriet: the horseguards, the life-
>   guards,
> the golden Lord Mayor's Chariot, Queen Bess—

---

1. See Table of Dates, 1970–1977, on pages xxxix–xlix for details. There was great concern in Lowell's circle that the system of support he had relied on during past manic episodes was unavailable to him in England.
2. Lowell to Hardwick, August 11, 1970.

true as anything else to fling a child . . .
In Maine, my country ~~as I loved to boast,~~ \where I ~~hoped~~
    wished to die,/
each empty sweater and ~~vacant~~ \idle/ bookshelf hurts,
~~the~~ \all the/ pretexes for their service gone.
I shout into the air, my voice comes back,
it doesn't carry to the farther shore,
rashly removed, still ringing in my ears.
Is a sound sleeper one ~~you~~ \who/ will not wake?[1]

In the letter there is hope that communion is still possible. The poem is far lonelier, with a sense of loss too big for the letter's containment and decorum. He repeats and varies the words he had addressed to her, as if his emotion could not be discharged in a single saying. In the sequence of poems, the speaker's pursuit of the dolphin will lead him to abandon his family, his country, his former life. Is it a pursuit of the beloved, of his sanity, of his own art (the dolphin a figure for one of its gods[2]), doubting yet hoping for its powers of divination? "I have learned what I wanted from the mermaid," Lowell writes in another poem, "and her singeing conjunction of tail and grace."[3] But in "Notes for an unwritten Letter" he has not yet crossed over, and feels unhoused and restless. The "farther shore" and the cancelled word "autumn" allude to the vast crowd of unburied souls in *The Aeneid* stretching their hands in longing for Hades, where they might finally rest, but which they cannot reach.[4] The poem resembles a familiar letter

1. "Notes for an unwritten Letter" [*The Farther Shore* 3], "The Dolphin" manuscript.

2. Apollo, god of poetry, healing, and divination. For more about the symbol of the dolphin in the history of poetry, see Peter M. Sacks, *"You Only Guide Me by Surprise": Poetry and the Dolphin's Turn* (2010).

3. *Mermaid* 1:1-2, *The Dolphin*. Cf. Milton: "Th' old Dragon under ground, [. . .] Swindges the scaly Horrour of his foulded tail" ("On the Morning of Christ's Nativity" 168, 172; the poem echoes elsewhere in *The Dolphin*, too). Cf also T. S. Eliot: "I have heard the mermaids singing, each to each" ("The Love Song of J. Alfred Prufrock," 124). Ricks and McCue's edition of Eliot also points to Donne: "Teach me to heare Mermaides singing" ("Song: Goe, and catche a falling starre," 5); and *A Midsummer Night's Dream* 2.1: "I [. . .] heard a mermaid on a dolphin's back | Uttering such dulcet and harmonious breath | That the rude sea grew civil at her song" (*The Poems of T. S. Eliot*, vol. 1, *Collected and Uncollected Poems*, ed. Christopher Ricks and Jim McCue [2015], p. 398).

4. Virgil: *"Tendebantque manus ripae ulterioris amore"* (*Aeneid* VI, 314). William Empson writes that the line "is beautiful because *ulterioris*, the word of their banishment, is long, and so shows

but breaks with those conventions by listening more to itself than to its addressee. It is, after all, an "unwritten" letter, a conversation in his own mind. Hardwick will never receive it in an envelope, only as a poem in a book—and not even that, since it did not appear in this form in *The Dolphin*.

In the final version, published in 1973, the poem is entitled "Letter."[1] It begins with the Lizzie character talking or writing to the speaker who then turns to his own thoughts. Does the title "Letter" refer to the lines spoken by Hardwick or himself, or to their mutually solitary communications? Does the ambiguity change our sense of his engagement with the addressee? Or does "Letter" lay claim to being a freestanding poetic form?

"In London last month I encountered only
exhausted traffic and exhausting men—
the taxi driver might kill us, but at least he cared."
Cold summer London, your purer cold is Maine,
where each empty sweater and hollow bookcase hurts,
every pretext for their service gone.
We wanted to be buried together in Maine . . .
You didn't, "impractical, cold, out of touch."
The terrible postcards you bought and stamped for me
go off to Harriet, the Horseguards, the Lifeguards,
the Lord Mayor's Chariot, Queen Bess who could not bear—
true as anything else to fling to a child . . .
I shout into the air, my voice comes back—
nothing reaches your black silhouette.

Lowell has dispensed by now with the allusion to Virgil, and the sonnet-like form is a narrow room in which he frets in solitude. The suspension and vacillation in the poem's first states of feeling have given way to a more clearly defined anger and sense of isolation. Gone is the hope that his old love will turn her face to him—he can

---

that they have been waiting a long time; and because the repeated vowel-sound (itself the moan of hopeless sorrow) in *oris amore* connects the two words as if of their own natures, and makes desire belong necessarily to the unattainable" (*Seven Types of Ambiguity*; reprinted in a New Directions edition [1966], pp. 10–11).

1. "Letter" [*Hospital II* 2], *The Dolphin*.

only see her outline.[1] What Lowell brings to the final version, which the good manners and hopefulness of his letter could not express, is the dissolution feared, and indeed realized (by the time of publication), in the real plot of their lives.

"Nothing worthy to answer your beautiful letters," Lowell had written to Hardwick upon his release from the hospital.[2] The poems in Lizzie's "rapier voice" in *The Dolphin* are "piercing and thrilling" to the poet. They arrive between Lowell's "sidestepping and obliquities,"[3] between poems that turn over the courage of his desires, his snail horn perception of feeling, his study of Caroline and the children, his tangle of loyalties and wit. They are unanswerable. Christopher Ricks compares Lowell's artistic achievement in *The Dolphin* to the dramatic monologues of Robert Browning and Alfred Tennyson. He suggests that Lowell had newly imagined "kinds of silence" that are "terrible challenges to the possibility of consolatory utterance." "You don't get the same feeling in Browning of contours of thought and feeling being shaped by the recipient in the way in which these tragically personal letters in Lowell are," Ricks remarks. There is a "dramatic tautness in the letter" by virtue of its being so hard to reply to, such as when the Lizzie character writes, "I hope nothing is mis-said in this letter":

> Of course it's imagining the receiving of the letter that's the great stretch, not the writing. The good ones in Lowell are not ones emanating from him, they're in letters arriving, so that the onus is on you to come up with something to say, and all you can come up with, say, is the re-working of the letter into poetry.[4]

～

Hardwick was at home in her apartment on West Sixty-Seventh Street on the afternoon of September 12, 1977, awaiting Lowell's taxi from Kennedy Airport. "The elevator man called me and I went down,"

---

1. Cf. Lowell: "Now twelve years later, you turn your back" ("Man and Wife" 23, *Life Studies*); "Dear Figure curving like a questionmark, | how will you hear my answer in the dark?" ("The Flaw" 31–32, *For the Union Dead* [1964]).

2. Lowell to Hardwick, August 27, 1970.

3. Lowell, "On the End of the Phone," *The Dolphin*.

4. Ricks also talks about Lowell's *Life Studies* poem "To Speak of Woe That Is in Marriage" in this context; in John Woolford and Daniel Karlin, "A Conversation with Christopher Ricks, Part Two," *Browning Society Notes* 10, no. 3 (1980): pp. 4, 7.

she told a journalist from the Associated Press, where she found Lowell apparently asleep and unresponsive in the cab. She got in beside him and drove eight blocks south to Roosevelt Hospital, where he was pronounced dead at six o'clock. As the informant on his death certificate,[1] Hardwick named his "surviving spouse" as Caroline Blackwood and described herself as a "friend." She identified herself as "Elizabeth Lowell." ("I go back and forth" between the two names, she had once written to Lowell, "as a commuter. Lowell to all the old trades, elevators, Castine, Harriet's friends as her mother, some of mine—and then the Hardwick train of profession, women, students, readers. Neither seems quite to belong to me and alas they both have a deceptively rooted and solid sound for one so much a mutation in all stocks, all 'roles' to use the unmentionable word."[2]) She tried to call Harriet with the news but had no change, and no one at the hospital would lend her a coin for the pay phone. She paid somebody ten dollars for a dime.[3]

When he died, Lowell was returning to Hardwick but was carrying in his arms a parcel wrapped in brown paper—"Girl in Bed," a 1952 portrait of Blackwood painted by her former husband Lucian Freud. Lowell's marriage to Blackwood was over, he had told friends the previous spring. Its end was initiated by Blackwood but accepted by Lowell, who saw the wisdom of the separation even after Blackwood changed her mind.[4] His illness terrified her, and exacerbated her depression and her drinking. "It's the effect my troubles have on you," he had written to Blackwood that summer. "It's like a nightmare we all have in which each motion of foot or hand troubles the turmoil it tries to calm."[5]

Those times were "a great sadness" for him, Hardwick told Ian Hamilton.[6] After Easter, he had "started coming down to New York" from Harvard, and with Hardwick's measured acceptance eventually

---

1. Reproduced in Jamison, *Robert Lowell: Setting the River on Fire*, p. 380.
2. Hardwick to Lowell, September 19, 1975.
3. As Hardwick reported to Darryl Pinckney at the time.
4. "I feel you ended things during my Irish visit, ended them wisely and we can't go back" (Lowell to Blackwood, May 3, 1977); the letter is now missing but quoted in Ian Hamilton, *Robert Lowell: A Biography*, pp. 460–72. Frank Bidart recalls Lowell telling him the marriage was over as early as November/December 1976 (interview with editor, January 29, 2017).
5. Lowell to Caroline Blackwood, July 17, 1977; the letter is now missing, but is quoted in Ian Hamilton, *Robert Lowell: A Biography*, p. 465.
6. Elizabeth Hardwick, interview with Ian Hamilton, October 26, 1979, Ian Hamilton Papers, British Library.

moved back into 15 West Sixty-Seventh Street, going between their old apartment and Hardwick's studio. "She felt he was worthy of care," Harriet Lowell recalls.[1] In the summer, they went to Castine and spent the season there, also traveling to Russia together. Letters at the close of the present edition give Hardwick's account to friends of what was going on. In one, she writes:

> About my "situation"—the whole thing is astonishing and I have no idea exactly what the shape of it all will turn out to be. Cal is going to Ireland on the 1st of Sept. for two weeks, returning the 15th to teach at Harvard. *They* appear to be friendly from calls and letters and I think Caroline will make an effort again to mend her too hasty surgery on the marriage. Who knows? As for me, I spoke of the astonishment, by which I mean as clearly as I can say that I don't feel vulnerable, don't feel sent out on approval, as it were, don't talk or care about contracts and commitments, whatever those are. It is very odd—we are just going along, having a very agreeable time. [. . .] I know this sounds strange, but as the thing has gone along day by day it seems real just as it is. Cal and I burst out laughing on July 28th—had it not been for the "gap" we would have been married that day for 28 years.[2]

Lowell's visit to Blackwood in Ireland was an unhappy one—he telephoned Hardwick on September 11 to say it was "sheer torture"[3]—and he flew back to New York on the twelfth, three days earlier than expected.

1. "On Robert Lowell," Oral History Initiative, Harvard University (September 29, 2016).
2. Hardwick to Robert Craft, August 4, 1977.
3. Ian Hamilton, *Robert Lowell: A Biography*, p. 472.

LOCATION OF MANUSCRIPTS

Robert Lowell was first approached by W. H. Bond, librarian of the Houghton Library at Harvard University, to sell his papers in 1966, "but Lowell felt uncertain and the matter was allowed to drop for four years," writes Rodney G. Dennis.[1] The letters in the present edition document what happened once the idea was again raised by Elizabeth Hardwick. Hardwick was thinking not only of the literary and financial value of the papers but also of protecting their daughter, Harriet Lowell, from having to sort through them after the deaths of her parents. In Lowell's absence at Oxford, Hardwick arranged for the papers to be organized and assessed. After three years of negotiations, Lowell sold them to the Houghton in 1973. The sale comprised his "family and literary correspondence generated before 1971 and literary manuscripts covering a period of about thirty-five years, beginning with school poems and ending with *Notebook*." It also included eighty letters written by Hardwick to Lowell and to others, and 168 letters from various correspondents written solely to Hardwick.

After Lowell's death in 1977, his remaining papers (written during his years with Caroline Blackwood) "were placed at Harvard on deposit," says Dennis. "The library was offered first refusal." But the

---

1. Rodney G. Dennis, introduction to *The Robert Lowell Papers at the Houghton Library, Harvard University: A Guide to the Collection*, comp. Patrick K. Miehe (1990), p. ix.

Harry Ransom Center at the University of Texas at Austin (HRC) "made an offer that Harvard could not match."[1] In 1982, the HRC came to an agreement with the Lowell Estate to buy the late manuscripts (including those for Lowell's last four books), together with his correspondence between 1970 and 1977. A selection of twelve letters, telegrams, and cards from Hardwick to Lowell was included in the sale.

Left out of the sale were 101 letters, telegrams, and postcards from Hardwick to Lowell, one letter from Hardwick to Blackwood, and Lowell's 1970 calendar, all of which Blackwood had previously set aside and mailed to Frank Bidart, Lowell's literary executor, on April 25, 1978. Bidart kept them in his apartment until 1988, when he deposited them at the Houghton Library, with a note explaining that they were the property of Lowell's Estate. "In the event of my death, they are to be returned to Caroline Blackwood, who entrusted them to me for safekeeping. If at that time Caroline Blackwood is dead, they are to be kept here at the Houghton Library until the death of Elizabeth Hardwick—at which time, they are to be returned to the Estate of Robert Lowell."[2] Blackwood died on February 14, 1996. Hardwick died on December 2, 2007. In May 2010, Bidart informed Evgenia Citkowitz (Blackwood's daughter) and Harriet of the existence of the letters. They are currently on deposit at the Houghton Library.

In 1991, the HRC separately agreed to buy from Hardwick her own papers, including "seven boxes of creative works, correspondence, printed material, articles and photographs," together with all of Lowell's letters to Harriet and to her.

Letters in this edition are mostly housed at three repositories: the Houghton Library; the Elizabeth Hardwick Papers at the HRC (all letters from Lowell to Hardwick and Harriet); and the Robert Lowell Papers at the HRC (twelve letters and telegrams from Hardwick to Lowell, and all letters from Blackwood to Lowell). Letters from Mary McCarthy to Hardwick are in the Vassar College Archives & Special Collections Library and the HRC. All other incoming letters to

---

1. Dennis, *The Robert Lowell Papers at the Houghton Library*, p. x.
2. Frank Bidart, July 1, 1988 cover letter to MS Storage 244, Houghton Library.

Hardwick and to Lowell in this edition are at the HRC. The locations of outgoing letters are as follows:

Robert Giroux to Charles Monteith	Archives and Manuscripts Division, New York Public Library
Hardwick to Elizabeth Bishop	Vassar College Special Collections Library
Hardwick to Blair Clark	Harry Ransom Center, The University of Texas at Austin
Hardwick to Ian Hamilton	Harry Ransom Center, The University of Texas at Austin
Hardwick to Harriet Lowell	Harry Ransom Center, The University of Texas at Austin
Hardwick to Mary McCarthy	Vassar College Special Collections Library
Lowell to William Alfred	Brooklyn College Library Archives and Special Collections
Lowell to Frank Bidart	Houghton Library, Harvard University
Lowell to Elizabeth Bishop	Vassar College Special Collections Library
Lowell to Blair Clark	Harry Ransom Center, The University of Texas at Austin
Lowell to Stanley Kunitz	Firestone Library, Princeton University
Lowell to Harriet Lowell	Harry Ransom Center, The University of Texas at Austin
Lowell to Mary McCarthy	Vassar College Special Collections Library
Lowell to Adrienne Rich	Schlesinger Library, Radcliffe Institute for Advanced Study, Harvard University
Charles Monteith to Robert Giroux	Archives and Manuscripts Division, New York Public Library
Robert Silvers to Lowell	Archives and Manuscripts Division, New York Public Library

A NOTE ON THE TEXT

AND ANNOTATION

Transcriptions are of primary sources except in a few noted instances, when I have had to rely on published versions.[1] Lowell and Hardwick typed most of their letters; any that were handwritten are noted as such.

Dates, addresses, and forms of address (given here in italics: *Mrs. Robert Lowell, Professor William Alfred*, etc.) are recorded when written or typed by the letter-writer on the letter or envelope. Dates and addresses gleaned from postmarks or from biographical or other sources are given in square brackets.

The pattern of dates (American or British) is not standardized but follows the practice of the writer or publication.

Except where noted, misspelled names and typos have been silently corrected, and any letter-writer's revisions for the sake of grammatical sense have been silently accepted. Significant revisions, marginal additions, and interjections are marked by sloping lines \for insertions/ or the use of ~~strikethroughs~~. Punctuation has been faithfully preserved, but punctuation typos (overstrikes, for example) have been silently corrected.

Editorial omissions have been marked with ellipses in square brackets [. . .] to distinguish them from Hardwick's or Lowell's own

---

1. On a few occasions, further scrutiny of manuscripts and other sources led to the correction of a transcription in previous editions of Lowell's letters.

ellipses (. . .), which they used to break off, drift, fall silent, or for other effects.

In the footnotes, quotations from poems are run-on, with line breaks indicated by a vertical bar (|) to distinguish them from this edition's convention of using \sloping lines/ to signal marginal insertion.

Annotations provide information: personal identifications (supplemented by the Index), the contexts of Hardwick's prose and Lowell's poems and prose, and their reading. I have also taken care to annotate what might be common knowledge on one side of the Atlantic but not the other (for instance, the SSAT, the American tax date, or such phrases as "forty acres and a mule" for readers abroad; or the eleven-plus, grammar schools, and O levels for readers unfamiliar with the British school system).

References to Lowell's poems and Hardwick's prose are to the first published editions, unless otherwise stated. For Lowell's "The Dolphin" manuscript (1972), refer to *The Dolphin: Two Versions, 1972–1973*. Individual book titles are given in full, except for the following abbreviations for the three editions of Lowell's *Notebook*:

Notebook 1967–68, first edition, published in 1969:   *Notebook69-1*
Notebook 1967–68, second printing, published in 1969:   *Notebook69-2*
Notebook, new edition, published in 1970:   *Notebook70*

In bibliographical citations, titles and year of publication are given in the first instance; titles alone are given thereafter. Citations of the *Oxford English Dictionary* (OED) are mostly to the 1933 edition (or the supplements published in 1933, 1972, and 1976), which Hardwick and Lowell would have known. In some instances, the OED's online definitions and quotations for the third edition are given.

Many sonnets in the *Notebook* editions, *History, For Lizzie and Harriet*, and *The Dolphin*, are gathered in sequences. In such cases, titles of individual poems are given in quotation marks, followed by the italicized sequence title and number in square brackets, thus: "Plane Ticket" [*Flight to New York* 1], *The Dolphin*.

Scholars who wish to consult the original letter manuscripts should apply to the Houghton Library for further information.

At the request of the Lowell Estate, the following letters silently omit references or passages that violate the privacy of families or living persons: Hardwick to Lowell, April 26 [1970]; Hardwick to Lowell, March 9, 1972; Lowell to Harriet Lowell, June 28, 1972; Lowell to Hardwick, March 5, 1973; Hardwick to Lowell, March 31, 1973; Lowell to Hardwick [April 4, 1973]; Lowell to Hardwick, April 5 [1973]; Hardwick to Lowell, April 9, 1973; Hardwick to Lowell, April 21, 1973; Hardwick to Lowell, May 5, 1973; Lowell to Hardwick, June 23, 1973; Hardwick to Lowell, July 20, 1974; Hardwick to Lowell, November 20, 1974; Hardwick to Lowell, September 19, 1975; Lowell to Hardwick, October 1, 1975.

TABLE OF DATES, 1970–1977

Outlining publications, travels, and major personal and world events alluded to in the letters.

1970

JANUARY–FEBRUARY—Lowell is on leave from teaching at Harvard University and continues to make revisions to the page proofs of *Notebook*, postponing its publication. He writes "1970 New Year." Harriet Lowell turns thirteen on January 4. Hardwick teaches at Barnard College. Lowell's planned trip to Russia is cancelled "at the last minute" due to the Soviet Union blocking a visa for Olga Andreyev Carlisle, his co-translator of Osip Mandelstam's poems. Hardwick publishes an article on Jerzy Grotowski and the Polish Laboratory Theatre in *The New York Review of Books*, and a review of the film adaptation of Horace McCoy's *They Shoot Horses, Don't They?* for *Vogue*. MARCH— Lowell turns fifty-three on March 1. Lowell accepts Elizabeth Bishop's National Book Award on her behalf. Lowell, Hardwick, and Harriet Lowell leave for Italy on March 18, visiting Florence, Venice, and Rome. APRIL—The family spends the final six days of their holiday in Rome. Hardwick and Harriet return to New York. Lowell travels to Amsterdam. Lowell begins fellowship at All Souls College, Oxford, on April 24. Lowell begins affair with Caroline Blackwood on April 30 in her house at 80 Redcliffe Square, Chelsea, London. MAY—U.S. invasion of Cambodia. Students protesting the invasion are killed at Kent State University and Jackson State College. JUNE—Working with Caroline Blackwood, Lowell finishes revisions to *Notebook*, which includes new sonnets written since March, "Left Out of Vacation" [*February and March* 12]; "Letter with Poems for a Letter with Poems" [*For Elizabeth Bishop* 3]; "America from Oxford"; and "Wall-Mirror" [*To Summer* 17]. Blair Clark meets Lowell and Hardwick in London on or about June 14 and discusses the options of telling Hardwick "it's true" indirectly or directly.[1] Lowell telegraphs Hardwick on June 20 that he will not be returning as expected. Lowell telephones Hardwick and Harriet on June 23 to say he is staying in Britain for the summer. Hardwick learns on June 25 that Lowell is seeing Blackwood. Hardwick drives Harriet to camp in Cornwall, Connecticut, on June 28. JULY—Hardwick publishes "A Useful Critic," a letter to the editor of *The New York Review of Books* defending Richard Gilman from an attack by Philip Rahv. She spends Fourth of July weekend in Connecticut, drives Harriet back to New York for school interviews, and then drives her back to camp. Lowell locks himself and Blackwood in one of the flats in her Redcliffe Square house for three days. Lowell is admitted to Greenways Nursing Home on July 8. Blackwood departs. Hardwick drives from New York to Maine on July 12. Blackwood turns thirty-nine on July 16, and is in Ballyconneely, Ireland, on July 17. On July 20, Hardwick and Blair Clark discuss the need for someone from Lowell's American circle to go to London to look after him (since they felt that, excepting Grey Gowrie, Xandra Bingley, and Jonathan Miller, few of his British friends had an understanding of his illness and its patterns). Hardwick asks Clark if he will go, but she cautions that they "can't do anything until he gets over this manic phase." On July 21, Blackwood is back in London. Robert Silvers tells Clark that Lowell had left the hospital and shown up at Blackwood's house. "Car[oline] can't stand it." Clark is urged by Jonathan Miller to come to England because everyone Lowell knows in London "is vanishing, including himself," and he is "troubled by the idea of Cal emerging" from the

---

1. Quotations from June 14 through August 9 are from Blair Clark's diary and notes of conversations with Hardwick, Lowell, Mary McCarthy, Robert Silvers, and Jonathan Miller (Blair Clark Papers, HRC).

hospital "with no point of real contact." On July 22, Silvers tells Clark that "Caroline is closing house in London—vanishing concerned that he not track her down—Car[oline] quotes 'I can't take responsibility' but 'hasn't thought through what ought to happen ultimately.'" On July 23, Clark speaks to Mary McCarthy, who says that Clark will have to go to London eventually. She says Lowell "is quite mad but [it is] masked by lithium—with lithium, he may stay up forever & never reach a manic climax." McCarthy also says that "Lizzie seems O.K.—certain euphoria (60%) about living alone." Hardwick turns fifty-four on July 27. Hardwick and Lowell's twenty-first anniversary falls on July 28. On July 29, Hardwick tells Clark she has heard the "most appalling news from London," that Lowell is "allowed to go out—in pyjamas—out to pubs," and that Sonia Orwell told her he "steals from handbags." Hardwick is especially alarmed by the reports of stealing, which he "had never done before," and that "he might keel over dead, with drugs and beer." Says that "he is a brilliant, proud, dignified man," "not this detached idiot," and that he is "not in emotional contact with his real personality (reserved and proud)." She has "made up [her] mind" to go to London with William Alfred, who will "go to pub, cut his hair, buy him shoes—until they can control him— sit there with him." "Car[oline] thing is secondary—he can marry her if he wants." AUGUST—Hardwick publishes review of Francine du Plessix Gray in *Vogue*. Hardwick and William Alfred leave for London via Boston, arriving on August 2. Hardwick later tells Clark that "the A.M. I arrived Car[oline] called & told Dr. under no circs. can I take him" home. Hardwick wonders if "maybe Car[oline] had some shame about neglecting him?" Hardwick says to the doctor, "What kind of love [is it] where you say 'you can't be sick.'" Hardwick and Alfred visit Lowell in the hospital daily, cut his hair "back to its usual poetic length," take clothes to the laundry, walk with him to a pub called the "George Washington," "both holding him up," take him to the movies. Hardwick had "one outburst against Cal"—"when he taunted me, I hit back, 'I'm not a nurse.'" Lowell "said he didn't want divorce" but also "doesn't seem to have any intention of coming back." Hardwick and Alfred return to the United States on August 7. "All 3 were weeping as taxi left." Blackwood returns to London. On August 9, Hardwick tells Clark that "he is still in hosp. Very glad I went—everything Sonia & others mentioned wrong," including the stealing story. Hardwick said Lowell was an "absolute invalid," "very drugged & hardly able to get across street." "He can hardly write, writing a few poems (they're all right)." "Cal back in touch with Caroline, my coming did that." Hardwick also said "Let this cup pass from me." "I don't want to know, day by day. Going to make a terrific effort to put Cal out of my mind." Hardwick drives to Connecticut to pick up Harriet from camp on 15/16 August, and they return to Castine. Hardwick and Harriet travel to Quebec. Six new *Notebook* sonnets are published in *Modern Occasions*. Lowell is released from hospital, hoping to stay in Redcliffe Square, but at Blackwood's insistence looks for his own studio. SEPTEMBER—Hardwick publishes review of Mary McCarthy's *The Writing on the Wall* in *Vogue*. Lowell moves into a studio at 33 Pont Street in Belgravia, London. Hardwick and Harriet return to New York over Labor Day weekend. Harriet starts the eighth grade at Dalton School. Hardwick is active in Democratic Party politics. Hardwick publishes essay about Zelda Fitzgerald in *The New York Review of Books*. OCTOBER—Lowell begins to teach at the University of Essex. Hardwick publishes a review of Muriel Spark's *The Driver's Seat* in *Vogue*. NOVEMBER—Publication of *Notebook*. Hardwick publishes a review of Nabokov's first novel, *Mary*, in *Vogue*. DECEMBER— Lowell flies to New York's Kennedy Airport on December 14, where Hardwick meets him. He gets off the plane wearing a ring given to him by Blackwood. Lowell, Hardwick, and Harriet celebrate Christmas at 15 West Sixty-Seventh Street.

1971

JANUARY—Lowell celebrates Harriet's fourteenth birthday on January 4 and leaves the same day, arriving in London on the morning of January 5. Hardwick publishes a review of Edward Bond's play *Saved* in *Vogue* and the essay "Militant Nudes" in *The New York Review of Books*. Lowell teaches again at Essex. Hardwick resumes teaching at Barnard College. FEBRUARY—Hardwick serves on the jury of the PEN Translation Prize awarded to Nadezhda Mandelstam's *Hope Against Hope*. Publishes a review of a play about the Manson murders and a meditation on the Metropolitan Opera's production of *Parsifal* in *Vogue*. She begins to write about Ibsen for *The New York Review of Books*. MARCH—Lowell turns fifty-four. Lowell tells Hardwick that he and

Blackwood are expecting a baby. Lowell travels to Norway. Hardwick and Harriet travel to South Carolina. Genocide in East Pakistan begins on March 26. Lieutentant William L. Calley, Jr., is convicted by court martial of murder for his role in the 1968 My Lai massacre on March 29. APRIL—Lowell gives up his studio in Pont Street and moves in with Blackwood at Redcliffe Square. MAY—Lowell visits the London Dolphinarium and buys stone dolphins, his behavior increasingly hypomanic, but manages to avert an episode. JUNE—Hardwick publishes "The Ties Women Cannot Shake and Have" in *Vogue*. She and Harriet go to Castine. JULY–AUGUST—Hardwick drives Harriet back to New York, and Harriet leaves for camp in Mexico on July 5. Hardwick returns to Maine. Lowell travels with Jonathan Raban to the Orkney Islands, home of his Traill and Spence ancestors. Moves with Blackwood and her daughters (Natalya, aged eleven; Evgenia, aged eight; and Ivana, aged five) to Blackwood's house Milgate Park, Bearsted, in Kent. Blackwood turns forty. Hardwick turns fifty-five. Lowell publishes "Excerpt from *The Dolphin*" (fourteen poems) and an interview in *the Review*. Hardwick writes about Sylvia Plath in *The New York Review of Books*. SEPTEMBER—Harriet begins the ninth grade. Hardwick teaches at Barnard, publishes an article about Edith Wharton in *Vogue*. Robert Sheridan Lowell born on September 27. OCTOBER—Lowell teaches at Essex. Hardwick publishes "In Maine" in *the Review*. NOVEMBER—Hardwick writes about Carson McCullers and Flannery O'Connor for *Vogue*. Gives the Christian Gauss Seminar at Princeton University. DECEMBER—Mary McCarthy and James West visit Lowell, Blackwood, and family for Christmas.

1972

JANUARY—Frank Bidart comes to England at Lowell's invitation to work with him on assembling *History, For Lizzie and Harriet*, and *The Dolphin*. Harriet turns fifteen. Death of John Berryman on January 7. British coal miners begin strike on January 9. Lowell teaches at Essex. Hardwick teaches at Barnard. British soldiers kill fourteen unarmed protesters on "Bloody Sunday," January 30, in Derry, Northern Ireland. JANUARY/FEBRUARY—Ivana, six years old, accidentally turns over an electric kettle of boiling water on herself; her life is saved by the burns unit at Queen Victoria Hospital in West Sussex. On the night of the burn, Lowell "found a small towel and spread it out on the cold hospital corridor floor outside my door," Ivana recalls, so that Blackwood and he could sleep near her.[1] MARCH—Lowell turns fifty-five. Harriet visits Lowell and Blackwood in England for the first time. *Time* publishes a special issue on "The American Woman" to which Hardwick contributed, including an unsigned piece on "The New Woman, 1972." APRIL–MAY—Hardwick publishes "Scene from an Autobiography" in the spring issue of the journal *Prose*, "Working Girls: The Brontës" in *The New York Review of Books*, and a review of Simone de Beauvoir in *The New York Times Book Review*. JUNE— Five men are arrested for breaking into the Democratic National Committee offices at the Watergate building in Washington, D.C. JULY—Hardwick publishes "Is the 'Equal' Woman More Vulnerable?" in *Vogue*. Goes to Connecticut for the summer. Bidart returns to England to work with Lowell on revisions to the manuscripts of *The Dolphin*, *History*, and *For Lizzie and Harriet*. Blackwood turns forty-one. Hardwick turns fifty-six. AUGUST—Hardwick begins publishing a six-part series of articles on "One Woman's Vote" in *Vogue*, with updates through to the November election. SEPTEMBER—Harriet begins the tenth grade. Hardwick teaches at Barnard. Sheridan turns one. OCTOBER—Lowell and Blackwood travel to New York, then to the Dominican Republic where Lowell divorces Hardwick and Blackwood divorces Israel Citkowitz; later the same day they marry each other. NOVEMBER—Death of Ezra Pound on November 1. Richard Nixon reelected; Hardwick writes about the election in *The New York Review of Books*. NOVEMBER–DECEMBER—Hardwick writes about Dorothy Wordsworth and Jane Carlyle in *The New York Review of Books* and an article on "Suicide and Women" in *Mademoiselle*.

1973

JANUARY–FEBRUARY—Harriet turns sixteen. Hardwick teaches at Barnard, writes about Virginia Woolf in *The New York Review of Books*. Lowell teaches at Essex. MARCH—Lowell turns fifty-six. Harriet visits England. MAY—Watergate hearings begin on May 17. MAY–JUNE—Hardwick publishes a review of Doris Lessing in *The*

---

1. Ivana Lowell, *Why Not Say What Happened?* (2010), p. 36.

New York Times Book Review. Travels to Castine to empty the house on School Street for sale. Publishes "Seduction and Betrayal" essay in two parts in *The New York Review of Books*. JULY—Lowell publishes *History, For Lizzie and Harriet*, and *The Dolphin*. Harriet visits England. Blackwood turns forty-two. Hardwick turns fifty-seven. AUGUST—Hardwick goes to the Rockefeller Foundation's Bellagio Center in Italy and writes fiction. SEPTEMBER—Lowell moves with Blackwood and family to Brookline, Massachusetts, to teach at Harvard. Harriet begins the eleventh grade. Hardwick teaches at Barnard. Sheridan turns two. Hardwick lectures at Smith College. OCTOBER—Hardwick publishes "Writing a Novel" in *The New York Review of Books*. Lowell begins writing new poems. NOVEMBER— Lowell gives reading at the Pierpont Morgan Library in New York. Harriet visits Lowell and Blackwood in Massachusetts. Blackwood publishes *For All That I Found There*. DECEMBER—Hardwick publishes "When to Cast Out, Give Up, Let Go" in *Mademoiselle*. Lowell visits New York. Lowell, Blackwood, and the small children return to Milgate at the end of Harvard's fall term. Death of Philip Rahv; Hardwick delivers a eulogy at his funeral on December 24.

1974

JANUARY—Harriet turns seventeen. Hardwick teaches at Barnard. She publishes "Philip Rahv (1908-1973)" in *The New York Review of Books*; and she serves on the jury that unanimously recommends *Gravity's Rainbow* by Thomas Pynchon for the Pulitzer Prize in fiction, which the Pulitzer board will reject in May when the prizes are announced. MARCH—Lowell turns fifty-seven. Harriet visits England. APRIL— Lowell goes on a reading tour of the South. Wins the Copernicus Award. Lowell returns to England. MAY—Israel Citkowitz dies on May 4. Hardwick publishes *Seduction and Betrayal*. Lowell wins Pulitzer Prize in poetry on May 7 for *The Dolphin*, recommended by a divided jury consisting of William Alfred, Anthony Hecht, and Gwendolyn Brooks. JUNE–JULY—Hardwick summers in Maine. She publishes "Sad Brazil" in *The New York Review of Books*. Death of John Crowe Ransom on July 3. Blackwood turns forty-three. Hardwick turns fifty-eight. AUGUST—Richard Nixon resigns on August 9. SEPTEMBER—Harriet begins the twelfth grade. Hardwick teaches at

Barnard. Busing to desegregate Boston schools begins. Sheridan turns three. OCTOBER/NOVEMBER—Hardwick travels to Paris. She publishes an essay about Thomas Hardy's *Jude the Obscure* in *The New York Review of Books*. DECEMBER—Hardwick writes about Peter Brook's production of *Timon of Athens* at the Théâtre des Bouffes du Nord in *The New York Review of Books*.

1975

JANUARY—Harriet turns eighteen. Hardwick teaches at Barnard. FEBRUARY—Lowell and Blackwood move back to Brookline, Massachusetts, and Lowell teaches at Harvard for the spring term. MARCH—Lowell turns fifty-eight. APRIL—Fear of an impending manic episode causes Lowell to take too much lithium. He checks into Mount Sinai Hospital in New York City for observation and to reduce lithium toxicity. Fall of Saigon on April 30. MAY—Lowell publishes three poems in *The New York Review of Books*. JUNE—Harriet graduates from the Dalton School. Hardwick summers in Maine. Lowell and Hardwick contribute to a symposium about "The Meaning of Vietnam" in *The New York Review of Books*. JULY–AUGUST—Hardwick publishes "Thomas Mann at 100" in *The New York Times Book Review*. Blackwood turns forty-four. Hardwick turns fifty-nine. Lowell spends the summer at Milgate, travels to Ireland for a festival organized by Seamus Heaney. SEPTEMBER—Harriet attends Barnard. Hardwick teaches at Smith. Sheridan turns four. Lowell prepares *Selected Poems* for publication and begins to work on a collection of his prose. Hardwick publishes "Reflections on Simone Weil" in *Signs*. NOVEMBER—Lowell suffers an acute manic episode and is hospitalized at the Priory in Roehampton. Discharges himself. DECEMBER—Lowell is hospitalized again at Greenways Nursing Home in London. Death of Hannah Arendt on December 4.

1976

JANUARY—Harriet turns nineteen, and Lowell is released from Greenways on 4 January. From January 4–20, Lowell receives twenty-four-hour nursing care at home in Redcliffe Square, London. In late January he is committed to St. Andrew's Hospital in Northampton. Hardwick teaches at Barnard. FEBRUARY—Lowell returns to Milgate in mid-February, writes more poems for *Day by Day*. MARCH—Lowell turns fifty-nine. Hardwick writes about Billie Holiday in *The New York Review of Books*. Lowell publishes *Selected Poems*. APRIL—Lowell and Blackwood travel to New York City for American Bicentennial production of *The Old Glory*. MAY—Lowell writes about Hannah Arendt in *The New York Review of Books*. Blackwood publishes *The Stepdaughter*. JUNE–JULY—Lowell attends the Aldeburgh Festival to hear Benjamin Britten's setting of *Phaedra*. Lowell and Blackwood summer at Milgate. Hardwick summers in Maine, writes about Jimmy Carter in *The New York Review of Books* and the election in *Vogue*. Blackwood turns forty-five. Hardwick turns sixty. AUGUST—Hardwick travels to London for a PEN International conference. SEPTEMBER—Hardwick writes about Maine in *Vogue*. Harriet returns to Barnard, where Hardwick also teaches. Lowell and Blackwood prepare to spend the fall semester at Harvard. Lowell suffers a manic episode; he is hospitalized at Greenways Nursing Home on 15 September. Blackwood leaves for Cambridge, Massachusetts, with Sheridan and Ivana. Sheridan turns five. OCTOBER—Lowell is released on October 27 and follows Blackwood to Cambridge, staying at the house on Sacramento Street that they have rented. NOVEMBER—Lowell removes himself to Frank Bidart's apartment on 63 Sparks Street. Jimmy Carter elected president. Hardwick publishes "The Sense of the Present" in American fiction in *The New York Review of Books*. DECEMBER—Blackwood returns to Britain on December 3 with Sheridan and Ivana. Hardwick visits Lowell in Cambridge. Lowell returns to Britain. Lowell, Blackwood, and the small children spend Christmas in Scotland.

1977

JANUARY–FEBRUARY—Harriet turns twenty. Hardwick teaches at Barnard; publishes "A Woman of Transcendent Intellect Who Assumed the Sufferings of Humanity," a review of Simone Weil's biography, in *The New York Times Book Review*. Lowell moves back to Cambridge, Massachusetts; suffers congestive heart failure. He is hospitalized for nine days in Phillips House at Massachusetts General Hospital on February 1. Teaches at Harvard. Hardwick participates in "An Exchange on Fiction" in a letter to the editors of *The New York Review of Books*. She serves as Advisory Editor to and writes introductions for the eighteen-volume series "Rediscovered Fiction by American Women: A Personal Selection." MARCH—Lowell celebrates his sixtieth birthday with Hardwick, Harriet, and Blair and Joanna Clark. Blackwood sells Milgate and moves to Castletown House, Ireland. APRIL— Lowell visits Ireland at Easter, and he and Blackwood agree to separate, at Blackwood's instigation. MAY—At the end of the Harvard term, Lowell moves back in with Hardwick at 15 West Sixty-Seventh Street. Receives the National Medal for Literature from the American Academy and Institute of Arts and Letters. Blackwood visits Lowell in New York to attend the ceremony. JUNE–JULY—Lowell publishes a poem "For John Berryman" in *The New York Review of Books*. Hardwick and Lowell travel to Russia, visiting Moscow and Pasternak's grave in Peredelkino among other places; on their return they stop in Boston for Lowell to undergo heart tests. They spend the summer in Maine. Lowell works on his prose, and Hardwick works on fiction that will become *Sleepless Nights*. Lowell publishes the poem "Executions" in *The New York Review of Books* on July 14. Blackwood turns forty-six. Hardwick turns sixty-one. AUGUST—Lowell publishes *Day by Day* and *Selected Poems* (revised edition). SEPTEMBER—Lowell leaves for Ireland on September 1 to visit Blackwood, Sheridan, and his stepdaughters. Hardwick returns to New York, begins to teach at Barnard and the University of Connecticut. Harriet begins her junior year at Barnard. Seamus Heaney recalls, of a Dublin visit from Lowell and Blackwood, "a quick coded exchange between us in the hallway before I drove them home, when Marie [Heaney] and Caroline were getting their coats. 'Will I be seeing you soon again?' I asked and he replied, with that high neigh that sometimes came into his voice, and one of his lightning-flicker looks over the glasses, 'I don't think so.'"[1] On the morning of September 12, Lowell takes a plane from Ireland to New York. Harriet visits Hardwick in her Barnard office to ask "what was going on"[2] with her parents and to find out about Lowell's health. Hardwick tells Harriet that Lowell is "coming home later that day."

---

1. Dennis O'Driscoll, *Stepping Stones: Interviews with Seamus Heaney* (2008), p. 219.
2. Harriet Lowell Interview, "On Robert Lowell," Harvard Oral History Initiative, August 2016.

She says that Lowell's heart disease and the recent recurrence of manic cycles are causes of concern. She is welcoming him back because "this is his house, and everything I have—you—is his, everything." She also says that she feels he is "worthy of care." Hardwick teaches her "Experiments in Writing" class from 2:10–4:00, then goes home to await Lowell's return. Harriet joins protests at Barnard and Columbia against the death of Stephen Biko, who had just been assassinated. Lowell has a heart attack in the taxi bringing him home from Kennedy Airport, and is pronounced dead at Roosevelt Hospital at six o'clock. Lowell's funeral is held at the Church of the Advent in Boston on 16 September. He is buried in the family graveyard in Dunbarton, New Hampshire. Blackwood stays with Hardwick. Sheridan turns six.

PART I

1970

1. Elizabeth Hardwick to Robert Lowell

[15 West 67th Street, New York, N.Y.]

Tuesday, April 7, 1970

Darling: Safely home, but quite tired and still not back on a schedule Americana, having waked up at 4:A.M. . . . However, the trip was heaven, every moment full of pleasure and interest and relief and food and good companionship, love, art, walk. . . . I never had a better time and thank you for it and miss you already. The apartment was beautiful and serene, clean and bright and filled with stupid mail and worthless books and bills and some good books, some communications necessary if not exhilarating. I will send off tomorrow a large envelope airmail to Oxford, all of it needing answers I fear. Also Nicole[1] found some old travelers checks which I will send, hoping you will use these first since they may have been around for quite some time.

A letter from the Sussex people, or person rather.[2] I don't know. I found I was so pleased to see our sinfully comfortable, heavily equipped apartment, our library, records, Harriet immediately settled in spite of the trip for three hours with her guitar. . . . then I thought of some cold, rented place, with no books or records, few rays of heat, gas logs,

---

1. Gomez, the Lowells' housekeeper.

2. Letter now missing, but from P. W. Edwards, chairman of the Department of Literature, University of Essex, inviting Lowell to teach there; see Lowell to Hardwick, [April 26, 1970], below.

the works and then I wondered. But still see how you feel about it. We needn't go next year, but might wait a bit until H. is in boarding school and would actually be nearly 15, quite old enough to come for Christmas in London. Then we'd be free, without all the cares of a real family "situation." I don't know . . . perhaps this is the fatigue of the trip home, the pleasure of Nicole and Sumner[1]!

Bob is fine and Mrs. Barbara[2] likewise. That is all I've had time for. Will write again in a few days, to Oxford, sending along the mail as I said. It is bright and sunny here today. . . . Be happy, be somewhat wise, and a little prudent. Enclose article on lithium.[3] Much love always to you and the fondest greetings to our Dutch friends.

Elizabeth

2. Elizabeth Hardwick to Robert Lowell

[15 West 67th Street, New York, N.Y.]

April 10, 1970

Dearest Cal: I will send off the mail in a few days. Please answer this enclosed request immediately.[4] . . . How, I miss you! I came home with

---

1. The cat, named for the abolitionist Charles Sumner. See Lowell: "Left Out of Vacation" [*February and March* 12] 8–11, *Notebook70*; and Hardwick: "Her skinny brown cat stared at her, hardly blinking. His yellowish-gray gaze was very like her own. They looked at each other, unseeing, into a mirror of eyes, before the cat fell asleep, his lids suddenly closing, tightly, quickly, strangely" ("Writing a Novel," *New York Review of Books*, October 18, 1973; see also page 461).

2. Robert Silvers and Barbara Epstein, editors of the *New York Review of Books*, which Hardwick, Lowell, Epstein, and her husband, Jason, had the idea to found at a dinner in 1963, during the New York newspaper strike. Jason Epstein: "the four of us that evening saw the opportunity wordlessly presented by the strike: either create the kind of review that Lizzie demanded [in her 1959 *Harper's* article "The Decline of Book Reviewing"] or forever stop complaining. [. . .] Bob was born to edit the review that Lizzie's *Harper's* article demanded. I called him the following day and, to our delight, he immediately accepted. He then called Barbara and asked her to be his co-editor. That morning Lowell and I visited my bank to open an account, to which he contributed four thousand dollars from his trust fund" ("A Strike and a Start: Founding the New York Review," NYRDaily, *New York Review of Books*, March 16, 2013, https://www.nybooks.com/daily/2013/03/16/strike-start-founding-new-york-review/). See also Lowell to Elizabeth Bishop, January 23, [1963], and March 10, 1963, in both *The Letters of Robert Lowell*, ed. Saskia Hamilton (2005) and *Words in Air*, ed. Thomas Travisano with Saskia Hamilton (2008).

3. Enclosure now missing, but probably "Long-Studied Drug Is Licensed for Treatment of Mental Illness," *New York Times*, April 7, 1970.

4. Enclosure now missing.

a terrible cold and have been feeling rotten and unreal, going to sleep at 8 P.M., waking up at five. It seems to be almost gone today and so perhaps things will seem more cheerful, instead of lonely, dark, broken up.

Poor Bill.[1] The play, as he thought, did not please. Clive Barnes and the N.Y. Post were all I have seen thus far, and they thought it was boring. Bill himself came out all right, with the reviewers wondering why they ever thought of reworking a good play in this manner.[2] It does seem such an ungodly waste. I sent him a telegram for all three of us and will call him today. I assume the thing will not run.

Isaiah B. popped over for a moment last night to tell me goodbye. They[3] are off today and looking forward to seeing you.

The mail groweth ever worse, even though I have cut down a lot of it.[4] I'm sorry to say I was too sick to go to Orestes. And I haven't seen anyone, except Isaiah for a moment.

I still look back with joy on the Italian trip—with you, especially. Dearest one, happiness and peace go with you and return—to turmoil and domestic rasp, which is kinda nice too.

Harriet is fine, full and fresh.

Elizabeth

3. Elizabeth Hardwick to Robert Lowell

[15 West 67th Street, New York, N.Y.]
Saturday, April 12, 1970

Dearest: I'm so sorry about the trouble you had at the Rome airport. I know you've forgotten it by now, but still the picture of the old bear . . . struggling . . .[5] It's too much. I'm at last, for the first time today, over that damned cold I got on the way home. All forgotten.

My first letter to you may have seemed lukewarm about England. I

1. William Alfred, friend to both Lowell and Hardwick since the late 1950s, also Lowell's colleague at Harvard.

2. *Cry for Us All*, a musical adaptation of Alfred's play *Hogan's Goat*, opened on April 8, 1970, and ran for nine performances. Clive Barnes, "Theater: Musicalizing 'Hogan's Goat,'" *New York Times*, April 9, 1970; Richard Watts, "Politics in Old Brooklyn," *New York Post*, April 9, 1970.

3. Isaiah and Aline Berlin.

4. "In the morning it flourisheth, and groweth up; in the evening it is cut down, and withereth" (Psalm 90:6).

5. See footnote 2 on page 146 (Lowell to Harriet Lowell, January 6, 1970 [1971]).

was under the spell of the clean, quiet apartment. But that is gone, once more. Cal I can't cope. I have gotten so that I simply cannot bear it. Each day's mail and effort grows greater and greater: we have left a little bit of ourselves in too many places. Writing, students, politics, friends, automobile, Maine, taxes, bills, house, Harriet, books arriving at the rate of ten or so a day. I give all my time to this and yet everything is in disorder, files mounting up like those of some monstrous institution, old checks, records, things in four or five places, since four or five "homes" are needed, and hours spent looking for a single bill, wondering if it was paid. . . . I feel the getting away for a year would push us backward to some more possible step along the way. Also I know the awful anxiety here. Harriet doesn't really like Dalton[1] anymore and it seems to me needlessly complicated and anxious-making in its organization, without truly giving very sound instruction. Also I have some concern about her deep-seated notions that such and such aren't "important"—grades, school, traditions, work. I feel as Esther[2] does that one can't do much, but must try to offer some variation on this dismaying theme.

Now, wait until you hear what I have gotten involved in. Jack Thompson happened to speak to the President of Stony Brook[3] about your papers. They are wildly interested: hoping to compete with Buffalo maybe.[4] In any case, he, the President, is arranging for an appraiser to come next week or so. I was rather taken aback by this, since you aren't here, etc. However, I will try to stir myself to get the things in some sort of shape and with a list, general outline. I don't see why you shouldn't have the appraisal. You needn't act on it, and you needn't sell the stuff to Stony Brook, but could then compare offers with other places. I feel that the papers should be sent somewhere because the whole thing would be an unbearable headache for Harriet. The money would be parcelled out in yearly installments. And perhaps we should have this "foundation" and really change our lives for awhile or forever. I, myself, feel that it would be a relief to dispose of as much back-log as we can, in the concern for simpling a life that has become too weighty, detailed, heavy—for me. If we don't do this I will have to have a secretary next year, or

---

1. Private school on the Upper East Side of Manhattan.
2. Brooks.
3. John S. Toll. John ("Jack") Thompson, Lowell's college friend who was also close to Hardwick, was at the time an English professor at the State University of New York at Stony Brook.
4. The Poetry Collection of the State University of New York at Buffalo Library.

else simply give up on any hope of writing or reading. I don't want a secretary. Another person to deal with, face, worry about, pay . . . But.

I'm also ready, as you are, to be d-mobilized! Darling, think of a cottage, as they call it, near Oxford or Cambridge, or near London. A garden, a library, a few friends. (What nonsense! Sounds like Katherine Mansfield and J. Middleton Murry.)[1]

Much love, my only one. I miss you amazingly! "Amazingly" only in that I thought it would be possible to use this time to catch up. But it is not you I need to be separated from but from all this nonsense here.

Sweetheart, I'm not planning to sell anything of yours or even to be very snoopy. There is not the time nor the inclination. The few letters I glanced at seemed to belong to another life, lived by two other fools. (These are letters in my own desk. I won't go through anything in your study. Just give a general idea.)

Answer this Harvard thing.[2] I am sending a packet of mail today. Nothing "important" as H. would say.

    Elizabeth

Horrors! The papers, the manuscript, the letters. I took one look at your studio. Really we must make an effort to get this vaguely organized and taken away. How do you open the filing case! Of course the appraiser can't come until something is done to organize all of this. I really think it would be worthwhile and I will do what I can.

4. Elizabeth Hardwick to Robert Lowell

[15 West 67th Street, New York, N.Y.]
April 14, 1970

Darling: How I miss you! I wrote the Brookses that if you stay married long enough you are bound to fall in love, and so I pass that on to you. It is so lonely without you. Everything since I've been back has been a

1. See *Katherine Mansfield's Letters to John Middleton Murry, 1913–1922*, ed. John Middleton Murry (1951). Hardwick: "Katherine Mansfield wrote in a letter to Middleton Murry: 'Did you read in *The Times* that Shelley left on his table a bit of paper with a blot on it and a flung down quill? Mary S. *had a glass case* put over same and carried it all the way to London on her knees. Did you ever hear such rubbish!'" ("Wives and Mistresses," *New York Review of Books*, May 18, 1978).
2. Enclosure now missing.

little disturbing. Poor Harriet is so far behind in Spanish and Latin she will never catch up, and that fills her and me with despair. Don't know quite how it happened. The Dalton system is unnecessarily complicated and nervous-making. Otherwise I think she's doing fairly well. There will be a report on Thursday. Also the poor dear has eczema on her face, around her eyes, even on the eyelids. I am sure we will be able to cope with it, but at the moment I suffer for her. She misses you also, dearest. We owed a lot of money to the income tax! I am absolutely bogged down in your "papers," and tempted to give up, but still if I can persist it will be valuable to you, to us, to those who come after us.[1] It is important to try to make some order at this point. I haven't heard from the appraisal man, and of course am not planning anything without your wishes.

I wonder if you are in Oxford yet. Do let me know several things. One, roughly when you will be returning. We have to make plans here for June appointments, going to Maine, preparing for camp, etc. Also give me some ideas about next year as soon as possible.

No mail of any interest. The political scene is very dark and mysterious here. It will just be luck if we come out of it without too much damage to the country. Both the left and administration are so profoundly threatening. Of course all our friends say the left has not enough power to be threatening, but I don't agree. I do believe that, powerless as they are, they have profoundly shaped the course of the country by their hysterical "revolutionary" games . . . The poor astronauts in the lunar nodule with failing oxygen[2]—aren't they the symbol? How I wish I liked nature and simplicity and isolation better than I do. That would be an escape from the low-oxygen nodule, but I love the hard pavements, the killing noise. There's so much I want to talk to you about.

Bill Alfred is trying to be brave, but the loss of so many years is great. He says he has another play almost ready and I hope he can have the courage to continue. The sadness of it all oppresses me. I'm

---

1. Cf. Lowell, "Those Before Us," *For the Union Dead* [1964].
2. Thus, for "module." On April 13, 1970, an oxygen tank exploded during the Apollo 13 mission to the moon, forcing the astronauts to evacuate the command ship for the Lunar Module Aquarius. See "Power Failure Imperils Astronauts," *New York Times*, April 13, 1970; and "Astronauts Face 2 Critical Problems: Keeping Spacecraft Cool and Its Air Clean," *New York Times*, April 14, 1970.

sure he needed money for the excesses of Old Mr. A.[1] He sends his love to you.

Write us when you have time. Find, somewhere in your pocket with a hole in it, a little prudence. May God keep you.

E.

5. Elizabeth Hardwick to Robert Lowell

[15 West 67th Street, New York, N.Y.]
Saturday, April 19, 1970

Darling: I hope to hear from you today. Really, I do miss you so and wish we hadn't embarked on this long separation. However, there is nothing to be done about it now. The morning is beautiful today and last night was warm and misty. Went to Jean van der Heuvel's party for Nicolas and Dominique.[2] It was rather dull, as these large cocktail parties spanning the human possibilities will be: from black to white, rich to poor, important to handsome, young to old, left to right. Can't quite remember who was "poor" but he must have been there. Greetings and love and expressions of wish for your presence were heard.

Marian Schlesinger there like a spectre, but quite a heavy one in purple satin. Arthur must have been out of town and so this moment was seized to include the poor *abbandonata*.[3] Misfortune and neglect have not improved Marian.

Blair[4] called, plans to be in London some time in May.

Harriet's report was very bad, except for English. I was quite unhappy about it and she seems very sullen and careless and although one knows that this is adolescence and sees it without alarm in other people's children, still it does worry. . . . She is trying to grow up and there is so much charming and lovable about it. I think it is the negativism that causes me concern and a lack of even normal ambition. They say at school that she could do as well as anyone, and I believe that is meant seriously. But she is sloppy. On the other hand, I have the idea that this

---

1. Alfred's father, Thomas Allfrey Alfred.
2. Nabokov.
3. Abandoned woman. Marian and Arthur Schlesinger were divorced in 1970 after thirty years of marriage.
4. Clark, Lowell's friend since St. Mark's School.

year she just wants to have fun in school, whenever one can sneak that in . . . and so she is busy sending notes, drawing pictures of the teacher . . . and that is nice. I wish I knew what would [be] best for her. The camp this summer could make a big difference.[1] We will go up to Putney.[2] In general I would like a less long-haired school, but I am not sure where she can get i[n], what she would like. This is such a critical year for her record, since it is the one that will decide. On the other hand, I hate to have her leave. If I could find any way to make New York really good for her I would like it best of all because then the dear one could be with us.

Sumner is pawing the typewriter.

I don't even know where you are. No doubt in London, going about every minute. No mail except worrisome requests from students for recommendations, or more recommendations. I write them and say that you are away and that it will be sometime before you can be settled and able to do that sort of desk work . . .

Do send us a line. I'll write again next ~~month~~ week, on Monday. Much love, darling.

> E.

6. *Robert Lowell to* Mrs. Robert Lowell[3]

[Postcard: Frans Hals—*Regentesses of the Old Men's Almshouse of Haarlem*, Frans Hals Museum, Haarlem]

> [Amsterdam]
> [April 21, 1970]

Dearest Liz—

After a beautiful sunlit day in Haarlem—something we never saw 20 years gone. How the old numbers turn up on the wheel! I've seen every friend and acquaintance of 1952,[4] except Roger Hinks, who is gone.[5] I've had such a good visit, I am dull. Oxford in a couple of days.

> Luv, Cal

---

1. Cornwall Summer Workshop in Cornwall, Connecticut.

2. Progressive boarding school in Putney, Vermont.

3. Handwritten.

4. Lowell and Hardwick lived in Amsterdam from September 1951 until June 1952.

5. Hinks had worked for the British Council in Amsterdam from 1949–54 and knew the Lowells when they lived there.

7. *Robert Lowell to* Miss Harriet Lowell[1]

[Postcard: Frans Hals—detail of *Regents of the Old Men's Almshouse of Haarlem*,[2] Frans Hals Museum, Haarlem]

[Amsterdam]
[April 21, 1970]

Dearest Harriet—

This picture is not a photograph of me, but of a fine man 300 years ago. I've seen many things you might like, but most a group of nonviolent radicals, called Kabouter,[3] elves \(this is true)/, the youngest your age, the oldest mine, break into an empty house. The police made them leave, but no one was hurt. Miss you terribly.

Daddy

8. *Elizabeth Hardwick to Robert Lowell*

[15 West 67th Street, New York, N.Y.]
April 24, 1970

Dearest Cal: Very distressed that I hadn't heard from you, but I suppose I couldn't expect it. One letter from Holland[4] and now today, at last, a post-card. I had the idea you were going to Oxford sooner, but don't see any reason why you should have. Last Sunday I had a call from Bep Du Perron.[5] I could hardly hear her and couldn't really think of anything to say. She was thanking me for a present I didn't know anything about, but I am happy if you gave her one and I only regret that the telephone was so useless and somehow we never really got together on it—you know how it happens sometimes.

---

1. Handwritten.

2. Hardwick: "And the long time in Holland, time to take trains, one to Haarlem to see the old almshouse governors painted in their unforgiving black-and-white misery by Frans Hals in his last days. The laughing cavaliers perhaps had eaten too many oysters, drunk too much beer and died a replete, unwilling death, leaving the poor, freed by a bitter life from killing pleasures, to shrivel on charity, live on with their strong, blackening faces" (*Sleepless Nights* [1979], p. 103).

3. Anarchist group founded by Roel van Duijn and named after the Dutch word "kabouter" ("gnome, pixie, [. . .] little people [. . .] fairies," *Van Dale Woordenboek Nederlands-Engels*, s.v. "kabouter").

4. Now missing.

5. Elisabeth du Perron-de Roos.

Darling: now I must have some idea about next year immediately. I would never have imagined how many things are waiting upon it, but it is quite serious. First of all, the car. I want to give it to Jack for a nominal fee (it is 1964) especially if we are going away next year and maybe anyway because of my worry about it, the terrible anxiety I have every year with insurance, registration, etc. I must know because I have to pay insurance next week or lose it . . . Ugh. Also, various things about Harriet's schooling depend seriously on our plans for next year. Also how on earth am I going to rent three apartments[1] when I am away in the summer and would want to come back only for a quick leaving for England. I don't know whether you should take the Sussex or not. One is naturally mixed—inertia, the problems of settling, \Sumner,/ no place to live and work that would be right for us. Yet—the idea of being out of the US is attractive, perhaps. I understand from Bob that Sussex U (sounds like a cheerleader) is in Brighton . . . I also understand that Quentin Anderson and family were there last year and hated it!

But do make some inquiries and give us an idea. Harriet is trapped in some sort of escalating warfare with the Spanish teacher and cannot get "signed off" on her work card of two months ago—like a suit in Chancery.[2] She has to go back to school on Sat. (her third); she is willing to do anything and yet somehow nothing advances her suit. . . . I am furious. . . . Will go over this afternoon trying to get some sort of way out for H. I can understand those parents (I know so many) after long years in a school, have a row and take their children out. I have no place to take her and so I'll try to be cool. She is fine, except for this; having a nice time with Lisa[3] on many occasions and is still your lovely little, big girl.

The mails bring nothing except tedious requests for letters to be sent in answer to something or other. I am trying to keep up, also still on your "papers." It will be a help to have them in some order, but

---

1. The family apartment and two studio apartments (which Lowell and Hardwick used for writing) at 15 West Sixty-Seventh Street.
2. See Dickens's *Bleak House* (1852–53), both generally and the preface: "There is another well-known suit in Chancery, not yet decided, which was commenced before the close of the last century, and in which more than double the amount of seventy thousand pounds has been swallowed up in costs."
3. Wager.

what a chore. The man is coming to see them on next Wednesday. I miss you, old man. I wish I were there to hang up your clothes, talk to you, think about things. How I loved Italy—dear Albergo di Londres.[1]

Take a little care, darling. I'm going out to have lunch with Bob before descending on Dalton. Bob has been in Zurich to a fantastic conference with bankers, etc., industrialists, prime ministers. I am curious to hear his report. Darling, I enclose this,[2] just in case. I've told him and various others that you are away . . . but. . . .

Please write!

Elizabeth

9. *Robert Lowell to* Mrs. Robert Lowell

All Souls College, Oxford

April 25, 1970

Dearest, here I am not quite a day yet, a half lost soul in All Souls about to have lunch with the Berlins. The first two people I met here were Charles Monteith and A. L. Rowse.[3] It's a bachelor world, but very beautiful. Oxford is rather like Bath—Bath and Yale, quite Italian. I have eaten in gown, handled a 14th century psalm book, not much else.

Thanks for your lovely letters (I had ~~lovely~~ \good/ ones from Elizabeth,[4] Farb[5] and Donald Davie, who is at Stanford and suggested

---

1. Thus, for Albergo di Londra, hotel in Venice.

2. Enclosure now missing.

3. Monteith was Lowell's editor at Faber & Faber, and a fellow of All Souls College. A. L. Rowse first met Lowell in 1960 in New York: "22 November [1960] [. . .] at one met Robert Lowell at Cerutti's, where I was giving him lunch. I had been rather apprehensive from the tone of his voice over the telephone—'Yah-Yah-Yah', just like Wystan Auden, off-putting. But he turned out to be *most* sympathetic, and we got on easily, without any trouble. We had no reserves with each other and came out with everything we thought. He, too, had a cold, a rather runny one, for which he stuffed menthol up his nose, rather unprepossessing, and recommended it to me. He was less bulky and shambling than I had been given to suppose, and less mad. In fact, he was sane, sensitive, perceptive and responsive, full of original thoughts, rather a dear, and obviously a man of genius. No-one in the United States came up to expectations as he did" (*The Diaries of A. L. Rowse*, ed. Richard Ollard [2003], p. 336).

4. Bishop; probably her letter of April 8th, 1970 (see *Words in Air*, pp. 671–72).

5. Peter Farb.

that I might like getting out of my country, just as he wished to leave England[)]. I'll go to Essex next week and phone or write you immediately, when I know a little more. I think we could live in London and I could do the sort of thing I did at Harvard.[1] London is fifty minutes by train. I think the change of air might be refreshing and clear the mind. In fact, if I like Essex and hear good things about it, I am inclined (if you and Harriet are willing). We could begin this October or next.

Holland. I stayed 16 days with Huyck and Judith[2] and loved it all. I think I saw literally everyone we saw before, except that strange couple with the lovely father who read *Finnegans Wake*. All sent their love, and Henk van Galen Last, three times. I suppose they are all what we would call Old Left, but without the unpleasant features of many of ours. They are all still friends but with many rifts.

Waiting me of course was a blistering letter from Allen, a rather paranoid reading of my motives. I wrote him a gentle, I hope, rather appeasing letter back.[3] I don't want to excuse my failure with his festschrift. Give H. my love. I miss you both so. This must go now.

Cal

P. S. We are now enjoying a hail storm, crystal peas bouncing off mouldy parapets. Winter is long. Huyck's Mother, old and sick, said "It's nice to have a nice guest since summer is late."

---

1. Lowell's teaching at Harvard began in 1963. His job was "two classes, two days a week [. . .] I'll commute from here [New York] and have the rest of the year to burn" (quoted in Ian Hamilton, *Robert Lowell: A Biography* [1983], pp. 303–304).

2. W. F. ("Huyck") van Leeuwen and Judith Herzberg.

3. Lowell had promised to edit and introduce a Festschrift for Allen Tate, but in March 1970 he feared he had lost the essays that were to be included in it. "Somehow all the Tate material has been lost. I brought it back from Maine in a special carton, then placed it on a shelf in my study bookcase, then back in a carton. When I was away recently, my study was cleaned all too thoroughly by the maid and she threw out the carton"; Lowell to Allen Tate, March 19, 1970. See *The Letters of Robert Lowell*, pp. 530–31 and 778–79. See also William Doreski, *The Years of Our Friendship: Robert Lowell and Allen Tate* (1990), pp. 193–94. The Festschrift, *Allen Tate and His Work: Critical Evaluations*, was edited by Radcliffe Squires and published in 1972.

10. *Robert Lowell to* Mrs. Robert Lowell

[All Souls College, Oxford]

[April 26, 1970]

Dearest Liz—I enclose Professor Edwards's letter[1] so you can see once and for all the college is *Essex* not Sussex—not much difference maybe, except that Essex has Donald Davie's rather special literature department; and demonstrations.[2] However, no one thinks I'll be bothered much. The question is whether you'd like to live in London or somewhere in Essex or Sussex. Cambridge is no farther from London, but apparently long by car, the only way of getting there while London is under an hour by train. The only reason to take the job is to be in England, which I am for.

Oh sell the car. I superstitiously feel no rented car will \roll/ without hitch as our dear old burgundy.[3] You mustn't sell any papers, tho I would be glad of an appraisal. I loathe the idea of their lying forever in the wastes of Stonybrook. Have you been there? Do *papers* include letters, or just my ms.? In any case I would have to have zeroxes.[4] But I don't want them to go to Stonybrook. Maybe, God help us, you'll come on Allen's material when you rummage. His letter was the worst I've ever had from him.

I know how vexing the decisions are, and how toilsome carrying them out. I think I can decide by ten days; then you must decide. Sorry not to have written more, but I had great trouble working Huyck's typewriter, the only vexation in a lovely visit. Nothing much to report.

---

1. Letter written on the verso of an April 2, 1970 letter from P. W. Edwards, chairman of the Department of Literature, University of Essex.

2. Comparative literature department founded by Davie at the University of Essex in 1964. Essex "had been the scene of some of the most fiery student riots of the 1960s" (Ian Hamilton, *Robert Lowell: A Biography*, p. 395). "Essex was, along with the London School of Economics, the place in England where 'revolutionary theatre' was most often played before the delightedly acquiescent television cameras" (Donald Davie, "The Responsibility of the English Department," *ADE Bulletin* 60 [February 1979]: p. 15). After Donald Davie's departure, "The morale of the department went right down, and tempers were very short. Our well-publicized student riots of May, 1968 made things worse, since Davie found himself on one side of the fence and most of his colleagues on the other" (P. W. Edwards to Robert Lowell, April 2, 1970). See also Lowell to Donald Davie, April 27, 1970, *The Letters of Robert Lowell*, p. 533.

3. Lowell: "our old Burgundy Ford station-wagon summer-car, | our fourth, and first not prone to accident" ("Cars, Walking, etc., an Unmailed Letter" 13–14, *The Dolphin*).

4. Thus, for "xeroxes."

All Souls is a club dressed up as a college. Delightful, but \I/ am both too old and too young for it.

Give H. my love and yours,
    Cal

P. S. Edwards (the author of the enclosed) just called; we meet at the National Liberal Club on the 29th. Maybe I'll know then.

11. Elizabeth Hardwick to Robert Lowell[1]

[15 West 67th Street, New York, N.Y.]
Tuesday, April 26 [1970]

Darling: I loved having a little talk with you and can't wait to get your letters, to hear from you by phone on Sunday. The call relieved me, because it had been such a long time and one does mind, does feel cut off and strange.

I see that I have been mixing up Sussex and Essex. Quentin Anderson was in Sussex and although Jack had had the idea it wasn't too successful, Quentin told me he had liked it very much.

I think we should go, if you feel after you've been around awhile anxious to return to England. I worry about details, such as renting our place and getting everything in order here. I'm sure we can find a London place. And I think we should take Nicole, who would I assume want to go. What a help that would be, for all of us, for Harriet. Cal, I feel the best thing about making a change would be the release from Dalton for Harriet. She is \"socially"/ happier this year, but the system is truly not suited to her nature. It is pressured and anxious-making in a peculiar way. Those month-long assignments are grotesque. I have watched Harriet these last years and I find that so far as getting the work done she is much happier with things like math that have daily assignment. She may not always do them well, but they are done the minute she gets home, and then one is free at least from the spectre of undone work. Then you don't learn anything at Dalton, unless you teach yourself. You, otherwise, simply flounder about in work for which you haven't the background, you fake, you blink in

---

1. Crossed with Lowell's letter of the same day.

confusion. . . . She will mind going away a little, but I feel certain in my heart that she will improve as a student. The camp this summer will help in making a new adjustment.

Otherwise, she is beautiful, practicing for the modern dance recital tomorrow night, playing "Blowing in the Wind" and "Donna, Donna" on the guitar,[1] using bad language, washing her hair, lightly dieting.

I have been so occupied with Harriet, making appointments with teachers to see what the trouble [is], trying to get her caught up so that she doesn't have Saturday school—but this last week I did see Bob, the Epsteins, some movies . . .

A grotesque thing is planned for Friday at Yale. Up to 30,000 people descending on New Haven to demonstrate about the Black Panther trial. (This one is Bobby Seale and the murder of a black informer.[2]) Yale hasn't had classes all week, accommodations are being set up. Brewster made a statement last week, saying that he didn't think the Panthers could get a fair trial and seeming to go along with the shut-down of Yale.[3] This seemed to me really suicidal. I agree the Panthers can't get a fair trial, but I can't see that Yale, as a school, can involve itself in this. What are the judges, the lawyers, the jurors to do. Watch the demonstrators and turn off the trial, acquit them? (There is a death and nearly everyone thinks some Panther is responsible— who else?) What is Yale to do if there is violence? I feel the demonstration is o.k., but I don't think the university should be seeming to promote it. I really do feel that if we want the university out of the CIA, the Defense Department, we can't have it involving itself in left-wing things, although individual teachers may do so and students will naturally want to do so. (I've made a mess of expressing what is on my mind. Sounds like a New York Post editorial. Much more complicated in fact.) Horrible rampaging at Harvard recently.[4] God knows over

1. Bob Dylan, "Blowin' in the Wind" (1963); "Donna, Donna," Yiddish song recorded on *Joan Baez* (1960).

2. Nine members of the Black Panthers, including Bobby Seale, were on trial in New Haven for the murder of Alex Rackley. Hardwick refers to Seale in prison in "Militant Nudes," *New York Review of Books*, January 7, 1971.

3. Joseph B. Treaster, "Brewster Doubts Fair Black Trials; Yale President is 'Skeptical' That Revolutionaries Can Obtain Justice in U.S.," *New York Times*, April 25, 1970.

4. Donald Janson, "Damage Estimated at $100,000 After Harvard Riot," *New York Times*, April 17, 1970.

what issue. Still if it weren't for the students there would be no protest anywhere. Worst of times and the best of times.[1]

Otherwise a sense of let-down here, generally. Spring . . . We'll go up to Olga's[2] toward the end of the month.

Darling, I must finish up the papers today. The man is coming tomorrow. I am happy that they will be in some disorderly order, at least. It is important. If anything happened to us this would at least makes[3] things easier. I haven't the time to read letters—thousands and thousands . . . And what a lot of papers, but I will write a list of interesting things. I am not throwing about[4] anything, "girls" or otherwise! As I told you, this is just a getting together. The selling would be very complicated, a long-drawn out thing—so don't worry!

I'll write soon. Sorry for this bureaucratic letter. I have to write some good ones for the "files"![5]

Love, my heart, always,

E.

If we go to England we can go during the year to France, Scotland, Ireland! Portugal!

P.S. I found some things of Allen's—articles, reviews, etc., telephoned him immediately and will send them.[6] I hadn't had your news then of his letter. Poor A. a little baby, in fever, crying in the background.[7] How the years came back! A. and H. are going to England in May.

---

1. "It was the best of times, it was the worst of times" (opening sentence of Charles Dickens's *A Tale of Two Cities* [1859]).

2. Olga and Henry Carlisle's house near Roxbury, Connecticut.

3. Thus, for "make."

4. Thus, for "out."

5. Hardwick: "Was that written for the archives? Who is speaking?" ("Writing a Novel," *New York Review of Books*, October 18, 1973). See also McCarthy to Hardwick, October 12, 1973 (below).

6. Tate acknowledged the return to Lowell on May 12, 1970: "As you must know, Elizabeth found the 'material' and sent it to me. My feelings are, of course, assuaged. What disturbed me was not so much the delay and cancellation of the book (one can live without *that*), as what seemed to me your indifference about the possible duplication of the articles. But now—never mind" (quoted in William Doreski, *The Years of Our Friendship: Robert Lowell and Allen Tate* [1990], p. 195).

7. Tate and his third wife, Helen Heinz Tate, had three children: the twins John Allen Tate (b. 1967) and Michael Paul Tate (1967–1968), and Benjamin Tate (b. 1969). Lowell wrote of the death of Michael Tate in *Father and Sons*, *Notebook 69-1* and *-2*.

12. *Robert Lowell to* Mrs. Robert Lowell

All Souls, Oxford
April 27, 1970

Dearest—

I haven't really noticed the calendar for weeks; now three days roll by in the space of one. In ways you might guess All Souls is too good to be true: windows on the Warden's garden close, roused by the knock of a maid, my gown taken from my back at Commons and rushed up two flights of stairs by my scout to my lodgings, food about as good as Mrs. Meyers's,[1] letters stamped and mailed for me. And anomalies: about twenty fellows occupy buildings as large as Quincy House, down my hall is a cell marked Q. Hogg (the former Conservative Prime Minister). And of course there are people who knew Churchill, Gaitskell and Attlee. And anomalies; I used to think there couldn't be too many, but it's like living on only old frosting. The second sex doesn't exist at All Souls, I feel fourteen again, vacationing at St. Mark's.[2]

I won't hear from Professor Edwards of Essex till tomorrow, but I've talked at length with Isaiah and John Wain. The main trouble seems to be rather disturbing student demonstrations, like Berkeley. On the other hand not living in the town would probably keep me disengaged and untroubled. Davie thinks the department one [of] the best he has ever seen (he chose it). Almost everyone understands how one would want to leave America temporarily. If it looks like we will accept, I think you should fly over for a week or so, when H's school is out and we will decide on where to live. Dear Harriet's school. I am unhappy \about her/ school troubles; they are so like mine at 13, 14 and 15, that I brush them off a little. I had the same record, but almost no one thought me humanly bright. Harriet is very stubbornly and humorously deep—God help her.

Living in a family[3] made it easier to be away from you, but \here/ I miss you both every minute. I may telephone for you to come and get me. But there's so much I like here; it's an education. For what?

All my love,
Cal

---

1. Agnes Meyer.

2. The boarding school in Southborough, Massachusetts, that Lowell attended from 1931–35.

3. At the van Leeuwens' in Amsterdam.

P.S. I've answered almost all my mail on this delightful rented type-writer.

\Cat for Harriet. This drawing is deficient because I have no live model in All Souls'./

13. *Robert Lowell to* Mrs. Robert Lowell

[Postcard: Caravaggio—*David with Goliath's Head*, Borghese Gallery, Rome]

[Oxford]

[Postmarked 30 April 1970 but written on April 29]

Dearest—

I am sorry I was so mute on the phone. At the start two others seemed competing with you[.] The stones here are beginning to soften.[1] Everyone is very kind and casual. All love to you both, I'm off to London.[2]

Cal

14. *Elizabeth Hardwick to Robert Lowell*[3]

[15 West 67th Street, New York, N.Y.]

April 29, 1970

Darling: I got your first letter today and happy was I to receive it. It is now boiling hot here, incredibly noisy outside with drills, dirty . . .

---

1. Ovid: "The stones (who would beleve the thing, but that the time of olde | Reportes it for a stedfast truth?) of nature tough and harde, | Began to warre both soft and smothe: and shortly af-terwarde | To winne therwith a better shape: and as they did encrease, | A mylder nature in them grew, and rudenesse gan to cease" (*Metamorphosis*, trans. Arthur Golding (1567), I: 476–80). See Lowell, "Ovid's *Metamorphoses*," *Collected Prose* (1987).

2. For a party hosted by Faber & Faber, Lowell's London publisher. Ian Hamilton: "On April 30 there was to be a party at Faber and Faber in Lowell's honor" (*Robert Lowell: A Biography*, p. 396). Among the guests was Caroline Blackwood.

3. Crossed with Lowell's postcard of the same day.

and upstairs Mr. Metzdorf, a very nice, very professional man has arrived and will be here several days! Some points I have "unearthed"—literally, since I am filled with dirt and dust and sneezing—which I'll just tumble out lest I forget them later. The papers! (Mr. M. goes to do Eberhart's in June.) As I told you he is paid by Stony Brook. . . . Now, he said, although I am not allowed to quote him, naturally, that speaking from the point of view of the papers, the only place "it fits" is Harvard![1] He said they wouldn't have as much money possibly as other newer places, but perhaps they could get a donor. Mr. Metzdorf, a truly good man, believes collections don't make sense unless they "fit." He said poor Marianne Moore, who recently was reported to have sold her papers to the Rosenbach Foundation, got very little, was talked into the thing by a young man, and worst of all her papers don't "fit" since the Rosenbach is very weak on literature.[2]

I am very happy to have done the work I have these last three weeks since H. and I got back. (I am not quite through yet, of course, and I have done what you would call merely primary or beginning sorting.) We have an astonishing collection here—or rather you have an astonishing collection. Actually, everything has been saved. Early notebooks, a whole box on Lord Weary's Castle,[3] worksheets, etc. Extensive worksheets on every book, not to speak of the unspeakable tons of *Notebook*. Each one in its place. Plays, autobiographical things that became Life Studies.[4] The letters are of course unbelievable. Far more than you realize, more Allen, more Williams, Eliot, Mary McC, Pound, Powers, Delmore, five from Claude-Edmonde Magny, strange long one from Ginsberg, Theodore Roethke (I'm reading from my list), a room full of Peter.[5]

Mr. Metzdorf just called from your studio, saying "Did you know

---

1. Harvard's Houghton Library for rare books and manuscripts.

2. Moore sold her papers to the Rosenbach Museum & Library in December 1968 for $100,000. She was introduced to Clive Driver, its director, by the bookseller Robert Wilson. See Linda Leavell, *Holding On Upside Down: The Life and Work of Marianne Moore* (2013), pp. 383–84.

3. (1946).

4. (1959). For autobiographical prose in addition to "91 Revere Street," see *Collected Prose*.

5. For the catalogue of letters to Lowell from Allen Tate, William Carlos Williams, T. S. Eliot, Mary McCarthy, Ezra Pound, J. F. Powers, Delmore Schwartz, Claude-Edmonde Magny, Allen Ginsberg, Theodore Roethke, and Peter Taylor, among other correspondents, as well as the list of papers and manuscripts, see Patrick K. Miehe, comp., *The Robert Lowell Papers at the Houghton Library, Harvard University: A Guide to the Collection* (1990).

you had two copies of *Land of Unlikeness*![1] Last one sold at Gotham[2] went for $1,000!" I said yes, I had actually put the two aside, listed them, one belonging to [the] library of Elizabeth Hardwick, one addressed to grandmother (Gaga)[3] by R.L.

I'm just writing all this nonsense for the fun of it, just so it won't go by without your knowing of the funny thing this excursion has been.

The most interesting things—outside of the really alarming number of E. Bishop, which are fantastic—are the Santayana and Randall.[4] You have the long letter Randall wrote about L. W. Castle,[5] very detailed, also a carbon of the manuscript with his handwritten notes, very extensive. (Mr. Metzdorf says that in the trade anything more than one is called "extensive!") Also those notes you and Randall made for an anthology, which are most interesting.[6] I haven't read the letters of all these people; there wasn't time to do anything except search for the signatures. Your letters to me,[7] mine to you, yours and mine to Cousin Harriet.[8] All your girl friends. Extensive!

I don't even know whether Mr. M will tell me what evaluation he puts on these things. I'll have to find out today how his work proceeds.

I hope you will decide to dispose of all of this and that we can gradually strip down our belongings a little and be a bit freer and less tied.

Harriet is fine, very tired from "modern dance" rehearsals, and looking forward to the performance tonight. Tomorrow she visits

1. (1944).

2. Gotham Book Mart on West Forty-Seventh Street in Manhattan.

3. Mary Devereux Winslow.

4. George Santayana and Randall Jarrell.

5. Jarrell to Lowell, [January 1946], *Randall Jarrell's Letters*, ed. Mary Jarrell (1985), pp. 144–48. See also Jarrell to Lowell [November 1945], *Randall Jarrell's Letters*, pp. 136–40.

6. "Randall and I are doing an anthology of modern poetry—we want things like fifty Yeats, fifty Hardy etc. that cost like hell"; Lowell to Elizabeth Bishop, Nov. 29th, 1953, *The Letters of Robert Lowell* and *Words in Air*. (The idea for the anthology was abandoned, but the papers are part of the Robert Lowell collection at the Houghton Library.)

7. Hardwick's letters to Lowell from 1949 to 1969 are part of the Houghton's collection. Lowell's letters to Hardwick were kept out of the sale to the Houghton, but Hardwick later sold them to the Harry Ransom Center at the University of Texas at Austin (HRC) in 1991. Most are published in *The Letters of Robert Lowell*.

8. For Lowell's letters to Harriet Patterson Winslow, see *The Letters of Robert Lowell*.

the eye doctor for the second time (once last week) to decide about reading glasses. She is not really in striking need of them, that we know already, but may get some for reading. Friday night we go to Boston and then up to Putney early Saturday morning, and, I hope, back to Boston and home Saturday night. I hope to talk to you on Sunday.

I'm sure your Faber party was exciting and how I wish I could have been there with you. Look around for a living place. Nicole, of course, wild to go with us if it should all work out. We'd have to go in September for Harriet's school. I want to find out the name of some schools, but will just settle for the American School in London[1] probably.

Dearest forgive all foolishness. Love, peace, good health to you,

    Elizabeth

15. Harriet Lowell to Robert Lowell[2]

[New York, N.Y.]
[n.d. April? 1970]

Hi Dad,

How is England? Do you want to teach there next year. I miss you very much. So does Sumner. Sumner is biting my pencil.

Love,
    Harriet

---

1. Housed in Mayfair and Regent's Park until 1971.

2. Handwritten.

16. Elizabeth Hardwick to Robert Lowell

[15 West 67th Street, New York, N. Y.]
May 3, 1970

Dearest: I loved talking to you today. England sounds delightful and I am completely happy about your decision. Harriet seems very agreeable to it, by which I mean there have been no tears or real resentment although she will say she is not sure she wants to go away. But how could she be sure? I think she is relieved. She was very good at Putney over the weekend and had I think a quite successful interview. She wants to go up to Abbot-Andover[1] and I will try it before school is out. So I incline to the belief that this shows a willingness to explore the world. She will miss Lisa the most I think, for they have become good friends. I also think the American School will be more what she has been used to at Dalton. The comprehensive schools are for those who on the 11 plus exams don't get into grammar schools.[2] I don't think the kind of education, the kind of pupil would be right. And also she has done well in recent years on the various standardized tests given at the end of each period. We will have the results of her SSAT's in June[3]—the standard prep school test, which private schools take, and which is required by the American School. She will do well, I imagine . . . I feel sure she only needs to begin to care deeply about a subject to be a very good student. I hope she will make friends and expect she will.

I would so like to be in a nice neighborhood, not a good place in a dreary neighborhood, or something out of the way. I don't want, if possible, to have too much trouble getting about—I hate transportation and being stuck somewhere. I will not live in the equivalent of Eric's place on Riverside Drive.[4] It was so dreary I nearly died. We

---

1. Abbot Academy and Phillips Academy, private boarding schools for girls and boys in Andover, Massachusetts; they merged as Phillips Academy in 1973.

2. "Students completing primary school at age 11 were required to take a series of examinations called the eleven-plus. Results of these tests determined a student's placement in a three-track secondary system. The highest scoring students were admitted to grammar schools and were likely to go on to university studies. The other students attended either modern schools [. . .] or technical schools [. . .] After World War II many 'comprehensive' schools, which combined elements of grammar, modern, and technical schools, were established" (Editors of the Encyclopaedia Britannica, "Grammar school," in *Encyclopaedia Britannica*, July 20, 1998, rev. November 27, 2014; https://www.britannica.com/topic/grammar-school-British-education).

3. Secondary School Admission Test.

4. The Lowells lived in Eric Bentley's apartment at 194 Riverside Drive in 1960–61.

have the money and so please, please don't be hasty. I can come over around June 10th or so. Harriet goes to camp on the 28th of June. I think we should take her and then go on to Maine, not go up to Maine and then come back to Connecticut.

. . . . I am so pleased you liked Essex.

I am telling them tomorrow at Barnard[1] and will tell Dalton also. You should write to Harvard. Otherwise I will take care of everything.

Your "papers" are in the most incredible \fine/ order and they are most interesting. Mr. Metzdorf gave me to understand Stony Brook was thinking of between $50,000 and $100,000. The very inflated prices one hears of aren't true, he says. For instance Susan Thompson said a letter of yours, nothing special, to a poet, she thought maybe Louise Bogan or ~~something~~ someone, was listed by a dealer in the Library Journal for $800. Mr. M. thought that was ridiculous, and said who would buy a letter for that? Anyway we will know his evaluation in a few weeks. I am writing to Harvard just to start that going, since the minute the evaluation (and it includes a complete inventory) comes, Stony Brook will want a reply. . . . All of this is so boring to write you about, even though the papers are most interesting. . . .

I hate going into all these book-keeping and housekeeping and child-raising details, because they leave out the real news of the day. But I have been absolutely overwhelmed with all this and just to be able to [g]o away, to get the taxes, insurances, houses, studies, papers, schools organized, mail answered, things turned down, will take every minute until we go to Maine. It is simply horrendous. The drive back to the airport from Vermont was very tiring and I have been all morning on the State Insurance Fund[2] (Nicole) which is required by law. . . . so it goes, and I can't wait to get away from some of it for a while.

I don't seem to have any mail saved for you. Some books of interest.

Darling, I'm so happy you're having such a nice time. I have to stop to send off some things today and I will write again, more interestingly, very soon. We're both fine and miss you sorely. And we miss you more and more and send our dearest love to you,

E.

---

1. Where Hardwick had been teaching an "Experiments in Writing" course since 1965.
2. New York State Insurance Fund, for workers' compensation insurance coverage.

17. Elizabeth Hardwick to Robert Lowell

[15 West 67th Street, New York, N. Y.]

May 4, 1970

Darling: Can you answer the enclosed?[1] I suppose you could go, if you liked. We will be going by boat, H & I & Nicole & I hope Sumner! Of course there is a lot to do.

Mary McCarthy here for a day from Japan—coming to dinner tonight.

Elated over England! More happy by the minute!

We're going up to Abbot-Andover next Wednesday.

Cal it is very sad and disturbing here. It's a matter of fundamental indifference to human destruction—and everything follows from that. Nixon & Mitchell like to think of thousands of N. Vietnamese killed in a single day, of "sanctuaries" bombed.[2] Every moral distortion seems natural, even good when you have crossed the field[3] and reached the other side without revulsion. What can we hope for?

Bill Alfred just called, they want you to name a winner of The S A Prize[4] for poetry immediately. Send to Warren House[5] immediately.

I love you, miss you. Will write soon.

E.

---

1. Enclosure now missing.

2. On April 30, 1970, the *New York Times* reported on a "Big Allied Sweep Aimed at Enemy's Sanctuaries," and in a televised address that evening, Nixon announced the incursion of American troops into Cambodia, explaining that "North Vietnam has occupied military sanctuaries all along the Cambodian frontier with South Vietnam" ("Transcript of President's Address to the Nation on Military Action in Cambodia," *New York Times*, May 1, 1970).

3. Lowell (translating Pasternak): "To live a life is not to cross a field" ("Hamlet in Russia, A Soliloquy," 35, *Imitations*); quoted in Hardwick, "Writing a Novel," *New York Review of Books*, October 18, 1973, and in *Sleepless Nights*, p. 11.

4. Possibly the Signet Society Medal for Achievement in the Arts (also known as the Signet Associates medal).

5. Location of the Harvard English Department in 1970.

18. *Robert Lowell to* Mrs. Robert Lowell

[All Souls College, Oxford. OX1 4AL]
May 5, 1970

Dearest—

What delightful letters you write! Your little jokes and Mr. Menzies (whatever the papers man is). I've seen the Carolyn McCullough movie,[1] and found it surprisingly good, tho I can follow myself always in print or picture with a certain suspension of disbelief and even of boredom. Everyone feels a strange feminine person, at first unseen and merely a Southern voice, crowns the show, or is the darling of the show. Mary is very good and I think about half the movie is that long wine dinner at Castine. \It's like life, only I'm allowed to talk enormously more./

I have accepted Essex and will receive confirmation in a day or so from the Vice-provost, or what ever the queer anomalous title of the head of the university is.[2] I get 4000 pounds about 8000 dollars, but \much/ more in buying power. A minimum this, but it will be more and go up. Appointment for two years, but I can make it one, or permanent—but then the taxes would be much higher. Apparently for two years it does \not/ have to be taxed (?)

Not [much] news since calling. I gave my first student reading last night, of me and others. In a little while I have dinner with Sir Maurice Bowra, very affectionate, loud and deaf. The Berlins have him for a guest each summer, and have two plans: to persuade him that the Hunta, Junta, is becoming liberal so he can go back to Greece[3] or marry him to Sonia[4] (my idea)[.] But he is very nice and distinguished. People shower me with offprints, nevertheless I've found time to walk under Arnold's Cumner Hills.[5] Everyone is

---

1. *Robert Lowell* (1970), a twenty-five-minute film, dir. Carolyn McCullough, was screened at the National Film Theatre in London.

2. Albert Sloman, Vice-Chancellor of Essex from 1962 to 1987.

3. L. G. Mitchell on Bowra: "The military coup in Greece in 1967 deeply distressed him, and he was happy to allow Wadham [College, Oxford University] to become a base for those trying to restore democracy" (L. G. Mitchell, "Bowra, Sir [Cecil] Maurice [1898–1971]," in *Oxford Dictionary of National Biography* [Oxford University Press, 2004; online ed., May 2005]).

4. Orwell.

5. Cf. Matthew Arnold: "And air-swept lindens yield | Their scent, and rustle down their perfum'd showers | Of bloom on the bent grass where I am laid" (*The Scholar-Gipsy*, 27–30); "the

keeping an ear open for a house or flat for us, if possible on one of the parks.

All love,
Cal

\Dear Harriet, this is me at the end of a dinner. Hope your eyes are forever O.K. Dad (DAD)/

19. Elizabeth Hardwick to Robert Lowell

[15 West 67th Street, New York, N.Y.]
Friday, May 8, 1970

Darling: It has been a week like no \(none?)/ other here. I am sorry you missed it because of the intensity, the peculiarities, the national shifts which one could almost feel like a violent rain storm, letting up, then crashing down again. Tears, radio on all night, new alliances, suddenness of reversals. *They did not get by with it* . . . The killing of those Kent State Students[1] (that's the place I went for the Arts Conference, where Ed McGehee teaches and all the students are in home ec or business or elem. educ.) and the escalation of the war was too much. What a monstrous error, all built on the ugly, selfish vanity of stupid men. Nixon, as you read in the paper, had to call in students, college Presidents, and it ended up with a crazy promise not to speak ill of students any more, to tone down Agnew, to get out of Cambodia in a matter of weeks, to have a volunteer army![2] Secretary Wally Hickel wrote a

---

warm green-muffled Cumner hills" (69); "some lone homestead in the Cumner hills" (101); "And thou hast climb'd the hill | And gain'd the white brow of the Cumner range" (126–27). Cf. Lowell: "We have climbed above the wind to breathe" ("America from Oxford" 14 [*Notebook70*]).

1. On May 4, 1970, the Ohio National Guard opened fire on students demonstrating against the Vietnam War. Four were killed and nine were wounded.

2. See Robert B. Semple, Jr., "Nixon Will Bar Hostile Comments on Students by Agnew and Others; Summons 50 Governors to Meeting," *New York Times*, May 8, 1970.

letter denouncing the tone of the Administration, people are quitting in various posts . . . [1] Now, if the students don't blow it tomorrow in Washington.[2] I am going, as of now, with Harriet, who insists, Barbara and Francine and Cleve Gray. I stood out in the street on Broadway for the funeral of one of the people killed in Ohio and thousands stood in utter silence crying. It was very beautiful. Spock spoke inside; Lindsay and his wife were there and Sen. Goodell.[3] I was wrong about Kingman Brewster . . . Everything worked there, the students seem to understand that they can only lose by being "revolutionary" and one of the interesting things is that the faculties, administration, and students are all united at last. Stephen S.[4] says it is like what happened in Czechoslovakia . . . Now, we will see. But what a strange, strange week it has been.

A few practical details: Carlos Fuentes, wife,[5] baby[6] and Mexican maid will take our apt. from Sept. to June. He is teaching at NYU and doesn't have much money. I thought it would [be] better to let him pay just what we pay $350 a month and of course all their expenses than to try to make another one hundred by renting to someone we don't know. Jack Ludwig's house was destroyed by "nice" tenants he let it to . . . J. Thompson has taken over the car and all the expenses of that. I have told Barnard, Dalton . . . Harriet is delighted and is a "heroine" at school. She has, like the national scene, taken a sudden turn in another direction and is going well in school, is suddenly quite astonishingly more confident, out-going, sure of herself, interested. She's looking forward to camp, serious about the boarding school possibility.

Darling, please, please right now look in the London Phone book for the address of the *American School in London*.

---

1. See Max Frankel, "Hickel, in Note to Nixon, Charges Administration Is Failing Youth; Protests Close over 80 Colleges; Agnew Criticized; Discontent Is Believed Spreading in Ranks of Government," *New York Times*, May 7, 1970.

2. To mark a nationwide student strike, over 100,000 people marched on Washington on May 9, 1970. See Robert D. McFadden, "Students Step up Protests on War; Marches and Strikes Held Amid Some Violence—200 Colleges Closed," *New York Times*, May 9, 1970.

3. Funeral service for Jeffrey Glenn Miller, one of the four students killed at Kent State University, was held in the Riverside Memorial Chapel on Amsterdam Avenue and West Seventy-Sixth Street in Manhattan on May 7, 1970. See Linda Charlton, "Spock Delivers Eulogy: City Closing Its Schools to Honor 4 Slain at Kent," *New York Times*, May 8, 1970.

4. Spender.

5. Rita Macedo.

6. Cecilia Fuentes Macedo (b. 1962).

Loved your letter which just came. I must run for more agitation! I'm longing to see the McCullough film . . . All our love, my darling one . . . We'll write soon. I'm so happy to be going to England! Nicole is going, and that makes four.

Love, love, and oh you are so missed,
Elizabeth

20. *Elizabeth Hardwick to Robert Lowell*

[15 West 67th Street, New York, N.Y.]
May 8, 1970

Darling: International telephone is not very satisfactory. My own voice kept echoing back in my ear and I kept screaming louder as a result. I had the feeling you were in a crowded hall, talking to two people at once. Anyway, I loved talking to you, even if the sense of it was muffled.

I can't believe I heard correctly about 75,000 pounds, which would be about $150,000–200,000. But I assume I misheard you. Maybe you said $75,000. Can you imagine what the mortgage rates would be on that? It would be way out of our range. Also the buying and selling of an expensive house for a 9 months stay is crazy. How would I sell it, except through very expensive brokers. Furnishing even Azuma style[1] would be $5,000 and we would be very uncomfortable and also it takes months to get curtains and things and minimal furnishings. Beds, lamps, tables, desks, rugs, chairs, curtains, dishes, pots and pans, knives and forks, equipment, sheets, towels, sofas, chairs, dining room . . . all very homely and uncomfortable would cost a fortune and take months to assemble. I am sure we can find some kind of furnished house or large flat for the winter.

True we may decide to stay on and we may not. That I can imagine, but we are much too deeply in here to make a decision like that after a few lovely spring-time weeks in England. You may want to come back after the long winter, or you may not . . . Anyway it is a big decision and why make it before we have to?

I thought of coming over for a week or so around June 12th at the

---

1. Inexpensive imports store in New York.

latest. That is "Arch Day,"[1] and since it may be Harriet's last at Dalton I might want to be here with her. She can visit Lisa until we come back about the 20th. I don't particularly want to come to London unless I have to, to find a place for the fall. . . .

This is just to say that I don't myself think it would be a good idea to buy anything. We will really be a bit hard up for ordinary expenses as I see it since neither of us will earn as much, but I think we will manage. . . . Anyway, darling, I will sign off. . . . Much love

Elizabeth

21. Elizabeth Hardwick to Mr. Robert Lowell[2]

[Postcard: Bernini—*The Rape of Proserpina*, Borghese Gallery, Rome]

[New York, N.Y.]

[Postmarked May 9 AM 1970 but written on May 8]

My third letter today

The American School is in Regents Park, very near Jonathan.[3] Remember our dream of H. being near school to make friends, to bring them home! The Spenders are far away—no?

Love, E.

22. Elizabeth Hardwick to Robert Lowell

[15 West 67th Street, New York, N.Y.]

May 14, 1970[4]

Dearest Cal: Everything has been in turmoil here—indeed since we got back over a month ago. The last few weeks have of course been whirling with "crisis"—that paradoxically permanent state. We went to Washington, Harriet, Barbara and I—and heat was paralyzing and brought me nearly to a heat stroke. It was also boring and yet necessary.

---

1. Annual school occasion at Dalton when students walk under an arch to mark passage to the next grade.

2. Handwritten.

3. Miller.

4. But probably written on May 15, 1970 (see reference to the Jackson State College killings below).

We rushed home as soon as we could. There are more student deaths this morning, these in a black college in Mississippi, where again the National Guard simply opened fire on them.[1] All strange, student (white) riots in University of S. Carolina[2] and such places for weeks! I do feel Nixon is breaking up. He is so clearly incompetent, fumbling, and now genuinely bewildered by the overwhelming devastation in front of him—stock market going lower and lower, unemployment rising, Congress balking, petitions, complaints. I think the country became conscious just in the nick of time. You could actually see someone like Nixon fumbling in his wooden, empty way to nuclear weapons against "the enemy" in Hanoi. Too bad Gene McCarthy quit, because the Senate and perhaps the leadership might have been his just now. Of course the war people will put up a terrible fight again, but I do feel Nixon, weak and empty to begin with, will never feel secure again.

But here at home, the sense of crisis never leaves me. I haven't been able to sleep since I got back and don't know why—terrific neurotic anxiety about everything. It just looms up as unmanageable. I think a lot of it is a sort of climacteric[3] at last reached, or hoping to be reached, in my violent love affair with Harriet. We are both anxious to get her settled in some way that will free both of us to be happy with each other again. She's really now—and rightly—only happy with people her own age. (Washington with me was just not it, for her.) We talk late at night, but going in the park together or trying to find something to do on the weekends is awful. She's outgrown that and yet hasn't too many friends and is too often alone and still too young to manage on her own. Also the mounting work and confusion at Dalton really threw me and that was bad for both of us.

She is absolutely thrilled about England, but I am determined not to let her down if possible . . . We can't! This is our last year with her[4] and it must be made good for her. I want to be in the center, near her school, or reasonably near so that she won't go off alone, friendless,

<hr>

1. Two students were killed and twelve injured at Jackson State College when Jackson city and Mississippi state police opened fire on demonstrators on the night of May 14/15, 1970. See Special to *The New York Times*, "Jackson Police Fire on Students," *New York Times*, May 15, 1970.
2. On May 7 and May 11.
3. Lowell: "gored by the climacteric of his want" ("To Speak of Woe That Is in Marriage" 13, *Life Studies* [1959]).
4. That is, if Harriet was to go to a boarding school on the family's return from England.

every day and to endless empty weekends. She will still be too young to go about London alone and to really manage her own life, but she will manage school so much better, naturally, than before. She is much more out-going and less shy suddenly. . . . Now for something really interesting. We went up to Abbot Academy this week. It is right next to Andover, at Andover, Mass. and they have more and more classes and meeting[s] together. I had written for the catalogue and when I got it I sensed something new and exciting. How right I was! It is the most impressive, beautiful and serious school I've ever been near. A new headmaster has transformed it. The girls first of all were in jeans, ponchos, afros, sandals, wearing red armbands (the present student strike insignia). The admissions officer was a young woman of thirty at the most. The place is alive, fewer rules than Putney, grown-up, serious, free and absolutely tingling with excitement. Bushy-haired boys roaming the incredibly beautiful old New England grounds, tall maples everywhere, great flowering bushes . . . Harriet fell in love with it. She made that step toward utter desire and longing and acceptance. I saw it in the enchanted way she looked around, her glowing eyes. I think her interview was very good, but I worry that her falling grades this year, her generally wilted record, her lack of activities will prevent her from getting in. I am going to try to speak to Mr. Casey[1] about being as optimistic as possible, but they aren't really smart. I have just filled out six or so different applications for my students this year saying that any kind of checking in the categories listed on the applications would be meaningless. . . . Well, you can imagine where H. would be on Leadership, Motivation, Participation. . . . And yet there is something so valuable and promising in her, I know it, something that really only needed to fall in love with a place, to get there on her own and find her way. She can pull up next year—up to December—in England and that will help. She means to do so I can tell you!

The "evaluation" . . . ! Mr. Metzdorf turned in his inventory, a complete listing and pricing. Conservative estimate, without Maine material, is $89,000. I have since telephoned Mr. Bond, Director of the Houghton Library and told him of the matter this far. I sent a copy of the inventory and he will perhaps send someone down next week. Also

---

1. Michael Casey, director of the Dalton Middle School.

I will be hearing from Stony Brook immediately and feel very uncertain because they have gone to all this trouble and yet you probably will not want to sell to them. The inventory fee, $420.00, can always be repaid. Oh, dear. I don't regret at all having all this behind us, but I do wish you were here to take over. Under no circumstances should it be left here now in case of fire, etc . . . Needless to say I am not making any decisions. You will do that when you come back and after Harvard has made a proposal. Maybe even Stony Brook won't have the money under present circumstances. . . .

Disappointing never to hear from you, but . . .

I am going up to Olga's next weekend, the 23rd, thank heavens, and probably to Castine, for Memorial Day . . . I wonder if you have any ideas about my coming to London. I can come and you needn't be there if it is inconvenient. I don't quite see that we can arrive in the fall, with a great deal of luggage, cat, all of that and no place to stay . . . On the other hand I am most reluctant to come, expense, etc. but suppose I must unless there is something practical before. Harriet has arranged to go to Lisa's if I do come to London. I might leave here the night of June 12th and come back the 20th or earlier. The 20th the latest. Everything is so unsettled and so many trips to be made, Maine, back to clean out the sanctuaries of accumulation here (horrid taste in that reference!)[1] and then off.

I will enclose a few things. Hope you are having a good time. We do miss you—it is all quite strange and unreal somehow, so hard to imagine what it is like to have you with us . . . And you must be going to Manchester just now, or Leeds or whatever.

Much love,

E.

23. Elizabeth Hardwick to Robert Lowell

[15 West 67th Street, New York, N.Y.]
May 16, 1970

I guess we'll never hear from you. I'm not even sure that you are still planning for us to come to England next year. Thinking that was the

---

1. See Hardwick to Lowell, May 4, 1970, and footnote 2 on page 26.

case I have been working day and night on these tedious school things for Harriet. Dalton has been cancelled, the apt. rented. Now I got an application from the American School in London today. It will be moving in Sept. to the same street Natasha lives on. . . . [1] That still does not mean, if you are planning to bring Harriet to England, that I feel at all interested in buying a house. I just wanted you to know and thought you might tell Natasha, so that she could keep looking in her neighborhood.

> E.

Of course, I don't even know H. will be accepted. So much to be done on all this. School sounds O.K. and she will not find it too hard scholastically, but it sounds also rather unimaginative.

24. *Elizabeth Hardwick to* Mr. Robert Lowell[2]

[Postcard: Raffaello—*Portrait of a Young Woman with the Unicorn*, Borghese Gallery, Rome]

> [New York 23, N. Y.]
> [May 1{6/17?}, 1970]

It has been suggested to me that Harriet *must* have a relationship with her father. She is not a baby & needs the respect [of] a serious letter about you, what you are doing, what next year could mean to her. If you don't want \to write/ me, O.K, but some communication with her would be decent.

---

1. Natasha Spender; the Spenders lived on Loudoun Road in St. John's Wood. The American School in London moved to Loudoun Road and Waverley Place in 1971.
2. Handwritten.

25. *Robert Lowell to* Mrs. Robert Lowell[1]

All Souls College, Oxford
May 17, 1970

Dearest—

I am sorry to write in long hand but my typewriter only runs one way.—Week of galleys:[2] I've been in London getting Grey[3] to help me, then a student, then tomorrow Burton Feldman (the guy who wrote the Dissent review accusing me of being New Left).[4] Next week, Manchester, Leeds & Bristol. All Souls—I can't describe it—not my life, but interesting. Old Boston customs, beautiful countryside, villages. I love it here—England.

The house 3500 pounds. Write the American School care of Natasha. It is near there. I do think we'll want to stay here 2 years.

If you'll trust me and specify I'll get a ~~American~~ house or flat. I'm enamored with the idea of something on a park, but you might rather be more central, whatever that is. I guess I can choose, guided by various experienced hands. ~~here~~.

Oh dear the last week. One boiled with it—then it boiled off. The very name of America disappeared from half the papers. Even at the height, people changed the subject to Oxford gossip. I suppose our hopes for change were heartless because callous with fact. Yet even I thought for a high moment that things might change, and just possibly for the better. How did dear Harriet take Washington? How did you, even staying out of politics is dangerous.

Dear—I miss you so. I've haven't been here or I would have tried to write. I've formally accepted Essex. I've written Harvard.

---

1. Crossed with Hardwick's letters of May 14 and 16, and Hardwick's postcard of May 1[6/7/8].
2. For *Notebook70*; corrections to the galleys in the Farrar, Straus and Giroux files (New York Public Library) are mostly in Lowell's hand and Caroline Blackwood's hand. Lowell was meant to have finished *Notebook70* in January 1970. Ian Hamilton: "[Frank] Bidart stayed in the studio at West 67th Street for a week in January 1970 and 'we worked all day for about a week ⋯ These pages of revisions were very complicated and Farrar Straus wanted cleaner copy, so he asked me to help him put it together'" (Ian Hamilton, *Robert Lowell: A Biography*, p. 392). Lowell added poems between January and June, including "Letter with Poems for a Letter with Poems" [*For Elizabeth Bishop* 3]; "In the Family" [*February and March* 11]; and "Left Out of Vacation" [*February and March* 12]. At least two new poems were written in May–June 1970: "Wall-Mirror" [*Summer* 17], which is dedicated "To Caroline," and "America from Oxford," which is dated May 5, 1970.
3. Gowrie.
4. Review of *Notebook 1967–68* in *Dissent* (November–December 1969).

Soon, we [will] all be together, and find, God willing, more leisure to breathe.[1]

Love,
    Cal

\Harriet ma[r]ching/

26. Elizabeth Hardwick to Robert Lowell[2]

[15 West 67th Street, New York, N.Y.]
May 19, 1970

Dearest one: I'm sorry I was so upset in my latest letters and notes, but it just seemed that you didn't care anything for us, and each day that would go by was so distressing. Do write a real letter to Harriet when you get time. She is, as I said, quite grown-up and quite critical of both of us, as I know from some notes she left on the floor[,] \notes/ that she and Lisa had exchanged. I don't entirely take the psychiatric view that they want you to find these things, but of course I did. She said I nagged her too much and she couldn't wait to be 18 and free forever! She said she never felt she was even your child and if you ever paid any attention to her it was just to pretend she was a baby! Please don't say, ever, that I saw this! Lisa—amazingly—said that she had just lied when she said she was happy at camp last summer, that everyone hated her, but it was better than being at home at least! I know these are passing things, but I have been nagging Harriet all spring and I mean to quit. It had to do

---

1. Lowell: "We have climbed above the wind to breathe" ("America from Oxford" 14, *Notebook70*). Matthew Arnold: "What leisure to grow wise? | Like children bathing on the shore, | Buried a wave beneath, | The second wave succeeds, before | We have had time to breathe" ("Stanzas in Memory of the Author of 'Obermann'" 72–76).

with that damned school work, because I felt so much was riding on these last months. Imagine making such a dumb mistake—interfering, worrying, all of that. I am trying to be better. I do think she adored Abbot and I hope that will come about, because she does want to be away from home. I went over to Dalton and Mr. Casey was wonderful. He says he will really do his best on filling out the recommendation. So, I will simmer down on all this. Our darling girl is really nice, honest, beautiful and brave. She has endured terrible loneliness here in New York with great stoicism, grown up in an essentially dreary household (for a child) with none of that young person's bustle and excitement that brothers and sisters and their life and their friends and their interests can mean, been given a barren summer life, desolate week-ends, often ~~alone~~ friendless. I do want to leave her alone, give her the support and love I can and try to find a better life for her. . . .

I miss you, we both do so terribly. It has been a very hard time for me. But I am eager for England. I don't know what to do about a house. You know there will [be] four of us[1]—it would be nice to have it well-heated and to have books and records, and for it to be near school and more or less central. Now, about the house near Natasha, don't know whether you mean what you wrote—3,500 pounds or 35,000 pounds. Of course 3,500 pounds would be another matter, something to consider. As for anything else I am sure Natasha or whoever would be a good guide and you could trust them and your own feeling if you found something.

Darling I didn't know you were in London working on the galleys of your wonderful book. I send you my love about it, and all of that. Sorry I complained about your not writing.

I have to go. . . . want to get this off. Love, darling

E.

---

1. Lowell, Hardwick, Harriet, and Nicole Gomez.

27. Robert Lowell to Harriet Lowell

All Souls College, Oxford. OX1 4AL
[May 25, 1970]

Dearest Harriet—

I don't know how to describe the England I am hoping you will see and love next fall. Think of a much larger New York State, thousands of green fields everywhere, stone house villages, taxis you can almost stand up in, people having tea sometimes for breakfast and sometimes small fish—a climate neither as cold or as hot as ours, too much rain. At every moment, I feel I am in some part of America, and at every moment some often small detail of accent or architecture tells I am in England. I think you'll find it lovely here, and less rushed. You can run about much more—more parks, fewer, almost no, thugs. The traffic in London is lousy, but nothing like Rome.

Glad you went on the march. I miss you. There are many beautiful walks we could take at Oxford when you ha[ve] the wish. I haven't been inside a single cathedral, except yesterday in Bristol when Mary McCarthy turned up beautifully and turned my mind to higher things. All Souls, where I live at Oxford, is like a boarding school without any students[1]—that is it's filled with a group of about twenty men, ages twenty-five to ninety, doing queer things like writing a four volume history of Sicily, or bookbinding—I mean, they write, of course, about bookbind[ing], they don't bind books.

I miss you. You have a deep look and a clear head at times, clearer than any of us, except Sumner—the most beautiful girl, soon to be more than a girl.

Love to Mother

Cal (Dad)

P.S. I want to hear about Abbot.

---

1. All Souls, a research college for advanced study, has had no undergraduate students since receiving its founding charter in 1438.

28. *Robert Lowell to* Mrs. Robert Lowell

All Souls College, Oxford. OX1 4AL
May 26, 1970

Dearest Lizzie—

What's up? Such boiling messages, all as public as possible on cables and uninclosed postcards.[1] It's chafing to have the wicked, doddering, genial old All Souls' porter take down your stinging cable.[2] It matters not; everything must be pressing you this moment in New York.

Grey and Bingo,[3] but mostly Bingo, are flat or house hunting. She is in touch with three or four agencies. I think something near Regent Park or Hampstead would be best for Harriet. Not too far from the center of the city, yet parkish. I crave not to look out on traffic, even here at Oxford, it goes on like the ocean.

I've just given a reading at Bristol for Christopher Ricks; Grey drove me over and Mary McCarthy took a train from London to arrive with a guide book of Gloucestershire. Lovely day of Bristol strolling and supper in the country.[4]

I've written Harriet a letter without funny pictures and animal jokes.

What else? Bingo thinks it will be perfectly possible \for us/ to find a place without forcing you to come over. They have three. Things can be found, nice places, tho probably their main heat will have to be supplemented with plug-in heaters.

About letters—I can't pour them out, Dear. Every mail alas brings in a new tide, and some must be answered. Today, a nice one from Desmond Harmsworth with a translation of Valéry's Cimetière.[5] Also letters from All Souls seem to arrive four or five days after mailing.

Miss you both—Luv,
Cal

---

1. See postcard of May 1[6/17/18?], but Lowell may be referring to other postcards that are now missing.
2. Now missing.
3. Xandra Bingley, Grey Gowrie's first wife.
4. At Ricks's house in Lasborough, Gloucestershire.
5. Paul Valéry, "Le Cimetière marin," trans. Desmond Harmsworth, *ADAM International Review* 35, nos. 334–36 (1969).

29. Elizabeth Hardwick to Robert Lowell

[15 West 67th Street, New York, N.Y.]

May 27, 1970

Dear Cal: There are so many things I don't know what to do about, but I hesitate to go on with so much to be done. The bare minimum facts I need:

1. Your return date.
2. Your studio. The rent is $160 per month and it is not actually so easy to find someone. Several people I knew thought they might use it, as you have, for writing, but the money is just too much. I am arranging to rent mine to two Juilliard girls, nieces of a friend of Chuck Turner's.[1] I'm not anxious to have the little places used full time, for cooking, etc., but the money is very important—I mean the fact that we won't have to pay the rent. I need to know about your studio because of the difficulty of renting anything in August when we come back, with no one around.
3. Money is very low here at home, home being America and here with us.
4. Facts on Stony Brook: they would want you to decide when you come back. Offer of $100,000 (not payable all at once). They also want to give me if I want it a good, high-paying one day a week job as curator of these papers and also ~~as a person~~ to suggest others to go with them . . . Many more details. You can be pondering it. No word from Harvard, not even an answer to my sending the inventory they asked for. If you don't want to sell them, we'll have to find some sort of storage or vault.
5. I wonder if you can call the American School in London. Ask if Harriet will be able to be placed in the 8th grade. Might speed up her admission. Mrs. Murdoch Admissions dept. The telephone in London is 01-486-4901[.] Also you might ask when school starts. The catalogue says middle of Sept. That would mean leaving here about the 1st of Sept., leaving Maine no later than the 20th. Or at least I would have to leave the 20th of August to get things ready for tenants. Carlos Fuentes wants me to write him in Paris telling him when the apt. will be free.

---

1. Charles Turner.

6. Harriet goes to camp on June 28th. We'll leave her off there, Cornwall, Connecticut and spend the night with Olga. Of course, if you wish.

This is a boring letter. I don't have much gossip. Stanley[1] is well. B. Meredith[2] called with the news that he had heard you were going into exile. Not so much "repression" as to follow in the steps of the Master, TSE.[3] I said the reason was much simpler—you were having a good time in England.

Sorry to have "crowded" you about letters. I have been frantic since we got home from Italy—flying to Boston, renting cars, visiting schools, driving back to airport at the rush hour. Visits to Dalton, letters of recommendation, mail, bills, shopping for camp, dentist appointments (braces off!). . . . Just now I am feeling better. I've been with Harriet almost every night trying to see her through at least some of the ridiculously hard school work, so that the end will not be catastrophic for her future. We've had rather a good time. Now on "Rime of the Ancient Mariner."[4] She's been reading it aloud to me at night. I've been sneaking into Jack Bate[5] by day in order to write—ugh—or help her to write a "precis".

Man coming now to look at my studio. We are going to Castine for the long memorial day weekend, with Lisa. Called Mrs. Wardwell,[6] who is opening up for us now, and she said all was "luuvelly".

Sorry about the questions.

We miss you, love mucho

Harriet isn't home from school yet, but will have your letter waiting for her.

    E.

P.S. Leave dress clothes, shoes, etc. with someone in London.

P.S. Apparently the two girls will take my studio, you suddenly realize there are no dressers, no curtains & you loathe the idea of two people there day & night. But—it's done!

---

1. Kunitz.

2. William Meredith.

3. Two expatriates to Britain: Henry James (the Master) and T. S. Eliot (TSE).

4. By Samuel Taylor Coleridge (1798; revised 1817).

5. W. Jackson Bate, *Coleridge* (1968).

6. Washerwoman.

30. Elizabeth Hardwick to Robert Lowell

[15 West 67th Street, New York, N.Y.]

May 29, 1970

Dear Cal: Just a few words, nothing to be answered. Harvard is interested in your papers and will send someone to look at them soon. When you get here you can then talk to both libraries. This, just so you can be thinking about it. Don't know what their offer will be.

After I wrote I got a letter from [the] American School and they will hold up Harriet's admission until the Dalton grades and SSAT scores arrive. I have written Dalton to hurry up on the grades and to be joyful about Harriet.

In an hour or so going to Dalton to pick up Harriet and Lisa and then off to Castine for a long Memorial Day weekend. Even New York is unbelievably beautiful today, clear, lovely deep green park, rustling in a gentle wind—and Connecticut last weekend was truly as beautiful as England, green, quiet, beautiful white frame houses in the little villages, and ~~feels~~ fields with a mist in the distance. Can't wait to see if the flowering crab we put in last August will have taken hold in the yard at School Street. Hope to have time to unpack your barn and get it more or less in order. Darling Nicole has to have another hernia operation. It opened up! She's all right, but it must be done, and so she will stay here. A friend will nurse her. With Harriet away and Mrs. Wardwell to open and close it won't be too bad for us. Also we will save Nicole's salary for two months and that is a help. She will get unemployment insurance.

It is expensive to go up to Maine, but Harriet is so gay about it, so eager with desire—and Lisa too is ecstatic, both of them making plans to dye T-shirts and all sorts of nonsense. I wouldn't go of course without Lisa or some friend since it would not be so much fun for H. otherwise. Must say I am eager, also, and remember the great joy we had in the deserted little place last year. I sent three huge bags up air freight, to cut down on our problems when we go. But what a chore that was and what a bother if they aren't in Bangor tonight.

There isn't too much news here. Wonderful about your book. I certainly hope something \an apt/ can be found without my coming over. I am disappointed that we weren't lucky enough to find a writer's place with books, records, pictures, etc., and dread the thought of the usual wasteland that most people call home.

Don't bother to write, except a card, with the answers to my last letter: when you're coming back, your studio, etc.

Love from here. Everything very worrying. I think Nixon is going to get by with it all. More and more talk of "tactical" nuclear weapons. Don't see how the N. Vietnamese can hold out in the South short of a World War . . . It is very distressing.

I think I'll go back to Coleridge. Feel "Mariner" breaks down in the end. Harriet visibly disappointed in final stanzas, but I explained they really didn't mean that! And so you can see literary studies are still going on! What a relief to grow up and learn that things mean what you want them to.

Off to Bangor. . . . love, again

Elizabeth

31. *Robert Lowell to* Mrs. Robert Lowell

All Souls College, Oxford. OX1 4AL

May 31, 1970

Dearest Lizzie:

Very Oxford day: in the crowds watching the bumping \(8)/ boat races on the Isis,[1] lunch with Iris Murdoch and her husband,[2] Aline,[3] Lord David Cecil, Father Peter Levi; funeral of Enid Starkie at St. Mary the Virgin; afternoon of reading Warden Sparrow's Shakespeare books[4]—and yesterday an immense walk from Godstow[5] to Oxford over a three mile meadow covered with buttercups, peacocks,[6]

---

1. Annual Eights Week regatta at Oxford.

2. John Bayley.

3. Berlin.

4. From John Sparrow's library of rare editions.

5. Matthew Arnold: "And, above Godstow Bridge, when hay-time's here | In June, and many a scythe in sunshine flames" (*The Scholar-Gipsy*, 91–92). See also Caroline Blackwood to Lowell, no date but summer 1970 (below): "As to the future—God knows—or does he? Please get better Cal. I love you so much[.] Love Godstow Marsh."

6. Lowell: "The cattle has stopped in the Godstow meadow, | a peacock wheels his tail to move the heat, | then pivots, changing to a wicker chair, | tiara of thistle on his shitty bobtail. | It's the feathery May and England, but the heat | is American summer. Two weeks use up three months; | at home, the colleges are closed for summer, | the students march . . . *Brassman* lances Cambodia, | he has lost his pen, the sword folds in his hand like felt—| Is truth ~~here not there~~ \here with you/, if I sleep well, | Bystander? The peacock spins, the Revolution hasn't ~~evolved to~~

cattle and skylarks. Blithe spirit[1]—but no, the skylark's nagging wearied twitter like stars in the sky above us. This I did with Sidney.[2] Brisk telephone conversation with Al Alvarez.

Bingo and I (if that's the right way to phrase it) are putting an ad in the Times for a house or less. We should hear next week. I'm steeling myself to do something about my teeth. There are now five holes I can stick my tongue in; none yet painful.

Not much happens. I read to the Oxford poetry society and answered questions. Much like home, only I was asked to read Marianne Moore. Oxford incredibly beautiful with all the flowers, I think, I've read about in English poetry—a bit too like a college. What's happening? I read as much as I could of the last exhaustive review[3]—Saturday I must do something with Ronnie Dworkin[4] \on the unreal world./[5] I must stop, my ribbon is screwy, high table dinner. I feel when I'm through here I'll receive my sixth form degree.

Love to both,
Cal

---

us \involved us/ . . . a heat that moves | air so estranged and hot I might be home . . . | We have climbed above the wind to breathe ("America from Oxford [May 5, 1970], *Notebook70*). Corrections "here with you" and "involved us" are written in Caroline Blackwood's hand. Cf. "America from Oxford, May 1970" and "Oxford" [*Redcliffe Square* 3 and 4], *The Dolphin*.

1. Percy Bysshe Shelley: "Hail to thee, blithe Spirit!" ("Ode to a Skylark," 1). Cf. also Matthew Arnold: "Thee, at the ferry, Oxford riders blithe, | Returning home on summer nights, have met | [. . .] And leaning backwards in a pensive dream, | And fostering in thy lap a heap of flowers" (*The Scholar-Gipsy*, 71–72 and 76–77).

2. Nolan.

3. The June 4, 1970 issue of *The New York Review of Books*, with articles about Cambodia, Nixon, the Black Panthers' trial in New Haven, and student protests.

4. Dworkin and Lowell discussed Vietnam, civil disobedience, Nixon, and "a host of other matters" at the request of Oxford students. "It was just the two of us together with a large room full of students. I don't remember many details of our conversations, alas, but I do remember being impressed both with Lowell's outrage and his knowledge of politics and events" (Ronald Dworkin, email message to editor, January 25, 2004). Their conversation was published as "Mud in the Blue Stream: Robert Lowell and Ronald Dworkin on America after Cambodia," *Isis* (June 8, 1970).

5. Lowell: "I lean heavily on the rational, but am devoted to unrealism" ("Afterthought," *Notebook70*).

32. *Robert Lowell to* Mrs. Robert Lowell

All Souls College, Oxford

June 1, 1970

Dearest—

A cool gray day. I sit with a big light on to see my type and wait for Charles Monteith to come for midmorning coffee. The weather here is between a good Castine summer and a bad Castine summer. All Souls is elderly and stiff, yet a pleasant seat on the sidelines to watch the storm, house of space and repetition.

To answer your questions. 1. I plan to leave here on the 25th. We have some kind of final round-up here on the 24th, then I want to be ~~here~~ in London to go over my pageproofs with a copy editor. As you can imagine my manuscript invites misreading. Then there's the dentist, which I'd like to put off . . . O forever, but shouldn't. 2. I guess we must rent my studio, tho it would be handy to have for a transAtlantic descent; I guess that would be above our means. 4. 100,000 dollars is unbelievable. How much would go into taxes? I feel numb about storing so much that is mine in the empty and remote Stonington. Like being buried in the Long Island Vets' Cemetery where Bill's mother[1] is. Will they zerox[2] everything for me? Will the public be kept out till long after my death—I mean will everyone be kept out? Certain personal letters will have to be subtracted—many? 5. Today is Sunday, but I'll call the American School early tomorrow. 6. You are right, I like it here. I'm not following in the wake of Ezra Pound.[3] 7. I'll store everything possible in London. Do you plan to come by air or boat? I feel sure we'll stay two years, long enough to let the wonder dull. Did I tell you Mary will be in Maine by midJuly. Poor dear, her essays have three slams out of four.[4] I know how these things hurt. I'll write Harriet this afternoon; she seems happy to move, thank God.

---

1. Mary Bunyan Alfred; Long Island National Cemetery in Farmingdale, New York.
2. Thus, for "xerox."
3. See Hardwick to Lowell, May 27, 1970.
4. Bad or mixed reviews of the English edition of *The Writing on the Wall and Other Literary Essays* (1970), including Francis Hope, "Unfinished Arguments," *New Statesman*, 28 May 1970; Julian Mitchell, "What's Going On," *Guardian*, 28 May 1970; "Making It New," *Times Literary Supplement*, 4 June 1970; and Christopher Ricks, "Mary and Martha," *Listener*, 11 June 1970.

Tell Bob, that I could spend months here never entering a room unilluminated by one of the Mag's contributors or admirers. One in Bristol was waiting for the next issue to know what to think of Cambodia week, breathlessly withholding his own thoughts. Miss \you/, Love,
Cal

33. *Robert Lowell to Harriet Lowell*

All Souls College, Oxford
June 1, 1970

Dear Heart—

I am thinking of you without braces; it's like a graduation—blinding white teeth, and you can talk more rapidly because your jaws will be lighter, but never say as much in quantity as your mother and father.

Today is cool and gray—I hope your trip to Castine on Memorial weekend was brighter, but what does it matter, it is all weather, all giving us something different to do. I am having lunch with someone really named Sir Isaiah Berlin, whom you have met and probably forgotten. The college where I am living is called All Souls, and they are very old souls, like Grace Stone you met in Rome, only all are men. A large maid gets them up for breakfast.

I don't know all about the American School. It's in the suburbs, half-country and much more green and airy than Dalton. I expect it is easier. Tomorrow I'll talk to the admission dean, and learn more. If we are lucky, we'll live somewhere nearby—this typewriter ribbon is the worst I've ever used, just good enough not to change! Then you wouldn't need a bus and could visit your friends at will. It's much safer here for little girls and for everyone.

I don't know how to tell you about England—the countryside is somewhat like Connecticut and what you drove through going to Putney and Abbot. Only everything is farmed—hedges, streams, trees, gardens. London is a little like a big Boston, but not very and greener. Love, Dear—I must leave space for a picture but of what? In our corridor is a Quintin Hogg, ex-member of the Conservative cabinet. When he comes in he snortles like a seal, and slams his door so that the house shakes. When he was out, another man, Lord Lever, took a hammer, tacks, strips of felt and fixed Hogg's \door/ so that it slammed without making a sound.[1]

\tack/   Dad
\hammer/ \felt/

34. *Robert Lowell to* Mrs. Robert Lowell

All Souls College, Oxford

June 2, 1970

Dearest Lizzie:

I am off to London to do a translation reading at something called ICA.[2] Fairly intelligent audiences I'm told. Then I go for a few days with Grey to the Lake Country, mostly to see the Wordsworth scene but also to call on one of Grey's idols, Basil Bunting. Ford[3] used to suggest that Pound must have made up such a name, but he is actually quite good, and it helps to know someone in a region.

I'll be in London in a few hours and will check on Harriet's school. Also will keep in touch with Bingo about the flat. There'[ll] be no trouble I'm sure.

I've been through "eights" week here, and am glad to be off.

Love to you both,

Cal

\Hope Maine was lovely./

---

1. Sir Jeremy Lever: "I think that I must indeed be the 'Lord Lever' to whom Robert Lowell referred despite my lack then, as now, of the title. Perhaps the confusion arose because there was at the time a Labour Party Life Peer who was a Lord Lever. Quintin Hogg, Lord Hailsham as he became, had the bedroom next to mine in the attic of the Warden's Lodgings [. . .] When he retired for the night, he would come into his bedroom in the attic and I would then hear a loud thump when he would throw across the room one of the two heavy boots that he wore; the worst outcome was then waiting for the second thump which sometimes inexplicably did not materialize. Because he had held the Ministerial office of Lord Privy Seal in 1959–1960, I sometimes joked about my neighbouring seal (an animal that barks loudly). However, I was sufficiently in awe of the great man that I would never have taken countermeasures of any description. I guess that Robert Lowell must have heard me joking about my seal neighbour and embroidered the tale" (email message to editor, October 7, 2014).
2. On June 3, 1970, at the Institute of Contemporary Arts.
3. Ford Madox Ford.

35. *Robert Lowell to* Mrs. Robert Lowell

[Telegram]

[London]
[n.d. May 1970]

MRS ROBERT LOWELL 15 WEST67THSTREET
NEWYORKCITY
SEND SCHOOL RECORDS WHN YOU CAN HARRIET ALMOST
CERTAINLY ACCEPTED
      CAL

36. *Elizabeth Hardwick to Robert Lowell*[1]

[15 West 67th Street, New York, N.Y.]
June 3, 1970

Dearest Cal: I am crushed by the news that you won't be coming back until nearly the end of June. I somehow thought you would [be] coming home any day now.

Thanks for the cable about the school. Yes, I know they are waiting for the grades, but Dalton has been late getting out this year.

The manuscript expert is coming from Harvard today. I guess he will go back and report and they will make you an offer, I hope. Yes, the thought of Stony Brook is grey. But, I suppose all this will have to be put aside. As I see it the negotiations, the study, by you, of the material, the final statement by you of what is to be done with various things, will take a good while. Then lawyers conferences, tax accountant conferences \the money not all at once/. It is quite an undertaking. I will ask about copying at Harvard, but of course everything can't be copied, nor would you wish it. I will have to see about how the files can be put—where—while we are gone? In any case, I know that I am relieved the manuscript and letters have at last been ordered. Only you or I could have done it, identified, pointed out significance, etc. So, that is behind us at least.

We are broke. The income tax this year was enormous. The withholding first quarter is now due and paid, rent and maintenance goes

---

1. Crossed with Lowell's letter of June 2, 1970.

on, Harriet's camp, expenses. I wonder if how you are holding out. Perhaps you have some royalties at Faber you can use to get your ticket back.

Very disappointing that an ad will have to go in The Times. Incredible running down of answers, etc. I had hoped a writer or painter or someone would turn up, leaving. You see, we are very well set up here with the work of 12 years in our arrangements. It will be hard without books, records, pictures, studios, dishes, space. I want you to stay as long as you like, but please don't make the arrangement for more than one year now. There is all this damned space here to rent again, all the things to be looked after.

I will see about the studio, yours I mean, right away. First an ad in the review,[1] but I fear it will be out too late to help. Don't know just what H. and I will do between now and the time you get back. Maine was glorious. I have your studio ready, all is ready, and it was exhausting but fun. The political situation changes so frequently, slightly this way, slightly that—not much point going into it.

I worry about your teeth.

Much love. I don't know where we will be when you finally get back, but I'll let you know. I'll write Stony Brook and Harvard and say you will be later than I thought. I had planned to go over by boat around Sept. 1st. People will be wanting the apartments and, as I wrote you, that will mean coming back from Maine on August 20th at the latest. Just now I am trying to get together the tax things I have to take with us. . . .

All of this is very tedious, I realize, and it is boring to write about, worse to read. So I'll just carry on as best I can. Love again

E.

---

1. *New York Review of Books.*

37. Elizabeth Hardwick to Robert Lowell

[15 West 67th Street, New York, N.Y.]
June 3, 1970

2nd letter today

Darling: Harvard is going to make an offer of $90,000! Can be paid in 10,000 and 15,000 lumps! Or however you like it. This is just for what you have to sell now. Later work will be bought as you collect it! Isn't this wonderful? They have just finished buying Cummings.

I'm so happy. I haven't done a lick of work since I got back to N.Y., but I have made $90,000 for you. That will help us next year over the hump of nothingness described in my letter!

Must stop immediately. Love. . . . You will be very interested to look over all of this when you get back and to make your decision.

In haste, with love,

E.

They will copy things as you need them, all very nice. Librarian ecstatic, thinks the material is so interesting and important. It is interesting and alas there is never anyone to write well about anyone. Sending off in haste, after calling Oxford to learn you are gone until Sunday! Have a good time wherever you are. Italian tv just called to ask for a statement about Ungaretti, on his death.[1]

If you felt you could make a basic decision now before your return, at least I could get Stony Brook off the fire. Harvard doesn't seem to care about restrictions, and even though the offer is less it is so much more in tune with the other ~~work~~ writers they have, and you can go there yourself to use any of your papers.

\Shall we keep your studio? The rent for the 9 months Sept–June would be

160

9

———

1,440-/

---

1. Ungaretti died on June 1, 1970. See Lowell's translations of Ungaretti, including "You Knocked Yourself Out," *Imitations*, and "Returning," *For the Union Dead*.

If you do decide to stay longer, you can rent it then, or if someone comes up really suitable, or a truly reliable visitor, could be done now. I could leave the key and terms with Barbara and if some writer needed it, and could pay, something like Naipaul did . . . [1] we would come out a little better.

Love,
Elizabeth

38. Elizabeth Hardwick to Robert Lowell[2]

[Card: Wm. J. Bennett—South Street from Maiden Lane, New York, ca. 1828, Aquatint][3]

[15 West 67th Street, New York, N.Y.]

[June 3, 1970]

I misread your letter this morning to say you weren't coming home until June 25th. I was distressed & surprised. Now I have read it over & I learn you are *only going to London on the 25th*!

I feel I have to write this, after my two other letters today, to say I am very much hurt & deeply upset. I will just have to think about it for a while.

Elizabeth

39. Frank Bidart to Robert Lowell

383 Harvard St., Apt. 508, Cambridge, Mass.

June 4, 1970

Dear Cal,

I just heard you won't be back this fall. Cambridge will be a forlorn place without you, but I'm glad England has worked out so well. Per-

---

1. Patrick French: "Keen to save dollars, he [Naipaul] jumped at the opportunity when the manic poet Robert Lowell ('the only American who has read my work') and his wife the critic Elizabeth Hardwick offered to lend him their book-lined studio apartment on West 67th Street while they were away on a trip to Israel and Europe [in 1969]" (*The World Is What It Is: The Authorized Biography of V. S. Naipaul* [2008], p. 274).

2. Handwritten.

3. On verso, in Lowell's hand, "[Isaiah] Berlin 6511[.]"

haps this forms the only natural conclusion to writing *Notebook*. Even if sections do keep coming, their character will change . . . Perhaps this will provide the new subject, new departure, you mentioned this spring. But you'll be missed!—

I have some news. Several weeks ago I sent my poems[1] to Richard Howard at "New American Review," and I just got a letter saying that he wants to publish them as a book. He's directing a new poetry series for Braziller, and wants me to be third on his list. I said in the original covering letter that there was a possibility Farrar, Straus may do them, and he understands this. In any case, it was incredibly encouraging to find someone so enthusiastic about the volume (which is still not quite finished)—he's the first person not a friend who has reacted so decisively, unequivocally. Of course, I'd rather have it published by Giroux.

Perhaps we'll see each other or talk this summer (are you going to Maine?), we can discuss what I should do about the offer. I don't think Howard has to know right away.

I'm anxious to see anything new you've written, and the final revisions of *Notebook*.

Give my best to the Gowries.

Bill Alfred says that Elizabeth Bishop may come next fall, which is fantastic, but won't make up for . . . Well, if you see an aerial photograph of Cambridge, and it has a great big hole in the center, know that it's because Mr. Robert Lowell is no longer at Quincy House.[2]

Best,
Frank

40. *Elizabeth Hardwick to Robert Lowell*

[15 West 67th Street, New York, N.Y.]
Thursday, June 5, 1970

Cal, dearest: Hate to load you down with all this mail from me, but there is no other way with so many things to be discussed, changes of

---

1. *Golden State* (1973).
2. Lowell: "'Your student wrote me, if he took a plane | past Harvard, at any angle, at any height, | he'd see a person missing, *Mr. Robert Lowell*'" ("In the Mail" 1–3, *The Dolphin*); see footnote 2 on page 293. Cf. Hardwick to Lowell, OCT 16 PM 5.13 [1970]; Lowell to Harriet Lowell [April 2, 1972]; and Hardwick to Lowell [no date summer 1972].

plans and feelings from the last letter. Actually a complete exchange of one letter, one answer, wait for an answer is almost ten days. I called, as I told you in letter two, but they said you were away for a week.

I am coming to London on June 29th, BOAC flight 594 arriving there at 9:50.P.M. I will somehow get Harriet up to her camp on the 28th and drive back and then take off the next morning. I have nothing else to do; it is very hot and dreary here and lonely. I will not under any circumstances, pack up, drive all the way to Maine, unload and settle, drive Harriet way back to Connecticut, and then drive back to Maine again. It is not possible and I never considered Castine a happy and possible way of life for me alone. I've had nightmare trips all spring, driving, managing alone. Actually, my one worry is what on earth Harriet and I will do for the more than two weeks she has here before camp. I hope she's invited somewhere, but otherwise it will be unbearable. It is full summer here. She also does not want a great trek to Maine and back with just us alone and feels it is too hard on me. If you were here and we all went together, stopping to see Aunt Sarah,[1] it would be different.

Can you borrow a flat for us, so that we can save money while I'm there. Then I can apt. hunt, visit the School, even bring over a few things. When we will be coming back? I want Harriet to know at camp and also to know where we ~~are~~ \will be, for emergencies/. Also, I really do, honey, need some ideas about the papers. We are flat broke and I will hope to write something for Vogue, whom I am calling this morning, to pay for the air trip.

Much love, dearest. . . . Also, shouldn't I try to get a prescription from Dr. Platman [f]or pills.[2] Also, here is the name of a dentist, from Harriet's dentist. (Can't find it right now, but will send it in an envelope when I do.)

Dear heart, so sorry to bother you. Can't wait to see you. It has been very lonely for both of us and we miss you sorely. I'm still sorry you aren't coming back before Harriet goes to camp, but I know you would if you could. Anyway I am so happy that I'll be seeing you just after she has gone because there wouldn't be any point in being here after that.

---

1. Sarah Winslow Cotting, Lowell's maternal aunt.
2. Lithium.

I won't write so much again. Just if something you need to know comes up.

Love, always
    Elizabeth

P.S. I'm doing a 600 word review of Francine's book[1] which was slaughtered by a rat Jesuit in the NYTimes,[2] and a 600 word of Mary's.[3] This will more than pay for my trip. For Vogue. Of no importance, but still they do have a lot of short critical things in the mag. and it will be a chance to say a few good words on both—and give me the means to come to see you! Must get to work. Much love, darling.

41. *Robert Lowell to* Mrs. Robert Lowell

All Souls College, Oxford
June 14, 1970

Dearest Lizzie:

Lovely to hear your voice, clear as tho it were across the yard \quad/. I'll reserve passage on the 24th or possibly the 23rd. This is a day or two later than I said on the phone. The reason is I ~~plan~~ \hope/ to go to Poland with Blair next Tuesday, or Wednesday. He is going to see his friend,[4] now separated from her husband. This is a stand-in trip for our age-old "ancestral" tour of Scotland.

I am going this morning to see Huyck and Judith at the Wains'.[5] Everyone I know knows someone else I know fortunately. Then on to Cambridge driven by Omar[6] to see D. P.[7] Not too much fun really, but something decided more than a month ago, and a debt to old times.

Wonderful drive through Cumberland, Lancashire and Northumberland and a visit to Basil Bunting. A Wordsworth fan and a Pound

---

1. Hardwick, *"Divine Disobedience,* 'Important Record'" (review of Francine du Plessix Gray's *Divine Disobedience*), *Vogue*, August 1, 1970.
2. Andrew M. Greeley, "The Newest Heroes in Catholicism-as-entertainment," *New York Times Book Review*, May 31, 1970.
3. Hardwick, "Books: *The Writing on the Wall*," *Vogue*, September 1, 1970.
4. Joanna Rostropowicz.
5. John Wain and Eirian Mary James.
6. Omar Pound, son of Dorothy and Ezra Pound.
7. Dorothy Pound.

disciple. (This trip to Europe seems to circle around Pound[.]) I told you about Empson, "I now find the glare at the end of the tunnel to the afterlife (his retirement) oppressive."[1] And "the afterlife is now assuming almost Egyptian proportions." About art critics writing catalogues, "a steady iron-hard jet of absolutely total nonsense."[2]

I think my study better be rented. We can't pay over a thousand dollars for storage. I trust Harvard will make out a catalogue so I can get hold of (know) what I have or want. I wonder if there are old lost poems, salvageable? Perhaps not.

You've had a terribly chafing stint of schools, Lowell "material." ~~Inavertently~~ \Tastelessly/ I used this word in my first letter to Allen, and each letter of his sends it back to me in quotes.[3] I wonder if colleges will have to buy this kind of stuff by weight rather than interest. It seems horrible to think of warehouses stuffed with papers and papers. When machines do all, pedants can spend lifetimes listing and living variants. Or will computers do this too?

I guess I've taken it easy. This is almost the first time since lithium[4] that I~~'ve~~ \am/ mostly unemployed—take leisure to be wise.[5] I'm not ~~quite~~ what I was when one groping and reaching summer I began Notebook.

Give all my love to Harriet, tell her I am bringing you both nice but modest presents.

Love from your soul among the "Souls,"
    Cal

---

1. Lowell: "if we see a light at the end of the tunnel, | it's the light of an oncoming train" ("Since 1939" 45–46, *Day by Day* [1973]).

2. William Empson: "A steady iron-hard jet of absolutely total nonsense, as if under great pressure from a hose, and recalling among human utterances only the speech of Lucky in *Waiting For Godot*" ("Rhythm and Imagery in English Poetry," *British Journal of Aesthetics* 2, no. 1 [January 1962], reprinted in William Empson, *Argufying: Essays on Literature and Culture* [1987], p. 148).

3. See, for example, Tate's letter of May 12, 1970, quoted above in footnote 5 on page 18.

4. Ian Hamilton: Lowell's lithium treatment "seems to have begun shortly after his discharge from McLean's in the spring of 1967" (*Robert Lowell: A Biography*, p. 359).

5. Ecclesiasticus: "The wisdom of a learned man cometh by opportunity of leisure: and he that hath little business shall become wise" (38:24); Samuel Johnson: "Deign on the passing World to turn thine Eyes, | And pause awhile from Letters to be wise" ("The Vanity of Human Wishes," 158–59). See also Matthew Arnold, "Stanzas in Memory of the Author of 'Obermann,'" 71–76, quoted in footnote 1 on page 37 (Lowell to Hardwick, May 17, 1970).

42. Robert Lowell to Mrs. Robert Lowell

[Telegram]

[Maidstone, Kent][1]

[Received 1970 | June 20—Sat | 10:40-P.M.][2]

MRS ROBERT LOWELL 15 WEST67STREET
NEWYORKCITY
PERSONAL DIFFICULTIES MAKE TRIP TO NEWYORK IMPOSSIBLE
RIGHT AWAY LOVE CAL

43. Elizabeth Hardwick to Robert Lowell

[15 West 67th Street, New York, N.Y.]

June 23, 1970

Dear Cal: I have no idea where you are, but I will just send this off to Faber and if it doesn't reach you it doesn't matter too much. I got your cable when I came home after a week-end. When I saw it lying there on the floor I knew what it would say.

I will take Harriet to camp this Sunday. She has had periods of saying she didn't want to go and I hate to have her away because I can hardly bear it but I know it is best for her and I will just count the days until she comes back to me. I will spend the night with Olga after taking Harriet and then back here and face the decision of what to do with myself.

I must say I feel rather like a widow. Your things, you, your life, your family, your clothes, your work, your old shoes, ties, winter coats, books, everything seems sitting about at every turn. Thinking you were coming back I had your typewriter over-hauled and took it up to your study for you and it was just as if you were there[,] all your little objects, papers, books, your desk just as you left it, your bed. I suppose just as you left it isn't accurate since it is a lot cleaner waiting to be dirtied "creatively." And I was spraying mothballs on your clothes, and looking about our living room, your family, your past everywhere. I feel you have totally forgotten us as with an amnesia, but we have not forgotten you.

---

1. Near Blackwood's country house, Milgate Park.
2. In Hardwick's hand.

I am sending this review by Cathy Spivack[1]—very sweet, if not interesting.

I sit here answering your mail, saying "my husband is away and will be so indefinitely. I do not think he would like to write on his concept of style, since this isn't exactly what he likes to do, but I will send along your kind letter." And so it goes. Anthologies pile up, telephones ring.

I don't know why I am writing this. There are so many absolutely pressing practical problems with Harriet and me. I have written them all to you I think and have no answer or even mention of them and so I suppose it would just be vexing to go into it all. And these are of course worrying but not my real grief and anxiety. Soon after the man was here from Harvard I wrote that I thought their offer would be agreeable to you, but you would get in touch with them when you came back. I haven't written Stony Brook, but I guess I will. I cannot proceed on my own with Harvard and they would not like it, nor can it be done in a casual way. The restrictions would need to be quite specific and thought out, for your own ease I think. Also the material—(ugh!) is very interesting and you will want to see it to know what you want to have copied and so you will certainly need to come back here one of these days. \Strange old manuscripts you will be interested in./

Did I tell you I sent Allen a second batch and I think now I have found one of his books he sent you.[2] I will send that to Allen—it is not a poetry book, exactly. I saw it a week or so ago and forgot about it and ~~will wait~~ yet I felt it was his not yours.

The end of Dalton was somehow just a catastrophe for our beautiful girl. She was so happy to say goodbye to it and to feel something new and hopeful ahead of her. If it is ahead of her. I have had to raise her and so I couldn't come to England with you as I so wanted to and to share all of that. And perhaps you would have kept your love for us if we hadn't been separated.

---

1. Kathleen Spivack, "In the Midst of Life: *Notebook 1967–68* by Robert Lowell," *Poetry*, June 1970.

2. Allen Tate, *The Hovering Fly and Other Essays* (1949); "Dear Elizabeth, Thank you for sending *The Hovering Fly*. I believe that completes the list of items, and I am most grateful" (Tate to Hardwick, July 17, 1970, HRC).

I will do the best I can. This is just to send undying love to you, a great sense of loss—from me and from your daughter.

Elizabeth

P.S. Dr. Annie tells me Elizabeth has signed a contract to do poetry reviews for a year for the New Yorker.[1] Isn't that marvelous? For poetry, if not for her,—a dog's life it is. But there is no one saying anything about poetry here and so I feel good about it. I hope she can review your new Notebook and ~~will write~~ give it the attention it truly deserves. One wants serious criticism, not just vague praise. When I was organizing your life's accumulation I read very few things except Randall and I feel more and more what a great man he was. Curiously, with his death something in the culture came to an end, something I can't define beyond just the obvious rare conjunction of great powers of mind and utter devotion to literature. But that isn't good enough. I feel, reading the English press, that they are even worse off than we are, since they have a longer tradition. No, they are not worse, but reviews, the weekly and monthly cultural scene is just as mediocre. Of course the old people are beautiful, here and there too. But I feel as if they were all dead, and also came out of a world never to be had again, like that world of housemaids downstairs. (It is not the maids I mean but the lost cultural depth.) Did it come from some bustling downstairs?

There are only two people in England I care to have my relationship with preserved: Sidney and Isaiah.[2] Please tell them how much I love them. I would grieve to lose their friendship and their company when they come here. Jonathan of course, but that's a little different.

We have a Demo primary today. Rather tedious examples of an

---

1. Bishop to Dr. Anny Baumann: "I think I'm taking on the job of poetry reviewing for *The New Yorker*—something I'd really like to do. It is just 4 or 6 times a year—and one can write about what one wants to, I gather, so I think I could do it all right, and it would be a small source of 'security' (much needed)" (Bishop to Anny Baumann, March 7, 1970, *One Art: Letters*, ed. Robert Giroux [1994], pp. 519–20). Bishop abandoned the idea; see *Elizabeth Bishop and* The New Yorker: *The Complete Correspondence*, ed. Joelle Biele (2011), pp. xl–xli, 306, and 314.
2. Isaiah Berlin: "I think the cleverest woman I ever met is [. . .] Elizabeth Hardwick. Elizabeth Hardwick has a feminine mind. Much more bitchy than Mary [McCarthy]'s, but sharper and more original" (Frances Kiernan, *Seeing Mary Plain: A Life of Mary McCarthy* [2000], p. 269).

uninspired political paralysis. But it will [be] fun to listen to some of the returns with friends tonight.

The recession here (depression) is truly frightening. The stock market is very low, gains a bit, goes back down. Penn Central railroad went into bankruptcy, leaving a lot of banks who had loaned the road millions in a very shaky condition.[1] I have no money at all and am going today to Harriet's savings account so that she can pay for her camp. I got 3,000 a week or so [ago] from Bob Giroux for the June 15th income tax installment, which just for the federal came to 2,800. The State and city together were over 2,000—so we have just paid out $5,000. I really need another 3,000 more immediately for back bills, like the going to Boston for schools, Maine, renting cars, the quarterly maintenance of over 1,000 that comes due this month. Bills in Maine. After I pay my 3,000 I need 3,000 more for from now to September. Then next year if you are leaving us or if I am leaving you I will have to have $20,000. I can't get by on less that first year and cannot even pay the taxes on that.[2] Later it would be of course be less.

I hate like anything to write these degrading money things to you. It seems to cancel out all of the love I want to send. But it isn't really true and so read it in the spirit simply of what we have built together, that we have had to ~~leave,~~ live, had to pay rent, had to spend money for Harriet, for phones, for getting places. I will of course try to economize and actually have spent almost nothing except for real household expenses. But they are awful. Nicole is in the hospital today after her second hernia. The insurance will pay her salary this summer, thank heavens. Everything is so damned expensive.

I am trying to write some little things and then hopefully this summer and next fall something more substantial.

As I said I really do not expect this letter to reach you and if it does God knows what will have happened by then. But here it is, with my love if you want it.

E.

---

1. Linda Charlton, "Penn Central Is Granted Authority to Reorganize under Bankruptcy Laws; No Cut in Service; Step Blocks Collection of $75 Million in Debt Due by End of Month," *New York Times*, June 22, 1970.

2. Lowell: "We can't swing New York on less than thirty thousand" ("Transatlantic Call" 1, "The Dolphin" manuscript); *"We can't swing New York on Harry Truman incomes—"* ("During a Transatlantic Call" 1, *The Dolphin*).

Another postscript . . . a letter just came from Sister B. Quinn which I will answer, saying My husband is away, etc. I feel like Edmund's card.[1] It, the letter, wasn't anything, except about some young man's interest in Prometheus.[2] Peter Farb's novel, Yankee Doodle,[3] . . . oh, dear. A bill for $350.00 from last year's income tax firm, very reasonable actually, and $125 for three months social security for Nicole or something. And insurance. . . . There are many good things, too, many days that are fun and even pretty and I am feeling pretty good. So . . . I send this off, wanting to wait a little, but for what?

I did say something funny the other day, which I knew you would never repeat because it was just that the opportunity came and I couldn't resist. I spoke of Blair Clark as a "tower of weakness."[4]

Dearest, dearest love,
    Elizabeth

44. Elizabeth Hardwick to Robert Lowell

[15 West 67th Street, New York, N.Y.]
June 23, 1970

Darling: I sent off a letter in the blue to Faber to be forwarded. I want to add this touching conversation I had with Harriet, who has been in

---

1. Engraved cards that read: "EDMUND WILSON REGRETS THAT IT IS IMPOSSIBLE FOR HIM TO: READ MANUSCRIPTS, WRITE ARTICLES OR BOOKS TO ORDER, WRITE FOREWORDS OR INTRODUCTIONS, MAKE STATEMENTS FOR PUBLICITY PURPOSES, DO ANY KIND OF EDITORIAL WORK, JUDGE LITERARY CONTESTS, GIVE INTERVIEWS, CONDUCT EDUCATIONAL COURSES, DELIVER LECTURES, GIVE TALKS OR MAKE SPEECHES, BROADCAST OR APPEAR ON TELEVISION, TAKE PART IN WRITERS' CONGRESSES, ANSWER QUESTIONNAIRES, CONTRIBUTE TO OR TAKE PART IN SYMPOSIUMS OR 'PANELS' OF ANY KIND, CONTRIBUTE MANUSCRIPTS FOR SALES, DONATE COPIES OF HIS BOOKS TO LIBRARIES, AUTOGRAPH BOOKS FOR STRANGERS, ALLOW HIS NAME TO BE USED ON LETTERHEADS, SUPPLY PERSONAL INFORMATION ABOUT HIMSELF, SUPPLY PHOTOGRAPHS OF HIMSELF, SUPPLY OPINIONS ON LITERARY OR OTHER SUBJECTS." See Jeffrey Meyers, *Edmund Wilson: A Biography* (2003), pp. 248–49; Lewis M. Dabney, *Edmund Wilson: A Life in Literature* (2005), p. 448.
2. Lowell, *Prometheus Bound* (1969).
3. (1970).
4. Nancy Schoenberger: "Blair Clark is a tall Boston aristocrat" (*Dangerous Muse: The Life of Lady Caroline Blackwood* [2001], p. 211).

Stockbridge with the Wagers since Friday and will now even not be coming home until tomorrow. She said she missed me, then sweet little voice:

"What is the news of Daddy?"

"Well, he sent a cable saying he couldn't come this week because of work. But I think he will be here next week at the latest."

"The minute he comes, after he is rested, drive up here to Connecticut to get me."

"Yes, darling. We'll go out for a picnic."

"No. I have to be with you, with Daddy, a couple of days."

So my darling, I am expecting you soon. Next week. There are just too many things to be settled. I don't know where you are. This isn't like you or anyone, really. I long to see you and will wait here in New York for the word. There is so much to be done.

Don't forget us! There was a life here and there still is, and love and we need you and need some relief from our troubling uncertainties.

Dearest love,
Elizabeth

Harriet needs you. \She is deeply worried as am I./

45. Robert Giroux to Charles Monteith

[Telegram]

[New York, N.Y.]
June 23, 1970

MONTEITH

FABBAF

LONDON W1

ELIZABETH HARRIET DISTURBED CALS NONARRIVAL NEW YORK. COULD YOU DISCREETLY INQUIRE AND CABLE ME WHEN HE WILL BE BRINGING BACK THE PAGE PROOFS. GRATEFULLY
Giroux
Farrarcomp

46. Charles Monteith to Robert Giroux

[Telegram]

[London]
[n.d. June 1970]

ROBERT GIROUX

FARRARCOMP

NEWYORK

HAVE JUST SPOKEN CAL STOP PROMISED HE WOULD RING ELIZ-
ABETH STRAIGHT AWAY STOP SAYS HE'S STAYING HERE FOR THE
SUMMER

CHARLES MONTEITH

47. Elizabeth Hardwick to Mary McCarthy

[15 West 67th Street, New York, N.Y.]
June 25, 1970

Mary, dear: I was talking, if you can call it that, to Cal this afternoon
and he said you were going to Maine on the 12th and that you were
going to write me. Then Bob[1] said you were coming here on the 8th.
I want to send this off, even if you have written me, to give you my
plans.

I am taking Harriet to camp on this Sunday, the 28th, and spend-
ing the night with Olga—then back here for a week to clear up things,
find a new school \in N.Y./ for Harriet[.] I will be here if you are
coming on the 8th and we can drive up in a big station wagon I have
rented for the summer, going whenever you want, and taking things.
So, I just wanted to let you know. . . . At first I thought I didn't want to
go to Maine, but I spent last weekend on Long Island. I had thought I
might rent something out there. However, I came back longing for my
own place and looking forward to Castine. I will miss Harriet terribly,
but I want her to go to camp because there is so little to do up in C.
Nicole, blessed one, had a very bad hernia operation last summer and
it all literally came apart this summer. I have had her sent to a proper
hospital with a top doctor and she will be home tomorrow. She has to

---

1. Silvers.

rest at least a month and I really don't need her. She is such a joy and comfort to me here that I want to get her well.

I knew Cal had a girl and had been distressed for some time, but it was just this afternoon that I knew it was ~~Carolyn~~ Caroline. I felt such relief and burst out laughing![1] I called him immediately at her house and he talked as if he were talking to me from his studio, for an hour, laughing and joking and saying you are spending all your alimony on this call.[2] Harriet had cried pitifully on the phone when he had told her he wasn't coming home. He said he wasn't worried about her, but about me, even though I had told him I was pretty good, which is true. And I told him I was better after I heard it was Caroline.

I cannot take her seriously for Cal. There is a comic element to me in it. Anyway I don't care . . . But, Mary, Bob Silvers is in complete misery. The day Cal called me, saying he had "somebody", apparently Caroline called Bob saying she couldn't go on a trip they had planned because she had Cal.[3] I hadn't spoken to Bob for a long time because I didn't want to bore him with my suffering. I chose one friend and called day and night, changing my mind every minute, and I felt one was enough. What I want to tell you is that Bob is crushed and cannot see anything funny in this. He doesn't want anyone to know it, poor dear. He thinks Caroline is the most intelligent, fascinating person in the whole world. He believes that the life she has organized in England is so beguiling that no one could ever leave it, that she and Cal will last forever. . . . I haven't seen Caroline since she was here and she was very silent and withdrawn, diapers on the floor, really frightening.[4] I

---

1. Lowell: "And that new woman—| when I hear her name, I have to laugh" ("From my Wife" [*The Farther Shore* 1] 8–9, "The Dolphin" manuscript; see poem on page 260); ". . . That new creature, | when I hear her name, I have to laugh" ("Voices" [*Hospital II* 1] 8–9, *The Dolphin*).

2. Lowell: "She tell\s/ me to stop, we mustn't lose your money" ("Transatlantic Call" 14, "The Dolphin" manuscript). Cf. "During a Transatlantic Call" 14, *The Dolphin*.

3. Robert Silvers objected "on factual grounds" to this and other statements in this paragraph (Silvers, email message to editor, December 22, 2016).

4. Nancy Schoenberger: "With her inherited share of the Iveagh Trust, Caroline [. . .] bought a brownstone at 250 West Twelfth Street" in 1959; "in 1964, Caroline gave birth to another girl [. . .] named Evgenia and called Genia. Soon, the beautiful townhouse [. . .] with its good furniture and paintings by Francis Bacon, began to look more like a bohemian household with young children—which is exactly what it was. It was chaos"; "Caroline first met the poet [Lowell] in 1966, the year of Ivana's birth [. . .] Silvers had brought Caroline to a number of dinner parties at the Lowells' as his guest" (Schoenberger, *Dangerous Muse*, pp. 139, 145, and 154). Caroline Blackwood to Ian Hamilton: "when I was with Bob [Silvers], he used to take me to dinner at

do believe Bob that she is better organized in England, and he says "all that is taken care of."

I didn't think Cal was in good shape, not at all. He got very angry, not with me, but with other people; he seemed very casual and filled with that amnesia about the past I know so well. However, I think he is more or less under control with the pills, but he should be taking more. I don't particularly want him back and had made up my mind to quit until I heard it was Caroline. I called him and told him I thought it was ~~worse~~ really a sort of joke and he said, "Oh, you think you are so smart!" I can't do anything and he doesn't want me to, he says over and over. Caroline isn't even divorced from Lucian.[1] What I am concerned about is her passion for having babies she can't take care of. . . . Oh, dear.

What I really want to say is that I am fine. I will not take Cal back unless this is over in a month or so. I have gotten my apartment back here in New York, done everything on the assumption that I won't be going to England. The person who is absolutely crushed is Bob and so I want you to know that, when you see him. What Caroline can do is break up my marriage—or what Cal can do, I mean—and then their thing will not last. It can't, I feel. But that will then be too far along . . .

I am writing tomorrow and the next day a little 600 word review of your book for Vogue. You can't say anything and even if you could that magazine isn't right. But everyone ~~rights~~ writes these things, because they pay well, and when I needed the money I called and asked to write something about you. They gave me four reviews and so I will have a little money. I am planning a lot of writing this summer, most of which is under way.

West 67th Street. And I couldn't speak. I'd been told—which was nonsense—that Cal couldn't speak about anything except poetry. That was the legend about him: everything else bored him. If you know that about anyone, it's terrifying. So there were these ghastly silences. I thought it was better, if he only wanted to talk about poetry, not to talk at all—better than to say, 'Do you like Housman?' or that kind of thing. So I just used to sit absolutely silent. I was always put next to him. And it used to be my dread. To break the silence once, I said I admired the soup. And he said, 'I think it's perfectly disgusting.' And then we had a silence" (*Robert Lowell: A Biography*, pp. 397–98).

1. Freud, whom Blackwood married in 1953; they were divorced in 1959, when she married her second husband, Israel Citkowitz (see Schoenberger, *Dangerous Muse*, pp. 138–39). In 1970, Blackwood was still married to Citkowitz.

I am looking at the news, drinking bourbon, as I write this and so it is mixed up. Dearest love to you and Jim.[1] And let me know whether I should wait—no, I couldn't possibl[y] leave before the 8th anyway and if you are coming then I can well and profitably wait until you want to go \to Castine/.

Love,
Elizabeth

48. Elizabeth Hardwick to Robert Lowell

[15 West 67th Street, New York, N.Y.]
June 26, 1970

Dearest Cal: You must give up Essex and come back in September. Harriet is destroyed, deeply depressed. She needs you to start a new year in school, to help her, to be a part of her life. I do not think she can survive otherwise.

You cannot treat people as you wish to, you and Caroline. Caroline is deeply destructive and neurotic. You are leading a parasitic life, just like her other lovers. Poor Israel, coming around to see the girls.[2] All the rich squalor, covering up for inability to feel and function. I was horrified that you asked Harriet to visit you in "your great country house."[3] It is not yours and I would never allow her to go into that kind of spoiled, negligent indifference. I do not like parasites. I feel astonished that you have become ~~like a queen~~ infatuated with England and as you said all the things \"easiness"/ a rich girl can give you. She will destroy you, just as without even thinking about it—or if thinking about it, not being able to feel—she would destroy Harriet. This kind of anarchy and nihilism will certainly ruin you.

You are a great American writer. You have told us what we are, like Melville, you have brought all the culture of England, and of course even America and other countries have something, to bear on us, on our land, on your past, your people, your family. You are not an English writer, but the most American of souls, the most gifted in finding the

---

1. James West, Mary McCarthy's husband.
2. Israel Citkowitz and their daughters Natalya, Evgenia, and Ivana.
3. Blackwood's house, Milgate Park.

symbolic meaning of this strange place. You are a loss to our culture, hanging about after squalid spoiled, selfish life.

You must, absolutely must, come back in September, help Harriet in school, give her love and a feeling of being wanted by a father, a man, get her possibly into what she wants more than anything—Abbot. A mother alone cannot do it. You must do this. And if you don't, not only will she be destroyed, but your own dignity will. You may feel very arrogant and combative now, but you are [a] person too and you cannot lead that life. When it breaks up as it will, you will have destroyed everything here you have built up. You cannot go on living with Caroline in that unreal world, year after year vaguely noticing her children, going about with people like Sonia, living vicariously, leaving what means a lot to you. I mean a lot to you and you know it. I not only saved your life but I gave you freedom and love and humor. I want you to come home, in September, start new work of which there is plenty among your papers, prose projects[,] everything. I have contempt for your situation. I am not jealous of it, but horrified. How could I be jealous of Caroline? She is charming and pathetic and unreal.

Poor Bob. I don't know whether their relationship was real, but he cared terribly and is suffering pitifully. I hadn't spoken to him for a long time and that is why I hadn't known it was Caroline. I had been talking to another friend a bit about my distress and troubling thoughts and I felt boring one friend was enough. He spoke very little, too pained and betrayed—no matter what illusion his love may have been based on. I love Bob with all my heart and I trembled for him. He, unlike you, couldn't pursue Caroline in London because in spite of his rather inexplicable and somewhat comic love of rich English girls, he felt he had work to do in America, that this was his. I don't mean to imply that he could have won her—although those are hardly proper conceptions with her, since the basic anarchic removal is so great. But he is working on, trying to do what is right, committed to what he knows, America, horrid place, but all that those of us who were born here and have minds can really make ours.[1]

I was astonished that you said you were worried about doing

---

1. Robert Silvers objected to statements in this paragraph (Silvers, email message to editor, December 22, 2016).

something for me instead of Harriet, that you \knew you/ could do something for her. What do I need, if I don't have your love? But she does need much. Were you thinking of a trip to your country house as doing something . . . a fantastic idea, in which she would be neglected and hardly fed if the servants were away.

I had thought of going to Long Island but a weekend there made me think I want for part of the summer my own house and my barn. At least now I can put up the pictures I like. I don't know that I will go on in Maine if you tell me you are not returning in September. There is much I don't like about it and I will have to discuss it with Harriet . . . I will miss her sorely . . . After speaking to you she didn't want to go to camp but she must. Both Olga and Francine are near and are going to visit her to make her feel wanted and not rejected. I will come down once from Maine, at least, and call and write her. The school is a hideous problem. To me everything depends on it. I know how late it is and wonder if she can find a place in any school. We had utterly uprooted ourselves. I miss Barnard, which would have meant a lot to me, but they have filled my post for the year. Crummy, cruel thing for you two selfish little people there to do.

I will do as I please about your studio. I have rented my own to two girls and I would rather have it because it is nearer to my apt. but there is so much more stuff in yours and somehow I think of you there and can't face two dreary girls in it. I have the idea of renting it off and on to people I know for a few weeks and using it for guests because I love having people but not in my apartment here.

I have, or will, write Harvard and Stony Brook that you are going to be away and will make a decision later since there is no rush. I would not consider having you sell the papers without having a week to delight in the study of them, but I cannot exactly agree that prices will go up. Your value will always go up, because you are a tremendous man. But the colleges are broke, libraries are broke, everyone is broke here.

Let's see. Alice Meade was around the other day.[1] Heroic, Women's Lib character she oddly turned out to be without wishing it, brave life in a 72nd Street hotel. However, she wants Everard to give one of their houses and he won't even speak to the lawyer and she wants some

---

1. Alice Winslow Meade, Lowell's maternal first cousin, who was married to Everard K. Meade, Jr. until their divorce in 1969.

more money. But she is nice, odd, very like Aunt Sarah I thought in a kind of gay femininity and curious discipline.

I am going to try to get in touch with Marietta Tree, who has pull at the UN school, and I have talked with Bobbie Handman, whose daughter was a top student there. She says it is very hard even to get an interview—and the year is over. But I have to try. If you never come back Harriet and I are going to Ivan Illich's place[1] next summer because she wants, she says, to learn Spanish really well quickly and then study the culture.

H. sat with Helen Epstein last night and it was a good thing perhaps for her to get out of the house. Barbara called me and said what a beautiful, really deep and special creature she thought Harriet was. I have a good daughter, although good is not the word, an original, beautiful, reserved, suffering girl of great moral beauty. I tremble when I think of the summer without her. She is the joy of my day and night, and the pain too because she is \hurt/. I have known real love and I am, I suppose, blessed in that.

I am writing my few things, doing the dumb Vogue thing for Mary's book today, having done Muriel Spark[2] and Francine. That is all of that. Bob has many projects for me and I am writing my book about home again.[3] Also, when I can't sleep I am writing about you, a journal,[4]—but rather hard to know what "role" to play.

You must leave that parasitic life and come home in September. I know you can work at Harvard. You cannot stay away from me and Harriet for a year and half, almost two and return, love\, I am not Caroline, unreal./ You know that. The choice you have made is ludicrous

---

1. Centro Intercultural de Documentación in Cuernavaca, Mexico; see Lowell, *Mexico* 1-12 in *Notebook69-1, -2*, and *Notebook70*; and *Mexico* 1-10, *For Lizzie and Harriet* (1973).

2. Hardwick, "*The Driver's Seat:* 'Purest Confidence,'" *Vogue*, October 1, 1970.

3. A writing project that emerged from Hardwick's "Going Home in America: Lexington, Kentucky" (*Harper's*, July 1969) and eventually became *Sleepless Nights*.

4. Hardwick: "Re. my 'Notebook,' I told Cal I was writing a sort of memoir, putting it in a handsome leather book with fine paper which had been given to me as a present by John Thompson. Cal had certain grandiose ideas about this 'Notebook,' also known as, my title, a joking one, 'Smiling Through.' I did very little of it, came upon it later and threw it away. Cal, I think, hoped it would be deliciously acerb and 'interesting.' Instead the little I wrote was sentimental and I tore it up like many another false start" (interview with Ian Hamilton, *Robert Lowell: A Biography*, p. 503). Cf. the title "Smiling Through" with "Those two eyes o' blue | kept smilin' through | At me!" (Arthur A. Penn, "Smilin' Through" [1918]); and with Jane Cowl's play *Smilin' Through* (1919).

and destructive and unreal. You will be destroyed by the unreality, the spoiled richness, the alien ground. I believe this and say it without regret, since I am not trying to impress anyone but tell the truth as I see it. You cannot live on Caroline, step into the sheets of Israel Citkowitz and all those weak people without diminishment. You cannot leave your responsibilities to your daughter without moral decay. You cannot continue your career as a fashionable London person,—that is all over \uninteresting/—and your talent is otherwise. I feel you are a loss to American literature and to the country, as well as to us.

Be ~~made~~ mad if you like, arrogant and above-it-all if you like, but this is the truth, or my truth.

No gossip or mail. I wish you everything with your book, old Zeus. I wish you health and dignity and serenity and moral beauty. I wish you a long creative life and a long life just for itself. I have contempt for your present situation, but love for you.

E.

Elizabeth

The mail just came. A few "My husband is away, but . . ." bits. Nothing from Mary. She didn't know I gather when you saw her that I knew "it" was Lady Caroline. But I have written her, hoping to drive up with her from here . . . I got an unexpected $500 for something I wrote and I am so happy. I want to earn money as a writer, as a woman. Harriet does too and in all her sorrow yesterday went to the Epsteins until 12:30! I received Noel Stock's book about Pound in the mail.[1] I am starting to do the Dreiser, Crane thing.[2] Can I add Pound who would fit, or do you not want me to.[3] If you are not returning in September

---

1. *The Life of Ezra Pound* (1970).

2. Unpublished. Hardwick had written about Dreiser in "Fiction Chronicle," *Partisan Review* 15: 1 (January 1948); and would later write about him in both "Mrs. Wharton in New York," *New York Review of Books*, January 21, 1988, and "Wind from the Prairie," *New York Review of Books*, September 26, 1991. She wrote about Crane in "Anderson, Millay and Crane in Their Letters," *Partisan Review* 20, no. 6 (November–December 1953).

3. Hardwick to Darryl Pinckney, who had asked whether Lowell commented on the "intellectual content" of her essays: "I must say he often looked discomfited on that score. Sometimes he thought I was too snippy [. . .] I remember in one of the first issues of *The New York Review* I wrote a piece about a biographical book on Robert Frost. It was more or less mild, but Cal was quite annoyed—annoyed for a short time. I noticed in Randall Jarrell's letters that he gave a bit of approval to my Frost essay and so I said to myself, Okay, Cal? On the whole, Cal was encouraging"

we won't be connected except legally, but not personally, and so I can do as I would. I'm not planning an assault, but a study of what the American scene[1] does to writers, what it is like. If you would rather I didn't, I won't, but I'm sure you don't really care. Anyway I won't get to him for some weeks.

Your loving wife,
E.

I have written the bank. Hope they could understand what I meant. I did it without regret & in our great need & in my relief that [you] have no need of money.

49. Elizabeth Hardwick to Robert Lowell

[15 West 67th Street, New York, N.Y.?]
[June 26, 1970]

I want to add my absolute horror that you two people have taken away something I loved and needed. My job at Barnard, which I tried to get back, but it is filled for this year and the budget is filled.

[. . .]My utter contempt for both of you for the misery you have brought to two people who had never hurt you knows no bounds.[2]

50. Elizabeth Hardwick to Robert Lowell

[15 West 67th Street, New York, N.Y.]
Saturday, June 27, 1970

Cal, dearest: I want to apologize for the terrible things I wrote in my last letters. My life this week has been a night-mare of inability to re-claim what I had given up, \& a suffering/ of Harriet's distress. And when I talked to you on the phone today I had just driven a rented

---

(Elizabeth Hardwick, "The Art of Fiction No. 87," interview by Darryl Pinckney, *Paris Review*, no. 96 [Summer 1985]).

1. Cf. Henry James, *The American Scene* (1907); and Hardwick, "On Washington Square," *New York Review of Books*, November 22, 1990.

2. Quoted in Ian Hamilton, *Robert Lowell: A Biography*, p. 399 (ellipses are Ian Hamilton's); original letter is now missing.

car across town. Even there they made me write a check of $400 for the summer rental which probably isn't good. Originally I had said we would pay with Diner's, etc . . . The UN School seemed so delightful a possibility and I will still try, but everything seemed closed and ruined and I just became furious.

I am all right, Harriet is all right. It took her a few days. We just bought her an adorable, long sort of granny, old-fashioned dress, she is excited about camp, more adults are looking after her, Barbara thinks she is the loveliest thing imaginable . . . everyone is going to visit her at camp from Connecticut[,] Olga, Francine . . . Of course she can visit you. We think of say, after Christmas day with me, a visit up until school,—if there is one—convenes again. It would be about 7 or 8 days. If that isn't good because you'll be too busy partying, as everyone is, another time can be worked out. Camp isn't a possible time. Not over until Aug. 15th and we are going to spend a few days with Aunt Sarah then, which Harriet very much wants, and maybe back here on the school matter, etc.

Forgive me. I am glad you don't need money. It would be a nightmare otherwise of poverty for all of us. I do hope the bank will act soon for me. I am very puritanical and I just haven't anything in the bank and worry when I write a check. . . . Then I'll be fine. I am looking forward to Maine. I don't feel embarrassed. I may have a friend to drive me up, if I don't go with Mary, but if not I'll stop in Boston. I hope the economy picks up because I would like to sell School street and using your barn as a kind of substitute for the School street barn build a small, cozy house attaching to it. But this is a bad year for selling and building costs are astronomical . . . Francis Goodwin's house on the beach is a masterpiece . . . I have a lot of writing to do. I am going to be content. My main love and anxiety is Harriet. She didn't have such a good year, but the odd thing is that she has suddenly really come alive and will be a superb girl and a really interesting person. You'll know what I mean when you see her.

This is just to ask for forgiveness. Love, don't worry, all is well here and I think you are well and I give you my hope for your happiness in England. Don't hate New York and the USA seriously—it is hateful but we don't really hate it. Can't afford to I guess[.]

Elizabeth

51. *Robert Giroux to* Mr. Charles Monteith

Farrar, Straus and Giroux, 19 Union Square West, New York, N.Y.

June 29, 1970

PRIVATE AND CONFIDENTIAL

Dear Charles:

Many thanks for your great help in the Lowell matter, and for your cable. Cal phoned Elizabeth some hours after your call here, obviously as a result of your calling him. Elizabeth learned the worst, but at least she knew where she stood. It was the uncertainty and the worry about Harriet that was the hardest for her to take. The next day she learned (from friends of theirs in London) the name of the person with whom he is staying. "I had to burst out laughing," she said.[1] She thinks from this and other evidence that Cal is probably ill, and she is consulting his doctor. She called him next day and described his telephone manner as low-keyed, "not vindictive and even solicitous." The previous day she was planning a divorce, but I would gather that this is not now her plan. At any rate, as you cabled, Cal is not returning this summer. I'm glad you persuaded him to phone, and Elizabeth is grateful to have escaped from the unreality and frustration of last week's limbo.

As I told you on the phone, I've just completed plans to visit London in August. I'll arrive from Paris on Wednesday, August 12th. Would it be possible to see you and Peter[2] and Matthew[3] on Thursday the 13th or Friday the 14th? I'm not sure at this moment whether I'll be staying at the Connaught or with a friend on Mount Street. But I'll have nine days in London, my first visit in five years, and I very much look forward to seeing all my friends at Faber.

With best wishes,

Yours ever,

[Bob]

Robert Giroux

---

1. See Hardwick to McCarthy, June 25, 1970, footnote 1 on page 64.

2. Peter du Sautoy, vice-chairman of Faber in 1970.

3. Matthew Evans.

52. Elizabeth Hardwick to Mary McCarthy

[15 West 67th Street, New York, N.Y.]

June 30, 1970

Mary, dear: I just got your letter and it was sweet. I don't know what I wrote you before because I was writing so many letters that day, like Herzog.[1] But I am well, resigned, and working day and night to pick up the pieces, which are terribly complicated. Harriet is very upset, because Cal spoke with all that detachment and gaiety you know so well, not meaning to, about \Harriet/ flying over, etc. She has gone off to camp without a school, having given up Dalton, hating it last year, saying goodbye. No place will even interview you, all filled, long waiting list, closed to September. However, I feel I will work something out and have decided not to worry and H. seems better, since I just talked to her on the phone at camp.

I will stay here—or so I think—until the 18th of [July] because then the first visiting day for camp comes,—it's in Connecticut—and I can stop there on my way to Castine and then not have to drive all the way back to camp until August 15th, when I'll be bringing H. up to Maine. I am going to visit Connecticut this weekend, visited the Carlisles last weekend and so I am not alone in the hot city too much. I will have all my affairs in shape here, getting at least one of the studios rented, and ready—getting things back.

I look forward to Castine very much and am so glad I spent a weekend in the Hamptons. That told me that I didn't want to go there—like a retired couple leaving their little town and taking a trailer to Florida for life—and really want my own place.

I thought Cal seemed well when I last spoke to him.[2] Everything is cooling down. It will be all right. Will see you in Maine or you can

1. Saul Bellow: "He had fallen under a spell and was writing letters to everyone under the sun. He was so stirred by these letters that from the end of June he moved from place to place with a valise full of papers" (*Herzog* [1964], p. 1).

2. McCarthy: "I saw Cal just now in London [. . .] and spent an evening with him. He talked a lot about you, with a good deal of rue and tenderness. [. . .] My impression as a veteran of all these wars, including Cal's bouts of psychosis, is that he isn't manic. Excited but rational and in some part of him calm. So far as I can judge, he is serious and Caroline too. The summer will doubtless show. The news was very shaking when I first heard it (by telephone). [. . .] I am so eager to talk to you. What wasn't clear from Cal's conversation was your state of mind. Maybe it is Panglossian to think so, but this could be looked on as a blessing. I hated to see you so unhappy last summer. But

call me here in New York if I am not there when you arrive. If there is anything you want to know. Much love to you both,

    Elizabeth

Beautiful Darby Betts house on [Route] 166 was for sale when I was in Maine on May 30—with the beautiful meadow, the pillars on the lawn. Let's get someone to buy it. We'll make a new community. Or Commune.

53. Robert Lowell to Mrs. Robert Lowell

[Telegram]

[London]
[July 1, 1970]

MRS ROBERT LOWELL 15 WEST67THSTREET
NEW YORK CITY
THANKS FOR YOUR SWEET LETTER AFTER CHRISTMAS OUR BEST
TIME[1]

    LOVE

        CAL

54. Elizabeth Hardwick to Mary McCarthy

[15 West 67th Street, New York, N.Y.]
July 1st, 1970

Mary, dearest: Foreign communication . . . What a confusion it is. I wrote you yesterday and then I got your letter today and learned your plans had changed or might change. Now mine are a bit changed.

I think I will also be driving up about the 10th or 11th or 12th. I don't at all need anyone to drive up with me and I plan to take some bits of furniture if I can. I have been in a nightmare of driving recently and ought not to be a road-menace by then. I am going tomorrow to

---

this is nothing to be talked about in a letter. I feel too much in the dark" (to Elizabeth Hardwick, June 25, 1970).

1. I.e., for Harriet to visit Lowell in England (see Hardwick to Lowell, Saturday, June 27, 1970, above).

spend the 4th with Francine Gray and I will pick up Harriet from her camp and bring her back to New York on Sunday, the 5th. After the most exhausting time I have gotten an interview at the United Nations School for Harriet on Tuesday, July 7th, then I drive her back to camp three hours up in Connecticut, then back here to fix my studio to be rented, pack up and go to Castine as soon as possible. It will be such a relief to have these unending practical problems over for a while. I won't know about the UN School until late August, because it is entirely filled and they have to wait for a cancellation, if it should come. Poor Harriet. It will be a difficult adjustment, but she is rather excited and hopes it comes off. I can't have her going back to Dalton, upset, not liking it, having said goodbye. They are also filled up. The UN School is much better and I think she will feel glamorous and proud of herself if she gets in.

She's fine, I think, and I was of course furious with Cal for all our problems and for what seemed to be brutal ways of handling things. But I have cooled down and pain can't be avoided and there is no way to do these separations without disruption and exhausting efforts to re-establish yourself. Naturally all of this fell to me since Cal is still, in a certain sense, right here in the house, all his things, his books, his mail, his business, his taxes, his clothes. He made a plaintive remark: "I'd write you and Harriet but I can't find any stamps since I left Oxford."

Being resigned doesn't turn you off immediately, but it is a state, a new one for me and I am very happy that it turned up, like a visitor at the right time. I saw Caroline last during what may have been just a low period for her . . . baby diapers in the living room, 40 bottles of milk and not a bit of food in the house, no maid. Bob says she is much better set up in England and I gather that is true. There is something missing, along with much there. And so who knows. And all that is not the point for me. Cal kept, as usual, the door open here, telegrams saying right up until two weeks ago, all my love and can't come *right now*. But it is closed forever, now. I guess it is just that strange thing that happens to you when you know you don't want it any longer. I am speaking of myself, and of course the same is true for him.

I look forward to Maine and know we will have a nice time. I am planning some guests too. I never thought about Jean on L. Island,[1]

---

1. Jean Stafford (Lowell's first wife) lived in Springs, East Hampton. McCarthy: "We're so pleased you're coming to Castine. Selfishly and unselfishly. Long Island would have been awful.

because I was in the other end, but I hated it. Just the drive, even with someone else at the wheel, on the Long Island Expressway, taking three creeping hours even though we left the city at 10 at night—it was horrid. I hated the 100,000 dollar shacks on the beach, the publishers, the people.

Am trying to get at least one term of my Barnard job back, because I love it. All will be well I'm sure.

I forgot in my haste to say how I grieve for Jim that his children[1] won't be there. I'm going to let Harriet go to see Cal if she is ready for it next Easter—and if they will feed her and not miss the plane! It is an awful deprivation to be separated from young children and I will be counting the days until my beloved is back up in Maine with me.

I'll see you soon, dearest one. Maybe it will be the 13th, but no later.
E.

55. *Charles Monteith to* Robert Giroux, Esq.

Faber and Faber LTD Publishers, 24 Russell Square,
London WC1B 5ED
3rd July 1970
Private and Confidential

Dear Bob,

Very many thanks for your letter of June 29th. I'm very glad that Cal telephoned Elizabeth—as he promised me he would when I talked to him after talking to you. I've met the lady in question myself a number of times and I can understand Elizabeth's reaction! She may well be right in thinking that Cal is ill; and if there's any way in which I can help don't hesitate, please, to let me know. Is he, I wonder, in touch with a doctor over here with whom his own New York doctor has been in contact?

It's most excellent news that you're going to be in London in August; Peter, Matthew and I all look forward very much indeed to seeing you. If it's convenient for you, could you call in here about 12.15 on Friday

---

I suppose you had thought of the presence of Jean, which for me in itself would have been a deterrent" (to Elizabeth Hardwick, June 27, 1970).

1. Daniel, Alison, and Jonathan West.

August 14th? We can talk about books in the office for half an hour or so and then go on to have lunch afterwards. Alas, I can't—as I'd much looked forward to doing—suggest you come down to stay with me at Oxford for the weekend since the College[1] is closed for the whole month of August. Try to plan your next visit for some other month!

Yours ever,
Charles.

56. Elizabeth Hardwick to Robert Lowell

[15 West 67th Street, New York, N.Y.]
July 8, 1970

My dearest one: Life being what it is in the fast set of London, I have heard that you are in the hospital.[2] Sweetheart, I just want to send you my love and Harriet's and Sumner's, et alia. All of us here, all of your friends, who love you and treasure you. Don't worry, baby, you'll be all right.

If you need money, tell them to write me and I will write the bank, or whatever you want. I only want to help you, not to hurt you. I value you so much and so does your daughter. Sometimes we can't believe you'll never be coming down from upstairs again, never, never, never.[3] Or going with pimento cheese to your studio on Water Street. But if that is your wish, never to have all of that, we will support you in any way we can.

I've driven back and forth along the west side highway four times

---

1. All Souls College.

2. Ian Hamilton: "On July 9 [*thus*—but compare date of Hardwick's letter, July 8] Lowell was admitted to Greenways Nursing Home in London's St. John's Wood. Hardwick was telephoned by Mary McCarthy (from Paris; McCarthy had heard the news from Sonia Orwell)" (*Robert Lowell: A Biography*, p. 400).

3. "Thou'lt come no more, | Never, never, never, never, never" (*King Lear* 5.3). Hardwick, reviewing a 1964 Peter Brook production: "The opening scenes of this play, with the three sisters, the questions and answers, are, as Coleridge said, a sort of fairy tale; at the end it is a devastating drama of power, old age, and death. [. . .] when you have seen this remarkable production, the accent given to the text seems, if certainly not the only one, a brilliantly possible one. All the existential 'nothings' and 'nevers' of the play take on a special meaning" ("*King Lear*, 'Brilliantly Possible,'" *Vogue*, August 1, 1964).

over the 4th of July. I went up on that Thursday and had a lovely week-
end at Francine's, with the Millers[1] for swimming, playing tennis with
Bill Coffin's wife,[2] driving Jean Van den Heuvel back. (I hear your
remarks in the Bobby Kennedy book are lovely.)[3] Then Harriet got an
interview at the UN School, but I worry so about her. She is very up-
set and yet, after crying the first time she spoke to you, says nothing,
which is worrying. I love her so. She is so, so smart, but so, so unlike
other people—dear little creature. I won't go into the school problems.
It is a sort of nightmare.

Have the apt. back o.k. Lovely note from Fuentes, saying, "I love
and respect you" and I barely know him. I'm o.k., honey. Guess what
I'm doing? You had it the first time. Having a bourbon and looking at
the news! I have written all those little things I planned and will start
on my book. I have such good ideas for it and it will save my life. . . .
There are, if I can do it, so many things in my past: commie stuff,
women's lib, all those horrid men I slept with, and the wonder what
I have really made of myself as a woman. I think if it hadn't been for
feeling that as a woman you owe it to yourself to preserve dignity and
honesty and integrity I couldn't have stood what has happened to me.
But I am really well I think and I will just write my book, started in the
"going home piece," and hope for the best, for a little prestige at least.

Thank you for the lovely poems to me and Harriet in *Notebook*.[4]
I read all of the book last night and it is really a strange, wonderful
work. It would be stupid to speak of "loving it"—I don't "love" really
good books in that easy way. But I know your book is everything. And
with the new ones, the additions[5]—Oh, God. I can't agree with you
when you said to me on the phone that you had 12 admirers in England
to one here. The students at Harvard, I know, worship your book—
and which twelve do you mean? It just depends on who it is . . . You

---

1. Arthur Miller and Inge Morath.
2. Harriet Gibney Coffin.
3. Jean Stein, *American Journey: The Times of Robert Kennedy*, ed. George Plimpton (1970), pp. 36,
192–93, 268–70, 304, 309–10, 318, and 340–41.
4. In *Notebook 69-1* and *-2*.
5. New poems forthcoming in the third edition of *Notebook*, published in the fall of 1970. "This
text differs from the first edition in May 1969 and the second in July. About a hundred of the
old poems have been changed, some noticeably. More than ninety new poems have been added"
("Note to the New Edition," p. 264).

have great love and the deepest belief in your genius here, from all of us who know what you are writing about.

Goodbye, my love. . . . I will always treasure you and do what you wish. Horrible book on Pound by Noel Stock, so, so boring. It just can't be. You would never know if you didn't look at the pictures that he was interesting. . . . It goes,

"Then Miss Rudge,[1] . . . Then Mrs. Pound . . ." As if they were secretaries.

Well, "many a noble heart mourned the loss of those old trees . . ." remember I got that from Palgrave, up in Castine.[2] Can't wait to get there. Going I think on Sunday to Maine . . . Just heard from Vinny McGee, a new friend, going to jail as a draft resister . . . Some people think Columbia won't even open, no money . . . I don't believe it . . . I really want to get a job at Yale, year after this, because I think it would be fun. Also Harriet and I have Francine's Connecticut house until New Year's, after New Year's really, and we plan to go up for weekends. She says she doesn't want to come to England at Christmas. Not ready. Maybe Easter. But she will come some day, when she can face it. . . . Dearest love, always,

Elizabeth

57. *Robert Giroux to* Mr. Charles Monteith

Farrar, Straus and Giroux, 19 Union Square West, New York, N.Y.
July 9, 1970
PRIVATE & CONFIDENTIAL

Dear Charles:

Shortly after your letter arrived this week, Elizabeth phoned to tell me that Cal was in a nursing home. The whole continental literary set is now in the act. It was Mary McCarthy who phoned Elizabeth from Paris; she had spoken to Cal the day before and thought he was "high" (it is not always so easy to tell). Then Sonia Orwell (I don't know her

---

1. Olga Rudge.

2. Wordsworth: "Many hearts deplored | The fate of those old trees" ("Composed at Neidpath Castle, the Property of Lord Queensberry, 1803" 8–9, in *The Golden Treasury of English Songs and Lyrics*, ed. Francis Turner Palgrave). Quoted as "Many a noble heart mourned the fall of those great oaks" in Hardwick's "In Maine," *New York Review of Books*, October 7, 1971.

present married name)[1] phoned Elizabeth and wanted her to come over and take Cal home; it's not that simple, however. Elizabeth knows she could not persuade him and that he might even react badly. His being in the nursing home is the best news of all. From my experience I would judge that the longer he stays, the better. It takes a little time for him to get down from the heights, and then the depression follows. If he agreed to go into the nursing home (this was not made clear), he's headed for recovery through insight about his own need for quiet and rest. It's when he's footloose, over-drinking and over-talking, encouraged by people who have no suspicion of the boiling volcano beneath the apparently controlled and sometimes even sweet exterior, that the fireworks begin.

Elizabeth said she phoned Mrs. Nolan, who refused to pass a message to Sidney. He of course works wonders with Cal, as indeed I saw with my own eyes that night at the opera some years ago. The doctors really don't seem to know what to do for Cal. Elizabeth is getting the name of the London doctor and will put Dr. Baum[2] (I believe that's her name) in touch with him. When Sidney and I delivered Cal to her on the memorable night at the opera, Dr. Baum said, "Cal, how can you act like this? Think what people will say *about me*."

I don't know of anything you can do, Charles, beyond what you've already done. Elizabeth is taking Harriet to Castine in Maine for the remainder of the summer. She feels she has to go on as best as she can for the girl's sake, and I know she'll do whatever is required. I'm writing Cal, in your care, by this mail merely to tell him I'm vacationing in France and will be in England. I'll see him (I'm giving Faber as my address) only if he wants it and there's something I can do.

Friday, August 14th, is fine for me, and I'll come by at 12:15 to see you and Peter and Matthew. As for Oxford, I'll make certain to plan for a better time than August on my next trip. Incidentally, I'm delighted that you are taking on the Peter Handke novel, THE GOALIE'S ANXIETY

---

1. Ian Angus: "On 13 October 1949 [Sonia] married [George] Orwell, seriously ill with tuberculosis, who died on 21 January 1950; subsequently she mostly used the surname Orwell. On 12 August 1958 she married Michael Augustus Lane Fox Pitt-Rivers (1917–1999), a wealthy farmer, but the marriage ended in divorce in 1965" ("Brownell, Sonia Mary [Sonia Orwell] [1918–1980]," in *Oxford Dictionary of National Biography* [Oxford University Press, 2004]).
2. Probably Dr. Viola Bernard, one of Lowell's psychiatrists (Lowell and Hardwick were also patients of Elizabeth Bishop's doctor Anny Baumann, but for general not mental health).

AT THE PENALTY KICK.[1] I'm sending Matthew the book of his we have already published, KASPAR AND OTHER PLAYS.[2]

Yours ever,

[Bob]

Robert Giroux

p.s. Thanks for corrected proofs—what a lot of work! It may well be his best book. Even that latest (and saddest) poem, "Wall Mirror," is very moving.[3]

58. *Elizabeth Hardwick to Robert Lowell*

[15 West 67th Street, New York, N.Y.]

July 11, 1970

Darling Cal: How strange it is, making calls from here at 6 in the morning. But that is the time I wake up, and I love the mornings. I am very anxious to go up to Maine. There were just so darned many things to be done here that I couldn't get away before. Mary tells me it is beautiful up there. The Thomases[4] called to wonder where I was . . . tennis doubles waiting. I played once as I told you in Connecticut, in a humid indoor place, like having a heat stroke, but it was fun. I must say I am no better. . . .

I found yesterday, in going over my papers, a portrait I had done of Dorothea and Ivor Richards.[5] It is quite good—oddly enough I have

---

1. Trans. Michael Roloff (1972).

2. Trans. Michael Roloff (1969).

3. Lowell: "Moonshine to say we can relive our lives, | beggging nature's clean-edge Roman roads | turn back full circle . . . from the byways of night, | day, seeing nothing, missing nothing, God. . . . | The paintings blow over the floor, crach\k/ and are free, | blown with the artist who gave them a color. | Your wall-mirror in a mat of plateglass sapphire, | mirror-scroll and claspleaves, holds our faces, | the style and the sitters dead like their portrait, unlearning. | Summer already looks further along than it is, | leaf blighted by streetdyes and the discard girl. | We are on the astigmatic crossroads. One summer, another—| and this one that. You. One life for \our/ two lives—| we stop uncomfortable, we are humanly low" ("Wall-Mirror," dedicated "To Caroline," typewritten insertion of [*Summer* 17] into *Notebook* page proofs, "to go after THE BOND and before STALIN [*Summer* 16 and 18]." Cf. with *Fall Weekend at* Milgate [1] in "The Dolphin" manuscript and in *The Dolphin*).

4. Mary and Harris ("Tommy") Thomas.

5. Now missing.

tried these posterity efforts before and they were ~~quite~~ always dull. It occurred to me that it had to do with the fact that I really was writing about people I knew too well, and somehow there was too little and too much, as Henry James said of writing about places.[1] Certain limits on the knowledge of the place are a genuine help . . . I may try a few more, although I am not especially in line for posthumous acclaim since I feel I need so much right this minute . . . not acclaim, but good work to be published to keep me going.

Saw Stanley on the bus a little while ago. He looked fairly well and then I spoke to them before they went away,[2] but that was some time ago. I enclose a card from Adrienne.[3] Just the usual dumb mail, anthologies—all being saved here somewhere or another, requests for interviews by absurd sociologists on insane projects, two poems sent for your criticism, as if God himself could say anything about a few lines . . . .

Dearest, don't feel that the lithium has let you down because of this set back. I guess you have put it to the ultimate test. It will work, it does work. . . . Bill Alfred said that if by any chance you should want to come back here this year, the second term at Harvard would be free since Elizabeth[4] and Fitzgerald[5] are both teaching the first term . . . I have no reason to think you would want that, but just wanted to pass the word along. You know how I am! I just found in an old notebook, also (all of these things are going with me to help with my Kentucky life of myself) the old baseball phrase: "Nice guys finish last!"[6] and that

---

1. James: "How can places that speak *in general* so to the imagination not give it, at the moment, the particular thing it wants? I recollect again and again, in beautiful places, dropping into that wonderment. The real truth is, I think, that they express, under this appeal, only too much—more than, in the given case, one has use for; so that one finds one's self working less congruously, after all, so far as the surrounding picture is concerned, than in presence of the moderate and the neutral, to which we may lend something of the light of our vision. Such a place as Venice is too proud for such charities; Venice does n't borrow, she but all magnificently gives" (Preface, *The Portrait of a Lady* [1908], p. vi).
2. Stanley Kunitz and Elise Asher, who summered in Provincetown, Massachusetts.
3. Rich; enclosure now missing.
4. Bishop.
5. Robert Fitzgerald.
6. Attributed to Leo Durocher (manager of the Brooklyn Dodgers), but possibly an editorial compression of his remarks as reported by Frank Graham: "The nice guys are all over there, in seventh place" (*New York Journal-American*, July 7, 1946; quoted in the *Yale Book of Quotations*, ed. Fred R. Shapiro [2006], p. 221). First appearance of the phrase in print is in Leo Durocher, "Nice Guys Finish Last," *Cosmopolitan* (April 1948).

would seem to fit me, at least at the moment and in certain respects. If I knew, right now, how not to be nice I would not be, but can't seem to find the occasions. (Naturally I am joking. My own awareness of the limits of my "niceness" is alive.)

Things have settled down here in the US, in a way at least, an odd way. There isn't anything to be done. Nixon is so empty and has so appallingly failed at everything. One just sits back. The economic difficulties everywhere are the most absorbing I guess, since we have made the world numb to destruction and death. Incredible story someone was telling me yesterday about all the rich people selling out in the Caribbean, leaving vast beach houses at Jamaica, etc. Bob tells me there is a charming piece coming in the next issue by Naipaul on Black Power in Trinidad. I read a line or two, which told of ~~their~~ the black people waiting for the great African chieftain, Hailie Selassie, the Lion of Judah, on his visit, only to find that he looked like a little East Indian![1]

Dearest, warmest greetings to you from me and everyone, if there were any one here to send his greetings. Much love, my dear old fellow. Will write or call you again soon.

> Elizabeth
> Castine, Maine
> 207-326-8786

59. Caroline Blackwood to Robert Lowell

[Unknown Address[2]]
[n.d. summer 1970]

Darling Cal—I think about you every minute of the day, and I love you every minute of the day. Have just got your letter. You are right to

1. V. S. Naipaul: "Recently the Emperor visited Jamaica. The Ras Tafarians were expecting a black lion of a man; they saw someone like a Hindu, mild-featured, brown, and small. The disappointment was great; but somehow the sect survives" ("Power to the Caribbean People," *New York Review of Books*, September 3, 1970).

2. Records and biographers differ as to where Blackwood was in mid- to late July 1970. Blackwood sent a telegram about Lowell to Blair Clark from Ballyconneely, Ireland (no date, Blair Clark Papers, HRC), and Ian Hamilton states: "'Caroline in Ireland'" (*Robert Lowell: A Biography*, p. 400). Nancy Schoenberger: "She packed up her children and left for the country, to an eighteenth-century house she had recently bought in Maidstone, Kent" (*Dangerous Muse*, p. 168). But cf. also Lowell: "Diagnosis: To Caroline in Scotland" (*The Dolphin*).

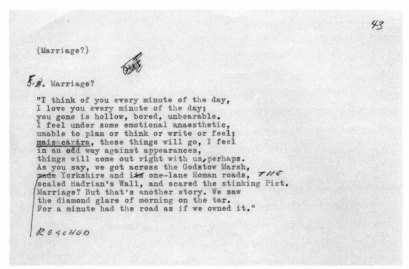

(Marriage?)

5.8. Marriage?

"I think of you every minute of the day,
I love you every minute of the day;
you gone is hollow, bored, unbearable.
I feel under some emotional anaesthetic,
unable to plan or think or write or feel;
maisacarira, these things will go, I feel
in an odd way against appearances,
things will come out right with us, perhaps.
As you say, we got across the Godstow Marsh,
made Yorkshire and its one-lane Roman roads, *THE*
scaled Hadrian's Wall, and scared the stinking Pict.
Marriage? But that's another story. We saw
the diamond glare of morning on the tar.
For a minute had the road as if we owned it."

RE-USED

"Marriage?" [*Marriage 9 5*], from "The Dolphin" manuscript, composed and re-vised between 1970 and January 1972 (cf. "Marriage?" [Caroline 4], *The Dolphin*).

object to me calling it "your" sickness.[1] It is mine. Or ours. That is the trouble. I know it is better if I don't see you or speak to you until your attack is over even though I really long to and without you everything seems hollow, boring, unbearable. I still feel as if I am under some kind of emotional anaesthetic and can't plan or think. But that will change. I feel in an odd way and against obvious appearances that everything is going to be alright. But not immediately[.] As you say we got across the Godstow Marsh and manipulated that endless Military Road, and we reached Hadrian's wall.

Are you working? Have you got enough books etc? I will get any letters that you send to Redcliffe Square. I enclose a copy of Wall Mirror that you said you wanted. At the moment I feel really sub-humanly low.[2]
 Love Caroline.

---

1. Blackwood, some days earlier: "I am going away. If I see you when you are so sick I know everything between us will become distorted and destroyed. Your sickness is so distressing to me and I am so bound up with you that I can't help you and will break down again myself—and that does not help. I love you just as much as ever—you may think this is hypocrisy but it is *not* as Grey tried to tell you. As to the future—God knows—or does he? Please get better Cal. I love you so much[.] Love Godstow Marsh" (Blackwood to Lowell, no date, but summer 1970, Robert Lowell Papers, HRC).
2. Lowell: "we stop uncomfortable, we are humanly low" ("Wall-Mirror" [Summer 17] 14, *Note-book70*). See footnote 3 on page 82.

60. Elizabeth Hardwick to Robert Lowell

[Castine, Maine]
July 14, 1970

Dear Cal: Just a word from Maine. Very hot and beautiful, clear and shining. Played tennis yesterday with the old group. The drive up was hard, but I went first to Boston to spend the night and dined at the Athens[1] with Bill Alfred and with Peter Brooks, who was back fixing up their house for rental a second year. That was wonderful and we almost walked back to Cambridge. But how strange Harvard Square is, so over-populated with dirty, naked kids this summer, with a glazed look about them. Filth in the entrance to The Coop, around the plaza at the Holyoke Center. I began to see what Esther meant, how because it is so small one could see it as menacing to the sanity of young children somehow[.] New York, Central Park, the village—it's all too big, people don't mix with strangers and so that seems different. Boston fascinated me.

Here, Mary is settled in gaily, the Dupees are arriving tonight, Rahv is coming in August. On the Vineyard, he sold Theo's beautiful house with a splendid garden, something she had always owned and which was a magnificent, expensive property right on the water, very much Theo. The day or two after the lease was signed, it burned to the ground. Chilling, isn't it? Not a thing of Theo is left was the thought of everyone.[2] She's gone, utterly.

Well, you are certainly not gone from here. Your red wool shirt, your black and white checked wool, your sneakers, your dungarees, your bed in the barn and up here, your field glasses, your old muddy boots . . . [3] It's all like a Hardy poem.[4] Birds are nesting in the house down there and up here. The trellis with the dutchman's pipe vine absolutely collapsed, something before I came, and I am just staring at it, thinking about the next step.

---

1. The Athens Olympia Restaurant on Stuart Street in Boston's Back Bay.

2. Theodora Jay Stillman, Rahv's second wife, was killed in a fire at their house at 329 Beacon Street in Boston on September 25, 1968.

3. Lowell: "In Maine, my country ~~as I loved to boast,~~ \where I ~~hoped~~ wished to die,/ | each empty sweater and ~~vacant~~ \idle/ bookshelf hurts, | ~~the~~ pretex[t] for their service gone" ("Notes for an unwritten Letter" [*The Farther Shore* 3] 8–10, "The Dolphin" manuscript; see poem on page 98); and "Letter" [*Hospital II* 2], *The Dolphin*.

4. See especially Thomas Hardy, "The Going" (quoted by Hardwick in *Sleepless Nights*, p. 151); and Hardwick to Lowell, May 24, 1973, footnote 2 on page 337.

I wonder how you are. The telephone calls to England became rather upsetting to me and they are unbelievably expensive and so I won't make them unless I'm asked to.[1] I write to support you, if you are feeling upset, and to say that Harriet and I feel millions of miles away, almost as if we had never known you. I am sure you feel the same about us. . . . I hope you get the Salmagundi I sent you, with the very good article by Robert Boyers.[2] I haven't much else to say. My mail hasn't started coming from New York, but I am busy and happy here, having a very good time, making the house cozy for that cold day that will surely come soon. I am working at writing and that is what I want to do. The weather is lovely. Can't wait until August 15th and Harriet comes back. Mr. Soper[3] wanders about, the Thomases have re-done their house, and it is very pretty. Your barn is beautiful. I'll have the Dupees for a drink in the sun there so that they can see it. Grass growing on the lawn, bulkhead standing after terrible storms, Sally's house lovely, Pat all over Water Street, with bikes and so forth. Bob's large boat in the harbor. Booths present and heavy somehow.[4]

Well, I would like some word from you, about you, if you care to send it.

With much love,
Lizzie

61. Elizabeth Hardwick to Robert Lowell

[Castine, Maine]
July 16, 1970

Darling: It was good to hear your voice. It is a rainy, or misty day, here and I can't say I mind altogether. Tremendous activity, as you can imagine, with Mary here. Cocktail party for the Dupees and then

---

1. In 1970, a three-minute telephone call from New York City to the United Kingdom cost $3.60 (approximately $23.33 in 2019 dollars, according to the Consumer Price Index Calculator [CPI]) ("Table 13: AT&T Residential Rates for Calls Lasting 3 Minutes to Selected International Points, 1950–1997" in Linda Blake and Jim Lande, *Trends in the U.S. International Telecommunications Industry* [Washington, D.C.: Federal Communications Commission, 1998]).
2. Robert Boyers, "On Robert Lowell," *Salmagundi*, no. 13 (Summer 1970), pp. 36–44.
3. Edward A. Soper, handyman.
4. Castine neighbors: Sarah Austin ("Sally"); Patricia ("Pat") and Robert ("Bob") Bicks; Philip and Margaret Booth.

I have them all back here for dinner. I had everyone, and the Dupees, after tennis at the barn yesterday, with the fire going, a great wind outside. Very nice. In addition now to the dubious liberation of feeling I can drive the freeways of the US at any hour, I now feel no worry at all about staying here alone at night. I just want a night at home, mostly, to read and go to bed early.

There isn't much to say today. If you ever need to telephone me do at 11 to 12 in the morning *your time*! that will be six or seven in the a.m. here and I will certainly be at home. . . . But we won't telephone unless there is something to say. I feel a bit strange sending off letters in the blue and I called you just to be sure they weren't a bother. I just want to give you any support, or whatever would be better to call it, that you might need right now.

Be sure to tell the hospital to send the bills here, and the doctor. You have a new man at the State Street.[1] I have his name written down someplace. Mr. Loring retired, and Mr. Nichols hasn't really been on your "account" for a while, some years. Darling, I'll have more to say in a day or two. Forgive this dull letter. But I send greetings and love and good wishes to you. Bear up and all will be well. I have faith in that and want you to have faith. Not cant, either, but based on my own knowledge and observation and rather large experience.

Dearest love,
Elizabeth

62. *Elizabeth Hardwick to Robert Lowell*

[Castine, Maine]
July 20, 1970

Dear Cal: I enclose this review, in case you haven't seen it.[2] I hope you are well. Castine is lovely, very warm and clear and I have had a lovely time so far. Senator McCarthy's secretary called today but I said you were in England and not expected back here. Didn't speak to him. Perhaps he is coming up. Mary and I would have loved to see him, but I didn't feel I could ask to speak to him personally.

---

1. State Street Trust Company.
2. Enclosure now missing.

You seem so far away, letters are becoming difficult. Harriet is having a good time at camp I think.

Love,

Lizzie

63. *Elizabeth Hardwick to Robert Lowell*[1]

[Castine, Maine]

Tuesday, July 21, 1971 [1970]

Darling: My typewriter is locked completely, carriage won't budge. I want to send this off early. Cal, dear, would you like me to come over to help you get back on your feet & do what you want? Honey, telephones are ringing day & night here, with calls for help (not ringing at my house, at others).[2] It is felt dearest that you are not well enough to come out of the hospital, that you are still very high & not the deep, serious Robert Lowell we all love. You will be all right, love—no one knows that better than I. If you want me—with so many people out of London—to sit with you, talk to you, make some order in your practical affairs there, and it must be made, I will, for a short time because I really haven't long before I get Harriet from camp. Cable or call me Friday or Saturday. I would do this as a friend, as help if possible for my child's father. Naturally I don't want to come, am happy here. But I know I can help, Dearest love & just forget this offer if you don't want it. Do call—*your time*—between 11 or 12 in the morning or send a cable. I could only stay ten days at the most but I could try to help & talk to

---

1. Handwritten.

2. Ian Hamilton, quoting Blair Clark's notes, July 21–26, 1970, gives the following account of this period: "*R. Silvers phone conv. with B.C. 21/7/70*—worrisome situation: Cal was at Caroline's in London, got cleaning woman to let him in—he was drunk—Car. can't stand it yet doctors say he can't be told. They won't answer for consequences. *E. Hardwick conv. with B.C. 21/7/70*—'I talked to Cal about 2:30 and he said she'd had a nervous breakdown just like [him] and will be in hosp. for 2 weeks.' *B. Silvers conv. with B.C. 22/7/70*—Caroline is closing house in London—vanishing concerned that he not track her down—Car. quotes 'I can't take responsibility' but 'hasn't thought through what ought to happen ultimately' [. . .] *E. H. phone conv. with B.C. 27/7/70*—(Cal) said as if saying he had a cold—'Trouble is that Caroline had had a nervous breakdown'" (*Robert Lowell: A Biography*, p. 401). In Clark's notes taken during a telephone conversation with Jonathan Miller on July 21, Miller says that everyone whom Lowell knows in London "is vanishing, including himself," and he is "troubled by the idea of Cal emerging" from the hospital "with no point of real contact" (Blair Clark Papers, HRC).

you about your general business arrangements—And bring you news of here, maybe talk about interesting things, your work, etc,

Dearest love,

E.

This is *good faith*, not wife-maneuver. If I had wanted to do that I could have months ago—at least tried.

64. *Elizabeth Hardwick to Robert Lowell*

[Castine, Maine]

July 28, 1970

Dear old heart: I liked talking to you.[1] My tears welled up when Phil[2] brought a great bouquet of flower-weeds, straight from the dump, as he said. Mary has been a devoted, imaginative friend, so sweet and good to me and I will love her always. It has been a perfect summer here, boiling hot, lively, gay tennis games, friends for drinks. Bob and Barbara calling me with kindness and love from New York. Harriet, too, has had the really astonishing devotion of her friends. Lisa went to the camp the first visiting weekend and last weekend, Melissa and her parents, who were visiting Melissa not far away went to see Harriet. Both people described her as looking very beautiful, with her face lighting up with gratitude for the visits, the efforts made, the loyalty. It is an 8 or 9 hour trip from here and of course I couldn't go. I dread going down and coming back on the 16th, when I go to pick up her to return to Castine for the rest of August, but I will go a day early and spend one or two nights with Olga or Francine. She \H./ is very distressed to live without a father, day in and day out, especially painful is to be deprived for ever of an extraordinary father, an unforgettable, strange man. Daddy is so funny, she says, with his silent laughter!

There is a black bear in town![3] Hanging about the manor![4] Rev.

---

1. July 27, 1970, was Hardwick's fifty-fourth birthday, and July 28th was the Lowells' twenty-first wedding anniversary.

2. Booth.

3. See footnote 2 on page 146 (Lowell to Harriet Lowell, January 6, 1970 [1971]).

4. A derelict house in Castine. See footnote 5 on page 422 (Hardwick to Mary McCarthy, January 29, 1976).

Ed Miller is puzzling over things, but I notice he withheld his perfect enthusiasm from a discussion of Bill Coffin and the wonderful Bishop Moore. Asking one saint about another is like asking George Ortman about Robert Motherwell. All my love, my dearest Cal.

Elizabeth

65. *Elizabeth Hardwick to Mary McCarthy*[1]

[London]
Sunday, Aug. 2, 1970

Mary, dearest: I'll just send off this note instead of a cable, since you have all the other addresses.

Clive Hotel
Primrose Hill Road
London, NW 3, England[2]

It is very depressing here somehow & I realize again how happy it was for me in Castine. Cal has several more corners to turn before the realization that he has had a bad time really comes to him, but I think the next two or three weeks will do that. He is in awful shape physically, can only go about for an hour at the most & then just collapses. I will see the Dr. tomorrow. I am sure the thyroid is a problem.[3] I was unable to hold back tears watching him creep along, exhausted. Sonia

---

1. Handwritten.

2. Ian Hamilton: "On July 29 Hardwick [. . .] decided she would go to London [. . .] She telephoned Blair Clark: '—made up my mind—Bill Alfred going with [me]'" and reported the gossip she had heard from London, that Lowell was "'allowed to go out—in pyjamas—out to pubs— steals from handbags [. . .] they don't understand—he drinks—I'll talk to doctors [. . .] —Car. thing is secondary: he can marry her if he wants —He might keel over dead, with drugs and beer —Bill will go to pub, cut his hair, buy him shoes—until they can control him—sit there with him. Cal is really a marvelous person, not this detached idiot—not in emotional contact with his real personality'" (*Robert Lowell: A Biography*, p. 402; Ian Hamilton's source is "Blair Clark's notes, July 29, 1970").

3. Thomas A. Traill: "previous medical history included treatment in 1968–69 for hypothyroidism. There was thyroid swelling, and his condition eventually seems to have improved (thyroid hormone was discontinued in March 1969), so one imagines he had thyroiditis" (in Kay Redfield Jamison, *Robert Lowell: Setting the River on Fire; A Study of Genius, Mania, and Character* [2017], p. 420).

is unbearable. She met us[1] at the town air terminal & between there & the hotel—quite nice, next to Cal's hospital—did not let me say *one word*. At hotel coffee ordered & I said I don't want coffee I want to see Cal for God's sake & went off next door where he was waiting. I just hope she will keep away while Bill & I are here, but I doubt it. Had the feeling she was rushing back to town in two days!

What is so dreadful is the whole world of mental collapse—in different degrees, I hope. Caroline, Israel, Bingo (Grey's lovely young wife, who had one previous breakdown). A world in which literally only Sonia is able to function. I find that very sad for Cal's future, no one ever really hits the point of anything.

Cal is quiet, much too tired to drink more than a pint of beer; trying to write. He still can only speak in terms of jokes & has no real notion of the efforts people have made, etc., but sometimes a look of unutterable depression flashes across his face for a moment & I want to weep—then he pushes it back with a careless joke.[2] But he has turned many corners, even if he has some left. That homely image is really the way getting over this seems to me. The "stealing" was all wrong—part of the telephone horror. Books from Sonia, a map of London she "thought" was in her handbag, later found on his bed![3] I said, "Books! they don't count." There is a nightmare quality here I hate & Bill feels it too, less in Cal now than in the hapless, helpless, unhelpful circle about him. God help him, I can't stay long enough—as I estimate it—to see him through this period & of course I haven't spoken to him anything about C. or "coming home." I don't even know what all the "telling him about Caroline" fear means, neither Bill nor I got the idea from Sonia's ravings of just what there was to tell Cal about Caroline or not to tell. I feel she will be an awful disaster for him with her own deep unbalance. Cal seemed so helpless, so needing love & openness & wifely care (indeed). But that is all for now. Will wire you when I am coming back.

Dearest love to you both

E.

---

1. Hardwick and William Alfred.

2. Lowell: "Your clowning makes us want to vomit" ("From My Wife" [*The Farther Shore* 1] 4, "The Dolphin" manuscript; see poem on page 260); "your clowning makes visitors want to call a taxi" ("Voices" [*Hospital II* 1] 4, *The Dolphin*).

3. Before she went to London, Hardwick told Blair Clark that she had heard (probably from Sonia Orwell) that while in the hospital, Lowell was "allowed to go out—in pyjamas—out to pubs—steals from handbags"; see footnote 2 on page 91.

66. Elizabeth Hardwick to Mary McCarthy[1]

Clive Hotel, Primrose Hill Road, Hampstead, London, N W 3

Aug 4, 1970

Dear Mary: I miss Castine. It is depressing here with so much illness & neurasthenia. I will not see Sonia, who is returning tomorrow. I think her hysterical reporting has done damage to Cal & I have no wish to hear her ideas. Cal is not well, but is certainly on the way. He is quiet, sober, honest. The hospital is charming & right for him, the doctor is good. I do not know what his future is, but I do know that by some odd good fortune I realized when I got here that I had no wish to start over again. One thing—not to do with Caroline, whom we have not mentioned—has quite released me. My only desire is to come home to my house & friends but the doctor wants me to stay as long as I can. I have said 14th at the latest. Have cut Cal's shoulder length hair, had his shirts washed, his trousers cleaned.[2] He is very weak & trembling & rather frail & needs help even to get around & is quite exhausted after an hour or so—even though we had a good time at *Patton*,[3] an extraordinarily interesting 3 hour oddity.

Love "Thanksgiving"[4]—not unlike "Patton" in a way. I hope to feel free to come \home/ earlier, but have a seat on the 14th. I may have to go to Harriet's camp from Boston, but may not if she has remained firm in her interest in the Canada trip.[5]

London is nice. Hampstead enchants me. I will not call anyone— too tired & also do not want to talk about Cal. I hope to stop all that by my own silence. Bill Alfred is dear, patient & infinitely helpful. We are like two old nuns running errands, doing washing, taking the air for a pint of beer with Cal. He accepts our efforts like an invalid Archbishop, seeing nothing extraordinary in the service.

But we will both be glad to get home.

dearest love,

E.

---

1. Handwritten.

2. Lowell: "your suit \is/ lazies\d/ to grease" ("From my Wife" [*The Farther Shore* 1] 8, "The Dolphin" manuscript; see poem on page 260); "Your trousers are worn to a mirror" ("Voices" [*Hospital II* 1] 8, *The Dolphin*).

3. *Patton*, directed by Franklin J. Schaffner (1970).

4. Mary McCarthy, "Thanksgiving in Paris—1964," *Atlantic Monthly*, August 1970.

5. Hardwick and Harriet Lowell went to Quebec from Maine for a brief visit in August 1970.

67. Elizabeth Hardwick to Robert Lowell[1]

Clive Hotel, Primrose Hill Road, Hampstead, London, N W 3

Aug. 5, 1970

Dearest Cal: Here with a rubber band are some stamped post-cards & envelopes for airmail.[2] Please don't erase Harriet! A child can destroy herself over that, I get the feeling that with you she is like a cottage that once was near but has been lost to memory when a new building went up.

Are you prepared, happy to give us up for the rest of your life? Do you remember, actually, our apt, your studio, with its bed, its books, your phone. Do you remember Maine, the fire in School Street, friends, wine, music? Do you remember your barn & your seals & your long, lazy days.

Do you want to kiss Harriet's cheeks again, hear her laugh, hear the guitar in her room?

You are going, irrevocably, to an emotionally crippled life, chaos, withdrawal, no support, no loving help, none of the effort made by a wife to create a life, everything for the man she loves. You are leaving private jokes, your \own/ life, to lead someone else's life, you need the reality, the energy I brought to you, the care, the humor.[3]

What are your values? Do they include loyalty, responsibility to those you love, since you have love for me. Sickness & shame will overcome you as your whole life sinks into that created by someone else, ruled by a new country & the English aristocracy & its helpless ways, by surrender of something beautifully old-fashioned & New England & pure in you.

Your writing will flourish I hope, but what will renew it without the sense of fresh life always there, sometimes irritating I know, \me, the family/, the news? English gossip, old subjects?

---

1. Handwritten.

2. Hardwick stamped and pre-addressed the postcards and envelopes to Harriet Lowell, but she left the postcards blank and the envelopes empty for Lowell to write his own messages or enclose his own letters. See "Notes for an unwritten Letter" [*The Farther Shore* 3], "The Dolphin" manuscript (see poem on page 98); and "Letter" [*Hospital II* 2] 4–12, *The Dolphin*.

3. Lowell: "You have left two houses, two thousand books, | a workbarn by the ocean, and a ~~woman~~ \slave/ | ~~who~~ \to/ kneels and waits ~~on upon~~ \on/ you hand and foot—" ("From my Wife" [*The Farther Shore* 1] 10–12, "The Dolphin" manuscript; see poem on page 260); and "You left two houses and two thousand books, | a workbarn by the ocean, and two slaves | to kneel and wait upon you hand and foot—" ("Voices" [*Hospital II* 1] 10–12, *The Dolphin*).

Do you want to know of deaths and sicknesses at home? Do you feel no need for continuity or are you expatriated, occasionally informed by random visitors?

You could go home with us, to us, if you wished now. Essex will not buoy like Harvard. I understand it is dreary, like Stony Brook with a few good faculty.

My heart is broken, but I must make a clean break. I am strong & still get joy out of life. I do not believe in destruction, though I am \often/ wild.[1]

    Love, hope for you
      Elizabeth

~~P.S.~~[2]

Cal: Inside is a letter from me, some envelopes & cards stamped, some cards from the \National/ Gallery, I am going shopping, Bill is trying to get our tickets to leave Friday morning, day after tomorrow. Perhaps you can call me this afternoon & we could meet at 5 before I go to Valerie's.[3] I will see you as much as you like tomorrow, my last day.

    Love,
      Elizabeth (Lizzie)

Bill \in 320/ [will?] see you for lunch, if you like[.]

68. Elizabeth Hardwick to Robert Lowell[4]

> Clive Hotel, Primrose Hill Road, Hampstead, London N W 3
> [n.d. August 1970]

Cal, darling: If you need me I'll always be there, and if you don't need me I'll always not be there.

    Salud & happiness, I wish you.
      Lizzie

---

1. Thomas Wyatt: "And wylde for to hold, though I seme tame" ("Who So List to Hunt" 14).

2. Handwritten on a paper postcard bag from the National Gallery.

3. Valerie Eliot (T. S. Eliot's widow), who lived at 3 Kensington Court Gardens, London.

4. Handwritten.

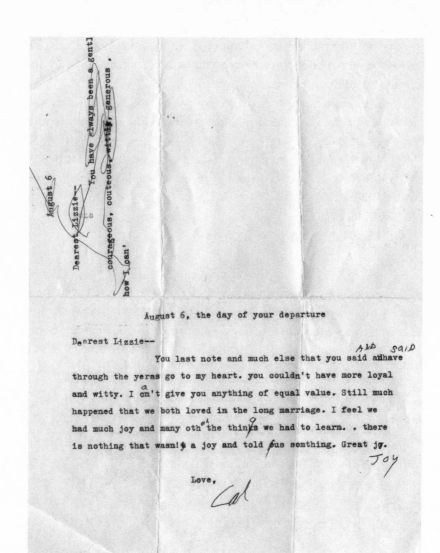

Robert Lowell to Elizabeth Hardwick, August 6, 1970

69. *Robert Lowell to* Mrs. Robert Lowell[1]

[Greenways Nursing Home, 11 Fellows Road, London]
August 6, [1970]

~~August 6~~
~~Dearest Lizzie~~

---

1. All typos in this letter are given as in the original. Addressed to "Mrs. Robert Lowell, Castine, Maine U!S!A!"

~~You have always been a gentl~~
~~courageous, couteous, witty, generous.~~
~~how I can'~~

August 6, the day of your departure

Dearest Lizzie—

You[r] last note and much else that you said \and/ ~~an~~ have \said/ through the years go to my heart. you couldn't have more loyal and witty. I can't give you anything of equal value. Still much happened that we both loved in the long marriage. I feel we had much joy and many oth\er/ ~~the~~ thin~~k~~gs we had to learn. . there is nothing that wasn!t a joy and told ~~ous~~ something. Great jy \joy/.

Love,
Cal

70. *Robert Lowell to* Mrs. Robert Lowell[1]

[Greenways Nursing Home, 11 Fellows Road, London]
~~October~~ \August/ 9, 1970

Dearest Lizzie:

Daily I send off those curious London sights photographs to Harriet.[2] I wonder what her fellow campers make of them. O O, the camp is running out, the yellow leaves are coming, even \here/ where I think of the climate as Norwegian. I bubble on,[3] saying nothing because I am thinking more contentedly tha[n] ever of your long and yet rushed visit. A heart here thinks of you always. I expect to leave here about a week from now (nothing since the rainbow of Noah's flood is certain) and already feel better in a way than I have for months.

All my love to you and all,
Cal

\P.S. All love to you./

---

1. Dated by Lowell October 9, 1970 (the correction "August" is written in Hardwick's hand). Addressed from R! Lowell.

2. Postcards now missing. Lowell: "Horseguard and Lifeguard, one loud red, one yellow, | colorful and wasteful and old hat. . . . | Americans can buy them on a postcard—" ("Walter Raleigh" [*Hospital* 5] 1–3, *The Dolphin*).

3. Thus. Cf. Lowell: "my hand tingled | to burst the bubbles | drifting from the noses of the cowed, compliant fish"; "Colonel Shaw is riding on his bubble, | he waits | for the blessèd break" ("For the Union Dead" 6–8 and 61–64).

71. *Robert Lowell to* Mrs. Robert Lowell[1]

[Greenways Nursing Home, 11 Fellows Road, London]

August 11, 1970

Dearest Lizzie:

There's cold in the the air, enough to make me rub my feet for warmth. And th\en/ a colder, perhaps truer air in Maine. Illusions, surely! The true Maine is always at [a] distance. You are there. And this morning I can reach to you. O I hope I have reached Harriet Lowell, To whom I have sent many postcards, terrible things like the horseguards which you were so gracious as to buy, stamp and leave me.

Goodbye, My Love,

Cal

```
(The Farther Shore)                                                    11

   3. Notes for an unwritten Letter
              IN THE AIR
      Ice of first autumn, enough to make me hold
Soels my feet for warmth. A purer cold in Maine---    IS a
      all things are truer there, truth's foreign langauge.
      The terrible postcards you bought and stamped for me
      are mailed to Harriet: the horseguards, the lifeguards,
      the golden Lord Mayor's chariot, Queen Bess---    HAVE GONE
      true as anything else to fling a child...                  WISHED
      In Maine, my country as I loved to boast,  WHERE I DARED TO DIE
      each empty sweater  and vacant bookshelf hurts, I OCE
      the pretexts for their service gone.     ALL THE
      I shout into the air, my voice comes back,
      it doesn't carry to the farther shore,
      rashly removed, still ringing in my ears.
      Is a sound sleeper one you will not wake?
                            WHO
```

"Notes for an unwritten Letter" [*The Farther Shore* 3], from "The Dolphin" manuscript,[2] composed and revised between 1970 and January 1972.

72. *Elizabeth Hardwick to Robert Lowell*

[Castine, Maine]

Aug. 12, 1970

Dearest Cal: I don't know that you will even get this, but I do want to write to say that your kind note to me meant a lot, more than a lot,

---

1. Addressed to "Mrs. Robert Lowell, Castine, Maine U!S!A!"

2. Cf. "Letter" [*Hospital II* 2] 4–12, *The Dolphin*.

more than I can say . . . Beloved Mary \Incarnatus!/ was waiting at the boiling Bangor airport, even though it was not certain I would be there. All is serene and beautiful here, tennis, friends. I leave in a few days for a couple of nights with Francine and Olga and then back with Harriet on the 15th. That will be a joy.

All my good wishes go with you always.

Lizzie

73. Elizabeth Hardwick to Robert Lowell

[Castine, Maine]
August 13, 1970

Dearest One: Letters, letters, letters. Now the bank calls that your signature is needed to get the money for the trip B. and I made. I dread the arrival of the bills from Faber[1] and the long passage, with many regurgitations for new information, through the intestines of the Blue Cross, but will try as hard as I can. Those \bills/ not taken by B.C. will be paid by the bank.

It is so much fun here. Up this morning writing a parody for the yacht club poetry contest (judges Mary McCarthy, Philip Booth, Frank Hatch). It is called Reminiscences of the Bay Poets and is a jumble of lines and moods from Lowell, Booth, Eberhart, Daniel Hoffman. Since I don't have Booth, Eberhart and Hoffman exactly at my finger tips a little digging was necessary. Tennis games are marvelous, lasting until seven. Somehow Castine is a lot livelier and gayer than it used to be; perhaps it's the hot summer.

Daniel Berrigan arrested last night.[2] He had been underground, hiding out. Barbara called me at ten. I had just come from the dock with Mary and Jim and their nice friend, Leonard Tennyson. I cried, even though of course he would be caught. It took four months.

---

1. Lowell's London hospital bills were covered by Faber & Faber as a loan until he could be reimbursed by Blue Cross Association, his U.S. health insurance company. See Lowell to Hardwick, May 6, [1971], below.

2. United Press International, "Fugitive Priest Is Seized by F.B.I.; Berrigan, Draft File Burner, Arrested on Block Island," *New York Times*, August 12, 1970; Special to The New York Times, "Father Berrigan Begins 3-Year Sentence for Burning Draft Records," *New York Times*, August 13, 1970.

Dreadfully worrying story in the Times recently, saying many of the gentlest Catholic C.o.'s[1] and resisters have been put in maximum security prisons, where they are at the mercy of assaults, sexual and otherwise, by the most incorrigible criminals. If you complain you may be killed. Philip Berrigan has been in one such, being held there as a hostage because of Dan we think . . . [2] It is all so sad. Old Spock[3] was around the harbor the other day, sent (over) greetings to you. Ann and Alfred Kazin have spent the summer near Blue Hill, which seems odd, and are coming over this afternoon. Alfred has been unkind about M.McC.[4] and so nothing communal can be planned, but I hear he is in good shape and she is predatory as ever.

Off at dawn for Connecticut. I am hoping Harriet will have a good time here and am planning reading and music evenings \for the two of us/ that may just go, people are having us both to dinner and I somehow think she will enjoy that in part. The Halls[5] will tune her guitar and a little solitude will be nice for her after the urban, teen-age torpor of the camp. Francine Gray visited Harriet in camp and wrote "what a stupendous beauty she is!" In a strange sense her suffering and loss have made everyone love her more and that comes at a time when she can receive it because she is older. I feel so guilty at times, because somehow I never made enough effort with the children of our friends, for her to take part in various families that she might have. But she is surrounded by love and sincere wishes for her happiness, and effort to provide pleasures and re-assurance. I am hopeful.

Olga just called with arrangements for my visit. I'm staying with Francine, because her house is bigger. I told Olga I was in the midst of writing you and she sent love.

Dearest Cal, I miss you sorely. You are loved here by me and Harriet and many others, by all of us, who have known you and who

---

1. Lowell: "I was a fire-breathing Catholic C.O." ("Memories of West Street and Lepke" 14, *Life Studies*).

2. See Joel Kovel, "In the Service of Their Country: The Young Men Who Say No to the Government," *New York Times*, July 5, 1970; and Homer Bigart, "Prison Denies Berrigan Is Mistreated," *New York Times*, July 30, 1970.

3. Dr. Benjamin Spock.

4. See the portrait of Mary McCarthy in "1940," the final part of Alfred Kazin's *Starting Out in the Thirties* (1965), pp. 154–59.

5. Bernice and David Hall.

will always miss your presence. Please, honey man, sign this \Sheet enclosed inside envelope. But needs stamp, Baby!/ and mail immediately.

> Dearest love again,
> Elizabeth

74. *Robert Lowell to* Mrs. Robert Lowell

80 Redcliffe Square, Kensington, London[1]

August 27, 1970

Dearest Lizzie:

Nothing worthy to answer your beautiful letters. I've been rambling about getting a studio,[2] toying with revisions, feeling the deadest poet as so often, and getting my textbooks ordered for Essex. Very cordial department \head/ who found an actually much better anthology for the one I'd ordered, also one much worse. No pressure. Also my students are already picked for me in very small numbers, so I avoid that agony. Not much else a lunch with Karl Miller, stay in Kent.[3] I don't feel very boastful, but I don't think I'm a bastard. I rather look forward to Essex; teaching is so much easier and more dependable than writing, tho so much less.

I've thought much and wonderingly about Harriet's picture. Since Venice she's turned into a woman, or is that only the photographer's angle? Then the profound in the second line and rather sad camp note.[4]

---

1. Caroline Blackwood's London address.
2. Caroline Blackwood to Ian Hamilton: "I told him he must get a flat of his own. Which he minded terribly—he was very wounded. But it was like it always was—he *wasn't* all right: he was terrified of being alone [. . .] But Israel said rightly, was saying, 'I really don't want a madman with the children.' I had to tell Cal that. Because Israel could have taken the children away from me" (*Robert Lowell: A Biography*, p. 403).
3. Location of Blackwood's house Milgate Park.
4. Lowell: "*You must be strong through solitude, said Fate,* | *for the present this thought alone must be your shelter*—| this in your yearbook by your photograph" ("In Harriet's Yearbook" 1–3, *The Dolphin*). There is no such page in Harriet Lowell's 1970 Dalton yearbook, though it may have been a yearbook from the Cornwall Summer Workshop. The quotation, which, according to Harriet Lowell, was chosen not by her but by a yearbook editor, is from Paul Klee: "You must grow strong through solitude, spoke fate. For the time being let thought alone be my shelter" (*The Diaries of Paul Klee, 1898–1918*, ed. Felix Klee, trans. Pierre B. Schneider, R. Y. Zachary, and Max Knight [1968], p. 54).

I wish I could be with her and let her let fly her random thoughts. We were good at deep jokes. When can I see you both? I thought of a trip leaving here around the 10th of December, or a little later. Would that confuse? Well, God bless you, all the sorrow in joy. Thanks for liking my revolutionary sonnet group.[1] They'll have a different arrangement in NOTEBOOK but this pleased me.

All my love,
Cal

75. *Robert Lowell to* Miss Harriet Lowell

80 Redcliffe Square, London
August 27, 1970

Dearest Harriet:

I don't \know/ what a father so far away can say to you. My life except for you and mother is naturally much as it always was. Writing teaching enjoying myself as much as I dare. This country is like a combination of country Connecticut and Boston, perhaps. Not much like New York maybe. I'm like myself, just as you are like yourself. But I know you are older. A girl your age must grow older and wiser, which isn't always true of the old. I want very much for you to talk and feel at ease with me. All is as was, tho never quite. I may come to New York sometime before Christmas, if you and mother ask me.

All my love,[2]

---

1. "Ulysses and Nausicaa," "Marching," "Romanoffs," "Robespierre and Mozart as Stage," "Saint Just (1767–1793)," "Death and the Bridge" [*The Revolution* I-VI], *Modern Occasions* (Fall 1970). Cf. with the titles and order of poems in *Notebook70*.
2. Unsigned.

76. *Elizabeth Hardwick to* Mr. Robert Lowell

[Postcard: Charles Osgood—*Nathaniel Hawthorne* (1840), Essex Institute, Salem, Massachusetts]

[Castine, Maine]
[September 3, 1970]

Sorry about that stupid phone call. Please don't call us. I'll write when I get time & hope all this will be better by then. I realize there is nothing on earth you can do or feel about our problems, small or grave. The call was a desperate reflex I guess. I'm looking after Harriet & time will help. I believe (this a.m.) the return to Dalton & seeing her friends was the trouble.

Lizzie

77. *Robert Lowell to* Mrs. Robert Lowell

[London]
[September 1970]

Dearest Lizzie—

I have been thinking about you most of the time and am very stirred up about Harriet, the vagueness about what happened of course making things almost ominous, though I think I know what happened, an extreme explosion of anger and tears, and sad thoughts about herself. I suppose it will pass, part of her age's whirlpool,[1] but one must never say this and rely more or less on nature, though there's little else.

Glad to have the checks and have added a thousand dollars to my small account. Saw Gertrude[2] two days ago, who was temporarily in the house of the man I rent from.[3] Somehow fated. We had a pleasant evening. She has a little job with a little publisher, which she complains of, though bravely. Yet, miracle, she is as she was twenty years ago to my dim eye.

School begins in two or three weeks. I've been assembling my

---

1. T. S. Eliot: "He passed the stages of his age and youth | Entering the whirlpool" ("Death by Water" [*The Waste Land* IV] 6–7).

2. Buckman, with whom Lowell had a love affair in 1946–48; see *The Letters of Robert Lowell*, pp. 53–86.

3. 33 Pont Street, owned by Desmond FitzGerald.

texts, and Essex had been helpful, a good American anthology, which costs ten pounds, more than any student can buy, and something made up of Ginsberg and the Black Mountain for the moderns. Am I a wolf in black fleece offering myself to the very advanced classes of Essex?

Not much more money will be needed; soon my salary will be rolling in. I would like what I get from royalties. Is that too much? When I come in Christmas time I'll clean up the papers business, which should set us up better. All love to you and Harriet.

Love,[1]

78. *Robert Lowell to* Mrs. Robert Lowell

33 Pont St., London SW 1
September 12, 1970

Dearest Lizzie:

Suddenly after mailing my letter I realized I hadn't thanked you properly for the checkbook and making the whole business of cashing so easy. Even if we think of ourselves (not practical) as still on the old basis of a joint account, still nothing could be done without your help.

No news here. This is one of those rainy dark European city days, pleasing at times, but at others they almost make one ~~see~~ \touch/ eternity as Baudelaire wrote. I am reading the Shakespeare I will teach, mostly the Roman plays. I rather need a library, but I've always more or less gotten on without using one, except for the random, accidental offering of Quincy House. But now instead of Hazlitt's characters, I have Professor Dorsch's defense of the character of Julius Caesar.[2] Professor Dorsch is the editor of my edition, and is too off even to effectively disagree with. Love to Dear Harriet.

Love,
Cal

1. Unsigned.

2. William Hazlitt, *Characters of Shakespear's Plays* (1817); Shakespeare, *Julius Caesar*, ed. T. S. Dorsch (1964).

79. Elizabeth Hardwick to Mary McCarthy

[15 West 67th Street, New York, N.Y.]

Sept. 17, 1970

Dearest Mary: Just a note to say I meant the quotation about Ivy Compton Burnett as an example of good writing. . . .[1] And as another example, your wonderful letter was such a joy to receive this morning and I read it over twice for the pleasure of it. Ah, Philip. I would much rather have your delicious account than meet that creature in the flesh.[2] He makes me so nervous somehow and leaves me with the feeling of my own insignificance that takes some time to cast off.

Here in New York it is actually very nice, cool, often bright, with something suspended, waiting . . . and not the revolution, as those inane young persons see it . . . but perhaps some return to sanity, or perhaps not. Seeing Nixon making a boring law and order speech, you realize that they are desperate and these vague banalities are all they have.[3] But thirty or forty boring hecklers keep it alive when obviously we should ignore, at least in so far as public attendance is concerned, both Nixon and Agnew, let them go on talking and then do your own talking, at your own time. I can't quite explain what I feel is different this fall. It may be fatigue with the peculiarity of our politics and it may not. Anyway it is very nice somehow, and all of a sudden different. One feels like trying to write well, trying to read again, trying

1. Hardwick: "Here is the opening of an essay on Ivy Compton-Burnett: 'A Compton-Burnett is a reliable make, as typical of British Isles workmanship as a tweed or Tiptree or an Agatha Christie. The styling does not change greatly from year to year; production is steady.' This is immediately arresting. It strikes one as true, well-said, as the phrase used to be. But just as Mary McCarthy has moved beyond the fashionable, so she has in her style gradually sloughed off the need for novelty and with it certain staccato, epigrammatic effects" ("Books: *The Writing on the Wall*," *Vogue*, September 1, 1970, p. 306). McCarthy: "I'm pleased and touched by your *Vogue* piece . . . One thing puzzles me about what you say. You quote from the opening of the Compton-Burnett piece, and I can't figure out whether you mean this as an example of the 'staccato, epigrammatic effects' you think (or hope) I've outgrown. Or the opposite" (to Hardwick, September 14, 1070 [1970]).

2. McCarthy: "Just to keep my stock down, he [Philip Rahv] made the following marvelous remark, shortly after arrival: 'I read your chapter in the *Atlantic*. People tell me the one in *Playboy* is better.' Total comment. He had the appropriate bane for everyone" (to Hardwick, September 14, 1970; also quoted in Kiernan, *Seeing Mary Plain*, p. 644).

3. On September 16, 1970, at Kansas State University. See Robert B. Semple, Jr., "President Urges End to Violence and Intolerance; Makes a Strong Appeal for Restoration and Civility in American Society," *New York Times*, September 17, 1970.

to be happy and calm. All of this sounds foolish, but it is just a way of saying that the "crisis" existence of the last few years seems to have died down even though the very conditions remain and may even be worse. I am hoping to write my book that will be about Kentucky, myself in college, a little, and coming to New York, etc. I will try to be as removed from myself as possible and try to get the feeling of the thing. I have been talking it over with Jason[1] or rather he called me to talk about my doing just this and what he thought were the possible themes that might make it a book of interest right now. Jason is a wonderful publisher in the sense of "exploiting" with great energy the things he likes and so I am somewhat buoyed up by the thought that, when I get the book done, he might "put me over."[2]

I've had some letters from Cal and talked to him on the phone the day we got back. He has his own flat, or maybe it is just a studio. I can't tell what mood or period, if that is the right word, he may be in and I try not to think about him. Every day brings new things of interest and painful as it is still I believe one cannot win with Cal. He will spare you nothing, least of all that terrible breeziness and casualness about the deepest feelings of your own life and, also, of his own.

Harriet is fine, I think. She's back in school and very busy and talks on the phone from five to six without stopping and all of that is nice. The summer was beautiful in Castine. I like it more and more there, because you are there I'm sure, and Jim. But all the others are dear to me too, and the town, all of it.

Well, dearest love, Mary[,] and take up your book with a happy heart—if one can ever take up the hard, hard task in quite that way.[3] What would be better is: take it up with confidence and pride.

    Lizzie

---

1. Epstein, who was an editor at Random House.
2. OED: "to put over (d) To convey or take across or to the other side; to transport: [. . .] c1595 CAPT. WYATT R. Dudley's Voy. W. Ind . . . 'To give them a faire gale to putt them over to the maine'" ("Put, vi." 49, Oxford English Dictionary Vol. VIII [1933]).
3. McCarthy was writing Birds of America (1971).

80. *Robert Lowell to* Mrs. Robert Lowell

33 Pont Street, London SW 1

September 18, 1970

Dearest Lizzie:

In a postcard you said you realized that there was nothing I could do about your problems.[1] I was sad of course when I read this, and knew in a way you were partly true. The distance is fa\r/ther than a hand can reach or mind can perhaps attend.[2] Nothing for me to do, and as for my feeling it's an acute, useless undifferentiated ache. I can't imagine the inside of your lives, yet I am not free at all of what I've done to you.

Very soon I'll begin my teaching and am pointing toward it— getting classbooks even reading them. It's all very shadowy but I guess my feet are on earth. I do miss you both and would ask to be forgiven, if that had active meaning. All's well. Do let us keep in touch, closely in touch till I come at Christmas.

Love to you both,

Cal

The last few days, after finishing Shakespeare's Roman plays, I've \had/ the London sights with a guidebook. The Tower is more Roman than Fellini's Satyricon[3] which I also saw.

81. *Robert Lowell to* Mrs. Robert Lowell

33 Pont Street, London SW 1

September 25, 1970

Dearest Lizzie:

I see we are using the same ornate letter-paper.[4] And if you were to \use/ my old typewriter, it would be the same type or at least the same

---

1. See Hardwick to Lowell, [September 3, 1970], above.

2. Lowell: "I shout into the air, my voice comes back, | it doesn't carry to the farther shore," ("Notes for an Unwritten Letter" [*The Farther Shore* 3] 11–12, "The Dolphin" manuscript (see poem on page 98).

3. (1969).

4. Typed on plain paper stationery.

machine. So much for continuity. I would have written sooner, but I've been spending a few days in Amsterdam with Huyck and Judith.[1]

Adrienne came up naturally often in our talk but no one knew of the separation.[2] I am sorry, knowing nothing about it. Mostly because Adrienne seems ~~so~~ \such a/ match~~stick~~, tho gloriously, to live by herself. Again, knowing nothing about the facts, I don't think the separation will last long and because Adrienne will need Alf if she goes to the hospital again,[3] and because after all they shared and agreed on many things. I don't quite know how to write into her confusion and don't know the address, but give \her/ all my love. What are Street Schools?[4]

When I first came to England, people gave me quite a few \old/ long pieces, so that naturally there seemed to be the world's abundance and enthusiasm. I suppose I'm liked in one country about as much as another. These buildings can fall in a minute.

I do want to hear all your communication and gossip. It could never be too much. I too can't state my feelings even to myself. The past is almost more with me than today. I look on it with all pride and joy, but it is piercing to look back, especially when I have no reproaches. Shall `I say that I, or rather we, are alright? There's much to be said at length at Christmas. Love to yourself and to my Harriet. She has gone into a void, but I can't imagine she would find writing to me pleasant. In your next letter, quote something she has said.

Love,
Cal

---

1. Huyck van Leeuwen and Judith Herzberg were also friends with Adrienne Rich and Alfred H. Conrad.

2. From her husband, Alfred H. Conrad.

3. For orthopedic surgery to treat her recurrent rheumatoid arthritis (Adrienne Rich, email message to editor, 2003).

4. Adrienne Rich: "In September, 1970, on a corner in the [West] 90s [in Manhattan], two school buildings stood across from each other. One was—and still is—the sleek new brick wing of an old established boys' preparatory school. The other, lodged in a (now demolished) storefront bordered by an empty lot full of broken bricks and glass, didn't look like a school at all . . . Inside the Elizabeth Cleaners a tuition-free, alternate high school was beginning to hold classes" ("The Case for a Drop-out School," *New York Review of Books* [June 15, 1972].) See also Elizabeth Cleaners Street School, *Starting Your Own High-School*, ed. David Nasaw (1972).

82. *Robert Lowell to* Mrs. Robert Lowell

33 Pont Street, London
September 28, 1970

Dearest Lizzie:

The enclosed is ambiguous.[1] I don't know whether I have \a/ rough five thousand *minus* three thousand or the whole $4,700. I've written Bob[2] to give you three in the probable second case, and one thousand in the first. Confusion infects; I am almost as muddled as Bob. I don't remember signing any check in June, but seem to remember that you drew the royalties, as was right. We can make this a little clearer at Christmas.

I have been sightseeing in the strangely oppressive heat, saw a very hard small baby elephant and now recognize most of the London place names in Vile Bodies.[3] Saw Poirier[4] with Karl Miller, smart enough but the evening was enlivened by a frank argument on homosexuals. Poirier backed your halfattack on Hemingway,[5] then went on at length to ~~defend~~ \glorify/ him in general. Tomorrow I go trembling to school for the first time,[6] and I hope \for a library with/ more than the weekly literary reviews which I have been gorging. If there weren't a paper strike, I fear I'd be reading the news down t[o] the sporting pages and movie ads. I want to get the money news off to you.

Love to you both,
Cal

---

1. Enclosure now missing.

2. Giroux.

3. Evelyn Waugh, *Vile Bodies* (1930).

4. Richard Poirier.

5. Hardwick, "Dead Souls," *New York Review of Books*, June 5, 1969.

6. "And then the whining school-boy, with his satchel | And shining morning face, creeping like snail | Unwillingly to school" (*As You Like It* 2.7).

83. Robert Lowell to Elizabeth Bishop

33 Pont Street
[October 5, 1970]

Dearest Elizabeth:

Didn't I write about your beautiful poem?[1] It's the nearest thing you've written to a short story in verse—an *I*,[2] you or not you, telling a naturalistic narrative, more heightened than prose fiction would accept, very personal, the way a short story can sometimes be, without too much stress, because you always, till well on in writing, seem to be just quietly talking. One of your poems that most stays with me. \My dentist, I feel!/

I've written thirty more poems in the meter of *Notebook*, but somehow unlike *Notebook* in tone—more strained, the Romantic romance of a married man in a hospital. Mostly I'm not very very forthright. A few may be good, but I am disheartened by the whole, and keep trying to comb out the unnecessarily grand obscurities I somehow began with.

Like you I depended on Bill for everything all my years at Harvard. Once I was a year behind on my health certificate. Perhaps much more, I depended on him for companionship. I could always drop in and have drinks or a dinner or meet students. Often they, not I, came to his house at four in the afternoon and left at four in the morning. Give him my love; today I am going to Essex to teach for the first time and dreading the undefined errors I am bound to make without Bill. Give him my love.

By now you will probably have fifty poet-appliers, manuscripts double at first meeting. I tried to cut them down to 12 but usually couldn't. Then I made the mistake of letting in auditors, usually wives of physics professors, who wrote better often than most of the students in worn styles that couldn't be digested by the students. Other classes were comfortably small but insultingly so. I had three for the Bible. Some were too large to talk, others too small. Yet the students mostly in the end were ideal, or at least in class they were. I don't think you'll \have/ troubles. I almost always left a class happier.

---

1. "In the Waiting Room" (later published in the *New Yorker*, July 17, 1971).

2. Bishop: "But I felt: you are an *I*, | you are an *Elizabeth*, | you are one of *them*" ("In the Waiting Room," 60–62).

Natasha Spender speaking of her husband teaching English students for the first \time/, says he is like a boy going off from home to school for the first time.

My "someone" is Caroline Citkowitz. She \is 39/, has published stories in the *London Magazine*, has three very pretty daughters, oldest ten, and was once years ago married to Freud's grandson, Lucian. You might have ~~meant~~ met; Caroline lived some time in San Francisco and later in New York, but you haven't or she would remember. However she reads you with great admiration and thinks you much brighter than Mary whom she knows. What a bare list, but how can I make the introduction? She is very beautiful and saw me through the chafes and embarrassments of my sickness with wonderful kindness. I suppose I shouldn't forget Harriet and Lizzie, anyway I can't. Guilt clouds the morning, and though things are not embattled, nothing is settled. I'll be back in New York for Christmas, then there will perhaps be more decision. I could be happy either way, if things could be settled. But nothing is. I am happy to be in presentable spirits.

This is somewhat in the mood of waiting [to] take a train to my new work later this afternoon. If only life \could/ be as manageable as teaching. Didn't Faust say this? England, I speak from the wisdom of a six months stay, is wonderfully unstirred after New York.

All my love,
Cal

84. Robert Lowell to Blair Clark

33 Pont St., London SW 1
October 9, 1970

Dear Blair:

When I first read your postcard, through some macabre mistake I read that Peter White had *raised* the list of class suicides to four—I only know of two excluding Al Clark.[1] What a grim way of holding the suspense then suddenly springing it. Glad he's alive.

I expect to come over to New York during the Christmas holidays. There's a problem whether to come with ~~Lizzie~~ \Caroline/. The only

---

1. From the St. Mark's School Class of 1936. See Lowell, "Alfred Corning Clark (1916–1961)," *For the Union Dead.*

time she can come is before Christmas, while Lizzie wants me to come later when Harriet like Caroline's children will be out of school. However, it seems callous humanly for me to *arrive* in New York, in Lizzie's home city, with Caroline. Or am I being meaninglessly scrupulous? Until the divorce is made, and it looks as though it will, and that I will marry Caroline—it still remains uncertain in my mind. When friends of mine have been in this dilemma, I've always thought they should stop torturing themselves and everyone else, and make a quick clean severance. But it's not easy, unless one becomes some sort of doll only capable of fast straightforward action.

I am beginning to teach and enjoy it, also getting away to London. Sometimes the change is small, tonight Caroline and I are having dinner with an angry young Hindu novelist whom I met in a pub near my sanitarium. Sunday, a higher life, the Spenders. Just talked to Mary finishing her novel and depressed; we'll see her here in a few weeks. Hope you'll \see/ Joanna and all moves toward, not heaven, but paradise. I miss you. Could I or we stay with you in midDecember? Love,
Cal

85. *Robert Lowell to* Mrs. Robert Lowell

33 Pont Street, London, SW 1
October 11, 1970

Dearest Lizzie:

This has been a gray warm Sunday until now at twilight it is cool and clear. For the last three or four hours, I have been home and on bed reading forty or fifty pages of Emerson's poems for ~~class~~ \teaching/. The unease of distance and severance are on me. He says of his child that his lips could pronounce "words that were persuasions."[1]

Why don't you write and tell me what is happening? I know it's hard in this uncertain, changing time. You wrote something—like so \many/ phrases and feelings in your letters, it stays with me—like it was hard to state your thoughts accurately, even in your thoughts.[2] I feel that too, and so find it hard to write, though not-writing I'm afraid

---

1. Ralph Waldo Emerson: "For his lips could well pronounce | Words that were persuasions" ("Threnody" 52–53).
2. Letter now missing.

was always one of my gifts. Let me hear of you and Harriet, and at length, if you can.

Essex, my part of it, is enough like Harvard to sometimes seem [a] mirage. The same students, tho half audible from their good manners and foreign idiom, the same old classes, the \same/ with fresh text-books, a taxi drive along the Thames that is like the East River and even the Charles. I suppose my low-toned, conversational teaching is safe from the falls of ambition, but I feel wobbling in talking. You can seldom tell what students think, or what is perhaps more important, what good you've said. It's all fairly pleasant. "The gentle lifesaver of routine," as Emerson might have said, if he had had less soaring comforts.

Did you get the three thousand dollars? It deserves a note, even if it has already melted into the flow of costs. I really haven't very much. I have enough, but wish I could hear.

Love,
Cal

86. William Alfred to Robert Lowell

31 Athens Street, Cambridge, Mass. 02138
15 October 1970

Dear Cal,

Please write Elizabeth something clearest about what you mean to do. Your letters, written in kindness though they are, only serve to deepen her conviction that you are of two minds about the years ahead. That makes her miss you more, and understandably resent the pain your absence is causing her. And please be careful with Harriet. Send her little things from time to time. London has wonderful shoplets where you can pick up pretty bits of jewelry reasonably (the alleys off the Charing Cross Road, near the train station). She is at the age now where she could lose faith in everything for good, if it isn't made clear to her why you won't be with her. They say the fear of death is at bottom only our childhood fear of desertion come of age.[1] I know you can bring her through that fear with your gift ~~of~~ \for/ love and words.

---

1. Cf. Lowell: "They say fear of death is a child's remembrance | of the first desertion" ("During a Transatlantic Call" 7–8, *The Dolphin*).

Frank Bidart tells me he has an advance copy of the book, and he thinks it is a towering achievement.

I miss you, and pray for your happiness and well being.

Love,

Bill

87. Elizabeth Hardwick to Robert Lowell

[15 West 67th Street, New York, N.Y.]

October 16, 1970

Darling: This is the last of the letters. *Please telegraph Harriet and me about when you are coming home for good.* That is the only question, the only reality . . . All the rest is just foolishness on my part. We are utterly miserable, unbelievably wounded. I do feel as I say again that this is like a death. We can't bear your photographs, anything . . . [1] What you have done is very, very serious. All we need to know is when you are coming back. If you aren't coming soon, then we absolutely must know. Please, please—tell us the answer right now. We cannot go on this way, and we will not.

I'm working and getting things in shape when I'm not writing. I feel as if I were preparing for my own death somehow. I can't, if anything should happen, leave Harriet with all this confusing junk about, all the mixed up drawers stuffed with old things.

How horrible this is.

I have told her that I am asking you to let us know once and for all. I know you understand, as anyone alive would, that you cannot stay away until the end of the school year. That is out of the question . . . But you realize that . . . Anyone who can leave his family and never return can certainly get out of a teaching job by explaining how dearly, painfully he is needed back across the ocean . . . We love you my dear . . . You'll be exhausted from these letters. But there will not be more unless you are planning to return to us. I cannot bear it other-

---

1. Cf. Lowell: ". . . I was playing records on Sunday, | arranging all my records, and I came | on some of your voice, and started to suggest | that Harriet listen: then immediately | we both shook our heads. It was like hearing | the voice of the beloved who had died. [. . .] " ("Records" 1–6, *The Dolphin*).

wise, it is degrading, unnecessary and quite destructive for me to keep writing to someone who doesn't care for me or for his daughter.

We long to have you open the door, to laugh, play music, have you call from your phone upstairs, have a bourbon, fuss, kiss you, have grape-nuts, clean up your studio, kiss Harriet in the morning, look at Sumner on the blue chair, have dinner ~~with~~ in our dark orange dining room, see your little white seal in its window, the crushed tin from the explosion on 11th Street,[1] your books, your poems, your writing, your oldest jokes and your newest,—and to look after you forever, and to have you look after us. WE NEED YOU. We really need you.

    Lizzie

When are you coming home?

88. *Elizabeth Hardwick to Robert Lowell*

[Telegram]

[New York]
OCT 16 PM 5.13 [1970]

ROBERT LOWELL

33 PONT STREET

LONDONSW1

MANY LETTERS ON THEIR WAY[2] STOP THANKS FOR THE MONEY STOP

HARRIET AND I ARE GRIEVING PITIFULLY STOP SHE IS ONLY 13[3] STOP PLEASE COME HOME LOVE

    LIZZIE

---

1. Members of the Weather Underground destroyed a townhouse in an accidental explosion on March 6, 1970. See Douglas Robinson, "Townhouse Razed by Blast and Fire; Man's Body Found," *New York Times*, March 7, 1970. Lowell "might have had a crushed tin of something and made a joke that it came from the Weatherman townhouse" (Harriet Lowell, interview with the editor, July 5, 2016).

2. Some now missing.

3. Cf. Lowell: "You insist on treating Harriet as if she | were thirty or a wrestler—she is only thirteen" ("In the Mail" 4–5, *The Dolphin*); see footnote 2 on page 293. Cf. Frank Bidart to Lowell, June 4, 1970; Lowell to Harriet Lowell [April 2, 1972]; and Hardwick to Lowell [no date summer 1972].

89. *Robert Lowell to* Mrs. Robert Lowell

33 Pont Street, London, SW 1
October 18
(Shortly after our phone-talk)

Dearest Lizzie:

I don't know whether I've said or written ~~that~~ I feel like a man walking on two ever more widely splitting roads at once, as if I were pulled apart and thinning into mist,[1] or rather being torn apart and still preferring that state to making a decision. Is there any decision still for me to make? After all I have done, and all that seven months have done, can I go back to you and Harriet? Too many cuts.

Time has changed things somewhat since we met at Greenways, I am soberer, cooler. More displeasing to myself in many little ways, but mostly about you. A copy of my new book came the other day, and I read through all the new and more heavily revised poems. A sense of the meaning of the whole came to me, and it seemed to be about us and our family, its endurance being the spine which despite many bendings and blows finally held. Just held. Many reviewers saw this; though it was something I thought pretentious and offensive ~~if claimed~~ \to push/ in my preface, I saw it too. I have felt as if a governing part of my organism were gone, and as if the familiar grass and air were gone.

I don't think I can go back to you. Thought does no good. I cannot weigh the dear, troubled past, so many illnesses, which weren't due to you, in which you saved everything, our wondering, changing, growing years with Harriet, so many places, such rivers of talk and staring—I can't compare this memory with the future, unseen and beyond recollection with Caroline. I love her very much, but I can't see that. I am sure many people have looked back on a less marvelous marriage than ours on the point of breaking, and felt this pain and indecision— at first insoluble, then when the decision has been made, incurable.

I don't think I can come back to you, but allow me this short space before I arrive in New York to wobble in my mind. I will be turning from the longest realest and most loved fragment of my life.

---

1. Cf. Lowell: "Just yesterday we passed from the northern lights | to doomsday mornings. Crowds ~~herd~~ \crush/ to work at eight, | ~~lamp-white like couples leaving a midnight show~~ \and walk with less cohesion than the mist;/" (~~Flounder~~" [~~London and~~ *Winter and London* 4\3./] 1–3, "The Dolphin" manuscript). Cf. "Flounder" [*Winter and London* 3], *The Dolphin*.

I'll arrive mid-day or so on Thursday. I'll probably stay with Blair. We won't feel tied together at all hours, but all my time will be yours. I don't expect to see anyone except Blair and probably Stanley.

I don't want to scrap over details.

My love to you both,

Cal

90. Elizabeth Hardwick to Robert Lowell

[Telegram]

[New York]

1970 OCT 19 03:45

ROBERT LOWELL

33 PONT STREET LONDONSWIENGLAND

CALL ME IMMEDIATELY SERIOUS[1]

ELIZABETH

91. Elizabeth Hardwick and Harriet Lowell to Mr. Robert Lowell[2]

[Postcard: Vittore Carpaccio—*St. Augustine in His Study* (detail)[3]—Venice]

[New York, N.Y.]

[Postmarked Oct 20 AM, 1970, but written Oct. 19?, 1970]

Be lovely to see you. I am not tense about it or expecting anything. Don't worry. Just want a pleasant visit. *Lizzie.*

I can't wait to see you. Love,

Harriet

---

1. Probably about the suicide of Alfred H. Conrad; see postcard from Hardwick to Lowell, October 20, 1970.

2. One of the twelve letters, postcards, and telegrams written by Hardwick that were included in the Lowell Estate's sale of papers to the HRC in 1982.

3. Detail of a dog looking in St. Augustine's direction.

92. *Elizabeth Hardwick to* Mr. Robert Lowell

[Postcard: Greenwich Village, New York City: "One of the most colorful districts in New York, a Bohemian atmosphere pervades this part of the city where artists, writers, sculptors, composers, actors and beatniks make their homes. Here will be found off-Broadway shows, nite-clubs, a great variety of restaurants, exciting Espresso shops and friendly people."]

[New York, N.Y.]
[Oct 20 PM, 1970]

H. just fine today. Her conversation with you cheered her up . . . and I don't think any of these crises will come again. The Conrad thing was horrible and everyone was in agony.[1] Dearest love & hope this didn't upset you. We are O.K.

     E.

93. *Robert Lowell to* Mrs. Robert Lowell

[33 Pont Street, London SW 1]
[October 21, 1970]
Wednesday

Dearest Lizzie—

I phoned you just before leaving for Essex, and now am writing just after returning and reading your letters. Alf's face was with me most of the time, large in the foreground, and what was nearer, you and Harriet and of course thoughts of Adrienne were peeping out behind, as if behind a poster. He always seemed in such full health and discipline, that nothing pointed this way. It's as abrupt as Randall's death, and these last days hits me with the same force, though we weren't close and my real friend was always Adrienne.

You have written so much and so many things, the same repeating contradictory things since last summer. Poor thing, what else could you do under the circumstances? The last letter is relaxed, more relaxed, and ends with more of an up-note. And the last sentence is "hell and damnation . . . Life is so terrible."[2] Even if I returned for good, if

---

1. Alfred H. Conrad, Adrienne Rich's husband, had committed suicide on October 18, 1970.
2. Letter now missing.

that has meaning, almost all would be unsolved. I realize all three of us (crushing realization) have lived a depression, lived through our darks, at more or less the same time. Mine, waking up pricked through with my guilt and hollowness; the same ache you have felt has hurt me, but with time the feeling lifts. It's the usual, once annual depression, lighter than most, but enough to make me peculiarly indecisive and useless to you now. I suppose I've made my choice, I and my seven months absence have ~~have chosen~~, and you are right to say you wouldn't have me back. I feel whatever choice I might make, I am walking off the third story of an unfinished building to the ground. I don't offer this as good description, it's too vague and grand, but to show you why my useless, depressed will, does nothing well. Just the usual somberness after mania, jaundice of the spirit, and yet it has so many absolutely actual objects to pick up—a marriage that was both rib and spine for us these many years.

Caroline isn't (if you really want me to be free to talk to you about her) one of my many manic crushes, rather \this/ and everything more, just as you were at Yaddo and after.[1] She is airy and very steady and sturdy in an odd way. She has been very kind to me. I think we can make out.[2] I love her, we have been together rather a long time—often and intensely. I have ~~fears~~ \doubts/ that I by myself, or anyway, can make \out/, that dear you and Harriet can make out. I think somehow that Christmas will help us all, great troubles but \no/ longer everyone unreal to everyone, and Christmas is the season to lighten the heart.

All my love to both—
Cal

Hold on my Dears. Making out is so much stiffer than making it.

---

1. Lowell and Hardwick fell in love at Yaddo in January 1949. He began to suffer his first major manic episode that winter and was hospitalized for acute mania in March 1949. After his recovery and release from hospital, he and Hardwick were married on July 28, 1949 (the day after Hardwick's thirty-third birthday).

2. Lowell: "'Ourselves,' you wrote, 'are all we know of heaven. | With the intellect, I always can | and always shall make out [. . .]'" ("To Margaret Fuller Drowned," 11–13, *Notebook 70*). OED: "to make out (b) To manage, make shift, to do something. Also *absol.* to make shift, get along; to succeed, thrive; to get on (well, badly). Also *to make it out.* Chiefly *U.S.* . . . 1776 ABIGAIL ADAMS in *Fam. Lett.* (1876) 180, I would not have you anxious about me. I make out better than I did" ("Make, v.1" 91, *Oxford English Dictionary*, Vol. VI).

94. Robert Lowell to Adrienne Rich

[33 Pont Street, London S. W. 1]
Wednesday, October 21, 1970

Dearest Adrienne:

I heard about Alf's death last Monday from Lizzie on the telephone and then went off to my teaching at Essex carrying the wound and a sort of composite picture of him, now short-haired now long and a gay green or blue turtle-necked sweater—accurate thoughts and figures and an ardent moonlight glow. His death seems to me the most tragic I have known since Randall's. In both, the end seems so unproportioned to the previous lives, full of health and promising its renewal. We knew him less well than you, but Lizzie and I have felt we lost part of ourselves, a part of our old lives of the last fifteen years.

You've heard of course from Lizzie about our situation. I am with another girl, Caroline Citkowitz. I love her and we've \been/ together a long stretch by now. Still, it's all somber and unreal. Both Lizzie and Harriet are disturbed, and so am I. Hard to tell what is right or even possible. There's an old picture somewhere, mostly as frontispieces, where Dante stands against an elaborate tapering tower with galleries[1]—it is Purgatory, and it seems to lean. That's how the last twenty-one years seem to me now. This week especially with its many letters. I'll be home for two or three weeks at Christmas. Perhaps things will [be] better and flatter then. Meanwhile the useless inescapable time of the two mutually exclusive choices. I imagine I'll get divorced, and all may be well, but the loss will never go.

I am talking for you in a way in your much greater trouble. I have thought of you much when I heard of your separation, and felt my ignorance was too great to express itself in a letter. Terrible things happen, that have causes of course, but which can't be answered. Maybe you'll try not to, as is best, and your marvelous courage will carry through these new obstacles as it has through so many of the old. At Christmas, I pray that we may have more of our vodka or saki luncheons. My love to the children and all to you.

Love,
Cal

---

1. *La Divina Commedia di Dante* by Domenico di Michelino (1465), in the nave of the Duomo (Cattedrale di Santa Maria del Fiore) in Florence; used as a frontispiece for the Temple edition of *The Purgatorio of Dante Alighieri* (1901).

95. Robert Lowell to William Alfred

[33 Pont Street, London S. W. 1]
October 21, 1970

Dear Bill:

I've just gotten back from Leicester and read your caring letter. Telling Elizabeth plainly and without ambiguity in a letter what I am going to do is hard. It's hard for me to be that certain even in my quietest thoughts. I am coming to New York over Christmas and stay two weeks or so. Then we can talk at leisure, then we can talk it out, which can't be done by letter or long distance phone. This helps no one I have said, and you more or less say. Still such an old and passionate love cannot be ended like slicing pie. The time hasn't been very long after all considering how much is still hanging. I have written Lizzie several times that I felt we would get a divorce, but that we should decide when w[e] met.

Oh yes, you are right about Harriet, I lie awake about her. Jewelry is a good idea. We talked the other day on the phone and things seem less frantic.

Love,
Cal

96. Elizabeth Hardwick to Blair Clark

[15 West 67th Street,
New York, N.Y.]
Friday, October 23, 1970

Dear Blair: I felt after I talked to you yesterday that I wasn't sure you understood what I meant.[1] I really do not want this unreal

---

1. Blair Clark to Lowell, October 22, 1970: "I phoned [Elizabeth] this morning [. . .] in the course of the conversation I found it natural to say that you had written to ask if you could stay with me when you came in December and that I had said of course, yes. To this I added that there was some possibility that Caroline might come too. I should have anticipated the reaction, which was very strong. She said that there were many practical things that had to be settled between you but that if Caroline came when you were here, she would leave town, taking Harriet with her, perhaps to the Caribbean. She would leave all the papers in order and a list of questions for you to answer and deal with, but she wouldn't be here" (Robert Lowell Papers, HRC).

Christmas visit from Cal, but I have asked all my friends, thought about it day and night, and I don't see how he can possibly get in touch with Harriet or she with him unless he sees her. I can't send her there, where she would be on unfamiliar ground—and I haven't the confidence in Cal at this point that would make me able to let a 13 year old go to him. But in re-establishing things I hope and expect to work out something \for them/ and even had in mind something about the spring vacation, if we can afford it. For my business with Cal a visit is not necessary. I do not expect that any of us, even Harriet, will get anything out of it really and I will be glad when it's over . . . Caroline would never come. That is his fantasy and his need to keep a sense of our competing over him going. She has never competed for anyone in her life and I do not want Cal back under any circumstances. But I don't see his coming here, supposing Caroline would, and having a honeymoon visit when the whole purpose of the trip was to spend a bit of the Christmas with Harriet, to make arrangements for the future. This is the last time he will see me—something I don't think he realizes, since he is reluctant just to face the lack of drama that the end of this would mean. Also I have the idea that he is afraid to budge one inch from Caroline—she might not be there when he got back. I don't think he is really well, and he is kept going on this false sense of people competing for him.

I could not put Harriet and me through the giddy unreality I know Cal would be sunk in if he came over with Caroline. I feel it would be the end of her \Caroline's/ feeling for him too, because she would see how he has to exploit and boast or else things aren't real. In a way I doubt *he* will come. In all the months he has been gone I've heard from him a lot and he has never answered one question that I have put to him, or discussed really anything, me or Harriet or practical things or Caroline—except himself.

I am not withholding Harriet from Cal. My aim is to get him to acknowledge her. He has to come home in a manly way, for \only/ a few days, settle up things, make arrangements and then leave forever. That is the only decent thing to do. Any other path of celebration would be disastrous for his own reputation with those of his friends I know, and I think immoral for his daughter.

I don't want you to be my emissary. I have no position. I just wanted *you* to understand what I mean. If Caroline should come with him I am sure Harriet would still want to see him and they would have a few afternoons I guess, but that would be something. I think it is very cruel as a method and quite unnecessary, but there is absolutely no chance, I believe, that Caroline would consider such a thing. As I told you they can move in next door for all I care after this is settled. Cal should have come in June before Harriet went to camp, talked to her, arranged things with me. Then it would have been done and over with.

    Love,
      E.

97. *Robert Lowell to Harriet Lowell*

[33 Pont Street, London SW 1]
[October 26, 1970]

Dearest Harriet:

    I am mailing you a small arrow covered with diamonds[.] At first I was going to send you a gold love-knot which would have meant *I love you forever*, but the knot was only a copy and not as pretty as the \really/ old arrow. I don't know quite what it means; both arrows and diamonds are something that goes to the heart like truth. Let it be our love.

    I'll be back Christmas. Whatever happens between Mother and me, you must never think of me as gone. Wherever I am you must come and stay as long as you wish. I haven't made the last months happy for you or Mother. I did the best I could and promise better.

    Love from your forgetful, not forgetting
    Father.
    Love,
      Dad

98. *Robert Lowell to* Mrs. Robert Lowell

[London]
[October 26, 1970]

Dear Lizzie:

I have had letters from Blair and Bill, rather different letters. Bill's was about Harriet and making my intentions absolutely clear.[1] Blair was about Caroline's coming to New York.[2] From \both/ I see I must be more open and certain. This was hard for me to do and seemed rough. I merely wrote out of my feelings, which was probably unkind and without purpose. I must say now that I definitely want a divorce whenever arrangements can be made. I don't see why you should veto Caroline's coming to New York. There wouldn't be much sense in my coming if you and Harriet were in the Caribbean. Harriet should meet Caroline sometime then, though this would have to be awkward, she would feel less bewildered by the possibility of visiting us.

Oh dear, these sentences seem stiff and unreal to type out.

I've sent you a charming little present along with one to H.

Love,
Cal

99. *Elizabeth Hardwick to Mary McCarthy*

[15 West 67th Street, New York, N.Y.]
October 29, 1970

Dear Mary: No advertisement for Senator Goodell and I don't suppose there will be one. One ad alone cost 8,000 and the Goodell people just don't have it. We had, the Arts and Letters Committee had, a party ten days ago at someone's town house to raise money but it didn't do much good. Now the polls have Goodell trailing badly—and Buckley ahead by seven points two weeks in a row and the election almost here. I gave money for G., everyone did, and I suppose I will still vote

---

1. William Alfred to Lowell, 15 October 1970, above.
2. Blair Clark to Lowell, October 22, 1970, quoted in footnote 1 on page 121 (see also Hardwick to Blair Clark, Friday, October 23, 1970).

for him although the Ottinger-Buckley business is very perturbing.[1] An unusually miserable thought to think of New York with the first Conservative Party senator, and old Bill Buckley half out of his mind with "wit" and hysterical crowing. However, perhaps one should do when he can what he would like or think right for everyone to do. In that case I think it would be Goodell who has quite literally been purged by Nixon and Agnew. I'm having some people in for dinner on Nov. 3rd to watch the returns—one couldn't go through it alone I guess . . . This is just a note since I have your contribution on my mind. . . . I have just written a short story of normal length, my first in over ten years. Golly, they are hard! as Randall J. would say in a high whine.[2] Worst was to break the junkie habit of rushing through, sending it off to Bob and having it in print the next morning . . . Indeed I can't see where this will find print since the possible places are so few. A gratuitous act, or so it will probably turn out to be although I hope not. Saw Edmund last night at the Epsteins. He has just finished a book on "Upstate"[3] and was worried. Shawn was reading it over the weekend but E. thought the N. Yorker most likely wouldn't take it. He says he fears they are trying to change their "image." Actually they have been advertising all over the place, even TV. And such peculiar unbeckoning ads they are.

I remember that I wrote very testily, or actually sadly, about Cal and Harriet. Someone got to him I suppose because he has been cor-

<hr>

1. On the death of Robert Kennedy in 1968, New York Governor Nelson Rockefeller appointed Charles Goodell, a Republican, to fill Kennedy's senatorial seat. Goodell's increasingly liberal and anti-war positions as senator provoked conservatives and the Nixon administration. In his 1970 reelection campaign, he faced not only a Democratic Party opponent, Richard Ottinger, but a Conservative Party opponent, James L. Buckley (older brother of William F. Buckley, Jr.). See Daniel Berrigan, Philip Berrigan, Malcolm Boyd, Robert McAfee Brown, and Noam Chomsky, et al.: "[Goodell] is one of only two national Republicans who deny Nixon the party unity behind his war policies that he seeks. Senator Goodell is rare also, in that he raises questions not only about the war, but about the kind of country that would allow such a war to continue. [. . .] [We] believe that it is in the interest of peace and the antiwar movement to keep Charles Goodell in the Senate" ("Senator Goodell," *New York Review of Books*, October 22, 1970). On election day, November 3, 1970, Ottinger and Goodell split the liberal vote, handing Buckley a victory.

2. A habitual exclamation of Jarrell's, but given that Hardwick had recently reread Jarrell's letters to Lowell and to her, see Jarrell to Lowell, [November 1951]: "Jesus, have you *seen Paterson IV*? Golly, golly" (*Randall Jarrell's Letters*, p. 284).

3. Wilson, *Upstate: Records and Recollections of Northern New York* (New York: Farrar, Straus and Giroux, 1971); two excerpts, "An Upstate Diary I: 1950–1959" and "An Upstate Diary II: 1960–1970," appeared in the *New Yorker* on June 5 and June 12, 1971.

responding with her and will come Christmas—with Caroline—as a sort of honeymoon, I ~~suppose~~ \reckon/, coupled with his visit to his daughter, the first it will be then in 9 months. I was annoyed when I heard Caroline was coming *from Blair* and wondered why Cal who has been writing very weirdly about this trip for weeks to me ("much trouble, but Christmas is the time of joy") \didn't tell me/ and said I would vanish, but I changed my mind the next day and I don't care at all. Cal is a terrible show-off and just couldn't come home, see Harriet quietly, settle up with me in a few days and then go away. (I am assuming Caroline wants to do this unlikely middle-class thing of coming here with him, meeting his "child" bit . . .)[.] He is such a childish torturer—that little side look of malice he gives you—and so spooky, more and more. I feel glad to be out of the torment and I am not at all frightened or upset about his visit and look upon it as a step along the way to the ending of my business with him as soon as possible. Harriet is all right, too, really marvelous, not expecting too much, saying quite sensibly they will get on better when she is older. I think maybe that is true and if Caroline is really going to marry Cal, as his idea goes, I think the sooner Harriet can add the Citkowitzes to her life the better. The only trouble is that I don't have any real confidence in Caroline— that isn't what one has "in" her—as a step-mother!

I am very well. Spoke to Philip R. on the phone and I found him almost unintelligible. He is unbelievably eccentric, isn't he? I told him Commentary was running in the next issue an entire article against the N. Y. Review,[1] the culmination of their obsessions, or Podhoretz's obsession. Philip grunted: Norman is Captain Ahab and Bob is Moby Dick!

Not a very interesting letter, but I just wanted to write to explain about the ad. I have done a bit of work for the Goodell campaign and Republicans are astonishing, just the office staff, the regular people. They are strangely ignorant, unimaginative, square. I must say I found it interesting, but—as we New Lefters say—"frustrating."

All my love to you both
    Lizzie

---

1. Dennis H. Wrong, "The Case of the 'New York Review,'" *Commentary*, November 1970.

100. Robert Lowell to Mary McCarthy

[33 Pont Street, London SW 1]
November 2, 1970

Dearest Mary—

I've put off writing because I draw back from seeing what I am going to say ~~in~~ type\d/. It's a kind of decision which I haven't yet talked about to anyone. ~~It looks as~~ \I think/ I'll end up by returning to Lizzie and Harriet. I've done great harm to everyone and bemused myself. To go on seriously toward marriage with Caroline against the grain, the circumstances, our characters etc. \is more/ than can be got away with. We don't think we can, and are in accord. Still—

I won't go on much. I do find though that even for such a careless person as me one is cemented in habits beyond belief. I had to come to England and live with practically a new wife \to learn/ my whole being is repetition of things once done. I don't mean quite that. With time we build up an organism, an artifact, that is mysteriously complex, quite beyond our intelligence. You most[1] have found that. Still, it seems nothing merely to know what one can do. As if that were ever enough, as if one ever did.

~~Well,~~ I'll see you on the sixth. Maybe *we*'ll see you. I love the idea of your naturalistic check-up in Rome. I've been writing furiously too. It's too far from publication for me to be \pierced/ with acute discontent, and good enough to ~~engage~~ \grip/ the day. Dying to see you, and love to Jim and you. I've talked on the phone to Lizzie and I ~~suppose~~ \know/ we can make up. I feel a little ~~someone~~ \like a Russian/ who has lost his own fortune and his uncle's at Baden Baden. ~~Other OK, pardon all this.~~

Love,
Cal

P.S. Excuse the pencilling.

---

1. Thus, for a probable "must."

101. *Robert Lowell to* Miss Harriet Lowell

[Postcard: Joshua Reynolds—*The Strawberry Girl*, Wallace Collection]

[London]
[n.d. November? 1970]

Darling Harriet—

Here is a small girl who might take the little dog[1] you sent me out for walks. I'll do that with you or something as delightful. Sometimes life isn't life without you and Mother. I'll be back about two weeks before Christmas with an offensive British accent.

Love
Dad

102. *Robert Lowell to Elizabeth Hardwick*

33 Pont St., London SW 1
November 7, 1970

Dearest Lizzie:

I wonder if we couldn't make it up? It's hard to put this in a letter, and no doubt will be far harder in fact. I have thought this might be for about ten days now, and people have noticed, and thought I was more like my once self, what I must have been.

A cold way of putting it is that long burned-in and accepted habits never leave us. One can make out with the family he has long endured, which has a long time suffered him and his ways. Maybe you could take me back, though I have done great harm. Maybe now that the possibility is really possible, you will quite rightly draw back, happily rid of your weary burden.

I don't know. I'll be back around the fourteenth of December, so soon we can almost reach out hand[s] and touch it. If we should come together, there's one hard problem, among many I would like you to consider. I don't think I can very honorably drop my Essex appointment which lasts into March—more self-inflicted messiness and alteration than I can face in myself. That would mean I would have

---

1. By Vittore Carpaccio; postcard from Elizabeth Hardwick and Harriet Lowell to Robert Lowell, October 19?, 1970. Cf. "Old Snapshot from Venice 1952" [*Hospital II* 3], *The Dolphin*.

to return etc. Things have reached a kind of tolerable balance for me here, that will continue, I think, but not conceivably forever.

My book is out and has had gratifying, and more than that, reviews from Alvarez and Connolly in the Sunday papers, not like Benito.[1]

Dying to see you and Harriet,

Love,

Cal

103. Robert Lowell to Elizabeth Bishop

33 Pont Street [London]
November 7, 1970

Dearest Elizabeth:

You are cheerfully grumpy about Harvard. You should see Essex. Queues for the only cafeterias, often no sitting space, long tan, narrow, uniform corridors, only manageable by eccentric numbers that go up to six figures—my room 603,113. It was built in the late thirties, the time of some sensational failure in architectural design, all asbestos-white without a red brick in sight.[2] My students, minute classes, small to the point of insult, are polite and inaudible. They would make yours seem like roughs from Seattle. Still, I like it at [that], wake up to thank myself for being in England.

I know Atlas[3] and Rizzi;[4] Miss Rizzi wrote quite sensitive, low-keyed poems for me, then met Robert Bly and wrote a flaming, eloquent lead-article in the Crimson, rather decently denouncing \me/. I lacked a feeling for large spaces—like your eastern seaboard students.[5]

---

1. A. Alvarez, "A Change in the Weather," *Observer* (November 8, 1970); Cyril Connolly, "The Private and the Public," *Sunday Times* (November 8, 1970). The March 1967 production of Lowell's *Benito Cereno*, directed by Jonathan Miller at the Mermaid Theatre in London, was poorly reviewed.

2. OED: "redbrick university *n*. [. . .] a British university founded in the late 19th or early 20th cent. in a major provincial city, typically having buildings of red brick (as opposed to stone); [. . .] any recently founded or created university; freq., esp. in early use, in contrast with *Oxbridge*" ("red brick, n. and adj.," OED Online. March 2016. http://www.oed.com/view/Entry /160174?redirectedFrom=red+brick [accessed March 25, 2016]).

3. James Atlas.

4. Thus, for Margaret Rizza.

5. Margaret Rizza, "Poetry for Galway Kinnell: Confessions, a Blessing," *Harvard Crimson* (December 1, 1969).

I think your students will brighten up, at least you will find two or three people you like to talk to—maybe out of class, I found my best were older and not even enrolled often.

I think Lizzie and I may come back together. It's impossible to give up my child and ~~some~~ \one/ I've loved most of my life, in my life that gave me most ~~of~~ habits and limits. Now that I am far away and detached here, they all come back, a creature of habit, as if my body were only spine and ribwork. Still, I can't think of America without shuddering. Have I grown allergic?

My book is just out with good reviews from Alvarez and Connolly, particularly from Alvarez. Too good maybe. I'll see you I hope when I come back in December, around the 14th through Christmas, a trial trip.

All my love,
Cal

104. Mary McCarthy to Robert Lowell

141 rue de Rennes, Paris
November 8, 1970

Dearest Cal:

I can't write much. I'm just back from New York. Heinrich is dead.[1] He died a week ago yesterday—suddenly, of a heart attack; Hannah will be writing you. Having gone over, when we got the news, to be with her, I still feel somewhat dazed and numb. The funeral was Wednesday, very affecting and in a not altogether somber way; his students and colleagues talked about him so as to almost make you believe in immortality.

I don't know what to say about your news. I saw Lizzie briefly while I was at Hannah's. She seemed agitated by letters and calls she'd had from you. I don't think she understood what they portended but feared more grief and torment at a time when she was finally in balance. Whether she will want you to come back now, I don't know. She had so firmly closed her mind against entertaining this possibility as a hope that it may not be easy for her to open it again. The coincidence

---

1. Heinrich Blücher, Hannah Arendt's husband, died on October 30, 1970.

of Women's Liberation with what she's been through, over Caroline, has played, I'd guess, quite a role. But probably you sense more of her feelings than I can.

As for Caroline, I'd already come to the conclusion that it couldn't work between you. I mean marriage. In fact, looking back, I'm astounded that I thought it could. Too much romantic faith in the power of the will for transcendence. Maybe what I think of as love can only transcend death and is not much good about life.

Anyway, however it comes out, I wish you will.[1] And I count on seeing you the weekend that ends the 6th.

Much love,
Mary

P.S. I can't make up my mind whether to tell Lizzie that I've heard from you or not. Jim too finds this a hard question to decide. Perhaps for the moment I won't write her anything, though I feel she ought to know soon what is in your mind.

105. Robert Lowell to Mary McCarthy

[33 Pont Street, London]
November 15, 1970

Dearest Mary:

Heinrich's death seemed on the horizon so long that one forgot. At least I did being out of touch. Poor Hannah! I suppose crossing bridges beforehand may make the final thing a little less jolting, less jolting anyway than the suicide of our friend \though mostly his wife Adrienne/, Conrad. Friends dying comes now like increasing raindrops.

Thanks for your remarkably clear letter. You rather sharpen the horns of my dilemma. Everyone has vacillated, though I the worst.[2] I hope you will write Lizzie. There's nothing you can tell her that she doesn't already know from me, but your sympathies and views would help. I think the jag that hit Caroline and me was whether to get mar-

---

1. Thus, for a probable "well."

2. Lowell: "From the dismay of my old world to the blank | new—water-torture of vacillation!" ("Pointing the Horns of the Dilemma" [*Doubt* 2] 1–2, *The Dolphin*).

ried, she not wanting to and I not wanting to go on *in perpetuum* un-married. Or maybe this was just the surface manifestation of some deeper unsurmountable gap. Pray God it all washes out.

My number here is 235-2270. Please let me know your plans. I hope we can do more or less as we intended to on your ghost visit last month. My love to you, hope your book is off. I almost have a new one, a small scale sequel to *Notebook*. It will probably be ages before it goes off to the publisher.

Love again to you both,
Cal

P.S. I have [been] puzzling \on/ your mysterious sentence about Lizzie and Woman's Lib. What's that? Do you mean it's in the air or something closer?

106. *Robert Lowell to* Mrs. Robert Lowell

33 Pont St.
November 16, 1970

Dearest Lizzie:

I didn't write sooner because I didn't want to ~~go~~ \fly/ off into crossed letters.[1] I will do all I can to make things work; I think \we/ can,—we have after all for more years than I have the wits to count, tho all remains remembered. Perhaps everyone involved will get in the end what was most deeply and secretly desired. I'm no better than I was, unless it's better to discover the hardness of old habits. I won't put you through more.

I have \been/ pouring out poems, and almost have a little book, in the same form as Notebook, but much smaller. I've even anticipated my landing in New York. You see I am back home.

I still don't get what happened with Alf and Adrienne, there must be some crude fact. You don't go off and leave all your children with someone going mad. Poor Adrienne!

I have a vague idea I knew ~~what~~ about "groupies," it's like some

---

1. The Hardwick letter Lowell refers to is now missing.

Greek or archaic English word, I once knew and forgot.[1] I guess the new idiom is here to stay; it keeps seeping in in tiny trickles when I try to write. You and Harriet seem to have been having a week of pre-Thanksgivings. Give my derelict love to Sarah and Cot.[2]

My classes are small and quiet, the Poetry Writing rather retarded after Harvard, a good one in Shakespeare, where I have twice spent two hours reading one act of Antony and Cleopatra aloud. The college looks like Brandeis, if Brandeis had been built on a fiftieth the money, and with no Jews. The people are young and lively, most of my colleagues being just beyond graduate student age.

I think about you and Harriet. I am jealous. Let me into your circle again, but not to see the groupies.

Love,
Cal

107. Robert Lowell to Blair Clark

[33 Pont Street, London SW1]
November 21 [1970]

Dear Blair—

It must be like migraine getting stuck with all my affairs, from all sides. Here's what's going on in me. I am haunted by my family, and the letters I get. There seems to be such delicate misery. Lizzie's letters veer from frantic affection to frantic abuse. Then somehow she and Harriet are fused as one in her mind. It's not possible, but I get the impression they really are in Lizzie's mind. It's crazy, yet I can't from a distance do anything about it, perhaps less on the spot.

The thing is I am ~~really much~~ \perfectly/ happi~~er~~y with Caroline. At first I was frightened of not being married—old feelings of being outlawed. But I see it doesn't matter much. We can go on permanently as we are. We are permanent no matter what our status. Caroline has always been afraid of legal marriage. Not being married, somehow loosens the bond, man and woman's mutual, self-killing desire to

---

1. *Groupies*, dir. Ron Dorfman and Peter Nevard (1970). See Hardwick, "Militant Nudes," *New York Review of Books*, January 7, 1971.
2. Lowell's aunt Sarah Winslow Cotting and uncle Charles E. ("Cot") Cotting.

master the other. Then we might get married anyway when we knew we didn't have to. I don't yet know what will happen, but I increasingly fear the blood I'll have to pay for what I have done, for being me. Anyway, I'll be coming to you around the 14th alone.

I want to hear all about you, and your heart if you wish. Long deep talks.[1]

Love,
Cal

108. *Robert Lowell to* Mrs. Robert Lowell

33 Pont St.
November 28, 1970

Dearest Lizzie:

I'm back from reading at Cambridge, and tomorrow it's a reading at the Mermaid, scene of Benito's triumph.[2] All went well enough at Cambridge and I was told I had a record small audience. Somehow it leaves one with a feeling of tarnish and fraudulence. Two lunches a breakfast and a dinner at various faculty tables and high tables—too much like St. Mark's, too much like college. Still good conversation, warmth of a kind. Essex on the other hand is in great disgrace, a protest with bonfires, then the next \day/ by accident, a long-prepared Daily Telegram[3] attack on our leniency. The protest was what is talked of a[s] pitifully non-political: pot. Not much to arouse the demons, or amuse them.

I may have been short about Jack's well-meant cable[4]—I was wor-

---

1. Blair Clark replied: "All this makes me think of one thing you might set yourself to thinking on until we meet—The one big agenda item: do you really want to live 'in the same room' with anyone? I think in the past you have never questioned much that this was the best and most natural arrangement for you. But is it, at our age? I, of course, have had a longer training period than you in the business of living apart while never being un-connected (sometimes with too many at the same time!). But I was very much married for quite a while, as you know, and mostly exclusively. Now—I don't know [. . .] Well, dear Cal, we'll stew about all this when you come, at length" (Blair Clark to Lowell, November 29, 1970). Cf. Lowell, "The Friend," *The Dolphin*.
2. See Lowell to Hardwick, November 7, 1970, footnote 1 on page 129.
3. Thus, for *Daily Telegraph*. See R. Barry O'Brien, "Campus Freedom Plan Crashes in a Wave of Violence," *Daily Telegraph*, November 26, 1970.
4. Now missing.

ried, unknown troubles for you in New York, and then I hate having friends tilt my hand. I have enough tangles now to occupy me for years, on top of my pills, a delicate matter to keep one from scumming up another. Nothing new though. Only new thing is I notice spreads in my teeth, rather like Mary's before her patching.

Not much that might interest you. Most [of] the people I see wouldn't even be names to you, my colleagues. Once [a] week I have lunch with Sidney, and come away with lines for poems. Poems at a great rate, even scribbling lines down during a dinner. I suppose I may have a book, a little notebook, ready by next fall. Then a new tune, a new meter, a new me. The last never, I guess[.] The surroundings here are not disappointing, I mean for the eye, but perhaps mostly humanly, the famous more mumbled and muffled pace.[1] Well, it will be very soon. All my love to you and Harriet.

Love,
Cal

109. *Robert Lowell to* Mrs. Robert Lowell

33 Pont St., London, SW 1
November 30, [1970]

Dearest Lizzie:

A line before I set off for Essex. The Mermaid reading was as good as I could make it and went over. Somehow, it's a show I can stage too easily. But why shouldn't it give the satisfaction of a well-played tennis game? I don't [know] what that would be, just a very occasional ace serve. I guess, reading gives more satisfaction than tennis. But who could face it daily, or weekly. I'm through for this year.

---

1. William Empson: "the delicious social hints and evasive claims-by-mumble of spoken English are a positive intoxicant though externally drab. One may agree that a poet should be enough in contact with the spoken English of his time, and also believe he has always needed to be free enough from it to sing. Taking for granted that mumbling is the only honest mode of speech is I suppose a fog which has thickened steadily for the last fifty years" ("Rhythm and Imagery in English Poetry," *British Journal of Aesthetics* 2, no. 1 [January 1962], reprinted in Empson, *Argufying*, p. 156). Lowell had been reading Empson's essay in June 1970; see Lowell to Hardwick, June 14, 1970.

I still do nothing much but bury my indecisions in many many poems. I think I have ninety now and a tall house of draft and discard. I am very bad company because I am so removed. You won't enjoy me. However I am coming to see you and dear Harriet, not Blair. So you'll hear from me at once. If I'm not hung up in red tape. The Home Office still has my passport, and my bank account is an impenetrable mist. No, I'll be there.

I thought you were better informed than I on my reviews, but later in the day, clippings came from Faber, the one new to me Elizabeth Jennings.[1] She is a sad, touching person, rather like Claude-Edmonde in appearance and habits—but shy, poor and poetic.

I dread the Review circuit and the buzz of American politics. An American isn't expected to \follow/ issues. He can miss the papers for days without being pulled up and informed. But even for Englishmen, all's mumbled and distant. Can't see us as Mary and Bowden,[2] even with my lack of engagement.

Love to both dear ones,
Cal

110. *Robert Lowell to* Mrs. Robert Lowell

33 Pont St., London SW 1
December 3, 1970

Dearest Lizzie—

My pay seems to be mostly old-age deductions, something that demands more optimism in me than in the government. I think I had 333 pounds a month, that is 666 pounds in all with another 333 pounds at the end of December, or more likely early in January. From this so far 191 pounds has been deducted with half as much again when I next receive my monthly pay. The whole salary is spread out over 12 months. I feel the government owes me money. Readings bring amounts like sixty dollars or unexpectedly nothing. In addition the Home Office still has my passport, necessary for acquiring a work certificate. A Mrs. McGlashan at Essex is trying to retrieve it for me[.]

---

1 "Poet's Chronicle," *Daily Telegraph*, November 12, 1970.

2. Broadwater, to whom Mary McCarthy was married from 1946–60.

I went to a great Vanderbilt game with Ben[1]; Caroline's[2] dachshund was lost; I think permanently, a tragedy Ben didn't rise to, nor did Caroline rise to the dangers she had put Ben in by letting me drive him back to Clarksville. I remember Allen and Ben yelling when the girl band came on, "Get those women off the field." O blessed old days before Woman's Lib. I liked some of John's poems in some British or Irish magazine; he had gotten rid of Henry, and good and tender things made up for show-off obscenities.[3] Can't believe it's all bad; it isn't. Folly to answer, even in a single sentence. I got a rather sour review from Denis Donoghue, who seems to think the book is about the breaking and final break up of our marriage.[4] That's not in the text. I wouldn't trust Carruth too much, tho he has a gnarled integrity.[5]

I'll be seeing people this weekend, Mary, Gaia,[6] Francis Bacon and Sidney.

I'll be with you both soon, if I can leave England.

Love to you both,
  Cal

P.S. I was a little testy about politics last letter. I feel like someone naked under his raincoat—though I guess that's always a girl[7]—coming back to be inspected.[8] I think Bob Silvers and I have become too entangled to meet with shared joy.

---

1. Tate, Allen Tate's brother.

2. Gordon, Allen Tate's wife from 1925–45 and from 1946–59.

3. John Berryman, "To B——E——" and "The Search," *Stand*, XI (Fall 1970).

4. "The events which he does not list as public are domestic misfortunes, notably a marriage breaking, then broken" (Denis Donoghue, "Lowell's Seasons," *Guardian*, November 19, 1970).

5. Direct reference not known, but see Hayden Carruth, "A Meaning of Robert Lowell," *Hudson Review* 20, no. 3 (Autumn 1967): pp. 429–47.

6. Servadio Mostyn-Owen.

7. "I come like someone naked in my raincoat, | but only a girl is naked in a raincoat" ("No Messiah" [*Flight to New York* 6] 7–8, in "The Dolphin" manuscript, and in *The Dolphin*).

8. "'You're not under inspection, just missed;'" ("Fox-Fur" [*Flight to New York* 1] 8, "The Dolphin" manuscript); cf. with "Foxfur," *The Dolphin*.

111. *Robert Lowell to* Mrs. Robert Lowell

33 Pont Street, London
[n.d. December 1970]

Dearest Lizzie—

I'm just off to lunch with Sidney, but yes it's a date for the Messiah on the 17th.[1] Hope you feel much better by the time this reaches you. Here in London, we've reached weather like one of the worst Maine summers. Less disturbing maybe because it's the usual thing. You a see[2] a streak of indirect sunlight some day at three and everyone hymns the weather.

Love to my two messianics,[3]
Cal

112. *Robert Lowell to Elizabeth Bishop*

London
[December 1970]

Dearest Elizabeth—

I fear I may owe you an apology for versing one of your letters into my poems on you in Notebook.[4] When Lamb blew up at Coleridge for calling him "Frolicsome Lamb," Coleridge said it was necessary for the balance of his composition. I won't say that, but what could be as

---

1. Lowell: "'Will you go with me to The Messiah, | on December 17th, a Thursday, | and ~~drink~~ \eat/ at the *Russian Tearoom* afterward?'" (*"The Messiah"* [*Flight to New York* 2] 5–7, "The Dolphin" manuscript); cf. with "Foxfur" 9–12, *The Dolphin*.

2. Thus.

3. Lowell: "I stop in our Christmas-papered bedroom, hearing | my *Nolo*, the non-Messianic man—" ("No Messiah" [*Flight to New York* 6] 11–12, in both "The Dolphin" manuscript and *The Dolphin*).

4. Lowell: "'You're right to worry about me, only please DON'T, | though I'm pretty worried myself. I've somehow got | into the worst situation I've ever | had to cope with. I can't see the way out. | Cal . . . have you ever gone through caves? | I did once . . . Mexico, and hated it—| I've never done the famous ones near here. | Finally after hours of stumbling along, | one sees daylight ahead, a faint blue glimmer. | Air never looked so beautiful before. | That's what I feel I'm waiting for now: | a faintest glimmer I am going to get out | somehow alive from this. Your last letter helped, | like being handed a lantern or a spiked stick'" ("Letter with Poems for a Letter with Poems" [*For Elizabeth Bishop* 3], *Notebook70*). Cf. Elizabeth Bishop to Robert Lowell, February 27, 1970 (*Words in Air*, pp. 663–67).

real as your own words, and then there's only a picture that does you honor. Still, too intimate maybe, and if so I humbly ask pardon.

The other night, part of a weekend alone, I was in a Knightsbridge Portuguese restaurant *Offado*, more people worked on the tables, half in the kitchen etc. than there were guests; even the guitarist and singer helped, then sang things like Girls from Mallorca, while I ate and consumed a carafe of rosé, their table wine.[1] After a while I expected you to come in the door any moment, even began nervously looking at my watch. So much I wanted to see you.

So much I do. I'll be in New York staying with Blair Clark about the time you get this. I think Lizzie and I are going to break. I should have done it much more cleanly some time ago. But I can't. I wonder if anyone in his right mind could. I am back to see Lizzie and Harriet, things are not even now quite settled, but they must be.

I must see you. I can easily come to Cambridge, or it could be New York if you'd like—you must be ripe to leave Cambridge by now, but I'd rather like to see it \Harvard/. Give my love to Bill. All my love to you,

Cal

113. *Caroline Blackwood to Robert Lowell*

[80 Redcliffe Square, London]
[December 14?, 1970]

Darling Cal—I've just got back to Redcliffe. Eliza[2] is sobbing about her dead mother and her hoover is wailing against the wall. Genia[3] is crying about you. Ivana is rather corruptly copying. London seems to be Chinese grey—oyster grey—every appalling shade of pitch, pitch grey. I miss you so much already and your plane probably hasn't even taken off yet. If I have had drunken hysterical seizures it's because I love you so much that I'm afraid sometimes it makes me rather deranged.

I have no news. Nothing has happened since I saw you go with those two bearded and yammering Rabbis.

---

1. Cf. Lowell: "At *Offado's*" [*Winter and London* 2], *The Dolphin*. O Fado was the name of a restaurant at 50 Beauchamp Place, London.
2. Blackwood's housekeeper.
3. Nickname for Evgenia.

```
  4. Departer for Departure
8 .  At the Air-Terminal

London a Chinese gray or oyster gray,
every apalling shade of pitch-pitch gray---
no need to cook up far-fetched imagery
to establish a climate for our mood---
anything's real until it's published.
"If I have had hysterical drunken seizures,
it's from loving you too much. It makes me wild,
I fear. I'll make the dining-room a bedroom.
I feel unsafe, uncertain you'll come back.
I know I am happier with you than before;
my pains were always girdled about with joy."
My signal flashes. My plane is at the door.   THE
Our gold rings touch. Surely, it was great joy
blaming ourselves and wanting to do wrong.
```

"\Departure for Departure/ At the Air-Terminal" [*Flight to New York* 2. \3 4./],
from "The Dolphin" manuscript, p. 48, composed and revised between late 1970
and January 1972.

I will get your books sent out and the other little chores etc and fix
the downstairs flat. I feel very unsafe. I don't know if you will really
ever come back—if I will ever see you again—if you should come
back. I just know that I have been happier with you than I have ever
been—ever. So even if the whole thing ends up for me with sadness, I
will always think that it was worth it.[1]
    Love
      C

114. *Robert Lowell to* CAROLINE CITKOWITZ

[Telegram]

BLAIR CLARK'S
229 EAST 48 STREET
NEW YORK NY DE2170
[December 21, 1970]

CAROLINE CITKOWITZ 80 REDCLIFFE SQUARE

LONDON SW1

THANK[S] FOR LETTER I'M NOT A CRIPPLE ALL MY LOVE
    CAL

---

1. Cf. Lowell, "Departure At the Air-Terminal" [*Flight to New York* 4] 1–11, "The Dolphin" man-
uscript; and "With Caroline at the Air-Terminal" [*Flight to New York* 2], *The Dolphin*.

115. *Robert Lowell to* CAROLINE CITKOWITZ

[Telegram]

BLAIR CLARK

229 EAST 48 ST

NEW YORK NY 10017

DE 24 70

[December 24, 1970]

CAROLINE CITKOWITZ

KIRRIEMUIR ANGUS SCOTLAND

ALL WELL MERRY CHRISTMAS LONG FOR YOU

    CAL

116. *Elizabeth Hardwick to Robert Lowell*

[15 West 67th Street, New York, N.Y.]

[n.d. December 1970]

Dearest: I came up to get some envelopes. I had the most pleasant evening, with several exciting things coming up about work. I took one of the Libriums[1] beloved Dr. B.[2] gave me and it helped enormously—took it about five, just before I saw you. So I think my trouble is "chemical," if not in origin in devastating effect. I don't want you to worry about me—if such a thing is possible! ?—because I do feel on the mend, very much so. And suddenly having this good evening, free of care and memory, was almost unbelievable. See you tomorrow.

    E.

---

1. Antianxiety medication. Cf. "The room is filled with double-shadows, | ~~librium~~ \sedation/ doubl~~ing~~\es/ everything I see . . ." ("Double Vision" [*Hospital* 4] 8–9, "The Dolphin" manuscript).
2. Dr. Anny Baumann.

PART II

1971–1972

117. *Robert Lowell to* CAROLINE CITKOWITZ

[Telegram]

BLAIR CLARK | 229 EAST 48TH STREET NYC

JAN 2 1200PM '71

CAROLINE CITKOWITZ 80 REDCLIFFE SQUARE

LONDON SW1

PANAM FLIGHT 2 730AM TUESDAY ALL LOVE

CAL

118. *Robert Lowell to Harriet Lowell*

33 Pont St., London

January 6 1970 [1971]

Dearest Harriet:

I can't really recommend my trip back to you. Forty-five minutes waiting for Jack Thompson to come to lunch; a line of cars that moved like snails for almost fifteen miles to the airport; a long line to weigh my baggage; a slow line to pay fifty-six dollars excess weight; a line to get into the lounge to wait for the plane; a wait in the lounge to be searched for dope and bombs; a long wait for the plane to take off; people ~~lined~~ seated up for seven hours eight abreast; a two mile trip by the airplane on the ground across the airport at a slow walking speed; a walk of a mile inside the airport; a mile trip on a very slow escalator;

a wait while three hundred bags came out of the plane before mine. Then no more waiting, but snow was on the ground and I could see my breath like smoke from a dragon streaming before my face \in my cold apartment./ Now I am at rest and very tired, too tired to write you a longer letter. Your redwood bear,[1] Arms of the Law,[2] sits in my bookcase and reminds me of you. I loved talking to you over Christmas. All my love, take care of mother. Don't boss her.

    love,

    Dad

119. *Robert Lowell to* Mrs. Robert Lowell

[33 Pont St., London SW 1]

January 7, 1971

Dearest Lizzie:

In my thoughts I planned a much more ample personal and bread and butter letter, but still feel the jar, loss of sleep etc. of the flight. If I'd taken a later or earlier plane I would probably have been diverted to Birmingham.

I thought of a lot of kind charming things you did[.] Above all you stand out at the airport with your curled hair and beautiful smile that survived the long dull wait. Then the blue wash cloths, the buttermilk, the calm Christmas day, and the wonderful wit and good spirits of Harriet, surely rather owing to you—I mean your old undeviating loyalty.

I haven't done much, rested, read Hamlet for class,[3] Henry Adams

---

1. A Christmas present from Harriet. Lowell: "The tedium and *deja-vu* of home | make me love it; bluer days will come | and acclimatize the Christmas gifts: | redwood bear, rubber-egg shampoo, home-movie-| projector" ("Christmas 1970" [*Flight to New York* 10] 1–5, "The Dolphin" manuscript; cf. "Christmas" [*Flight to New York* 12] 1–5, *The Dolphin*).

2. Lowell: "I was learning to print. I wrote in ugly legible letters: 'Arms-of-the-Law, A Horrid Spoof. Arms-of-the-Law was a horrid spoof most of the time, but an all-right guy on the 29th of February. He was also a Bostonian, an Irish policeman, and a bear'" ("My Crime Wave" typescript, "Autobiographical prose," Robert Lowell Papers, *73M-90 bMS Am 1905, folder 2223, Houghton Library), quoted in Ian Hamilton, *Robert Lowell: A Biography* (1983), p. 15. While a student at Kenyon College in 1938, "Lowell had dreamed up a world peopled by 'bear-characters'—or 'berts' [French pronunciation], as he called them—and his favorite off-duty sport was to invent bear-dramas or bear-parables, which incorporated caricatures of friends and relatives. Each friend would be given a bear-name and an appropriate bear-voice. Lowell himself seems to have been the chief bear, known as Arms of the Law (the hero of his 'horrid' childhood 'spoof')" (Hamilton, *Robert Lowell: A Biography*, p. 55).

3. Lowell: "I feel how Hamlet, stuck with the Revenge Play | his father wrote him, went scatolog-

on the English,[1] a mountain of mail asking \me/ to read various places without fee. I worry about your blood-pressure. Mine went back to 180, due to the journey no doubt. I'm sure both our pressures will go down. Would that all pressures might. And thankyou \for breasting/ the problems and trials of my visit, so often turning trial into joy.

Love to you both,
Cal

120. Elizabeth Hardwick to Robert Lowell[2]

[15 West 67th Street, New York, N.Y.]
Jan. 8, 1971

Dear Cal: My financial situation is desperate and is going to be for the rest of my life. But I will manage that; the taxes for the coming year obsess me. I have paid $15,000 since we parted in April of last year. Now I obviously can't have $21,000 and pay $15,000. You \(one)/ are forced to pay quarterly. . . . All of this leads me to say that the \tax/ check of $5,290 which Mr. Brooks mentioned must not be turned into pounds, but put into our account here, which I pay the tax with, or else they can hold it at the State Street Trust for you. Then, you must ask F. and Straus to hold, since they can't withhold and send to the government, in a tax account for you 25 % \of your earnings/ and then at the end of the year they can put it on our final \tax/ accounting. I will send you a receipt for the $5,290 check.

I won't go on about this, since the two letters[3] are all anyone can take in I guess . . . I haven't done anything about the papers. Exhaustion, trying to get my own affairs in shape. But I will. I am looking for a spring teaching job because I just haven't enough money to pay the rent which, just went *up* over 100 per month . . . bringing the apartment maintenance to $500 per month.

Harriet is fine. I am fine. We miss you and hope, dearest, all is well

---

ical | under this clotted London sky" ("Plotted" 7–9, *The Dolphin*); "*If it were done, twere well it were done quickly*— | to quote a bromide, your vacillation | is acne" (*Artist's Model* [3] 1–3, *The Dolphin*).

1. In *The Education of Henry Adams* (1907); see among other passages Adams's account of meeting Swinburne (pp. 139–44), given Lowell's allusion to Swinburne's "tears of time" below (Lowell to Hardwick, January 9, 1971).

2. Crossed with Lowell's letter of January 7, 1971.

3. Possibly a reference to a second January 8 letter from Hardwick that is now missing.

and happy with you. I thought when I finally knew you would never be with us that I would have that empty space gradually to fill up with something new, but it is filled up with nothing but money worries. Still they are different, better, a challenge rather [than] a grief. I hate to send off a \business/ letter but it is just to say that you should keep the tax on your earnings in dollars and to try to suggest how to do it.

Love from here, as always,

Elizabeth

121. *Robert Lowell to* Mrs. Robert Lowell[1]

33 Pont St., [London]

January 9, 1971

Dearest Lizzie:

I trust you have Mr. Brooks's statement. The Agency Fund gives us both a little over 13,000 when some $5000 is deducted for capital gains. I've suggested that this sum be sent to you to pay with all the other taxes. I hadn't thought we had gained so much, but I guess we at one time reduced the fund to about $15000. The government scoops us like a steamshovel.[2]

Looking for an address this morning, I came on *Lowell, Harriet, Summer Workshop, West Cornwall.*[3] How swiftly gone; the tears of time![4] Called the Nolans and was greeted by Cynthia, a mirthless laugh.[5] I've recovered from flight, but have spent three days reading Hamlet and am rusty for next week's teaching.

Love and miss talking with you,

Cal

---

1. Crossed with Hardwick's letter of January 8, 1971.

2. Lowell: "Behind their cage, | yellow dinosaur steamshovels were grunting | as they cropped up tons of mush and grass | to gouge their underworld garage" ("For the Union Dead" 13–16, *For the Union Dead*).

3. In Connecticut.

4. Cf. Ezra Pound: "Then from my sight as now from memory | The courier aquiline, so swiftly gone!" ("Canzone: Of Angels" 29–30); and Swinburne: "Us too, when all the tears of time are dry, | The night shall lighten from her tearless eye" ("Tristram of Lyonesse" 231–32).

5. Lowell: Sidney Nolan "and I are very close friends and have frequent lunches, but his wife, described by Kenneth Clark as a German abstract expressionist painting of the angel of death done without passion, refuses to see us. An embarrassment" (Lowell to Frank Parker, [March 20, 1973], in *The Letters of Robert Lowell*, p. 605).

122. Elizabeth Hardwick to Robert Lowell

[15 West 67th Street, New York, N.Y.]
Wednesday, Feb. 10, 1971

Dear Cal: The Listener check, changed into dollars (100.00) came here. I felt if I sent it to you—it was drawn on an American bank—and it had to be sent back to the BBC to be redigested and finally months from now passed through the computer intestines. . . . well, it would never show up again. I had it changed into pounds and also added another pounds worth of 100, making it 200 dollars in pounds. I am sure you have no money and am sure you should have. I haven't received the money from the Agency Account yet, and of course you haven't. . . . But, not more book-keeping.

Love,
Lizzie

Enclosed 81 pounds—$200.00

123. Elizabeth Hardwick to Mary McCarthy

[15 West 67th Street, New York, N.Y.]
Feb. 19, 1971

Mary, dearest: I wrote you a letter a few days ago which was returned for insufficient postage—and just as well, because now I have had the joy of a letter from you today. I was writing to say that the *Literary Guild* publicity magazine—a little hard-sell advertising for members—asked me to do a "personality" piece on you—400–600 words. I asked for a copy of [the] novel, which they said was not available yet, but in any case not necessary—they want just a "friendly" picture. We'll both be deeply embarrassed I guess but I have agreed, even though I am bewildered by the sample of past work they sent me: Budd Shulberg on Irving Stone. I was writing to say how delighted I am that *Birds* has been chosen and to send my love and congratulations that the book is soon to come out, and my hope, nay, belief, it will be read, loved, admired and bought and that everything good will come to you . . . As for the horned owl present,[1] I stared off into the distance at your mention of it in your letter. Yes, it came, Cal was here on the red sofa, we looked at it and I said I remembered some version from the Southern Review[2] and then—blankness. I looked and looked yesterday and did not find it until this morning, still in a box, a sort of Christmas box of things not put away, a leather belt of Harriet's, a drawing pad, a sheep bell from Greece and underneath, lo, the lovely owl cover, the paper around it, the beautiful print. I have just been on my couch, reading, and it is a beautiful moment in \our vanished/ life, bringing back so much that seems gone forever—when people took houses in Rocky Port, the *feel* of things. When the mother leaves the house, there is more than simply taking up her work again; you feel everyone has left \forever/ that kind of house, and a possibility of a year in New England—and neither the house nor New England really quite exists any more. Very moving. The "psychology" is very true, especially at the end between the mother and the boy.

I hope you are coming soon for your book. Do let me know. If you would like to stay in Cal's studio—just vacated by Florence Malraux and Alain Resnais—it would be splendid. It is very comfortable, you can fix your own breakfast, there is a phone; you would miss telephone messages but nothing else. For awhile it was more than a little *triste* because dear old Cal seemed to be in the very woodwork writing poems, the air still alive with his cigarettes—but I have changed it about a bit. I haven't given it up because of some intricate problems, or advantages I hope, coming about when our house goes cooperative, as we plan in the next six months . . . But that is too tangled to go into. . . .

My Harriet has been accepted for a first-class Spanish language camp in Mexico for July and August. Quite a bit better than that Arthur Kober camp[3] I found for her last year. At the moment she and I plan to go to Castine around June 12; then I'll come to N.Y. to see her off early in July and then back. I think of your chimneys standing nobly in the snowy, wintery sky, and the staircase and the wall paper will

---

1. Limited edition of "Winter Visitors" (the first chapter of *Birds of America*), with pictorial boards, "published as a New Year's greeting to friends of the author and the publisher" (Harcourt Brace Jovanovich, 1970).

2. Mary McCarthy, "Birds of America," *Southern Review* (Summer 1965).

3. Playwright of *Having Wonderful Time* (1937) about a camp in the Catskills.

soon be longing for you and Jim, and so will I. I rather like being alone up in Castine, although I expect to have more visitors this year.

I'm doing pretty well, feeling a great deal better in every way. The article Mary T. mentioned[1] was a sort of "popular culture" reflection and I don't know that it is anything special. I'm writing on Ibsen now. One piece will be in the next Review and it will be followed by a second.[2] I have my Barnard job for the second term and I find it terribly pleasant and easy, and while it doesn't pay much small sums are the only way to big, or bigger, sums. Next year I have been asked to give the Christian Gauss lectures at Princeton, just three, and that made me happy; and I may have another teaching job, since of course the Princeton is just an \a temporary/ addition, of a day a week. I don't mind teaching at the most three days, preferably two, and I feel one can do just as much work if the soul is determined. All in all, this "getting on my feet," has been the "cure."

I have talked a number of times on the telephone to Cal, but I don't have much of a picture of him or anything that is really "news." To me he seems neither sick nor well and I feel a great sadness about him, but what can one do? I will sometime tell you about the three-week Christmas visit. Nothing dramatic, but more \often/ foolish. I was shocked when I saw him because the person I had been missing so painfully was the rare, glorious person of at least a decade ago and when I saw him at the airport, disheveled, that darting wild look in his eye, heard the eternal jokes, it was just so pitiful. I'm afraid I feel Caroline is a sort of wicked goblin and my poor old dear giant has been turned cross-eyed and is running backward. Cal told me she slept most of the day and fell into long periods of apathy and depression. . . . As for Sonia, I haven't a clue as she would say.[3] I don't think Cal and I mentioned her; I haven't spoken to her ever about Caroline since I didn't talk to her in England and had only one conversation up in

1. "Militant Nudes," *New York Review of Books*, January 7, 1971; Mary Thomas.

2. "A Doll's House," *New York Review of Books*, March 11, 1971; "Ibsen and Women II: Hedda Gabler," *New York Review of Books*, March 25, 1971.

3. Mary McCarthy to Hardwick: "All I've heard from England . . . was an hysterical letter from Sonia, accusing you, me, and everyone of having put false stories in circulation about her: typical denials of charges never made, such as that she had talked to you against Caroline, her *dearest* friend, and how could one be so *wicked* as to think she would . . . ? I answered this with a quite sharp letter that's never been mailed, since the day after I wrote it, the [postal] strike started, and the p.o. here wasn't accepting anything for England" (February 15, 1971, Elizabeth Hardwick Papers, HRC).

Maine about the doctor. I think Caroline may have wanted to drop her or something and she thinks *we* have done her in. On the other hand, Cal has become a rather active liar! I know when he is lying but not everyone does. He will, if questioned, pass it off as a joke—or as his "joking"—and so there is no telling what he may have said . . .

No matter, dears, just love to both of you and longing to see you both.

Lizzie

124. *Robert Lowell to* Mrs. Robert Lowell

[33 Pont Street, London SW 1]
[March 8, 1971]

Dearest Lizzie—

I think our letters on the agency tax-money must have crossed.[1] I wrote as soon as the States Street[2] letter arrived.

Through long hours of revising, a leisurely bath and a quick dressing, I have been thinking about our long past. What shall I say? That I miss your old guiding and even chiding hand. Not having you is like learning to walk. I suppose though one thing is worse than stumbling and vacillating, is to depend on someone who does these things. I do think achingly and bewilderingly about you and Harriet.

Tell Harriet that last Tuesday[3] my taxi was twenty minutes late. I missed my train, got another taxi at Essex that took someone in the opposite direction, reached my class half an hour late, just as it had been dismissed. However, I made it up in the afternoon. Even muddlers survive, though shaggily.[4]

Do miss you both. All my love,

Cal

1. Hardwick's letter of January 8 and Lowell's letter of January 9, 1971.
2. State Street Trust Company.
3. March 2, 1971, the day after Lowell's fifty-fourth birthday.
4. Lowell: "Sometimes the little muddler | can't stand itself!" ("Child's Song" 17–20, *For the Union Dead*).

125. Elizabeth Hardwick to Caroline Blackwood

[15 West 67th Street, New York, N.Y.]
March 12, 1971

Dear Caroline: I have told Harriet that you are having a baby by her father. It seems to me that she will have to meet her new family, to be with you and Cal and your children before the baby comes in order to make real everything that seems unimaginable to her—England, a new family for her father. She knows that she will have very little of him from now on and that he belongs to you and all of your children, since his physical presence there and absence here is the most real thing.[1] I am bringing Harriet to England on June 14th, to stay maybe a week or ten days, or at least enough days to visit you and Cal. I cannot have her continue to be entirely cut off from her father and to receive a letter when the baby comes, because of course the new child and all of the new situation are a part of her life. She does not want to go alone and as I imagine it, she and I will stay in a hotel in London and I will see my friends while she is seeing you and Cal and your family in the evenings, as it suits you; and perhaps spending a weekend in the country with all of you if you invite her. But she would be with me in London. Also, I hope she will be able to spend the week between Christmas and New Years visiting her father and you and your new child, this time without me since she would have made some acquaintance with it all previously.

As I said, she does not imagine very much of Cal but I feel that I must make definite arrangements for at least a few days with him each year and I hope you won't mind these brief and rare occasions. The June visit seems the only sensible time. She will be out of school then and waiting to go to Mexico, where she is going to spend the summer in a Spanish language camp. The only other time would be a week in late August, but she will just have come home from a very special summer, will be getting ready for school early in September; the pregnancy will [be] very advanced by then and it might be a little tiring for all of you. So, I will take for granted that June is agreeable. If necessary only a very few and brief meetings are required. We will just see how it works when she gets

1. Cf. "Green Sore" [*The Burden* 5] 11–14, "The Dolphin" manuscript (see poem on page 154) and "Green Sore" [*Marriage* 7] 10–13, *The Dolphin*.

there, but I feel I must arrange the meeting. I frankly don't know what else to do and this seemed the only way to manage.

Yours truly,
Elizabeth

(The Burden)   54

4 5. Gold Lull

This isn't the final calm...as easily,
as naturally, the belly of my breeding   *THE MOTHER LIFTS*
lover is swalling to every breath of sleep--- *IN*
Rubens' nudes needed no anaesthetic at childbirth.
In this gold lull of sleep, two muzzled mother   *< cover*
lies open and takes the world for what it is,   *lies takes*
a minute less than a minute...as many a writer   *HERE*
S suffers illusions that his phrase might live:
power makes nothing happen, deeds are words.   *words are deeds.*
President Lincoln almost found this faith;
once a good ear could almost hear the heart
murmur in the square thick hide of Lenin....
If only successful statesmen had a chance,
courage to be merciful to the young.

5 6. Green Sore   *THE MORNING MAIL*
                                                 BRINGS THE FAMILIAR
The too early squeaking country birds fatigue, *VOICE TO KENT:*
uxorious rattling of the pinhead rooks,   *and like o*
war of words, lung of infinitude...   *those*
The postman brings America to Kent: *expose first*
"not that I wish you entirely well, far from it." *NEW*
The new spring fields extend like a green sore.
We'll We pack and leave Milgate, in a rush as usual
for the train to London, leaving five lights burning---
to fool the burglar? Never the same five lights.
Sun never sets without our losing something:
books, keys, letters, or"Dear Caroline,
I have told Harriet that you are having a baby
by her father. She knows she will seldom see him;
physical presence or absence is the thing."

THIS
the
2) It was one green life, even heard through tears....

1) The morning mail brings the familiar voice to Kent:

"Green Sore" [*The Burden 6.* ↘5./], from "The Dolphin" manuscript, p. 54, composed and revised between 1971 and January 1972.[1]

---

1. Corrections in Lowell's and Frank Bidart's hand.

126. *Robert Lowell to* Miss Harriet Lowell[1]

80 Redcliffe Square, London SW 1[0]

March 14, 1971

Dearest Harriet—

It's hell trying to talk easily on the transAtlantic phone, and we're not the talkative types at best. Or maybe we are.

I don't know whether Mother has told you what I am going to write. I want anyway to tell you myself and try and keep you from feeling lonely and hurt. Caroline and I are going to have a baby. It is already visible and will be born according to the doctor (God willing) on the ninth of October. There can't ever be a second you in my heart, not even a second little girl, to say nothing of a boy.

You are always with me, you and mother. I want you to visit us whenever you wish and can. We're not ogres or bears. I think you may find that you will love Caroline. She has never been harsh to her own girls. You may even take delight in having a step brother or sister; one so much younger she is almost of another generation. Talking British and having my face or something of me, of you.

I'll see you around the sixth of May, when I'll be returning from giving a talk against technocracy in Purdue Indiana. I know nothing about technocracy, but suspect it's bad, and would not give the talk but for wanting to come to you both.

Dear Heart, give all my love to mother and to your self—alas, we can never give all. I try.

Love,

Dad

127. *Robert Lowell to* Mrs. Robert Lowell

80 Redcliffe Square, London SW 10

March 20, 1971

Dearest Lizzie:

Overjoyed that you intend to bring Harriet here in early June. I think coming alone would be hard and perhaps impossible for her. She

---

1. Crossed with Hardwick's March 12, 1971, letter to Blackwood.

will be long looked forward-to and embraced with warmth. So very much by me. There are many things, good weather, sights, country-side, my play etc. to make her stay happy. And I hope yours.

I am flying to Norway in a few hours. Meticulous letter from Per,[1] all numbers: every plane schedule down to the minute, how many cro-nin I'll be paid 20 minutes after arrival, how many after two days, how many students in each meeting, the seven poems of mine that have been read in Bergen, and a somewhat different seven in Oslo. Norway as I approach embarkation hour seems like Newfoundland, but I liked Newfoundland, they had never seen an American poet and came with tastes uncloyed.

I think it bold and generous of you to undertake the trip. I have a feeling that you will actually enjoy yourself. So will Harriet after we both get over the first stiff, shy minutes. I mean we *all* will. It's good, I think, that I will see you on the fifth or sixth of May for a few days. I think we have all gotten through the narrows of the worst. I think this, and am not saying it in a mood of callous and shallow euphoria.

Love,
Cal

128. *Adrienne Rich to* Robert Lowell

333 CPW,[2] NYC 10025, NY, USA
New York, 21 March 1971

Cal dear: I had thought of writing you for your birthday, but here it is almost three weeks later. In the meantime I've been to Ohio and seen Kenyon College at last and imagined, or tried to imagine, you and Peter[3] and Randall frisking like young lambs on those green and unpolluted hills.[4] They have girls there now, very attractive and

---

1. Seyersted, whom the Lowells had met when he was a student at Harvard in 1956. They were introduced by Huyck van Leeuwen.

2. Central Park West.

3. Taylor.

4. *The Winters Tale* 1.2: "We were as twinn'd lambs that did frisk i' the sun, | And bleat the one at the other"; Milton: "For we were nurst upon the self-same hill, | Fed the same flock, by fountain, shade, and rill" ("Lycidas," 23–24).

intelligent-looking ones, who would have done you & Peter & Randall a lot of good.

I think of you often, with a sense of loss. Even when we didn't see much of each other, you were part of New York for me, as you were part of Boston back in those distant days when you marveled at being forty and I was swamped with infants and wearing Lizzie's cast-off maternity clothes and you and Elizabeth were the strongest link I had with the reality of poetry, of my world, as against the domesticities and professorialities of Cambridge. I often think of you, and her, as having flung me a lifeline in those days. Well, they were simpler times; now it feels that we all have to be lifelines to each other, if we're to be anything.

I see a lot of Elizabeth, and love and admire her very much. Women are more interesting now than they've ever been, and even women like E. who were always interesting have become more subtle, more searching. So many of us through one thing or another—choice, divorce, suicide or death, chance of some kind—are living more autonomous lives, and it's like a second youth, only with far more sense of direction, of one's real needs and longings, as opposed to the heady confusion of first youth.—I have cycles of feeling swamped, still, with grief over Alf—not just over the manner of his death but the manner of his life recently—and with a kind of anger at him for walking out on a conversation which had grown difficult.[1] But on the other hand I'm enjoying my life; there's a kind of zest in it, even the difficulties, with concerns about money, the children, etc. My book will be out in April and I'll send you a copy. I'm writing again, after a nearly six-months' total silence. No, longer.

Your piece on Stanley[2] was out today and by all accounts has made him very happy. I thought it was lovely on Stanley but strange on poetry. I don't know what you really mean by obscure poetry;[3] you talk

---

1. Rich: "your eyes are stars of a different magnitude | they reflect lights that spell out: EXIT | when you get up and pace the floor | talking of the danger | as if it were not ourselves | as if we were testing anything else" ("On Trying to Talk with a Man," 35–40 [1973]).

2. Review of Stanley Kunitz's *The Testing-Tree* (1971) in the *New York Times Book Review*, March 21, 1971.

3. Lowell: "Now that obscure poetry is perhaps out of fashion, one must pay homage to its supreme invention and exploration. I remember Empson years ago with a group discussing one of his poems, 'To an Old Lady.' Was it about the moon described as an old lady, or an old lady as the moon? Was it physics or metaphysics? Empson said, 'It's my grandmother. The old girl

as if obscurity were a trick one could pick up and lay down, a matter of choice. I think it goes to the core of where one is, what one is able to say and what one is only able to dream. Some poems are closer to letters and others to dreams. A letter is intended for someone else primarily, a dream is first of all for the dreamer, but both kinds of poem have their place, and I love best the mixture of the two.

I know from Elizabeth that you are going to be a father again, and I wonder why—having children must be a profound thing if it's anything, and right now in history it is a strange thing to do, even though very common. Men & women are having such a hard time with the intense fragility of their own relationship that adding a complication seems foolhardy, except perhaps for the very young, who don't know what it is like.[1]

Ted Hughes is here, being hailed as a kind of second Shakespeare. I haven't read CROW,[2] as Ah don't know. I'm interested in a poetry of the future, that will be ahead of where my sensibility can take me unaided. This poetry would have to concern itself with the breakdown of language and the breakdown of sex, with politics in its most extreme sense, now & then I read a poem that seems to be doing it, but not many. Of course, I'm trying to write a few.

I realize that I don't have an address for you, so I'll send this to Essex. I'd love to hear from you. I think of you with a warring affection—but the affection is true.

Adrienne.

---

would have been furious if she had known I was writing about her.' Wasn't he right? Think of the simple, heartfelt, offensive poems that have been written about friends, wives, children. What hope for the half-poet? The frank, open and vulnerable, the voice of a generation, fades as soon as the elitist incantations of the hermeticist" (*New York Times Book Review*, March 21, 1971). But compare Empson's own account of "To an Old Lady," in which he says that it was about his mother. She had said to him, "'I will say, that poem about your Granny, William, now that showed decent feeling.' And I was greatly relieved by her saying this; I thought the situation was very embarrassing. She thought it was about her own mother [. . .] and I meant it about her" (*The Ambiguity of William Empson*, BBC Radio 3 [22 October 1977]; quoted in William Empson, *The Complete Poems* [2000], p. 193).

1. Lowell: "It's strange having a child today, though common, | adding our further complication to | intense fragility" ("Overhanging Cloud" [*Burden* 3] 4–6, "The Dolphin" manuscript); cf. "Overhanging Cloud" [*Marriage* 14], *The Dolphin*.

2. Ted Hughes, *Crow* (1970).

129. Elizabeth Hardwick to Robert Lowell[1]

[15 West 67th Street, New York, N.Y.]
March 21, 1971

Dear Cal: Just a note to say Harriet and I are going off at noon on Saturday the 27th and will not be back until April 7th. The Adventure Inn, Hilton Head Island, South Carolina . . . a place Walker Percy told me about, when I happened to meet him. We fly to Savannah and during our time will go to Charlestown, S.C. I am very tired. I have been doing all this writing day and night to make a living and I begin to feel like Dwight McDonald, except that he doesn't do it anymore and has sort of disappeared into various colleges. I made money last week for the trip, but our finances here are acute—so, man, be prepared in May for some shocks from the tax man and from the lawyer I am seeing on Wednesday, who goes by the name of Mrs. Gentleman! Tuition, rent, clothes, dentist, everything has gone up.

Your review of Stanley appeared today and I will say as someone said about Christianity: "Important, if true."[2]. . . . Very Calish, nice, delicious writing, but I have read Stanley's book twice and thought it very, very thin and disappointing. Your part of the review is lovely, very good and special.

Hope you sent Harriet some cards from Norway \Per-Laand!/ She will send you some poor nigger scenes . . . [3] She is planning to take movies, with the famous camera. Harriet is in great form, looks wonderful, and is very happy about Mexico. I'm very happy with her; she is very gay, alive and busy . . . I hope you get the NY Review. I

---

1. Crossed with Lowell's letters of March 14 to Harriet Lowell and March 20 to Hardwick.

2. Madame Olga Novikoff: "[Alexander] Kinglake interrupted me. 'Pray, remember I am a heathen. I dislike churches and, had I my way [. . .] I would write on every church, chapel, and cathedral only one line—"Important if true."'" (*The M. P. for Russia, Reminiscences and Correspondence*, vol. 1, ed. W. T. Stead [1909], p. 151).

3. Satirical. Cf. Hardwick: "What a sad countryside it is, the home of the pain of the Confederacy, the birthplace of the White Citizens Council. [. . .] [T]he whole region is fiction, art, dated, something out of a secondhand bookstore. And this, to be sure, is the 'Southern way of life,' these dated old photographs of a shack lying under a brilliant sky, the blackest of faces, the impacted dirt of the bus station, the little run-down churches, set in the mud, leaning a bit. [. . .] Life arranges itself for you here in the most 'conventional' tableaux. Juxtapositions and paradoxes fit only for the most superficial art present themselves over and over. [. . .] These Southerners have only the nothingness of racist ideas, the burning incoherence, and that is all" ("Selma," *New York Review of Books*, April 22, 1965).

think my piece on *Rosmersholm* is the best of the three.[1] Had a letter from Esther Brooks and get news of you from various people who have seen you, also from newspapers who list you along with movie stars as having abandoned the ship here. Well, perhaps you are all wise. I don't know. It still seems to me just as it always was and the passing scene, as you know to your sorrow, means a lot to me. . . . Adrienne's book is out, very good I think, especially "Shooting Script."[2] I had dinner the other night with, of all people, Richard Howard. He gave a brilliant lecture at Barnard that I attended, and I don't think it was my lack of knowledge that made it seem better than it might have been had it been about English matters. (French criticism was the subject.)

I am playing the Dvořák Cello Concerto with Rostropovich[3] and finding, such is the tyranny of taste, that I love for the moment rather second string romantic things. It's like the revival of old forties show tunes, I guess.

I hope Prometheus is the great, splendid success it deserves to be.[4] It's a wonderful, wonderful play—with some of your greatest speeches in it. I understand Irene and Kenneth[5] are both in [the] cast and so I can't imagine you won't be filled with glory. I hope so. This is our wish of hope, since we don't know exactly when it is coming on . . . Also Harriet has a March 1st birthday present for you, held back by the strike and saved for your visit here.

Dearest, do take care. Nothing is worth destroying yourself.[6] You have worked hard, led a good life and you have the right to nothing I'm afraid. But it is always nice when there is not justice but good luck and you have happiness and what you want. I don't entirely wish you well, far from it, of course.[7] But I still feel less angry with you than

---

1. "Ibsen and Women III: The Rosmersholm Triangle," *New York Review of Books*, April 8, 1971.
2. In Rich's *The Will to Change: Poems 1968–70* (1971).
3. Mstislav Rostropovich's 1969 performance with the Berlin Philharmonic (cond. Herbert von Karajan) of Antonín Dvořák's *Concerto in B Minor for Cello and Orchestra* (Op. 104, s), released by Deutsche Grammophon.
4. *Prometheus Bound*, dir. Jonathan Miller, opened at the Mermaid Theatre in London on June 24, 1971.
5. Irene Worth and Kenneth Haigh.
6. Hardwick: "there is a radical undercurrent to the realistic plays. If they have any moral it is that, in the end, nothing will turn out to have been worth the destruction of others and of oneself" ("Ibsen and Women III: The Rosmersholm Triangle," *New York Review of Books*, April 8, 1971).
7. Lowell: "~~The postman~~ \The morning mail brings/ ~~America~~ \the familiar voice to Kent/ to Kent: | 'not that I wish you entirely well, far from it'" ("Green Sore" [*The Burden* 5] 3–4, "The

with those who have used you for their own childish, destructive purposes. Write to Harriet. That is very easy, just nothing, and God will curse you if you do wrong when it is easy to do right. \He may just curse you anyway if He feels like it!/

Love, \darling,/
　　Elizabeth

Heredity! Harriet's story for school is a mad thing about a fish named Gabino (name of Spanish teacher) who likes to live in the sink. "Aside from an occasional egg on the head and bacon behind my fin and corn-pudding on my tail, life was very calm and nice." Who does that remind you of?

130. *Elizabeth Hardwick to Robert Lowell*

[15 West 67th Street, New York, N.Y.]
March 22, 1971

Dear Cal: Don't you hate it when letters cross? I had written you last night because Harriet and I had been talking about you and I just wanted you to know we were thinking of you. It was H. who read out that fantastic bit about the sink-fish and said, "Isn't it just like Daddy?" Now today your sweet letter to her arrived. \It took a week!/ By now you know that I had told her even before we spoke on the phone over a week ago. And I had made, with her, the plans I wrote Caroline about. We don't talk about the baby, but we do say, "I'll need the raincoat for England," and that sort of thing. I will be on a program about reviewing at the American Embassy. It doesn't pay my way, but it will give me something of an honorarium and a few days['] room and board. We won't stay long, but I think it must be.

What a year this has been. We will be taking off now as we took off with you last year for Italy, but this time alone and to S. Carolina. Harriet seems quite well and I think she will be all right if she doesn't feel that you don't care about her. I have tried to take the most optimistic attitude possible with her and while it is awful not to have a father, one

---

Dolphin" manuscript; see poem on page 154); "words of a moment's menace stay for life: | *not that I wish you entirely well, far from it*" ("Green Sore" [*Marriage* 7] 3–4, *The Dolphin*).

who is around a little at least, I think we will all manage. When I told her you would be coming to Harvard a year and a half from now, she said, "Oh, good, then I'll get to see him!"

Much love, dearest. We will work things out. Did you get the money from Blair, the bank, the NYTimes? May God keep you, now and for a long time. Forever is only for the world or for Him, isn't it.

Lizzie

\We look forward to May 6th. Dine here with us that night. How eager we are to see the dearest soul in the world./

131. *Robert Lowell to* Mrs. Robert Lowell

80 Redcliffe Sq., London SW 10

March 29, [1971]

Dearest Lizzie***

Letters are very slow, but this and an earlier one[1] (if you haven't got it) will be waiting when you return. I almost wept over yours. Ah we must keep it so. Our time on this earth is so poignantly short. Two additional lives would be too little to cleanse my character, to go the rounds of amends.

In Norway, someone came up to me and said that your Hedda piece had solved the problem they had been debating for a hundred years. It was at a party, and I never could discover what problem. Hedda's ~~soul~~ nature, good and evil? I guess there was more.

Reed Whittemore's letter seemed strained, pushed by something unexpressed. A *nasty instance*, or whatever he said my review was. I answered cordially, I think.[2] Miss van Duyn writes witty and intelligent \reviews/, I guess her verse is witty and intelligent. She *must* be better than Corso, but I haven't read him for years.[3]

---

1. Lowell to Hardwick, March 20, 1971.
2. Letter and Lowell's reply now missing. But Lowell wrote to Blair Clark in 1973: "I have something of a grudge against Whittemore. A year or two ago he wrote a six page letter protesting against a review I'd written of Kunitz—log rolling, praising mediocrities etc. at the expense of Reed etc. Very hysterical, almost unhinged, but well-meant I suppose" (Lowell to Clark, July 31, 1973).
3. Mona Van Duyn won the 1971 National Book Award for *To See, To Take*, which "was hotly disputed by Allen Ginsberg, the poet [a judge for the award]. The book [. . .] was on the long end of a

A haunting letter from Adrienne. Woman seems to have ousted the blacks. I thought of a made-up folk saying, A man whose profession is finding needles in haystacks will soon see them everywhere except in pin-cushions. I don't know who this applies to.

Can I say that Caroline's children are already planning things for Harriet? Ones a little below her age perhaps like the Hyde Park maze. She is warmly awaited.

Oh dear, Scandinavia. Per is improved by [h]is homeground, warmth under the ice. Norway is a country country, a bit of Oregon, Colorado and Vermont. Bergen partly made of wood and cliff-hung is one of the most beautiful cities I've seen. Oslo is one of ours, Boston in the setting of Portland. Then Copenhagen, and Amsterdam, but I was tired and knew no one, and had recommendations to people withdrawn by flu. My hotel was like a Volkswagen, efficient, uncomfortable, cheap and uncomfortable\small/. My shower was a hole in the ceiling separated by a movable board from the basin but not from the toilet. At breakfast, a cheerful middleclass man in spectacles chanted Danish hymns.

I think you are heroic to make the trip to London. It's you who is the dearest soul that ever breathed. Or is it Harriet. Again my eyes water. All must be for the best.

Love,
Cal

132. *Robert Lowell to* Mrs. Adrienne Conrad[1]

80 Redcliffe Sq., London SW 10
March 29, 1971

Dearest Adrienne:

How lovely to hear from you at the beginning of my 54th year of grace and pardon. I haven't read my Stanley piece in print and forget exactly what I wrote about obscurity. I think I was putting in [a] plug for the difficult poetry I grew wise and confused on in the thirties. I

4-to-1 vote, with Mr. Ginsberg, the lone dissenter, supporting Gregory Corso's 'Elegiac Feelings American.' Mr. Ginsberg called the choice of the other four jurors 'ignominious, insensitive and mediocre'" (George Gent, "Bellow Wins 3d National Book Award," *New York Times*, March 3, 1971).
1. Adrienne Rich.

don't think obscurity can be put on like an overcoat, any more than the style of the Rape of the Lock[1] can be. Still there's always an effort of will \whose other name is choice/. I'm uncertain what you mean by dream, but I am sure you don't mean sleep walking. The poetry of the future? I'm not sure I have read any, then again I think I've read a lot—Rimbaud, Othello, wherever poetry is straining to its uttermost. Most art, even the best hardens to a convention, yet the very best can't be imitated by the future, no second Moby Dick,[2] and hundreds more.

Women? Randall and Peter and I found them even in our Kenyon exile, we were all more or less engaged. I know too much about women to be entangled into an argument. We are having a child because we stumbled into it and then found we dearly wanted one, and had a moral horror of abortion—I mean for ourselves, not for others. We feel a calm and awe. I don't think you know what you are talking about. Why shouldn't our having a child be profound? The times are difficult, almost impossible today, yesterday, always. If one lived in East Pakistan, Biaffra either[,] Vietnam. Character and private conditions may make having children fearful, but I don't \believe/ the *times* make it ~~very~~ hard\er/ for anyone we know.

Oh well, dearest Adrienne, it's lovely you are writing. I hope to be briefly in New York around the first of May. I'll spare you a lecture on repetition and change based on a trip to Norway and reading the Burnt Njal Saga. What could be less like our lives than theirs of honor and ~~hacking~~, yet at every point a responsive cord is struck. In sad moments it seems that man and woman advance from one black bog to another. ~~A~~ \To/ look at the worst, as Hardy says.[3] And the joy is incredible too. Please forgive my chaffing, my heart is with you.

Love,
Cal

---

1. By Alexander Pope (1712).
2. By Herman Melville (1851).
3. Thomas Hardy: "Let him in whose ears the low-voiced Best is killed by the clash of the First, | Who holds that if way to the Better there be, it exacts a full look at the Worst, | Who feels that delight is a delicate growth cramped by crookedness, custom and fear, | Get him up and be gone as one shaped awry; he disturbs the order here" ("In Tenebris II" 13–16).

133. *Harriet Lowell to* Mr. Robert Lowell

[Postcard: Land's End. Looking out from Hilton Head Island onto the Intercoastal Waterway.]

[Hilton Head, S.C., but postmarked Savannah, GA]

[March 29, 1971]

Dear Daddy,

Hi. I am having a great time. We are very sunburnt. The water is warm. I hope you are having a good time. There is not enough room on this card to say anything interesting.

Love, Harriet

134. *Robert Lowell to* Miss Harriet Lowell

80 Redcliffe Sq., London SW 10

April 2, 1971

Dearest Harriet:

I have gone and come back from Norway, very "scenic" like Maine or Aspen, \snow-topped/ mountains near large cities, pretty wooden houses on cliffs, an amber-colored drink that tastes of caraway seeds and is called the "water of life." In Oslo, the capital, I went to a famous park where a man named Vigeland got a contract in the 'twenties to put up naked statues, then no one could legally stop him and he put up four hundred before he died. Everyone in Norway speaks English as well as we do, but they aren't as bright, at least some of the people teaching American literature weren't.

I started a story: "Aside from an occasional egg on the head and bacon behind my fins and cornpudding on my tail, life was very calm and nice. It rapidly grew much less nice, when a small chocolate-brown cat without foreclaws, but with terrible hindclaws and the bark of a police man began to haunt my sink, sniffing for fishblood. "You pig," I screamed, flipping my tail, and hitting the beast on the head with a wet lump of cornpudding. "Your round," replied Charles Sumner Lowell in a surly voice, "but wait till Old Missus has to wash dishes, then you'll be left high and dry." "I hope you croak on catfood," said the sinkfish. "Why don't you just stop breathing," said Sumner. (You finish[.])

I'll be in New York on the first or second of May, and will fly on to
Indiana, then spend a few days on my way back.

Love,

Daddy \(what a pretty signature)/

135. *Robert Lowell to Robert Silvers,* New York Review of Books

[Telegram]

LONDON
[received April 2, 1971, 2:45 PM]

ROBERT SILVERS

NEWYORK REVIEW

250 WEST57THSTREET

NEWYORK

I CANT TAG THIS TO A REVIEW COMMA BUT IT SEEMS MEANT
FOR THE NEW YORK REVIEW OF BOOKS PERIOD

POISONED BY MY FRESH IMPRESSIONS COMMA I FUMBLE FOR
MY FIRST WORDS—NO ONE HAS A GOOD CASE AGAINST LIEU-
TENANT CALLEY[1] PERIOD WHY SHOULD THE BAIT BE EATEN
WHEN THE SHARKS SWIM FREE QUESTION MARK[2] OUR PUBLIC

---

1. First Lieutenant William L. Calley, Jr., was convicted on March 29, 1971, for the premeditated murder of 22 South Vietnamese civilians during the 1968 My Lai massacre. On April 1, President Richard Nixon ordered him released from jail. For British coverage, see "Calley Guilty of My Lai Murders" (*Guardian*, March 30, 1971); Michael Leapman, "Lieut. Calley jailed for life amid wave of U.S. protest" (*Times*, 1 April 1971); Louis Heren, "Lieut Calley, a cog in a war machine" (*Times*, 1 April 1971); and Fred Emery, "Nixon order to free Lieut. Calley from prison pending review" (*Times*, 2 April 1971). Cf. Lowell, "Women, Children, Babies, Cows, Cats," *History* (1973).

2. Lowell: "I hoped to gamble with unloaded dice . . . | like Racine, no enemy of craft, | drawn through his maze of iron composition | by the incomparable voice of Phedre. | As for this writing . . . flowers for the dead, | faulty things once written as best I might, | when I sat in service to the too many | words of the collaborating Muse, | and plotted perhaps too freely with my life, | not avoiding injury to persons, | not avoiding injury to myself—| we ask compassion. Why should

UNDER THE HEAD OF STATE HAVE EXPRESSED SYMPATHY FOR
CALLEY COMMA MORE THAN HUMANIZED HIM COMMA MORE
THAN CONDONED HIS ATROCITIES——A SMALL STUMBLE COMMA
PERHAPS FATAL COMMA [ON] OUR HURRIED ROAD FROM HIRO-
SHIMA TO NOW PERIOD WE ACT IN DAYLIGHT SEMICOLON NO
GROPING CIVILIAN CAN CLAIM TO SEE NOTHING PERIOD WEVE
NO NEED TO WORRY ABOUT RETRIBUTION COMMA IT IS NEVER
AN EYE FOR AN EYE COMMA ETC SEMICOLON IT NORMALLY FALLS
ON SOMEONE ELSE PERIOD WE PLANT THESE TREES FOR OUR
GRANDCHILDREN SEMICOLON WE DARE NOT HYPOCRITICALLY
OSTRICIZE PRESIDENT NIXON COMMA OUR OWN HUCKLEBERRY
FINN WHO HAD TO SHOOT EVERYONE ELSE ON THE RAFT[1]

    ROBERT LOWELL

---

the bait be eaten | when the sharks swim free? This book is fiction, | an eelnet made by man for
the eel fighting" ("Fishnet," from "Excerpt from 'The Dolphin,'" *The Review* 26 [Summer 1971]).
Cf. "Dolphin," *The Dolphin*.

1. Silvers replied on April 6, 1971 that "We certainly want to publish the message you sent
me," sending Lowell a fair copy of the "badly transmitted" text (silently corrected here; for the
original, see Manuscripts and Archives Division, New York Public Library). Lowell replied
by telegram on April 13, 1971, with corrections. The statement was published as "Judgment
Deferred on Lieutenant Calley" (Lowell's title), *New York Review of Books* (May 6, 1971):"A
principle may kill more than an incident. I am sick with fresh impressions. Has no one the
compassion to pass judgment on William Calley? His atrocity is cleared by the President, pub-
lic, polls, rank and file of the right and left. He looks almost alive; like an old song, he stirs us
with the gruff poignance of the professional young soldier. He too fought under television for
our place in the sun. Why should the bait be eaten when the sharks swim free? I sense a cold-
ness under the hysteria. Our nation looks up to heaven, and puts her armies above the law. No
stumbling on the downward plunge from Hiroshima. Retribution is someone somewhere else
and we are young. In a century perhaps no one will widen an eye at massacre, and only scat-
tered corpses express a last histrionic concern for death. We are not hypocrites, we can learn
to embrace people outside society—President Nixon, our own Huckleberry Finn who has to
shoot everyone else on the raft."

136. Elizabeth Hardwick to Robert Lowell

[15 West 67th Street, New York, N.Y.]
April 9, 1971

Cal, dearest: I am not bringing Harriet to England. It more and more doesn't seem the right thing to do to her. You are our only real concern in this and I am looking forward to your visit to us.

S. Carolina was a disaster. Rootless, village-less, condominium (whatever that is) country-club development on a lovely old island that was given to the Negroes after the Civil War—forty acres and a mule.[1] The wind blew, many retired couples, many hot biscuits. Went to Savannah and Charleston for quick visits, each a long drive and the drives, flat, empty and not even a cabin with its wisp of smoke along the road.

There is a lot happening here, but all too complicated to go into. H. and I went to S. Carolina on the plane with Isaiah B. and Aline, who were enroute to Columbia Dickey-land.[2] Had lunch with Stephen Spender yesterday. Bob S. and I went to Stravinsky funeral,[3] but didn't actually get into the chapel, all the seats having been taken.

Did I tell you Flavio committed suicide.[4] Poor Elizabeth[.] She and Ted Hughes hear the tolling of the bell over and over.[5]

I must get to my work. Harriet is fine, but she doesn't like to talk about what is happening to you, even though she does talk about you, as you were, with much pleasure and pride.

It is nice of you to come over to see us, no matter for how brief a

---

1. "The islands from Charleston, south, the abandoned rice fields along the rivers for thirty miles back from the sea [. . .] are reserved and set apart for the settlement of the negroes now made free by the acts of war and the proclamation of the President of the United States [. . .] each family shall have a plot of not more than (40) forty acres of tillable ground" (General W. T. Sherman, "Field Order No. 15," January 16, 1865, from sections I and III). Eric Foner: "Sherman later provided that the army could assist them with the loan of mules. (Here, perhaps, lies the origin of the phrase 'forty acres and a mule' that would soon echo throughout the South)" (*Reconstruction, America's Unfinished Revolution, 1863–1877* [1988], pp. 70–71). The Field Order was overturned in the fall of 1865 by Andrew Johnson.
2. James Dickey was professor of English at the University of South Carolina in Columbia, S.C.
3. On April 9, 1971, at Frank E. Campbell's Funeral Home on Madison Avenue in Manhattan.
4. Flavio de Macedo Soares Regis, nephew of Bishop's lover Lota de Macedo Soares.
5. Lota de Macedo Soares committed suicide in 1967. Ted Hughes's first wife, Sylvia Plath, committed suicide in 1963, and his lover Assia Wevill committed suicide in 1969 (also killing their daughter, Shura, in the act).

time. Until then I am thinking about you with love and a good deal of worry. I have just written something about myself that says, "All I know I have learned from books and worry."[1] So, just think of my "worry" as the pursuit of knowledge.

Again, dearest love, \to you always/
    Lizzie

137. *Robert Lowell to* Mrs. Robert Lowell[2]

80 Redcliffe Sq., London Sw. 10
April 9, 1971

Dearest Lizzie:

You must be just returned from your southern trip, tanned and weary. These trips rather get one down, I'm still aching back into form from mild Norway. Tomorrow we go to the Hebrides. I think I may steal out of going to Purdue, since I'll be seeing you and Harriet about a month later here. I really wish to see you both in New York, in \expectation/, but the trips are hard, require weeks to sink back to one's true self. So, I think not, but will wait ten days or so to make sure. Why take a lot of money just to break even talking about something I'm incompetent on?

Don't you think everything is moral chaos now? Liked and immensely admired your Ibsen, maybe rawly near home. Or is it? So many phrases come back to me from letters in other \foreign/ contexts, yet seem to ~~stick~~ \glue/ to Ibsen.[3] I think you should be vain of having put so much of yourself into the classic plots; I'm envious. Pardon this letter, I'm coming out of mild flu and irritatedly intuitive\, or stupid./

Love to you and Harriet,
    Cal

---

1. Hardwick: "All my life I have carried about with me the chains of an exaggerated anxiety and tendency to worry, an overexcited imagination for disasters ahead, problems foreboding, errors whose consequences could stretch to the end of time. I feel some measure of admiration for women who are carefree, even for the careless; but we work with what we are given, and what I know I have learned from books and worry" ("The Ties Women Cannot Shake and Have," *Vogue*, June 1971, p. 86). Cf. Hardwick: "A lifetime of worrying and reading may bring you at last to free trips you are not sure you wish to take" (*Sleepless Nights*, p. 129).

2. Crossed with Hardwick's letter of April 9, 1971.

3. See footnote 6 on page 160 (Hardwick to Lowell, March 21, 1971); cf. also Lowell to Silvers, April 2, 1971, with Lowell's early draft of "Dolphin" (pages 166–67, footnote 2).

138. *Robert Lowell to* Mrs. Robert Lowell

[33 Pont Street, London SW 1]
April 13, 1971

Dearest Lizzie—

Our letters seem doomed to cross. I woke up this morning silently saying *Flavio*, and for the first time in the twenty-four hours since I'd read your letter—realized how deeply terrifying his death must be for Elizabeth. Where is she? I've sent a cable to [her] Brazil address, saying "Dearest Elizabeth, can I help?" I do hope she is in this country. How almost like something in Hardy would it have been if the little group in Rio could have looked eight years ahead.[1] Even Keith[2] has had vicissitudes.

Think carefully about not bringing Harriet to London. Are you coming yourself? Of course it is all delicate and uncertain, and the success of her trip would have to depend on the moods of so many persons, so many swayed persons. Maybe you have been getting the wrong advice, from yourself among others. Anyway, it's [a] great blow to me. I suppose I'll make the early May flight, though the flying is like six hours of giving blood. \For you and Harriet too!/ And isn't really a serious and honorable assignment.

You seem to have found a curious new stylistic trick, the phrase, uncertain between two meanings, id est, ["]Harriet's not interested in what has happened to you."[3] Happened has two meanings, but I don't suppose you knew that you couldn't have both. Poor Carolina South! It is nature wearing the mask of city slum. Sorry you didn't have a better trip. Love to you both. I'll be seeing you.

Love,
Cal

---

1. The Lowells visited Bishop and Lota de Macedo Soares in Brazil in 1962. See *Words in Air*, pp. 415–25; and Elizabeth Bishop, *One Art: Letters*, pp. 405–13.
2. Botsford.
3. See Hardwick to Lowell, April 9, 1971 (above): "Harriet is fine, but she doesn't like to talk about what is happening to you, even though she does talk about you, as you were, with much pleasure and pride."

139. Elizabeth Hardwick to Robert Lowell

[15 West 67th Street, New York, N.Y.]

April 19, 1971

Dearest Cal: I despair of letters. Apparently mine do not say what I mean or feel and I'm sure I read yours wrongly also. No matter. If you say I wrote "Harriet isn't interested in what is happening to you," I suppose I did, but it is a fantastic untruth, misprint, something. I do know that sometime not so long ago I said *you* were the main concern, not London, the scene or anything else. I want more than my life to do what is best for everyone. Harriet is absolutely wonderful, beautiful, gay, doing well in every way. I have a horror of upsetting this before she goes off to Mexico, alone, brave, all that. Children her age, Cal, just don't sit around talking about things about their parents that upset them. Adrienne says her children never mention Alf. But I do talk to Harriet about you, gaily, friendly, never denying that I miss you, but no longer bitter. I have been absolutely candid about everything, clear, sure, and she knows you are not coming home, everything. But after some longer thought I do feel that a short trip to England, back to the same for months, years, whatever, is rather bad just now. No, I will not be coming. I got the invitation after I had decided to bring Harriet—rather a strange coincidence. But, another thing, I couldn't possibly pay for our trip, couldn't begin to. The income tax is a nightmare; tomorrow 1969 will be audited and they always charge. . . . I feel the trip is much too expensive right now.

I very much agree about the exhaustion of your coming here, the general uselessness of the astronaut conference. It seems for such a short time, so dislocating, tiring. Do what you like and we will certainly understand. Harriet is fine, busy. All is well here. So it is up to you, but please believe that I see every reason for you not to come and I am being absolutely honest, honestly.

I guess we will go to Washington this weekend.[1] It is a dedication and like dedications, repetitious, gratuitous often, not specially interesting or fresh—merely necessary.

I hope there is nothing askew in this letter![2] May God keep you[.]

E.

---

1. For the *Vietnam War Out Now* rally on April 24.
2. Cf. Lowell, "'I despair of letters . . .'" [*Burden 6*], "The Dolphin" manuscript (see poem on page 172); and "Letter" [*Marriage 8*], *The Dolphin*.

```
.(The Burden)

6. "I despair of letters..."

"I despair of letters. You say I wrote H. isn't
interested in the thing happening to you now.
So what? A fantastic untruth, misprint, something;
I meant the London scene's no big concern, just you...
She's absolutely beautiful, gay, etc.
I've a horror of turmoiling her before she flies
to Mexico, alone and brave, half-Spanish.
Children her age don't sit about talking out
the thing about their parents. I do talk about you,
and I have never denied I miss you...
I guess we'll make Washington this weekend;
it's a demonstration, like all demonstrations,
repetitious, gratuitous, unfresh...just needed.
I hope nothing is mis-said in this letter."
```

"'I despair of letters . . .'" [The Burden 6], from "The Dolphin" manuscript, p. 54, composed and revised between 1971 and January 1972.

140. Robert Lowell to Stanley Kunitz

[London]
April 25, 1971

Dearest Stanley—

I wrote the review knowing that many of the poems were written when death was near enough to you to put out your hand and touch it, and that you might be in that position when you read it. How lovely to know you feel tough again, back to your lifelong state.[1] Once or twice, I felt I was likely to die. Can't say I enjoyed the realization much, yet what a relief to have been there. Have we though? Someone said death isn't an event in life, it isn't lived.[2] Thank God. You must be sick of people bothering you about my review. I wanted to put you dramatically, and think (without exactly admitting it to myself) \I/ was angling for a good place in the Review.

Several of my books, especially Notebook, I assumed might be my last. Now with this one (No doubt it will be) I don't. It's about done,

1. Kunitz to Lowell: "A few months ago, at Lenox Hill [Hospital], I thought I was really through with my body. But in the springtime I seem as tough as ever" (April 23, 1971).
2. Wittgenstein: "Death is not an event in life. Death is not lived through. If by eternity is understood not endless temporal duration but timelessness, then he lives eternally who lives in the present. Our life is endless in the way that our visual field is without limit" (*Tractatus Logico-Philosophicus* 6.4311, trans. C. K. Ogden [1922]). Lowell: "Death's not an event in life, it's not lived through" ("Plotted" 14, *The Dolphin*).

many taken out, many put in, total a little under 120, title Dolphin (a very different title than Crow[1]—which by the way I don't like at all, tho I like him personally better than any other poet here)[.] I'm playing \with/ the idea of bringing out the book in a limited edition, in a sort of Cummington Press run by Ted Hughes' sister,[2] about 500 copies, printed any way I want, expensive. That might be the most tactful thing I could do for Elizabeth short of burning the Ms. Then in a year or so I'd bring out commercial editions. I'd hate to leave the book in type if I were run over or something. Lawsuits between Lizzie and Caroline etc. Lizzie is the heroine, the eel I try to ensnare and release from the eelnet,[3] but she will feel bruised by the intimacy. She should win all hearts but what is that when you are left, and left again in print?

Everyone in America seems to think this is too dire a time to breed. I had an impertinent lecture from Adrienne, but for us it's a calming joy. We already have three rather lovely little girls, so the coming of another child is not alarming—tho always there is a frightening mystery and uncertainty. Caroline is comparatively physical, healthy, we breathe now as the cattle breathe. Caroline sleeping and eating double, looking as though she'd deliver tomorrow, tho it's not till October 9[.] We mustn't talk as if we were living in East Pakistan.

We live in the same house now, next week Caroline will take my name—this isn't marriage yet, I don't want to jostle Lizzie at all. Will the hailstones of the gods fall on me,[4] if I say I've never been so happy, nor knew I could be?

Don't know when I'll reach America. Maybe in September. It

---

1. Kunitz to Lowell: "When exactly is your revised Notebook coming out here? The books of verse that stand out for me this season are Ted Hughes's nightmarish *Crow*, which has been extravagantly praised, and Jim Wright's beautiful but unsung *Collected*. Adrienne's *The Will to Change* has just arrived in the mail" (April 23, 1971). Ted Hughes, *Crow* (1970); James Wright, *Collected Poems* (1971); Adrienne Rich, *The Will to Change* (1971).

2. Olwyn Hughes, who managed the private Rainbow Press that she and Ted Hughes had founded together. Cummington Press was the publisher of Lowell's first collection, *Land of Unlikeness* (1944).

3. Lowell: "this book is fiction, | an eelnet made by man for the eel fighting" ("Fishnet" 12–13, "An Excerpt from 'The Dolphin,'" *The Review* 26 [Summer 1971]; see poem on pages 166–67, footnote 2.); "yet ~~asking~~ \ask/ compassion for this book, half fiction, | an eelnet made by man for the eel fighting" ("Dolphin" 12–13, "The Dolphin" manuscript); "this book, half fiction | an eelnet made by man for the eel fighting— | my eyes have seen what my hand did" ("Dolphin" 13–15, *The Dolphin*).

4. Lowell: "You have done too much. This hailstorm of gifts is poverty" (*Prometheus Bound*, page 24).

seemed too jolting to come this spring. The plane trips in themselves are murder,—and so much else added! Oh my Dear, who to talk to? I love it here, but the English are generically horrible, just like New York Jews and New Englanders. Alas, I've been all three.[1] But the countryside, and the ~~eccentric~~ \changeful/ slowed pace of life here are lovely, not that feeling one sometimes gets in New York of screaming, metallic, poisoned ice.

all my love to you and Elise.

Cal

PS. We can't make it to the Cape, either. It seems best to spend a quiet summer in Kent, where patterns can be repeated in a house Caroline has lived \in/, broken in. The guy in the Tribune was as you say.[2] Two errors. I really said that Shakespeare was such a success that he couldn't [be] regarded as a model or typical of other writers.[3] Also at the end, I meant to say that my living in England was *not* \a/ symbolic gesture.[4]

---

1. Lowell had Jewish ancestors on his paternal and maternal sides. They had similar names. His Lowell grandmother descended from Mordecai Myers (1776–1871), mayor of Kinderhook, New York, and Schenectady, New York. His Winslow great-grandmother, Margaret Devereux (née Mordecai) of Raleigh, North Carolina, was descended from Myer Myers (1723–1795), a New York silversmith. See Lowell to Ezra Pound, October 24, 1956: "I have no mind for your gospel, and don't let us talk about the Jews. I have several on my family tree" (*The Letters of Robert Lowell*, p. 263). About his father's side: "The account of him is platitudinous, worldly and fond, but he has no Christian name and is entitled merely Major *M*. Meyers in my Cousin Cassie Myers Julian-James's privately printed *Biographical Sketches: A Key to a Cabinet of Heirlooms in the Smithsonian Museum* [. . .] he was Mordecai Myers. [. . .] a German Jew [. . .] Mordecai Myers was my Grandmother Lowell's great-grandfather. His life was tame and honorable" ("91 Revere Street," *Life Studies*, p. 11). About his mother's side, see Nicholas Jenkins, "Beyond Wikipedia: Notes on Robert Lowell's Family," http://arcade.stanford.edu/blogs/beyond-wikipedia-notes-robert-lowells-family.
2. Kunitz to Lowell: "The interview with you in the NY Times a few weeks ago troubled me a bit. I had the impression that you were being pestered and badgered by an insensitive clod—no pal of yours, I hope" (April 23, 1971).
3. Lowell: "Shakespeare was an unusual playwright and not typical of his age. He was much less successful than Ben Jonson and I imagine people who saw his plays were a very small number, and the playhouse was very small, and the plays ran for a very short time; and I imagine the people who bought his first folio when it came out were a very small number. I don't have the figures but I'm sure that his sales weren't anything like the hundredth best seller this year" (Dudley Young, "Talk with Robert Lowell," *New York Times*, April 4, 1971).
4. "Young: *What about the speculation that you are in flight from America? Is that a myth you want to endorse at all?* No, I've been here the best part of a year and I'd quite like to stay another year and it is a vacation from America which has no sort of symbolics. I'll go back to America and be American and I'm not comparing the countries. *So we're not to see you as a disenchanted pilgrim, returning*

141. Elizabeth Hardwick to Mary McCarthy

[15 West 67th Street, New York, N.Y.]
April 26, 1971

Dearest Mary: I keep expecting copies of your novel, but haven't received any yet. Bob of course had one but it went off to Pritchett immediately.[1] Anyway I hope it is coming soon. I had put off writing you in the thought that the book was just around the corner. The Review people tell me that [they] have a splendidly interesting piece from you, the introduction to *Neither Christ nor Marxism*.[2] I haven't seen that either since I haven't been on the premises for a few weeks.

Harriet, Barbara, Francine Gray, Rose Styron and a few others of us went to the demo. The church service, with the veterans, the night before was very nice, the march itself tiring but, well, at least there. There was no way to look upon it except as a personal dedication—repetitive, not especially interesting, merely necessary. It was a nice day, the numbers were pleasing. Then late Sunday night some idiots, Rennie Davis group, did the one thing that would drive the harassed American wild, held up traffic for four hours on the Pennsylvania turnpike. Counter-productive indeed. The march had been a wild success and I don't think this last foolishness, over a day later, made any sense. Not that one couldn't think of times when such actions would be proper, but not just now. The veterans were the main thing. And one young man, John Kerry, sane, intelligent, attractive really emerged with all his wounds and decorations from the crowd, suddenly providing that mysterious thing: leadership. He spoke before Congress and Senate, brought tears to old elected eyes. Otherwise, the slaughter goes on. It is, isn't it, just like *The Iliad*, as S. Weil sees it.[3] The fighting just can't stop.

Long to see you. I have the feeling that from abroad poor old

---

to *European sources*. It's an American theme . . . the discovery, the pioneer going into the wilderness. After a while the wilderness changes into the Europe of Henry James and Eliot—a freehold almost barbaric in its newness" ("Talk with Robert Lowell," *New York Times*, April 4, 1971).

1. V. S. Pritchett, "Ironical Aviary," *New York Review of Books*, June 3, 1971.

2. Mary McCarthy, "The American Revolution of Jean-François Revel," *New York Review of Books*, September 2, 1971 ("*The following will appear as an Afterword to Jean-François Revel's* Without Marx or Jesus, *to be published by Doubleday*").

3. See Simone Weil, "The Iliad, or The Poem of Force," trans. Mary McCarthy, *Politics* (November 1945).

Babylon seems truly lost. And the Nixon people of course surpass anything we could have imagined. But still, the country is perhaps turning around in slow, hesitant steps. I feel hopeless about government but not about the people. Even the prospects for summer of 1972, for the Democrats, seem backward, but I guess we will need just to continue. It is interesting here, in any case, and doesn't feel the way I imagine people living abroad think it feels. I ponder the whirling changes that seem to take place here over night, those quick, unaccountable shifts of attitude and feeling. Perhaps being attuned to such things is in itself a distorting talent, but it does seem to me that every six months is different from the six before. Some people think the students are apathetic from despair, but I believe, or try to believe, that they are radical, genuinely troubled but no longer foolishly destructive. There seem to be ~~less~~ fewer drug scenes, among the sensible at least. The March was much more calm, gloriously less stoned. The Panthers, the guns, the bravado seem wiped out, by the trials, the hopelessness of the whole strange gesture. It is horrible in its end, just as the beginning was horrible—like a peculiar dream in some awful African-Congo village.

Maine—when will you be coming? I guess Harriet and I will go up on June 14th, then I will fly back down for the weekend of the 4th of July to put her on her way to Mexico. She is very well, dieting with great courage and tenacity, has had a good year in school, and announced to me last night with a frown that we really had to start building a Socialist Party in this country. And I felt how sad it was that the Socialist Party didn't exist, after its very brief—not so brief—blossoming around World War I. It is a strange lack; I guess the dear old New Deal really is the answer . . . About Non-Socialist Maine. It is about as far from what I need in my life now as anything could be. We have no place for vacations, holidays, Harriet doesn't like it at this point. If it weren't for you I think I would pull the cover over my head, after calling out an order for sale. But I can't face it now. Instead, writing Link Sawyer to repay the inevitable damage of the foul winter.

I spoke to Cal this morning. He seemed quite together and so I hope he is well. Time is gradually liberating me from the pains of the past, by giving me new ones I guess. The only thing I worry about now is Harriet, but she seems so extraordinarily well that I accept that with trembling gratitude. I have \been/ candid with her, have taken a positive attitude about the baby and Cal's future and for the rest we talk about him only in joking and friendly memories of his odd ways. Children her age don't \seem to/ like to talk about their parents' troubles—all that will come soon enough. So for the moment all is very well. I want her to get through Mexico happily without too much concentration on what has happened this year. We have a good time together, she has friends. I think everything is going to be perfectly all right for her.

Can't wait to get *Birds* and to see, whole and plain, you and Jim. I look forward to the summer because of you two enormously—and of course I like Castine itself, and wish it were nearer. Much, much love

Lizzie

142. *Robert Lowell to* Miss Harriet Lowell

80 Redcliffe Sq., [London SW 1]
May 4, 1971

Dear Little Harriet—

Little, for so I think of you through all the years since the day when I carried you a limp almost boneless lump from the maternity hospital to Aunt Sarah's car and the long times when I could carry you a squat-nosed snubbles refusing to walk home from our walks in Central Park. Now you are not small at all, though I think I can call you young. It breaks my heart that you are so far away so hard to get to. Sometimes when I am thinking a little absentmindedly and sadly, it seems almost as though I were a clay statue and part of my side had dropped at my feet \like a lump/. My dearest joy is picturing how you might some-day, sooner or later, spend a long time with us. You wouldn't be sorry. You could remind me that I am a great American moral leader, and not a reactionary sybarite.

How was the Washington Demo? Will the War ever end? It's now dragging toward the end of its second ten years. How will things be when you enter college, if you so choose? Quieter? Unhappier? Or maybe better? I can't see ahead.

Happier things. I've been to see two performing dolphins, Baby and Brandy, in a tank on Oxford St. They can jump twenty feet, bat a ball back to their trainer, pretend to cry for a fish. Smart as Sumner, bigger-brained than man and much more peaceful and humorous. It's like summer outside today. Glorious, though for some time I've been troubled with a low virus. Little shivers. I am taking antibiotics, and it will go. It's mainly why I decided not to fly to America. We have many pets. A hideous large white rabbit, Snowdrop, a beautiful small black rabbit, Flopsy, a tiny gerbil named Gertrude Buckman, two kittens. So, a zoo. Wish I had you with me to talk to and laugh with. Give Nicole my love, and most of all Mother.

> Love,
> Dad

143. *Robert Lowell to* Miss Harriet Lowell

[80 Redcliffe Sq., London SW 10]
May 5, 1971

Dearest Harriet:

I have been thinking all day about writing you since getting your wonderful postcard. I could perhaps zip over to New York before you fly to Mexico, but it is difficult. My play is coming out on the twenty-fourth of June, and Jonathan Miller who is directing it has come down with *chickenpox* (!) and won't \be/ able to go to the first four or five rehearsals. I can hardly skip the opening night. The last days in June mightn't be a very good time \for me/ to drop on your excited household, marshalled for your trip. This isn't the best time to leave Caroline who is five months pregnant but looks nine. Still? Another time is September, when you would have more leisure, but this is even closer to the birth of our child.

Could you come here at any time, now or September before school? We would so love having you, and could promise an unrushed varied stay for you—unplagued with churches and heavy sights. The children aged ten, seven and five await your coming like Elvis Presley. The oldest, Natalya, particularly, who treats her youngest sister with the same stern smiles that you gave Angela, the marvelous fat little Spanish girl who stayed with us in Castine. How I would love to see you!

Our two cats, Tabby and Tiger, sisters, have nervous troubles when either is in the room with the other, but each sends her love to Charles, so sure she would be his favorite.

(If you came here in June, I am sure you'd enjoy seeing my Prometheus, a play in which a man is tied to a rock \and talks/ for two hours.)

You know I am a very unresponsive, humorless, conventional man, seldom giving voice to my emotions, so you can guess what it costs me to tell you I more or less wept with joy reading your card. It was at the end of a long day's journey home from Italy—\to/ your letter the one letter in a pile of complimentary books, bills, requests to do things I didn't want to do—to Tabby and Tiger too stupid even \to/ talk like Sumner at his most unwilling. Dear Heart, my Love,

> Dad

P.S. This is the longest letter I've written on this kind of paper.[1]

144. *Robert Lowell to* Mrs. Robert Lowell

[80 Redcliffe Sq., London SW 10]
May 6, [1971]

Dearest Lizzie:

Radiant report from Stephen on you and Harriet. Or rather he found you both radiant. Nothing could be more consoling to me. The air is full of returning Englishmen and American visitors. Yesterday I heard Poirier in a labored perverse lecture blast Saul Bellow at the embassy. I don't think going to the embassy would have made your trip, a small familiar audience of the local critics. I'm doing something in Rome at the end of the month, some sort of Fulbright symposium. I'll speak on American poetry of the sixties. I won't try to cover it and will just read people I like, such as Wallace Stevens, Randall etc. It pays planefare and lodging, nothing—but the trip will be fun and I'll take my long planned trip with Rolando[2] to Ravenna and Urbino.

I had a letter from Bob Giroux about my royalties etc. I think I will for the moment put them in a savings account but in my name alone.

---

1. Aerogram.
2. Anzilotti.

If you are desperate I can give you something. We aren't flush and the child brings on all kinds of expenses. By the way, is there some way of getting the trust fund to pay for the hospital. I seem to still owe Faber over a thousand pounds, which means I won't get a cent of royalties from them during my lifetime. The Blue Cross payed, I think, less than a third. And then what can we do about the manuscript? I delay because I hate the idea of people pawing through it. The other day I got a letter from a guy at Harvard writing a doctors on Ted Roethke. He enclosed three of my letters to Ted that I forgot having written[1]— also requested that I return them in the next mail.

Not much news. I'm glad to be done with teaching for a spell. Also am throwing off a low virus. Also have a young man who trout fishes eagerly and badly.[2]

One grows lazy with deep spring. I read the Scarlet Letter trying to anticipate your comment, but failed[.][3] Loved the book as much as ever. He invented New England.

Hope you and Harriet weren't on the second and rougher demo.[4] I am going to my first woman's Lib on Sunday. Kate Millett and Sonia co-chairmen![5]

Love,
    Cal

1. Lowell to Theodore Roethke, June 6, 1958; September 18, 1958; and July 10, 1963 (copies, with notes and queries by a researcher, HRC). See also *The Letters of Robert Lowell*, pp. 427–28.
2. Possibly Jonathan Raban.
3. By Nathaniel Hawthorne (1850); Hardwick, "Seduction and Betrayal I," *New York Review of Books*, May 31, 1973, and *Seduction and Betrayal* (1974), pp. 180–84.
4. The May Day protests in Washington (May 1–6, 1971). See Richard Halloran, "30,000 Anti-War Protesters Are Routed in Capital," *New York Times*, May 3, 1970; Richard Halloran, "7,000 Arrested in Capitol War Protest; 150 Are Hurt as Clashes Disrupt Traffic," *New York Times*, May 4, 1971; and James M. Naughton, "Protesters Fail to Stop Congress; Police Seize 1,146," *New York Times*, May 5, 1971.
5. Panel discussion with Sonia Orwell, Edna O'Brien, Anne Sharpley, and Jill Tweedie following a production of Jane Arden's *A New Communion for Freaks, Prophets, and Witches* (also known as *Holocaust*) by the Holocaust theatre group at the Open Space Theatre in London. Millett did not appear. Caroline Blackwood: "As though a Women's Institute fete had been expecting a visit from the Queen and had only been informed after it opened that she was confined to her bed with a heavy cold, a feeling of let-down hung over the Women's Lib rally . . . 'Where's Kate Millett?'" (Blackwood, "Women's Theatre," *Listener*, 3 June 1971).

145. *Robert Lowell to* Mrs. Robert Lowell

[80 Redcliffe Square, London SW 10]
[May 12, 1971]

Dearest Lizzie—

Such good reports of you and Harriet. Both Jonathan and Stephen used the word radiant of Harriet, and reported you were in fine confident spirits, electric. I'm sorry to have sent you that fussy letter about money. I really can't make out on my Essex salary. At our age it's hard to live on nothing, taxis etc. I think the only article of clothing I've bought in a year is an overcoat. If you need money at any time from the Farrar royalties I'll give it [to] you. I am keeping the fourteen thousand as a reserve. I admit this sounds like an anticlimax to my money groans, but I think you can understand the mental relief just having it gives me.

Rather homesick for America now in the heavy summer weather, Americans arriving like summer birds, returning Englishmen. I had some sort of virus without fever that made my head and bones ache. The antibiotic cure of course brought a slight nausea and depression. Otherwise all is well. I'll go to Rome at the end of May. Then my play comes out on the 24th of June. I've been through it three times, brisking it up, making Zeus a little more like God or nature and less like a gestapo boss. Elizabeth Bishop is coming here I think in the second week of June. I don't know how she has taken the boy's suicide and dread knowing. I think I'll spend the summer revising my imitations.[1] I made two or three much better I thought by being more quiet and accurate. I am tired by so much original writing, almost four years without stop.

I think of you constantly and long in a way for America, but not just a hurried glimpse. Maybe next Christmas would be best. Or I could dash over in September. I am beginning to get habituated to being here, really quite a job but it brings peace. I think a writer never for long feels he has done well. One of the most exciting things here has been Borges' visit. I've had two nights more or less alone with him,

---

1. Lowell revised his earlier translations of Homer, Sappho, Leopardi, Heine, Hugo, Baudelaire, Rimbaud, Rilke, and Annesky from *Imitations* (1961), and of Juvenal and Góngora from *Near the Ocean* (1967), for *History*.

talking about Tennyson, James and Kipling, and almost wept when he talked "without pity" to an audience about his blindness.[1]

I started this letter meaning to talk only about missing you, but that though true would be boring. I guess all is well as far as mortality and one's large failings allow. Jealous of you and everyone else seeing Harriet.

Love,
Cal

146. *Robert Lowell to* Miss Harriet Lowell

[Postcard of two dolphins]

[London]
[May 17, 1971]

Dearest Harriet—

Here are two friends, Baby and Brandy. They can jump 20 feet and laugh at things humans don't even know are funny. I miss you too much!

Love,
Dad

147. *Elizabeth Hardwick to Robert Lowell*

[15 West 67th Street, New York, N.Y.]
May 19, 1971

Dearest Cal: Hot summer, lovely day. I'm back from a long period with the tax man, eating a pineapple yogurt (Mary McC. could hardly forgive me) and still trembling because these tax things make me very, very nervous. Now: here is the situation. Please write immediately to Bob Giroux asking them to send me $3,750.00

With that you will be paid up on Federal, State and New York City taxes for *1971*. You can then ask them to send you the rest of what they are holding and that will give you some thousands. My heart bleeds

---

1. Jorge Luis Borges was awarded an honorary D.Litt by Oxford University on April 29 and then spoke for the ICA in London on four evenings from April 30 to May 13, 1971.

that you haven't any clothes, and I worry foolishly. *Then you should have another 7,000 \from F, S & G,/ or so in the fall, around Sept. which is all yours and all the money from Janet Roberts' office[1] is yours and all the tax will have been paid. (Did I tell you before that the money from the State Street Trust, the $5400 was to pay only the capital gains on what we got from it, not the other taxes.)* Our taxes are less this year because I overpaid last year, driving myself almost out of my mind. I hope you understand, dear. I mean what I am saying about the taxes. *You are only paying on American money that is yours for your private, single use.* I know it is hard to realize, but at the tax man's this morning it turned out that with your English earnings you have exactly the same amount of money—in total—that I have. Our American bracket is 50% and so I pay just as much tax here as you pay to Essex. I just want you to know that and I am paying all the rent, all the tuition, clothes, doctors, vacations, everything, for your child. I don't want any more money, but I feel you don't realize this. Actually you will now be much better off than you have been . . . I am glad for you, really. The reason you are paying \tax/ now is that we have to pay in advance, quarterly, or be penalized. I thought it best just to get the whole thing now instead of nagging you for it again in Sept. and next Jan. . . . This is for a 1971 joint return, which is cheaper I assure you by far, and seems the best thing at the moment. Please send the letter to Bob immediately. I have to finish off everything soon.

Dear Mary has been getting bad reviews. I read the book with enough pleasure. There is nothing cheap or commercial or strained about it and if it isn't a "good novel" that doesn't seem altogether unusual since few write good novels. She is coming to Maine in July and Hannah will be there in August. I will be there off and on.

I am so relieved to have the tax thing clear in my mind. I have written something for Vogue saying everything I know I have learned from books and from worry.[2] But what a price the latter is. I would

---

1. Theatrical agent at Ashley Famous Agency.
2. Hardwick: "I have never felt free. I do not speak of the constraints of society but of the peculiar developments of my own nature. All my life I have carried about with me the chains of an exaggerated anxiety and tendency to worry, an over-excited imagination for disasters ahead, problems foreboding, errors whose consequences could stretch to the end of time. I feel some measure of admiration for women who are carefree, even for the careless; but we work with what we are ("The Ties Women Cannot Shake and Have," *Vogue*, June 1, 1971, p. 86).

like to sail the Greek islands today or do something daring. Oh, to be young and free as we once were. But still I like being what I am, at least today, unwillingly liberated, going to a concert this evening, thinking of you, still with pain, but believing it will grow less some day. Goodbye, my dear one.

Lizzie

\Did Janet Roberts reach you?/

\If you sell your papers, get it all cleared up this year, but start payment in 72 because of Capital gains (agency account) this year already having sent us soaring. That is a suggestion. Nat Hoffman[1] said he thought Véra Nabokov was the world's greatest tax expert, but he saw that I was second only because of having far less money to deal with!/

148. *Robert Lowell to* Mrs. Robert Lowell

[80 Redcliffe Square, London SW 10]
May 20, 1971

Dearest Lizzie:

Thanks for writing Harvard. I'll wait till I hear from Stonybrook before deciding. The protection given such collections seems rather vague. A few weeks ago I got a letter from a young man writing a PHD on Roethke. He enclosed zerox's[2] of three of my letters to Ted, and asked me to mail them back to him at once, with an OK for quoting them. The letters mostly critical, had things about breakdowns.[3] I

---

1. Accountant.

2. Thus, for "xeroxes."

3. For "mostly critical," see Lowell to Theodore Roethke, July 10, 1963, in *The Letters of Robert Lowell*, pp. 427–28. About "breakdowns," Lowell writes: "Getting out of the flats after a manic leap is like our old crew races at school. When the course is half-finished, you know and so does everyone else in the boat, that not another stroke can be taken. Yet everyone goes on, and the observer on the wharf notices nothing" (Lowell to Theodore Roethke, June 6, 1958, copy in Robert Lowell Papers, HRC); and "You sound yourself and clearly must be. For months (perhaps always) there are black twinges, the spirit aches, yet remarkably less as time passes. I fell almost in a thanksgiving mood—so much of life is bearable. I've quite stopped wanting to turn the clock back or look for a snug hole" (Lowell to Theodore Roethke, September 18, 1958, copy in Robert Lowell Papers, HRC).

had so forgotten them, they seemed like someone else's. I don't want mine open during my lifetime.

Your letter to Harvard made me very sad,[1] more than your letters to me. An air of aristocratic poignance and distance. I can understand your not wanting your letters mingled with the pile, but if you'd like to, & take that part of the money, or more, do. I don't think my early notebooks are more interesting. Please don't wish to erase our long dear years from the blackboard.

I go to Italy Sunday for my Fulbright conference. It feels like our old "CIA" days.[2] Americans come. I had an evening with Hannah and another tonight at the Spenders. It will be pleasant for you to have her in Maine. Quite a different presence than Sonia.

Please tell me about Harriet, if you are in the mood. I am. Everyone says she is radiant, and that you are writing like Dreiser.

Love to you both,
Dad

149. *Robert Lowell to* Mrs. Robert Lowell

[80 Redcliffe Sq., London SW 10]
May 22, 1971

Dearest Lizzie:

I am falling in love with these one page stamped air mail letters.[3] Now that I've almost mastered the mechanics, they are so easy.

I've written Bob about the 3750 dollars. You describe my finances

---

1. Letter now missing.

2. Lowell and Hardwick traveled to Brazil in 1962 for the Congress for Cultural Freedom. A 1966 *New York Times* article reported secret, indirect C.I.A. support for academic and cultural organizations, including the C.C.F., explaining how the C.I.A "may channel research and propaganda money through foundations—legitimate ones or dummy fronts [. . .] Through similar channels, the C.I.A. has supported [. . .] anti-Communist but liberal organizations such as the Congress for Cultural Freedom, and some of their newspapers and magazines. Encounter magazine, a well-known anti-Communist intellectual monthly with editions in Spanish and German as well as English was for a long time—though it is not now—one of the direct beneficiaries of C.I.A. funds" (T. Wicker, J. W. Finney, M. Frankel, E. W. Kenworthy, others, "Electronic Prying Grows: C.I.A. Is Spying from 100 Miles up; Satellites Probe Secrets of the Soviet Union" *New York Times*, April 27, 1966). See also Matthew Spender, *A House in St. John's Wood: In Search of My Parents* (2015).

3. Aerogram.

of course accurately, more than I could. Whenever you think I can afford it, have some of my money. I have a man here named Henshaw supposed to be even better than Vera Stravinsky. He manages William Burroughs, and can deduct money for shoes and penknives.

O to be young! I was reading a review by Pritchett of the Magny dinners.[1] The people were young when they began, and ten years later dead or very old. I've been seeing the old lately. Two delightful almost alone evenings with Borges. A long afternoon in the hospital with David Jones. Hannah has been here and seems on the verge of old and frail. Oh dear. Life is much too short.

I yearn for your letters, and hope you won't give up the habit. I have always prayed I were two people (one soul) one here, one with you.

I rather dread Mary's book. Hannah feels it's a new sympathetic Mary. She is a lovely person, or a "corker" as David Jones said about Shakespeare. Some of the reviews of her Essays were venomous. I've only seen one of birds, in Newsweek, I think, not venomous, but disheartening.[2]

Something that will half-amuse you—Allen wrote me volunteering as a godfather. I miss you always to joke with, reason with, unreason with. Do you think you could dictate a postcard to me from Harriet? I've a notice to wire her in my datebook.

Love,
Dad

You're writing like the wind. Lovely. I'm written dry, after about four non-stop years. Or is it ten? Now nothing, except maybe translation.

1. V. S. Pritchett, "How They Talked" (a review of Robert Baldick's *Dinner at Magny's* [1971]), *New Statesman*, 21 May 1971. Hardwick had written about the dinners in "Memoirs, Conversations and Diaries," *Partisan Review* 20, no. 5 (September 1953).
2. Peter S. Prescott, "Candide without Voltaire," *Newsweek*, May 24, 1971.

150. *Adrienne Rich to* Robert Lowell

W. Barnet. Vt.

June 17 [1971]

Dear Cal, I feel we are losing touch with each other, which I don't want. Perhaps part of the trouble is that the events of my own life in the past 4 or 5 years have made me very anti-romantic, and I feel a kind of romanticism in your recent decisions, a kind of sexual romanticism with which it is very hard for me to feel sympathy. I guess I could have written nothing or written only about "ideas" etc but I feel we would then be completely out of touch. Also my affection and admiration for Elizabeth make it difficult to be debonair about something which— however good for her it may ultimately be—has made her suffer.

Still, I really do care about you—we have had a long friendship with many problematical & mysterious aspects but one which I would not surrender easily to indifference or misunderstanding. There is a certain depth in simply having cared about someone's existence for a number of years.

I'm in Vermont now, with the kids & 2 of their friends & a former Columbia student of mine who has become a kind of brother to us all. It's very beautiful here, lush & green & still. It was painful coming back the 1st time but the pain has drained away & we are all terribly glad to have this house. Last winter, thinking I wouldn't want to be here all summer, I rented it for July & August, now I am almost sorry. But we are going to the West Coast for July and part of August. I've rented an apt. in San Francisco for July & in August we'll drive or bus down the coast to L.A. where I have old friends.

My life is coming back together again. In many ways I feel my marriage to Alf was still unfinished when he died & there \are/ all kinds of pain connected with that. But I like being a separate woman—though I wish it had come about differently. Alone, one allows oneself to see clearly many things one dared not look at when one was tied to another life. And it's a different relationship, altogether, one has with the world. I don't think I could ever live with a man, in the old way, again.

How are you? What are you doing? Whom do you see? Your Norwegian friend Per-?—wrote me he was coming to NY but I leave for California the same day.

I've been cleaning the house & swimming & lying in the sun and feel an almost sensual tiredness such as one doesn't get in New York. Goodnight—and love—

Adrienne.

151. *Robert Lowell to* Miss Harriet Lowell

[80 Redcliffe Sq., London SW 10]

June 23, 1970 [1971]

Dearest Baby—

I am thinking of \a/ moment six or seven or eight years ago, when you were having some sort of difference with Mother, and she threatened to let you do the cooking, order the groceries and answer the school report, and you suddenly collapsed and said, "I'm just a bay-bee." You are not; but I don't know how to order suitable presents for you. If I send you jewelry, it arrives with import duties for you to pay, duties higher than what I originally paid here. Then there are clothes, but the mistakes I might make terrify me, something small enough for a doll, or big enough for an elephant, or worse something tacky. So I have cabled you twenty-five pounds, about sixty dollars. Not very much, but something to stretch your pocket-money, and to be spent on something delightful and colorful and absolutely useless.

I worry a little about Mexican diseases, though I'm sure the camp takes all precautions. When I was in Mexico, I was never sick to my stomach, and only suffered two or three rather purifying, stunning days of fever. I think about Mexico, the volcanoes, the old Aztec temples (better than European churches)[,] the flowers,[1] the awful, wonderful Spanish \language/ and Indian faces. You'll lose Nicole's Castilian accent. Will you see our friend, Ivan Illich? And will you give him my love?

Tomorrow, my play opens, the one you saw four years ago at Yale—Jonathan Miller directing as before, the same lead actor, all the same almost, only it's being done in a former warehouse called the Mermaid theater on the muddy Thames River, and we are doing

---

1. Lowell: "the Aztecs knew these stars would fail to rise | if forbidden the putrifaction of our flesh, | the victims' viscera laid out like tiles | on fishponds changed to yellow flowers" ("Oxford" [*Redcliffe Square* 4] 6–9, *The Dolphin*).

without scenery, except for a bucket and a rag. It's about the half-god Prometheus chained to a rock. I saw a God-awful woman's Lib avant garde, all woman cast play last month which you might have enjoyed more. Do you remember Mrs. George Orwell from three years ago in Castine? She presided, and couldn't keep the women in the after-play discussion from talking all at once and shouting obscenities at each other.[1] Aren't you glad you are a lady?

Dearest, bless you through the Mexican summer and always. I die to see you. I am writing Mother, but please give her my love personally.

Love,
Dad

152. *Robert Lowell to* Mrs. Robert Lowell

[80 Redcliffe Sq., London SW 10]
June 23, 1970 [1971]

Dearest Lizzie:

I've just cabled Harriet a small sum of money, an unadventurous, impersonal gift, but I couldn't face the disaster of import duties, delays, choosing the wrong thing. At least this can't wholly miss fire.

Tomorrow Prometheus opens at the Mermaid, once more beautifully directed by Jonathan. The Wernicks (!) went last night to the preview and liked it. I've only seen the dress rehearsal, very finished, except Ocean improvised his lines—maybe he should, but we hope he won't. Io very good, but less than Irene, and young.[2] Hermes better.[3] Gulls better. Kenneth the same. Reading the text and speeding it with little changes, I kept coming on suggestions of yours like a *hailstorm of gifts*.[4] This happened many times because I was following with the lines to see that the actors got my emendations. Feelings of tender and lonely gratitude to you. I can't judge the play. How did I get into so much Greek? And I may finish up the Oresteia. Jonathan says

---

1. See Caroline Blackwood, "Women's Theatre," *Listener*, 3 June 1971.
2. Angela Thorne.
3. David Horovitch.
4. "You have done too much. This hailstorm of gifts is poverty" (*Prometheus Bound*, p. 24).

Sir Bernard Miles who runs the Mermaid Theater is like old Cronus. Quite a change from Bob Brustein.

I think strangely about Harriet's summer, and the sublime, probably arid, Cuernavaca scenery. Hope she gets none of the Mexican diseases. I imagine the camp is extremely careful. Will she be at sea and alone? I think she'll love it. The new Harriet. Still this moment of departure must make her shiver a little.

I may go to Russia to see Madam Mandelstam who wrote me a touching letter in reply to mine on her book.[1] But O the filthy Russian regime and the maddening precautions one must take, such as not writing her before I arrive. I've conferred with such Russian authorities as Gaia, Weidenfeld and Mary. They all agree, but of course no one knows what the government intends to do with Madam M.

I keep looking for your Scarlet Letter. I like almost all of it, tho perhaps the non-fictional historical shadowing most. I see I learned all I know about the Puritans from Hawthorne. I'm reading Hogg's Justified sinner,[2] a similar very Scotch book, only the women are in the background, Chillingworth is the hero-fiend. No use to say how much I think of you. My blood-pressure is down.

Love,
Cal

Could you mail me Ivan's address and Harriet's. I expect to give my stuff to Stonybrook by the end of the month[.] They offer more and show more interest, a man is coming here next week. Do you want to be secretary?[3]

---

1. Nadezhda Mandelstam: "Dear Robert, Do come here. I want to see you so much. Soon you'll be late—I am old and can't last long. And it is not a novel (imagination!), it is life. It is far more difficult to live one's life than to write about it. Do come . . . As to you, I think that the second marriage is always better than the first. I am greatly for divorces. I hope you soon will be through it. [p.s.] If you want to make a call - my number 126-67-42. But I am rather deaf. Do speak slowly" (to Robert Lowell, June 1, [19]71, HRC; quoted in Michael Watchtell and Craig Cravens, "Nadezhda Iakovlevna Mandel'shtam: Letters to and about Robert Lowell," *The Russian Review* 61, no. 4 [October 2002], p. 524). *Hope Against Hope: A Memoir*, trans. Max Hayward (1970).
2. James Hogg, *The Private Memoirs and Confessions of a Justified Sinner* (1824).
3. Postscript typed above the date and address to Hardwick. See Hardwick to Lowell, May 27, 1970, in which she writes that Stony Brook had offered "to give me if I want it a good, high-paying one day a week job as curator of these papers."

153. *Robert Lowell to* Mrs. Alfred Conrad[1]

80 Redcliffe Sq., London SW 10

June 23, 1970 [1971]

Dearest Adrienne:

I wonder if this will reach you before you leave for California? I trust it will trail you there. O I think you might want to live somewhere else this summer, and then return to Vermont in the cool of another year.

I mustn't advize[2] or judge you, but I feel an air of relief in your letter, as if you had emerged from a very long fever. As indeed you have. The loneliness and freedom of a new life. We are never born again I think, nor would want to be. Yet there are new starts. A marriage ends, and nothing stays unchanged. We face the freshness and fears and release of looking at what we really are. \(What is THAT?)/ And the awful pains of improvisation and invention.

It wouldn't be correct for me to defend myself to you, but you \may/ be able to see that we are in somewhat the same position, by different paths. You know a lot about me but nothing about my situation. You hold half the broken eggshell and see things thru Lizzie, not exactly through Lizzie's eyes. The only important thing wrong with marriage with Lizzie was our unending nervous strife, as tho a bear had married a greyhound.[3] We were always deeply together and constantly fascinated and happy together, and constantly sadly vexed. When you talk about romantic sexual love, Dear, you are surely talking through your hat. I doubt if you are through with it. And anyway, it is only very partially true of me. No one sees a woman steadily for over a year and remains only romantically in love. I think you are thinking of people like Sandra.[4] This has nothing in common with that. It's not for nothing that in the old days I always came back to Lizzie. Sometimes I think you\r sense of justice/ want\s/ Lizzie to be happier and me to be unhappier. But you can't wish that—and I do think she will be happier, tho to say so sounds like cant. I think you will be happier, and now are. These are hard sayings and life is hard, but only fatal in the end.

---

1. Adrienne Rich.

2. Thus, for "advise."

3. See footnote 2 on page 146 (Lowell to Harriet Lowell, January 6, 1970 [1971]).

4. Hochman, with whom Lowell had an affair during a manic episode in 1961.

I see the people you can imagine and a few you can't. Our weekends are much like yours—sun, grass[,] children. Sometimes I go trout fishing and fail to land them. God go with you on your summer. I wish you weren't so far.

Love,

Cal

154. Elizabeth Hardwick to Robert Lowell

[15 West 67th Street, New York, N.Y.]

June 28, 1971

Dear Cal: I am enclosing Harriet's addresses, as you asked, and will sometime, when I get it, send Ivan's. Yes, I do worry about dysentery, but the camp, the group (Experiment in International Living) are very experienced and first-class. Harriet has never seemed to waver in her wish to go. The idea gives her a feeling of self-esteem and adventure; I have heard nothing but good things from children who have done the thing. I pray it will be well and feel no worries beyond the same awful Mexican sicknesses you mention. She was pleased with your 60 dollars, very unexpected and nice. I hope she will write you this week, but don't be disappointed if she doesn't. She finds writing letters very difficult and puts them off and I have resigned \myself/ to not hearing from her in Mexico even though I have made both stern demands and tearful pleas. How I will miss her! She is an enchanting companion, witty, brave, very firm about how she feels, sulky in the morning, quiet in the afternoon, and talkative, gay, fascinating by dinner-time. At the moment she wants to go to law school! (But I wouldn't mention it because it might embarrass her to have her parents talking about her. And no doubt that will change.[)] She isn't a child at all any longer—going into high school, 9th grade, in September. I think her grades will be quite good for the past year—we don't seem to get them until mid-summer . . . We've been up to Castine— Lisa Wager with us—and it was warm and beautiful. I will be on my way back up there soon after this reaches you. However, when Harriet comes back on August 24th I'll meet her and we are going to have Francine Gray's house in Conn. until Sept. 7th—with swimming pool, Olga, the lovely countryside. I rather think we won't go to Cas-

tine next summer and I am planning to rent my house in advance . . .
When we got back from Castine yesterday the usual "surf" of mail,
a lot of it stuff for you—waves from every old shore still quietly ~~lapping~~ tiding in and out. The Newman Press (Catholic), Peace Groups,
Common Cause (McCarthy)[,] Boston College (Father Sweeney), a
strange, repentant, religious note from the guy who wrote that fatuous piece in Esquire . . . [1]

I felt something on the day *Prometheus* opened, but ruthlessly
kept down too much memory and nostalgia; it is \for me/ so pointless and hurting. I thought of a telegram which would have said:
"Zeus is the best we have." . . . Mary due any moment. We are all
very much concerned about Dan Ellsberg, a strange, sweet young
man (a former Hawk), married to (do you remember?) Patricia Marx
who used to be John Simon's girl friend—a "hawk" in the sense that
Hemingway spoke of Zelda F. as a hawk.[2] Poor Dan gave himself up
this morning, admitted that he revealed the Pentagon Papers.[3] He is
now arrested, but he had made the decision and now I believe acts on
it with a whole heart and as much courage as [he] can muster. The
awful thing is that these court cases go on and on, draining body and
soul. The papers are fascinating, immoral, arrogant, treacherous, full
of betrayals of trust. Power does corrupt absolutely, of course, and
the false courtesy that allows men in power to accept the most outrageous situations without exploding. I think you were right to cut
Billy Bundy at Yale[4] . . . I am interested in your travels. Esther wrote
me that you and Caroline had visited her; and now you are going to
Russia. I was on the PEN Club translation prize committee and we

1. Donald Newlove, "Dinner at the Lowells'," *Esquire*, September 1969.

2. Hemingway: "It was only Zelda's secret that she shared with me, as a hawk might share
something with a man. But hawks do not share" (*A Moveable Feast* [1964], p. 185). Hardwick:
"Hemingway is smug and patronizing to Fitzgerald and urges upon us forgiveness by laying
Fitzgerald's weaknesses and pains at the feet of his wife. Hemingway sees Zelda as a 'hawk'"
("Caesar's Things," *New York Review of Books*, September 24, 1970; and *Seduction and Betrayal*,
pp. 89–90).

3. *The New York Times* and *The Washington Post* began publishing the Pentagon Papers during
the week of June 13, 1971 (*The New York Times* on June 13 and the *Post* on June 18). See Paul L.
Montgomery, "Ellsberg: From Hawk to Dove: Ex-Pentagon Aide Now Outspoken Critic of the
War," *New York Times*, June 27, 1971; Robert Rheinholds, "Ellsberg Yields, Is Indicted; Says He
Gave Data to Press," *New York Times*, June 29, 1971.

4. In June 1968, when Lowell received an honorary degree from Yale; William Bundy (a distant
Lowell cousin) was a Fellow of the Yale Corporation at the time.

gave it to M. Hayward for the Mandelstam book—really to her, or at least that was my idea. I can see that with all of this a short trip here in May, just before Italy, would have been too much. Fortunately I had not at all stressed the coming visit to Harriet because I thought you might change your mind and so she didn't notice it. She would like you to come, but the circumstances of your break from us are so drastic \and/ complete it leaves one numb after a while. In any case, we are both very fit, very busy. I am totally absorbed by the life here, dismaying as it is,—America I mean . . . I haven't written Hawthorne yet, but am saving it for the Princeton lectures which terrify me. I am writing about Sylvia Plath.[1] What an awful girl! What rage and hatred—out of sheer hate so much of that intense burst of genius came. But investigation turns me against the Hughes family too. *The Bell Jar* is a best seller; they are dribbling out her work, cleaning up. She would have slit Ted's throat instead of her own! What a horrible irony it all is. I said to my informant, "But they are surely just putting all the mon[ey] in trust for the children?" Mmm . . . came the reply. And Lois Ames[2] given a contract by Faber and Harper's to write a biography for which she has no gifts, nothing.[3] Sylvia will slit her, also. But I feel bewildered by her violence, even though vengeful feelings can unleash powerful expression. What a brilliant writer she is! What a strange "career" this was.

I hope the play was well received. . . . About the "papers,"—"Aspern"[4]—which I have not looked at since I first and last went through them. Have I the strength? I hate them and hate to let them go; the damned things are my life also. Did you write Harvard about Stonybrook's offer? They know nothing about Stonybrook, except

1. Hardwick, "On Sylvia Plath," *New York Review of Books*, August 12, 1971.

2. See Sylvia Plath, *The Bell Jar*, with a biographical note by Lois Ames (1971). Ames was under contract for a full biography with Harper & Row, but the book was not completed (see Doug Holder, "Lois Ames: Confidante to Sylvia Plath and Anne Sexton, Interview (2005)," November 13, 2009, http://dougholder.blogspot.com/2009/11/lois-ames-confidante-to-sylvia -plath.html).

3. "Whether [Plath] was anything like the creature her hasty biographer, Lois Ames, seems to be patching together we will never know. Mrs. Ames follows the Indian trail of the natural wherever a hint of a footprint can be found. Thus, we learn that 'she played tennis, was on the girl's basketball team, was co-editor of the school newspaper . . .' and so on" ("On Sylvia Plath," *New York Review of Books*, August 12, 1971).

4. Henry James, *The Aspern Papers* (1888; revised 1908).

that they are interested. Perhaps they will meet ~~it~~ \the offer/. I don't know, dearest. There are your Harvard students—especially if you plan to return occasionally, who are writing about you all the time. Harriet and I had a good evening with Frank Bidart on our way to Maine. You would be teaching at Harvard—although you will probably want to can that when the time comes—but you *might* be teaching at Harvard and all your papers, all the things that will go into "work" on you will be at Stonybrook. I don't want to interfere and Mr. Lusardi is desperate. Please don't mention that I have said anything. I would feel bad and out of order. It is just that I think you could write Harvard, if you did not do so, telling them of Stonybrook's offer. Then see what happens. Please do not arrange for any payments this year, because of our tax! Then sometime we will have to get together to talk things over at length, make our final decisions and arrangements.

Meanwhile, all is well with us, your lovely daughter is blooming and thinning and I at least am deeply blessed by her being and thank God for her and for my love of her which is the greatest thing in my life. . . . Off to Castine on the 5th.

    With love,
      Lizzie

P.S. Thinking perhaps you hadn't written Harvard saying you had had a better offer I called Mr. Dennis. He was horrified at the thought that they wouldn't get the papers and had assumed that if you had a better offer you would have let him know. I did this only to clear the way for you to make the choice that would really suit your heart. It is of some importance—I glanced fearfully into the pulsing grey tin drawers and felt sick. Ugh, our Lois Ames is out there waiting to say, "meanwhile Elizabeth was writing to Harriet Winslow in Washington saying that 'Bobby'—"—Oh, F—! Please I'll kill you if you let Lusardi know I alerted Harvard. But I \knew Harvard cared very much!/

155. *Robert Lowell to* Harriet Lowell

[Telegram]

[n.d. but July 1, 1971]

HARRIET LOWELL 15 WEST67STREET
NEWYORKCITY
GOOD LUCK FOR MEXICO DEAR HEART
    DADDY

156. *Robert Lowell to* Mrs. Robert Lowell

[80 Redcliffe Sq., London SW 10]
July 1, 1971

Dearest Lizzie:

Very rushed letter; I am off in a couple of hours for a six day trip to Edinburgh and the Orkneys (Home of the Spence negligence).[1] A quick trip but it gives me a chance to meet McDiarmid, see my ancestral islands, and Edinburgh.

Spence negligence! I don't need it. Somehow I mislaid the Harvard man's name and wrote Bill Alfred a couple of weeks ago for it, and hadn't heard. Harvard rang up just after I had had dinner with Lusardi, clumsy very touching type. In half a minute Harvard had upped their price to 130 thousand from 90. Then two days later Lusardi went up to 150. I'm not keen on the auction, at least I don't admit I am. My

---

1. Ferris Greenslet and Bruce Rogers: "In 1806 Charles Lowell [Robert Lowell's great-great grandfather] married Harriet Traill Spence, an indirect cousin and a childhood's sweetheart. Both her father, Keith Spence, and her maternal grandfather, Robert Traill, were born in the Orkney Islands, and the imaginative Mrs. Lowell and her more imaginative son [James Russell Lowell] liked to trace their descent to persons no less portentous than Minna Troil and Sir Patrick Spens. At any rate, Mrs. Lowell possessed much of the wild beauty of the people of those windy northern isles, and her mind showed an irresistible tendency toward their poetic occultism. This tendency became irretrievably fixed by a visit which she made to the Orkneys in company with her husband early in their married life. Thenceforward until 1842, when her tense brain became disordered, she was a faerie-seer, credited by some with second sight [. . .] there was a certain dreamful languor in the blood that blent queerly with the characteristic Lowell effectiveness. Throughout his [James Russell Lowell's] early life, whenever he failed to do any of the things which, for his academic or domestic health, he should have done, the Lowell connection was prompt to attribute it to this deep quality, which they mis-called 'the Spence negligence'" (*James Russell Lowell: His Life and Work* [1905], pp. 9–10).

lawyer here thinks nothing should be decided till after the divorce and birth of the baby. I suppose the bidding might have come out the same way anyway, but my heart-felt thanks for your timely intervention. I don't \think/ the colleges should be jewed up[1] too much; what I want is an annual income that could replace if need be my part-time teaching, say from 8 to 12 thousand, an independence, my retirement fund. I will go on teaching, but hope not to do it steadily till sixty-five. I seem to be in excellent health for blood-pressure etc. but Oh me we well-in-our-fifties have lived ~~so~~ \too/ much of our lives already. Peter Taylor and I humorously mourn about this. Most writers if they don't survive into hopeless ill-health and senility die at fifty-seven.

Thrilled about Harriet's law vocation. Do you think law and the Supreme Court will replace Eldridge Cleaver, the Beatles, and even Jesus with the young? I've just wired my little cable to H. God bless you in Maine this summer. I think Conn. is a good idea for you and H. Will Mary be stranded?

Love,
Cal

157. Elizabeth Hardwick to Robert Lowell

[15 West 67th Street, New York, N.Y.]
July 3, 1971

Dear Cal: I am still here in New York until Harriet leaves in the morning. I got a copy of the letter Mr. Dennis of the Houghton Library sent to your agent or lawyer, with his offer, etc. Now that I have managed to do all of this for you I find, as I want to say quite frankly, that I am very disturbed. I have from the first acted as a very efficient agent and of course as someone who knows the value and meaning of all that is concerned. A lot of the stuff in the inventory is mine—not just your

---

1. Satirical, as against "to jew down." OED: "Phr. *to jew down*, to beat down in price [. . .] These uses are now considered to be offensive." Among the examples given by the dictionary of the phrase in print from 1825–1972 is "1970 R. Lowell *Notebk.* 69 This embankment, jewed—| No, yankeed—by the highways down to a grassy lip" ("Jew | jew, v.,"OED Online. March 2016. http://www.oed.com/view/Entry/101211?rskey=Br5XvE&result=2&isAdvanced=false [accessed March 27, 2016]; from the Second Edition [1989]). See Lowell, *Charles River* [7] 4–5, *Notebook70*.

letters to me which I don't want to sell, but letters to me from everyone, your parents, hundreds from Cousin Harriet, from our mutual friends. I only plan, I guess, to take out, your letters to me. Also I do not think I can make you a present of the copy of Land of Unlikeness, with my maiden name in it, which I bought before I met you. I plan to give that to Harriet instead. I really don't know how to put into words all the strange feelings I suddenly have. It was I who set the Stonybrook price at $125,000 and who called Harvard and told them to bid on their own, etc. That and for so many other things I have never even been thanked. It worries me that I should have at this late date taken on so much for you. You and Caroline have treated Harriet and me with unremitting meanness. But then, what else has she to do with herself? She drifts about, has babies, destroys lives of both men and women who are really serious and deep by her carelessness and spoiled indifference to consequence and the feelings of others. However, with you—it is a different matter. You have been a person of the deepest moral yearnings and it was that person I loved. I hate your life and what you have done to those who cared so deeply for you. But that I feel is just the beginning of your suffering and decline. You will not be allowed to survive but will be sacrificed to the emptiness of Caroline, her shallow, narrow existence.

Nothing can be done about the papers until at least Sept. 15th. Then the list will be gone over. Whatever is mine that will stay in I have to ask you to pay me for from what you get. I am in no position to give you anything. I cannot live on the $20,000 you have set aside for us. I pay $6,000 rent for the apartment, Harriet's school is 3,000, this summer alone 2,000. That almost takes up what you have given us after taxes.

I do not know what caused me to take action when you carelessly wrote, "What have we done about the papers." I noted "we" but somehow was seized ("I" as always) with the desire to do what you wanted. The papers are yours, but they were here and you would probably have waited to accomplish all this if I had not answered and done it for you, and I must say so well. Why? For Caroline? For my memory. I don't know. But I feel stupid and upset. I have not done well by Harriet or myself. ~~We are both~~ You risked, without a thought, the sanity and stability of a young creature on the brink of life. I am not impressed by Caroline's "maternal" qualities; they do not extend to my child or to her responsibilities to me as another woman. These things are part of being a decent person.

I hated the reviews of the play[1] I saw; just as I hated the English reviews of Notebook. I say that as a critic, as someone who knows how beautiful and rare *Prometheus* is.

I am very angry with myself, with the incredibly stupid way I behave almost without thinking toward you, writing letters, getting better arrangements. I loathe Caroline and silly little Tories like Grey Gowrie and their destruction of the dear Yankee genius they will never understand. Anyway, I hope you begin to understand Daddy Lowell better and his empty smiling and "happiness."[2] Sometimes it is the only way one can bear a ruined life. And I think you have ruined your life for a mess of potage—a mess.[3]

Harriet is all packed and very calm about her trip. The other night, sharing a rather feeble fan, we talked until 1:30 in the morning. She is tougher than anyone knows in a way—at least at the moment—but the shocks of her life that have made her tough have also turned all her thoughts in a noble and serious direction, not toward selfishness as sometimes happens. Her direction in life is much firmer—she actually used more or less that phrase. She wants to be independent, she told me, and to have worthwhile work to do. Her grades were all B's, very good I think. Next year it really counts since it is the beginning of high school and she seems determined suddenly to work hard because of her interest in her future. I think my really feeling confident about her instead of just "praising" her is one of the main things. She has lost 12 pounds and now, of course, I want her to give up her newly found powers of resistance to pleasure for a goal. She is just right and looks wonderful. I took her to lunch with Mary, who has come and gone back for a week. M was wonderful, incredibly simple and pure suddenly,

---

1. Reviews as of July 3, 1971: Benedict Nightingale, "By Jove," *New Statesman*, July 2, 1971; Kenneth Hurren, "God the Father," *Spectator*, July 3, 1971.

2. Lowell: "Smiling on all | Father was once successful enough to be lost | in the mob of ruling-class Bostonians" ("Commander Lowell" 62–64, *Life Studies*); "He smiled his oval Lowell smile"; "After a morning of anxious, repetitive smiling, | his last words to Mother were: | 'I feel awful'" ("Terminal Days in Beverly Farms," 9 and 44–46, *Life Studies*). For "smiling," see also Hardwick to Lowell, June 26, 1970, footnote 4 on page 69.

3. Lowell: "Luck threw up the coin, and the plot swallowed | monster yawning for its mess of pottage" ("For John Berryman" 4–5, *Notebook69-1*).

with dinners for all her old friends every night—Fred,[1] Wm Phillips, Hannah and me almost every night of her stay, lunch with Harriet. We didn't mention you and that was a relief. Mary has written me many times how much better off I am. Everyone insists that I am. But can it be true? I know they mean it but I am not sure. I enclose the Vogue picture and article.[2] I told them we were separated and am only sorry they mentioned you at all, but I guess I haven't been "solitary in the field" all these years.[3] I suppose this letter will enrage you, but I am enraged today—by what strange little or great events—my getting all this arrangement for your papers to be profitably concluded—can one suddenly be stabbed by emotion. Well, be enraged in your turn. I don't care. I believe what I say and know it to be true. You will never be free of the ~~dreadful~~ thing you have killed in yourself and of your ingratitude and lack of loyalty and love. And no child you produce can be more splendid than the one you abandoned

    Lizzie

158. Elizabeth Hardwick to Harriet Lowell

Castine, Maine

July 11, 1971

Dearest: You have now been away only one week and it seems months. How I miss you. Nothing new up here, except incredibly wonderful weather, very very hot. Apparently New York has been in a terrible heat wave and so I am happy to be in sunny, clear, but not unbearable Castine. They have had a theatrical group playing here, quite young, not very inspiring but o.k. They seemed very forlorn and so I had them all down at the barn last night. There was a wonderful moon, the high tide rose, we played records and they danced until 3!—nearly

---

1. Dupee.

2. "The Ties Women Cannot Shake and Have," *Vogue*, June 1971. Photograph of Hardwick by Cecil Beaton.

3. *Vogue* biographical note: "With her daughter Harriet Lowell, Elizabeth Hardwick lives in a rambling two-story studio-apartment [. . .] filled with the paintings and books she and the poet Robert Lowell collected during the twenty-one years of their marriage" ("The Ties Women Cannot Shake and Have," *Vogue*, June 1971, p. 87). Wordsworth: "Behold her, single in the field, | Yon solitary Highland Lass!" ("The Solitary Reaper," 1–2).

breaking the place up. Then the lady in charge said, that's enough, and they scurried about like little soldiers, cleaned up the whole place, put back together the bed that had broken down and went home. The thing they danced to—there were several blacks—was that awful Ike and Tina Turner record which I brought down for want of anything else to do with it.[1]

I do so much want to hear how you like the Experiment. I hope it is fun and that you have found some friends here and there. And I hope you are well. I just can't let myself think about the Mexican diseases—like la turista,[2] which is intestinal. I think Sumner is alright. I was out by the barn door this morning and heard a little cry and there he was, looking very frightened. He had been out for about a minute and wanted back in! I find him wanting to sleep on my stomach but I have to say no.

Nicole must be taking off today. No news my dearest except that you are in my heart. And so send your old mother word of you.

All my love
Mommy

159. Elizabeth Hardwick to Robert Lowell

[Castine, Maine]
July 13, 1971

Dearest Cal: I'm sorry I wrote you in such an angry manner. I feel all that, from time to time, and often I just don't feel anyway now. However, I do want to say a few things. I won't be able to do anything about your papers until the fall, maybe October. There is so much still that I want to go through, and there is a question of just which things are actually addressed to me, etc., and are actually my property. It was all thrown together. I am up here; I go back; school starts, my lectures start and so I personally feel I will need a little time—perhaps October. Whichever University you honor will then come over and we will get the whole thing accomplished.

A second thing: last spring Mary Jarrell called wanting to be able to

---

1. *Workin' Together* (1971).

2. Sam Shepard, *La Turista*, introduction by Elizabeth Hardwick (1968).

make copies of Randall's letters to you for a volume she wants to edit. I said I didn't think she should edit the volume—speaking as a critic—and that I don't particularly believe in one little volume of letters, then another. These things tend to preempt the field for quite sometime to come. She would make casual statements about, "Oh, I'll take out anything personal," and I informed her that the question of taking out was the great question—it is more than a matter of not hurting people's feelings, etc. I looked over a few of Randall's letters. The ones I saw are fairly impersonal but they do say Randally things like: "Wouldn't you hate to be Eberhardt or Nemerov." Anyway, I talked to the Taylors who do not want to give their letters and who are very much opposed to what Mary may try to do. They—way back there—simply didn't answer. Now, Michael di Capua[1] has called again. Last Spring when I demurred—also saying to Mary you hadn't really had a chance to see the correspondence—he became very rude and said "The letters aren't yours," etc. I said, well they are in my apartment.

But when he called the other night I did feel the justice of his remark that none of this was really mine and I said to write to you. I don't know what you will want to do, but I think you could stall, not answer, or whatever until you've had time to think about it.

No word from Harriet. Mail is very slow there, I hear. Sumner was out all last night with a white cat. I nearly died, but he came back this morning. I fear he will never be the same. . . . Castine is heaven, very warm and clear. We are all up at the tennis court, drinking cocktails in the evening. I go two days from now to meet Mary at Bangor. The Coris[2] are here, planning a big musical party for Alexander Schneider on Sunday. It is very, very pleasant. I have a friend visiting.

I just write this so you will have some picture of the situation with me here about the papers and to make those remarks about the request that will be coming from Mary Jarrell.

Much love,
Lizzie

Fond memories of the old grey head going down Water Street! The swallows miss you.

---

1. Jarrell's editor at Farrar, Straus and Giroux.
2. Anne and Carl Cori.

160. *Elizabeth Hardwick to* Miss Harriet Lowell

Castine, Maine 04421 USA

July 19, 1971

Dearest, dear Harriet: What a joy to go [to] the p.o. this morning and to see there a beautiful airmail letter. But the best was still to come. It was such a gay, witty, real letter, which actually told me about everything there and about you. I was completely delighted to get it and enjoyed it immensely. It seems to be fun and that made me happy. I hope to go to Mexico with you sometime because I've never been there.

Beautiful Maine weather, perfect; but I've been busy writing and had to work all weekend and then yesterday race up to Bangor to put my piece on the plane for New York.[1] Still getting it done made me happy. I have no human news but amazing cat news—if that doesn't sound too childish. It turned out to be impossible to keep Sumner in the house; he found ways to get out and so I gave up. It is perfect. He is friendly with a big white cat, goes and comes, nicely cautious. At night now because of rain I usually keep him in. But oddest of all is how he has changed in his character. He will eat any kind of food—all sorts of different cans, and he purrs like a steam machine and wants to be in your lap all the time. So, you can see!

The summer is racing by. Nixon made headlines by saying he will be going to China to visit Mao! Bet Señor Roche is furious![2] Nixon a Maoist! Mary McCarthy is here. My routine is fairly much the same as always—and I think you would have been especially miserable here this summer. It is nice in many ways and perhaps you will like it later, perhaps not.

I am cut off from New York except for New York Review and so have nothing interesting to send you except my dearest love. Tell me more if you have time. I truly adored hearing from you. Relieved you got through the first days at least without beings ~~sill~~ \sick/. Many greetings, darling,

Mother

---

1. Hardwick, "On Sylvia Plath," *New York Review of Books*, August 12, 1971.
2. Harriet Lowell's Spanish teacher at Dalton, who was politically conservative.

161. *Robert Lowell to* Mrs. Robert Lowell

[Milgate Park, Bearsted, Maidstone, Kent]

July 25, 1971

Dearest Lizzie—

I don't want to say anything about your "angry" letter, even if you hadn't followed it with a kind one. But your Vogue piece is a tirade in the best sense,[1] every feeling, every cadence alive—all too alive for me, beautiful, and shakes my being. Too good for Vogue. Rather sorry Cecil Beaton did the picture, still it gets the old room in all its manifold objects and shine.

We are moving permanently to Maidstone, but keeping some of Redcliffe Square to visit. A big country house used only for weekends and the short English summer \vacation/ was backbreaking for commuting and upkeep. I think this is the way I want to live—*mostly* in the country. Anyway the strain is immediately much less.

I miss so many people in America. Give my love to the Thomases, the Booths, Bishop Scarlett, Sally and Helen Austin, and of course Mary and Jim. We have, probably fortunately, no neighbors here. But I miss the old country community. Do you still have the French readings?[2] (I've just read the Education Sentimentale,[3] shamefully in English[.]) Does the tennis still have its shaggy excellence? Do you have drinks and gossip in the barns?

I've mislaid your letters (not lost) and don't know how we agree on the correspondence, ms. etc. I don't think any thing should be finished till January. Probably Stonybrook. They seem willing to offer a lot more, and to have more interest in figuring out the best financial dole. Still what a meaningless place to leave the stuff, if place matters? It's not like one's grave. OH talking about letters, I've just read [the] best

---

1. Lowell: "The merciless Racinian *tirade* | Breaks like the Atlantic on my head" ("Holy Matrimony" 39–41 [draft of "Man and Wife"]; Houghton Library, bMS Am 1905, folder 2204, p. 1); cf. "Your old-fashioned tirade, | Loving, rapid, merciless, | Breaks like the Atlantic Ocean on my head" ("Man and Wife" 26–28, *Life Studies*).

2. Lowell: "Once a week, we have our old French readings with our friend, who teaches French at Exeter. But we've been rather frighteningly improved by Mary, who always does her homework... and knows the language" (To Adrienne Rich [August 1967], *The Letters of Robert Lowell*, pp. 489–90).

3. By Gustave Flaubert (1869).

novel in English, Jane Welsh's letters.[1] Dickens said she was of another order than all the great literary women he knew. The best Victorian marriage, in a way the only one, and miserable.

All my love,
Cal

Prometheus got the worst and most superficial and most reviews of anything I've written. Only one good one, in the TLS.[2] However, it filled much of the theater for its six weeks, unlike Benito. What's any good in the play is Io and the bit right after. I might cut it to that for my collected poems or something.

162. *Robert Lowell to* Miss Harriet Lowell

Milgate Park, Bearsted, Maidstone, Kent
July 25, 1967 [1971]

Dearest Harriet:

I am shocked to see how many days are gone since I wrote you (how many are gone since you wrote me?) and now it's too late to address a letter to your camp. I hope you will find this one waiting for you when you open Senorita Gomez's door[3] (porta?) \puerta?/ Is she a cousin of Nicole's?

Since I last wrote you, we have been up to our eyes moving from London to the country. And now we are moved in in a raggedy way. You know how I used to blow off about wanting to spend a winter in Castine. Now that has come true, only it's not such a severe step—we are only fifty miles from London, and can reach it in less than two hours. This house—let me boast—is bigger and older and *much* shaggier and messier than Mary McCarthy's. We have a trout stream about five inches deep at its deepest, a lake? about as big as my Castine barn area and solid reeds right now, herds of cattle and sheep can be seen from my study window (a neighboring farmer's—I'm not trying to

---

1. First published in 1883, but the edition that Lowell was reading is not known. See Hardwick, "Amateurs: Jane Carlyle," *New York Review of Books*, December 14, 1972.
2. "Rhythm in the Voice: Lowell's 'Prometheus Bound,'" *Times Literary Supplement*, 9 July 1971.
3. Letter addressed to "Miss Harriet Lowell, c/o Senorita Eda Gomez, Portofirio Diaz no-I-E, Ixtalahuaca, Mexico."

rival Uncle Cot)[,] hundreds of birds with harsh, horrid early morning voices—pigeons, rooks, sparrows. Things repeat. I have a bed to write on, about half the books I need, the same time commuting to where I teach as it was from London or New York. Our first two visitors come this week (not together) Bob Silvers! and Senator McCarthy.

I think of you away from me with deep sorrow. Maybe (I hope so much) you'll come to us on Christmas vacation. You can split your time between here and London. I wonder how the summer has gone for you. Can you still speak English, or only English, or are you bilingual. Still more I hope you've had good friends, and intelligent happy things to do. I've been writing hard for a long time, and now I'm just reading, rereading old things I loved. A time to cool off before I dry up. I hear such wonderful things about you. I weep that I cannot see the new Harriet, or just the old.

All my love,
Daddy

PS. What do you think of my living in a place called Bearsted? AH, BUT MY BEARS have all hibernated since I last saw you. My last sentence looks so haywire because I've just untangled a typewriter ribbon that's been tangled for two months. It may be worse.

163. Elizabeth Hardwick to Robert Lowell

[Castine, Maine]
July 29, 1971

Dear Cal: I was much blessed this morning at the p.o. A letter from you and one from Harriet, my second from her. She is having a very, very good time and her letters are quite detailed and interesting. The mail is very slow there and she doesn't seem to have heard much from me. But I am beginning to miss her terribly and she seems to feel the same way, although the summer is a wild success even with 6 hours a day of study! When she comes back on August 24th we will go immediately to Francine's and stay there until about September 7th. Your letter—I hadn't really expected to hear from you again and so that was nice . . . Castine has been green and blue and luminous all summer, utterly breath-taking. It is all exactly the same, tennis, drinks, dinners, fires, records. One night last week was heavenly. Chuck Turner was visiting and I had Mary and Sally; a wonderful clashing storm came up, thunder, lightning, and we had the fire and played Elisabeth Rethberg and Fischer-Dieskau and then all got out Cousin Harriet's old umbrella and finally got Madame Mary to Sally's car. The group is studying Montaigne this year, but I have asked off. I am studying Charlotte Brontë for my Princeton lectures. *Villette*[1] is a wonderful novel—I have two young girls who work at Harper's (Pub.) and they want me to write a preface to go along with an incredible 38 page essay by Queenie Leavis, not the kind that makes me tremble, but quite good.[2] [(]Her letter to the editor says: "I have left Miss H. the biography, but let me know if she feels I have taken up too much space and too much content otherwise. I am a very agreeable person!") Actually, her ideas and mine never once cross—a bit disconcerting . . . The Review has my Sylvia Plath piece in it this issue—don't know what you will think of it. . . . Hannah is here, all set up in Mary's garage apartment, and seems very grateful and happy to be here. She hadn't, I think, realized how much she would miss Heinrich. She was gone a great deal—Chicago,[3] etc.,—but still there was a whole great space he was in the center of. Phil Booth is largely, brownly present, with some new yearnings I cannot name stirring inside him. Well, though. I had a marvelous letter from Adrienne in San Francisco. She speaks of herself as a "manic" free-way driver and is contemptuous of S.F. for "charm," saying that "charm is the canker at the heart of civilization." Also she is horrified by the healthy, sun-tanned profs at Berkeley, etc. Dear frail creature of such baffling strength—Adrienne. I always feel a bit back-sliding and unreliable with her and yet she makes me filled with love because I know that one of the things among the thousands she has on her mind is "helping" me to be strong and sure. Sometimes her brown eyes brighten with danger and I see she has sensed my unconquerable ambivalence, my imperishable weaknesses. . . . I feel I ought to have more news. Everyone we know is as he or she was. I will

1. (1853).

2. Charlotte Brontë, *Villette*, with an introduction by Q. D. Leavis (1971), pp. vi–xii. Reprinted in Q. D. Leavis, *Collected Essays*, vol. 1, *The Englishness of the English Novel*, ed. G. Singh (Cambridge: Cambridge University Press, 1983).

3. Arendt was on the faculty of the Committee for Social Thought at the University of Chicago from 1963 to 1967.

give your greetings to everyone. I miss you terribly and always will until I die.

With love,
    Lizzie

Quotations from H.'s letters. In Oaxtepec they are in a huge government resort, worker's vacations, national sports events and so on are held there. The Experiment has a floor.

"I arrived in Oaxtepec today. The hotel is beautiful but very touristy. There are 13 swimming pools. All that kind of garbage . . . Getting here was awful. We had a 5 hr. bus ride to Nuevo Laredo, a border town. 5 hour wait in the heat, then a 27 hr. train ride. I am having a great time. I went swimming instead of eating breakfast. We sleep in a big dormitory with about 20 girls. Mexico is beautiful and very poor. My hands are very sore from carrying our bags. As they say we are not here to be pampered."

2nd letter:

"We have 6 hours of classes a day. My first teacher was very strict. He is nice out of class. The teacher I have now is really nice. I don't really like my group leader, nice but a little stupid. She looks like a Salvation Army woman. She wants me to read some chapters in a book and make a report. Don't think I will. Too nice a day. The kids are nice, but a little conventional. Oaxtepec is really gross! So touristy. We had a group of athletes here and now a religious group. I am having a wonderful time and hopefully learning some Spanish . . . Mexico is nice, but I like the USA. More freedom. You can wear what you want. In our families we will have to wear dresses, probably shoes and nylons. I prefer my way of life. Why shouldn't I. I haven't been able to get too many American newspapers and so you kind of forget all the bad things. Adios."

(By the time this reaches you, she will be at her homestay. I hope they aren't too "conventional.")

Did I tell you H. had lost 12 pounds before she left home and looked beautiful? I'll take some photos in Connecticut and send them to you.

Again, much love and good wishes to you,
    E.

164. *Robert Lowell to* Mrs. Robert Lowell

Milgate Park, Bearsted, Maidstone, Kent

August 3, 1971

Dearest Lizzie:

It's hard to believe letters cross the Atlantic in less than the months of the old ships at sea in the nineteenth century. It does something to smother expression maybe. Or is it that I feel you would \not/ much welcome details of my daily life? Not that we have drama. I've been mostly settling in, and am now fairly at ease and glad to \be/ out of the press and smother of London. It's easy to go there, but the call isn't strong this summer. And summer so queer and cool and short. The children's school ends the sixth of July and begins the sixth of September. Another reason to be here instead of a[n] interrupted almost ten months in London.

Events—this morning two swallows flew in my window and out . . . those old friends who used to scare me into my old barn. I have a rabbit who dogs me around the house, and can't be housebroken. I've just corrected a thirty-five page interview for a little magazine called The Review.¹ It's mostly shop, though we took care not to repeat Seidel's old one.² It seems double its ten years or so ago, I'm very valetudinarian, free with ~~the~~ \my/ wisdom of age. Last weekend, separately Bob Silvers and McCarthy were here, Gene rather pricking up his ears toward campaigning, or backing someone. Bob told me about your letters from Harriet. I rub my eyes—suddenly from cats and pigs to full adolescence. Liked particularly the garbage and newspaper bits. I had one lovely \card/ from her before she left—tender and gracefully humorous.³ We hardly bring out the most severe and ideological in one another, tho I write her like another grown-up—almost. Funny, just yesterday, I took Villette out of the bookcase—and put ~~it~~ her back. I'm deep in Dombey⁴—almost to where I left off in Maine four summers ago. I am terribly proud of Harriet—the flower has come to her, about

---

1. Ian Hamilton, "A Conversation with Robert Lowell," *the Review* 25 (Summer 1971).
2. Robert Lowell, "The Art of Poetry No. 3," interview by Frederick Seidel, *Paris Review*, no. 25 (Winter–Spring 1961).
3. Card now missing.
4. Charles Dickens, *Dombey and Son* (1848).

five years earlier than anything came to me. Whatever else, she won't be a wooden lady.

Bob brought your Sylvia—dazzling, as usual. In a way I want to see it in contrast with your book's other heroines—you feel strong attraction, strong ~~repulsion~~ \disgust/. *Daddy*[1] is too much for me, and I think it [is] weakened by being too much Sylvia—Oh stridently! Some \of her/ new poems (not the intermediate book) but more *Ariel*[2] are terrific—one on unfaith. Remember how Dr. Eissler said Freud ~~shifted~~ \transferred/ from the benign Joseph to the far more dangerous Moses?[3] Don't.

Love,
Cal

165. Elizabeth Hardwick to Robert Lowell

[Castine, Maine]
August 12, 1971

Dearest Cal: Yes, letters are strange. There is no answering in the true sense in our correspondence, since no answer or information is called for. There is just *writing a letter.* Yes, I did mind hearing about your daily life, but I don't ~~much~~ any longer. Actually I am at last glad that you are so happy, have found exactly how and where you want to live. Kent sounds lovely and the fantastic, extraordinary life one has with a new baby, all the dream-like, peculiar new rhythms—that should be much easier for you and Caroline in the country.

I have had a really fine summer, strange in many ways, in others exactly the same. In the afternoons the light drops suddenly, the day waits and you feel a melancholy repetition, as though you were living moments lived before, maybe long ago by someone else. I will be going to get Harriet in about a week and so if you want to write one or both send it to 67th Street. I will write you all about her just as soon as I see the beloved girl. Only going to the airport to meet you could com-

---

1. *Ariel* (1965).

2. "new poems": *Winter Trees* (1971); "intermediate": *Crossing the Water* (1971).

3. See Sigmund Freud, "The Moses of Michaelangelo" (1914) and *Moses and Monotheism* (1939). Cf. Lowell, "Freud" [~~London and~~ *Winter and London* ~~3\4/~~ \5/], "The Dolphin" manuscript, and "Freud" [*Winter and London* 5], *The Dolphin*.

pare with the emotion I feel about re-uniting with our daughter. But, honey, we don't talk "ideology!" as you sometimes seem to think; we laugh and gossip about people and experiences not at all about politics! There are no "politics" around anyway; nothing much is happening. I forgot to tell you Harriet wanted the 25 pounds you sent her used for the East Bengalis. She had just read something about them in the paper and her eyes were tearing. I said, "It will just go down the drain." Later in the day she came to me and said, "Yes it will go down the drain. But spending it at Bloomingdale's is down the drain, too." And so I sent the money.

I am not a law-giver (your little admonition about shifting from the "benign Joseph" to the "dangerous Moses." I agree with that.)[1] It's funny about my piece on Sylvia Plath. Most of the letters I have had speak of \my/ "compassion" and actually I don't quite feel that for her. I find her very unattractive as a woman, so hard and cruel, with herself and with others. I dislike "Daddy" intensely (I compare it with "Terminal Days at Beverly Farms") and also "Lady Lazarus."[2] But so much else is fantastically beautiful, isn't it. . . . I have a sort of trembling, sick feeling when I think of the fall coming up. I have been asked to speak at various places, to write things and of course I want to do so, but I feel so inadequate and so pressed for time. "Little" essays take me such a bloody long span to write.

Ah, well, darling Hannah was over for a drink yesterday and I was playing lieder, this time your old Schwarzkopf record, which has been through many a scene of your life, and she became very happy in a strange agitated way, listening to An die Musik, Gretchen, etc.[3]

---

1. "How often have I mounted the steep steps from the unlovely Corso Cavour to the lonely piazza where the deserted church stands, and have essayed to support the angry scorn of the hero's glance . . . But why do I call this statue inscrutable? There is not the slightest doubt that it represents Moses, the law-giver of the Jews, holding the Tables of the Ten Commandments" (Freud, "The Moses of Michaelangelo," trans. James Strachey, in *The Standard Edition of the Complete Psychological Works of Sigmund Freud*, vol. 13 [1955], p. 213).

2. Lowell, *Life Studies*; Plath, *Ariel*.

3. Franz Schubert, "An die Musik" (D 547) and "Gretchen am Spinnrade" (D 118/Op. 2); very likely the 1952 Schwarzkopf recording (Columbia 33CX 1040). Hardwick: "When I visited him in the hospital [. . .] we were always ordered rather grandly to bring the Vergil, the Dante, the Homer, the Elisabeth Schwarzkopf record" ("Cal working, etc.," from a letter to Ian Hamilton, n.d., 1981 or 1982; see pages 473–75). See also Lowell, "Elisabeth Schwarzkopf in New York" (*Midwinter* 5), *Notebook69-1, -2*; (*Midwinter* 7), *Notebook70*; and *History*.

I suppose it was the German. Suddenly I felt close to her for the first time in my life. She is happy here, Mary and Jim are well. I have given Tommy[1] your address and he will be writing you. Bill Alfred is going to Ireland in Sept., paid for by PEN club and I will also give him Kent, with phone number, etc. Gene McCarthy—I don't think he can rally any forces. It will be interesting to see . . . You know, Sarah Orne Jewett is wonderful. I am doing a sort of Maine thing[2]—"creative"—using my old notes. I began to look at her stories and they are stunning.

> "A man ought to provide for his folks he's got to leave behind him. 'Be just before you are generous:' that's what was always set for the B's in the copy-books."

> "'As for man, his days are as grass' that was for A—the two go well together . . . My good gracious, ain't this a starved-looking place? It makes me ache to think \them/ nice Bray girls has to brook it here."[3]

For some reason I am immensely moved by that use of "brook."[4]

I had been hoping for a letter from Harriet today, but I probably will have to be satisfied with the two I quoted you. In Mexico I think they sort of throw away the mail, South American fashion. I did have a card from Jean Valentine and so I hope that means she's all right. As I got to know her better last winter I saw how unbearably hard life is for her at times and how she won't or can't accept help. There are weeks when you call, no answer even though you know she's there; or at 6 p.m. the children say she is sleeping. Then it passes, but one worries and yet there is nothing you can do except let her know you're there, not so many blocks away, if needed. We made a wonderful friend, both of us, in a student Jean had at Barnard when she had my course last fall and I had in the spring. I know how one treasures these students when they are right, witty, smart, nice.

---

1. Harris ("Tommy") Thomas.

2. "In Maine," *New York Review of Books*, October 7, 1971.

3. From Sarah Orne Jewett, "The Town Poor," *Stranger and Wayfarers* (1891), pp. 43–44.

4. OED: "To put up with, bear with, endure, tolerate [a fig. sense of 'to stomach' in 2]. Now only in negative or preclusive constructions" ("Brook, v." 3, *Oxford English Dictionary* Vol. I).

This one, Mary Gordon was also much liked by Harriet and now the girl is going off to Syracuse to study with Snodgrass. She told me she and her boy friend used to walk up 67th Street, sighing, "*He* lives there!" You, of course . . . Barbara told me Phyllis Seidel had been disturbed this summer. Strange, she called me often and would ask me to dinner parties; when Jonathan was here I had her at a little dinner I gave. All these last years she has seemed beautiful, busy, very much on top of things, quite dismissing about Fred, indifferent.[1] And then, or so I gather, everything sort of flooded over her and broke and it turned out she had very complex and hurting feelings still. She's all right now, and I will call her when I get to New York. I feel like the voracious Lillian Hellman with my "young" friends; but these aren't things I pursue. They just happen. The only thing I can see that has come from Women's Lib is that women seem more able to lean on each other, be free to. The rest is bad writing, bald simplicity and simple-mindedness, ~~or~~ usually. I look forward to New York, shameless urbanite that I continue to be, even edging the grave. I will see Bob on the 23rd for dinner. He gave a nice account of you and Caroline. He had or has—don't know—a new "Lady"[2] someone to while away the hours, or are they minutes, that he can spare from the never sleeping Review. \Goodbye Lizzie/

166. *Robert Lowell to* Mrs. Robert Lowell

[Robert Lowell | ~~15 West 67 St~~ Milgate Park, Bearsted,
Maidstone, Kent]
August 18, 1971

Dearest Lizzie:

May I say it? The last is the sweetest of your letters—only one crack. How could you compare my gentle Flaubertian elegy on my father to *Daddy?* Oh how I too wish that in some turning of time and doubling of matter you might be meeting my plane in New York this late summer. I don't see how I will get to America sooner than Christmas or Easter. The date of the child's (Lowell-Guinness, I've been

1. Phyllis Munro Seidel (née Ferguson) was married to Frederick Seidel from 1960 to 1969.
2. Grace Dudley.

holding this back from you) [birth] is little more than six weeks off. Yes, the country is already much better \for/ the children, and will be for the next one's entrance. They have so much more at their age to do \distract them—much/ most of it will last through winter: indoor swimming (at an awful country hotel, The Great Dane)[,] various horse things, and even ballet, and mostly running about the house, indoors and out. Pets go on snowballing, Bosun, a miniature, long-haired dachshund, liable to be eaten by the cats, Tigger and Kitty—and Goldie and Carpie, liable to be eaten by everyone. Oh this is like one of Harriet's old letters.

Guests pile in—the Empsons, Sonia, and now perhaps Alice.[1] I don't think McCarthy is doing much—that makes him refreshing after the other polls. Sorry about Phyllis. Fred was here last fall—much better than the Humphrey evening,[2] but rather too torpedoeing around town. Could he be called a snob, but then an intelligence\?/ Everyone knows the name and frame of Bob's Lady romance, but no one has seen them together. When he came, I'm sure all three of us felt scared and embarrassed, it went off with kindness, awe, and even much humor. He's been a friend. Sorry too about Jean V. It was the same last year. It seems rapid to say \think/ she must be tough in her weakness. Give her my Love. Your book seems a big thing: a more passionate, personal style, Woman, a subject hardly \un/touched in our time by anyone of critical and literary vocation. Are [you] going to use any of your old women pieces, particularly Emily Brontë,[3] and maybe La Deuxieme?[4] You've given that \this/ out of the way subject quite a little time. The one advantage I find in Woman's Lib is that I can start off humorous or angry argument with *any* woman. Last winter, a Lady

1. Meade.

2. Hubert Humphrey; cf. Seidel: "I miss the dry-ice fire of Bobby Kennedy. | I met McGovern in your living room. | Hubert Humphrey simply lacked the lust" ("The Former Governor of California" 15–17, *My Tokyo* [1992]).

3. Possibly Hardwick's biography of Emily Brontë in *Atlantic Brief Lives: A Biographical Companion to the Arts*, ed. Louise Kronenberger and Emily Morison Beck (1971). Hardwick would write further about her in "Working Girls: The Brontës," *New York Review of Books*, May 4, 1972.

4. Simone de Beauvoir, *Le Deuxième Sexe* (1949). Hardwick: "The Subjection of Women," *Partisan Review* 20, no. 3 (May/June 1953), reprinted in *A View of My Own* (1962). Hardwick would write further about de Beauvoir's *The Coming of Age* in *The New York Times Book Review* (May 14, 1972); see also remarks about de Beauvoir in "The Art of Fiction No. 87," interview by Darryl Pinckney, *Paris Review*, no. 96 (Summer 1985).

Norwich stopped speaking to me with the furious remark, "I have as much right as a man to crank a car." I said I had always prayed for such a woman.[1] ~~I'm very low. I~~[2]

\How co/[3]

167. *Robert Lowell to* Miss Harriet Lowell

Milgate Park, Bearsted, Maidstone, Kent
August 18, 1971

Dearest Harriet:

If you'd write me oftener, I'd write you oftener. However, mother told me about two of your letters, the "thirteen swimming pool hotel" and "such garbage" and about your preferring America to Mexico because you hadn't "read many American papers lately." Well, now you are home ~~to~~ \and with/ the papers. Three come to us at breakfast (over my dead body) one, even flatter than the New York Times, \the/ London Times, one easier to read but irritatingly conservative, and one much more violently conservative, and constantly smoking into editorials calling for reform of the young \and Irish Catholics/—each issue of this paper is gayed up with photos of four new half naked girls with considerable figures.

I hope you have a lot of Spanish. And it gives me pride to hear that you have serious \thoughts/ about life and education. Does it spoil it ~~all~~ for me to say so? None of us do what we might; that's almost a definition of life. How many though thicken their minds and tear the nerves to tatters when they might \not/ have? Have you met ~~met~~ more silly grown-ups or more silly persons roughly your own age. I've ~~met~~ \find/ more grown-up\s/, but then I see more.

I intended to write you about our pets. They increase at the rate of one a week. Last one, a wooly miniature dachshund. It made our most

---

1. Possibly Anne (née Clifford), Vicountess Norwich. John Julius Norwich: "V. odd. In 1971 Lady Norwich would have been my first wife Anne. (My mother never used the title.) But neither of them ever cranked a car in her life. Nor does that strangely defensive remark ring true. I think he got the name wrong!" (email message to editor, October 14, 2014).

2. Page torn.

3. Page torn.

terrifying cat, Tigger the killer of voles, almost jump threw[1] a window. Now Tigger and Kitty and an Irish terrorist cat, Kelly, have drawn the outline of a dog on the flint of the driveway, and then jump for its throat.

I am glad you gave the twenty-five pounds to East Pakistan—one of the few issues like Biaffra, where there's only one ~~right~~ side.

Goodbye and love,

Daddy

168. Robert Lowell to Mrs. Robert Lowell

Milgate Park, Bearsted, Maidstone, Kent
September 2, 1971

Dearest Lizzie:

We've had two weeks much like the famous Brooks' summer in Castine. And hanging over the clouds, the birth, now little less than a month off? No troubles, but frightening at best. The other day we went to a vulgar new movie of Wuthering Heights.[2] I had forgotten the plot.

Alice has just left from a swift over-night visit. She had rhapsodic pictures of you and H. You seemed to be *growing* more than Harriet. Indeed Harriet had lost weight. Do you think Harriet would like to come here for Easter vacation. Things could be split between here and London, maybe more of London, she is young to retire. I'd like her to see the other children—the oldest thinks of her as a model, but is more involved with pets than politics. And the new child\, involved too./

Maybe because Alice left rather early in the morning for her plane, the moment was melancholy. I've known her since four, but somehow it's ~~the~~ more recent years that flash and trouble my immediate vision of her—drives with Everard etc. to Mount Desert lakes, the Boston Hospital. We don't get younger, tho you may. She is over the excited stage about her divorce, can't regret Everard, ~~but~~ a little sad with her outlook. Very sweet.

---

1. Thus, for "through."
2. Dir. Robert Feust (1970).

You see, I have nothing to write, but wished you to know I was thinking of both of you this Maine morning. I think Bill Alfred is coming in [a] few days.

Love,
Cal

(I do hope your hip has healed—what I meant to say, but the letter was sealed.)[1]

169. *Elizabeth Hardwick to Robert Lowell*

[15 West 67th Street, New York, N.Y.]
September 21, 1971

Dear Cal: I have seen my lawyer, Mrs. Barbara Zinsser, and she will be writing you about my intention to start divorce proceedings.

I have never tried to deny my grief and pain and my love for you. For me at least the amputation will probably always hurt, but I am resigned to that. The recent shocks have added something new. I don't know what to call it—the intolerable, I guess. All the more sad in that there is in what you plan to do no element of necessity.

About Harriet. She finds it hard to write you, anyone. I got only two letters this summer and she said she wrote one to you. However, so many people speak of letters returned, months later, from all your old London addresses. Harriet is definitely not up to handling her feelings about all of this. She just turns off, naturally. I hope you will set up some sort of regularity and your own relationship, writing at set intervals, cards, even a monthly telephone call. She is a child and the relationship cannot be on a reciprocal basis with you any more than it can with me. We talk of you occasionally, but only in friendly, smiling terms. We were remembering the other night those freezing mornings in Spain and your inevitable cry of disappointment when, instead of orange juice and a freshly boiled egg, you got a tepid bottled orange soda with a raw egg floating in it. Actually my own memory of you is \of/ about 15 years ago. You and Harriet are on your own now, with your own arrangements and relationships to make.

---

1. Typed on the verso of the aerogram.

For the rest, I believe getting my own life into order, protecting myself from further sorrows is the best I can do for myself and for Harriet and even for you.

Love,

Elizabeth

170 . *Robert Lowell to* Mrs. Robert Lowell

Milgate Park, Bearsted, Maidstone, Kent

[September 24, 1971]

Dearest Lizzie—

I only partly understand your second paragraph about "recent shocks." One of course is my book,[1] but it doesn't have a publication date, need not come out ever. It's not defamatory, \it's/ like your *Notebook*,[2] probably less astringent. My story \is/ both a composition and alas, a rather grinding autobiography, what I lived, though of course one neither does or should tell the literal or ultimate truth. \Poetry lies./ I'll send it to you if you wish (when it's in neater shape), you won't feel betrayed or exploited but I can't imagine you'll want to scrape through the sadness and breakage now.

I can't write much. Everything has fallen on us this week—false labor pains, rushed midnight trip to hospital, discovery that the child is upsidedown, feet-first\, and must be turned./ For over a week I had continual nosebleeds (high blood pressure?) now stopped and cured by an expert ~~stuffing~~ \wicking/ my nose.[3] No more worry? Our whole household seems to be catching \scabies/ from Bosun the ~~pet~~ \toy/ dachshund.[*] What a moment! I guess all will be well.

Mail is queer. Some reaches me. I guess more doesn't. Harriet's didn't. I'll write her soon. Mary and Jim were here, sad over your illness and gloating over the reactionary Dr. Russell's[4] misdiagnosis. Poor Mary! She got some of the worst reviews I've ever read—worse

---

1. "The Dolphin" manuscript.

2. See Hardwick to Lowell, June 26, 1970, footnote 4 on page 69.

3. Lowell: "Today I leaned through lunch on my elbows, | watching my nose bleed red lacquer on the grass; I see, smell and taste blood in everything" ("Ninth Month" [*Marriage* 11] 4–6, *The Dolphin*).

4. Castine physician.

than my Prometheus, \more/ ~~all~~ inconsequential entertainment jour-
nalists. She seemed shaken; but \a/ brave soul never shows it except
involuntarily.

I can't write more; all my love to you and Harriet.

*All must be washed \boiled/, all us, ~~and the~~ \clothes,/ rabbits
and *hedge*. ~~Could you give Blair some proof, like a library card, that I
can exist and recover my/~~

Cal

171. *Elizabeth Hardwick to Robert Lowell*

[15 West 67th Street, New York, N.Y.]
Sept. 27, 1971

Dearest Cal: I am sorry, actually much distressed, by your ill health.
I pray it is all gone and will not return. Caroline seems to have had a
rough time, but that will inevitably be temporary and I hope all will
go well. You will have the letter from Mrs. Zinsser by now. It will be a
tedious, difficult and expensive thing, infinitely complicated—money
paid to me taken off your income tax, some that can't be \etc./ I don't
know all the details. I can't speak about the book. I know only the
shocked reaction of our mutual friends. As for my journal—something
I haven't written in since last Feb.—I looked at it recently and it is
nothing, alas, except a rather masochistic eulogy, explaining your tre-
mendous efforts at survival, your heroic working life, your humor,
etc.[1] Also it is entirely in my own hand, first draft, just a diary really. I
may tear it up; it doesn't seem very much to the point any more. There
is a good portrait of Merrill Moore and a not bad one of your parents
and Dr. Bernard, Dr. Eissler . . . But nothing much.

This is just to say that I \am/ frightfully worried about you, al-
though I do believe you will be all right. I hope someone will let us
know if anything goes wrong with you. I would bring Harriet right
over.

---

1. Hardwick: "Strange, what I have written about the working habits, the coming out of the hos-
pital is not new. It is what I wrote in the 'notebook' I tore up, which did not seem to have a proper
context for such reflections. It turns out that one has very few ideas finally and I have written
more or less these same things to friends over the years in letters that also contained my distress
over Cal's actions" ("Cal working, etc.," n.d., 1981 or 1982; p. 475).

I have to go now. But to cheer you up—a fantastic little exchange I had with Bill A. on the phone.

E: Did you know J. Berryman has called his new book Agnus Dei?[1]

B: I don't know her.

E: She's terribly nice.

A. Well, that's good because we all know what a long suffering person Berryman has been!

E Yes, Agnus will be his fifth wife just as soon as she gets divorced from Mischa Solemnis.*

B Good, that will be a happy marriage.

I gather you need some sort of paper for some reason—whatever you scratched out of your last letter. I will send it. What is it? And when you get time let me know, or Mrs. Zinsser, about the lawyer. ~~Whenever you get time to think about it.~~

Dearest love, & salud, always
    Elizabeth

*I must confess to that terrible pun![2]

172. Robert Lowell to Blair Clark

[Telegram]

[London]
[Received Sept 28 1971, 707 AM]

MR BLAIR CLARK 229 EAST48TH STREET
NEWYORKCITY
BOY ROBERT SHERIDAN BORN LAST NIGHT LOVE
    CAL

---

1. "Opus Dei" (an eight-poem sequence) was published in *Delusions, Etc.* (1972).
2. Beethoven, *Missa solemnis in D major*, Op. 123 (1819–1823).

173. *Harriet Lowell to* Mr. Robert Lowell

[Telegram]

[New York]
[Received Sept. 29, 1971]

MR ROBERT LOWELL MILGATE PARK
BEARSTEDMAIDSTONEKENT
DEAR DADDY I TRIED TO CALL TO SAY THE NEWS IS GREAT STOP
LOVE HARRIET +

174. *Robert Lowell to* Miss Harriet Lowell

Milgate Park, Bearsted, Maidstone, Kent, England
October 1, 1971

Darling Harriet:

I feel . . . I mean to say that your lovely cable was like having another new child born. I remember Mother writing me last spring just telling you of our child's ~~existence,~~ \appearance,/ its coming existence—that she didn't want you to hear the news in a telegram, she meant *first* hear of it ~~existence~~ that way of course; but I trembled a little at sending my cable to you.[1] Forgive me, if this is clumsily said, but I am so tired I've half-forgotten English.

The last twenty days before Robert Sheridan Lowell's birth were rough. Twice labor pains that stopped but were real and forced us to hurry in the middle of the night in an ambulance [to the] local hospital, then a last minute shift from the Maidstone Hospital to London, because here it took 12 hours to see a doctor—medicare not at its best. Just before all this, I had continual nosebleeds for 8 days, and had to suddenly go to London because of mistakes at Maidstone. It was as though we (Caroline and I) were in a basket of \our/ blood. But all's well.

After 12 hours of labor pains, Robert was born in thirty-seconds, no time to go to the delivery room. He looked like a lobster-red \stiff/

---

1. Now missing.

gingersnap man, in a ~~crimson stream~~ \mud/.[1] His first sentence was (I had been praising you) "Isn't Harriet a girl?"

We have two other babies: a taffy-colored Burmese kitten and a very floppy childish miniature long-haired dachshund: Moonlight and Bosun. Both are childish, Bosun incredibly so; Moonlight has his Uncle Sumner's lovely voice, but unlike Sumner, an undignified fawning needling way of using it. The boy is much more dignified, despite looking like a bar tender, one who imbibes as well as sells.

What I want is for you to come to us as soon as you can. Christmas wouldn't be too soon. There's a famous progressive, casual country school in Devon that my oldest step-daughter goes to—Dartington. You might like it for a year or two before college, much less clamping than Dalton, and a change of scene. Ask Mother[.] It's the one school in England almost that ~~everyone~~ \anyone/ likes. My loveliest daughter, please come and stay.

Love,
Daddy
X

Love,
Daddy
X
(SOME JOHN HANCOCK)

(some John Hancock)

175. *Robert Lowell to* Mrs. Robert Lowell

[Milgate Park, Bearsted, Maidstone, Kent]
October 1, 1971

Dearest Lizzie:

We had to dash from Maidstone to London \on the next to last

---

1. Lowell: "in less than thirty seconds swimming the blood-flood: | Little Gingersnap Man, homoform" ("Robert Sheridan Lowell" 7–8, *The Dolphin*).

day/ in order to get proper medical attendance; then after *inducement*, twelve hours of labor. Even fathers get tired, but all is well. Not enough to write ~~much.~~ \letters./

Whatever you do, don't burn *your Notebook*! I hope to live in it long after I'm dirt. What you showed me was some of your tenderest, and easiest writing. I wrote you that mine need not be published ever. It won't be published, but kept. I won't burn all but a few \blue/ parts so you mustn't. Maybe in calmer times we can publish the two books in one volume. I think in time to come, if \we/ are still here, my poems will seem less disturbing to you. It's my best \last/ work maybe—isn't an author always his own best critic? Particularly of a lately finished book.

My blood survives the tense last two weeks, two midnight ambulances etc. \Not for me!/ It's my old high wavery bloodpressure. Now I'm back on aldomet,[1] have had and will, all sorts of tests. All's well, heart, liver etc. Only the blood goes high then drops—not with inner anguish, but mysteriously. I guess it's not too serious. Like me.

Oh the will—I mean the settlement—can't your friendly lawyer draw up what seems right, and then I without a lawyer will object to what I wish to. I'd like to avoid lawyer costs. Though I pay less than my share, my expenses for the baby are heavy, will be. Also my royalties for this half (?) were only a little over $4000—with $7000 last spring this give[s] me only 11 or 12 thousand. \A drop?/ Or is there some catch? On the other hand, I'll have 140 thousand \in trust/ from Harvard. Oh I'm well enough off. Of the common possessions, I'd like [a] few family ~~possessions~~ \tokens/ for *Robert*; I'd naturally like to leave him something—maybe royalties. For myself, a few of the books. I have much of what I want in paperbacks. Thankyou for your *dear* concern.

> Love,
> Cal

---

1. Antihypertensive drug.

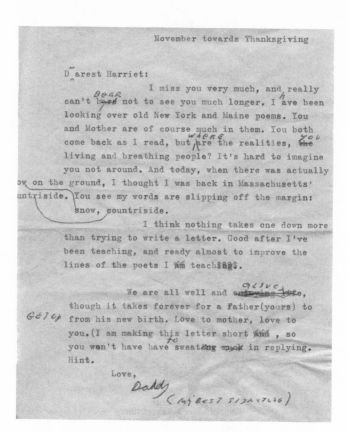

Robert Lowell to Harriet Lowell, November 20, 1971

176. *Robert Lowell to* Miss Harriet Lowell

Milgate Park, Bearsted, Maidstone, Kent, England
November towards Thanksgiving
[November 20, 1971]

Dearest Harriet:

I miss you very much, and really can't ~~bare~~ \bear/ not to see you much longer. I \h/ave been looking over old New York and Maine poems. You and Mother are of course much in them. You both come back as I read, but \where/ are the realities, ~~the~~ \you/ living and breathing people? It's hard to imagine you not around. And today, when there was actually ow on the ground, I thought I was back in Massachusetts' untriside. You see my words are slipping off the margin: snow, countriside.

I think nothing takes one down more than trying to write a letter. Good after I've been teaching, and ready almost to improve the lines of the poets I ~~am~~ teaching.

We are all well and ~~enjoying life~~ \alive/, though it takes forever for a Father (yours) to \get up/ from his new birth. Love to mother, love to you. (I am making this letter short ~~and~~ , so you won't have have \to/ sweat~~ing much~~ in replying. Hint.

Love,
    Daddy
    \(my best signature)/

177. Robert Lowell to Frank Bidart

[Milgate Park, Bearsted, Maidstone, Kent]
[December 6 or 8?, 1971]

Dear Frank:

We've been having problem[s] of someone working for us suddenly going violent, somewhat insane, with many unpleasant side-effects. We were left with two little girls, a baby still at the breast and a large somewhat remote country house—all rather spooky for a week or so, but now over, I think.

I am writing to take you up on a favor. Could you come here after Christmas or early January? Here's the agenda, as Pound would say. My new book, The Dolphin, about eighty poems, shorter than when you saw it, but with many new poems (it now ends in a long pregnancy and birth (one poem) sequence) everything endlessly rewritten, and about 40 poems about English statuary, demos etc. taken \out/, not because they are bad, but because they clog the romance 2) \To find/ something to do with the rejected poems; they can't be a narrative, but could have a mounting \drive/ of similarity. 3) Here's where I need you most: I've tried to reduce *Notebook* to personal narrative. Mostly the Historic, the metaphysical and the political go, tho it keeps bits of each, then \go the/ personal poems that fit well enough but are inflated, uninspired or redundant. I've done ~~this in~~ a sort of jerry-built first draft, and am not sure whether it works (half my new revision will go? etc.) You can see how your advice and care would be unique and invaluable. This all began by trying to get around the mounting pressure on me not to publish The Dolphin (For moral reasons). And indeed, it must wait.

Now my confession, I haven't yet gotten around to your book[1] and will in a few days and will write you. I've done nothing but schoolwork and my own work for a month—uneasy to have so much unfinished on my hands unfinished\ing./

Anyway Caroline and I would love to have you here. I of course want to pay your passage. Do see if you can come. Miserable about Elizabeth B.[2] I think With asthma you think you cannot breathe at all. I'm writing her but give her my love.

Affectionately as ever,

Cal

178. Mary McCarthy to Elizabeth Hardwick

141 rue de Rennes, Paris 6

December 9, 1971

Dearest Lizzie:

News: we are going to spend Christmas Eve and night with Cal and Caroline in Kent. I'll write about this, them, and the baby on our return. This will be a stage on a Christmas trip to visit English cathedrals, going up as far north as Durham, southwest to Wells and Winchester and south-east, probably to Canterbury. Cal says all these are "only a stone's throw" from Maidstone, but look at the map. This pilgrimage is a strange notion in the cold season, especially since some of these cathedrals are supposed to be dank and chilling even in full summer. But it strikes a common romantic chord in us, and practically we'll take sweaters, wool socks, and above all fleece-lined boots.

The trip, I hope, is a prelude to my finally getting started on the book on the Gothic I've been planning for so many years. Meanwhile I'm still slogging away on Medina and doubt whether I shall get out of

---

1. The manuscript of Bidart's *Golden State* (1973).

2. Bishop had an asthma attack in late October 1971, and "on November 9 she collapsed and was taken by the university police to the Harvard infirmary. Transferred immediately to Peter Bent Brigham Hospital, she remained in an oxygen-deficit fog for eight days." She was then "back at Stillman Infirmary at Harvard, where she remained for three more weeks, until December 6" (Brett C. Millier, *Elizabeth Bishop: Life and the Memory of It* [1993], pp. 454–55).

those trenches for Christmas.[1] It's my first experience with something like writer's block, and God knows what exactly is the reason.

We had a letter from Elmer Wardwell saying that Tommy had been operated on twice but that he had seen the Missus[2] downtown after the second operation and all was going well. Do you know anything about this? I shall write her.

Bob says you're in splendid form, very much in demand, collecting your essays. This must mean the Gauss lectures finished well. How is Harriet? Here it's been a rather gloomy late fall (I mean morally), perhaps partly connected with the Medina syndrome and partly with Jim's troubles in Alabama, which are too long and complicated to detail now. But beyond these specific causes I feel wrapped in a dark heavy cloud, which may be just the world. I keep thinking about Dante. But we're past the middle of life's journey.[3]

Dear Lizzie I wish you, Harriet, and all friends a Merry Christmas and hope our attendance at Cal's crib and fireside won't give you pain.

Much love,[4]

179. Elizabeth Hardwick to Mary McCarthy

["Season's Greetings" card, Albrecht Dürer, "Mouse (detail from ADAM AND EVE)," Cleveland Museum of Art]

[New York, N.Y.]

[December 1971]

This doesn't seem altogether suitable as a Christmas greeting. It was personally bought at the Cleveland Museum. Bob, Grace Dudley and I flew out here on Saturday to see the Caravaggio show.[5] It is quite an astonishing museum, large, important, and all down there in the middle of the tracks, smokestacks, waste—we almost went on to the sights of

---

1. McCarthy covered Captain Ernest Medina's trial for his role in the 1968 My Lai Massacre. See her study, *Medina* (1972).

2. Mary Thomas.

3. Dante: "Nel mezzo del cammin di nostra vita | mi ritrovai per una selva oscura, | ché la diritta via era smarrita" ("In the middle of the journey of our life I came to myself in a dark wood where the straight way was lost" [Temple translation, 1900]; *Inferno*, I:1–3).

4. Unsigned.

5. *Caravaggio and His Followers*, The Cleveland Museum of Art, October 22, 1971–January 2, 1972.

Toledo and Kansas City, both actually supposed to be excellent muse-
ums also. It was rather a fantastic day, starting at 8 a.m. when Bob and
Grace emerged from their suite at the Pierre![1] I don't suppose I'll forget
the details and so they can be saved for a meeting sometime. There is
one thing I finally get very nervous about with rich people—they like
themselves far too much. Otherwise, fantasy land drifts about them
like a dream I guess. I must say Bob is having real fun; she likes him,
she takes care of him—he blinks with the newness of such attention,
goes on talking, putting out the essays, telephoning, dining. Incred-
ible. . . . New York is not bad right now, but I haven't been feeling well,
very, very tired. How awful that is. I have always had the habit of say-
ing I was tired, but it meant something else. It will pass—I have pills
and I am sure there is nothing at all wrong. Harriet seems fairly well.
I had been wanting her to go away to school, thinking it would enrich
her life, and I spent a lot of time on it—but she doesn't want to. I would
have missed her terribly of course and it is great fun having her in and
out. I suppose my Princeton lectures went well. I enjoyed dashing over
there; I'm going to Chicago and Univ. of Wisconsin in the spring—
not for anything important, but just profitable enough to make it pos-
sible. I do wish you and Jim a good Christmas in Kent; it will be nice
for Cal and so that pleases me. Much love, dear ones.

    Lizzie

180. *Robert Lowell to* Miss Harriet Lowell

Milgate Park, Bearsted, Maidstone, Kent
December 14, 1971

Dearest Harriet—

    Almost an abstract Christmas present, but solid and the exchange
value of the pound is rising. If you kept this till you were 100, who
knows what it would be worth? Would to heaven I were with you in
its place.

    Love to you and mother,
      daddy

---

1. Hotel in Manhattan.

181. *Robert Lowell to* Mrs. Robert Lowell

[Card from the Scotch House, Knightsbridge, London S.W.1 X 41PB]

[Milgate Park, Bearsted, Maidstone, Kent]

Christmas 1971

Dearest Lizzie—I tried to choose something modest and sharp[.]¹
With my love
Cal

182. *Robert Lowell to* MRS. AND MISS ROBERT LOWELL

[Telegram]

[Maidstone, Kent, England]

[Received] Dec 23 3 51 PM '71

MRS AND MISS ROBERT LOWELL15 WEST67ST
NEWYORKCITY
LOVE AND MERRY CHRISTMAS COULDNT PHONE LOVE
AGAIN
DADDY

183. *Harriet Lowell to Robert Lowell*

[Card: Peyote Chief (ca. 1930) by Jack Hokeah, Kiowa, Museum of the American Indian: "A beautifully costumed ceremonial leader kneels on a colorful blanket, holding his gourd rattle, beaded staff and feather fan as he prays in Peyote rites. Hokeah was one of the original 'Five Kiowa' painters."]

[15 West 67th Street, New York, N.Y.]

[January 2?, 1972]

Dear Daddy,

Thank-you for the check. I just got it cashed. I still haven't decided what to spend it on. Christmas was very nice. I went to the country with the Browns. School starts tomorrow, back to the old grind. My Robespierre paper is due tomorrow and I am typing it on an electric

---

1. See Hardwick's thank-you letter of January 23, 1972.

typewriter. Some girls who lived in mommy's studio left it, instead of the rent. Well, I must be getting back to work! Dalton won't leave me in peace on my last day of vacation. Thanks again.

Love,
    Harriet

184. *Robert Lowell to* Miss Harriet Lowell

Milgate Park, Bearsted, Maidstone, Kent
[January 10, 1972]

Darling Harriet:

If you had consulted me on Robespierre, Dalton would have left you in peace on the last day of vacation. I transcribe my 14 line masterpiece on this subject.

Robespierre and Mozart as Stage[1]

Robespierre could live say\ing/, "The Republic
of Virtue without *la terreur* is a disaster;
loot the chateaux, have mercy on Saint Antoine;"
or promise Danton, "I'll love you till I die—"
both discovered the guillotine is painless.
La Revolution, old Jacobin, kept repeating,
"This theater must remain and remain theater,
play ~~her~~ \my/ traditional, barren audience-drama,
play back the revolution." Ask the voyeur
what blue movie is worth a seat at the keyhole.
Even the prompted Louis Seize was living theater,
sternly and lovingly judged by his critics, who knew
Mozart's operatic slash could never
cut the gold thread of the suffocating curtain.

There it is in my usual uneccentric and clear style, every word in need of a "footmark" except for you a recent scholar on Robespierre. Oddly enough everyone writes well on odious Robespierre

---

1. Lowell: "Robespierre and Mozart as Stage" (*The Powerful* 14) *Notebook70*; and "Robespierre and Mozart as Stage," *History*.

(and even with sympathy)[,] Carlyle, Michelet, Büchner.[1] He only killed two or three thousand, while Napoléon must have killed a million, still Robespierre knew the people he killed, he killed most of the people he knew and respected in parliament, the French Convention.

My last day of vacation is getting too near. My students are gentle but many couldn't get into a good American high school. In the past our college has had rather pitiful little demos (for pot) and as a result, the County gives ~~them~~ \us/ as little money as is legal; ~~and~~ so new teachers can't be hired, secretaries, etc. Going back to work is a slightly wet experience.

What about Easter? I would like to fly over and get you, if you'll come. When is your Easter vacation. I think it's early with us, but probably Dalton doesn't acknowledge Easter. A former principal, Dr. Abram Straus[,] asked why Dalton should celebrate the resurrection of a renegade Arab mystogogue. Seriously, I am dying to see you. You'll meet few people of all ages here, and I'll dictate all your history papers. Give my love to mother; I think she was gypped on the apartment.

All my love,
Daddy

185. Harriet Lowell to Robert Lowell

[15 West 67th Street, New York, N.Y.]
[n.d. but January 1972]

Dear Daddy,

I sent you a card earlier, but addressed it wrong. Anyway, I want to thank you for the check. I am trying to find something extravagant to spend it on. I am now fifteen, whatever that means.[2] At school we are reading Donne & ~~Johnson~~ Jonson. Tonight I have to write a paper on *anything*. I am not sure I enjoy all the freedom. I saw the movie of *Macbeth*.[3] The witch scene was done in the nude, which didn't seem much like Shakespeare. At Christmas time I went with the Browns to

---

1. See Thomas Carlyle, *The French Revolution* (1837); Jules Michelet, *Histoire de la révolution française* (1847–53); Georg Büchner, *Dantons Tod* (1835).
2. Harriet Lowell's fifteenth birthday was on January 4, 1972.
3. *Macbeth*, dir. Roman Polanski (1971).

a hotel on the Hudson. We had a New Year's party here, which wasn't very exciting. Well, bye.

Love, Harriet

186. Robert Lowell to HARRIET LOWELL

[Telegram]

[Maidstone, Kent]

[Received] 1972 Jan 18 PM 2:18

HARRIET LOWELL 15 WEST67STR

NEWYORKCITY

APPALLED I LOST YOUR BIRTHDAY I BOAST YOU ARE 15 TO
EVERYONE IT MEANS THE EDGE OF WHAT IS TO COME AND GO
IN LIFE GLORIOUS FOR YOU I TEACH DONNE PLEASE COME HERE
LOVE

DADDY

187. Elizabeth Hardwick to Robert Lowell

[15 West 67th Street, New York, N.Y.]

January 23, 1972

Dearest Cal: A morning of amazement! I came in and saw on the chair a package and I looked at it and thought, quite truly, "Who in England would be sending me a gift?" Dorothy Richards? I opened it to find the astonishing surprise. A beautiful dark green cashmere which I love, which fits perfectly, and is grand and elegant and something I could never afford for myself. How happy I am with it and I thank you very much, very much.

The morning mail, also there alone[1] with the sweater, brought sounds from another long silent voice. Fred Seidel, a long poem, dedicated to me and Norman Mailer! I think it is very, very brilliant except for the part within that mentions me and Norman Mailer—not "together" but just as names.[2] How strange. I will write him and ask to

---

1. Thus, for "along."

2. Seidel: "He took an office just like Norman Mailer. | He married a writer just like Lizzie Lowell. | He shaved his beard off just like. Yes. Exactly" (manuscript draft of "What One Must Contend With,"

have my name out of the poem because I think it sort of ruins it for Fred, as a poem I mean. I haven't seen him for ages.

Ah, ages. Well, I have been \reading/ Sir Gawain and the Green Knight in bed and I love it and Renaissance poetry this a.m. to help Harriet study for an examination Harry Levin couldn't pass. But I mutter to myself, "Gosh, that's good!" as if it were all sprung new from a Village pen and going off to Poetry.[1]

Harriet is marvelously well. I sort of gave up writing before and after Christmas and find it hard to start again and instead do housekeeping. However, I am back, of various necessities. "The Wife of Bath"—isn't that the very best ever? I am using it in a lecture I have to give this week-end on men and women, a subject like the air if I ever heard of one.[2]

All is well here, rather busy. I went to a party at William Phillips' this past Saturday,—depressing and distressing. I never saw so many looking so awful. Dwight[3]—the first time in over a year—simply fallen apart, or so I felt, terrible color, vague; faces, blown up, of Will Barrett and his wife Julie—remember—also blown-up and silent. Years of suffering and calories and spirits seem to have taken their toll.

24–26, dedicated to Elizabeth Hardwick; Elizabeth Hardwick Papers, HRC). In the version published in *Sunrise* (1979), the dedication was removed and the lines read: "He took an office just like Norman Mailer. | He married a writer just like—yes exactly. | He shaved his beard off just like—et cetera."

1. An allusion to Randall Jarrell. Peter Taylor: "I remember once at Kenyon there was a student who had done a painting, a landscape, and had it proudly displayed in his room. When Randall came in and saw it there, he exclaimed, 'Gosh, that's good!' He pointed out all the fine qualities. The painter sat soaking up the praise. They talked of other things for a while, and when Randall got up to leave he said, putting his fist on his hip and frowning, 'You know, I've changed my mind about that picture. There's something wrong, awfully wrong, about the light in it. You ought to work on it some more, or maybe you really ought to just throw this one away and do another'" ("Randall Jarrell," in *Randall Jarrell, 1914–1965*, ed. Robert Lowell, Peter Taylor, and Robert Penn Warren [1967], pp. 246–47).

2. Hardwick: "Women, wronged in one way or another, are given the overwhelming beauty of endurance, the capacity for high or lowly suffering, for violent feeling absorbed, finally tranquilized, for the radiance of humility, for silence, secrecy, impressive acceptance. Heroines are, then, heroic; but the heroism may turn into an accusation and is in some way feared as the strength of the weak. The Wife of Bath, coarse, brilliant, greedy, and lecherous as any man, tells a tale of infinite psychological resonance" ("Seduction and Betrayal: I," *New York Review of Books*, May 31, 1973). The essay "was read at Vassar College in 1972" (*Seduction and Betrayal*, p. vii). See also Lowell's "To Speak of Woe That Is in Marriage" (*Life Studies*).

3. Macdonald.

Judy Feiffer, shrunken, but all right. Adrienne and Hannah the only joys intact.

Blair is married,[1] but I haven't seen him. N. Chiaromonte died. And John Berryman's death was simply awful.[2] I just couldn't try to find out details, if there are any. The desperation stands for itself, without any footnotes being needed. And where did it come from and why did it stay forever? We never know much I guess. I met him in 1945 and knew him a little better than I ever told anyone. He was beautiful and dear and brilliant and afraid.

Again my thanks for the staggering gift, coming truly from the blue.

With dearest love,
    Lizzie

\I shall go out in my new green sweater & my winter dunce cap to mail this and—guess what?—buy *the New York* Post. So doth habit keep us happy./
    E

188. *Elizabeth Hardwick to Robert Lowell*

[15 West 67th Street, New York, N.Y.]
January 31, 1972

Dear Cal: I am sorry we got cut off on the phone, but I think most of the information from both sides got through. However, I do want to write a few new ideas. There is no necessity for you to come \to/ get Harriet. She has no hesitation about going off alone. I've just talked with her at length about it. And in addition just to get the picture a little bit clarified I called BOAC. Things are very crowded at that time. I am assuming that you understand that you will have to pay Harriet's fare because I cannot in the most literal sense. Well, youth fare round trip, which she is eligible for is $190 and the other fare is $452—almost $260 \more/! But each flight only allots a few for youth fare and so I went on and made a reservation; it had to be Qantas, BOAC filled. She feels

---

1. To Joanna Rostropowicz.
2. Berryman committed suicide on January 7, 1972.

that a week, actually about 8 days it is, would be about right. I made her reservation for March 25, returning April 2. Her actual vacation starts as yours does on March 20 and ends April 4th. We don't need to go into the details; this is just a quick note to say that it is not necessary for you to make a trip here in order to have Harriet go to England. The reservation is very tentative, but at least I have it.

I feel very sorry for Ivana; the first blow of pain never leaves you as long as you live.[1] However I am encouraged from what you said and what I have read about the new methods of treatment.

This is in haste, and I will probably hear from you about how all of this appears to you and then we can correspond further about the plans.

Love from both of us,
    Lizzie

189. *Robert Lowell to* Mrs. Robert Lowell

Milgate Park, Bearsted, Maidstone, Kent
Feb. 5, 1972

Dearest Lizzie:

Just a note of delight about Harriet's trip. I enclose the check \(in another envelope)/. Of course I would be glad to come and escort her here, but plane trips kill me—two in about two days! Also this isn't a moment when I feel like a swift, a rapid motion \glimpse/ of all my dear New York friends. So I sigh with relief. I'll be at Heathcliff[2] airport with a car at the exact hour.

I can't write much. This week was hell, just ending. Ivana's case was and is very grave; doctors' reports conflicted; no point was reached when we could feel she was out of danger. Then difficult drives through one of England's worst snow storms (nothing to ours, but looking like Napoleon's retreat from Moscow to the English eye). Then the skin-

---

1. Ian Hamilton: "In January 1972 Lowell's stepdaughter Ivana (now aged six) overturned a kettle of boiling water and was badly burned; she spent three months in the hospital" (*Robert Lowell: A Biography*, p. 428). See Lowell's "Dolphins" and "Ivana" [*Another Summer* 2 and 3], *The Dolphin*, and Caroline Blackwood's "Burns Unit" (*For All That I Found There* [1973]). For her own account of the accident, see also Ivana Lowell, *Why Not Say What Happened?* (2010), pp. 34–40.
2. Thus, for Heathrow.

stripping operation; then next the plastic surgery. I think she [is] out of danger (but for the unforeseen) but will be two more months in the hospital—one of the best in England and with manners like Miss Elsemore.[1]

I will write Harriet either today or tomorrow. Tell \her/ the thought of her coming has been to me the happiest of all happy thoughts. (Do I sound like Wordsworth?[)][2] I am Thrilled and half-marveling that you and Harriet are reading *poetry*. To me *poetry* means poetry written before 1906.

I appreciate your accommodation.

All my love,

Cal

190. *Robert Lowell to* Miss Harriet Lowell

Milgate Park, Bearsted, Maidstone, Kent
February 6, 1972

Darling Harriet:

The best news on earth you are coming. I would have loved the Gallantry of flying over to escort you here, but I find in my green old age such trips are murder; especially one within days of another. Last time I sat between a Canadian \insurance man/ and a woman from Newark. For about fifteen minutes, I found each more interesting than the other. Then they were both death. I waited in a line for an hour to get to the toilet and then gave up. Something had gone wrong with the lighting, so that at times when things were meant to be dimmed for sleep, the lights were so brightly blazing they gave me a sunburn. All the while I heard the voices of the electricians by some error amplified like rock and roll, while they conferred on repairs. I won't comment on the TV movie. Dearest, don't come on a super-jet and if you do sit by a window or the aisle. What a handsome sacrifice you are making to see us.

I'll be waiting at the \London/ airport and won't let you daw-

---

1. The babynurse hired by the Lowells after the birth of Harriet in 1957. See "Home After Three Months Away" (*Life Studies*) and *The Letters of Robert Lowell*, pp. 270, 278, 281.

2. Wordsworth: " a voice | That seemed the very sound of happy thoughts" ("The Wanderer" 734–45, *The Excursion*).

Robert Lowell and Elizabeth Hardwick in the 1950s

(Courtesy of Harriet Lowell)

ABOVE Harriet Winslow's house on School
Street in Castine, Maine
(Courtesy of Harriet Lowell)

RIGHT Robert Lowell on the steps of the
barn on Water Street in Castine, Maine,
in the early 1960s (Courtesy of Harriet Lowell)

BELOW Robert Lowell, Elizabeth
Hardwick, and Harriet Lowell in the
"old Burgundy" car in the late 1960s
(Courtesy of Harriet Lowell)

Harriet Lowell at
15 West 67th Street in
New York, circa 1971–72
(Courtesy of Harriet Lowell)

Robert Lowell and Caroline Blackwood with Ivana (left, holding Snowflake)
and Evgenia (right, holding Flopsy) at Milgate Park in 1971
(Photograph by Fay Godwin)

Adrienne Rich outside the New Yorker Theater on Broadway in 1973

(Photograph by Nancy Crampton)

Frank Bidart and Elizabeth Bishop on the ferry to North Haven in 1974

(Photograph courtesy of Archives and Special Collections, Vassar College)

Barbara Epstein and Robert Silvers in the office of *The New York Review of Books*
on West 57th Street in 1963

(Photograph by Gert Berliner)

Mary McCarthy in her house in Castine, Maine, in 1980

(Susan Wood / Getty Images)

Elizabeth Hardwick in her apartment on West 67th Street in New York City in 1971

(Photograph by Cecil Beaton for *Vogue* magazine)

Robert Lowell beneath a portrait of Charles Russell Lowell, Jr., in the house of
Mrs. Alfred Lowell, Boston, Massachusetts, February 19, 1965

(Photograph by Steve Schapiro for *Life* magazine)

Elizabeth Hardwick,
Robert Lowell, and Harriet
Lowell in the mid-1960s.
This photograph was among
those Lowell was carrying
in his briefcase on
September 12, 1977,
the date of his death.
(Courtesy of Harriet Lowell)

Elizabeth Hardwick outside the renovated barn in Castine, Maine, circa 1974. This image
was also among those Lowell was carrying in his briefcase on the date of his death.
(Courtesy of Harriet Lowell)

dle about there lost for 8 days. I plan to make your visit unplanned. Six country days here with children and animals (not more than one church a day—or at all)[.] Then a couple of days in London. The children want you to bring your guitar even more than Caroline does. Bring it. Bring your poetry book; your lessons were the first poetry written before 1900, except for mine, that Mother has read. I'm sure I can add to her very expert teaching.

Ivana, our six year old, has made a wonderful turn for the better in the last day or so, though she still must have plastic surgery and may well be in the hospital when you arrive. The plasma-intravenous feeding has ended. She is free from the plastic tubes that Caroline called her rosaries. Her life is no longer in danger. We had eight days without a sky but now it's just gruelling.

Dear Heart, I can't wait. Give my love to Mother, and thank her.

Love,

Daddy

191. Robert Lowell to Elizabeth Bishop

Milgate Park, Bearsted, Maidstone, Kent

Feb 6(?), 1972

Dearest Elizabeth:

You seem to have been here during Frank's visit, both by voice and reference (if Caroline had met you, you would have been as here as we are). (Change in type caused by my disastrous stopgap of putting an Olympia ribbon on a Hermes, meaning rolls stop rolling every five minutes and have to be exhaustingly switched.[)]

You are so here that I started to phone you about Marianne.[1] The end of her life already ended by infirmity—she was a star in my sky 35 years ago when I first read Dick Blackmur's essay.[2] Last week I was teaching her to my poor dim students, along with Cummings whom they of course liked and got much better. For you, tho, it's losing *the* person. What can I say? Maybe you'll write a little book of memory

---

1. Marianne Moore died on February 5, 1972.
2. R. P. Blackmur, "The Method of Marianne Moore," in *The Double Agent: Essays in Craft and Elucidation* (1935).

and thoughts. I have never heard anyone describe her so well—or anyone else. Her death has made little stir, unlike Berryman's—on whom each English week or arts page has a bad elegy. This is right, tho I thought him doomed too ever since I ate with him last year ~~but~~ then it was drink, later he must have died from not drinking. She was much more inspired—his heroism was in leaping into himself in the last years, ~~amazingly~~ \bravely/.

I think Frank and I revised 405 poems in a month. That's no way to write, but it was made more sensible by Frank's amazing filing code and total memory for my lines. Even for rejected versions. The three books are my magnum opus, are the best or rather they'll do. Are they much? Read *Dolphin* when you have leisure. I'll send the other two fairly soon. I am going to publish, and don't want advice except for yours. Lizzie won't like the last. What else can I offer her? There's something creepy about deliberately writing something posthumous. \(Love, Cal)/

I have no heart to write about Ivana's accident. We have been a lost ship.

192. *Robert Lowell to* Miss Harriet Lowell

Milgate Park, Bearsted, Maidstone, Kent
Feb. 22, 1972

Dearest Harriet:

We've just come out of the dark tunnel of the miners' strike.[1] You probably didn't hear much of it in New York, but here it held the whole stage. You'd be cooking an egg or reading Shakespeare or absorbing an interesting news reel about the strike on television, when all would fold into darkness. As this continued into the second hour, a chill settled down, you went to look for your overcoat. Other resources were tried, coal fires, wood fires, oil lamps, very dangerous, but which \made/ the night like day with their luminous, glowing "mantels." Doom snowballed in the daily news, 2 Million unemployed, armed pickets,

---

1. In Britain, coal miners downed tools on January 9, 1972. On February 16, the BBC reported that the Central Generating Electricity Board had announced "many homes and businesses will be without electricity for up to nine hours from today."

polluted water, deaths in stopped elevators, dentist drills stopping mid-tooth. Worst for me, threats of a total milk cut-off. We were nearing the dark ages, when it all suddenly stopped.[1] In two days, it disappeared even from the back pages of the newspapers.

I'll be meeting you at the London airport at ten p.m. on the March 25. We may spend the night in London, since the trip here is twice as long. I think Mother wants to prepare a guide for me, step by step with Harriet—turn left for the baggage counter with her suitcase, bring money for extra charges, see that she brushes her teeth,[2] help her two hours a day with the new math, read Milton aloud, don't make up ~~facts~~ \imaginary/ facts about Milton's life, that he adored buttermilk.[3]

Dear it's rather a long dark journey into a blaze of new faces. I know you'll find my Heart is warm. The little girl is better, having her last operation today and will be home in 3 weeks. She can even be funny about it now, but it wasn't funny. Love to you and Mother,
    Daddy

193. Elizabeth Hardwick to Robert Lowell

[15 West 67th Street, New York, N.Y.]
February 28, 1972

Dear Cal: A beautiful, warm day here. Sumner snoozing on the window sill among the begonias brought from Maine years ago and still bravely enduring . . . I have finished my essay on the Brontë girls[4] and am writing something for Time Magazine for a lot of money which I hope they won't print since they will pay me most of the money anyway.[5] After Christmas I had a too long bout of not getting down

---

1. The miners ended their strike on February 19, 1972.
2. Lowell: "She\'s/ a friend to *Mom* now, not an enemy, | except for my yelling, *Dammit, brush your teeth!*" ("Fox Fur," 11–12, "The Dolphin" manuscript, p. 47; see poem on page 249).
3. Harriet Lowell: "One time [my mom] was drilling me—I had a spelling bee and I guess I misspelled 'strange' and [my father] would say, 'Well, Ben Jonson spells it that way, so she can,' and she was furious because, [as she said,] 'We don't need this now, we want her to pass the test!'" (Harriet Lowell Interview, "On Robert Lowell," Harvard Oral History Initiative, August 2016).
4. "Working Girls: The Brontës," *New York Review of Books*, May 4, 1972.
5. For "The American Woman: A Time Special Issue," *Time Magazine* 99, no. 12, March 20, 1972, which is unsigned, as was *Time Magazine*'s practice. See especially "The New Woman, 1972."

to work, but that has passed and I seem to have a number of things going. There are always parties and people coming and going and Nixon and Chou[1] on the telly. I am trying to think of some gossip for you, but all the good things are rather long and take too long to tell. Not that I have such a bit of news or speculation on hand just now.

Some new plans for Harriet and some "advice"—since you have already credited me with it I might as well produce it! She is coming on Thursday the 23rd of March and returning the following Friday, March 31. The change to the first Thursday is to give me a free week-end and I will be away from Friday until Sunday night. The second Thursday is to give Harriet a weekend before she goes to school; she has some plan with a friend. I will put all of the information on a card enclosed here.

I was talking to Harriet recently. Here are her wishes; you can honor them or not as you ~~wish~~ \like/. The trip—for her—is to spend time with you after this long stretch of a year and a half. Also she is very keen to see London, go to the galleries, to restaurants. She said rather wistfully that she hoped the trip would be like her last one to Venice. She would like to stay in Kent from Friday until Monday and then come up to London and be alone with you until she leaves for home on Friday morning. You will let me know about this, will you? Is Redcliffe Square open, possible?

You and Harriet and I aren't the same people we were last year. What kind of life one lives, who you live with, what you value—that is everything. Harriet will be a strange surprise—if you recognize her at the airport. But she is still vulnerable and shy and full of deep feelings and some hurts I imagine. Very proud, though, and sure of just who she is. I think you will have a wonderful time getting to know her, being with her alone and I want it to work well so that sometime she can go on a beautiful, far-away trip with you and learn from you and have the delight and honor of all the old experiences I still value. I know it will be a deep, lasting love for you both if you can give yourself to her. I have had a marvelous time this year with her, her wit, her sympathy and loveliness and humor give me joy every day. I truly want the same for you and, of course, for her on her part.

---

1. Zhou Enlai; Nixon visited China from February 21–28, 1972.

I go out all the time and seem to be on everyone's list[1] like the man in Dickens who is folded in and out like a leaf in a table.[2] Dinners are dull often, but then again fantastic, peculiar things happen to you . . . I am glad life has taken a turn for the better there. Let me know your thoughts.

Love,
Elizabeth

Can you send me some information about where you will meet H. and what to do if you somehow miss each other for some minutes. The London airport is awful!

[Card enclosed]
These are *youth fares* and her flight back has to be reconfirmed from there or else she won't be on it; state that it is a youth fare when you call Qantas on Friday, after her arrival.

Very important, Dad:

Arriving London 10:25 P.M. Qantas flight 530 . . . Thursday, March 23

Leaving London, Friday March 31 at 12:15 P.M. . . . Get to airport early. Flight 531

Qantas

194. *Robert Lowell to* Miss Harriet Lowell

Milgate Park, Bearsted, Maidstone, Kent
March 1, 1972

Dearest Harriet:

I am fifty-five today. I thought I would be yesterday, I had forgotten leapyear. A day has been added to my life. What's wrong with that addition? Or that if you take a fast plane you arrive here before you left? You can't come soon enough. I've decided all Americans are

---

1. Among the chronicles of New York literary social life in 1972 is Robert Craft's: "On February 21, I shared a table with Lincoln and Fidelma Kirstein [. . .] for the Random House-*New York Review* Auden testimonial dinner, a combination birthday party and Last Supper [. . .] I saw Elizabeth Hardwick home afterward" (*An Improbable Life* [2002], pp. 306–307).
2. Twemlow in Charles Dickens's *Our Mutual Friend* (1865).

terrific, that a dull or limp American is by definition impossible. But I've only seen four since Sheridan was born. He gets more and more distressingly extravert, lifts up heavy steel standing lamps, races past speed-limits on down corridors in his walker, and talks an unintelligible mash and gulp which he considers great conversation. He only smiles at me, though, because I never hold him over my head, and say, "You're so manly, manly." He has so many bigger women to survive.[1]

I hear through Blair, through some Dalton mother you've written a good poem—and I am in it. If this is so, we write the same way; I've put you in \mine/—and you said every poem would need a footmark to be intelligible. Don't sadden over the uncertainties of the trip and our meeting. Nothing will be quite the same, but you will find a second home, a second family. Everyone will love you, though you may find many of us childish.

The climate is getting colorful and warm for you—crocus and snowdrop, more birds, noisier birds, invisible leaves like the hair on Sheridan's head.

All my love, and to Mother,
Daddy

195. *Robert Lowell to* Mrs. Robert Lowell

Milgate Park, Bearsted, Maidstone, Kent
March 4, 1972

Dearest Lizzie:

Sweet of you to remember old times, even my now rather rusty sight-seeing: the "horrors of the Vatican,"[2] the mosque at Cordoba that didn't look like a church, the Carpaccio with the dragon Harriet pitied,[3] the poets' feast, Grace Stone, and the many walks when we didn't arrive quite where we intended, or when. Don't worry, I have

---

1. Lowell: "a mother, unlike most fathers, must be manly" ("Dolphins" [*Another Summer* 2] 12, *The Dolphin*).
2. Harriet Lowell: "I remember my mother saying [. . .] [that] he asked for an art book called *Horrors of the Vatican* [for Christmas] and my mother went all over looking for it but it was just a joke" (interview with the editor, July 5, 2016).
3. "Old Snapshot from Venice 1952" (*Hospital II* 3), *The Dolphin*.

many things to go, *romero*,[1] with Harriet. More than the pitifully short time will allow. I'll make out a loose schedule when she comes. I had no intention of marching her in a caravan of small children.

Huyck van Leeuwen read of a theory in an Italian historian, Guglielmo Ferrero, that Napoleon's mobile Italian Campaign was controlled by fast dispatches from *The Directoire* in Paris.[2] But they must have left something to Napoleon who was there. I'm here. The plans will be alright. But is anything alright? We make so many mistakes and age rubs them in, almost indelibly. God rest us all, and Tiny Tim.[3]

You must change the departure date. I teach till very late on Thursday afternoon, and then again \on/ Friday morning. Friday night will be alright, tho the earlier plan would have been better. I know how hard and dark Harriet's trip is for you. I mustn't go into this. When she comes back you will wonder at some of your fears. When things loosen up, I'll try and get to America—*North* America as my Essex Literature classes call it.

Love to you both,
Cal

196. *Robert Lowell to* Mrs. Robert Lowell

Milgate Park, Bearsted, Maidstone, Kent
March 9, 1972

Dearest Lizzie:

Sorry to scuffle with you on the phone. I have plans made ~~out~~ roughly that are much like what you and Harriet suggested. I don't want things set much more than that—a London of a play, museums, the Tower, Regent's Park, the City, nothing maybe a must, lots of solitary me, as much as . . . I know all the dark thickets of feelings; the visit must be a happy one. It will.

I thought maybe, and almost certainly I'd try to make a New York trip in late May or early June, before the colleges close and people

---

1. Pilgrims; both "Pilgrims" and "Romero" were draft titles for "Marriage?" (*Caroline* 4), *The Dolphin*.

2. Guglielmo Ferrero, *Aventure. Bonaparte en Italie. 1796–1797* (1936).

3. Dickens: "And so, as Tiny Tim observed, God bless Us, Every One!" (final sentence in *A Christmas Carol* [1843]).

scatter, so as before I could combine seeing you all, and look up old friends and cronies. I really haven't been able to travel at all for a long time; except for my weekly drive to Essex. I don't think I've been to London more than four times since Sheridan's birth. All's easier. Ivana comes home today, after two months I think—hard to tell because she lived in the hospital under constantly changing release-dates. Now she is learning to walk again, and should be back in school in a month.

By the way, I got a furious illiterate letter from a Johnny Milford, who had offered to become my assistant and apprentice, and who had been firmly declined by "my New York Secretary." She only gave her title and typed signature, but I recognized the hand of the old rejector.[1] The postcard was enclosed and an insulting dollar bill—"hey Cal." I'll spend the money in New York—to live off one's parasites!

Want to read your Brontës. I do nothing but read books on subjects I've just taught without sufficient preparation, and won't teach again. Only three more weeks teaching thank God—the load is light but the nervous burden heavy. Principally because when I ask an Essex student, if he doesn't think act 2 scene 4 in Lear has most of the play's struggles, the students start mutely thumbing their text. How do you teach, if the students don't do your work? So, in life, in all things.

I lie awake, think of Harriet (and fear I'll prove unworthy) in hope. All love to you both,
　　Cal

197. Elizabeth Hardwick to Robert Lowell[2]

[Barnard Hall, 3009 Broadway, New York, N.Y.]
Thursday, March 9 1972

Dear Cal: I am sitting here in my Barnard office waiting for Caro-lyn Kizer who has been on campus for a week or so & is coming to my class. She is just as memory will bring her back to you—large, exhausting, energetic, predatory, blonde, inclined to recitation of her "firsts"—first feminist, first n'west woman, etc. So . . . I haven't seen

---

1. That is, Hardwick herself.
2. Handwritten.

your Berryman.[1] Bob was to have brought it over last night when he came to dinner. Harriet sits on the floor barefoot at all my parties now, listening & talking. She sat through Marshall Cohen saying what John Rawls' theory of a just society was & how Stuart Hampshire hadn't understood it![2]

Later

Sunk after lunch with C. K. who was drunk on vodka & then ordered a huge Chinese meal & so she is even more expansive & expanded than an hour ago!

Harriet will be on her way and I am sure all will go well. I am absolutely worn down with work, people, so many large & small deadlines.

Home, very tired, have cystitis (kidney infection) which Dr. Anny's pills will have fixed up before this reaches you. Your Berryman epitaph here. I like it; it honors both of you. John was—I think—not a "character" that goes right down on the page; there aren't too many details actually. He wrote; he drank. It was good to read it.

I am pleased about H's chance to be with you. I have always kept that alive with her. You are her dear father. You say it is "hard and dark" for me. Something is "hard and dark" but not her trip to England. I do hope things will go well with your life there and that there will be some rest & peace accrued from Essex being behind you for another year. With love, Elizabeth P.S. Don't forget to reconfirm Qantas home flight.

198. Elizabeth Hardwick to Robert Lowell

[15 West 67th Street, New York, N.Y.]
March 17, 1972

Dear Cal: I got the tickets today. The return is left open—the rules about the youth fare—but they will paste it on when you get to the airport for her return. Please be sure to call Qantas to confirm the flight

1. "For John Berryman," New York Review of Books, April 6, 1972.

2. John Rawls, A Theory of Justice (1971); Stuart Hampshire, "A Special Supplement: A New Philosophy of the Just Society," New York Review of Books, February 24, 1972. See also Marshall Cohen, "A Theory of Justice by John Rawls: The Social Contract Explained and Defended," New York Times Book Review, July 16, 1972.

back. Harriet will have the return flight number in her case and you have it. I am sorry she gets there so late for you in the evening, but I'd hate for her to be up all night also. Either way has some distress. She seems pleased to be going and will meet you at the door as they come through the customs. Bob says there is only one door. She's very grown-up and will surprise you since she suddenly looks about twenty-one.

We are going to "Le Chagrin et la Pitié"[1] tomorrow, four and one-half hours of documentary about Occupied France. Everyone says it is fascinating. I've been explaining to Harriet who Mendès France and Pétain are. On the night she leaves I am going to *Othello* at the Metropolitan.[2] Englishmen are in town suddenly—Stuart again, Richard Wollheim. The elections, the primaries are very dispiriting.

I always feel I have a lot of gossip to tell you, but things never seem quite worth the "creative" effort, the typing. Gossip has to be awfully good to stand up to the page and I like it when it isn't so ravishing, just faintly interesting.

I seem to be absolutely snowed under by mails, bills, phone calls, duties of all kinds and so I can truthfully say that I'm glad you're not here! How did I ever do it? Right now I am getting ready to answer a courteous letter from the Polish Ambassador about rights to the Old Glory. I throw lots of Robert Lowell envelopes into the basket, and feel I've made a goal on the basket-ball court[3] and am full of self-satisfaction; however, I do answer those that absolutely need it and the ambassador is writing because I didn't answer so many times before. When one begins to have a little pleasure from his work then the duties pile up, mocking you. Remember Marianne Moore saying, "Not one has compassion!" Much love, dear, and have a good visit with Harriet. Send her back, even though I know you won't want to.

Lizzie

\So she will see you Sat. night at 10:30!/

---

1. Dir. Marcel Ophüls (1969).

2. Giuseppe Verdi, *Otello* (1887), dir. Franco Zeffirelli, Metropolitan Opera, March 25, 1972.

3. Lowell (speaking in Hardwick's voice): "'My sister, Margaret, a one-bounce basketball | player and all-Southern Center, came home | crying each night because of "Happy" Chandler, | the coach, and later Governor of Kentucky. | Our great big tall hillbilly idiots keep | Kentucky pre-eminent in basketball'" ("The Graduate" [*Summer* 12] 5–11, *Notebook69-1, -2*; [*Summer* 20], *Notebook70*; and [*Late Summer* 7], *For Lizzie and Harriet*).

199. *Robert Lowell to* Mrs. Robert Lowell

Milgate Park, Bearsted, Maidstone, Kent
Sunday March 19, [1972]

Dearest Lizzie—

This probably won't arrive before Harriet, but I have put in for a call to you this afternoon. Thanks for your lovely letter. Poor old Caroline Kizer, sharp as a thistle when we first met, now wallow, Seattle's Sonia who is appearing today, quite gay if sober?

Sorry about your kidney. I live on mutually antagonistic pills. Nothing much wrong though but teeth. I feel my mouth is falling to chalk but the dentist will find only one urgent hole.

Ivana to the doctors' surprise is already climbing the stairs. Because most of the water boiled on her middle it's hard for [her] to stand straight like a ramrod, or rather walk upright. She's to go back to school next month. In six years, she'll have to have another plastic operation (less bad than this one) because she will outgrow her surgery. All done in half a second!

I wait for Harriet like a bridegroom, or a sinner waiting the priest. The weather has been heavenly for nearly a week, so warm it's a relief to go in the windowless hall and cool from the heat. I know we'll have a happy time. She comes ~~with~~ in the awe of full spring.

I can't judge my Berryman. It looks denser in proofs. It's fiction in a way, but may not be far from the truth. Anecdotes about John could be made up for miles by his cronies and students, monotonous, wearying, like Dylan Thomas's, because the escapades even when they happened, lived on the imagination. I was on a program for him in London. It centered on a movie interview with Alvarez—John, close-up, just off drunkenness, mannered, booming, like an old fashioned star professor. His worst. I think of the young, beardless man, simple, brilliant, the enthusiast . . . buried somewhere with the older ~~man~~.

Goodbye, my love. One seems to have no age in this season—I don't mean I feel twenty.

Love,
Cal

200 . *Robert Lowell to* Mr. William Alfred

Milgate Park, Bearsted, Maidstone, Kent
[March 20, 1972]

Dear Bill:

Many thanks for your letter bringing home the loneliness of being here without you. I wonder if you got the poems on page 47 right.[1] They are meant to be about Caroline and me, in a sort of pastoral analogue.[2] If you took them [to] be about Elizabeth, they might be better . . . sadder and about more.—Food for thought, when I get a little more time.

On the Auden, I have been indiscreet. How could he stop speaking to me about a book he hadn't seen.[3] I think he's not a snubber and has never stopped talking to anyone, except Rudolf Bing even then I think it was the Met he stopped talking to. Pretty rough to me, unpleasant too to wait for his appearance in England . . . to be cut. So, about ten-thirty at night, a too ardent hour, I sent him this cable: "Dear Wystan— astounded by your insult to me with William Alfred." I didn't mean to get you involved, but without naming you it seemed impossible to rescue my charge from complete vagueness. Well, now it seems Auden has been behaving this way lately when drunk and then doesn't re- member. I probably should have done nothing, but sending the cable made my life sweeter. I apologize to you. Poor Wystan, still marvelous and calm in things he writes. I think it's desertion not marriage that cuts him. For some reason, though once warm, not intimate, friends,

---

1. "Frank has given me *The Dolphin* to read. It is beautifully made, every line won hard, and it is sad and comforting at one and the same time. But 1 and 2 on page 47 will tear Elizabeth apart, im- portant though I agree they are to the wholeness of the book. I have to say that" (William Alfred to Lowell, March 12, 1972, Texas). In "The Dolphin" manuscript, the poems on page 47 are "Fox Fur" and "*The Messiah*" (*Flight to New York* 1 and 2). (See poems on page 249.)

2. Lowell mistook the page number (see footnote immediately above), but he may have been thinking of the poems on page 46 of "The Dolphin" manuscript, "Before the Dawn of Woman" and "Dawn" (*Before Woman* 1 and 2). Cf. *The Dolphin: Two Versions, 1972–1973*.

3. William Alfred: "I met Auden for the first time at Kronenbergers. He looked a dirty snowman with a boys' wig on. He spoke of not speaking to you because of the book [*The Dolphin*]. When I said he sounded like God the Father, he gave me a tight smile. I write to warn you" (Alfred to Lowell, March 12, 1972, Texas; quoted in Ian Hamilton, *Robert Lowell: A Biography* p. 425). Robert Craft: "On January 11 [1972], Wystan Auden, rumpled face now resembling that of a shar-pei, and Chester Kallman came for dinner. Conversation was like old times [. . .] W.H.A. was indignant about 'Cal' Lowell's treatment of Elizabeth and Harriet in his last poems" (Craft, *An Improbable Life*, p. 306).

we have cooled more and more for the last four or five years. He has cooled, I haven't and would be glad to stop it.

I am going to do everything not to make my book offensive to Lizzie; the poems you name could go with\out/ too much loss, but others couldn't.

Love as ever,
Cal

Sonia Orwell is a few feet away waiting for a picnic; Harriet arrives Saturday.

47

FLIGHT TO NEW YORK

I. Fox-Fur

"I have recruited the services of good
old Farrar, Straus and Giroux, and even if
the taxi strike is off, their limousine is ours.
I met Ivan in a marvelous fox-fur coat,
his luxurious squalor...and gave you one...your grizzled
knob rising in the grizzled fox-fur collar... ;
But\In fear rejection and will stall...
You're not under inspection, just missed;
and you'll be pleased with Harriet:
in the last two months, she's stopped being a child,
she's a friend to Mom now, not an enemy,
except for my yelling, Dammit, brush your teeth.
She says that God is only a great man, another
a ape with grizzled sideburns in a cage."

2. The Messiah

"I love you so, Darling, there's black void,
as black as night without you. I long to see
your face and hear your voice and take your hand,
laugh with you, gossip and catch up...or down.
Will you go with me to The Messiah,
on December 17th, a Thursday,
and drink at the Russian Tearoom afterward?   C9 T
I am going out for the tickets this morning,
your dear, longed-for presence going with me.
I wait for your letters, tremble when I get none,
more when I do. Nothing new to say;
I've not been feeling too well; it will have passed
by the time this letter arrives---just cold and nausea;
when I mail this and get The Messiah tickets, I'll rest."

"Fox Fur" and "*The Messiah*" [*Flight to New York* 1 and 2], "The Dolphin" manuscript, p. 47, composed and revised between late 1970 and January 1972.[1]

---

1. Compare "The Messiah" 1-4 with "In the Mail" 8-10, *The Dolphin*; see footnote 2 on page 293.

201. Robert Lowell to Christopher Ricks

Milgate Park, Bearsted, Maidstone, Kent—phone Maid. 38028

March 21, 1972

Dear Christopher:

My book problems are complicated and I would like to ask your advice. My new book is a small one, some eighty poems in the meter of Notebook—the story of changing marriages, not a malice or sensation ~~book~~, far from it, but necessarily, according to my peculiar talent, \very/ personal. Lizzie is naturally very much against it. I am considering publication in about a year; it needn't be published, but I feel fully clogged by the possibility \of not/. ~~My~~ \This/ awkward exposition shows my painful embarrassment.

I have two other books that are re-arrangement and rewriting 1) *Notebook*, now about 300 poems, ~~and~~ is called *History*, ~~going~~ through the ages from the reptiles to 1970. It takes me a hundred poems or so to get to Verdun, so the bulk of *History* is in my lifetime, ~~often~~ \sometimes/ heavily autobiographical—The Twenties are mostly seen as my adolescence. 2) \A/ short book, 60 poems, called For Lizzie and Harriet, which also comes from Notebook and is about my marriage. ~~The~~ \My/ three books are related, though not in sequence exactly. The new one, The Dolphin, would come out by itself; the other two would come out as separate books under one cover. All ~~would~~ \to/ be published at the same time.

I know so much published revision is silly, but the confusions of my composition, looking for my form etc. made it necessary. I am still making small changes on a fairly clear manuscript, and almost feel that I have made the improvements with \in/ my powers and gifts. Afterwards, something new, but not before I get ~~this~~ \my/ great load published.

I wonder if we could confer sometime toward the end of April? \We'd love to have you stay here. / You see how all this involves your article.[1]

Affectionately,

Cal

---

1. "The Poet Robert Lowell—Seen by Christopher Ricks," *Listener* (21 June 1973).

202. Elizabeth Bishop to Robert Lowell

[60 Brattle Street, Cambridge, Mass.]
March 21st, 1972

Dearest Cal:

I've been trying to write you this letter for weeks now, ever since Frank & I spent an evening when he first got back, reading and discussing THE DOLPHIN. I've read it many times since then & we've discussed it some more. Please believe that I think it is wonderful poetry. It seems to me far and away better than the NOTEBOOKS; every 14 lines have some marvels of image and expression, and also they are all much *clearer*. They affect me immediately and profoundly, and I'm pretty sure I understand them all perfectly. (Except for a few lines I may ask you about.) I've just decided to write this letter in 2 parts—the one big technical problem that bothers me I'll put on another sheet—it and some unimportant details have nothing to do with what I'm going to try to say here. It's hell to write this, so please first do believe I think DOLPHIN is magnificent poetry. It is also honest poetry—*almost*. You probably know already what my reactions are. I have one tremendous and awful BUT.

If you were any other poet I can think of I certainly wouldn't attempt to say anything at all; I wouldn't think it was worth it. But because it is you, and a great poem (I've never used the word "great" before, that I remember), and I love you a lot—I feel I must tell you what I really think. There are several reasons for this—some are worldly ones, and therefore secondary (& strange to say, they seem to be the ones Bill is most concerned about—we discussed it last night) but the primary reason is because I love you so much I can't bear to have you publish something that I regret and that you might live to regret, too. The worldly part of it is that it—the poem—parts of it—may well be taken up and used against you by all the wrong people—who are just waiting in the wings to attack you. One shouldn't consider them, perhaps. But it seems wrong to play right into their hands, too.

(Don't be alarmed. I'm not talking about the whole poem—just one aspect of it.)

Here is a quotation from dear little Hardy that I copied out years ago—long before DOLPHIN, or even the *Notebooks*, were thought of. It's from a letter written in 1911, referring to "an abuse which was said to have occurred—that of publishing details of a lately deceased man's life under the guise of a novel, with assurances of truth scattered in the newspapers." (Not exactly the same situation as DOLPHIN, but fairly close.)

"What should certainly be protested against, in cases where there is no authorization, is the mixing of fact and fiction in unknown proportions. Infinite mischief would lie in that. If any statements in the dress of fiction are covertly hinted to be fact, all must be fact, and nothing else but fact, for obvious reasons. The power of getting lies believed about people through that channel after they are dead, by stirring in a few truths, is a horror to contemplate."[1]

I'm sure my point is only too plain . . . Lizzie is not dead, etc.— but there is a "mixture of fact & fiction," and you have *changed* her letters. That is "infinite mischief," I think. The first one, page 10, is so shocking—well, I don't know what to say.[2] And page 47[3] . . . and a few after that. One can use one's life as material—one does, anyway—but these letters—aren't you violating a trust? IF you were given permission—IF you hadn't changed them . . . etc. But *art just isn't worth that much*. I keep remembering Hopkins' marvelous letter to Bridges about the idea of a "gentleman" being the highest thing ever conceived—higher than a "Christian" even, certainly than a poet.[4] It is not being "gentle" to use personal, tragic, anguished letters that way—it's cruel.

---

1. Thomas Hardy to James Douglas, November 10, 1912, published in the *Daily News* (November 15, 1912); quoted in Florence Emily Hardy, *The Life of Thomas Hardy, 1840–1928* (1962), pp. 358–59.

2. "From My Wife" [*The Farther Shore* 1], "The Dolphin" manuscript; see poem on page 260. Cf. "Voices" [*Hospital* II], *The Dolphin*.

3. "Fox Fur" and "*The Messiah*" [*Flight to New York* 1 and 2], "The Dolphin" manuscript, the same poems that William Alfred objected to in his letter of March 12, 1972, to Lowell; see poems on page 249.

4. Hopkins: "This is the chastity of mind which seems to lie at the very heart and be the parent of all other good, the seeing at once what is best, the holding to that, and the not allowing anything else whatever to be even heard playing the contrary. Christ's life and character are such an appeal to all the world's imagination, but there is one insight St. Paul gives us of it which is very secret and seems to me more touching and constraining than everything else [. . .] It is this holding of himself back, and not snatching at the truest and highest good, the good that was his right, nay his possession from a past eternity in his other nature, his own being and self, which seems to me the root of all his holiness and the imitation of this the root of all moral good in other men. I agree then, and vehemently, that a gentleman, if there is such a thing on earth, is in the position to despise the poet, were he Dante or Shakespeare, and the painter, were he Angelo

I feel fairly sure that what I'm saying (so badly) won't influence you very much; you'll feel sad that I feel this way, but go on with your work & publication just the same. I also think that the thing *could* be done, somehow—the letters used and the conflict presented as forcefully, or almost, without *changing* them, or loading the dice so against E. \but you're a good enough poet to write *anything*—get around anything—after all—/ It would mean a great deal of work, of course—and perhaps you feel it is impossible, that they must stay as written. It makes me feel perfectly awful, to tell the truth—I feel sick for *you*. I don't want you to appear in that light, to anyone—E, C,—me—your public! And most of all, not to yourself.

I wish I had here *another* quotation—James wrote a marvelous letter to someone about a *roman à clef* by Vernon Lee—but I can't find it without going to the bowels of Widener, I suppose . . . His feelings on the subject were much stronger than mine, even.[1] In general, I deplore the "confessional"—however, when you wrote LIFE STUDIES perhaps it was a necessary movement, and it helped make poetry more real, fresh and immediate. But now—ye gods—anything goes, and I am so sick of poems about the students' mothers & fathers and sex-lives and so on. All that *can* be done—but at the same time one surely

---

or Apelles, for anything in him that shewed him *not* to be a gentleman [. . .] The quality of a gentleman is so very fine a thing that it seems to me one should not be at all hasty in concluding that one possesses it. [. . .] By and by if the English race had done nothing else, yet if they left the world the notion of a gentleman, they would have done a great service to mankind. As a fact poets and men of art are, I am sorry to say, by no means necessarily or commonly gentlemen" (Gerard Manley Hopkins to Robert Bridges, February 3, 1883, *The Letters of Gerard Manley Hopkins to Robert Bridges*, ed. Claude Colleer Abbott (1935), pp. 175–76). Quoted in Bishop's posthumously published "Efforts of Affection: A Memoir of Marianne Moore," *Collected Prose*, ed. Robert Giroux (1984).

1. Henry James: "Receive from me (apropos of extraordinary women) a word of warning about Vernon Lee. I hope you won't throw yourselves into her arms—and I am sorry you offered to go and see her (after she wrote to you) first. My reasons are several, and too complicated, some of them, to go into; but one of them is that she has lately, as I am told (in a volume of tales called *Vanitas*, which I haven't read), directed a kind of satire of a flagrant and markedly 'saucy' kind at me (!!)—exactly the sort of thing she has repeatedly done to others (her books—fiction—are a tissue of personalities of the hideous roman-à-clef kind), and particularly impudent and blackguardedly sort of thing to do to a friend and one who has treated her with such particular consideration as I have" (Henry James to William James, January 20 [1893]; Henry James, *Letters*, vol. 3, *1883–1895*, ed. Leon Edel [1980], p. 402). See Leon Edel, *Henry James: The Middle Years*, *1882–1895* (1962), pp. 332–35, which quotes from the letter and is likely the source of Bishop's knowledge of the incident.

should have a feeling that one can trust the writer—not to distort, tell lies, etc.

The letters, as you have used them, present fearful problems: what's true, what isn't; how one can bear to witness such suffering and yet not know how much of it one *needn't* suffer with, how much has been "made up," and so on.

I don't give a damn what someone like Mailer writes about his wives & marriages [—] I just hate the level we seem to live and think and feel on at present—but I DO give a damn what you write! (Or Dickey or Mary . . . !) They don't count, in the long run. This counts and I can't bear to have anything you write tell—perhaps—what we're really like in 1972 . . . perhaps it's as simple as that. But are we? Well—I mustn't ramble on any more. I've thought about it all I can and can't reach any more lucid conclusions, I'm afraid.

Now the absurd. Will you do me a great favor and tell me how much you earned for a half-term, or one term I guess it is, when you left Harvard? They have asked me to come back—when I was so sick I didn't think it through very well—for the $10,000. I got last year, & last fall, and a "slight raise." (This may be $500. I learned from Mr. Blumfield.[1]) Of course I shd. have insisted on some sort of definite contract then and there but I didn't even think of it until later. I have rented this place for a year and another year—but I must plan ahead and I am getting fearfully old and have to think of what I'm going to do in the future years, where I'm going to live, etc. At present I'm afraid even to get a cold because I have no hospital protection—thank god I did have when I was sick. The Woman's outfit—whatever it is here—has been after me, too—asking me if I am getting the same salary that you got—and I don't know. This sounds very crass—but it's true I could earn more at other places—but prefer to stay here if I can . . . but must have some sort of definite contract, obviously. Forgive my sordidness (as Marianne wd. call it).

I had a St. Patrick's Day dinner for Bill—a few days late—and Octavio Paz, etc—very nice. We dine off the ping-pong table . . . Now I have to go to the dentist and I'll send this without thinking. Otherwise I'll never send it.

DOLPHIN is marvelous—no doubt about that—I'll write you all

---

1. Thus, for Bloomfield.

the things I like sometime!—I hope all goes well with you, and Caroline, and the little daughters, and the infant son—

With much love,
Elizabeth

[Enclosed:]
(Later—this is all pretty silly. The only good point is on page 2.)

1. These will be very petty comments—but things that held me up a bit when reading or possibly one or two small mistakes—Frank & I have argued a lot about most of them!

p.6. "machismo" is accurate for the peacock,[1] of course—but it is such an over-worked word at present . . . a fad-word, here, at least. I thought it useful when I 1st learned it, in Brazil, about 20 yrs ago; right now I can't bear it.

p.10. 2. I find the *lion* (Torcello. I remember it, too) confusing, with C's poodle (that little white dog?) in the Carpaccio, in *Venice*.—and can't make out which one is in the snapshot (possibly). I don't think you can mean "tealeaf" color which would be almost black after all[2]—or is just "strongtea color" implied? I'm fiddling & quibbling—but I am so fond of the images in this one I want to get them right—

p.12. 1. "count"—must mean *realize*? or "are worth"?—no, "realize"? or both (as F wd. say, because he loves ambiguities)[3]?

p.13. 3. "no friend to write to . . ."[4] Oh dear, Cal! The poem be-

1. Lowell: "Nothing but dung of the marsh, the moan of cows, | the machismo of the peacock" ("Oxford" [*Redcliffe Square* 3] 3–4, "The Dolphin" manuscript). Revised to read "nothing but the soft of the marsh, the moan of cows, | the rooster-peacock" ("Oxford" [*Redcliffe Square* 4] 3–4, *The Dolphin*).

2. Lowell: "The saint and animal | swim Carpaccio's tealeaf color" ("Old Snapshot and Carpaccio" [*The Farther Shore* 2] 9–10, "The Dolphin" manuscript). Revised to read "The courtesans and lions | swim in Carpaccio's brewing tealeaf color" ("Old Snapshot from Venice 1952" [*Hospital II* 3] 9–10, *The Dolphin*).

3. Lowell: "But surely it cuts the toll more than men count—" ("Flashback to Washington Square 1966" [*Caroline* 1] 12, "The Dolphin" manuscript). Revised to read "though we earn less credit than we burn" ("Flashback to Washington Square 1966" [*Caroline* 1] 12, *The Dolphin*).

4. Lowell: "I have no friend to write to . . . I love you" ("July-August" [*Caroline* 3] 13, "The Dolphin" manuscript). Revised to read "I have no one to stamp my letters . . . I love you" ("July-August"

ing remarkable for its carefulness about the emotions, and its courage, etc.—I can't quite see this—

4. "thump"—I wonder if C likes this . . . but because of *carpeted* maybe the *thumps* are all right . . .[1]

p[.]14—"vibrance"? I think you made it up—but suppose it works all right—[2]

15. 1. I'd like a comma, after cows I think—because I tend to see the "huddle" of cows & leaves all together—one lump—but maybe I'm supposed to?[3] Not just the cows under the autumn-leaved tree or trees?

17. the "his" in the last line . . . one has to think & think & think—and then the genders don't seem to come out right . . .[4]

23. 5. (Mermaid) I can't bear "grapple in the aspic of your flesh"[5]—Frank & I have argued at length about this . . . It's supposed to be violent and jealousy is a hideous emotion, etc.—but aspic is a *cold* jelly—all right—but "grapple *in*" well, it is supposed to be horrible, too, perhaps. Frank is so totally bewitched that he even argued for an ambiguity—"aspic" suggesting also Cleopatra's colloquial word for "asp." Well, I pointed out to him that this isn't possible—an

---

[*Caroline* 3] 13, *The Dolphin*). Cf. Hardwick to Mary McCarthy, July 1, 1970: "He made a plaintive remark: 'I'd write you and Harriet but I can't find any stamps since I left Oxford.'"

1. Lowell: "Up the carpeted stairway, your shoes thump," ("Morning Blue" [*Caroline* 4] 9, "The Dolphin" manuscript). Revised to read "Up the carpeted stairway, your shoes clack" ("Morning Blue" [*Caroline* 5] 9, *The Dolphin*).

2. Lowell: "a vibrance in the news and fat of my legs" ("Summer Between Terms" 7, "The Dolphin" manuscript). The line was deleted; cf. *Summer Between Terms* 2, *The Dolphin*. OED: No entry for vibrance in the 1933 edition but an entry from the 1993 supplement "vibrance n. = vibrancy n." gives two examples in print before 1972, including "1934 in Webster *Dict.*" ("vibrance, n." OED Online. March 2016. http://www.oed.com/view/Entry/243291?redirectedFrom=vibrance (accessed March 28, 2016).

3. Lowell: "\Here/ a huddle of shivering cows and feverish leaves | \burying old lumber without truce./" (*Fall Weekend at* Milgate [1] 11–12, "The Dolphin" manuscript). Revised to read "I watch a feverish huddle of shivering cows; | you sit making a fishspine from a chestnut leaf" (*Fall Weekend at* Milgate [1] 11–12, *The Dolphin*).

4. Lowell: "love vanquished by his mysterious carelessness." ("'I Was Playing Records,'" 14, "The Dolphin" manuscript; cf. "Records," 14, *The Dolphin*.)

5. Lowell: "I've wondered who would see and date you next, | and grapple in the aspic of your flesh" (*Mermaid* [5] 1–2, "The Dolphin" manuscript). Revised to read "One wondered who would see and date you next, | and grapple for the danger of your hand" (*Mermaid* [5] 1–2, *The Dolphin*).

"ambiguity" has to work equally well, or at least work, both ways . . . and you can't "grapple in" a tiny black snake, but I couldn't convince him.[1] Perhaps I'm just prejudiced from the feminine point of view, having made eggs in aspic, etc etc.—I feel sure you'll never change this, but it does make me feel sick.

31. I am pretty sure it's Ernest Thompson Seton—he used to be my favorite author. (I saw "Rolf in the Woods" at the Coop—so I'll check on it.)[2]

33. "thirty thousand"—(Frank says it was originally forty . . .)[3] This is the sum Fitzgerald needed annually, I remember.[4] But oh dear, it reminds me of that unfortunate remark of Mary's in an interview a few years back "Of course we're all much richer now."[5] Well, many of us aren't and I feel such sums not only tell against the writer of the letter but wd. be held against *you*.— Of course in time they'll prob-

---

1. Cf. Lowell: "Rough Slitherer in ~~the~~ your grotto of haphazard" (*Mermaid* [5] 10, "The Dolphin" manuscript). "Rough Slitherer" may have suggested the "asp" in "aspic" to Bidart's ear.

2. Lowell: "What ~~were~~ was the lessons of the wolverine, | the Canada of Earnest Seton Thompson" ("Wolverine" [*More London Winter* 1] 1–2, "The Dolphin" manuscript). The poem was removed from *The Dolphin* and added to *History* as "Wolverine, 1927." See also Ernest Thompson Seton, *Rolf in the Woods* (1911).

3. Lowell: "'We can't swing New York on less than thirty thousand,'" ("Transatlantic Call" 1, "The Dolphin" manuscript). Revised to read *"We can't swing New York on Harry Truman incomes—"* ("During a Transatlantic Call" 1, *The Dolphin*). Hardwick to Lowell, June 23, 1970: "next year if you are leaving us or if I am leaving you I will have to have $20,000. I can't get by on less that first year and cannot even pay the taxes on that." ($20,000 in June 1970 is approximately $130,296 in 2019 dollars [CPI].)

4. F. Scott Fitzgerald, "How to Live on $36,000 a Year," *Saturday Evening Post*, April 5, 1924; Thomas Caldecott Chubb: "In a short career, even now amounting to only five years, Scott Fitzgerald has already found time to do a great many things [. . .] He has told,—and presumably based the telling on his own experience,—how it is possible to live on $30,000 a year" ("Bagdad-on-Subway," *Forum* 74, no. 2 [August 1925]). Fitzgerald's 1924 figure of $36,000 is approximately $532,160 in 2019 dollars; Lowell's 1972 figure of $30,000 is approximately $184,508 in 2019 dollars (CPI).

5. Mary McCarthy: "But to speak of my doubts about the radicalism of the Thirties, what did we accomplish? Almost nothing that I can see [. . .] Some of us (you and me included) were OK on [Senator Joseph] McCarthy, but again history took care of that, and I would not like to claim that our disputes with [Sidney] Hook and others had any influence on events. Meanwhile, like most American writers, professors and editors, we were getting richer. And less revolutionary. Not just because we had more money, but because we were getting older, and because, according to our analysis, it was not 'a revolutionary situation'" (Philip Rahv, "The Editor Interviews Mary McCarthy," *Modern Occasions* 1, no. 1 [Fall 1970], p. 22).

ably seem absurdly small, too, but they don't now— But perhaps it is *meant* just to tell against the correspondent . . . it certainly does, to me, anyway. But it gives the sonnet— so moving otherwise—a sort of Elizabeth-Taylor-whine air . . .

39. Really *palate?*[1] I always thought that meant the small piece of flesh that hangs downaway at the back of the throat—the OED says it can be the "roof = etc of the mouth" so maybe it's all right—[2]

Somewhere—I can't find it right now—you wrote "with my fresh wife"—and that seemed just too much, somehow—the word "fresh," again, had a sort of Hollywood or Keith Botsford feeling that I'm sure you didn't intend—you've avoided it almost completely.[3]

2. Well, I could go on, of course. Most of these are trivialities & some I forgot to mark as I read through the book—many times, now. You know I am quite fiendish about trivialities, however . . . But right now they don't seem worth it. I am having trouble trying to decide how to divide this letter, but I think I'll put all my technical remarks on these pages. *This is the one big criticism I'd make*:

As far as the *story* goes—of course you haven't stuck exactly to the facts, & didn't have to. But starting about page 44, I find things a little confusing. Page 44 is titled LEAVING AMERICA FOR ENGLAND—obviously, about the idea of that. Then 47, FLIGHT TO NEW YORK. (I wonder if "Flight" is the right word here? (even

---

1. Lowell: "'My mother really learned to loathe babies, | she loved to lick the palate of her Peke, | as if her tongue were trying a liqueur . . . | What I ~~am saying~~ \say/ should go into your *Notebook*: | I'd rather ~~have~~ my children on morphine than religion'" (*Artist's Model* [3] 1–5, "The Dolphin" manuscript). Revised to read "'My cousin really learned to loathe babies, | she loved to lick the palate of her Peke | as if her tongue were trying a liqueur—| what I say should go into your *Notebook*. . . . | I'd rather dose children on morphine than the churches'" (*Artist's Model* [2] 1-5, *The Dolphin*).
2. OED: "Palate 1. The roof of the mouth (in man and vertebrates)" ("palate, n. and adj." *Oxford English Dictionary* Vol. VII).
3. Lowell: "I sit with my fresh wife, children, house and sky—" ("Later Week at *Milgate*" [*Burden* 7] 12, "The Dolphin" manuscript). Revised to read "I sit with my staring wife, children . . . the dour Kent sky" ("Late Summer at *Milgate*" [*Marriage* 10] 12, *The Dolphin*). Cf. Lowell's use of "unfresh" in "'I despair of letters . . .'" [*The Burden* 6] 13 in "The Dolphin" manuscript, and in "Letter" [*Marriage* 8] 13, *The Dolphin*).

if you do fly.) Then New York, and Christmas. "swims the true shark, the shadow of departure."[1] That's all about that. (The N Y poems in themselves are *wonderful* . . .) (Can the line about the "play about the fall of Japan" *possibly* be true.?!)[2] But after the "shadow of departure" comes BURDEN—and the baby is on the way. This seems to me a bit too sudden—there is no actual return to England—and the word BURDEN and then the question "Have we got a child?" sounds almost a bit Victorian—melodramatic.[3] This is the only place where the "plot" seems awkward to me, and *I* can fill it in of course—I think it might baffle most readers—

The change, decision, or whatever happens between page 51 & 52 seems too sudden—after the prolongation of all the first sections, the agonies of indecision, etc.—(wonderful atmosphere of life's *stalling* ways . . .)[4]

You've left out E's trip to London?—that's not needed perhaps for the plot—but it might help soften your telling of it?—but I somehow think you need to get yourself back to England *before* the baby appears like that. (Frank took violent exception to the word bastard, I don't know why—I think it's a good old word and even find it appealing & touching. He must have worse associations with it than I have.)

---

1. From "Christmas 1970" [*Flight to New York* 10] 14, "The Dolphin" manuscript; cf. "Christmas" [*Flight to New York* 12] 14, *The Dolphin*.

2. Lowell: "A ~~thick~~ \heavy/ book, sunrise-red from Lizzie, | with, 'Why don't you try to lose yourself | and write a play about the fall of Japan?'" ("Christmas 1970" [*Flight to New York* 10] 5–7, "The Dolphin" manuscript); cf. "Christmas" [*Flight to New York* 12] 5–7, *The Dolphin*.

3. Lowell: "Have we got a child . . . | Our bastard, easily fathered, hard to name?" ("Knowing" [*Burden* 1] 6–7, "The Dolphin" manuscript). Revised to read "We have our child, | our bastard, easily fathered, hard to name . . ." ("Knowing" [*Marriage* 5] 6–7, *The Dolphin*).

4. In "The Dolphin" manuscript, the protagonist learns that the Caroline character is expecting a child after his return from New York, and after his decision to leave the Lizzie character for Caroline. For the published version of *The Dolphin*, Lowell revised the order of the poems away from the actual chronology of events, fictionalizing them. He moved poems about Sheridan's conception and birth to a sequence titled *Marriage*, which occurs before *Flight to New York*. The visit to New York takes place a full year after his birth, and after the protagonist and the Caroline character have married.

```
THE FARTHER SHORE

   1. From my Wife

"What a record year, even for us---
 last March, we hoped you'd manage by yourself,
 you were the true you; now finally
 your clowning makes us want to vomit---you bore,         ,
 bore, bore the friends who want to keep your image  WISHED TO SAVE
 from your genteel, disgraceful hospital.   THIS
 You tease the sick as if they were your friends;
 your suit lazied to grease. And that new woman---  is
 when I hear her name, I have to laugh.
 You have left two houses, two thousand books,
 a workbarn by the ocean, and a woman SLAVE
TO who kneels and waits on you hand and foot---  upon (s 767/
 tell us why in the name of Jesus. Why
 are you clinging here so foolishly from us?"   there
                          /

   2. Old Family Snapshot and Carpaccio

 From the salt age, yes from the salt age,
 courtesans, Christians fill the barnyard close;
 that silly swelled tree is a spook with a skull for a cap.
 Carpaccio's Venice was wide as the world,  was
 Jerome and his lion scoot to work unfeared...  LOPED
 In Torcello, the lion snapped behind you,    Keeps his poodled
 venti anni fa, still peodles his hair---
 wherever you moved your snapshot, he has moved, I
 twenty years. The saint and animal   FOR
 swim Carpaccio's tealeaf color. Was he
 the first in the trade of painting to tell tales?..  [3 dots after question mark]
 You are making Boston in the early A.M.,
 dropping Harriet at camp, old love,
 eternity, us you, mothbitten time.
                  you and us,
                 YOU AND US,
```

"From my Wife" and "Old Snapshot and Carpaccio" [*The Farther Shore* 1 and 2], "The Dolphin" manuscript, p. 10; composed and revised between 1970 and January 1972.[1]

203. *Robert Lowell to Elizabeth Bishop*

[Milgate Park, Bearsted, Maidstone, Kent]
March 28, 1972

Dearest Elizabeth—

Let me write you right away . . . thoughtlessly, casually, my first scattered impressions—my thanks. The smaller things. Most of your

---

1. For Lowell's substitution of "slave" for "woman" in "From my Wife" [*The Farther Shore* 1], cf. Hardwick: "We are as good and useful as men. Equality is self-evident. We do not want to be slaves or married to slaves—but this is the condition of so much of the suffering world. When that happens, human beings can only cling together, huddling under the blanket" ("The Ties Women Cannot Shake and Have," *Vogue*, June 1, 1971, p. 87).

~~questions~~ \reservations/ seem likely to [be] right and useful. I can't tell from a quick reading and haven't checked your remarks with my lines. I think they will help; please give me more. I am talking about your brief line to line objections. 2) The transition back to London is a hard problem maybe. I'd like to do [it] in two or preferably one sonnet. The pregnancy isn't meant to come on \New York/, tho it was only a month later, i.e. \when/ we knew or suspected. It's [a] problem of finding inspiration for a link, I think ~~I can~~.

Now Lizzie's letters? I did \not/ see them as slander, but as sympathetic, tho necessarily awful for her to read. She is the poignance of the book, tho that hardly makes it kinder to her. I could say the letters are cut, doctored part fiction; \I/ thought of it (I attribute things to Lizzie I made up, or that were said by someone else. I combed out abuse, hysteria, repetition.[)] The trouble is the letters make the book, I think, at least they make Lizzie real beyond my invention. I took out the worst things written against me, so as not to give myself a case and seem self-pitying. Or maybe I didn't want to author them. I promise I'll do what I can to answer your piercing ~~objections~~ \thoughts/. I've been thinking of course these things for years almost. It's oddly enough a technical problem as well as a gentleman's problem. How can the story be told at all without the letters? I'll put my heart to it. I can't bear not to publish Dolphin in good form. I am in no hurry for time, and would love to spend the summer working if the muse lets me.

Salary is complicated. I got $9500, I think eventually at my highest. After three years, I was given rooms at Quincy House free for two or three days a week[,] the expense of commuting. I think all salaries must be higher now. Every two or three years I got a little $500 raise. I may have started at $8500. Also I wasn't around when I was teaching. I'm sure you will get more. Maybe the best thing is to have someone practical and forceful to handle it for you, but even lambs like us can kick \the bucket over/.

Harriet is with us now, and tho the weather is now suddenly wintry, think it is May with us.

I feel like Bridges getting one of Hopkins's letters, as disturbed as I am grateful.

Oh, I forgot. If you can get the revised Notebook from Frank, particularly the section For Lizzie and Harriet, but also the latter part of History, you might get a slightly different slant on the meaning of Dolphin. The three books are one heap, one binding, so to speak, though not one book.

All my love,
Cal

204. *Robert Lowell to* Miss Harriet Lowell

Milgate Park, Bearsted, Maidstone, Kent
[April 2, 1972]
Easter, 5 P.M.

Darling Harriet:

I meant to write you as soon as I got home, but my hand moves slowly, and my mind slower. It's gray at Milgate, though the pastures are green, and more things have leafed out since you left four days ago. Two fields have even mysteriously managed to mow themselves.

If you've slept as much as I today, you hardly need [to] go to bed at all tonight.

I can't write how much we, I, loved your visit. I think maybe you are all you ever were only grown up (almost). You are all I asked. Do fathers and even the most brainy mothers have blind eyes? You mustn't trust them. I am beginning to ramble. . . . (The four dots are Frank Bidart punctuation)[.] When you hunt chocolate Easter eggs, you can find them by putting your ear to the ground and listening for them to cackle like chickens.

I love you for liking both your father and mother—(another Bidart punctuation) that\'s/ why they are such extraordinarily normal, healthy and modest people[1]—(B. punctuation) and for never talking too much except on women and politics, particularly your theories on socialism.

Loved your being with me.
Daddy

---

1. Lowell: "She is normal and good because she had normal and good | parents" ("In the Mail," 6–7, *The Dolphin*); see footnote 2 on page 293. Cf. also Frank Bidart to Lowell, June 4, 1970; Hardwick to Lowell, OCT 16 PM 5.13 [1970]; and Hardwick to Lowell [no date summer 1972].

205. *Robert Lowell to* Mrs. Robert Lowell

Milgate Park, Bearsted, Maidstone, Kent
Easter Monday, [April 3, 1972]

Dearest Lizzie:

The trip, the visit, is sadly over. I am more happy than I can say to have seen Harriet in bloom, all that has been indicated for many years, all I hoped. Oddly, though now almost grown-up, she reminds me more of how she looked four or more years ago. Thinness? Or something in the character? Joy, amusement, awe and pride.

I'd like to come over for a week near the end of May. Isn't June tropical? I'd like to avoid that. Each year I grow less tolerant to heat. Talking about weather, we had England's worst weather during the whole of Harriet's stay. Today it's beautiful, as it was the day before she arrived. People are pouring in, Peter and Eleanor[1] tomorrow; the Brookses next week.

Thank you for so \lovingly/ sending Harriet.

Love,
Cal

206. *Robert Lowell to Elizabeth Bishop*

[Milgate Park, Bearsted, Maidstone, Kent]
Easter Tuesday, [April 4], 1972

Dearest Elizabeth:

Harriet has come and gone, and I'm left in a mood of wonder, so well she carried off what had to be difficult, impossible I almost thought. We talked more freely than we ever have (this is age only partly\)/ yet not too much, and no sides had to be taken except humorously. And things went well with Caroline, Harriet's brother and the other children. \A m/oment not to come again, for there never can be such a moment again, but it is a promise of future happiness.

Let me \re/phrase for myself your moral objections. It's the revelation (with documents?) of a wife wanting her husband not to leave her, and who \does/ leave her. That's the trouble, not the mixture of

---

1. Taylor.

truth and fiction. Fiction—no one would object if \I/ said Lizzie was wearing a purple and red dress, when it was yellow. Actually my versions of her letters are true enough, only softer and drastically cut. The original is heartbreaking, but interminable.

I thought of doing this. It's just a sketch, because I've really only had yesterday to read through *The Dolphin*, and scribble and sketch. *First*, the entire "Burden" section should come after "Sickday," after "Burden" come "Leaving America," and "Lost Fish," then all the "To New York" (new title).[1] This leaves rough edges, and falsifies the actual time sequence, but gets rid of the rather callous happy ending, and softens E's role in the New York group—she seems rather serenely gracious (I overstate) about my visit after the birth. I can go this far, but won't bring any post facto business about the baby into the New York section. *Two*, I take your moral objections are confined to the letters, and not to all of them. Several can be handled and perhaps improved by using some of the lines in italics, and giving the rest, somewhat changed, to me. *From my Wife* would be called "Voice."[2] Other poems do not need change maybe. "Fox Fur" and "The Messiah" become gentler when the reader assumes the child is born.

This is a sketch and not exactly what I'll do. The problem of making the poem unwounding is impossible, still I think it can be made noticeably milder without losing its life. It might be much better, for who can want to savage a thing. How can I want to hurt? Hurt Lizzie and Harriet, their loving memory? Working my poem out is a must somehow, not avoidable even though \I/ fail—as I must partially.

What are your plans? I hope to come to New York for a week at the end of May. I wish I could talk to you face to face about this and everything. The cloud of winter seems to have lifted.

Love,

Cal

---

1. The poems in *Burden* [1-10] (the penultimate sequence in "The Dolphin" manuscript) were revised and added to a sequence newly titled *Marriage* [1-16] (*The Dolphin*); "Sickday" [~~Sickday~~ *Leaving America for England* 3] was retitled "Sick" [*Leaving America for England* 5]. The idea to change the title of *Flight to New York* [1-10] in "The Dolphin" manuscript to *To New York* did not last; Lowell went back to *Flight to New York* [1-12] for the sequence title when he published *The Dolphin*.

2. "From My Wife" [*The Farther Shore* 1] in "The Dolphin" manuscript was rewritten as "Voices" [*Hospital II* 1] in *The Dolphin*.

207. Elizabeth Hardwick to Robert Lowell

[15 West 67th Street, New York, N.Y.]
April 9, 1972

Dear Cal: Harriet had a nice visit and came home in good shape, slept for a couple of days almost and now is back at school. New York is alive, sunny chill today, rainy warmth tomorrow. Last week was under the unbearable cloud of the death of Jack's son, Peter, in an automobile accident.[1] Jack's life has been built upon catastrophic losses in childhood, and now this. I believe he is all right, but I worry about him. He hadn't been doing the distressing drinking for sometime and so that is a help—or I hope it is.

One thing I wanted to say to you—rather difficult, but I will try. It seems that agitation about your book has come up again among your friends. I haven't seen any of the poems based on my letters and I know nothing about the book,[2] but I feel a little sad by the vigor of the defense of me and even somewhat bewildered by the terms of it as I understand it. I don't know what you should or should not do, but it seems to me that you have been writing for thirty years and publishing for nearly the same number. The matter of your work is yours entirely and I don't think you have it in your power to "hurt" me. I suppose that is something I control since the feelings are mine and perhaps my feelings are not as simple as my friends think. I mean that I cannot see what harm can come to me from a poem by you. Why should I care? The credit or discredit is entirely yours. I don't see any of this as having anything to do with me in the long run. I just wanted to "go on record" in this. It is certainly a wearisome business by now and I feel strongly that you should do what you wish. I went to Princeton last week with Hannah to hear Nathalie Sarraute. She, N.S., made a deep impression of the most exhilarating kind on me. Very handsome, elegant English, utterly strange and intense ideas of the novel. "You see, I do not believe in zese characters. Zee miser?[3] He ees impossible!

---

1. See John Thompson to Robert Lowell, May 24 [1972], Robert Lowell Papers, HRC.

2. Hardwick to Ian Hamilton, that before the publication of *The Dolphin* in 1973: "All I knew, and this from everyone visiting at Milgate, was that he was using my letters" (Elizabeth Hardwick Papers, HRC); see also Hardwick's remarks in footnote 1 on page 366 (Lowell to Giroux, July 26, 1973).

3. In Honoré de Balzac's *Eugénie Grandet* (1833).

No?" Last night I had dinner at a friend's house with Elliott Carter and Charles Rosen—most fantastic conversation about Rousseau's *Confessions* and someone's ideas—a French scholar—that he fabricated the whole thing about sending his children to an orphanage, and even about the existence of the children.[1] I got up this morning looking for the *Confessions* and have found an old copy.

Englishmen are coming here as we are going to you in England. Alvarez is coming or may already be here. I think I will go to the publishing party for him,[2] the strange little shark. I have always liked him, but somehow one must be prepared not to like him I suppose.

Another thing—May is looming up as a very busy and inconvenient time for me. In June it will be hot, as you feared, and I think you'd do well to stay at home then. I don't know how much importance you give to the visit, or how much difference it makes about my own plans—I mean I know you are coming to see friends, publishers, etc. But I am not sure I can spare my studio at the end of May. We can talk further about it, sometime. It isn't all that near.

I must sign off. Love, from here

Lizzie

208. Elizabeth Hardwick to Mary McCarthy

[15 West 67th Street, New York, N.Y.]

April 9, 1972

Dearest Mary: To have your own typed letter made me very happy because it meant you were well again.[3] Thank heaven it is over. Your courage through it all shouldn't surprise but yet it always does.

---

1. Cf. Hardwick: "There is some dispute about Rousseau. Perhaps he did not abandon his children to the foundling hospital. What a base lie. Not to have abandoned the children, all five of them. But of course he sent the children to the foundling hospital. Everything we know about him and Thérèse Levasseur makes it 'work.' That is if there actually were children born. There's always that" ("Cross-Town" [1980] in *The New York Stories of Elizabeth Hardwick* [2010], p. 159).

2. For the American edition of Alvarez's *The Savage God* (1972) (published in the U.K. in 1971). Hardwick: "A. Alvarez does make her alive and real to us and his chapter on Sylvia Plath in his book about suicide is very moving. Alvarez is restrained, but he manages to suggest many of the private sufferings that were there at the moment of suicide" ("On Sylvia Plath," *New York Review of Books*, August 12, 1971).

3. Carol Brightman: "When the Wests returned to Paris from [Nicola] Chiaromonte's funeral in

New York is lovely today, cool and sunny. But what will tomorrow bring? I had the most exhilarating visit to Princeton with Hannah to hear Nathalie Sarraute. We were driven by a young pansy named, wrongly, Mr. Bland,[1] who is Hannah's secretary at [the] New School. "I share him with Jonas!"[2] I feel in love with N.S.—first her presence, the little wing of grey-black hair falling over the right spectacles, her beautiful English, and the elegant intensity, turning page after page of her lecture, looking up slyly. I was gasping with the pleasure of it. Question period: Hannah: "But when you take the invisible and put it into words then it is in the realm of 'appearances,' no?" N.S. "Not precisely." Hannah closed in, circling, narrowing . . . finally, N.S. "Ah, as always you are too clever for me,"—sly little smile . . . We are going back next Thursday, motored by the wild Bland. Even though I teach all day and will have left home at nine to return at midnight the chance, the pleasure are too great to miss.

I hate the idea too of not being in Castine. Mostly because of you, but also I love the whole place. It is very inconvenient, expensive, difficult for me alone. I go up late May to finish the opening—terrible \costly/ airplane, rental car expense—and Harriet gets nothing from it during vacations or in the summer. I have no plans about it. Just as soon as my tenants leave in August I will abandon Olga's house and come up until school starts. I don't know how long they will stay, but perhaps they won't stay all of August. I hope not. And I do plan on Jim touring you to Washington, Conn., to visit me. (When I said I had no plans about it, I meant about selling it. The chance to see you and Jim can hardly be weighed against anything else, alas.)

Oh, Cal's book.[3] Yes, I guess that is agitating friends again. I

Rome, Mary had noticed a black speck in her right eye [. . .] A torn retina was diagnosed, and McCarthy had checked into the American Hospital at Neuilly for laser surgery. Recovering at home, her eyes bandaged, [she was] unable to move her head for weeks" (*Writing Dangerously: Mary McCarthy and Her World* [1992], p. 566).

1. Robert Bland.

2. Hans Jonas.

3. McCarthy: "About the ms. he gave to Faber he knows I don't commend him for it. I think he might have made the sacrifice, for the time being, of those poems. But Cal is not a sacrificing man, least of all, I suppose, where his poetry is concerned, which means more to him than any people. People in fact are sacrificed to *it*, to keep the flame burning. It is a Jamesian subject, I guess—the Moloch-artist. I just had a note from Gaia, saying, among other things, that Roger Straus told her that Cal had given him *two* manuscripts, and that he and Giroux didn't know what to do. I suppose

haven't read any of the letter-poems, but I don't care at all. The whole thing, Mary, seems to me to have that awful silliness about it—and to think it has been well over a year that Cal has held forth with his friends on the matter, everyone has read the "poems" and Olwyn Hughes even had the whole foolishness in page proof. I cannot imagine anyone else of Cal's gift and thirty years of writing and publishing being sent telegrams, letters of plea about his work. (Lots of agitation from Bill Alfred, Esther Brooks.) I truly think Cal is in a half-mad state, one I know well, and which I think is his permanent condition. You can function quite well (yes, I like his Berryman piece very well[1]) and then again you do very foolish, self-loving things, marked by that hypo-manic inappropriateness of feeling. This whole thing is a sort of half-manic caper and always has been. He hasn't the intention of "hurting" and hasn't the intention of the reverse—that doesn't enter in. He has some idea that there may be one person, reader, who needs to be informed of the background to the Caroline poems; without me he feels—foolishly I think—that it is "incomplete." I feel very strongly that he has to take his own chances. I can't see that I can be hurt. He will publish the whole thing someday. The one Bill Alfred read me over the phone was grotesquely bad, as a poem, and I confess I felt I was having some strange, unasked for revenge, instead of the other way around. I truly feel indifferent to it all. Credit or discredit is entirely his. I have written him that I don't care a fig. I agree with what you said many months ago that his sanctimoniousness were he to refrain is worse than any "betrayal," if that is what it is. I have the idea the second book Gaia mentioned . . . hold on . . . is a re-writing of *Notebook*, a re-arrangement, now called *History*! Do you see what I mean about his state of mind, poor old boor. I feel sad about that sort of happy dust[2] he seems to get up and inject himself with every day, because he was once the most beautiful and interesting man. I can't tell

---

that means publish or don't publish; Gaia is always elliptic. Perhaps the poems aren't so bad; I mean, from your point of view as, so to speak, co-author. I don't know. I saw only one or two, long ago, when he had the place on Pont Street. It wasn't hard to recognize your voice, certainly. Have you seen them and what do you feel?" (to Elizabeth Hardwick, April 5, 1972).

1. McCarthy: "Incidentally, I thought his Berryman piece was quite good. Patronizing, but he did not try to hide that. To my mind, Berryman, though, has been overrated; I don't feel he *does* compare to Cal, which people were tending to do more and more" (to Elizabeth Hardwick, April 5, 1972).

2. Figurative (OED: "happy dust n. *slang* [orig. *U.S.*] = cocaine n." ["happy, adj. and n.]," OED

from letters and the phone perhaps but he seems repetitive, ~~rather~~ lacking in any kind of true moral concerns, rather a fallen angel.

Harriet paid \Cal/ a week's visit. It went perfectly well. I haven't questioned her too much, as I understand you aren't "supposed to."

Much love. I can't wait until some way of getting together in the summer. I am certainly coming to Paris the next time I go anywhere. Things look a little possible here politically and I guess we are all prepared to find that McGovern has "charisma" and whatever. I would do anything to get Nixon out. What can we do. All of us are full of hope however.

Dearest greetings to you both,
　　Lizzie

209. *Elizabeth Bishop to Robert Lowell*

[Cambridge, Mass.]
April 10th (Monday) ? [1972]

Dearest Cal:

I have two letters from you here now—& I was so relieved to get the first one, especially—I was awfully afraid I'd been crude, rude, etc . . . Look—I do see how when you have written—one has written—an absolutely wonderful, or satisfactory, poem—it's hard to think of changing anything . . . However, I think you've misunderstood me a little.

I quoted Hardy exactly, & the point was that one *can't* mix fact & fiction—What I have objected to in your use of the letters is that I think you've changed them—& you had no right to do that (?)

April 12th—

Well, I was interrupted there and have stayed interrupted for two days, apparently . . . It was—is—as I was saying—the mixture of truth & fiction that bothers me. Of course, I don't know anything about your possible agreements with E. about this, etc . . . and so I may be exaggerating terribly—

Online. March 2019. http://www.oed.com/view/Entry/84074?redirectedFrom=happy+dust [accessed March 29, 2016]).

To drop this painful subject and go on to the rest—I think the re-arrangements you are thinking of making will improve the last part of the poem enormously—and I see what a lot of hard work they entail, too. The idea of the italics and your saying some lines—sounds fine.

I am so glad Harriet's visit apparently went off so very well. After all, she has two very bright parents and so must have inherited a good deal of intelligence!

I am getting read[y] to go to New York; the Brazilian anthology,[1] or vol. I of it, is to be launched tomorrow at a huge, I gather, party, and I must be there. I don't want to be especially, but must. This is no real answer to your letters—and thank you for being so frank about the poems—

Just rec'd an ad for a book about you called *"Everything to be Endured"* . . . [2]

I just wanted to get some reply to you in the mail before I left. I'll be back the 17th or 18th and then I'll write again. I even have some more of my niggling line-comments, too, if you can bear them. I read your Berryman piece with sadness—also wonder that you could do it all so fast and spontaneously. I have the new book here but haven't had time really to study the poems yet.[3] It is awful, but in general his religiosity doesn't quite *convince* me—perhaps it couldn't quite convince him, either . . . He says wonderful little things, in flashes—the glitter of broken glasses, smashed museum cases,—something like that.

I am still struggling to put down all my Marianne Moore recollections.[4] I've also done a couple of poems—one a pretty long one, still being furbished a bit—the first of this batch maybe I'll enclose.[5] It is very old-fashioned and umpty-umpty I'm afraid—but I'm grateful to get anything done these days and one usually starts me off on 2 or 3 more, with luck. Frank has also asked me for a blurb[6] and I strug-

---

1. *An Anthology of Twentieth Century Brazilian Poetry*, ed. Elizabeth Bishop and Emanuel Brasil (1972).

2. R. K. Meiners, *Everything to Be Endured: An Essay on Robert Lowell and Modern Poetry* (1970).

3. John Berryman, *Delusions, Etc. of John Berryman* (1972).

4. "Efforts of Affection: A Memoir of Marianne Moore" in Bishop's *Collected Prose* (1984).

5. Probably "Poem," which Bishop enclosed with "In the Waiting Room" (see Lowell to Elizabeth Bishop, April 24, 1972, below).

6. For *Golden State* (1973).

gle with the phrases for that in between everything else. It is terribly hard. His poem[1] is so personal, so conclusive—so definitive, almost (for Frank)—I don't see where he can go after that, really. I wish he'd try something easier. He has such amazing taste and sensitivity about other people's poetry . . . I wish he were a happier young man. I do think we've become very good friends, however. The Paz-es have also been very friendly and we had—I had—an Easter breakfast party—a great success, I think, with Frank doing [his] best at egg-dy[e]ing, and Octavio madly searching my bedroom and bathroom for eggs—all brand new to him. \—these Easter rites—/

It's spring—first one I've seen in many years. I had one wonderful last skiing week-end in Stowe—unbroken fields & mountainsides of snow—and then back here where everything looks very bare and still brown—and the brick walks are still bleached white by all that salt they use in the winter.

I'll really write again as soon as I return. Elizabeth *Cadwalader* is arriving to vacuum my house, thank goodness—I hope you're all well and that Robert Sheridan sits up & takes notice . . .

    With much love,
      Elizabeth

210. *Robert Lowell to* Mr. Frank Bidart

Milgate Park, Bearsted, Maidstone, Kent
April 10 [1972]

Dear Frank:

In the confusion of Harriet['s] visit and the arrival of the Taylors, I have mislaid your letter—left it in London. So I start again from scratch.[2] It's import\ant/, since I am your friend, to state the thing soberly. Blurbs tend to stiffen into honorary degree citations, a form, unlistenable, unbelievable, even when true. I think they exist to make reviewers seems intelligent and, natural and brilliant.

Here goes:

---

1. "Golden State," *Golden State* (1973).

2. Letter from Bidart now missing. Lowell had written an earlier draft of a blurb for Bidart's *Golden State* in a letter to Bidart on March 25, 1972.

\"/For three or four years, I haven't forgotten the story and atmosphere of Frank Bidart's California sequence; it is very painful, and moves in a \dry,/ gruesome glare, heightened—perhaps this is my anti-Californian bias—by flashes of a modern "western", when the gunslingers are fossils. Bidart's poetry, unlike most, doesn't distort or glaze or stand between the reader and the subject.\"/

I've read and long thought on Elizabeth's letter. It's a kind of masterpiece of criticism, though her extreme paranoia (For God's sake don't repeat this) about revelations gives it a wildness. ~~Yet~~ Most people will feel something of her doubts. The terrible thing isn't the mixing of fact and fiction, but the wife pleading to her husband to return—this backed by "documents." So far I've done this much: 1) Most important—Shift *Burden* before *Leaving America* and Flight to New York. This strangely makes Lizzie more restful and gracious about the "departure." I haven't changed a word to this effect, but one assumes she knows about the baby's birth. *Burden* now begins with *Sickday*, and I think gains much by the baby's birth not being the climax. 2) Several of the early letters, From my Wife, are now cut up into "Voices" (often using such title) \changing mostly pronouns/ as if I were speaking and paraphrasing or repeating Lizzie. Most of the later letters I haven't been able to change much or all. 3) Changes for ~~my wish and~~ style, not to do with this business.

Now the book must still be painful to Lizzie and won't satisfy Elizabeth. As Caroline says, it can't be otherwise with the book's *donnée*. However, even fairly small changes make Lizzie much less a documented presence. A distinct, even idiosyncratic voice isn't the same as some one, almost fixed as \non-fictional/ evidence, that you could call on the phone. She dims slightly and Caroline and I somewhat lengthen. I know this doesn't make much sense, but that's the impression I get reading through the whole. Then Sheridan is somewhat a less forced and climactic triumph; as Ed.'s \~~wrote~~/ problem of \the/ getting back to England and into pregnancy is gone; and the very end of *Flight*, with the shark is less Websterian and Poeish.

Harriet's visit scared me to death naturally beforehand. But never have we been able to talk so easily. One age. Surprisingly, she both knew about and liked Blue Nun, Irish coffee and champagne. Then she and Caroline would argue with me about socialism and women, both pitifully incoherent \to a man/, especially Caroline, but to my delight agreeing.[1] I want to get this off in the car, so will stop. Trust you'll come sometime in June.

Affectionately,
    Cal

Give my love to Elizabeth and Bill[.]

211. Elizabeth Hardwick to Robert Lowell

[15 West 67th Street, New York, N.Y.]
April 21, 1972

Dear Cal: My last letter probably sounded like a mood or a pose of some sort. The crazy thing is that it wasn't. I have gone over my calendar for May. The only part of the month that I am free of deadlines, visitors, engagements is the week starting Sunday, May 21st. At that time I believe you could stay in your own old studio, the last week before it goes. That would be better for me because I work in my studio, the telephone there is connected with the main one in my apartment, and the whole thing is the only privacy I have. Also, last mention of your book. I was being quite genuine, not angry or ironical. Everyone has seen the poems, a manuscript or two must be floating around. I really don't see, as I said, that it matters to me one way or another. We always think we are writing our autobiography, but life is not willing to ~~tell~~ \assure/ us which part of ourselves is the main one, which action is telling and what it tells. In that way I guess it is folly to see your life as a book—and such a clue for clever people who come after us to

---

1. Among Lowell's papers, typed by Lowell: "A Cursory list of | Errors with Harriet: | 1. Staying too long at Maidstone and bringing C. to London | 2. Dinner with Grey and Neiti | 3. Gold ring | 4. House of Lords? | 5. Waterloo and Original? | 6. Late hours, Blue Nun and Irish Coffee? | 7. C. and H. wildly arguing women and socialism against Harriet's father. | 8. Swanly College, Duckworth | 9. Having Ivana and Jenia around too much; not having Ivana and Jenia around enough. | 10. Failure to buy clothes | 11. Uninventive present to Harriet of a check | 12. Failure to pick up two registered letters | 13. Failure to take H. to call on New York Book Review elders | 14. Paltry stop-gap presents from Cal to H. and E. | 15. English weather | 16. Meeting with Lady Dufferin | 17. Introducing of Israel, the norm, humorously into talk. | 18. Lady Caroline Lowell" (HRC). ("Israel" is a reference to Israel Citkowitz.)

try to pierce our defenses and let out the pus. I am writing something on this—in June!, such is the way I have to plan out everything—in connection with Robert Craft and Stravinsky.[1]

Naturally, I am a little fearful of seeing you, of reawakening the great hurt that has at last subsided, thank God! I think you will find me more than a little ahead of where I was—I hope so. I started to say that if the week of the 21st didn't suit Himself, then September. But I looked at the calendar, both of us start school the first week. And speaking of heat!

With Love,
    Elizabeth

212. Robert Lowell to Elizabeth Bishop

[Milgate Park, Bearsted, Maidstone, Kent]
April 24, 1972

Dearest Elizabeth:

I seem to have left your last letter and poem (much turned to) in London, (I almost wrote New York) in a coat left there for another taken. I can't be as accurate as I'd like. The picture poem and the dentist one are in the clearest of narrative styles, of the best short stories . . . if quite a long one could be written on a page.[2] The picture is more mysterious—when the R.A. turns up I still jump—your relative seemed more of a failure than that—then you see the painting is good enough, that the poem is a life, yours, his, going to age.[3] I want to see more of these poems. I'm sure they roll up, a huge story maybe like "In the Village," gaining in what can be held on to, in graspableness by being poetry.[4]

---

1. About Robert Craft's chronicle of Igor Stravinsky in the *New York Review of Books*; see "Pages from a Chronicle" (February 25, 1971); "Stravinsky: End of a Chronicle" (July 1, 1971); and "Venice: Paragraphs from a Diary" (October 5, 1972). If Hardwick ever did write about Craft and Stravinsky, she did not publish it.

2. Elizabeth Bishop, "Poem" and "In the Waiting Room" (*Geography III* [1976]).

3. Bishop: "Your Uncle George, no, mine, my Uncle George, | he'd be your great-uncle, left them all with Mother | when he went back to England. | You know, he was quite famous, an R.A. . . ." ("Poem" 40–43, *Geography III* [1976].) R. A.: Royal Academician.

4. Elizabeth Bishop, "In the Village," *New Yorker* (December 19, 1953); reprinted in *Questions of Travel* (1965). See also Lowell, "The Scream," *For the Union Dead*.

Kunitz has similar reservations about Dolphin. But don't say this; everything seems to get back to Lizzie. There must be heavy changes. But Peter Taylor, a kind soul, has seen my *revised* Dolphin and saw nothing wrong, except that it needed to be read with the earlier poems about Lizzie and Harriet. I think I've at last turned the thing, though there's still file-work.

I'll be in New York the week beginning the 21st of May. Will you still be in North America?

From the shattering strength of your letters and your skiing, you are in huge health. Never more force! I hope to get back to tennis, but skiing—the last time I tried about eighty years ago during the war, I failed to stop on a low mound when my skis stopped and fell on my head with my thumb under a ski—broken. Do you believe in Woman Power? I do, the shadow at the end of history. However my son feels the opposite, has broken a kitchen chair, shovels everything (rugs, blankets, silver toys, the little dachshund, Caroline and my fingers) into his two tooth mouth. Our family of women braces itself.

Dear, how I hope you'll still [be] in Cambridge!

Love,

Cal

213. Robert Lowell to Stanley Kunitz

[Milgate Park, Bearsted, Maidstone, Kent]
April 24, 1972

Dear Stanley:

I have meant to do something about your book, but had the impression that Witness (bad slip) Testing Tree[1] had been to Faber. However my editor Charles Monteith knows about you and is unaware of having been sent Tree. I'm mailing both book and my review this morning. I should have acted ages ago, but the winter has been outwardly troubled and somber for us. Now full spring weather, Ivana back at school,

---

1. Stanley Kunitz, *The Testing-Tree* (1971). Cf. Robert Frost's title *A Witness Tree* (1942); and his lines "One tree, by being deeply wounded, | Has been impressed as Witness Tree | And made commit to memory | My proof of being not unbounded" ("Beech," 6–9).

Sheridan eating everything in sight: blanket, rug, small dog, our fingers—a microcosm of James Dickey but on the wagon. Lovely.

About your criticism.[1] I expect to be back in New York for a week beginning the 21st of May, and hope to unwind over drinks with you. Dolphin is somewhat changed with the help of Elizabeth Bishop. The long birth sequence will come before the "Flight to New York," a stronger conclusion, and one oddly softening the effect by giving a reason other than \new/ love for my departure. Most of the letter poems—E. B's objection they were part fiction offered as truth—can go back to your old plan, a mixture of my voice, and another voice in my head, part me, part Lizzie, \italicized,/ paraphrased, imperfectly, obsessively heard. I take it, it is these parts that repel \you/. I tried the new version out on Peter Taylor, and \he/ couldn't imagine any moral objection to Dolphin. Not that the poem, \alas,/ from its donnée, can fail to wound. *For Harriet and Lizzie* doesn't go with *History*, it goes before *Dolphin,* but I thought it was too sensational, *confessing,* to bring the two books out together. I think you are right, \tho,/ and I'll do something. History somehow ~~relates~~ \echoes/ and stands aside from the other books. Do you think I could comb out enough excrescencies from History to do much good? The metal too often reforged wears out. Maybe you could put your finger on a few of the worst. It must be as good almost as I ~~can~~ \will/ make it.

How are you and Elise? I have sort of a feeling from your letters that this has been a much healthier winter. You can't picture our complicated ménage. One thing we've discovered, Never employ men, they are forever trying to surpass themselves and everyone else.

Love to you and Elise,
Cal

Thankyou as ever for giving so much time and kindness.

---

1. Kunitz: "As for *Dolphin,* I should be less than honest if I didn't tell you that it both fascinates and repels me. There are details that seem to me monstrously heartless. I will grant that parts of it are marvelous—wild, erotic, shattering. (Who else has the nerve for such a document of enchantment and folly?) But some passages I can scarcely bear to read: they are too ugly, for being too cruel, too intimately cruel. You must know that after its hour has passed, even tenderness can cut the heart. What else need I say to you, dear Cal, not as your judge—God save me!—but as your friend. In any event, these are matters that I have not discussed with another soul" (Stanley Kunitz to Lowell, April 19, 1972; quoted in Hamilton, *Robert Lowell: A Biography,* p. 422).

214. Frank Bidart to Robert Lowell

[2 Ware Street, Apt. 508, Cambridge, Mass.]
April 30, 1972

Dear Cal,

I've just re-read *Dolphin* in the new order. Let me re-state this new order, in case I have misunderstood: "Sickday," then all the sections of "Burden" (from "Knowing" through "Robert Sheridan"), then "Leaving America for England," "Before Woman," "Flight to New York" (from "Fox-Fur" through "Christmas 1970"), then "Dolphin."

To my immense depression, I don't think it works. On the level of "plot," of course, it does—but it drastically changes the meaning and resonance of a great many of the sections, and ultimately of the whole book.

Lizzie, for example, simply *would not* write a letter like "The Messiah" after Sheridan's birth. Knowing about Sheridan, it seems far more pathetic of her to say "I long to see | your face and hear your voice and take your hand." She doesn't seem "restful and gracious," but far more desperate than in the original order. Similarly, she can't later say "I cannot tell you | the things we planned for you this Christmas season" (plans she had to abandon) if she had known from the beginning you would probably return to England.

But far more important, one's sense of where you are in the drama, and thus of the emotional meaning and resonance of so many of the lines, is thrown out of whack. It's hard to pinpoint this in specific lines (though I'll try). The whole "Burden" section breathes a kind of emotional resolution that seems to say you *have been through all the alternatives*; the lines have a resonance and rhetorical weight which *feel* like the end of a poem:

It's happy to find love with you at last,
now death has become an ingredient of my being:
bloodclot and hemorrhage, today, tomorrow,
like Mother and Father, their youth struck dead at sixty;
I have saved their blood, and hand it on. . . .[1]

---

1. "Morning Away from You" (*The Burden* 9) 8–12 ("The Dolphin" manuscript). Revised: "Good-morning. | My nose runs, I feel for my blood, | happy you save mine and hand it one, | now death

Without "Flight to New York" preceding this, the sense of resolution comes too abruptly; in the original, there is the sense that you have fought through much more to get here. Even more frustratingly, in the new order, *after* "Burden" one goes back to the relative bewilderment and emotional thinness (with respect to the relationship with Caroline) of "Flight to New York":

a feeling,
not wholly happy, of having been reborn.[1]

Surely, it was a great joy
blaming ourselves and wanting to do wrong.[2]

There's nothing wrong with these lines, except that they seem inadequate, even a little unfelt, after the intensity and complexity of "Burden". *I don't feel you would have written them in this order.*

For me, the whole ending of the book went out of focus. After the birth of Sheridan, it's hard to know what the flight to New York means to you; in the original, because the relationship with Caroline at this point is so much less resolved, there is the sense that you *have* to go back to New York to see if anything is left. (And Caroline feels the threat—e.g., "Departure at the Air Terminal".) This seems largely gone in the new version—even Lizzie has acknowledged it (she has already told Caroline that Harriet "knows she will seldom see him"[3]). The whole process of going back, implicitly searching for something and not finding it (especially in "No Messiah" and "Sleepless"), now has much less force, much less pathos.

It's true, as you say in your letter, that in the original order the birth of Sheridan comes to have a tremendous symbolic weight—one wonders if any child can mean the "death-fight" fought throughout

---

becomes an ingredient of my being—| my Mother and Father dying young and sixty" ("Morning Away from You" [*Marriage* 16] 7–11, *The Dolphin*).

1. "Plane-Ticket" (*Flight to New York* 3) 13–14, in "The Dolphin" manuscript; cf. "Plane-Ticket" (*Flight to New York* 1) 13–14, *The Dolphin*.

2. "Departure at the Air-Terminal" (*Flight to New York* 4) 13–14, "The Dolphin" manuscript. Revised: "Surely it's a strange joy | blaming ourselves and willing what we will" ("With Caroline at the Air-Terminal" [*Flight to New York* 2] 12–13, *The Dolphin*).

3. "Green Sore" (*The Burden* 5) 11, "The Dolphin" manuscript; see poem on page 154. Cf. "Green Sore" (*Marriage* 7) 11, *The Dolphin*.

the book is over. But for all the reasons I've been trying to give—especially in sections like "Morning Away From You," where the sense of resolution and happiness is bound up with feeling the "ingredient" of your own death—Sheridan's birth doesn't have to do all the work. If there *is* a problem here (and it doesn't bother me) I don't see that the new order satisfyingly solves it.

Also, the seasons get terribly confused. After the "summer" sections early in the book, Sheridan is born; can "Christmas" then be the *first* Christmas after you have gone to England? Somehow, in the new version, one still feels it is the first Christmas; but then all the emotions, turmoil and sense of emotional resolution in "Burden" happen in the nfew months of fall after the "summer" poems. They then seem too abrupt—it trivializes them. If "Christmas" is a full year and a half after the "summer" sections, it seems too far away. I'm not saying at all that one consciously counts the months when reading the poem—just that something seems disjointed about the passage of the seasons. I miss the suffocating uncertainty and intensity of Christmas after the vacillation, the pain of the fall, followed by nine months of pregnancy, where a kind of order and peace is slowly found again.

The abruptness of "Burden" after "Flight to New York" (Elizabeth's worry) just doesn't bother me. Perhaps in the title of this section you could make it clear you're back in England (though the poem is clearly addressed to "Caroline"). In fact, I *like* this abruptness—the poem isn't a chronicle, and after the departure from New York the next crucial event, through which all of your conflicting emotions begin to be worked out, is the fact of[1]

215. *Robert Lowell to* Mrs. Robert Lowell

Milgate Park, Bearsted, Maidstone, Kent
May 6, 1972

Dearest Lizzie:

I don't think I am going to be able to make the trip this spring. Ivana sometime soon is going to have another operation. One of her grafts has grown tight and woodlike, so that she has to bend when she

---

1. Third page of letter now missing.

walks, and has pains. We hoped to put this off for a year, but it now seems unlikely. It's not a major operation, but a tense and painful one.

Also the other day when we were driving to Maidstone in a taxi, a car about twenty feet in front and going in the opposite direction turned without looking into a filling station on our side of the road— that awful few slow seconds when you know you'll—and we hit. No injuries except I soon had a huge lump on my shin. It will last far into summer, but is not dangerous or painful. I still feel shaken.

I've talked to Stephen Spender who brought me good news of you and Harriet's visit. Has her French tour come off? She might, as I so wish, stop off here, either going or coming. I dearly wish I could come to New York very soon. I trust my nerves ~~though~~ \saying "don't."/ My teaching schedule will be improved (less work for less pay) and I will teach four days a month ~~all at once~~ \in sequence./ So I will be free to fly almost any time in the fall, avoiding the steam and rush of September.

Michael Henshaw who manages my taxes etc. will shortly be in New York and will call on you about the Harvard papers. Anything reasonable will suit me. I do want to end life financially independent. I suppose Henshaw is too "rough diamond."

Good times with the Brookses and Taylors. Talk sightseeing etc. The Taylors have seen so much, they are ready to drop from ~~fatigue~~ \over-knowledge/, yet no one can discover which of the family drives them on and on. I was nearly killed by both Peters independently, looking to the left when they should look right. I don't think I'd last a day driving in England.

Good remarks of yours about "autobiography[.]" In the best art, as in life, all the blood-veins go to the heart.

All my love,

Cal

P.S. The Brontës is one of your best portraits.[1] Very superior to the New Wuthering Heights I saw In Maidstone.[2] Excited to read your whole book.

---

1. Hardwick, "Working Girls: The Brontës," *New York Review of Books*, May 4, 1972.
2. See Lowell to Hardwick, September 2, 1971, footnote 2 on page 216.

216. *Robert Lowell to* Miss Harriet Lowell

Milgate Park, Bearsted, Maidstone, Kent

May 6, 1972

Darling Harriet:

As I have just written Mother, I don't think I can make New York this spring. Ivana will soon have to have another operation, not dangerous but tense and grueling. She has already outgrown one of her important grafts, and walks stooped.

I will write you in slightly more detail than I wrote Mother about our car accident. We had slipped off a mid-Sunday afternoon to an adults only \Maidstone/ crime movie, after twice narrowly missing death with Peter Taylor and Peter Brooks, neither of whom understood English left side driving. A taxi man was driving us, one of the safest. Suddenly about the length of the big parlor in your apartment, a car (not American!) and going in the opposite direction, turned fully across the road ahead. For a forever of fifteen (?) seconds I saw us in slow motion about to hit. Not a thing I could do. My whole life didn't pass before my imagination, no brilliant deep thoughts, no blood-gush of new compassion—I did stretch my arms in front of Caroline to break her fall. The cars hit and stopped with wrinkled fenders, I felt a small pain in my shin, and saw a slight scratch. Threequarters through the crimefilm (full of accidents much like ours) I felt a stretching tight of my leg-skin and some pain. I touched my leg, and found a bump like a second knee on the side of my leg. The bump will bulge for a long time, but doesn't hurt much and isn't dangerous. It's handy to persuade people to fetch my things like a cigarette lighter.

Now I will certainly be home in the fall. I wonder—we beg you— to consider stopping off here a few days on your European circuit. Sheridan has just had a terrible half-hour of taking a bath with Genia and her friend Kay, both saying "you are so manly." A few days ago, he mistook (?) Bosun's ear for a blanket, and might have eaten him— so Bosun says. I think he needs your mature touch. So do I.

All my love,
Daddy

217. Robert Lowell to Frank Bidart

Milgate Park, Bearsted, Maidstone, Kent

May 15, 1972

Dear Frank:

I've neglected answering because I was waiting for your History notes, and also because I imagined it I would soon be in America. But Ivana will have to have another operation in the next few weeks, and the time doesn't seem very fortunate with Lizzie before the divorce gets planned.

Your remarks on Dolphin are too profound and detailed for me to handle them in a letter. Besides you would have to see the new text before we would have our feet on the earth. The thing is I *must* shift the structure and somehow blunt and angle the letters. The new structure, with the alteration of a few lines here and there, seems a big improvement to me. I had meant to end with The Flight to New York sequence, even after R.S.'s birth conception, but feared I would be lying. Now The "departure" is the real, though not chronological ending; it will of course seem to be *both* the real and chronological ending because I place it at the end—not from anything I say. Sophistry? No, not entirely. this \This/ is the real truth of the story and is in a way happening again now. The letters are not really changed to improve—the most I can hope is to lose nothing . . . to both lose and gain. I do think Elizabeth is mostly right, though is peculiarly (almost unintelligibly) sensitive to private exposure. Her letter to me was as powerful criticism as I've ever gotten—usually she writes me about this phrase or that.

Affectionately,

Cal

P.S. What can we say of the War! Sorry you've been ill. We've had a rather hard winter; it's better now.

218. Elizabeth Hardwick to Robert Lowell

[15 West 67th Street, New York, N.Y.]

June 1, 1972

Dear Cal: I tried to phone you on this urgent, perplexing matter. Here it is. Starting in Feb. I wrote Michael Henshaw that we needed simple material for the 1971 income tax, the year ending Dec. 31, 1971. He never answered and then I wrote again and he said that he was coming in May, early. I wrote back that we had to file on April 15th; he wrote back saying we should get an extension until June 15th. I wrote back saying that was a bit risky—pay interest on months beyond April 15, have more and more meetings, quite expensive, with my accountant, make an audit more likely and I am not really in good shape for an audit since I've had to "improvise" expenses, etc., these last years. But we asked for the extension. No Henshaw; two cables, no answer. Here it is now June 1, weekend will pass; I will be going away the 15th. All of this is very, very distressing and quite frightening to me.

I told Henshaw I did not need any money because I have it from what you gave me the year before. *All I really must have are the earnings, deductions, English taxes paid on Essex Jan. 1971–Dec. 31, 1971 and a listing of miscellaneous earnings, a few readings, Ashley Famous.*[1] \Very simple./

As for this year, that is another matter. I hope we will be legally separated by the end of Dec. and in that case you will do your own American earnings taxes—royalties, I think \also/ you list what you give Harriet and me but I pay the taxes. However until then I have been paying or will, when I get the information, the estimated 1972 tax for both, which we will adjust later. You would have to pay it to three sources quarterly otherwise. Actually you'll have to get a tax man for here.

But all I need now are the records for the year well gone by. Cal, if you can't get Henshaw you must ask Essex to mail the day—airmail— you get this letter the records for the year 1971, starting Jan. ending Dec. And send a few other statistics, like a few readings. I can get in terrible trouble here, fines, months of investigation, trouble for signing your name, etc. I must get this before June 12th and so it must be acted on immediately.

Harriet is marvelous, taking exams now and next week. She will go to Washington, Connecticut[,] with me and in July go to Choate School[2] for a summer program—boys and girls in dorms, studying things they are interested in. She's taking "Choate Film Institute"— and maybe something else, history. This is just for fun. We couldn't

---

1. Talent agency that handled Lowell's plays.
2. Private boarding school in Wallingford, Connecticut.

begin to afford the Europe trip and both of us have the electoral frenzy and wouldn't want to be away this summer in any case. I am having a good time, feel wonderful. Will give a lecture at Harvard Summer School (that does not contribute to my "wonderful," but I guess I'll get through it). Esther and Dixey[1] were here and will be coming back. Everyone is very well that I know about. Your studio has at last been dismantled; the books go out today as soon as I get up to the dust infested upper reaches here and move everything to make room for your books. Was up in Maine last week to open up my house for tenants. The town was shining and blue-sparkling, house and barn lovely, grassy, sunny. The Thomases very well. I don't mind not goin[g] up, though. It is too far and Connecticut, going back and forth a good deal from the city, sunning, writing, having friends visit is just what I want. Love,

    Lizzie

After June 15th—Washington, Connecticut 06793 Phone 203 UN 8-2545

219. *Robert Lowell to* Miss Harriet Lowell

Milgate Park, Bearsted, Maidstone, Kent

June 28, 1972

Darling Harriet:

I am up early this morning to write you. I have been working like a steamshovel, if a steamshovel works, for the last month and have been too slothful, unversatile or self-indulgent to do anything else, I mean to write letters, I mean to write you. Devie[2] was here yesterday for the night. [She] reminded me of you, too much so that it was painful to me, and I knew how terribly I miss you. I could have given the money for your trip to Europe.

How are politics? It's hard for old Eugene McCarthyites to rave about McGovern—it's the sentimental Irish lost cause passion that's somewhere in all of us. I suppose, I know McGovern is all we'll get,

---

1. Brooks.

2. Devie Meade, daughter of Lowell's cousin Alice Winslow Meade.

and maybe that even isn't likely. I wonder what Miami will be like. In the last Democratic Convention, I never left my Chicago hotel, but police and demonstrators were all about us. This won't be that way.

Today we set off for Norwich to get, for me to get a doctor's degree.[1] It's a lot of trouble ~~getting~~ \training/ there and the degree has no money value, of course, and not much honor—but here in this far country, away from so much, I am rather touched.

Devie thinks you have your head screwed on—I wonder where you inherited that, not from Cousin Natalie or the Winslows. But what has Sheridan inherited? He is now so overnordic looking that he makes Willi Brandt look like Jason Epstein. And he has devoled[2] alarmingly, can crawl wide rooms and long halls in seconds, and also loves to destroy—the more irreplaceable the object destroyed, the better it pleases him—a dear unanswered letter on a window seat. He is very beautiful. Yesterday he stuck his tongue out all day, with a meditative profound, or stupid expression. H[e] has redgold hair now and dark questioning eyebrows, like Devie's. I am at the end of the page, I think. Goodbye. Caroline sends all her love, give mine to Mother.

All my love,
Daddy

220. Robert Lowell to Elizabeth Bishop

[Milgate Park, Bearsted, Maidstone, Kent]
July 8, 1972

Dearest Elizabeth:

We've been working like steam-engines; no, very hard \but/ like human beings. Pardon me for not answering. I think of you every day, and of course Frank is a constant reminder of you.

The work is rather peculiar and sounds[3] almost insane. We've gone over almost 400 old Notebook poems, with an average I suppose of 4 changes a poem, tho often the whole poem torn up trying to get rid of

---

1. The University of East Anglia awarded Lowell an honorary Doctor of Letters (Litt.D.).

2. Thus, for "devolved" or "developed."

3. Bishop marked this word with an asterisk and the rest of the paragraph with a line. At the bottom of the page, she wrote to Alice Methfessel, to whom she gave the letter: "*Coitado!* one can see what comes first! SAVE, please—"

muddy lines, dead lines etc. I dictate the changes to Frank. Often there are many alternates, and more come to me as I talk. He remembers everything, and keeps me from throwing \out/ silver spoons. Notebook was such a wilderness, now I think you'll [like] it better. Kunitz thinks it's transformed. Why boast? But I do think Frank will stay here a little longer. We just can't get through by the 15th. That's why I've given you this formidable account of my methods. I do feel guilty about his not going to Brazil, but think he wants badly to finish what's so largely done.

Not much news. Caroline is off to an all-day school picnic and circus with Ivana, the little girl who was burned. I think we'll \go/ to Ireland for two weeks or so in August. When are you coming to Europe? I gather it will be early August. We do so wish you'd stop off here with \us/ on your way. I could time the Ireland so as to be here. You and Kunitz are the only close American friends we haven't had. I want you to meet Caroline. She has gotten as bad as I about revising and sits on her bed all day with long foolscaps in front of her. She almost finished a book of short stories this winter—along with looking after, with help, three children, and in vacations four.[1] The nicest more or less new person I've met is Angus Wilson. Met when I got a degree at Norwich, as beautiful in its way as Ouro Preto, at least when we came on it from a distance, and saw it during the long English twilight.

I like all your poems—most the Night Flight,[2] another of your best and one I might just not have known was by you. Very directly grim. Moose[3] has *lovely* moments, but others maybe too close to light verse. The midnight prose poem[4] is eerie, hard to compare with the others, because it couldn't have been written in verse. Then the marvelous RA painting poem.[5] You're sailing! I can't send you anything quite finished. I'm trying to be simple sensuous and garceful[6]

---

1. That is, Sheridan, Ivana, and Evgenia, as well as Natalya when she was home from boarding school.

2. "Night City (from a Plane)," *New Yorker* (September 16, 1972). See Bishop to Lowell, July 12, 1972, *Words in Air*, p. 719.

3. "The Moose," *New Yorker* (July 14, 1972).

4. "12 O'Clock News," *New Yorker* (March 24, 1972).

5. "Poem (About the size of an old-style dollar bill)," *New Yorker* (November 11, 1972).

6. Thus, hand-corrected by Lowell to read *graceful*. Milton: "And now lastly will be the time to read with them those organic arts which inable men to discourse and write perspicuously, elegantly, and according to the fitted stile of lofty, mean, or lowly. Logic therefore so much

\bad word for a typo/. My new poems, about four are additions to the long poems. I'm sure you'll \find/ Dolphin less excruciating; it can't I'm afraid entirely come clear of that. The new order, due to you, helps everything.

All my love,
   Cal

Ps. I haven't read your anthology really,[1] but have gone over the Drummond religiously and find him one of the best living poets—a quieter Montale.

221. *Elizabeth Hardwick to Robert Lowell*

[Washington, Conn.]
July 25, 1972

Dearest Cal: Did you receive a copy of the letter I wrote to Mr. Henshaw soon after he left? I have a great many business matters, some very pressing, that I wish to write to whatever person is representing you. Is it Mr. Henshaw? Do you have a lawyer there in England who knows your affairs. You will probably need an American accountant and perhaps your representative could write the one we have been using, who does know your business pretty well. As I told Henshaw I have not paid any of your \quarterly/ 1972 American taxes, only my own.

I want to get our divorce \over/ as quickly as possible. I will start the minute I get back to New York and hope it will go through \smoothly/. It will not be what it has been in the way of money. The only reason I can say now that I am glad I waited before filing is that I have had two years in which to straighten things out, two years in which I have worked constantly. I haven't enough to live on and can't

---

as is useful, is to be referr'd to this due place withall her well coucht Heads and Topics, untill it be time to open her contracted palm into a gracefull and ornate Rhetorick taught out of the rule of Plato, Aristotle, Phalereus, Cicero, Hermogenes, Longinus. To which Poetry would be made subsequent, or indeed rather precedent, as being less suttle and fine, but more simple, sensuous and passionate." (Milton, *Of Education* [1644].) Cf. *The Letters of Robert Lowell*, p. 25.

1. *An Anthology of Twentieth-Century Brazilian Poetry*, ed. Bishop and Brasil.

pay Harriet's tuition this fall. But I do not wish to go into all of this with you, by mail. It just isn't a good idea. Also there are many things about the Harvard papers that disturb me. The papers themselves, some very damaging to both of us, my own work on them, the fact that I included everything of my own except your letters to me—my correspondence with Mary McCarthy is a good example—and a great deal of other material. I should have had my own arrangement with Harvard, but the actual selling, the removal from the house came about so quickly—and in some funny way I just wasn't able to take a stand on my rights and was a bit too sentimental I fear. . . . But, as I said, I just can't deal with you personally about this in letters. Please let me know with whom I can communicate, and it must be someone who will answer promptly and efficiently. I need $1600 right away for the FIRST HALF of Harriet's \yearly/ tuition. All of this will be written into the separation of course. Also I think I should remind you that you will have to pay the lawyer's fee in total—that is usual—and this is not a simple case. Thank heaven, your situation is so extraordinarily good financially that you won't have to suffer at all. I would hate it otherwise—and indeed I see no reason why you should be bothered about any of this. The only thing that I want to be sure of is that you know what is ahead. I will ask for $10,000 as my part of the Harvard papers, my work on them, selling them, looking after them, all of that goes in. Actually I am still in correspondence with the library and I imagine they will \confirm/ my idea of what my contribution has been in this.

Sorry to have to write this, but I am very eager to go ahead and I know that makes you and Caroline happy. I do not want any disagreement or resentment. It would be bad for Harriet and I feel nothing at all right now except that Harriet and I must be dealt with fairly because we are very vulnerable. Otherwise I'd say we had survived very well and no one need feel guilty.

I have had a nice summer, but very busy. I don't like Connecticut much and I am glad to know that. Actually I haven't been here all the time, far from it. In late August I will go up to Maine for ten days or so. I love the community there, but I plan, as a part of my reorganization to keep from going broke, to sell the house and keep the barn for renovating into a small, easy place for whatever part of the summers I will spend there. It probably won't be all summer any longer. I long, though, for the tennis, the Thomases, Mary, Ken's Market, Phil Booth.

Harriet is fine. She has been in Choate Summer Program for three weeks and will be back with me in about four days. I was at Harvard last week, saw Bill Alfred, Bob Gardner, went to Manchester[1] for a few days, past the gray "terminal days" in Beverly Farms house,[2] talk of Rock, Dunbarton, Grandpa.[3] It seems like a century ago, doesn't it. In a way it was a little bit like going back to Kentucky for me; I mourn the ~~loss~~ \sudden diminishment/ of nostalgia and sentiment for the loss of the place. What is sad is that finally things are just as if they had never been. Of course if it were otherwise we couldn't live I suppose. Much love, dear, and good health.

Lizzie

222. *Robert Lowell to* Mrs. Elizabeth Hardwick Lowell

[Milgate Park, Bearsted, Maidstone, Kent]
[July 28, 1972]

CARPACCIO'S CREATURES: Separation[4]
To Elizabeth

From the salt age\s/, aye from the salt age,
courtesans, Christians, they filled the barnyard close.
The tree with a skull for a cap is a silly swelled tree;
Carpaccio's Venice is broader ~~by~~, the world, \soured saint/
~~than the life Jerome w\c/ould taste and pass.~~
\And honeyed lion mutter to work unfeared./
In Torcello, *venti anni fa*,[5]
the lion, snapped behind you, has poodled hair,

---

1. To visit Lowell's aunt and uncle, Sarah and Charles Cotting, who had a house in Manchester-by-the-Sea, Massachusetts.

2. See "Terminal Days in Beverly Farms" (*Life Studies*).

3. Lowell: "'Rock was my name for Grandfather Winslow's country place at Rock, Massachusetts" (*Collected Prose*, p. 359). See also "My Last Afternoon with Uncle Devereux Winslow," "Dunbarton," and "Grandparents" (*Life Studies*).

4. Cf. "Old Snapshot and Carpaccio" (*The Farther Shore* 2), "The Dolphin" manuscript; and "Old Snapshot from Venice, 1952" (*Hospital II* 3), *The Dolphin*.

5. Twenty years ago.

whernever you move, no sooner he has moved.
Lion marblewhiskers. Priest and beast
leap in Carpaccio's tea-leaf color. Was he
the one in the trade who wished to tell tales? . . .
You are making Boston alone in the early A.M.,
~~having left Harriet~~
having left Harriet at camp. . . . Old Love,
Eternity, Thou, mothbitten time!

Dearest Lizzie—I really was going to write, and thinking of some enclosure to fill out the letter because I am \too/ groggy with mental \health/ pills to write much. Will you like it? This is an awful new Czech machine that bites my fingertips each [time] I touch it. The poem? As I \descend/ deeper in reality and age I seem to write with Mallarmean simplicity. I really did\n't/ know what [day] or month it was. Happy birthday, happy anniversary.[1] What I feel most is your writing about \me/ etc.[2] I've ~~thought~~ \always known/ it was one [of] the things you do best. Why not publish, then I could read a copy? Or can I any way. All my [love] to les deux

    Love,
      Cal

223. *Robert Lowell to* Miss Harriet Lowell

Milgate Park, Bearsted, Maidstone, Kent
August 2, 1972 (?)[3]
It's the day, not the year I'm
Unsure of.

Darling Harriet:

    I guess you're just beginning your vacation at last. I hope you love it. I can't pity you too much, a writer works like a woman, not just from

---

1. Lowell and Hardwick were married on July 28, 1949, the day after Hardwick's thirty-third birthday.
2. See Hardwick to Lowell, June 26, 1970, footnote 4 on page 69.
3. Postmarked August 4, 1972.

sun to sun, his work is never done. Just last night when half asleep two inspired lines came to me:

"The monologuist tries to think something out
while talking, maybe thinks fine things, yet fails."

Oddly enough I was writing about myself.

We have a noisy disturbed life. Sheridan managed to do something to a light connection that instantly short-circuited a third of the house. Frank Bidart is here and a great comfort to me, but the other day he came quite shaken into my study holding up a thick black sock, one of mine that had mistakenly been put in his drawer—and one of his was missing. To my nearsighted eyes there was no difference, but to his it was a tragedy. Also he has gained 12 pounds from drinking four thermos bottles of bitter black coffee and eating two icecream and cake cobblers a day. We had our car stolen again, now recovered. Genia and Natalya have just gone off to camp, much missed but leaving with the feeling of an army evacuating. We have two minute childish dogs named Sonnet, and Nerva. I went to a party in London and met a man who knew Kay Meredith, but not Susie Keast, or Bill Meredith.[1]

Gosh I miss you. Though somehow after your visit you seem so closer, I can almost talk out loud to you—even when you don't answer. O, trivia again, last week I got a manly bluejean suit and four leather slippers, the first unsleazy man's clothes I've found in England.

What happened to Devie Meade, she was supposed to come back here? Sheridan has her eyebrows. He can crawl about as well as a small puppy now, and follows better, and has one intelligible word: *Dada*. I'm the only man he has ever seen except for Peter Taylor and Frank Bidart, Caroline handles him like a fish-puppy.

My dearest love to mother and
You.
　　　Daddy

---

1. Katherine Meredith Keast (sister of William Meredith) and her daughter, Susan Meredith Keast, who was a childhood friend of Harriet Lowell's.

224. *Robert Lowell to* Mrs. Elizabeth Hardwick Lowell

Milgate Park, Bearsted, Maidstone, Kent, England

[August 11, 1972]

Dear Lizzie—

Here's the check. It was lovely talking to you the other day. Will write more later.

Love,

Cal

I've cancelled the Harvard till [I] can talk with you in October. It's like willing one's gristly bones to posterity.

225. *Elizabeth Hardwick to Robert Lowell*

[Card: "Warrior in the Costume of the Dog Dance," from Wied-Neuwied's *Travels in . . . North America*. London, 1843–44. Rare Book Division. The New York Public Library.]

[Washington, Conn.]

[n.d. summer 1972]

Am leaving Connecticut. Will be off and on in New York until August 24, then up to Maine until Sept. 4. I wish we could stay longer in Castine—can hardly wait for Mary who is offering dinner when [we] arrive, the courts at four, cocktails and music. Harriet is off visiting a friend in L. Island; I enclose Choate "Film Institute" report as a nice joke.[1] She is going to [the] Republican Convention with me—just for the Miami Beach fun, if such it can be called.[2] The Democratic was rather gay because every writer you knew in the world almost was in the Doral Bar all day, where waitresses in black leather hot pants and plastic boots look about twenty years from the back and prove to be their authentic seventy when they turn a sun-tanned, dentured, fantastic ~~taste~~ face toward you with the bloody Mary. The Fountain Blue (Fontaine-bleu Hotel) is a Jewish brothel fantasy, beefy Cubans, for

---

1. Enclosure now missing.

2. Both the 1972 Republican and Democratic Primaries were held in Miami Beach, Florida, the Republican from August 21–23, the Democratic from July 10–13.

Wallace, drive all the cabs. I hope the "kids"—Dave Dellinger!—do not insist on some sort of confrontation with Nixon, but I fear they will. I have been working hard all summer at sundry "free lance" unnecessary articles,[1] but I have made enough money to turn down everything I don't want to write for a while . . . Am watching a scruffy, seal colored woodchuck graze on weeds, then lift a greedy snout, listening, then back to the speedy feeding. He weighs a ton and alas has the human aspect in certain munching profiles.[2] Am reading ~~Clive~~ Bell's *Virginia Woolf*;[3] gets fairly good toward the middle, but why must they recreate the nursery, the early scenes, when they never seem the least bit like what a rare person could be as child. I find contemporary biographies really trapped in a bad tradition. It is so hard to take this when you've been reading Rousseau all summer. The only thing contemporary I like in this vein is my beloved Bob Craft's work. This intense, rare gift of his, the daring of it—that is what is necessary to bring a life into being on the page. Then the egotism of Bloomsbury weighs a little. Somehow it makes you think back with pride on the frontier intransigence, the eccentric provinciality that made Randall's aesthetic snobbishness so passionate and valuable.

No more! I've had a good summer; the best part of it going in and

---

1. In 1972, Hardwick contributed to the unsigned article "The New Woman, 1972" and perhaps others in "The American Woman: A Time Special Issue," *Time Magazine* (March 20, 1972); wrote seven articles for *Vogue*, including "Is the 'Equal' Woman More Vulnerable?" (July 1, 1972); and "Election Countdown '72: One Woman's Vote," a six-part series published between August 15 and November 1, 1972; wrote four articles for the *New York Review of Books*, "Working Girls: The Brontës" (May 4, 1972); "On the Election" (November 2, 1972); "Amateurs: Dorothy Wordsworth and Jane Carlyle" (November 30, 1972); and "Amateurs: Jane Carlyle" (December 15, 1972); and published "Scenes from an Autobiography" (*Prose* 4, 1972).

2. Lowell: "Your student wrote me, if he took a plane | past Harvard, at any angle, at any height, | he'd see a person missing, *Mr. Robert Lowell.* | You insist on treating Harriet as if she | were thirty or a wrestler—she is only thirteen. | She is normal and good because she had normal and good | parents. She is threatened of necessity. . . . | I love you, Darling, there's a black black void, | as black as night without you. I long to see | your face and hear your voice, and take your hand—| I'm watching a scruffy, seal-colored woodchuck graze | on weeds, then lift his greedy snout and listen; | then back to speedy feeding. He weighs a ton, | and has your familiar human aspect munching" ("In the Mail," *The Dolphin*). Cf.: Frank Bidart to Robert Lowell, June 4, 1970; Elizabeth Hardwick to Robert Lowell, OCT 16 PM 5.13 [1970]; and Robert Lowell to Harriet Lowell [April 2, 1972]. Cf. also lines 8–10 with "The Messiah" [*Flight to New York* 2] 1–4, "*The Dolphin*" manuscript, on page 249.

3. Quentin Bell, *Virginia Woolf: A Biography* (1972); Quentin was the son of Clive Bell and Vanessa Stephen.

out of New York where, as usual, you find everyone you thought was away. And what a relief to know that I do not want to live in Connecticut. Can't see the point of it for me, nothing to do, although there have been many friends about. I like Castine, at the moment, but want to simplify it and not feel so much committed, to use it when I feel like it. Goodbye fer now, as Mrs. Farley used to say.

see note below.[1] Love,

Elizabeth

\Please write asking him to give material to me, my lawyer or your lawyer. Otherwise they won't.

Creighton Gatchell
State St. Bank & Trust
Boston, Mass. 02101/

226. Elizabeth Hardwick to Robert Lowell

[15 West 67th Street, New York, N.Y.]
September 16, 1972

Dear Cal: I tried to get Blair in Princeton, where he lives now, so that he could pass on my progress to you about legal matters, but he has been in Washington working for McGovern and I guess has *muchas problemas* on that score. I have my lawyer, Mr. Ben O'Sullivan, and have had a long talk with him and am getting all the material together. Next step—you and I will talk, then you will talk about what you have talked to me about with your lawyer, then they will talk, then B.O'S. will draw up a ~~separation~~ divorce agreement, then it will go back and forth from there. These are not easy matters, the lawyers are busy, but I will do everything possible to keep them at it. I hope Blair will find someone for you not too high-powered and bitchy because that will hold things up. I plan to present not outrageous demands but exactly what I will not budge from. Anyway, when you all get here call me and we will talk over all of it, which I will have clearly in my mind by then.

I am swamped with work of all kinds, but I am trying to fit in first

---

1. Postscript written by hand.

some tedious stuff the lawyer wanted me to draw up for him. I fear if I wait a week it will not set the tone of speed I wish to impress upon him. Otherwise, let's see. Harriet starts school at last next week, but has a really horrifying schedule of six full academic courses, also required art and dance (exercise). On Fridays she doesn't even have lunch. This is not the school's fault. In the high school there everyone is taking his own schedule just as if it were college. But she is getting off her requirements in science, math, and what with two languages, English (now also an elective and for her "Greek Tragedy and Comedy["]) and History—ach! Poor little creature.

Esther Brooks' brother died in a drowning accident and she has been back in America—stayed with me[1]

227. *Charles Monteith to* Mr. Robert Giroux

Faber and Faber Ltd Publishers, 3 Queen Square,
London WC1N 3AU
September 21st, 1972

Dear Bob,

ROBERT LOWELL

Last week I went down to Maidstone to see Cal and Caroline and to stay the night with them. Cal handed over what he optimistically describes as the "final" version of his *three* new books: HISTORY, FOR LIZZIE AND HARRIET, and THE DOLPHIN.

As you'll see from this, NOTEBOOK has now been split into two: 1) HISTORY—which in its present form consists of 155 pages of typescript. It includes 80 new poems which didn't appear in any of the \previous/ versions of NOTEBOOK, and in addition, of course, he's reworked quite a number of the poems that have already been published.

2) FOR LIZZIE AND HARRIET. The title is self-explanatory. It's a short book—34 pages of typescript; and *all* the poems have already appeared in NOTEBOOK.

THE DOLPHIN. 61 pages of typescript—a sequence of love

---

1. Second page of letter now missing.

poems written to Caroline. None of these have yet appeared in book form anywhere.

All three have now been handed over to our production department, and our very approximate production schedule is as follows:

Galleys: early December
Page proofs: early February
Shee[t]s (and repro pulls): early April
Publication date: it looks as if the very earliest we could publish would be mid or late June. We fully appreciate of course that you must publish before we do; so when we get nearer the time, perhaps you could fix your publication date and let me know what it is to be. We'll then fix ours.

I do stress that this timetable is extremely approximate. Mr Peter Moldon—who'll be looking after all three books in our production department—will keep in touch with you when dates become more definite.

Format. As agreed with Cal, we'll be following the format of the earliest Farrar Straus edition of NOTEBOOK for all three volumes.

Proofs. We'll be sending you galleys and page proofs when they're ready—but these of course will simply be for your information. Cal warned me that he would probably rewrite quite a bit in galley—I'll be very surprised indeed if he doesn't—but he promised to be a good boy about page proofs. Let's see what happens! We'll arrange of course for Cal to read proofs here and they'll also be read by our own proofreader.

I expect you'll be seeing Cal very shortly—if you haven't done so already. He's going over to the States for six weeks or so, mainly I think to see to the divorce proceedings.

Robert Sheridan Lowell, whom I met for the first time, was in fine form. He's walking already—and walking very expertly too—though he's still not quite a year old.

With all best wishes,
Yours ever
    Charles
    Charles Monteith

P.S. I suppose we shall have a separate contract for LIZZIE AND HARRIET. Would the same terms as those we agreed on for THE DOLPHIN be all right? They were: a royalty of 12½% to 2500, 15% thereafter, and an advance of £200 on publication.

If these are agreeable to you, perhaps you could ask Gerald Pollinger to send me a contract.

228. *Robert Lowell to* Miss Harriet Lowell

Milgate Park, Bearsted, Maidstone, Kent
Sept. 28, 1972

Dearest Harriet:

I'll be seeing you very soon, on the 9th of October. Never has time moved so fast. I've been writing rather steadily all summer, and now when I look up the tops of trees are yellow, and it is cold to get up sometimes in the morning. Sheridan is now one. He surpassed himself at his party. The birthday cake with its one candle was unwisely put on the floor, soon he had rammed into it with his musical lawnmower. Almost every inch of the mawner¹ was sticky with cake and its music had stopped. Then he was given a large ball and sent to a far corner of the room. Suddenly through three large women, he dropped the ball on the middle of the cake. But there is worse. Last he met his first girlfriend-guest, Olivia Pearson, age eight months. He was gently patting her hair (his own is tangly now and rather better) then suddenly she was blushing red and alas crying. There's such a thing as being too healthy, as you will see when you see him.

Ah me, it seems unimaginable to be back again in New York, but it always did from Maine, and I guess in a few hours I'll feel I never left. Or will I?

Caroline sends her love. Mine to Mother. Rather an awful visit, but it must be.

all my love,
Cal

---

1. Thus.

229. Robert Lowell to Elizabeth Bishop

[Milgate Park, Bearsted, Maidstone, Kent]
[October 31, 1972]

Dearest Elizabeth—

I'm so glad you wrote because I didn't think we parted on the right note—so much so I didn't quite know how to write. The trip has left us bone-tired, not in spirit so much as physically—I could use one of Mailer's irritating metaphors, a boxer who has been punished for ten rounds.

I am sore about my alimony, though it's quite bearable and more or less what I outlined in my mind two and a half years ago. I keep what I make: salary, manuscript sale, royalties, I lose everything inherited, all trust interest, NY apartment,[1] Maine house and barn—I thought they were Lizzie's in Cousin Harriet's will, but as I had forgotten, they were half mine by Maine law—all this is OK, but it's the small things, the difficulty of getting personal or family things, my books, silver spoons etc. I have no need of furniture, but all of ours I paid for, and some pieces were in my parents' house when I was five, or seven or eight. Well, I want little, not even many books; there's a clause in the alimony agreement saying we should agree on what should be mine—and doubtless when emotions are less keen we will agree, since not more than a couple of thousand dollars at most is in question. What really bothers me though is that Harriet will receive nothing of consequence from me—the alimony provides for her tuition through graduate school and further, but to be handled by Lizzie. I feel Harriet has been stolen from me like the dozen silver spoons. Of course, there are provisions for mutual consultation on her life and education—unenforcible if we are in a temper, as we are now, and

---

1. Hardwick: "My lawyer drew up the settlement in consultation with Cal's lawyer. It was complicated by provisions for Harriet and so on and it is wrong to say the money was 'given' to me, since she was 13. It was for both of us. It was the income from the trusts, amounting to about $20,000 dollars, on which I paid the taxes and sent Harriet to school, maintained the house and so on. This at the time was about the same amount Cal had from his royalties, plays and so on. There were provisions for death, illness, and the usual legal requirements. [. . .] I think the fact that Caroline had a good deal of money made Cal wish to pose as a man who would have been rich had he not been 'wiped out.' He wasn't rich at all and the divorce was financially hard on him and on me, according to our previous income when we were together" (Hardwick to Ian Hamilton, copy in the Elizabeth Hardwick Papers, HRC).

mustn't be later when our blood cools—for everyone's good. So it will be, God willing—today I am enjoying the luxury of steaming.

Frank's dedication[1]—here's what happened (but no one concerned can tell the same story about something even as simple as this). I think I said to Frank last winter that I ought to dedicate History to him, but that this seemed odd because he was really a collaborator. Anyway I totally forgot and dedicated it to Kunitz, who had written me a powerful letter about it,[2] had recently nearly died, to whom for ages I had wanted to dedicate a book, etc. Frank was so upset, I made a double dedication, a solution like splitting a Bollingen, that no one quite relishes, but the only possible way out for me. I haven't dared tell Kunitz and meant to if I had had a chance to see him, not just talk to. Now I will. It's hard to express how much Frank's work with me was worth, and is—without giving an immodest evaluation to my poem. There's no other book to dedicate—the For Lizzie and Harriet is itself a dedication, and the Dolphin must be to Caroline. I'm so glad you really like her—I assumed so somehow—perhaps Frank has copies of some of her things.[3] He must have. We're so bad about parcelling and mailing, and only have one copy of most things.

Oh God, Dear one, I do feel you must have security. I don't think I've undermined you, cannot remember not being open about my return—somehow Bloomfield assumed I had resigned when I hadn't.[4]

If I weren't still tired I'd tell you humors of our San Domingo days—I'd say with my whole heart, we (you & I) are together till life's end,

All my love,
Cal

---

1. *History* is dedicated to Stanley Kunitz and Frank Bidart.

2. Kunitz: "I could enumerate for pages the things that are wrong with *History*—its rhetorical excesses, its hints of vainglory, its clutter, its trivia, etc.—but it would be a silly enterprise, for this is a monumental poem, your monument, a generation's book of days, and great enough to make its flaws inconsequential. You have made vast improvements with your rearrangements and revisions of *Notebook*, and some of the new sonnets are among your best. But if you intend to complete the book with *For Harriet and Lizzie* [thus], I wish you would think twice about it. They are separate structures and don't belong together. The main work is diminished in its grandeur by the juxtaposition: the whole dwindles to pathos, domesticities, and anti-climax" (to Robert Lowell, April 19, 1972).

3. That is, Blackwood's writing.

4. Morton Bloomfield was the chair of the Harvard English Department from 1968 to 1972. Bishop was anxious that Lowell's return to teaching at Harvard would displace her. See Lowell and Bishop's exchange of letters in *Words in Air*, pp. 728–33.

230. Robert Lowell to Harriet Lowell

Milgate Park, Bearsted, Maidstone, Kent, England
November 3 \6/, 1972

Dearest Harriet:

This letter is dated wrong because somehow I got an *idée fixe* that the election day was November 4 instead of 7. The last days are an agony to read about, it will be merciful when it's ~~all~~ over.[1] McGovern must feel that he is living a waking nightmare that he can't stop. It's strange to be writing you such things. I remember when my letters were all jokes. Better that way.

Yesterday a herd of twenty very handsome and very stupid cows got into our grounds. I think they are dumber, more harmless and stupider than guinea pigs.[2] I would chase them away from the garbage cans, then they'd slowly shuffle away and attack what was left of the roses. The worst was when they leapt a barb wire fence, putting one hoof on the top wire and bending it down. After a while, and slow as glue, I got them all uninjured back to their pasture. Cows are the same as little animals, only less bright. Size doesn't mean anything unless it sits on you.

We went through our divorce and marriage on schedule—a few errors such as not having any passports or identification when we stood before the divorcing judge. Santo Domingo where it all happened is much like Porto Rico, only the Spanish speaking people are at least half negro, and the blessing and disadvantages of America are hidden. Also hidden is the body of Christopher Columbus buried there. Miles of beaches ~~but~~ unswimmable because of barracudas and sharks pursuing sewage.[3] I quite enjoyed the swimming pool; actually cooler than the air.

---

1. Among many articles covering the 1972 U.S. presidential elections in the British newspapers, see Adam Raphael: "President Nixon, riding the crest of a 23-point gallup poll lead, came here [Chicago] to consolidate what his aides are now predicting will be one of the greatest landslides in American political history" ("Nixon sets out on triumphal progress—in advance," *Guardian*, November 4, 1972). See also "The meeting of St George and the Godfather: How President Nixon swung the tide of unpopularity," *Times* (London), November 6, 1972.

2. See Lowell, "Words for a Guinea-Pig" (*Eloges to the Spirits* 4), all three editions of *Notebook*; and "Words for Muffin, a Guinea-Pig" (*Circles* 7), *For Lizzie and Harriet*.

3. Lowell: "a barracuda settlement. (Santo Domingo, | quick divorces, solid alimony, | its dictator's marina unsafe because of sharks | checking in twice daily like grinning, fawning puppies | for our sewage" ("Alimony" [*Another Summer* 4] 7–11, *The Dolphin*).

Somehow I miss you even more than ever, and brood about it, and even wake up brooding. You must (I mean we invite you) to come here Easter. Maybe bring a friend and see more movies in London. Or all kinds of things that aren't movies. We plan to be at Harvard beginning in September, in the country if possible. I'll only be an hour or so away from you.

A miracle happened with Sheridan at Bill Alfred's. You know how every inch of his house is covered with reachable breakables. This was doubled by the Brooks's using his house as storage for part of the furniture [from] the Cambridge house they just sold. Sheridan somehow got interested in doing vaudeville with Bill's hat, a carrot-grater and a milk bottle. Just as we were leaving, the last hour, he realized what a chance he had missed and rushed for the dishes on low shelves. We stopped him. So much stronger are years than youth.

But what is strong? I miss you so. All my best to mother.

Love,

Daddy

231. Robert Lowell to Harriet Lowell

Milgate Park, Bearsted, Maidstone, Kent, Eng.

November 21, 1972

Dearest Harriet:

I sharpened the brown pencil for about five minutes in order to do my first Sumner, though you may not recognize him. Then confident

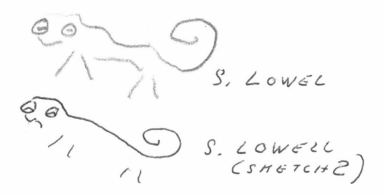

with failure, I tried my second in blue ink. I see that though I hate non-representation in all the arts, I will never be a lifelike painter. However, the purpose of my drawings is to make it easy for you to write me a letter. It's hard to write; it's harder for your father not to have an answer, not ever to hear.

For some crazy reason, we have had five sunny days out of six here, a record for southern England. On the sixth, a heavy rain fell blown by winds that bent large trees double. It left a lake on the flat roof over my study, and for twenty hours a steady heavy drip, caught by six dishpans and a rubber wastebasket. Then a man who knew came and the leaks stopped.

The Academy of American Poets is putting on a small memorial for Ezra Pound on January 4, and will pay my passage.[1] I plan to come (if I can get my passport back from the Home Office). I particularly promise myself that I will see you.

My teaching has turned out to be rather fun this year. The sun is setting now at four, and soon I'll be setting off on my longish dark drive to Essex. I dare not tell you or even myself how short my teaching hours are. Nothing like your daily homework, but think of the great mind, the courageous modesty etc. I put into it.

Caroline is still losing things right and left, and writing reams, and sends her love. I send mine to you and Mother.

Love,
    Daddy

---

1. Ezra Pound died on November 1, 1972. "A Quiet Requiem for E.P" at the Donnell Library Center (20 West 53rd Street), with Lowell, Leon Edel, Robert Fitzgerald, James Laughlin, and Robert MacGregor.

PART III

1973

232. *Robert Lowell to* Mrs. Elizabeth H. Lowell

Milgate Park, Bearsted, Maidstone, Kent

[January 10, 1973]

Dear Lizzie:

Back at last to teaching, my sixth term of teaching Modern North American Poetry. How different it seems than the poets of Philip Larkin's Oxford Book of 20th Century[1]—even when Eliot and Auden are in both lists. I'm doing a review of the Larkin because it might give me an opening to write unpretentiously about the poetry of the century—some of it, all British, Americans only used to point up differences.[2] I suppose we all thought of ourselves as more modernist than we really were, our tastes were more experimental than our own ~~chosen~~ styles. But in Larkin (a felt anthology, in no way defiant, but a sign of the times) modernism might never have been.

Why have I gone on this way? It was good to see so much of you and Harriet.[3] Sad, too because at best nothing is repeatable for us. ~~in time.~~ I felt when Harriet came here a year ago, that this would never be again—I mean that no matter how many times she came, and how happy the visit was, we would be different persons, at a different moment

---

1. *The Oxford Book of Twentieth Century English Verse*, ed. Philip Larkin (1973).
2. "Digressions from Larkin's 20th Century Verse," *Encounter* 40 (May 1973).
3. During Lowell's visit to New York for the Pound memorial (on January 4, 1973).

in our lives. I felt that with you. What did Peter Ross Taylor say after we left Columbus so long ago?

I am out of work now. No more of my old—6 or 7 years,—can be written. Nothing much new comes even as a desire. Maybe my prose bits. They'll need more—small stuff and too hard to do, but probably better than play or verse at the moment. Could I call my few essays *Men*. I see to my embarrassment, they all are.

Give all my love to Harriet, and tell her I'll write soon—very. Liked Mary's using Stalin, almost no one who is against Vietnam violently makes this qualification.[1]

Love,
    Cal

\P.S. (writing with Edel's pen)[2] Has Harriet's check arrived. If not, I [will] write another./

233. Elizabeth Hardwick to Robert Lowell

[15 West 67th Street, New York, N.Y.]
February 2, 1973
Dearest Cal: Your Christmas check arrived for Harriet. She was well pleased with it and felt, coming by ship, it had traveled a long way to arrive just when it was needed . . . As for me, I have not done any

---

1. McCarthy: "Where the G.I. in Vietnam out on patrol felt he was really a civilian that nobody had the right to snipe at, the counter-culture is convinced that all Americans except themselves are war-makers, *i.e.* indistinguishable from war criminals. Such virtuous 'indictments' of a whole culture in its ordinary pursuits are politically sterile. The VC and the North Vietnamese are always careful to distinguish 'the American people' from 'the U.S. imperialist aggressors.' By the American people they mean not the proletariat (whose general support of the war they are aware of) but some larger, vaguer entity—America's better self, still found throughout the whole spectrum of classes. The assumption that everybody *has* a better self is indispensible to those working for change. The opposite assumption, of equating individuals with social categories, most of which are treated as criminal *per se*, when it does not lead to Stalinist-style mass liquidations or assassination commandos, conduces to despair and is anyway patently false" (Mary McCarthy, *Medina* [1972], p. 83).
2. Leon Edel had appeared with Lowell at the Pound memorial. Lowell: "This morning I've lost my only English checkbook, my only legible pen, my silver ballpoint stolen from Leon Edel" (Lowell to Peter Taylor, no date but early April? 1973, Vanderbilt University Library Special Collections).

of your bidding. Not out of will, negative, but willessness, positive. I called energetically to a packer and shipper soon after you left and they were surly, disconnected. I looked long in the yellow pages and then retired never to take it up again. But I will do so. I have about a hundred pages to write this month and then I will turn my head to housekeeping, arranging, shipping.

Let me see, what from the tens of explosions, the dozens of gossips, the real and false events—what to pass on to you? A lovely banging rain today, dark at midday. . . . Last week I was on a program at the Y about Sylvia Plath; rows of radical lesbians, screaming something about Robert Lowell. I gathered it had to do with your introduction and laughed, southern syllables into the cracking mike, "Why are you'all against that—uh? I think it's kinda good, you know."[1] Chaos!

I need very quickly the name of the accountant who has your earnings from last year. I guess you want it done here by Mr. Hoffman. We won't \(can't)/ sign a joint account, but all of the money we have from you is in your name still—and still!—and so it goes to the govt. under Robert Lowell but those taxes will have to be paid by me. You will have to pay some. It is sheer horror, thinking about it. I hope this will be the last year for me and that I shall be utterly only on my own, but they are still having trouble getting "opinions" on putting the money in my name. Lawyers fees (and I do not mean the rest of Mr. O'S) are mounting. In heaven there is no marriage,[2] hence no divorce.

Otherwise we are altogether fine here. Harriet is very happy and busy and has just taken her mid-terms and done a paper on *Alcestis*.[3] Adrienne spent two nights with me and then drove Miss Bishop back to Cambridge. I did not see E. Adrienne is all over the place, very

---

1. Sylvia Plath, *Ariel* (1965), with an introduction by Robert Lowell. Hardwick appeared with Erica Jong and Robert Bagg on "The Works of Sylvia Plath" panel at the 92nd Street Y on January 22, 1973.

2. Matthew: "For in the resurrection they neither marry, nor are given in marriage, but are as the angels of God in heaven" (22:30). Lowell: "We might have married as Christ says man must not | in heaven where marriage is not, and giving | in marriage has the curse of God and Blake" ("Gruff" [*Marriage* 3] 9–11, *The Dolphin*).

3. By Euripides. Cf. Lowell: "All night I've held your hand, | As if we had | A fourth time crossed the kingdom of the mad— | Its hackneyed speech, its homicidal eye— | Alcestis! . . . Oh my *Petite*" (draft of "Man and Wife" 8–12, Robert Lowell Papers, Houghton Library).

much in vogue, lots of poems, a new book coming out.[1] Pablo[2] was with her one night and he is a beautiful boy, quite won our H.'s approval and liking. There is a review in Commentary which says John Ashbery's new book, *Three Poems*,[3] (long prose poems) is one of the dozen or so of the century, can stand with the *Four Quartets*.[4] So the moving finger writes.[5]

Reading "Visions of the Daughters of Albion" this a.m.[6] Strange poem that fell upon me like some wonderful cloud—obscure, heavy, soft. He—Blake—knows things we do not know.

So, addio once more. Harriet would send love if she were not out in the storms. From within, lamplight, Emily Brontë and E. Wilson on my crowded desk I send my own greetings.

Love,
　　Elizabeth

234. Robert Lowell to Elizabeth Hardwick

[Milgate Park, Bearsted, Maidstone, Kent, England]

[February 13, 1973]

Dearest Lizzie;

I am in a stupefying muddle of mind from several weeks of work and now a touch of flu. This letter will show it. Then I'm in a snarl on how to get money out of England. Living in two countries almost doubles the forms and stops. The money thing will work out, but it'll take two weeks or so to clear. As it stands, I can't pay the lawyers' bills. I don't know if I can pay anymore \than that./ I'm putting off Frank's painting as a wild extravagance[.][7] My check to him made out at the gallery after a Parker lunch had three inconsistencies and errors in it.

---

1. *Diving into the Wreck: Poems 1971–1972* (1973).

2. Conrad, one of Rich's sons.

3. (1972); Stephen Donadio, "Poetry and Public Experience," *Commentary*, February 1973.

4. By T. S. Eliot (1943).

5. Edward FitzGerald: "The Moving Finger writes; and, having writ, | Moves on" (*The Rubáiyát of Omar Khayyám*, lxxi, 1–2).

6. By William Blake (1793).

7. Francis S. Parker, "The Wave," which Lowell bought for $1,500; "The Great Wave has been on the wall above the bed where I work for five days now, rain and shine etc. it changes with the weather and glows most on dull days. It's somehow much like the pasture outside, stern before the leaves come. It has lost nothing of the glow my drunkenness gave it that afternoon at the Ath-

My accountant will be someone that Caroline's lawyer Henry King (Denton, Hall etc.) 3 Grays Inn Place will find for me. Meanwhile I see Henshaw tomorrow, the only person who knows my ramifications. I left (?) my marriage license with Bill Alfred, and in any case it will have to be rewritten by Iseman[1] in English. Harvard \papers/ at a standstill. Debts, immigration—I expect to be deported from England, refused entry to America, jailed or fined in both countries. This sounds wild.

I see I have no Blake in my library, but isn't Daughters of Albion one of those vague bombastic long-lined Ossianic things? His only long poem I find wonderful [i]s Marriage of Heaven and Hell,[2] as good as Nietzsche or Rimbaud's Saison.[3] My library doesn't have my preface to Sylvia Plath. As I remember, it was quick and tender. There was a similar ghastly Plath meeting here last spring, with Greer who could read poetry to illustrate her points. I've hardly met the real Lesbian storm troops, but I think they talk like hysterical Negroes and other fanatics—the meaning of words, the object they denote mean nothing. Glad you saved me, if you could ~~bare~~. Your Woolf has something people will quote on her—rather Bloomsbury writing (university people with a style) on Bloomsbury.[4] Can't understand you on Carrington and Strachey (Have you read her letters?)[5] Then Strachey's best books are more inspired and readable than anything by the group[6]

---

enaeum" (Lowell to Frank Parker [early April 1973?], collection of Judith Parker; see also *The Letters of Robert Lowell*, pp. 604–605).

1. A lawyer.

2. (1790/1794).

3. *Une Saison en enfer* (1873).

4. "Bloomsbury and Virginia Woolf," *New York Review of Books*, February 8, 1973.

5. Hardwick: "The worst thing before the present exhaustion of Virginia Woolf was the draining of Lytton Strachey. This is a very overblown affair, right down to his friend Carrington, who committed suicide forty years ago—an unreclaimable figure, fluid, arrested, charming, very much a girl of the period, with the typical Bloomsbury orderly profligacy and passionate coldness. Her marriage and her love affairs are held in the mind for a day or so after hard study, but they soon drift away to the Carrington haunt" ("Bloomsbury and Virginia Woolf," *New York Review of Books*, February 8, 1973). See also *Carrington: Letters and Extracts from Her Diary*, ed. David Garnett (1970).

6. Hardwick: "Back to the far too well known Lytton Strachey. The latest issuance holds out some hope of a pause with its advice that 'the most important of Lytton Strachey's literary remains are now in print.' But the sentence before mentioned 'the mammoth exception of his correspondence.' Surely that can wait for our children, who can then gather their brows once more over Ottoline, Ham Spray, Ralph, Pippa" ("Bloomsbury and Virginia Woolf," *New York Review of Books*, February 8, 1973).

except Passage to India.[1] And then Leslie Stephens,[2] admired by Leavis and J. [R.] Lowell? But more startling, what are your 100 pages? More of *woman*? It's your most passionate writing and therefore best.

What about Harriet coming here in her vacation? I'd love so to have her. Our local antique dealer is looking for a beautiful old \picture/ frame. If she comes I'll have to know the dates as soon as possible. I wonder if she wouldn't enjoy an early April trip to Italy, Brookses, Anzilotti, poets etc.

I so sympathize with your positive will-lessness. I've had none for anything practical for weeks.

Love,[3]

Let me know if I can sign anything to help with the Trust transfer. Do they think I am not in my right mind? Ever? But maybe that isn't anything to do with it. It's like a very cold end of April American day here—green with no leaves, a great shushing gale blowing outside that could move a sailboat if one were in my room.

235 . Elizabeth Hardwick to Robert Lowell

[15 West 67th Street, New York, N.Y.]
February 16, 1973

Dearest old Caligula:[4] Yes, the vacation is drawing near. And indeed Harriet will spend it with you. She is delighted at the possibility of Italy or whatever you decide. Just let me know by a soon mail.

---

1. E. M. Forster, *A Passage to India* (1924).
2. Hardwick: "One of the things that make *To the Lighthouse* interesting for the reader who is also a writer is that, in this case, one can bring things in from the outside. If Mr. and Mrs. Ramsay are in some way Virginia Woolf's mother and father, then you have Leslie Stephen as a character. And upstairs you have his *Hours in a Library*, *Studies of a Biographer*, the thin, green *George Eliot*. These are books I have used, but I have not learned greatly from them. Still when Mr. Ramsay appears in his being as a writer we are watching something real, immensely affecting—the poignancy of a long, hard literary life" ("Bloomsbury and Virginia Woolf," *New York Review of Books*, February 8, 1973).
3. Unsigned.
4. Lowell: "My namesake, Little Boots, Caligula, | you disappoint me. Tell me what I saw | to make me like you when we met at school? | I took your name—" ("Caligula" 1–4, *For the Union Dead*). Cf. also Lowell: "Dear Elizabeth, (You must be called that; I'm called Cal, but won't explain why. None of the prototypes are flattering: Calvin, Caligula, Caliban, Calvin Coolidge, Calligraphy—with merciless irony)" (to Elizabeth Bishop, [August 21, 1947], *Words in Air*, p. 7).

Here we are: Leave here Thursday Morning, March 22, get to
London that night. (Ha!)
Return Saturday March 31st (that is the latest).
When you let me know your plans I will get the tickets.

No, the boring, expensive business with the trusts has nothing to
do with you, but merely with the question of whether all that was de-
cided at the divorce can really be carried out . . . I do need the name of
your tax man in order to do your American tax, but I guess all I need
from them are the Essex things, anything from Ashley-Famous, etc.
I am very distressed for you that your F, S. and G. earnings were so
low this year; however with the flooding of the market you are plan-
ning[1] perhaps that will be altered! I am trying to get an extra teach-
ing job for next year. My great worries are daily things, the enormous
maintenance for the apartment, food, house-hold things, tuition . . .
One thing we managed was for both of us to feel poor. However, I
refuse to consider that for very long and find I am skidding along from
day to day extraordinarily well.

. . . I don't like Carrington's letters as well as you do, I guess. I
like her devotion, but the rest just seems too cut off from anything ex-
cept the immediate. Also I have as I said not learned much from Leslie
Stephen; he just isn't quite right on C. Brontë or George Eliot, a little
thick somehow.[2] But I will look again, as I trust what you say more
than any idea of my own. Lytton Strachey is a good writer, but Emi-
nent Victorians[3] is less so than I once thought—lighter. Yet it is one of
those things that brings something new to you and makes you think
you have always known it, even grown tired of it, later.

I had a wonderful long letter \about my Woolf article/ from *Mrs.*
L. C. Knights and a real masterpiece from Mary McC. about James's
punctuation.[4] Gosh, I read something beautiful last night: Blackmur

---

1. The simultaneous publication of *History*, *For Lizzie and Harriet*, and *The Dolphin* on June 21,
1973.
2. Leslie Stephen, "Charlotte Brontë," *Cornhill*, nos. 108–109 (December 1877); *George Eliot*
(1902).
3. (1918).
4. Hardwick: "I wonder about the 'morality' of certain marks of punctuation used by James in 'In
the Cage.' [. . .] In the midst of her upward longings, her rising misconnections, the girl pauses
unexpectedly, in a clause, at the end of the most externally conceived, impudent Jamesian depic-
tion of her—she pauses and 'made up even for the most haunting of her worries, the rage at mo-
ments of not knowing how her mother did "get it."' 'Get it' is alcohol, gin probably. The down,

on Emma Bovary![1] Also I am reading W. S. Merwin's new book,[2] very bare, stripped, plain, and moving in a peculiar way. About *Daughters of Albion* there are the cumbersome Oothoon and Theotormon and other mighty personifications I can't understand at all, but some of the passages are absolutely striking and were I not edging toward 6 P.M. I would copy out some for you.

My 100 pages are mostly adding, almost doubling each essay, and doing one long new one and then finished.[3] I am fed up with Woman and Women and want to write something utterly different. . . . Violet Parker was here on Sunday, very lovely and dear.[4] I am going to visit Dr. Arendt this evening. Mary McC. is coming again soon. She and Susan S.[5] go back and forth very often and that is nice both ways I think. Mary has a number of lectures, one in S. Dakota—not a tour, just single things. You will be here in the fall, so that if the old countree[6] brings forth any stab of longing[7] I suppose it will be more than assuaged then. It will be nice for the old country, too, and so . . . let

---

down mother ('never rebounded any more at the bottom than on the way down') drinks. [. . .] To put 'get it' in quotations is a moral failing; it pretends it is a mere colloquialism identified, or asks that we in our minds put some peculiar stress on it that will equal the accentual patterns in the author's mind, or wants to indicate an affectation on the girl's part—any of those things the mimicry of quotation marks may suggest. But this is wrong. [. . .] Even a second of an impoverished mother's pursuit of gin cannot be put on the page in that way. It accomplishes only a stylistic diminishment of the possibility of pain, of real feeling" ("Bloomsbury and Virginia Woolf," *New York Review of Books*, February 8, 1973). McCarthy: "I agree with you nearly 100% in what you find to condemn or rather blame or regret in Virginia Woolf, Forster, James [. . .] And yet I wonder about *In the Cage*. Most of my 10% disagreement is located there. In my memory, *In the Cage* is rather an exception—as though, in that instance, he was trying to peek out of *his* cage. [. . .] To me, he felt sympathy for the girl and for the awful expressions she used, which themselves expressed her deprivation and imprisonment. She was caged up in her narrow vocabulary. And I don't see how that could be rendered without *showing* it. [. . .] As for 'get it,' no, there, I really jib; he *had* to put it in quotes to flag the reader's attention; what was behind those two neutral little words would have slipped by otherwise. And in a certain way it's in quotes in the girl's mind, being her euphemism for her mother's habit, which she can't bear to name" (to Elizabeth Hardwick, January 22, 1973).

1. R. P. Blackmur, "Madame Bovary: Beauty Out of Place," *Kenyon Review* 13, no. 3 (Summer 1951).

2. *Writings to an Unfinished Accompaniment* (1973).

3. For *Seduction and Betrayal: Women and Literature* (1974).

4. Frank Parker's mother; see *The Letters of Robert Lowell*, p. 35.

5. Sontag.

6. Alfred Comyn Lyall: "Never a story and never a stone | Tells of the martyrs who die like me, | Just for the pride of the old countree" ("Theology in Extremis," 124–26).

7. Given the discussion of *Visions of the Daughters of Albion*, see Blake: "Enslav'd, the Daughters

me see. Yes, I saw a reprint in an anthology of your essay on Randall:[1] absolutely beautiful and I thought to put up my own pen in shame and take up sleep. Let me know immediately if you want H. in London, etc. and about who can send me the meagre tax information we will need. Much love,

    Elizabeth

236. *Robert Lowell to* Mrs. Elizabeth Hardwick Lowell

Milgate Park, Bearsted, Maidstone, Kent
February 23, 1972 [1973]

What a lovely letter!
Dearest Lizzie:

I think the Italy with Harriet is almost impossible because the Italian colleges have vacation at the same time as she, and then open again in April. Also all of our children (including Sheridan who is on perpetual vacation) come home or are off from the Convent then. I think we should do as we did last year, a few days here and a few days in London. Sightseeing, tho less rigorous. A few people under fifty for her to meet. Plays, movies, talk. I am coming to admire the depths of reality open to even the wooliest person past fifty and under sixty, but that's an acquired taste not attainable at sixteen. How I will love having her. I thought she'd forgotten. Leslie Stephen certainly is not Arnold, as Housman points out somewhere[2]—nor is he Bagehot. His pieces seem all one material, which makes for monotony and, even now, a graceful encyclopedic usefulness. Blackmur, when you break the crust[,] has a

---

of Albion weep; a trembling lamentation | Upon their mountains; in their valleys, sighs toward America. | For the soft soul of America Oothoon wandered in woe" (1–3).

1. In *Randall Jarrell: 1914–1965*, ed. by Robert Lowell, Peter Taylor, and Robert Penn Warren (1967).

2. A. E. Housman: "I will not compare Arnold with the mob of gentlemen who produce criticism ('quales ego vel Chorinus'), such woful stuff as I or Lord Coleridge write: I will compare him with the best. [. . .] I go to Mr Leslie Stephen, and I am always instructed, though I may not be charmed. I go to Mr Walter Pater, and I am always charmed, though I may not be instructed. But Arnold was not merely instructive or charming nor both together: he was what it seems to me no one else is: he was illuminating" (from a typescript of "a paper of the 1890's on Matthew Arnold," *Selected Prose*, ed. John Carter [1961], p. 198).

wonderful love of what he is writing about[,] a strange grace of style forever troubled and cleared.

I'm reviewing Larkin's Oxford Modern anthology, and have done a draft yesterday—at the moment and maybe in the end—my worst prose. The anthology is only the English, but my main throw is a comparison of English and American. I start finding no difference and end with the opposite, though I have no ingenious theory or desire to prove. It's more like knowing two people apart.

We see Mary tonight and Esther and Peter Tuesday. Mary thank heaven got rather a rave on her Medina from Roy Fuller in the Listener or New Statesman.[1] She must have thought once with the Birds that any notice would be a knock. I expect this with my outpouring.[2] If the[re] were two, not three, I could subtitle them Two Rights can't make a Wrong. O talking of Ashbery, tho I can't penetrate his expert verses to much ~~substance~~ \enjoyment/, I like his reviewing. Whether he's right—Wheelwright *is* eccentric, but Whitman and Stevens even aren't particularly—he makes one determined to reread and reconsider.[3] I've just been thru Derek's long autobiographical[4] and on the first blush of enthusiasm, wrote him a rave. I daren't read a second time, there's a lot of unsteady poetic soaring, still the book has dazzling local color, and perhaps more important gives the feeling of having arrived open red-eyed at middle-age.

You seem to be working at a white heat. While you can you should, as you are doing, pack all you can without making a very big book. Did you read Fiedler's silly Shakespeare ~~book~~, not big, not good, vulgarizing every current issue?[5]

Two things should show in this letter: my gratitude for yours, for

---

1. Roy Fuller, "Deeds and Words," *Listener* (February 22, 1973).

2. *History, For Lizzie and Harriet,* and *The Dolphin.*

3. Ashbery: "The pure products of America don't always go crazy: Dr. Williams himself is a demonstration of this. But the effort of remaining both pure and American can make them look odd and harassed—a lopsided appearance characteristic of much major American poetry, whose fructifying mainstream sometimes seems to be peopled mostly by cranks (Emerson, Whitman, Pound, Stevens), while certified major poets (Frost, Eliot) somehow end up on the sidelines [. . .] Both John Wheelwright and A. R. Ammons are full of tics and quirks [. . .] Both are American originals (in the French sense of *un original* as someone who is also quite eccentric)" ("In the American Grain," *New York Review of Books*, February 22, 1973).

4. Derek Walcott, *Another Life* (1973).

5. Leslie A. Fiedler, *The Stranger in Shakespeare* (1972).

Harriet, and that I'm in the middle, tied in knots in the middle of my review.

Love,
Cal

237. *Robert Lowell to Harriet Lowell*

Milgate Park, Bearsted, Maidstone, Kent, England
February 23, 1973

Dearest Harriet:

I'm so happy you are coming! This trip won't be so new or so strange. You'll be able to picture what you are coming to and choose a little. You won't have to resee Canterbury, that red brick school (Or was that with the Taylors?)[,] Waterloo, the flea-market. On the other hand, Sheridan is much faster, badder, heavier, noisier—he continuously makes a sound like a pot of boiling water filled and wheezing and thumping and china mugs. The expression everyone uses about him is He's so tiring. A month ago he had five words, now he has none and puts the energy into forever running (he never walks) refusing to go where we want him, and bringing ~~one untimely~~ \us the wrong/ objects. He just brought me a letter I'd finished to Mother and which he had started to crumble[1] to make it smaller and more convenient.

I think we'll split the time between here and London. There's enough to do and a lot to see. Anything you can think up, I'll try to fulfill.

When you came a year ago, I'm sure you had many clashing thoughts, and many questions that couldn't be answered ahead of time or on the plane. I think I lay awake most of some of the nights before frightened and wondering if you would like what you found. It was something one was unaccustomed to[,] like riding a horse or climbing a tree for the first time—like going to a new country, but much more than that. We can't have that year again. This visit will be more like the rest of our lives. It's strange, after these three years of swimming the ocean to be walking on land.

All my love,
Daddy

---

1. Thus, for "crumple."

238. *Harriet Lowell to Robert Lowell*

[Telegram]

[New York]
[Received] 1 March 1973

MR ROBERT LOWELL MILGATE PARK
BEARSTEDMAIDSTONEKENT
= HAPPY BIRTHDAY FROM THE LITTLE MUDDLER + LOWELL[1]

239. *Elizabeth Hardwick to Robert Lowell*

[15 West 67th Street, New York, N.Y.]
March 2, 1973

Dearest Cal: Here, in haste, are the facts of Harriet's visit[.] It will be only one week because that is all they have, with a day or two on either end. She will come on Friday, March 23rd and return Friday, March 30. I will write all this once more, but I just want you to have the exact dates so that you will be free. Again she won't be getting in until nearly 11 your time.

Arrive, BOAC, Flight 213 at 10:40 P.M. London Time. Friday March 23rd. Since she is going youth fare, considerably cheaper than regular[,] she cannot have a definite confirmation back, but must absolutely confirm from London when she gets there.

Unconfirmed return: Leave, March 30, BOAC, Flight 501
at 11 a.m.

Can you please tell me who can give me information about your English earnings, *immediately*. Henshaw or who? I will be doing your tax for you this year; it is immensely complicated and I must start. Please send me the name and address by return mail. I have to have everything from there quite soon and haven't even sent the request yet.

I have looked into the Larkin anthology. Where will your piece appear? I understand there is some disappointment in his selection. I have also received Derek's book. Very moving isn't it? He's truly a lovely soul and he has brought all his possibilities together: the traditional poetry, West Indies, black, all of it . . . It has been a somehow

---

1. Cf. Lowell to Hardwick, [March 8, 1971], footnote 4 on page 152.

strange winter here in New York: a sense of rush has so wormed itself into my being that I suppose a sense of leisure would come down upon me as unwanted, a sort of depression. And yet I feel I can't experience anything as fully, purely as I would like. Perhaps it is just as well to fly about as lie about. And yet when you awaken to a blue, clear icy day, as this day is, it surrounds you like a soothing water and you wonder if it isn't all a dream and what joy to sink silently into it.

So! Anyway heartless, grey March dawn for tomorrow, with the truck grinding the night's paper from ABC.[1]

The accountant, and address. And you will be seeing Harriet just three weeks from today! Addio.

Love,
    Elizabeth

240. *Robert Lowell to* Mrs. Elizabeth Lowell

Milgate Park, Bearsted, Maidstone, Kent
March 5, 1973

Dearest Lizzie—

It's still Henshaw, Michael, 22 Park Sq. East, London. I'm in the process of shifting to Caroline's lawyer, but this takes time. Henshaw absolutely promises to get the figures to you as soon as he has them and quickly.

I've finished the Larkin in a way but see that I hardly mentioned either Larkin or the English. It's a responsible carefully weighed rather thrilling anthology, more names than can be counted, too much justice ~~rather than~~ \not/ too little.

Thrilled to have Harriet's business settled. I had a sweet wire from her, "Happy birthday from the Muddler* Lowell." Tell her her father is so muddled he can hardly put anything down—paper, cigarette-lighter and find it again.

Esther is here from visiting Dixey in Wales. I'll get this off.

Love,
    Cal

---

1. From the ABC News studio in the Hotel Des Artistes at 1 West 67th Street.

Saw Mary who finds your Jane C. as exciting as I do.[1] Now that your book is near I've grown careless of saving your pieces—could you send me copies of your two women and also to Esther ~~who has just arrived and~~ whom I disappointed by having lost my Reviews.

241. Elizabeth Hardwick to Robert Lowell

[15 West 67th Street, New York, N.Y.]
March 16, 1973

Dearest Cal: Harriet will be there as planned, 10:40 \BOAC/ your time, Friday night, at Heathrow. Here is the problem I want you to have in mind. She has no reservation back. Again it is the youth fare problem, but the saving is several hundred dollars. The night she arrives please go to the BOAC counter with her ticket and get the reservation back for the next Friday, March 30th. I hope she can get on the 1 o'clock plane: they seem to be rather crowded and it is very important to get space back that night, or call the next morning if something goes wrong. I'll have to be cabled so that I can meet her, flight number and time. On Saturday, the day after she goes to you, I am going to Nassau for a few days with Grace, but I'll be back in the middle of the week. It isn't necessary to call me from England[—]just so that I know when H. will be arriving, by cable. Harriet seems very pleased to be going off, pleased to see you, and she says she loves London.

I hope Henshaw will answer me immediately. Our taxes are very difficult this year and I must have all the material by April 1st. Money is an incredible problem for me. I hope to have another teaching day next year—both terms—and I think it will be in Columbia College, where I will teach a real course in Modern British Literature. I hope after this year to get something rather fancy lined up with a big salary. I have lots of offers but away from New York and I can't take that. I never want more than two days anyway; this is the last period in my life in which I want to stop writing. Did you get a letter or a call from City College—the figure they were talking about for you was $37,000! I said there was some possibility you might be interested for year after

---

1. "Amateurs: Jane Carlyle," *New York Review of Books*, December 14, 1972.

next (it would be the whole year, I think) but anyway I gave them your address and phone.

Frank Parker and Judy are coming for dinner. I haven't asked anyone else and I look forward somewhat to the meeting, but also with a feeling of oppression too. I haven't anything to say to Frank. He hasn't taken in anything new for so long and dear, eccentric as he is I can't look forward with a whole heart to trying to catch murmurs of our common past. I do think he's attractive in every way, of course, rare, but he's troubling too—not that I feel vulnerable anymore. Just a bother to try to project to him what you are, through his haze of wine and nostalgia and something very fixed, like a wall, about his relations.

Mary was here. I didn't have any real talks with her, always at parties and lunch toward the end, but never alone. She is grand as always. Stephen is coming, but I am going to be in Nassau most of the time he is here. Hope for the end of the week to have him for dinner. (Why I go into these small social notes I don't know.[)] Let's see for ["]something higher . . . ?" Higher, nobler? Jan Hughes[1] died and I felt sad indeed. I am still reading a lot of poetry. Perhaps I will write about it one of these days. Have even written three poems, but they aren't "finished!" I am not sure how poems are put together and reading doesn't really tell me what I wish to know. I hardly think I will flower and flourish on this. The trouble is how to make it new![2] I have been corresponding with Merwin—hysterical chapter in Alone in America about him, with a vocabulary of some mad talking machine. Merwin the Preterist—then faineance, aporia, fewmets(!) and lagniappe.[3] Look those up in your pocket thesaurus. I must say, knowing how you feel otherwise, that I like Howard. Sat next to him at dinner the other night and we talked of what we had learned from Cal! Und So. Goodbye, do the reservation, send the cable, needle Henshaw, enjoy Harriet, have a lovely, lovely time.

Elizabeth

---

1. A Maine friend.

2. Ezra Pound, *Make It New: Essays* (1934).

3. Richard Howard, "W. S. Merwin: We Survived the Selves That We Remembered," *Alone with America: Essays on the Art of Poetry in the United States since 1950* (1969), pp. 349–81; for the words Hardwick quotes, see pp. 357, 360, 366, 373, and 375.

242. *Robert Lowell to* MRS ELIZABETH LOWELL

[Telegram]

[Maidstone, Kent]
[March 24, 1973]

MRS ELIZABETH LOWELL 15 WEST67STREET
NEWYORKCITY
HARRIET ARRIVED SAFELY MATURELY AND GLORIOUSLY LOVE
CAL

243. *Elizabeth Hardwick to Robert Lowell*

[15 West 67th Street, New York, N.Y.]
March 31, 1973

Dearest Cal: Harriet had a really lovely visit, came home her dear self to her waiting Mother. I'll try to get her to write a note, but she goes back to school almost immediately, has been on the telephone all the rest of the time. I suppose it will take a few more years before the demands of politeness become a pleasure—at least after one has done them. But, in any case, she was utterly pleased and happy with her trip. I will be in touch with you about the summer. The month of August in Ireland with a group is definite. It isn't the worst kind of cycling which our very own muscleless, lazy dear nymph would take to less well than she imagines. One week on a barge, all very nice and yet simple hosteling. That does leave, for her, the rest of the summer. But I am not at all sure what form that will take. I like her to have a good time, she has a really nice, bright friend at last,[1] most of the old ones being sort of bound in one way or another. Still neither the other parents nor I will want them altogether "free" and so don't worry. I am in favor of some sort of English visit if it suits all of you and works with the group. For a couple of weeks before the month in Ireland. But later.

I am writing this about the infernal taxes. Naturally no word from Henshaw. The day grows near.[2] I am not at all sure that you want us to do yours. I simply cannot explain it all, but Nat H. tells me I can

---

1. Catherine Grad.
2. April 15 (American tax deadline).

do mine and be rid of it immediately. You see you do have to list the money you pay us as your income and then deduct it, etc., etc. You and I are not on a joint return; I was just willing to help this year here. But I think it would be better for you to get in touch with the situation (inwardly in touch) because I naturally can't bother about this, the reminder year after year. Nat H. doesn't even know whether he is supposed to do it or not. If the English material isn't in by this week do you want an extension until June—some fines, etc.—but that is what you did last year, waiting. Also, for the future I hear there is an international tax firm in London who might do it for you. But here is Mr. Hoffman's address for your books.

Mr. Nat Hoffman
41 East 42nd St.
New York, New York

This is just to say that I will not be worrying about your return and that you are on your own. I will give figures if you want to do it. (All of this always sounds like a rebuke. It isn't. I just want you not to get in trouble about this—and it is trouble I assure you.)

I spent a few *luxe* days in Nassau. Grace was very nice, but oh! She wants I think to sell her place there, but it isn't easy. Bob is fine. Stephen S. has been here, but I saw him only once.

Let's see. Elizabeth Bishop had a poem in the N. Yorker. "Evening News" I think it was called.[1] Obscure, but brilliant indeed. I wish I had time to write more or had more that seemed needful of communication. But anyway forgive the last tax tirade. I feel like a retiring civil servant! Much love and thanks for Harriet—if that is not an insult. I mean thanks for sharing our oh-so-nice creature with me.

Elizabeth

---

1. "12 O'Clock News," *New Yorker* (March 24, 1973).

244. *Robert Lowell to* Mrs. Elizabeth Lowell

Milgate Park, Bearsted, Maidstone, Kent

[April 4, 1973][1]

Dearest Lizzie:

Now Harriet has gone and come back to you, leaving me with two days of acute heaviness—not unpleasant like growing pains—hers. What do I mean? It's that we remain the same, and she changes, almost while one watched. But which moves, the rushing train or the still station? It's that her character and characteristics are now somewhat as they must be, yet her next years are lost in fog.

I think her summer needs more planning. Just to stay on her own in London doing nothing but following impulse might be confusing. It wouldn't be responsible or entirely safe to leave her alone in Redcliffe Square for a month. London's not like New York; it's safe enough to stroll at night. Still two young girls alone in an often empty house—they could be followed by an unknown interested man, as one of our nurses was—when we were there and she could threaten to scream. I would like her to have someone she knows to come back to. I think some sort of sculpture class would help too. Then let her be on her own. I'm sure I can find something, if I have her desires and dates. I think she set her heart on being on her own in London—even more than the bicycle trip.

We saw the Doll's House,[2] and I turned back to your review. Act 3 bothers me—first the uninspired coming together of Mrs. Linde and Krogstad then Torvald's drunkenness, the most amusing moment in the play, then Nora's tirade—it's a Browning outpouring. Like you I can't fit it to the earlier, subtly drawn Nora, but life is like that and feminine hysteria[3]—but it's all so badly written. Wasn't it

---

1. Postmarked, but probably written on April 1, 1973; this letter crossed with Hardwick's of March 31, 1973.

2. *A Doll's House* (film), dir. Patrick Garland (1973).

3. Hardwick: "The change from the girlish, charming wife to the radical, courageous heroine setting out alone has always been a perturbation. Part of the trouble is that we do not think, and actresses and directors do not think, the Nora of the first acts, the gay woman, with her children, her presents, her nicknames, her extravagance, her pleasure in the thought of 'heaps of money,' can be a suitable candidate for liberation . . . Claire Bloom in the present New York production plays the early Nora with a great deal of charm and elegance. But neither she nor the director, Patrick Garland, has any new ideas about the play. They struggle on in the traditional fashion

even when first done *shock or force expressed by stereotype?* Or is it the translation—this one[1] seemed worse than the old Archer.[2] I think Ibsen loved her and intensely hated her—to the point of glamour, to the point of irony.

Well, another woman, Harriet. We loved the moments. Everyone who saw her was struck by her beauty and intelligence—some more by one, some more the other.

Several things I've enjoyed. Somebody's piece on Pound, much better reasoned than I could do; Alfred's nostalgic but beautiful picture of the New York that has disappeared; the Brodskys quoted by Auden.[3] I got a new magazine in which 23 poets review 63 poets, all in one issue.[4]

All my Love to you. What are your plans?

Cal

245. Robert Lowell to Harriet Lowell

Milgate Park, Bearsted, Maidstone, Kent, England
April 5, 1973

Dearest Harriet:

We've found two art schools in London that have sculpture (rather a lost art compared with painting). I think both have lodging and can be taken by the week. They are not ~~especially~~ just for youths such as you, and won't have stern rules. Cleaning my study this morning, I carefully tucked the brochures in a special place for them—and now they are utterly lost. I can see the large prospectus page and the little application slips.

Tidiness must be the happiest of virtues—wash, sort, write down numbers—but it's no way to get rich. Life's a little empty without you.

---

with the early Nora and the late Nora, linking the two by an undercurrent of hysteria in the first part. This is not sufficient and will not really connect the two women" ("A Doll's House," *New York Review of Books*, March 11, 1971).

1. By Christopher Hampton.

2. Henrik Ibsen, *A Doll's House*, trans. William Archer (1889).

3. Michael Wood, "Ezra Pound," *New York Review of Books*, February 8, 1973; Alfred Kazin, "Melville the New Yorker," *New York Review of Books*, April 5, 1973; W. H. Auden and George L. Kline, "The Poems of Joseph Brodsky," *New York Review of Books*, April 5, 1973.

4. *Parnassus: Poetry in Review* 1, no. 2 (Spring/Summer 1973).

I am going on a short fishing trip to Westmoreland (Lake District in the North) around Easter. Oh the next best virtue to tidiness is foresight, always have double what you need, cigarette lighters, money. So I give you the name of the agency for art schools, Gabbitas Thring Educational Trust, 6 Sackville St. London W1. The art schools might be crowded, so you should apply before you come.

I'd write you more and more interestingly, but a day of tidying and sorting has deadened my mind. Your visit was an even greater joy than last year, maybe in a way because I can't remember much of anything we did, except two plays, the Old Colony Club,[1] the wait for land-reports. The farmer is asking about twice what the land is worth; and then, more important, it looks every day harder to get people to work in country houses. If I did it, think what a valuable man I'd be, able to work any where!

All our love,
Daddy

246. *Robert Lowell to* Mrs. Elizabeth Lowell

Milgate Park, Bearsted, Maidstone, Kent, Eng.
April 5 [1973]

Dearest Lizzie—

You may get this letter before one I wrote five days ago, took to London for quick mailing, and finally left with a friend when I rushed for a train. It crossed with yours and said some of the same things. Yes, it seemed as though Harriet much enjoyed herself without being pressured. It wasn't possible or perhaps desirable to introduce her to someone her age in so short a time. Sixteen year-olders seem a dying species, so few do I see—only rumors of someone who turns out on examination to be twenty.

It would be better to go to jail than disentangle the income tax. I stare at the forms like a catatonic. Yes, I do want an extension.

The agency that handles Art Schools is Gabbitas Thring Educational Trust, 6 Sackville St. London W1. I just got the forms, carefully stowed them away, and can't find them. If all three of us make an ef-

---

1. Thus, probably for The Colony Room.

fort, something should happen. I like Cathy[1] and like the idea of their coming here.

Help is beginning to get as difficult here as in America and may make it impractical to live in this wonderful quiet big house. However, summer brings floods of students (college)[.] I wonder if Cathy and Harriet . . . But baby-sitting is harder than bicycling.

The demands of politeness—I must thank the people who got us tickets.

Blair has just had a son.[2] Elizabeth Bishop is buying a wharf-apartment overlooking Boston Harbor. I'm spring-fever stricken, or maybe it's just things like the income tax, many of them,

all love as always,

Cal

247. Elizabeth Hardwick to Robert Lowell

[15 West 67th Street, New York, N.Y.]

April 9, 1973

Dear Cal: I was supposed to go to the Univ. of Wisconsin today for a lecture, but it was cancelled because of a blizzard! So the old country goes on in its wild, frontier ways. And yet once more on the taxes. This is the "transitional year" and I have done mine, but they are nothing because I have only listed what I earned myself. You see we have single returns this year and all the money you have given us is filed with the government under your name and will go into your single tax form. Of course when that is done I will pay the taxes, pro-rated, on the part of your return I owe. We have asked for an exten-sion for you until June 15th. Nat says he must have everything well before that. All the forms sent you from here, all your English earn-ings, etc. So will you please advise Henshaw. I wish to get it done as soon as possible. Next year you will list the things the same, but I will not be concerned with that because whether you file or not I can, next year, (this year, 1973) just put on my own return what I got from you and pay the tax on it, without caring whether you have filed or not.

---

1. Catharine Grad.

2. Ian Clark.

I can't do that this year because I am not allowed to except for the period after our divorce.

I had a long, heart-breaking letter from [X.Y.]. I do grieve for them and for their children. I know so well how devastating all this can be, trying to call doctors, wondering what to do, waiting, grieving, suffering. We never know what's ahead of us. Perhaps all you can stand on is love and compassion; they expose you to pain, but who would want to be empty and free. I feel very lucky in so many ways. These last years have in the end dealt very kindly with me. I am closer to more people, care more for them, feel more happiness somehow. It is quite strange, stranger than you can really imagine.

The Peter Taylors and son were here and we went to see, with Harriet, a not very good production for Pirandello's Henry IV.[1] Harriet was not inclined to any approval of "Ross" Taylor! His long hair and his little man version of his father's clothes, down to the hat, with the little white shirt, loafers . . . I am sure he must be quite all right, nice, good, intelligent, but to her he came from the moon, with the bit of a dwarf, square astronaut in him.

I see today is Monday. Wednesday I am going to Elizabeth's reading and then to a large party afterward, given by the Hollanders. Will save this until then.

Tuesday[2]

Your letter about Harriet was lovely and filled me with happiness. I showed it to her and she was blushing with pleasure, especially at "intelligent." About the summer: we are in complete agreement. Of course she and Cathy can't stay alone in London in Caroline's house; they aren't old enough or capable enough and I don't think they would really want it. At the moment the plan seems to be, in so far as England is concerned, maybe a week in Kent at the end of July if that is convenient for your family. They can bike around during the day. At the end they will meet their group in London and go with them for the Ireland trip and then home with the group.

I do hope she will have a week or so in Amsterdam with Cathy's family. C.'s father[3] will be at the University of Amsterdam for the sum-

---

1. Dir. by Clifford Williams at the Ethel Barrymore Theater on Broadway (opened on March 28, 1973).
2. April 10, 1973.
3. Frank P. Grad, a law professor at Columbia University.

mer. Amsterdam: Adrienne was here to spend the night recently, bearing a letter from Judith Van Leeuwen[1] saying Huyck had left her for someone "younger," blonder. She was distressed (Judith) and Adrienne was depressed. I saw them on my trip; she absolutely beautiful, he, thin, rather dry as always. I have never found him attractive as a "man"—whatever we women mean by that. I guess it means you would never want him as a lover. And there is something rather unimaginative about him, even if a great deal that is very intelligent and handsome. He must be sixty, since I always think of him as older than we are. As a man with women I think of him as "abstract"—working out some picture of himself in his affairs and changes. Awful that Judith should suffer and worst of all to suffer in Holland where there is never any room between you and your "betrayer"[2]—an incestuous country, narrow, over-crowded, small intellectual class. . . . Did I tell you the great? Arthur Lehning (Madeleine's of yore) called on me recently. He was at the Institute in Princeton; wildly at dinner with Isaiah I mentioned him (where he lay in my memory I do not know); Isaiah gave him my number. He is here with his Kropotkin collection and work. It was a Sunday. Harriet, anarchist, Kropotkin lover, agreed to appear. Lehning would have kidnapped her on the spot, even if there were an amiable number of and "why should she not be. . . . with a mother who . . ." But H. found him a dour anarchist, with his long underwear peeping out of his short nylon socks, his prim little ways, his rather green face and oily eyes.[3] I walked him to the bus to send him on his way to his next appointment. Much gay holding of my arm and drawn-out good-byes. Fantastic!

After your letters: Harriet won't be going to art school, will only be in England about a week. We will work it all out properly or she won't have to go at all . . . am sure the shorter time is more practical.

---

1. Judith Herzberg.

2. Hardwick: "In Holland the coziness of life is so complete it can not even be disturbed by the violent emotional ruptures that tear couples and friends forever apart in other places. Instead, there, first husbands and first wives are always at the same dinner parties and birthday celebrations with their second husbands and wives. Divorces and fractured loves mingled together as if the past were a sort of vinegar blending with the oil of the present. Where could one flee to? New alliances among this restless people were like the rearrangement of familiar furniture" (*Sleepless Nights*, p. 100).

3. Hardwick: "Dr. Z. met a mild New York winter day clothed in Siberian layers. He was wearing a heavy black overcoat, a woolen vest, a dark-gray sweater, and when he sat down in the waiting room off the lobby gray winter underwear appeared above his sock" (*Sleepless Nights*, p. 113).

Went to the reading of Elizabeth and Jimmy Merrill. Tous New York present and also present later at the Hollanders. Barbara thought three rooms of aging fag poets a bit effortful, but I didn't mind. Merwin, Strand, John Ashbery added to the Howard, Kalstone, etc. Elizabeth read well and looked special in a sort of flowing soft silk pants and top. She is very large and I hope that means happy. I had a talk with her and was pleased to exchange a few words as she stood in the center of Dr. Baumann, Louise Crane, her old friend some connection of John Dewey,[1] and, alas, Loren MacIver, who must have some utterly unfair disease, as she has shrunk and is like some pitiful, broken, shrinking dwarf. . . . Then, the flagrant Frank Bidart, atremble,[2] but ever obsequious. I avoided his glance forever, but he captured me and began his breathing inanities. I hope he understands your work better than he does mine, but I doubt it because he seems to have no knowledge of life, a touching condition if one has a sort of innocent sense of moral truth, but less moral than life I feel. He kept praising that old Vogue piece of mine with the photograph[3] and I felt like saying—influence of Harriet's decade and style—"Fuck you!" What could he know about all that? I truly dislike him deeply, do not trust him and think he is boring in that special way that only those without any depth or real character can be. Except for that, the evening was quite fun. I love Jimmy M. and I like his writing—of course it reads brilliantly aloud.

Farewell. I can't tell you my plans just now because I don't really know them. I will write a little about the Maine property sometime later.

With love,
Elizabeth

---

1. Jane Dewey, daughter of John Dewey.

2. Cf. Bidart to Lowell, a year previous on March 15, 1972, in which Bidart described a telephone call with Hardwick on his return from England after helping Lowell with "The Dolphin" manuscript: "[I]t was one of the most unpleasant and painful conversations I've ever had. She seemed to feel I had betrayed her by going there, or staying so long, or helping you. My hand still shakes when I think about it. She had heard from Bob Silvers that *Dolphin* was going to be published in a year; perhaps she blames me for that. I said as far as I knew no decision about *Dolphin* had been made. . . . It's terrible to be the object of her anger. Later Bill Alfred talked to her, and said she feels she had been wrong and went too far, and would write me an apology. . . . I haven't gotten one. I really like Elizabeth, and find this unutterably depressing" (Robert Lowell Papers, HRC). Lowell replied, "Sorry about Lizzie, she's been incredibly sweet to me lately, as we talk about Harriet's coming" (Lowell to Bidart, March 25, 1972, Houghton Library).

3. "The Ties Women Cannot Shake and Have," *Vogue*, June 1, 1970.

248. Elizabeth Hardwick to Robert Lowell

[15 West 67th Street, New York, N.Y.]
April 21, 1973

Dear Cal: I never in a million years thought you were trying to do the income tax yourself. No, no. Henshaw never answered my letter, not saying he wouldn't do it, would do it later, wasn't your accountant, didn't care. Now, most businessmen answer mail and especially when it is a natural and urgent request.

All that is needed here is for your accountant to send

1. Essex with all withholdings, taxes pd., etc.
2. Royalties, but not FS&G, whose statement I have
3. Readings, writings, International Famous
4. Some idea of deductions, studio, etc.

More or less what we finally got last year. I have the State Street Trust, but you must have Grandchildrens.[1] Didn't you get some tax material from Eisman,[2] if so send it to [your] accountant to send to

Mr. Nat Hoffman
41 East 42nd
New York, New York 10017

Please do this immediately. Call whoever is your accountant, then call back in a week to check if they have done it. That's all, really. You have to file an income tax or go to jail and so it must be done immediately. If there is an audit you will have to come over, but let's hope not.

Harriet fine. Mastering the bike—a tremendously masculine, speedy affair. She and Cathy go all over town and do twenty mile work-outs in the park. She is reading *Sons and Lovers* for school.[3] And how blessed you and I are, for the moment at least, that hippiness is more or less dead here. Too many disasters in the long run and, I suppose, really too boring, too expensive, too painful. I worry terribly about all the [X.Y.s] and feel so dreadfully for them.

Watergate: the patter of little rat feet leaving the ship. The cor-

---

1. Name of one of the Lowell trusts.
2. Trust manager.
3. By D. H. Lawrence (1913).

ruption in this country is incredible. Every day a governor, a district attorney, cops uncountable (mostly the most decorated) . . . But the Attorney-General.[1]

Harriet and I played St. Matthew's Passion[2] during Easter week and compared the Gospel Stories. She went to the Easter parade and reported nothing except drag queens, one in a granny dress and roller skates. No, no. Not even a flowered hat on revered grey hair.

Rats to your assertion that we never like the same people! . . . Adrienne has published her new book, *Diving into the Wreck*. Some are very beautiful and the propagandistic ones are a mistake. Lovely seeing the Taylors and I am truly sad that Elizabeth must put up with the ravages of cortisone.[3] "Every cure alerts a nerve that kills"[4] or some such words from the bard. I am so happy to know that she is sorted out and more or less content. I liked seeing her . . . All is the same here in Babylon. Went to the Epsteins for the weekend and Jason and I cooked six ducks and innumerable potatoes.

Ah, let me see. Nothing in my head this morning, although I always have a store of things I plan to write if I have occasion to do so. Whence are they fled?[5]

Much love to you,
    Elizabeth

249. *Robert Lowell to* Mrs. Elizabeth Lowell

Milgate Park, Bearsted, Maidstone, Kent, Eng.
[May 1, 1973]

Dearest Lizzie**

When I read your letter, I called Henshaw and he promises to collect the material over the weekend—if he lacks anything he will

---

1. On April 19, 1973, Attorney General Richard G. Kleindienst removed himself from the Watergate investigation owing to conflicts of interest. He resigned as attorney general on April 30, 1973.
2. By J. S. Bach (1727).
3. For asthma.
4. Lowell: "each drug that numbs alerts another nerve to pain" ("Soft Wood [for Harriet Winslow]," 42, *Near the Ocean*).
5. Keats: "Ah! Where | Are those swift moments? Whither are they fled?" (*Endymion* I, 970–71). Felicia Dorothea Hemans: "The boy stood on the burning deck | Whence all but he had fled" ("Casabianca," 1–2); cf. with Elizabeth Bishop's "Casabianca," *North & South* (1946).

call \me/ Monday. England is a little like Maine, no one ever does anything within the promised time. I guess this will go through. God knows, I'm rather like Maine too.

I was exhilarated by Watergate and by the old southern senator.[1] It gets to be rather too much doesn't it—the dull endless roster of German names and advertising experts. And the really much greater war crimes of Nixon and Johnson passing by unatoned. The only human touch so far among the accused is the Mitchells.[2] I wonder if the last election can't be declared fraudulent—that would get around Agnew succeeding. Or maybe Nixon will ride it—I don't see how, except maybe that the actual bugging seems secondary to the perjuries. Augean stables—are they ever clean? The country is \so/ close to moral ruin . . . and \it/ might get better.

Glad to hear of Harriet's bicycle drill. We've had hippies working here; the women work like beavers, but the men are languid. They vary a lot. Did I tell you Dean (?) Crooks of the Harvard summer school\'s daughter/[3] comes in daily to clean—very nice and works like a beaver.

It seems so natural writing to you, like breathing, an organic part of my life. May it ever be. \Last week,/ I went fishing up north in Westmoreland a sort of inland New England draining population county. After a while one *is* older—stiffness, cold fingers and toes.

Love to you and Harriet
Cal

250. *Elizabeth Hardwick to Robert Lowell*

[15 West 67th Street, New York, N.Y.]
May 5, 1973

Dearest Cal: First, business of what is called our "transitional year." Naturally the "transition" is merely the legal designation of last year. Mr. O'Sullivan's office reminds me that [the] second half of his fee was

---

1. Sam Ervin, chairman of the Senate Select Committee to Investigate Campaign Practices (Senate Watergate Committee).
2. John Mitchell, who was attorney general from 1969 to 1972 and then chaired the Committee for the Re-election of the President, and his second wife, Martha Beall Mitchell.
3. Thea Crooks Bray, a friend of Dixey Brooks; see Roxy Freeman, *Little Gypsy* (2011), p. 15.

due in March. You are to make out $1,750 to me and I send it to them. That will be over, but I have no idea when if ever I will be over paying fees to Boston lawyers about the trusts. And they did not pay Harriet's tuition, saying they still don't have \legal/ authority to do so. . . . I hope Henshaw will send the records to Nat soon because I must have that cleared away.

Now, after a request for forgiveness on the above matters. To remind someone of money is unforgivable and I long to be able to write a letter with no taxes (will do so if Henshaw will "close") and I hope no money matters of any sort.

I called the Thomases this morning about the matter of going up to Castine soon to empty the house on School Street, send everything to storage. They have started work on the barn, but I do not believe it will be ready this summer. I said to someone the other day that Maine was precious to me, you, Cousin Harriet, poems, our Harriet as a little summer girl. But I will not be dishonoring, erasing, you and Cousin H; the barn will always be a shrine to me, and the streets of the town, the water, the dock.[1] I am very glad not to have the house[.] New addition to the school next door, basement flooded all the time, more dampness, incredible expense. The barn, with a wing, upstairs and down where the shed was will be beautiful, easy, and I think Harriet will love it, as a truly pleasant, easy place to visit with friends when she is older. Warm, bright; and the water is something to do, if only to look at, think about, remember, cherish.

Terrible news, like a novel. First, Bishop Scarlett died during the spring. But second. You remember that Leah left Clark about two or more years ago.[2] It was one of those two couple affairs; the other a Bar Harbor family, he the director of Acadia National Park. He and Leah finally got married after the two divorces, and they went to live in Yosemite where the man, named Mr. Good, (remember the old Boston joke, *Was* Good!) was appointed director. Leah went out to pick wild flowers last week, was found dead in a gorge. Her husband and her sister say it was not suicide. What a ghastly, searing end. Bishop

---

1. Harriet Winslow left her Castine properties to Hardwick (not to Lowell), but Hardwick felt it was "for reasons of practicality" and "was not meant as a rebuke to Cal." See footnote 3 on pages 337–38 (Hardwick to Lowell, May 24, 1973, second letter) for a detailed explanation.
2. Leah and Clark Fitz-Gerald; Leah Fitz-Gerald was the stepdaughter of Bishop William Scarlett.

Scarlett's heart had been broken, his old heart, by Leah and the frightening collapse of Clark's family. Clark behaved in the most childish, undisciplined way that was truly unforgivable, complaining, unable to take hold or even pretend to, to carry on. One looks back on their \the Fitz-G's/ somewhat accusing purity, making do, capabilities of an old-fashioned sort. The awful thing was that people began to hate Leah and yet Clark gave them nothing to respect with his self-pitying deterioration. I sympathize because of the house in Maine, the cold, the emptiness, the winds, the rains. And poor Leah's happiness, what all of this was meant to be about, in honor of! The wild-flowers are too much. Nature does betray the heart.[1]

Send the check, please, for the last of the divorce bill and please check once more with Henshaw about the taxes. All must be here soon because Nat needs time and may be going away.

Love,
Elizabeth

251. Elizabeth Hardwick to Robert Lowell

[15 West 67th Street, New York, N.Y.]
Thursday, May 17, 1973

Dear Cal: In Haste. I hope you have sent back the deeds signed by you and Caroline and notarized, as requested. Sent to Veague in Bangor. I am going up for a week on May 23 to empty the School Street house and send everything to storage. I hope to sign the sale deed on May 31st, as I agreed long ago. Work has started on the barn and yet I do not expect it to be finished by this summer. I may go to the Rockefeller villa in Lake Como, but it is not clear just yet because I only asked about it a few days ago and naturally everything for the summer had been settled long ago. However, more about that when I come to write you about Harriet's trip, a rather mixed up affair. Also the final check for my lawyer's bill, please, if you have not already sent it. Also I have not heard of any progress on the taxes, a really foolish unnec-

---

1. Wordsworth: "And this prayer I make, | Knowing that nature never did betray | The heart that loved her" ("Lines, written a few miles above Tintern Abbey, on revisiting the banks of the Wye during a tour, July 13, 1798," 122–24).

essary situation since so little is involved from England and so much from us here is waiting.

Will write in less business-like a manner after all of this is settled. I am at my desk working, with the little tv on a stool next to me. First day of the Senate Watergate Hearings!

Harriet is fine, except for examinations coming up.

Love,
Elizabeth

252. *Robert Lowell to* Mrs. Elizabeth Lowell

Milgate Park, Bearsted, Maidstone, Kent
\(A first letter, a week earlier than the second, and almost the same I'm afraid.)/[1]
May 21, 1973 [postmarked May 28, 1973]

Dear Lizzie:

Back from Italy—with O'Sullivan's bill, bill for $300 from Iseman, ten thousand out of Harvard when contract is signed for you, five thousand I've decided to give Elizabeth Bishop.[2] However she is intelligibly murky on whether she will accept it. This is all expected, but I have an illusion of paying more than I earn; my money is in small bits, with different ~~checks~~ \rules/ on them—and the amounts seem to change. And then the new vat[3] system, and then the income tax. My fault. I'll send the lawyer's, tho he seems to be paid more than than four carpenters working three weeks.

I have questions of the "dower" deeds. I've mislaid the divorce agreement, so I can't cite the minute particulars on which truth lies. But it's inconceivable that Cousin Harriet who unlike us knew all there

---

1. See Lowell to Hardwick, May 26, 1973 (below).

2. Lowell to Elizabeth Bishop: "My ms. sale to Harvard is coming to a conclusion, though there are still details. Your letters are the most valuable and large single group. I would like to have them pay you $5000. Of course they are yours, your writing, just as Miss Moore's letters are hers, but convention gives letters to the recipient. [. . .] I've seen a few of my own letters (to my mother, Roethke, incongruous couple) they aren't too much, but have words and sentences written seriously and unlike what I print. Yours have the startling eye and kept-going brilliance of a work to print. I hope you do" (*Words in Air*, p. 740).

3. Value-added tax, introduced in the U.K. in 1973 after it joined the European Economic Community.

was to know ~~on such matters~~, wasn't aware of this, and didn't intend to protect the Maine property for me and Harriet. I am interested in Harriet's part. If the house is sold, she should have some half (delayed) ownership in the *restored* barn, or a sum of money to be given her at eighteen or twenty-one. This might be worked out in several ways, all a little complex. Also I must have things, personal things, like the eagle, country clothes etc. Not worth much but dear, if I were to see ~~and~~ \them I would/ recognize them ~~again. Or maybe~~ I have no legal right to ask this?

I keep phoning Henshaw and he keeps promising. I will again this afternoon. But why can't your lawyer deal directly with him?

France and Italy, Paris and Pisa. Though my French and Italian have certainly rotted somewhat, I had a strange feeling that [I] could master both in six months. No. It's that after twenty years, city, country and tongue seem less foreign. Again the twenty course dinners with the poets; again Giambologna—Orcagna restored, the halls of the Campo Santo we saw in 1950 covered. Wish we were arriving again. Peter Brooks and I half-seriously imagined flying to the US to watch Watergate on TV. I don't intend to hold up the deed, \much,/ but it's naturally sad for me to have the house sold. What are you getting? Should I let it go without worries and suggestions, as if it had only been air to me?[1]

253. Elizabeth Hardwick to Robert Lowell[2]

[Castine, Maine]
May 24, 1973

Dear Cal: I'm writing you immediately after my call. I understand the feeling of deprivation very well and the emotional torrents about Maine. I am here all alone, trying to get things together in a week, and it has been a trauma, one that started weeks ago. I do want you to understand that nothing is being destroyed, thrown away, either here or in New York. True this house is being sold and I want to explain that it has been increasingly expensive to run it, there has been an addition

---

1. Signature not visible.

2. Letter crossed with Lowell's letter of May 21, 1973 (which wasn't posted until May 28).

to the school, flooded basement, the house increasingly damp, and very, very hard to keep up, roof, etc. I wasn't even in the barn last year, because I just never got around to opening it, cleaning it and that too is terribly expensive—taxes, mowing, burglary. It seemed to me that I couldn't begin to afford both, that I was exhausted with the work involved, Harriet at this stage doesn't like either. All the advice I could get, everything that seemed right, indicated selling this, adding a wing to the barn. We are putting the barn itself on a foundation; the wing will have a cellar, will go upstairs from the barn with a balcony, two bedrooms with one bath. Downstairs, kitchen facing the sea, and a guest room. I will put all I get for the house on the Commons into that and some more. But Harriet will have a place she can drive up to from May through Sept., with her friends, open the door, sweep out, close the door—nothing. All on the sea, compact, and very beautiful. Coming into the Commons House is a three week job. It is increasingly damp and mildewed. I could sell both and give H. the money, but how would she invest it? The thing is that real estate is the best possible investment. I am assured that this is in her interest. The Commons sort of house is not very desirable now; I feel I got a top price and for the last time. When I got here, the sidewalk was all torn up from new sewers, the yard in front destroyed, etc. I am keeping everything. If you and your family ever want to use the barn house you can do so with joy from me. Nothing of yours is being destroyed. In New York I am even more careful because I feel very strongly. About some money for Harriet I agree. I will look at our agreement, talk to Mr. O'Sullivan and see before you come in Sept. how it should be done. We will talk then. I just want to ease your mind about this and also offer it to you for any possible time. It won't be done this year. I won't be up here, or you could come up for a weekend in September.

Do take care of yourself. I hope to receive the lawyer's money, the tax figures (absolutely minimal) and then we can do your last year's tax. When you come in the fall, I think perhaps you can go and talk to Mr. Hoffman and arrange something. Our situation is complex, indeed, and I am prevented from paying taxes on the money you have given me because the money is listed as your income still in Washington. How boring it all i[s]. I assure you I don't go on about this in my life except for these letters to you, which are a grief to me, with all their business. I am fine, saw briefly in NYR office your Encounter piece,[1] very good, but I will have to get the magazine. No notice or news here of your books yet. Had lunch with Bill Merwin in New York and sat all afternoon looking at Watergate. I will write again. Will be back in New York very soon after this reaches you. Here is Mr. Veague['s] address. If you get this in time, airmail to him, otherwise to me. If Caroline has to sign please have her do it, at the Consulate. Mr. Arnold Veague, 6 State Street, Bangor, Maine.

I hate having a conversation like the one we had. Much love, \good health/

Elizabeth

The seals, the swallows miss you & so do I. How awful life is in some ways, with its swift passage![2]

254. Elizabeth Hardwick to Robert Lowell

[Castine, Maine]

May 24, 1973

Dearest Cal: Another letter, written after our conversation this morning, written at night. I was very distressed and I do know how you feel. I feel a great deal about Maine, but I know you feel many things in addition: the deprivation of the past, the idea that *I* have everything that belongs to you, money, houses, everything. You always felt very strongly about Castine, about its not being really mine—and I agree to that.[3] I even asked Mary if she thought you and your family would

---

1. "Digressions from Larkin's 20th Century Verse," *Encounter* 40 (May 1973).

2. Thomas Hardy: "Why did you give no hint that night | That quickly after the morrow's dawn, | And calmly, as if indifferent quite, | You would close your term here, up and be gone | Where I could not follow | With wing of swallow | To gain one glimpse of you ever anon! [. . .] O you could not know | That such swift fleeing | No soul foreseeing— | Not even I—would undo me so!" ("The Going" 1–7 and 40–43; 40–43 are quoted in Hardwick's "Writing a Novel," *New York Review of Books*, October 18, 1973, and in *Sleepless Nights*, p. 151.)

3. In a letter to Lowell dated January 25, 1956, Harriet Winslow wrote that she was going to leave the lifetime use of her Castine properties to the Lowells, together with a small income to cover taxes and upkeep. "I left the life income to Elizabeth instead of to you so that if she outlives you she can have it" (Houghton Library, Harvard). Lowell replied on January 31, 1956: "I feel an improper, but probably immemorially Bostonian squeamishness about acknowledging your

ever come here and she didn't think it would be likely. Summer is very brilliant in England, etc. But I cried after I talked to you, cried because I do have nice relations with others, as you do, never acerb, argumentative.[1] I called Harriet when she got home from school and had a long talk. She has professed utter hatred of Castine for the last few years, but I don't take that as permanent but as a just feeling about the deadness for her age. She said that she felt I was doing the right thing and that she could really imagine liking it, coming up without me with her friends later, when a truly interesting manageable place was made of the barn. The last years have been so much work for me and I want something simpler, and indeed this house, on School, is very expensive and difficult. I told Harriet that if she didn't like Maine when she was in college, I would sell it and she could have the money to invest and live on. I myself actually would not have too many regrets about disposing of the whole thing. What I would do I don't know, but I truly can't feel that would be right \now/. The furniture, the barn, the whole thing still seems a part of whatever it is a part of and I will come up after this year; also I can rent very easily with my new easy place . . . But it is awful. I have not and never will throw out anything of yours, your family's, anything, Harriet Winslow's. I have just dusted off your

---

kindness in your will. We are grateful for the life-hold on the brickyard house, and the generous yearly subsidy . . . and what touches me to the heart is that you have always seen Elizabeth as Elizabeth, and not just Elizabeth née Hardwick Lowell, a sort of Winslow in-law at one remove, though of course she is that too." See *The Letters of Robert Lowell*, pp. 253 and 724. When Harriet Winslow died in 1964, both the houses and the income were left to Elizabeth Hardwick. Hardwick: "Maine property. Was left in its entirety to me by Miss Winslow. Cal had no claims at all on it, but I always felt it was left to me for reasons of practicality and was not meant as a rebuke to Cal. When we were together, he and I decided that I would sell part of it in order to improve the barn on the water where he worked. That was done. When we were divorced, I wanted to live in the barn as more suitable for me and Harriet. I had to sell the house on the Commons in order to make a house of the barn. Under Maine law, Cal, as my former husband, was required to sign. Only his signature was required, but he refused for a good while, seeming to think the signature indicated that the property had been left to both of us. I explained, the Maine lawyer explained, but he would not for a long time accommodate and I almost lost the sale of the other house. Behind this was, in my view, his sadness, not his greed, that Cousin Harriet, much loved by both of us, had done what she did" (Hardwick to Ian Hamilton [n.d.], Elizabeth Hardwick Papers, HRC).

1. For "acerb" see Hardwick to Ian Hamilton on an early draft of his biography: "Throughout I seem to be little more than a nurse, and an early 'acerb' critic"; and on her "Notebook": "Cal, I think, hoped it would be deliciously acerb and 'interesting'" (Hardwick to Ian Hamilton [n.d.], HRC).

Harvard degree to take to New York. You have no real idea about how much I do feel the custodian of everything. I know you have no money, neither do I. I work very hard, and just as soon as Harriet gets to college I will be doing things like a term at Berkeley, everything I'm asked. I am enclosing these photographs. Will send you some more from New York from various periods, places—mostly without me if possible.

I am so sorry you are distressed about this. I suppose if you were here you would see how difficult it is. I have written a little thing I will send you about this move, the houses.[1] I do feel it all strongly. ~~If you call me when you get this letter I will not sell. . . .~~ Please forgive me. Life is very difficult in many ways for Harriet and me and we do try to keep going. I will definitely do what you think about money going directly to her, will talk it over when I see you in the fall. . . .

The Thomases are fine, Castine is lovely. I will probably be abroad most of the summer—but more of that later. I just feel utterly sad and upset about my talk with you.

     Elizabeth.

---

1. Enclosure now missing, but possibly a passage from Hardwick's "Writing a Novel": "*1972* Dearest M: I have sold the big house in Maine and will make a new place there, beginning with the old barn on the water. 'Existing barn,' the architect's drawings say. But I fear the metamorphosis, the journey of species. The barn, or so I imagine of all barns, once existed for cows and hay. Then later it was—well, a place. (For what I do not like to say. Too much information spoils the effect on the page, like too many capitals within the line, or the odious exclamation point. Anyway, you have the information.) Will the barn consent to become what I have decided to make of it? I don't know. Sometimes I am sure that I am building for a tire salesman from Bangor whose wife will not be kind to the sacred wounds of such a building—the claims, the cries of the original barn, the memories of the abandoned place. The claims and cries of Lightolier, Design Research, turkey carpets. As for the other, sluffed-off house, I mourn and regret much. The nights long ago with H. W. and her glorious 78 recording of Alice Raveau in Glück's *Orpheo*. I hear the music, see H. W. very tall, old, with her stirring maidenly beauty. The smell of the leaves outside dripping rain, the fire alive, the bowls of nasturtiums everywhere, the orange Moroccan cloth hanging over the mantle. What a loss. Perhaps my memories, being kind, betray me and bleach the darkness of the scenes, the agitation of the evenings. I am as aware as anyone of the appeal, the drama of the negative. Well, we go from one graven image to the next and, say what you will, each house is a shrine" ("Writing a Novel," *New York Review of Books*, October 18, 1973; see pp. 461–71.). Revised and included in *Sleepless Nights*.

255. *Robert Lowell to* Mrs. Elizabeth Lowell[1]

Milgate Park, Bearsted, Maidstone, Kent, England
May 26, 1973 [postmarked May 28, 1973]

Dearest Lizzie:

I've spent the forepart of this afternoon looking for the divorce agreement, and fail to find it though once there seemed to be three or four, various versions, in drawers.

I've been in a rather inactive mood since coming back from Italy, but also I am reluctant to act quickly on the "dower." The first I heard was a letter out of the blue from Iseman. I'm not happy about the common's house being sold, but of course feel that it is practical . . . necessary for you. I am assuming that Cousin Harriet, who was very up on such things, must have counted on the dower as some protection for me and Harriet. I am my own protector? Still it's a desolate thought that all I have from the past is Grandpa's gold watch and some fifteen books. I suppose that isn't something for us to fight about, ~~that~~ in convenient time, books, articles, furniture (a small share) will come. I do think Harriet must have something of her own while we are still alive. I suggest that out of the trust she be given at eighteen say, $1500 \a year./ I was eager to arrange this last fall in New York, but there were legal or tax obstacles. The houses were, maybe in Cousin Harriet's eyes, a certain protection for her; a yearly independent allowance would be a\n/ ~~better~~ equivalent.

I am not trying to hold you up more than I have written (except why should I sign away my claim to *all* \my/ Castine property?) The barn isn't being sold.) I am rather irritated about this being sprung on me in an instant.

Strange, this morning I was planning a friendly dawdling gossipy letter to you. We still can't get a house for four months at Harvard, but I suppose we will and it would be more satisfactory for me to pick out the books myself. It's cramped, almost illiterate not having them.

Write me about Harriet's summer. I keep trying to stir Henshaw.

Love, ~~Cal~~
\Cal/

---

1. Letter crossed with Hardwick's two letters of May 24, 1973.

256. Elizabeth Hardwick to Robert Lowell

[Castine, Maine]
May 30, 1973[1]

Dear Cal: I'm still in Maine and will be here two more days. Rain, storms, tornadoes, utterly dead, silent weekend. What a ghastly chore all of this has been. I write this, early morning, to say that I hope you sent off the notarized deed yesterday. I signed a contract in the fall to sell on May 31st and they to buy. Of course that won't be possible and I have a horror of the people backing out because of the delay— and all the furniture in storage at great expense. Having been here completely confirms me in the wisdom of my move. The house is impossible, much more activity at the school, yard a mess, fence destroyed, house so cold and damp. In a way I wish I didn't have to have anything here, because it is so far away, only practical for at least a three-month summer stay which I don't necessarily consider I will be sure to want, hideously expensive to fly up and back for chores, opening. However, Castine is very beautiful and I will persevere with it. Harriet is very much in favor of what I am doing, at least in getting rid of this house. I expect she will love Castine at some later period in her life. I hope so.

A special evening with the Coris and the Thomases, most of it spent talking about Gilgamesh—or listening to Carl C. Went to Frank Kneisel's funeral Saturday at the Trinitarian Church; little voices in the choir, organist (Mrs. Coombs) playing "Going Home" and Liebestraum;[2] very cold, grey day, all the old folks there. Came out into the gloom utterly melancholy and so drove to Bucksport and bought a copy of The Village Voice. Restored to urban idiocy as against rural spiritual blight. Today a memorial service for Bishop Scarlett. The Booths are here for a few days; had a drink with them yesterday. Leah and Clark haunt the town still. A sort of wasteland up there. Old Mrs. Fitzgerald dazed and lonely as a crippled eagle; all the rest gone into a world of light.[3]

---

1. Crossed with Lowell's letters of May 21 and May 26, 1973.
2. William Arms Fisher (words), Antonín Dvořák (music), "Goin' Home" (1922/1893); Franz Liszt, *Liebesträume* (1850).
3. Henry Vaughan: "They are all gone into the world of light! | And I alone sit lingering here" (*Silex Scintillans II*, 1–2).

I can't wait to get back home. Nine days for this! Why was I born a woman I asked myself once or twice. I want to shed as many burdens as possible and a lot of things have no meaning for me now and the effort seems unreal. New York is a struggle, but I do like it. It is the present for both Harriet and me, very alive, happy. Maine is a tomb. Perhaps it is only the weather, the anguish of this packing, moving, the anxiety of making the barn, the expense. I don't really know just what is involved in my present state of feeling about it here. I truly wonder if I will ever be eager to spend a whole summer here again. I have no clear picture right now of this coming summer. I want to spend August at the Rockefeller villa in Lake Como, but I thought of it just a few weeks ago and of course it is full. However they are trying to work something out and I should have word soon.

Meanwhile, this is a sort of adieu to Castine from me, dour and foggy and final. I hope the deed, executed as they asked, has gone off to Mr. Veague. Be in good health. I send my love as always

Elizabeth

257. *Robert Lowell to* Mrs. Elizabeth Lowell

Milgate Park, Bearsted, Maidstone, Kent, England
June 1, 1973 [but postmarked May 31, 1973][1]

Dearest Lizzie:

It was miraculous to have your letters and pictures. It always seems to have been an unfulfilled craving in my life to have a scrapbook—as the drawers overflowed with unsorted photos. I had just bought one, and now it's filled, artfully arranged pages, sequences, like my long poems, full of profundity for me if no one else. Way back, I have Allen and Mrs. Ford Madox Ford, Peter and me and Jean in New Orleans, looking hung over, except unbelievably for Jean. I have no old ones of you because two and a half years ago I left my billfold in a restaurant or taxi—early in the evening going home—and lost about eight small snapshots and a hundred dollars (?) in Per's Norwegian money. What I miss is that wonderful wild one of you smoking, taken on the Loire (?) by Robie. Please send me more. We can call it *Notebook's Scrapbook* and

---

1. Crossed with Hardwick's letter of May 30, 1973.

sell it [to] the Sunday Observer like Waugh's Diaries[1] . . . No, I really want more. Do send lots of you!

My books? I've written Bob to send you all three and just History to Harriet, so as not to force them on her. They'll be out June 20, almost three weeks late due to some unaccounted delay by Farrar—tho they may have had to because of Frank's drawings.[2] They please me very much. I mustn't write of your feelings about the book. I wish the publication and reviews were over; I seem to be a mark for all sorts of dissimilar people in both America and England. The books are so many and they cost ~~more~~ so much, less here than in America.[3] It would have been slovenly to have brought them out in one volume, though cheaper.

The sale of the commons house is a kind of death, but I think it was unavoidable. If you are willing, since you write the house is mine to use, we might make some sort of *access* agreement, something less binding than with children and really meaningless except psychologically. I would be too shy to live there until after my death. Maybe Sheridan could come as a visitor. I don't think he and Harriet are likely to become intimate—if he were five years younger he could easily be her son. When you write me, I'll sign the dower. It came too quickly and undescribed.

I am having a hell of a time with Henshaw. First he didn't call back, then came the long weekend bank holiday. Now he is incommunicado somewhere in Europe till the week end. You must feel everyone in America is a Nixon bugger; we feel everyone here must have a title and sordid photographed sexual orgies, a long suffering wife and a thousand acres[4]—Somehow aided or hindered by Henshaw. I'll try again to get some one else.

---

1. Cf. Lowell, "The Literary Life, A Scrapbook" (*Notebook69-1*, *-2*, *Notebook70*) and "Picture in *The Literary Life*, a Scrapbook," *History*. Waugh's diaries were published for eight weeks in the *Observer Colour Magazine* from March 25–May 13, 1973.

2. Frank Parker's frontispieces for the American editions of the three books. Their official publication date became June 21, 1973.

3. In the U.S., the list price of both *The Dolphin* and *For Lizzie and Harriet* was $6.95 (approximately $39.66 in 2019 dollars [CPI]) and *History* was $7.95 (approximately $45.36 in 2019 [CPI]). In the U.K., the list price of *The Dolphin* was £1.75 (approximately £22 in 2018, according to the Bank of England Inflation Calculator [BoE]), *For Lizzie and Harriet* £1.40 (approximately £17.50 in 2018 [BoE]), and *History* £2.95 (approximately £37 in 2018 [BoE]).

4. A reference to the Lord Lambton and Lord Jellicoe sex scandals of May 1973; see Our Political

Don't tell me about house decay. In the last month we've had two flooded cellars, the remov[al] of a partition, leadshallows stolen from an outbuilding, a dog lost, an unfindable fuse, a skylight leak, the disappearance of all our napkins and handkerchief, a plastering job done by Dixey's husband's brother,[1] a three days' cook with a son who went insane—the mother, Dean Crooks of Harvard's marvelous daughter married to a hippy[2] buying a donkey without asking us—the donkey had a bad cold and had the vet for six pounds, the dryer stopped, and so on. Houses really ail more than we do, they never cure themselves. I watch time go too, and love thinking about you and writing.

All Love\, and H. All day I've lived thru her life in your pictures./
Cal

258. Elizabeth Hardwick to Robert Lowell

[15 West 67th Street, New York, N.Y.]
June 3, 1973

Dear Cal: This goes off in great haste. I really must urge you to send the properly executed deed to Mr. Veague immediately. The house is empty. It took me nine, lonely, cold days, with bones and heart aching; all has gone to storage in Bangor for the year. Your eagle, your fish, your father's pearl-handled sword, everything. It will be sent back, all the furniture, everything to the completed barn this time next year. I have spent $2,000 just on that. I have great fear that this delay will cause my people to back out. They will not sign until the deed comes and they have had a chance to go up to inspect the premises, which alas seemed to me full of flaws and fears. I have grave doubts about the practicality of Maine for me; the expense, the distance—the fact that I can only make it practical by spending at least three months there. But I can not,

---

Staff, "Resignation of Lord Lambton as Minister," *Times*, May 23, 1973; "'I have no excuses . . . I behaved with credulous stupidity,'" *Times*, May 23, 1973; David Wood, "Mr Heath orders Security Commission inquiry after Lord Jellicoe resigns in call girl scandal," *Times*, May 25, 1973; and Wilfrid Kerr, "My wife and family are standing by me, Lord Lambton declares," *Times*, May 25, 1973.
1. Dixey Brooks married Dik Freeman, a gypsy (his brother was Bob Freeman); see their daughter Roxy Freeman's memoir, *Little Gypsy* (London: Simon & Schuster, 2011).
2. Malcolm Bray.

never will, let the barn go. I am making a very rentable, salable, valuable property for Harriet. As it is, just keeping all of it would be impossible for us and this is at least the ~~proper~~ getting in order. It will also be smashingly beautiful . . . As for the deed, that has nothing to do with Harriet Winslow, but with the amazingly backward State of Maine. It is only that since we are still married (there!) you have under Maine law the rights to half anything of mine, but I also have the right to anything of yours (England, elsewhere). I am doing something about all of that, but the signing of the deed, the only thing that concerns Maine law \now,/ is the first thing. I have been grieved and worried about it for sometime, since I knew you didn't understand. If I lost my sale and had an empty house there it would be a disaster! I cannot go up, at vast expense, to wait for another sale. . . . Please have it properly executed, as they asked, and sent to Veague immediately. I thank you. What a bore and a sadness.

I enclose the pictures I had around. There are almost none of me here, and I have only one nice one of the three of us taken in Santa Fe and one of you and me on Fred Dupee's steps a few months after we were married. I'll try to get a copy sometime because I somehow want to keep the ones I have.

I cannot do anything further about your filing a tax return for 1972. This is a thing that will go on until you die and so I guess this year is the time to get in touch with it. No one, Cal, writes you about filing income taxes; *you* have to *ask* an accountant to do it. Nat agreed, but it is not the sort of business where they check to see if you have paid, if you have filed or not filed. They simply take the figures, sit down with the person, talk it over, do the computing, filling the forms. It is immensely expensive for me—over $600 last year to the accountant. I think you will have to meet with him in September, set up something for the future. I don't say this in any kind of criticism. It really has nothing to do with me. I am always saddened to hear of any practical problems, a sadness deepened and sharpened by my own never finished practical problems.

I hate these business letters, hate writing them, as if I were a truant officer, which indeed I am not. I have just come home from what seemed like a lonely, breaking year in a house, dark and cold, and what a joy to see Harriet, to be back in the security of New York. Watergate starts up tomorrow. I go out to vote for some losers in the city Democratic primary, my desk is stacked with mail, my back hurts, my hands are cut (so much rusty iron in Maine) and I cannot sleep until the deed is with Veague and the thing done!

Here, to think on:

All things fall and are built again,
And those that build them again are gay.[1]

I went to a memorial service for Bishop Scarlett. A mad evening with Carl Cori telling me about Gilgamesh! He has a new hearing aid, but we all discovered that he has no intention of learning to listen. Greetings from one home to the sullen streets[2] after the sullen north.[3]

Elizabeth

259. *Robert Lowell to* Mrs. Elizabeth Lowell

Milgate Park, Bearsted, Maidstone, Kent, England
June 7, 1973

Dearest Lizzie***

Heavenly day, blue, gold, green and shadows. Till recently, a man downstairs vibrantly taking out pipes; poor Sheridan steadily crying with chickenpox of the *mouth*, now on the mend we hope, though his trouble was prolonged by the breezy local doctor, more or less prescribing the same cures for all diseases.

I am waiting for your reply to your[4] letter to sign the dower—I do

---

1. W. B. Yeats, "Lapis Lazuli" 35–36 (1936).

2. Cf. Moorfield Storey: "Some of us remembered the crowded sullen streets of Boston, through which by military force Anthony Burns was carried back to slavery. We had heard the news of battle and outrage on the plains of Kansas, and we had burned with fierce indignation, when Sumner was beaten in the Senate for daring to denounce the crimes committed against that unhappy territory [. . .] We had walked with tingling veins beside the Sixth Massachusetts as it marched through Boston on its way to the front, and had felt the sharp shock when the telegraph told us that the first blood of the war had been shed by those very men" ("Harvard in the Sixties" [1896]; reprinted in *Harvard Graduates Magazine* 5 [1897], p. 334).

3. Cf. Herman Melville: "Heavy the clouds, and thick and dun, | They slant from the sullen North" ("Admiral of the White" 15–16 [1885]).

4. Thus, for "your reply to my letter."

have the rather desolate feeling of staring at the bare floor of a once furnished house, but I don't intend to hold you up. Finally got Henshaw, first his phone was busy an entire day, then came the bank holiday, then he was incommunicado in France or Turkey, resting from overwork; now he promises to have [the] income off to you on Monday. The catch is that it has to be accurate and identical with my British returns.

I feel your seduction mounts and gains when both parts are read.[1] Also that one should not take them as exactly a critical essay, but a sort of reverie or monologue on the "situations." I had many of my own to write you—reflections, rambles, but now they flee me[2]—the sadness of putting off writing when one is full of it. Bob S. is coming here Saturday with the Grosses—I've seen several Americans, the Rosenthals, the Cowleys . . . and many more in letters. We still have no house in Cambridge. I resolve to see movies, but somehow have seen none except an atrocious Maidstone Western. What sticks most in my mind is \one part of/ Shirer's book on the fall of France,[3] General Gamelin, when all was falling, infinitely solicitous (tenderly) that he get eight hours sleep, and that everyone else get them, and eat unhurriedly—that his incompetent subordinates be fired only by hints they could never hear. The French were as bad as Nixon's staff in betraying and blaming each other. Are real books being written any more, are there any ~~more~~ we haven't read?

Love to Harriet and to

you,

Cal

---

1. "Seduction and Betrayal: I," *New York Review of Books*, May 31, 1973; "Seduction and Betrayal II," *New York Review of Books*, June 14, 1973.

2. Sir Thomas Wyatt: "They fle from me that sometyme did me seke" (1540).

3. William L. Shirer, *The Collapse of the Third Republic: An Inquiry into the Fall of France in 1940* (1969).

260. *Robert Lowell to* MRS. ELIZABETH LOWELL

[Telegram]

Milgate Park Bearsted Maidstone Kent
[Received] June 11 4 25 PM '73

MRS ELIZABETH LOWELL 15 WEST67THSTREET
NEWYORKCITY
SORRY FOR MORE DELAY LAWYER WANTS TO KNOW MEANING OF
DESCENDANTS RIGHTS BEFORE NOTARIZING WITH GODS SPEED
THIS WILL BE OVER IN A WEEK WISH IT WERE NOW LOVE
CAL

261. *Robert Lowell to Elizabeth Hardwick*

Milgate Park, Bearsted, Maidstone, Kent Eng.
June 11, 1973

Dearest Lizzie:

When we went to Caroline's lawyer to look over the quitclaim and have it notarized, he was unable to decide what she was signing, what rights of the descendant. I suppose this is all nothing, but I can't very well sign what I don't understand. I will have to consult the divorce statement which for some reason I don't have on hand here. No one's rights seem worth a hassle with Maine law, and I don't exactly see how the Maine property could be usefully divided between Harriet and Sheridan.

I think everything could be cleared in about a week. Maybe O'Sullivan could get in touch with King through Iseman who has a copy of the divorce. I've thought about this business with desultory heat and confusion. I assume it's all air and nothing is at stake, and nothing is worth keeping you from selling the house and getting on with your plans. Giving Harriet some share in it makes me happy. But just as I'd like to give her some independence at 21, I can't sign away something that might be Sheridan's inheritance—I can't sign it away without even knowing if I am.

We have the best of talks and I've worried for hours about this thing. I've no excuse for not acting a month ago, except that the quitclaim came without warning and unexplained .to me. Iseman sent the quitclaim without interpretation.

Let's trust the whole thing will be settled before the month is out.
Love,
    Cal

PS Sheridan has just emerged from chicken pox and everyone in the house has had a sort of mild almost poxless pox. I am infected with a rambling mind. I think the crux of the matter, what I wished to say, was that Mr. King can't tell what the quitclaim means, and I can't tell him because I don't know.

(Kelley, Drye
350 Park Ave. N.Y.C.)
Mr. Conway at the firm is the person to get in touch with

262. *Elizabeth Hardwick to* ROBERT LOWELL[1]

[Telegram]

[New York, N.Y.]
[Received June 12, 1973]

MR ROBERT LOWELL MILGATE PARK
BEARSTEDMAIDSTONEKENT
RIGHTS OF DE\S/CENT[2] MEAN AS MY HUSBAND IN MAINE YOU
COULD CLAIM 1/3 MAINE PROPERTY AT MY DEATH STOP WOULD
NOT STAND UP IN COURT BECAUSE OF SEPARATION AGREEMENT
STOP YOUR BOOKS LEAVE THE HOUSE TOMORROW I BEG YOU
    ELIZABETH

---

1. The first of the twelve letters, postcards, and telegrams written by Hardwick that were included in the Lowell Estate's sale of papers to the HRC in 1982.
2. "S" written in Lowell's hand.

263. *Elizabeth Hardwick to* ROBERT LOWELL

[Telegram]

[New York, NY]
[Received in Kent June 19, 1973]

ROBERT LOWELL MILGATE PARK
BEARSTEDMAIDSTONEKENT
=DO YOU FEEL WE ARE MARRIED? DO YOU AND CAROLINE CON-
SIDER SHERIDAN MY SON? IF NOT YOUR TREATMENT OF ME IS
STUPID STOP NOT EVEN HARRIET HAD LEGAL RIGHT TO THE
HOUSE STOP YOU HAVE RIGHTS ONLY AS MY HUSBAND BUT WE
ARE NOT MARRIED THE SIGNATURES ARE A TECHNICALITY
PLEASE SEND SIGNED DEED
     = ELIZABETH + ? ? +

[*The Dolphin, For Lizzie and Harriet*, and *History* were published on June 21.]

264. *Elizabeth Hardwick to Robert Lowell*

[15 West 67th Street, New York, N.Y.]
June 21, 1973

Dear Cal: Harriet and her friend will not be coming to London for the first visit in early July—just as well, since it was only for a few hours and to accommodate the bicycles. They are going with bicycles direct to Amsterdam. They plan to be coming to London and Kent around the 19th of July to stay until they meet their group in London on the 29th. They will call or write you or cable from Amsterdam, where they will be with Cathy's parents. I am assured by Harriet that they will in England look after themselves[,] cook for themselves, help with the house. They want to hike around in Kent and wander around London and both are very responsible, but I agree that they shouldn't stay in the house alone in London. They understand that their plans are real only in so far as they are easy and convenient for you and Caroline. They leave New York with the Grads for Amsterdam on July 6th. So if you feel the 19th is out you can let her know here, or if she is gone I will relay it on to Amsterdam. I don't have the Amsterdam address yet. They will probably come from Holland to England by train, but I don't know. In any case, after they join their group that will be the end for you since they will fly back to New York with [the] group and I will be here waiting.

I have to believe that by the time this letter reaches you the deed, signed, will be in the airmail to Mr. Veague. It is mid-summer, I have spent hundreds and hundreds of useless dollars on lawyers, calls, special insurance, etc. The people naturally want the house, which they have to furnish. There has never been anything at stake in this matter. The only reason you are required to sign is Maine "custom" and also you agreed to sign documents about this in the separation agreement; but that was all a technicality since this was the only thing in the agreement that was incontestably mine. Mr. O'Sullivan will be writing you—I have had to hire him along with Mr. Veague, an unbelievable situation to me. His letter will say nothing that I haven't said all along. There is nothing to say. I guess we can ultimately get some sort of Maine court order but that goes into the fall, the empty house, the withdrawn sale, the whole thing utterly bewildering and breaking to me.

Meanwhile, mysterious beyond belief, you have given extraordinary time and concentration to this matter which can only, after all, remain where it is since there is truly nothing at stake for you and Sheridan—and you have not been able to get a simple paper about your income tax for last year sent here. A deed every citizen has to do every year of his life. I am bewildered.

The books[1] go out next week they say. I found a few more after I sent them. It is not easy to find these things, all confused after years. The bill will come next week to me and I will send it. (I have just heard from the shipping office and the bill coming to me will be $140.20. That gets the books to London. They will bill you for from London to Maidstone. There are two hundred books. You can send the $140.20 as soon as possible because I am very low, what with Harriet's expensive summer and our terrible expenses.[)]

Elizabeth

---

1. From Lowell's library in the West 67th Street apartment.

265. *Robert Lowell to* Mrs. Elizabeth Lowell

Milgate Park, Bearsted, Maidstone, Kent

[June 23, 1973]

Dearest Lizzie:

The point of the delay is this that Caroline has no idea what she is signing. ~~away.~~ I'M sure the whole is merely formal, and would have signed long ago, but Caroline can't renounce what looks like (tho no doubt just for the moment) Sheridan's legal rights. I wired Iseman over a week ago and haven't heard. Maybe you can get in touch with him. Henshaw promised me to have off the information to you a week ago today. Apparently your figures have to be precisely the same as [those] I turn into the British collectors. Everything sticks—we still don't have a place at Harvard, despite everyone's efforts.

Sorry not to see Harriet sooner, tho I dreaded the bikes. I long for her so much, and am vaguely planning for the girls' country and city visit. I should think they could do anything they wished in London, if I were in the house. Can't they let us know, at least the day of their arrival from Amsterdam before they leave New York—just for my ease.

Just back from a visit to Rotterdam for the poetry festival. The old center of the city, just a messy, grassy open space in 1951 instead of the miles of old 17th century city destroyed by bombs[,] is all sleeplessly new, very pleasant, tho inhuman, of its kind, yet one felt that after the festivals and conventions it would be carted away like the world fair. High point of incongruity, meeting of Ginsberg and Günter Grass on a poetry barge. Grass, "Why he doesn't even have cymbals." Judith very distraught and active, but within hours receiving invitations to visit both Grass and Mali. MacDiarmid looking and drinking like Allen Tate. Isn't poetry terrible? Note my tactful avoidance of an Exclamation mark.

Brookses here for two nights now off to Ireland and Dixey. Melanie is studying. I've never seen Peter better or more fun to be with.

It's been too hot to have a fire at night, and really greasy during the day. I dread to imagine America.

Could you call Iseman and see if he can send us an exact definition of what Caroline is signing? Her lawyer advised her not to \do so/ in ignorance. She is not interested in sabotaging your sale.

Look forward to the books, those old friends in their hard backs of another age. I do feel I have nothing more of the past than I can hold in my hands. The photos are all in a photobook.

We do so want Harriet. Are you going to Lake Como?

Love,

Cal

266. *Elizabeth Hardwick to Robert Lowell*

[15 West 67th Street, New York, N.Y.]

June 29, 1973

Dear Cal: Your letter saying Caroline didn't understand what *she* was signing away has driven me nearly to the brink of suicide. I have written, cabled, done all I can. Please read this to Caroline:

1. You have rights at my death as my husband. (Descent means descending, the property, from wife to husband. Nothing in the world to do with descendants.)
2. If Caroline is your wife you are not my husband.
3. If you are not [my] husband you have no rights at my death and Caroline has no rights either.

The complications are with Maine law, mostly about the Dominican Republic. Had I known you and Caroline would hold me up on this I suppose I would not have agreed to the Dominican divorce without everything cleared up, and all of that. But you did agree, as every separation agreement does, that my property was mine, and if you find the agreement you will see that it is usual to sign a document. Speed prevented O'Sullivan from getting it from Maine and so you went off without it, my assuring him you would not ever think Maine was yours. It never occurred to me that Caroline and her lawyers would enter into it.

There won't be any Maine property after you all are through with me. I believe this has cost about $10,000. The people tell me I must make the basement dry, something you and I could never face financially. I have stopped work on the barn and suppose I will never take it up. I can't afford it, perhaps never could. Mary McC. Harriet, anyone will corroborate what I am saying.

I will have one more business letter to write you next week about what we have decided on the taxes since Mr. Hoffman is going off for sometime. I will write that, then I will be entirely out and will never take part in it \your taxes/ again.

Harriet thinks they will be coming from Amsterdam about July 18th or 19th. Probably by train, with odious bikes, from the Hook.[1] She is very excited; I showed her your welcoming letter. She likes London, looks forward to seeing you very much, likes Kent. Maybe she and Cathy should be encouraged to take those day trains to Bath, Cambridge. Anyway I know they will have a marvelous time with you.

Will write the tiresome letter next week.

E.

Mr. O'S. by way of Iseman has sent off new documents. They require consul, alas. It would have been better to sign the first, but they are no good now. I have three lawyers in my employ on this small transaction. But when O'S. got on the case he then wanted it done correctly.

267. *Robert Lowell to* Mrs. Elizabeth Lowell

Milgate Park, Bearsted, Maidstone, Kent

July 4, 1973

Dearest Lizzie—

Fourth of July—the only sign of it here was an article in the London Times by Ralph de Toledano explaining that the Declaration of Independence was not revolutionary, but that George III was the revolutionary.[2] Maybe there'll be banners for Red George and Red Mao. The two \lost/ American Holidays, This and Thanksgiving, leave a funny sort of present-absence here.

I'll take the deed to the consulate and mail it off probably Friday,[3] not later. We have guests coming and the trip to London and back in one day is somehow too much. Harriet is on the verge and by the time you get this she'll be in Amsterdam. You had better send me her ad-

---

1. Hoek van Holland.

2. Ralph de Toledano, "A Text for Reaction, not a License for Revolution," *Times* [London], 4 July 1973.

3. July 6.

dress and phone number. Everyone is turning up, Jean Valentine, the Eberharts, Mac Rosenthal. Are you going to Lake Como?

Love,
Cal

\Good summer!/

268. Elizabeth Hardwick to Robert Lowell

[15 West 67th Street, New York, N.Y.]
July 5, 1973[1]

Dear Cal: I have no heart for this letter and it appears to me that lack of communication is literal and complete, but I am deeply grieved by your accusations. I answer for the last time and beg you to desist in your defamation, but I have little hope that you will.

1. About all of the past possessions. They are here, they are yours, a truck could arrive tomorrow and I would feel that were everything in the house out by nighttime that you would be acting properly. I do not wish an answer on this, but I cannot figure out what I could have done except keep your things for you until you came or sent for them. I very much feel everything is yours; care has been taken to preserve them for you. I sent the books when you told me what you wanted. The entire house, apt. contents are yours.

2. About not building the barn. I have stopped everything. I told you that I have no deed and it is midsummer; the people are making me fill in the basement. Caroline's objections, all answered in my first letter and many times over and over, have caused me to hire new lawyers, take on expenses which I know are over $5,000, maybe more. There was never anything to all of this. I sold the house because it was an expense, terrible work every year, falling apart, the school expanded next door; the barn was deteriorating. I felt only one could be preserved and I thought the barn the most practical for us. Just what I will now have the money to do I don't know. On

---

1. Crossed with Lowell's letter of July 4, 1973.

the 14th Mary McC. and I are going up for a few days and I will make the decision.

3. Taxes: for the hundredth time. I have never in a million years wanted you to pay taxes on the trust funds. You naturally would not. I have said a thousand times over and over until I am in tears that you must *file*, file that you gave the money to us, file so that I can pay, file even if you had no trusts. If you remember you have not paid anything since you left the country. I paid on the 15,000 from FS&G in 1970 and 1971. I have this year \for you/ only the $7,900 or so from FS&G, but I will pay that and pay all the accounting fees in order to get out. Also I do not want the money for the shipping of the books, since you seemed not to notice that the shipping order was a bill to me. I have gone into all my savings, my only desire now is to be free of all this business and I will, or indeed am now, if you have sent O'Sullivan's deed and if indeed Henshaw has sent the English figures and they arrive before tomorrow afternoon when the accountant is going away.

I cannot write all of this again. I have not taken everything from the past; *it was left here* and I didn't throw it out. I have very little money each year; about $12,000 after taxes and Harriet's school comes to nearly $4,000. I am working very hard. We both wish you didn't have to give us anything, but that would simply mean starvation. In no way whatsoever do you need the fantastic defenses of leaving me. I feel that our marriage has been a complete mistake from the beginning. We have now gone down in history as a horridly angry and hateful couple. A review is coming out in which Harriet is called "the fictional Terrible Child" . . . [1] She knows nothing of all this. I am near breakdown and also paranoid and frightened about what you may next have in store, such as madly using this letter. I do not wish to write you again. Your life is your own and has nothing to do with me.

Elizabeth

I would be grateful if you would show this letter to Caroline so that she could know what the situation is. I have written it many times, each part. I will not write it again. Do, say, feel what you wish.

---

1. See Marjorie Perloff, "The Blank Now," *New Republic*, July 7 and 14, 1973.

One more possibility. If you send a list of furniture, objects, whatever you want, clock, desk, sofa, beds, anything[,] they can be sent to England or put into storage here under your name. \Please never accuse me again over this!/

269. *Elizabeth Hardwick to Robert Giroux*

[15 West 67th Street, New York, N.Y.]

July 5, 1973

Dear Bob: I am writing you to give my thoughts on the publication of *The Dolphin* and will send a copy of this letter to Mr. Monteith at Faber. I am deeply distressed that both of you would have seen this book through to publication without asking my permission for the prodigal use of my letters, for the use in the most intimate way of my name and that of my daughter. I have since the publication been analyzed under my own name in print, given some good marks as a wife and person by some readings, general disparagement and rebuke by other readings. I know of no other instance in literature where a person is exploited in a supposedly creative act, under his own name, in his own lifetime. The facts are not in the nature of facts because of the disguise as poetry and so cannot be answered. My young and shy daughter is also quoted under her own name, spoken of in a most unnerving way.

I know of the existence of these poems using my name and my letters because they are not a spontaneous act, coming suddenly and with the indiscretion of haste, into print. They have been shown to many, many persons, but never to me. I felt it was undignified for me to insist before. When I actually received the book, anxious as I had been from reports, the reality was disturbing far beyond anything I could have imagined. Had I seen the poems, the letters of mine, those using my name, I do not know what I would have done. I do hold you and Mr. Monteith, as distinguished publishers, in dismay for your heartlessness in concealing this from me. I do not think the decision was rightly left altogether up to Cal. He is the author, but publication is an intricate action, involving many other considerations and one of those was certainly, from the publishers['] view, the effect upon persons exploited. I have always understood that publishers had lawyers to advise them about the indiscretions of authors. There are so many wrong impressions in the book—nothing about my willingness to divorce, my acceptance of the separation, the good spirits of myself and the utterly gratifying contentment of my daughter. I have found in the book letters from the very early period of my distress, attached to a sestet written long after.[1] I am very eager to go on record with you as saddened and deeply resentful of not only one, the use of my letters without permission, but many, many ill-effects upon me of your consent to publication without any consultation with me.

    Yours truly,
        Elizabeth Hardwick

270. *Robert Lowell to* ELIZABETH LOWELL

[Telegram]

[Maidstone, Kent]
[Received] Jul 8 12 24 PM '73

ELIZABETH LOWELL 15 WEST67STREET
NEWYORKCITY
CONSULATE CLOSED WEEKEND CANT GET TO LONDON TILL TUESDAY[2] THINK OF DEED AS NOW SIGNED SORRY FOR VEXING DELAY LOVE CAL

271. *Robert Lowell to* ELIZABETH LOWELL

[Telegram]

[Maidstone, Kent]
[Received] 1973 Jul 10 PM 6 42 Jul 10 PM 6 50

ELIZABETH LOWELL 15 WEST67STREET
NEWYORKCITY
DEED MAILED TO MAINE THE REVIEWS FRIENDLY OR UNFRIENDLY ARE MORE OR LESS ONLY CRUEL PUBLICITY POSTERS GOD HELP US AND SPARE US LOVE CAL[3]

---

1. "In the Mail," *The Dolphin*; see footnote 2 on page 293.
2. July 10.
3. Written on telegram in Hardwick's hand: "Cal's answer to Mrs. Perloff's review in *The New Republic*."

272. *Robert Lowell to* Mrs. Robert Lowell

Milgate Park, Bearsted, Maidstone, Kent

July 12, [1973]

Dearest Lizzie,

I think of you all through these \five/ sultry days, and haven't called again lest I further trouble things. I swear I never in all this business have wanted to hurt you—the very opposite. The gloomy picture of us in Newsweek[1] is due to Richard Howard and his friend Victor who took pictures here for some poetry anthology, and must have sent this one to Newsweek without our knowledge. Ivana's not at her best; nobody is, . . . a family from Utah.

Most of the hurting reviews are flashed up for news and will look very dim by September. Miss Perloff I would guess to be an instructor or young professor, earnestly, waspishly, pursuing her career, too stiff to be much of a critic. The Hopkins comparison is so eccentric, one thinks someone wrote it into her paper when she wasn't looking. I suppose one shouldn't blame her for stupid cruelty that mistook itself for truth.[2] I'm sorry I brought this on you, the ghastly transient voices, the lights.

Love,
Cal

---

1. Walter Clemons, "Carving the Marble," *Newsweek*, July 16, 1973; photograph by Thomas Victor.
2. Marjorie Perloff: "it is Lizzie who becomes the dominant figure in the sonnets, and she is depicted, perhaps unwittingly on Lowell's part, as Dark Lady or Super-Bitch par excellence. In her letters and phone calls, she is forever patting herself on the back for running to Dalton to pick up Harriet's grades or driving her to camp, and she dwells irritatingly on Harriet's goodness [. . .] Poor Harriet emerges from these passages as one of the most unpleasant child figures in poetry; only Hopkins' Margaret, grieving over Goldengroves unleaving, can rival her cloying moral virtue. It is therefore difficult to participate in the poet's vacillation, for Lizzie and Harriet seem to get no more than they deserve. And since these are, after all, real people, recently having lived through the crisis described, one begins to question Lowell's taste" ("The Blank Now," *New Republic*, July 7 and 14, 1973).

273. Robert Lowell to Elizabeth Bishop

Milgate Park, Bearsted, Maidstone, Kent

July 12, 1973

Dearest Elizabeth—

I suppose you've seen some of my American reviews, a lampooning! I think they all have a jarring effect on Lizzie, but one by a Miss Perloff in the New Republic has been a calamity for Lizzie—what it says about her and Harriet. ~~Her~~ \The/ distortion of the "fictional" characters becomes a ~~kind of~~ slander on the people themselves. I have been talking to people who are seeing her and to Lizzie herself. Last weekend she seemed to be suicidal, and ~~people~~ \friends/ had to drop in and telephone to see that she didn't take too many pills. All was confused and increased by her having total insomnia. Now her mood has quieted, but I have no certainty. We dread the telephone.

In Newsweek, in an otherwise discreet review, an unflattering photo of Lizzie was published, and above it a family portrait photograph (taken by Victor when he was here and given without our knowledge to Newsweek)[,] Caroline, I, \a wild/ Ivana (labeled *Harriet*) and Sheridan looking like a secret polygamous poor white family. This was so grotesque that Lizzie seems to have thought it funny. Unfortunately, she reads all the reviews, though no possible one could be pleasant ~~to her~~.

The weather for the last three days has been close and sultry. My study is a very long room with a view of cows, fields, trees—all becalmed. If I stroll up and down, I can feel Lizzie with me, and no escape but arguing, though the past all in all gives a more joyful picture . . . and the future is only dread of what will happen. My intuitions hope, but what is that?

Your old letter of warning—I never solved the problem of the letters, and there and elsewhere of fact and fiction. I worked hard to change the letters you named and much else. The new order somehow makes the whole poem less desperate. And the letters, as reviewers have written, make Lizzie brilliant and lovable more than anyone in the book. Not enough, I know. And then I didn't want to imagine reviews in magazines with big circulations that would ~~treat~~ \reduce/ my plot ~~as~~ \to/ news or scandal, politicians or actors.

My immorality, as far as intent and skill could go, is nothing in my book. No one, not even ~~me~~ \I/, is perversely torn and twisted, nothing's made dishonestly worse or better than it was. My sin (mistake?) was publishing. I couldn't bear to have my book (my life) wait ~~hidden~~ inside me like a dead child.[1]

All the while I've been writing, I've thought of you in the heat, and been happy to think of Alice's room among the air-conditioned trees.[2] We could use air-conditioning here in the middle of the day, but at night it's ~~pleasant~~ cool.

all my love,
Cal

We still have no house.

274. *Robert Lowell to* Mrs. Elizabeth Lowell

Milgate Park, Bearsted, Maidstone, Kent
July 16, 1973

Dearest Lizzie:

I enclose my check for the book-shipping. I'm guessing at the cost from memory, but suppose this is enough. If not, I'll mail more. I have a notice of the books['] arrival in England.

I have been under a cloud thinking about you this week. The publicity is very poisonous; I think I should have have foreseen it more clearly. Except for Miss Perloff, they are what one might have anticipated. She can hardly make a statement without some erroneous and hurting inference. I fear she has brooded on us for ~~a~~ \too/ long [a] time.

I can't defend myself too much, or anyway shouldn't at this moment if I could. Nothing in the books was dishonestly intended. ~~There's~~ \I feel/ something febrile, ~~hard to avoid feeling oneself. So it seems, in America.~~ \about my American publication./ Here it is just another book of poetry. I think I am living through many of your feelings. I suffer.

Love,
Cal

---

1. Lowell: "always inside me is the child who died" ("Night Sweat" 11, *For the Union Dead*).

2. Alice Methfessel's apartment at 16 Chauncy Street in Cambridge, Massachusetts.

275. Harriet Lowell to Mr. Robert Lowell

[Telegram]

[Amsterdam]
[received 17 July 1973]

MR ROBERT LOWELL 80 REDCLIFFE SQUARE
LONDON/SW10/ENGLAND
ARRIVING LONDON ON 20TH 1.55 FLIGHT 127 KLM
    HARRIET LOWELL

276. Robert Lowell to Robert Giroux

Milgate Park, Bearsted, Maidstone, Kent, England
July 18, 1973

Dear Bob:

I don't know where the business with Lizzie will go to.[1] After the divorce our relations were as good as one deserved. For the last month or so we were having a complicated unimportant little dispute about Caroline signing a quitclaim to the Maine property. On the same day as your letter, I had one in her old delirious style (I had said something about being sorry to have nothing left from the past except my grandfather's gold watch and a few books) rhetorically offering to give me "everything." I think what she says about her feelings is more or less true. What most set her off was the Perloff review, published two days later than her letter to you.

On the 7th, my Cousin Devie Meade called up saying that Lizzie was suicidal. Later that night she called saying the seizure was passing. I talked to Lizzie, Bob Silvers, Mary McCarthy. For a week I've heard nothing and have a feeling things are better. She is supposed to be staying with Mary in Maine—the best thing she could do perhaps.

Of course I can't clear myself from one angle: publishing "versions" of her letters (I hope no reviewer will call them Imitations). They are

---

1. Robert Giroux to Lowell: "Enclosed is another batch of reviews [. . .] I felt I should send you a copy of Elizabeth's letter, in order to keep you advised of the position she has taken, and also because you may be hearing from Monteith. She has not taken a 'legal position' precisely, but she may be building up to it. We don't propose to do anything precipitous; I will simply acknowledge my surprise at her letter [. . .] p.s. I haven't seen *The Listener* interview. Can you send me this?" (July 11, 1973, Robert Lowell Papers, HRC).

made up of a mixture of quotes, improvisation, paraphrase. The *revelation*[,] particularly in the glare of reviews, ~~must be~~ is shocking, but the portrait is very careful and affectionate, the essence of her charm and bravery, her own words[,] humor and sharpness . . . out of the outpouring of her actual letters and conversation. The number of sentences quoted is a fraction of the whole Dolphin, though to me very clear and wanted.

I think this will blow off without a lawsuit—who knows? We did become very friendly again after the divorce. I have nothing left really to pay for a lawsuit; any further wrangle would be a tragedy for Harriet, Lizzie and me. The letters are the legal, arguing problem—the real trouble for Lizzie is the picture of Caroline . . . the two things combine. I did everything I could to make my book ~~inoffensive~~ kind without killing it.

The best reviews here are on a higher level than the American ones so far—their technical suggestions are almost more galling than the ~~hints~~ grin of scandal. I wonder if you could send the following to The New Republic (under your signature or the Firm's, because I mustn't pour my ~~own~~ fuel on the fire).

The lines, "from the | dismay of my old world to the blank | now" are misquoted by Professor Perloff who also flaunts them for her title *The Blank Now*. The lines actually are "From the dismay of my old world to the blank | new." The tone and meaning have been lost by changing the letter *e*.

I am asking Karl Miller to airmail you the Ricks review, it's [a] kind of lawyers summation of the defense in a difficult but just case.[1] It's not meant for court of course.

Well, I pray none of us get further entangled. Harriet is arriving in two days, greedy for London.

As ever gratefully,
Cal

---

1. Ricks: "the recreation of Lizzie's letters—which could be the most monstrous and is likely to be the most disliked part of Lowell's undertaking—is unsentimental and movingly just. These letters, lucid and poignant, show her as not reducible to the wronged woman or a martyr, and show that though Lowell speaks of himself as 'fired by my second alcohol, remorse,' he is enabled, by speaking so of remorse, to break its addictive elation and to achieve instead some lovingkindness" ("The poet Robert Lowell—seen by Christopher Ricks," *Listener*, 21 June 1973.)

277. *Harriet Lowell and Robert Lowell to*
MRS. ROBERT LOWELL

[Telegram]

[Maidstone, Kent]
[n.d. but July 20, 1973?]

MRS ROBERT LOWELL 15 WESTSIXTYSEVENST
NEWYORKCITY
HERE SAFE LOVE HARRIET AND CAL

278. *Elizabeth Bishop to Elizabeth Hardwick*

Sixty Brattle Street, Cambridge, Massachusetts 02138
July 20th, 1973

Dear Elizabeth:

I hope you won't think it intrusive or impertinent of me to write you a note . . . I have been absolutely appalled at the stupid, stupid reviews of Cal's—well, "trilogy" I suppose it is. Particularly that Marjorie Perloff's, whoever she is—cruel as the poems are, I think she has deliberately misinterpreted them—as I'm sure you see, too. (I've seen only that one and Time, Newsweek, & the daily Times—)[1] Bill and I talked on the telephone yesterday and he said he'd talked to you and thought you were feeling better, possibly,—I myself tried to telephone you last Thursday[2] and again on Wednesday,[3] but the line seemed to be busy. Anyway—this is just to send you all the sympathy I can and to say that awful as it is I am sure that anyone's, everyone's, sympathy is entirely with you. You've always been notably brave and strong and so I hope those qualities will come to your rescue again—\(/and stupid reviews—even cruel books—*do* fade away fairly soon\)./

As I think you may know, I did my damndest to stop Cal's writing a lot of that—in fact after my letters (that were hell to write) he did change ~~some~~ \a few/ things around for the better—whether because of them or

---

1. Martha Duffy, "Survivor's Manual," *Time*, July 16, 1973; Walter Clemons, "Carving the Marble," *Newsweek*, July 16, 1973; Anatole Broyard, "Naked in his Raincoat," *New York Times*, June 18, 1973.

2. July 12.

3. July 18.

not I don't know. I think a good many of his old friends did exactly the same thing . . . But—nothing could stop him, obviously. Please believe I really grieve for you and I do hope things will soon be better—

Faithfully,

Elizabeth

279. *Robert Lowell to Robert Giroux*

Milgate Park, Bearsted, Maidstone, Kent, England

July 26, 1973

Dear Bob: Dear Old Bob (You might guess from this that I have just been reading the Bostonians by James)[.][1] We've just had a visit from Harriet and her friend Cathy and they are now bicycling through the English countryside and will be back in two days. We didn't of course go into this controversy, but talked merrily enough on most other personal things such as the drama of packing the bikes under Lizzie's "supervision." Lizzie's off today to Lake Como.

I've asked Charles to send you offprints of the more interesting English reviews including Ricks. They are much more enthusiastic and even seem about another book. I'm sick of the American formula of "America's greatest poet," then slamming the books, then praising the language—tho I guess being called America's worst poet with an uncertain command of English would be worse.

Lizzie's letter reads to me as if a lawyer had looked it over. On the same day she mailed me one (written many times) in the same tone but irrational and incoherent[.] About the letters, the ones you named[2] are based [on] real letters and several more—also at random I quote from actual conversation and telephone calls—there are several in *For Lizzie and Harriet* previously printed in *Notebook*. Lizzie wasn't *shown*

---

1. (1886).

2. Giroux to Lowell: "Elizabeth is still very much upset, and I don't really know what to do or what in fact can be done. One point of fact you can help me with, if you will. Isn't it true that letters have been used in your poems in previous books? In *Life Studies* is 'To Speak of Woe That Is in Marriage'—even though it is obviously a dramatic character speaking—making use of someone's written phrases? Certainly in the two previous editions of *Notebook* poems like 'Heidegger' and '1968' are based on letters, and 'Letters from Allen Tate' couldn't be more explicit. It may be beside the point giving a rational explanation of your previous use of this device, but I can't understand why it came to her as such a surprise" (July 23, 1973).

the Dolphin, but she read quantities of it when I was staying in my study at Christmas 1970.[1] Almost all the letters except for the *woodchuck* quote are from that period.[2] Is her use of the word *shown* the advice of a lawyer? On the other hand her reviews and public writing are much more carefully phrased than her talk and letters of the same moment. I have a strong unsupported hunch that presently the furor will die down. God knows, I didn't mean to show her up or satirize. I trust (because we must) time and distance.

> Affectionately,
> Cal

PS. Our trouble at the moment is still no place to stay at Harvard, tho everyone is looking.

280. Elizabeth Hardwick to Elizabeth Bishop

[15 West 67th Street, New York, N.Y.]

July 27, 1973

Dear Elizabeth: Your letter was very kind and I was very moved that you took the time to write me. I have felt truly awful about all of this—somehow it has hurt me as much as anything in my life. I was anxious about the books from what I knew, but I did not expect what I found. And in the end, after having I guess some idea of what was behind Cal's need to do this, it seemed so sad that the work was, certainly in that part that relies upon me and Harriet, so inane, empty, unnecessary. I cannot understand how three years of work could have left so many fatuities, indiscretions, bad lines still there on the page. That breaks my heart, for all of us.

I am going to Europe tonight and will be back the end of August. I know I will gradually feel better. What can one do? I loved seeing you and hearing you at the Y; seeing everyone connected with you at the

---

1. Hardwick to Ian Hamilton, referring to a draft of his biography of Lowell: "p. 388—last line quoted from Cal's letter to Bill A. 'She had roughly seen the contents . . .' Completely untrue. I had no idea at all until the printed book came into my hand at publication. All I knew, and this from everyone visiting at Milgate, was that he was using my letters. I was genuinely shocked and appalled when I saw the book, the use he made, the distortion of the letters, the writing of some for me, putting lines unwritten by me, in my voice" (Elizabeth Hardwick Papers, HRC).
2. "In the Mail," 11–14, *The Dolphin*; see footnote 2 on page 293.

party. I like reading you, too, and always tremble at the sight of a new poem. May there be some soon.

Have a good summer, be in as good health as medicine, love, luck can give you. With gratitude,

Love,

Elizabeth

281. Elizabeth Hardwick to Mary McCarthy

[Bellagio Center, Rockefeller Foundation, Bellagio, Italy]

August 14, 1973

Dearest Mary: I am sure you and Jim are happily in the noble mansion, together at last. I missed some of your Watergate articles—the last I saw was "Exit Mutt, Enter Jeff," a wonderful piece of writing and observation.[1] All of your watergating was much admired among everyone I saw in Rome.[2] It was a good idea to go and there did turn out to be nothing at all like what you tried to do, even if of course there couldn't be anything in the press like what you would inevitably, naturally write.

I went to Rome earlier than I planned and tried Carmen's[3] phone without response. Barbara E. was there and Gore[4] entertained, wined and even more dined us, and then we all drove off to Ravello, up a thousand "scali" to his villa for a long weekend, a boat trip to Capri, and then here in Bellagio. I am feeling rather low, even more so than before I came. The villa, all of its luxuries known to you from Hannah, seems to me like the most beautiful, expensive hospital in the world, and I suppose I am lucky to be here. I can't seem to write anything, but I have read a good deal, go swimming and walking, and with everything possible given freely to one, all cares, all burdens lifted, I think this is the best place to be depressed in, among the pines and views and sunsets. I am sure I will be recovered when I return on the 29th.

How glad I am to have gone ahead with Castine—I am merely taking on faith that my barn is "going ahead" against all experience. I don't at all

---

1. Probably "Lies," *New York Review of Books*, August 9, 1973. "Exit Mutt, Enter Jeff": Bud Fisher, *Mutt and Jeff* (comic strip).

2. "Watergate Notes," *New York Review of Books*, July 19, 1973; "Lies," *New York Review of Books*, August 9, 1973.

3. Angleton, a friend of McCarthy's.

4. Vidal.

like spending the summer abroad. I hate rented houses, without books, records, anything except the place itself. And, more important to me, I adore Castine. So I am already in one August dreaming of the next. I don't know what Harriet's plans will be, just when I start teaching, what my bank account will show; but when I return I would like a few days amongst the fogs and folk and will call you about the possibility.

No mail ever arrives here, causing me uneasiness and adding to the hospital feeling I secretly have—only from my inner condition, not from the play-place itself. So [do] not give a thought that a word should be posted. It couldn't possibly get through the postal clog of Italy until Christmas.

What an extraordinary collection of dull people are assembled here. Strangely torpid, aging academics from at home and [the] U.K.; sly, dead eyes, darting away from an idea; envious sighs, and as much intellectual vivacity as a woodchuck.[1] And the wives, of all sizes, yet somehow one size in their heads! They mutter about typing His manuscripts, and they have not made one single demand upon themselves, whether of mind or body, and go forth without any effort or artifice as if they were dogs adopted by their *professore*. They are mostly kindly, but there is this thorough acceptance of their nature and they seem to have lived in a world without mirrors. Needless to say the only two women one can talk to at all, and also the only two given to any "dressing" have Ph.D's in their own right. It is a perturbation—the laziness of wives.

I am thinking again, "re-thinking," as our conversations run here—of the old American-Italian colony, or Anglo-Italian. The villas, the gardens, the *cultivation*, in all its aspects, the special discipline of the mornings, the walks, the visitors in their time-slot, the ritual. Books written, trying to connect Italian culture and English studies, English language. I have been thinking that the ritual discipline of the exiled rich is a particular thing—not like the discipline of Flaubert or George Sand. It lacks the Bohemianism, the driven, the exorbitant perhaps, and is a dedication of a smoother, more worldly sort. I am reading Santayana's autobiography[2] again and would like,

---

1. Cf. Hardwick to Lowell [summer 1972?]; and Lowell, "In the Mail," 11–14, *The Dolphin*; see footnote 2 on page 293.

2. George Santayana, *The Last Puritan: A Memoir in the Form of a Novel* (1935).

if my own dog-like torpor could lift, to write some thoughts about the matter.

Much love, dearest two, and all greetings to my friends. I long to return and when I do your 326 phone will ring from me.

Ever,

Lizzie

282. *Robert Lowell to* Mrs. Elizabeth Lowell

Milgate Park, Bearsted,
Maidstone, Kent
August 24, [1973]

Dearest Lizzie:

Yesterday the books arrived after waiting fuming for ages at the customs. I made room on my shelves and waited all day in anxiety as if for a distant person, uncertain of coming. All came picked as if I had had our library in front of me to choose from. No error except two Loeb \Sophocles/ classics volume I,[1] but that was my error first in buying them. Now that I'm old and scatter-minded, I constantly buy things I have. Thanks for taking so much accurate pains.

Harriet and Cathy had a pleasant visit here, at least for us. I took them to Jonathan's Seagull at Chichester[2] (more hours of travel almost than flying the ocean)[.] At dinner with Irene Worth she wrote a note saying that Harriet had a prophetic beauty. Then we had trouble locating the group, and for a day were in a confusion without plans, except for aimless ones like buying tent and staying on the Vondel Park.[3] All came out right, tho I imagine the trip was a sweat—five companions, a boy of 14 who looked 12, a boy of 16 who looked 14, and a girl who kept saying everything drove her crazy, and Mr. Karp.

We will arrive on the 7th, and our address is 18 Maple St. Brookline care of Connell. Tell Harriet that this afternoon, in an unused

---

1. Sophocles, Vol. 1, *Oedipus the King | Oedipus at Colonus | Antigone*, ed. Hugh Lloyd-Jones, trans. F. Storr (1912).

2. Anton Chekhov, *The Seagull* (trans. Elisaveta Fen), dir. Jonathan Miller, Chichester Festival Theatre, opened on May 23, 1973.

3. In Amsterdam.

drawer, something turned up I thought long lost, a picture of her fearfully peering and clutching Teddy in Trinidad with the Walcotts' son behind her.[1] Give her my love. I will call soon.

My love to you—shall I say as always.

Love,

Cal

283. Robert Lowell to Harriet Lowell

Milgate Park, Bearsted, Maidstone, Kent, Eng.

August 26, 1973

Dearest Harriet:

I have been imagining you and Cathy for many days now exhaustedly biking winding military roads, the kind in which you end up after hours of work some twenty feet higher than where you started. Then developing Caroline's Chichester illness, then losing your group, then the Karps disappearing into Dublin spending the fees for your trip on pubs and Irish watercolors. As I write, you are coming to the end, and this letter will arrive in New York about when you do.

Genia and Ivana have come back from camp tanned and matured somewhat—Genia talking much more slowly, and Ivana talking much, much more. Sheridan talks just the same, except that the other morning asked what he had broken, he said, "egg cup." Natalya shouts when she wants to say something like, "I don't want a purple door to my bedroom."

So, another summer. Just ten days ago, we finally got an American house, 18 Maple St. Brookline. We are in a mess of packing, school, visa plans. We will arrive on the seventh. England seems populated with weary American professors booking home to teach. I see that I am wild to taste America again, even though I fear Nixon will last it out. It's the leaving

---

1. Peter Walcott; the photograph was taken on a visit to Trinidad in 1962. Derek Walcott: "I've described the sundering that put me off Lowell for a long time—during which he went into a hospital and I cursed and told everyone, yes, I too was tired of his turmoil. But I want to record, tears edging my eyes when he invited me years later to his apartment on West Sixty-seventh Street, the dissolving sweetness of reconciliation. He opened the door, hunched, gentle, soft voiced, while he muttered his apology, I gave him a hard hug, and the old love deepened. The eyes were still restless, haunted. A phantom paced behind the fanlight of the irises. He reached into the inside pocket of his jacket. I knew why. For a snapshot of his daughter and my son, who are the same age, that had been taken at a beach house in Trinidad" ("On Robert Lowell," *New York Review of Books*, March 1, 1984).

and the settling (the uncertainty of whom and what we will see) that hurts. I suppose coming back to England in due time will be like rest, a vacation.

I loved seeing you and making Cathy's acquaintance. She is a good friend to you, and (despite appearances?) a good influence. I'll take you \both/ out to dinner in New York. You must come to Brookline. All I can remember about our house, (there were so many others we didn't get,) is that it has three bathrooms and a crib, a washer and no drier. There must be room.

So glad the bikes didn't have to be loaded on a plane. I was pleasantly sad when you left as always. Give my love to Sumner and Nicole and Mother.

Love,
Daddy

284. Adrienne Rich to Elizabeth Hardwick

[Unknown location]
[n.d. but summer? 1973]

Dearest E.— I'm still feeling bloodyminded about those poems[1]—& think of Ibsen's *When We Dead Awaken* for the 100,000th time.[2] When

---

1. See Rich, "Caryatid: A Column," which includes a review of *History*, *For Lizzie and Harriet*, and *The Dolphin*: "Finally, what does one say about a poet who, having left his wife and daughter for another marriage, then titles a book with their names, and goes on to appropriate his ex-wife's letters written under stress and pain of desertion, into a book of poems nominally addressed to the new wife? If this kind of question has nothing to do with art, we have come far from the best of the tradition Lowell would like to vindicate—or perhaps it cannot be vindicated." She comments on lines 8–15 of "Dolphin": "I have to say that I think this is bullshit eloquence, a poor excuse for a cruel and shallow book, that it is presumptuous to balance injury done to others with injury done to oneself—and that the question remains—to what purpose? The inclusion of the letter-poems stands as one of the most vindictive and mean-spirited acts in the history of poetry, one for which I can think of no precedent; and the same unproportioned ego that was capable of this act is damagingly at work in all three of Lowell's books" (*American Poetry Review*, September/October 1973, pp. 42–43). Lowell to Stephen Berg, editor of the *American Poetry Review*: "I started a letter a year or so ago saying I couldn't honestly blame you for Adrienne's slash. I don't see how you could have turned it down, particularly for your magazine whose lifelines ~~were~~ are opposing prejudices and judgments. However, Adrienne in her pre-prophetic days and for more than ten years was one of my closest friends. I could say she has become a famous person by becoming cheap and enflamed; but that isn't it. Her whole career has been a rage for disorder, a heroic desire to destroy her early precocity for form and modesty. And wasn't she right? And wasn't she unrecognized mostly when she first became a better poet and before the time of her fevers? And who knows how the thing will turn out—such a mixture of courage and the auctioneer now?" ([1976?], published in *The Letters of Robert Lowell*, p. 647).
2. Henrik Ibsen, *When We Dead Awaken* (1899); see Rich, "When We Dead Awaken: Writing as Re-Vision," *College English* 34, no. 1 (October 1972).

2 people have had something together, however difficult & painful, it is *not* the right of one to choose to "use" it in this fashion. I think people are ultimately more important than poems (I know you do too!)[.]

However ultimately I think all that will last of this is a sour taste in the mouth—many mouths.

It's strange that women artists have not seemed to need to use other people in quite the same way as men, in order to create—at all events the best ones.

I don't know that this is ethical at all: but if Bob is looking for a reviewer for *Diving* . . . I wonder if he's thought of Nancy Milford? (Did you see her excellent review of Juliet Mitchell in PR)?[1]

Will call you as soon as I make a beach-head at WEA[2] again—love to you & to H.—

Adrienne.

285. *Mary McCarthy to Elizabeth Hardwick*

191 rue de Rennes, Paris 75006

October 12, 1973

Dearest Lizzie:

This has to be a fast note. The *New York Review* came finally this morning, and I plunged into the pages of your novel.[3] Or toward your novel? Will there be a real, i.e. an old-fashioned, one or will it continue this way with multiple approaches? Talking to oneself. It is something new—fresh and exercising a kind of fascination. It isn't the same as the old Quaker Oats box of the novel in which someone is writing a novel in which someone is writing a novel, with infinite regression. Jimmy Merrill used that once more and in parts very brilliantly in *The Diblos Notebook*.[4] But this is different. I loved the ending,

---

1. Nancy Milford, "Women's Estate by Juliet Mitchell," *Partisan Review* 40, no. 1 (Winter 1973). *Diving into the Wreck* was reviewed by Rosemary Tonks in "Cutting the Marble," *New York Review of Books*, October 4, 1973.

2. West End Avenue in Manhattan.

3. Hardwick: "Writing a Novel," *New York Review of Books*, October 18, 1973; "*(This is the opening of a novel in progress to be called The Cost of Living.)*" Revised for *Sleepless Nights*. See page 471.

4. *The (Diblos) Notebook* (1965).

not being able to decide whether to call "myself" I or she.[1] Charming and poignant. And there are so many true and delightful things in it. I like least the "she" novel you reject but assume you intend one to be a bit cloyed by it.

"M." You spoke of that to me this summer. But "M." of course isn't me. It isn't anybody. It's you. I thought that was wonderfully done: I started thinking to myself "But, Lizzie, this doesn't sound like a letter. More like a diary or thinking aloud." And then it turns out that's what you were doing with it. "For the archives." It is not even like a diary, either, nor like thinking aloud or onto paper \exactly/. You are very much alone throughout this, my dear. Well, that pain or that predicament is the originality of it. Persevere and *brava*!

I have to go and cook. Maria[2] is away in Poland on her month's vacation, and I'm much at the stove or in the markets. How much time it takes. I think I must move more slowly than I used to.

One point I take issue with you on. Just as a factual matter. For me, in a memoir the problem isn't myself; it's other people.[3] Perhaps I delude myself but I don't find it so hard to be honest about myself. But to be honest about others or one's feelings toward them is too cruel. This wasn't a problem in *Catholic Girlhood*, because the people I might have been hurting were far away in the past and the only ones I cared about, really—my grandparents, Preston—were dead. Yet even there I had some twinges of pain for them, for instance when I wrote about my grandmother's face-lift operation: she wouldn't have liked that. If you are cruel to yourself, you can make it right with yourself. And your thoughts hurt you a lot anyway. Shame, remorse. You're used to that. The reason I bring this up is that I have been thinking of doing something that would have elements of a memoir in it, and the point, in that particular work (for reasons too long to go into) would have to be absolute honesty. And as soon as I start thinking of the other people who would be involved in

---

1. Hardwick: "Now, my novel begins. No, now I begin my novel—and yet I cannot decide whether to call myself I or she" (final sentence of "Writing a Novel").

2. Fourrier.

3. Hardwick: "The troubles in a memoir are both large and small. Those still living do not create the longest hesitations. I am sure no one makes an enemy without wishing to do so. The need is sometimes very pressing; the relief rather disappointing. No, the troubles are not with relatives, lovers, famous persons seen at a deforming angle. The troubles are all with yourself seen at an angle, yourself defamed and libeled" ("Writing a Novel," *New York Review of Books*, October 18, 1973).

the utterly honest bits of personal history, I immediately start saying to myself: "But you *can't* write that. You'll have to leave that out." Excision after excision. Fiction is different, at least for me.

Now, are you coming up for Thanksgiving? You promised. Or all but. Bring Harriet, if she'd like to come. Hannah is definitely coming, and the DuViviers. I don't know yet about Kevin.[1]

With love and pleasure,

Pseudo M.

Mary

286. Elizabeth Bishop to Elizabeth Hardwick

Sixty Brattle Street, Cambridge, Massachusetts 02138

October 16th, 1973

Dear Elizabeth:

I saw Aileen Ward last night & she told me she had just heard you give a very good ("lively", I think she said) talk at Smith. Also yesterday I sent a permission to F,S, & G for your quotation from the poor old "Fish" in your piece on Sylvia Plath—about to be published in a book, I gather.[2] I don't believe I ever told you I liked that piece very much, and the agreeable things you said about me in it, too.[3] And also yesterday I read the 1st chapter of a new novel by you in the NYRB, and I liked *that*. I especially liked the very last sentence![4]—and the apt. that looked like "Edinburgh"[5]—

---

1. McCarthy.

2. *Seduction and Betrayal: Women and Literature* (1974).

3. Hardwick: "Sylvia Plath has extraordinary descriptive powers; it is a correctness and accuracy that combine the look of things with their fearsome powers of menace. It is not close to the magnifying-glass descriptions in Marianne Moore and Elizabeth Bishop, that sense these two writers have of undertaking a sort of decoding, startling in the newness of what is seen. When Elizabeth Bishop writes that the 'donkey brays like a pump gone dry,' this is a perfectly recognizable and immensely gratifying gift of the sort we often get also in Sylvia Plath. But the detail in Elizabeth Bishop's 'The Fish' is of another kind: "I looked into his eyes | which were far larger than mine | but shallower, and yellowed, | the irises backed and packed | with tarnished tinfoil | seen through the lenses | of old scratched isinglass." [. . .] In Marianne Moore and Elizabeth Bishop we are never far away from the comic spirit, from tolerance and wisdom— qualities alien to the angry illuminations of *Ariel* [. . .] " (*Seduction and Betrayal*, pp. 122–23).

4. Hardwick: "Now, my novel begins. No, now I begin my novel—and yet I cannot decide whether to call myself I or she" ("Writing a Novel," *New York Review of Books*, October 18, 1973).

5. Hardwick: "Dearest M: Here I am in New York, on 67th Street in a high, steep place with long, dirty windows. In the late afternoon, in the gloom of the winter lights, I sometimes imagine it is

many of the bits about places and abodes are awfully good, I think . . . I am waiting for the next installment . . .

All these reminders on one day have given me the courage to write to you about something I'd thought of asking you long ago— something very trivial, and of importance only to me—but I'll ask you, anyway. I wonder, if, in this new collection, you're going to publish the piece on Maine?[1] (I'm not sure when it appeared; I'm convinced that teaching destroys the brain—certainly the memory.) I liked it— in fact I thought it was one of your very best pieces, evocative, poetic, even—except for two or three sentences that bothered me. I don't have the review here so I can't quote exactly, but (I think) you referred to the trip Lota & I made with Cal in the summer of 1957 or '58, up the coast of Maine and to Gardners' Island? (Unless I am completely mistaken, and you went again to Gardners' Island with another Latin-American friend—if so, ignore all this.)

If I am right—you maybe went by Cal's account of our visit, or maybe Lota & I talked about it on our return, too—the sentences are about Lota, and they misrepresent her & what she said, etc.[2] Actually her reactions to Maine & Gardners' Island were even funnier. She didn't complain of G I's bareness or ugliness, etc—in fact she adored New England colonial architecture, Shaker furniture, and so on. But she didn't approve of the Gs' *décor* at all, & loathed things like "Harvard chairs" (there were some of those); of course she was ~~rather~~ a fanatic on the subjects of architecture and interior decoration. The house & buildings at G I are *not* beautiful or interesting—compared with Castine, for example—but I don't think Lota commented on them—and she did appreciate New England architecture—I still have several of her books on the subject.

Edinburgh in the Nineties. I have never been to Edinburgh, but I like cities of reasonable size, provincial capitals" ("Writing a Novel," *New York Review of Books*, October 18, 1973).

1. "In Maine," *New York Review of Books*, October 7, 1971.

2. Hardwick: "A fantastic love of difficult, awkward islands gripped the heart of rich people at the turn of the century. Grandeur and privation, costliness and discomfort. Some years ago we took a friend from South America to an island quite a distance off Machias, Maine. The launch pulled up to a long, wooden pier to which the owner's sloop was moored. The house was a large yellow frame with two graceful wings and inside there were beautiful dishes, old maps on the wall, fine painted chests, and handsome beds. We lived there in silence and candlelight for a few days, stumbling about with our guttering tapers, coming upon steep back stairways where we had been expecting a closet with our nightgowns in it. 'This is madness! No, it is not one bit amusing!' the Brazilian lisped in fury" ("In Maine," *New York Review of Books*, October 7, 1971).

What she didn't like were the furnishings, our hostess's inappropriate clothes, the *lists* pinned up telling who was to stay in the house when, etc., and the fact that everyone was expected to *help*. That affectation of the American rich she considered just "romanticism." Also, she may have been the first or only guest who refused to get up for breakfast, since she never did. I felt I created a small scandal when I asked for a tray at breakfast so I could take hers up to her. If we made our own beds, or folded up the bed linen—I undoubtedly did that for her, too.

And Lota didn't "lisp." (That made me think it may have been someone else you had in mind.) Spanish-speaking people *seem* to be lisping, of course, because of their s's and z's—but they aren't pronounced that way in Portuguese and Lota wouldn't lisp in either Portuguese or English, of course.

On the trip we discovered that she thought all the fir trees had been *planted*, and she kept asking where the "beaches" were. Cal & I kept trying to make the difference between "beaches" and "coastlines" clear.

I'm afraid, as I said, that this will seem utterly unimportant, and of course it has nothing whatever to do with your really excellent piece. And it may have been someone else—I don't remember whether you specified Brazilian or not—if so, please disregard this. Someone else may have found things bare and ugly and someone else may really have lisped . . . It is just that I thought you meant Lota and I hate to have her, even incognito (a?), misrepresented. She already has been enough. I didn't think it would harm your piece at all to change those phrases—since her actual reactions were equally amusing and even more Latin.

⌒

What I'm speaking of \now/ isn't the same thing at all, of course, and you are completely innocent of it—but recently it seems to be the smart thing to use inaccurate personal references—we both know two or three famous poets guilty of this—and I think we should protest whenever we can . . . I just received proofs of a book of poems by a supposedly very bright young poet in which he has a poem about me (I've never met him)—appearing in a "dream" of his, singing about "death" and doing other unlikely things, in my nightgown, no less . . . [1] I was asked to write a "good word" for this book! When I wrote asking why on earth I should, given that poem, he was contrite, or pretended to be, and said that although the poem started off with me (a real quotation) it was really about *another* E.B., a woman of the same name. I don't believe this for a minute; no change of person was indicated . . . Again—your Maine piece has absolutely nothing to do with this kind of thing. I know you know better than I do how cruel and irresponsible it is and I think someone who can write that type of an article—(not you, probably—but an equally good journalist—) should attack it.

As to your piece—I am probably the only person in the world who could feel disturbed by those few sentences and you mention no names, etc.—and it may be too late to change them now—but I did feel disturbed.

I hope the novel is progressing easily. If you see Adrienne will you please tell her I'm sorry I didn't see her before she left & I'm still waiting for the letter she said she was writing me. I hope Harriet is blooming and that you are feeling much better and up to the rigors of a New York winter—

Affectionately,
Elizabeth

287. Elizabeth Hardwick to Elizabeth Bishop

[15 West 67th Street, New York, N.Y.]
October 18, 1973

Dear Elizabeth: I hasten to answer your letter about my description of Maine. It will not be in my new book of essays and I have no thoughts of republishing it, but the basic thing remains and I will definitely take out the paragraph (or the very end of a paragraph) about the rich and

---

1. David Shapiro: "The night I decided to paradoxically intend | I had the wished-for bad dreams. | Elizabeth Bishop, whose "2000 | Illustrations" this shows I had been reading | was whistling in a nightgown and playing and | singing to her family, | 'I am the death tree, | I grow spontaneously, | I grow in the round, | Plant death in the ground' | after which duet | was played on the $59 Sony cassette | she became lugubrious, dramatic, | or conversely lubricated, and mellow, | and sighingly said, | Now I am going to bed, like a good girl!" ("On Becoming a Person," 1–16, *The Page-Turner* [1973]).

their love of a luxurious privation. I did certainly have Lota in mind and it was a memory of a trip all of us were on to Roque Island.[1] The Brazilian only appears in two sentences at the end, but I know to my very bones what you mean. It is one of the most peculiar and terrifying sensations to have yourself or someone you have really loved and deeply known suddenly lighted up in a way that seems so far from the real, the true. I remember reading a book last year by a wife of a diplomat we must have met on our trip to Egypt and we are referred to sneeringly as not at all interested in what was going on around us but only in the past. That is calm enough, but it was hideously upsetting and untrue since we were crazily interested in everything. I can't tell you how I dread the future with biographies and *Lizzie*; to say nothing of "Cal" who will never be even touched with the truth of his own being and nature. Fortunately I'll be dead before most of them come. It is such a violation, like a wound. In the end it doesn't matter whether these things are "true" or "unfavorable" in the usual sense; you just can't help but weep with pain as you are tossed in someone's work, especially creative work. Opinion, analysis, can be unfair but the reader has the right to propose his own estimate and judgment at the moment he is reading—the other is simply an appropriation. I do understand your horror at the "dream poem" and I am glad you protested. Also glad \to be reminded/ that my friendly remark about the "Brazilian" and her feeling that wandering around in the dark was "not amusing" is not very interesting in itself and doesn't get right the whole infinitely complicated attitude Lota had or might have had. I will just remove it entirely. I think something new is at hand in these appropriations of one and \even/, as in the dream poem, under his own name. It must have to do with a sort of escalating need for and belief in publicity as a value and with the idea of attention. If you want it for yourself on almost any terms you cannot imagine that others would not share this. You keep saying, what's wrong with what I said? It's not against you! As if there were only one measure of that. I do feel Andy Warhol's idea that everyone will be famous for fifteen minutes is at the bottom of it.[2] In the end it just means that you don't think anyone is real.

---

1. In 1957.
2. Warhol: "In the future, everyone will be world-famous for 15 minutes" (*Andy Warhol: this book was published on the occasion of the Andy Warhol Exhibition at Moderna Museet in Stockholm*

I am sure you got the documents finally.[1] I regret deeply having assembled these \papers/ at one time without going over them. I know I will come to grief, more grief; but then it was simply too hard to draw back, too difficult to go over them. Well, I will not suffer future pain. . . . I am very well, having a good time, working, listening to music. I like my life a lot most of the time. Harriet is very well, busy smoking cigarettes and making fun of everyone. She told me that she didn't want to apply to Radcliffe because all of those students were dreadful, "all with their *interests*." Don't repeat this to Cal because he will repeat it in front of her and she loathes that more than anything. She is coming up to Boston next weekend and perhaps you will see her. Again, be in good health and happiness—as much as you want of the latter and more than you want of the first. Love,

Elizabeth

288. Elizabeth Hardwick to Mary McCarthy

[15 West 67th Street, New York, N.Y.]

October 28, 1973

Dearest Mary: I was happy indeed to have your letter and I thank you for it—tremendously. I have written a little more on my new book, but like you I am sunk in housekeeping, going to the market, cooking, going downstairs to the washing machines. The saintly Nicole hasn't been well at all, unable to work, with many painful illnesses all stemming from deafness.[2] She has gone to Spain for a month or so with the hope of getting well. I have a woman who cleans a bit but that hardly helps. However, I expect to have a little more support soon, but nothing could take the place of my beloved Nicole. Harriet and I miss her, every day. And the mail, the business—if that is what it all is . . . Other-

February to March 1968, ed. Andy Warhol, Kaspar König, Pontus Hulten, and Olle Granath, Olle. [1968]).

1. Documents agreeing to the $5,000 Lowell wished to give to Bishop for the portion of her letters that were included in the sale of his papers to Harvard. (Hardwick was overseeing the completion of the sale.) Hardwick: "Dear Elizabeth: You are to sign all three of these and return all three to Mr. Iseman, whose address is in the letter I enclose" (Hardwick to Elizabeth Bishop, October 16, 1973, Vassar College Special Collections Library).

2. Hardwick: "When I think of deafness, heart disease and languages I cannot speak, I think of you, Angela" (*Sleepless Nights*, p. 119).

wise I am very well, having a good time in what has been a strangely beautiful fall here in New York, clear skies, cool and yet summery. The Nixon affair keeps one almost literally breathless. I fear he will slide by again and noted with pain that his truly abominable, meaningless press conference last night on his plight and the Middle East got some very good "notices."[1]

I wish I had the word about Thanksgiving. I have written Aunt Sarah to say that I think they should give up the ordeal of sharing the board with Harriet and me and assorted Winslows at/in the Cotting farm. She has written back, not saying yes or no alas, just saying that if it takes place it will be because [of] the chance of another year with me and Harriet. I cannot do more to these people who have been kindness and love to me beyond my deserving. I hope you will let me come up with the New York group even if I can't let you know too early in advance. About Harriet I don't know either. I think I will come to Castine Friday in any case, if you can find a crash cot for me. I very much want to have Thanksgiving there, with you and Jim, with Hannah, the DuViviers. It is the most appealing engagement I can imagine. Will let you know soon.

Last night, about 11, I got a call from Tommy—the second time I think since all of this happened.[2] But this time he seemed really desperately lonely and I grieve for him. He is so vulnerable to painful feeling, always has been, and I think has always struggled with depression. He spoke of the "bleakness" and what could one say. He is coming down this weekend, a few days with Julian[3] in Poughkeepsie and here in my Studio Saturday. It seemed to me good that he was moved to action of some kind and I will be happy to see him. I guess it just has to be lived through. I can't bear the miserable years toward the end so many people seem to have to endure. Wystan, for instance, was very unhappy in many ways I think, worn, lonely, in the grip of iron habit that wasn't especially cheering to him.[4]

I have read so many rotten things recently, all of a personal nature. The Nicolson book seems to me a nothing, the letters bad, the com-

---

1. See James Reston, "Provocative President: Control Vanishes, Emotion Underneath," *New York Times*, October 27, 1973.

2. Referring to the sudden death of Mary Thomas on September 2, 1973.

3. Julian Thomas, son of Harris and Mary Thomas.

4. Auden had died on September 29, 1973.

ment by N.N. fatuous.[1] I loathe it when people write: perhaps she was cruel, but magnificently.[2] And then there is a boring thing by Hannah Tillich about the porn interests and sexual aberrations of herself and Himself, Paul.[3] It is a shame that it should be just as hard to write about sex as about anything else. And very hard to write about your private life, no harder than anything else perhaps, but the idea of these books is that it is easier, the whole effort really sort of done for you by experience.

I have been going to the opera, buying and playing records. My house is always crowded with people coming and going—even a recent Radcliffe graduate I know has been staying here. I feel that I would like to end up like Dr. Johnson with his crowd of paupers, but I fear their dirt. And of course Johnson had to go out every night.

Much love to you and Jim. I am obsessed with the Thanksgiving hope and want only to be there cracking chestnuts and washing dishes.

    Lizzie

---

1. Nigel Nicolson: "The story is told in five parts, two by her, three by myself. Parts I and III are her autobiography verbatim [. . .] Parts II and IV are my commentaries on it, to which I add essential new facts and quotations from letters and diaries" (*Portrait of a Marriage: Vita Sackville-West and Harold Nicolson* [1973], p. xi).

2. Nicolson: "She [Sackville-West] fought for the right to love, men and women, rejecting the conventions that marriage demands exclusive love, and that women should love only men, and men only women. For this she was prepared to give up everything. Yes, she may have been mad, as she later said, but it was a magnificent folly. She may have been cruel, but it was cruelty on a heroic scale. How can I despise the violence of such passion?" (*Portrait of a Marriage*, p. 194).

3. Hannah Tillich, *From Time to Time* (1973).

PART IV

1974—1979

289. *Robert Lowell to* Elizabeth and Harr[iet] Lowell

[Telegram]

Milgate Park, Bearsted, Maidstone, Kent
[no date, but January 1, 1974?]

LOVE AND FRENCH FOR THE NEW YEAR ITS WELL THE OLD YEAR
IS OUT LOVE

CAL

290. *Robert Lowell to* Mrs. Elizabeth Lowell

Milgate Park, Bearsted, Maidstone, Kent
[January 18, 1974]

Dearest Lizzie—

Sorry about the unexpected call. I had forgotten that cable in England means "telephone." I was caught by surprise having just telegraphed what I thought was a "cable."

Delighted with your Philip.[1] It seems to say everything for and against imaginable in your short space—and more than what is possible in a funeral speech. Yet I don't imagine anyone is hurt. I started

---

1. Philip Rahv died on December 22, 1973. Hardwick: "Philip Rahv (1908–1973)," *New York Review of Books*, January 24, 1974.

a piece on him for Commentary and had actually written a little less than two pages . . . when I read you. I felt a great relief of not having to go on, you made it unnecessary; mine was a rambly reminiscence beginning during the War with going with the first Rahvs to hear Randall lecture at Princeton with Allen very himself presiding.

I suppose the drop into the void is always a few weeks ahead, but for the moment we are so much more at ease than we were in Brookline that no hardship can be felt. I wonder if Harriet would like to come for a week or so at Easter. We have two, not first rate, but safe horses. And surely something more wide ranging, like London, can be arranged. When is Easter. I may come home to go to Skidmore and Vanderbilt sometime in April!

Nothing much with us. I write without much steam on me—quite a few free verse poems now, redrafts of some of my perversely wild translations (it's a mistake to invent something of one's translating *only* if faithfulness does better; the trouble is a *faithful* may do nothing, be undistinguishable from another of the kind). And then I have a prose book (*Occasional Criticism and Reviews*, like poor Philip's last magazine)[.][1] All the youthful stuff would have to be not just revised but re-imagined. It never ends.

Have I thanked you for the relief of my visit?[2] I had that settled-in fever-cold that's run through all my family, and psychologically and through physical weakness could hardly make my trip. Through physical complication and pinchedness Brookline was like one of these vexing dreams where innumerable little objects will never stay in place. All to disappear. I hope so I didn't leave my cold behind. How much briefer letters are than words.

> Love,
> Cal

---

1. *Modern Occasions*, edited by Philip Rahv. Lowell's prose was tentatively entitled "A Moment in American Poetry" in his American publisher's files (see Farrar, Straus and Giroux Inc. records, Archives and Manuscripts Division, New York Public Library); it would become the *Collected Prose* (1987).

2. Paul Mariani: "Mostly it was a low-keyed autumn [in 1973]. In early November he gave a reading at the Pierpont Morgan Library [in New York] [. . .] Harriet came up to Boston for a visit, and at term's end he went back down to New York for a short visit. By then Lizzie had relented enough that Cal could talk to her before flying back to England" (*Lost Puritan: A Life of Robert Lowell* [1994], p. 424).

I like best almost Philip not being particularly autobiographical, and his refusal to accept his friends['] versions of their actions being complete.[1] I am bugged about "provincial."[2] Almost no English or American intellectuals (except sometimes Jews and the foreign-born) have ever *tasted* another country or culture. It's not a matter of dipping in other languages, though this could help—it's their spirit which can't be ours, and isn't.

291. Elizabeth Hardwick to Robert Lowell

[15 West 67th Street, New York, N.Y.]
March 6, 1974

Dear Cal: Harriet is arriving Saturday night March 23 at Heathrow, 9:40 P.M. Flight BOAC 594[.] She is coming back on Thursday April 4, BOAC Flight that leaves at 11 A.M.—that in case you want to book the same flight if you are coming with her for your readings.

I am off to Rio the same day[3] but will return here a few days before Harriet's return. I don't see how I can possibly write anything. What a large, brilliantly imperfect subject for such a small, "perfect" talent.[4] I have met two delightful, engaging Brazilians and will stay in Rio with

---

1. Hardwick: "Thinking over the life and the nature of this extraordinary person, I remember that he had a large number of friends and maintained an intimacy with many of them. And yet we must respect the fact that Philip was not especially autobiographical. Of course this was something of a puzzle because his curiosity about the biography of his acquaintances was relentless, just as his refusal to accept their version of their actions and their motives was complete" ("Philip Rahv [1908–1973]," *New York Review of Books*, January 24, 1974).

2. Hardwick: "The outstanding theme of Rahv's efforts was, I think, a contempt for provincialism, for the tendency to inflate local and fleeting cultural accomplishments. This slashing away at low levels of taste and at small achievements passing as masterly, permanent monuments was a crusade some more bending souls might have grown weary of. But he was not ashamed of his extensive 'negativism' and instead went on right up to the end scolding vanity and unworthy accommodation" ("Philip Rahv [1908–1973]").

3. For the *New York Review of Books*. Hardwick: "I had been here for some months in 1962 and now in 1974 I returned—to see what? It was a time of celebration for the military regime. *They* had ruled for ten years [. . .] Prosperity flows to the chosen and to those who have more shall be given. For the rest, the huge remainder, their time has not yet come" ("Sad Brazil," *New York Review of Books*, June 27, 1974).

4. Hardwick: "Largeness, magnitude, quantity: it is commonplace to speak of Brazil as a 'giant,' a phenomenon spectacular, propitiously born, outrageously favored, and yet marked by the sluggishness of the greatly outsized" ("Sad Brazil," *New York Review of Books*, June 27, 1974).

one of them & his family. I will have my own room and bath (section I think where Elizabeth's Rio apt. was) and when I enquired about the condition of the beach he said, oh, that doesn't matter, we have a pool. I was pleased I admit. I understand Lacerda is immensely rich and immensely fat from drinking it up, but I intend to try to see him.[1] The people I will see are part of the legal opposition, pressing censorship as far as it will go, etc. They seem, Brazilian style, quite exhilarated, joyfully predicting a collapse of the celebrated economic growth. Apparently there are so many cars in Rio and St. Paulo that you have, literally, five hour waits. People get out of their cars and shoot each other![2]

Let me know if you are not returning with Harriet and I will meet her—no, I have to teach that day and she will take a cab home. Let's see—I am saving a little stack of blows and kisses for you (printed ones) of little importance but alive to the curious ego I guess.[3] Blows such as L.W.'s Castle no good, L. Studies better.

I know my darling's visit will be lovely for all of you. She is very much looking forward to it. I will not write again I guess and so you can put the arriv[al] time in the band of your hat.

Love,
  Lizzie

292. *Robert Lowell to* Mrs. Elizabeth Lowell

Milgate Park, Bearsted, Maidstone, Kent
May 1, 1974

Dearest Lizzie—

Here I am in the country half-frozen and out of touch with Mayday. Tomorrow I start a final performance of reading, & discussion of

---

1. Carlos Lacerda (friend of Elizabeth Bishop and Lota de Macedos Soares), whom Hardwick and Lowell met in 1962.

2. Hardwick: "it is not uncommon to hear that torture has become 'boring.' One brave old lady predicted that it would be replaced by murder, disappearance, gun shots in the streets. So it has proved to be. The idea of human sacrifice—a profane and secular purification rite, practiced in the name of progress, investment, and the holy 'Growth'—has left the country a ruin. The land is rich in heroes created by the military Will. A small card sent out by the family of a young student killed by the police: [. . .] (Having lived little [1946–1973] he accomplished the task of a long existence)" ("Sad Brazil," *New York Review of Books*, June 27, 1974).

3. See Lowell to Hardwick, May 1, 1974 and Hardwick to Lowell, May 6, 1974.

translation at Essex, amid the dying embers of a month-old strike.[1] I'm still tired from travelling about America.[2]

Sorry things blew up with us just at the very end last Thursday—I can't believe almost a week has passed. I'm sending the Clive James[3] to Michael Rubinstein my lawyer—still unread. I suppose only a lawyer knows what is libel and what isn't.

Letter from Wynn Handman wanting to do the whole Old Glory on some kind of grant.[4] Also someone here wanting to do Phèdre at Edinburgh. Ah, the old flowers of last year!

Except for the end, nothing could have been more tender and considerate of old "patriarchal" than your treatment of me—your treatment and Harriet's[.]

What do you think turned up here from Paris? A letter from Giovanna Madonia,[5] taking her ten years child to Glyndebourne. Oh where is Sidney Nolan who used to go there this time of year?

Love to you both,
    Dad-Cal

My first day I slept 18 (?) hours.

293. Elizabeth Hardwick to Robert Lowell[6]

[15 West 67th Street, New York, N.Y.]
May 6, 1974

Dear Cal: I'm glad you got back safely and I am just now, after all these weeks, finding the time to write you and to say that I am sorry

---

1. Power shortages were still in effect after the end of the strike by the National Union of Mineworkers on March 6, 1974.

2. Paul Mariani: "In April 1974 [. . .] he returned to the States for three weeks of readings, an itinerary which included Vanderbilt, the universities of Virginia and South Carolina (where he visited with James Dickey), then north to Washington, Skidmore, and Harvard" (*Lost Puritan: A Life of Robert Lowell*, p. 425).

3. Clive James, "Big Medicine," *the Review* 27 [Autumn–Winter 1971–2]; reprinted in *The Metropolitan Critic* [1974]. For Lowell's response, see *The Letters of Robert Lowell*, p. 631.

4. For a Bicentennial revival of *The Old Glory* (1965) that opened at the American Place Theatre on April 9, 1976.

5. With whom Lowell had an affair during a major manic episode in 1954. See *The Letters of Robert Lowell*, pp. 211–39.

6. One of the twelve letters, postcards, and telegrams written by Hardwick that were included in the Lowell Estate's sale of papers to the HRC in 1982.

the misunderstanding about various things in print occurred.[1] I had no idea I was the bearer of bad news, but I do remember the wisdom of the ancients in regard to those things . . . Aside from that, life has just been horrible. I had to fly last weekend to Lexington because my brother Robert, younger than I am, died;[2] now I fly back again this weekend for the long-arranged honorary degree.[3] We learned of Israel's death yesterday[4] and Harriet expressed the desire to send a cable and did so. Then yesterday news that Hannah had had a heart attack in Scotland. Jovanovich was there at the very moment and Mary soon arrived. But we are all in tears over it. That whole generation and its learning, the kind of thinking it did, the greatness of the lives and the persons. I cannot bear to think of the loss, cannot bear to have Hannah sick in this way.

My little book is out and got a huge review with a huge picture in the N.Y. Times.[5] The review was very boring I thought but I suppose I should be happy. Having a small dinner in its honor tonight—or a dinner is being had. Harriet and Devie as my escorts.

I haven't written my piece on Brazil[6] because of all the aching interruptions. Death and loss everywhere around us. So I write in that spirit of forgiveness and honor of all we have touched in our lives. Harriet is very well.

 Love,
  Lizzie

---

1. Possibly a reference to Clive James's *The Metropolitan Critic*, among others; see Lowell to Hardwick, May 1, 1974, footnote 3 on page 389.
2. Robert Hardwick died on May 1, 1974.
3. The University of Kentucky awarded Hardwick an honorary Doctor of Letters degree in May 1974.
4. Israel Citkowitz died on May 4, 1974. Lowell: "he was nearer to us than ex-husbands usually are—close to the children like an uncle, and made the best of me even to the extent of being a partisan. He wasn't mentally or physically well at the end, but he died rather gaily with oysters and champaigne (R months were just about over) and visits from Lord Gowrie's beautiful German nobility girlfriend" (to Stanley Kunitz, [May 14, 1974]).
5. *Seduction and Betrayal* (1974); Barbara Probst Solomon, "Of Women Writers and Writing about Women," *New York Times Book Review*, May 3, 1974.
6. "Sad Brazil," *New York Review of Books*, June 27, 1974.

294. Elizabeth Hardwick to Robert Lowell

[15 West 67th Street, New York, N.Y.]

July 20, 1974

Dear Cal: I'm sorry not to have written for such a long time. There is actually not all that much to say, or much that can't somehow get thrown into your occasional calls. Harriet is fine I think, even if she and all her friends often, at home at least, seem weighed down by adolescent torpor. In spite of that they will be off on August 1st to bike around Holland, through Germany to Copenhagen. Some of the trip by train, I hope. I naturally have some misgivings about something so vague, about Cathy and Harriet sweating out thirty miles a day on the roads of Europe, alone. I tell them to give up if it isn't altogether pleasant. The probability is that it will be great fun, with lots of people like themselves in hostels, in the public parks, etc. She is still a wonderful companion and delight to me when she is at home and was a brick about our time in Maine, when of course there wasn't a soul her age to be seen with a telescope.

I love my new house absolutely. Somehow the site is even more splendid and encompassing than we knew since it now opens in all directions, the windows are wider and in many ways the barn idea has disappeared although the dear structure is still there. My bedroom is overwhelming. The first night there I fell on the bed in exhaustion; there was a full moon, high tide, and the water seemed to be at the foot of the bed. It is indeed not just a view, but true living on the sea.

I saw Jack T.[1] the other night, the first time in nearly a year. He is in better shape, looked rather beautiful after so many homely, drunken years. And what a nice friend. He went to Robie and to Peter, in their troubles.[2] The description of Peter as he came home from the hospital, weeping, too weak to move, was awful. However he improved quite strikingly in a few days. The pain and the weakness of these attacks are fearful I understand. Poor Peter. The change is inevitable and

---

1. Thompson.

2. Robie Macauley's wife, Anne, died in 1973 (see *The Letters of Robert Lowell*, pp. 620–21). Peter Taylor had a heart attack in late May–early June 1974, and "as soon as Peter left the intensive care unit, he went into a deep depression that lasted for a month [. . .] 'I never before had such dark thoughts or such terrible nightmares,' he confided to Cal" (Hubert H. McAlexander, *Peter Taylor: A Writer's Life* [2001], pp. 222–23).

great, the inner change. But people do get stronger, live quite well and for many years. I am in New York with Harriet and left Castine just as Mary got there. But I talked to her by phone and will see her this week. She said Hannah was quite surprisingly well—and so that can be.

Bob told me you had written some poems or a poem about Israel.[1] And of course I thought he was talking about the beleaguered state and puzzled over it. Was later told it was about the deceased person. I haven't seen the work.

There is not much news. New York is not unpleasant and I have been in and out a lot but I look forward to the month of August in Castine. My number there is 207 326-4856.

Much love to you and good health,
    Lizzie

295. Robert Lowell to Harriet Lowell

[Telegram]

[London]
[July 31, 1974]

HARRIET LOWELL 15WEST67ST
NEWYORKCITY
MAY MY LOVE GO WITH YOU ON YOUR ADVENTURE
IVE TRIED TO PHONE THROUGH TO YOU REPEATEDLY LOVE
    DADDY

296. Elizabeth Hardwick to Robert Lowell[2]

[Castine, Maine]
Saturday, August 9 [August 10, 1974]

Dear Cal: I have written Harriet about the lovely telegram you sent her, which just missed her departure. She seems to be having a good time in Holland and I hope the bicycle trip to Denmark won't be hard.

---

1. "In the Ward (for Israel Citkowitz)"; see also "Burial (for—)"; both in *Day by Day* (1977).
2. One of the twelve letters, postcards, and telegrams written by Hardwick that were included in the Lowell Estate's sale of papers to the HRC in 1982.

Anyway, the long summer waiting was not good for the spirits. She came up with me in June to get my house settled, but Castine was a desert. The house is utterly beautiful. Incredible views on all sides, very bright colors, quite special and exhilarating. The grounds were like the entrance to a motor court but the grass is struggling up and the joy of life here is very great. Mary and Jim are wonderful. All of us, with Frankie FitzGerald, watched the incredible exit of Nixon.[1] For two or three days here the tension and excitement were like being drunk.

Cousin Natalie died in New York this week—of cancer. She had been quite ill all winter, but still rather the same "girl" and very hopeful and cheerfully distant from what was happening to her. I do not have further passages forward or backward to report.

I have done nothing but get the house ready for months and now will try to proceed with a few things. I have to see if I can indeed go forward with my novel, because I must recover having spent every penny in the world on this barn. I suppose it was worth it, but can one be self-esteeming enough to know that he deserves such as this. I do know I mustn't get sick until I have put some "capital" back in the bank. In the long run I think Harriet will like and use the house— actually she adores it, even if the town isn't alive enough for her . . . How nice it must be in Kent. I haven't seen any of your new work, but I hope it goes along to your liking. Much love from here.

Elizabeth

297. *Robert Lowell to* Mrs. Elizabeth Lowell

Milgate Park, Bearsted, Maidstone, Kent
August 16, [1974]

Dear Lizzie:

I am so happy you liked and sent off my cable to Harriet; I wanted it to be in the nick of time, if I failed to get her on the phone. By the time you get this the girls' trip will be largely over I suppose. Lovely and slightly scary to think of them orbiting without directors through northern Europe.

---

1. Frances FitzGerald; Nixon resigned the presidency at noon on Friday, August 9, 1974.

My feeling about Nixon is that a great pollution has been removed from our country, almost in a Biblical or Greek classical sense. Wasn't Nixon good on *au revoir*, the smallest citron ranch, and his mother who was a saint?[1]

Sad about Natalie. I just failed to write her a note at Alice's suggestion. Hope her cancer wasn't the unbelievable torture it can be. I pray to have suicide pills near when the hours come.

It makes me so happy the barn makes you so happy. Three people, you and I and Cousin Harriet made it as it is. A tradition. I have about half a book of "short" poems,[2] and have stopped for time—more or less at desire, though nature must help in these things.

Much love back from me.

Love,
Cal

298. *Elizabeth Hardwick to Robert Lowell*

[15 West 67th Street, New York, N.Y.]
September 23, 1974

Dear Cal: Your Ransom elegy is absolutely beautiful.[3] No one does these things as sweetly, oddly, brilliantly as you. I don't know why the magazine included the two other additions.[4] In fact I don't in general understand the magazine and its way of seeming to be made up of the most provincial gossip. The deadly bore of the old poetry festival; academe or journalism. Two pieces on Boston. (Ehrenpreis and Raban.)[5]

---

1. Nixon: "You are here to say good-by to us. And we don't have a good word for it in English. The best is au revoir. We'll see you again. [. . .] I remember my old man. [. . .] He was a streetcar motorman first and then he was a farmer and then he had a lemon ranch—it was the poorest lemon ranch in California, I assure you—he sold it before they found oil on it. [. . .] Nobody will ever write a book probably about my mother. Well, I guess all of you would say this about your mother. My mother was a saint" ("Transcription of Nixon's Farewell Speech to Cabinet and Staff Members in the Capital," *New York Times*, August 10, 1974).

2. For *Day by Day* (1977).

3. John Crowe Ransom died on July 3, 1974. Lowell: "John Crowe Ransom, 1888–1974," *New Review* 1, no. 5 (August 1974).

4. "John Crowe Ransom: Four Tributes" by Lowell, Denis Donoghue, Richard Ellmann, and Roy Fuller, *New Review* 1:5 (August 1974).

5. Irvin Ehrenpreis, "The Arts in America"; Jonathan Raban, "One American City"; *New Review* 1, no. 4 (July 1974).

I slipped and broke a bone in my foot and have been miserable, impatient, exhausted, helpless, bored, pained. It is now better and by the time this reaches you the cast will be off and I expect to be free, gliding, smiling. Do not break anything! Especially in your foot.

It is fall, rather nice after a long imprisonment in hot city humidity. Harriet's summer was good, she is quite thin, very nice, back in school reading Don Quixote[1] in Spanish, the Odyssey in English. It can't all be damaging I tell her.

I don't have this morning any great news or gossip for you. Mr. Alfred[2] died, as you probably know. The story of Donald[3] is worse and worse, now guns and a hideous (true) rape charge. Bill does not seem quite to understand that this last is the crossing of a barrier into hell. The sadistic, prolonged assault on another person is ~~another~~ \a different/ thing from car thefts. Donald is in jail after an escape, and Bill is at last free of his presence. But I feel he will still hang on to the idea of redemption, will remain responsible for the boy, true to him. It would not be right to wish it otherwise I suppose because one can't ever hope that anyone will be utterly abandoned. And yet I worry about Bill himself and the punishment of the entanglement. Right now he is all right, especially with the relief of jail.

Well, be in good health and courageous sobriety. I'll send this off now. It is a mere toast to your Ransom remembrance.

With much love,
Elizabeth

299. Elizabeth Hardwick to Robert Lowell[4]

[15 West 67th Street, New York, N.Y.]
October 2, 1974

Dearest Cal: I am sure you are all right by now, but I would like to know for a certainty and also what the doctor said. After I talked to you I began to think that the antabuse, and an inadvertent whiff of

---

1. By Miguel de Cervantes (1605).

2. William Alfred's father.

3. Donald Bourasa, William Alfred's foster son.

4. One of the twelve letters, postcards, and telegrams written by Hardwick that were included in the Lowell Estate's sale of papers to the HRC in 1982.

alcohol, were the real causes. But what a violent reaction.[1] It makes one wonder about the drug, just as one wonders a little about all of them. Do take care, although you have indeed spent the last year in a state of great prudence and courage.

Life in New York is violently expensive and worrying. I feel very tired after my siege with the broken bone in my foot. It was only a two-week thing, but I felt such impatience that even now, recovered, I seem exhausted and still impatient.

Harriet is fine, I think. It is a hard time for her. The college applications, worries, inevitably descend, but she seems to push them away. She won't make a special effort as many people do to prepare for the exams, or take the tutoring seriously the school offers. She feels that she can get into Barnard. I hate for her to stay in New York and, as you realize, one never approves of anyone you love engaging in anything you know well. Still it will be all right. I think we must wait a little for the final marks on the college boards to see if there is a remote possibility about Radcliffe. Harriet, as everyone I know truly believes, is terribly smart and wonderfully skeptical, observant, witty. I am pleased with her and I think of the college business because I believe in education and also because I can't see that society has another plan for an 18 year old. Oh, God, I saw Alida White somewhere who reported that Dixey was "radiant!" Will leave you on that & what I pray is good health. Dear love,

E

---

1. See Lowell to Harriet Lowell, October 9, 1974, below. Ian Hamilton: "In October 1974 Lowell was at a party given by the London publisher George Weidenfeld. He was not drinking; indeed, to aid in this latest of several efforts to renounce alcohol, he was taking the drug Antabuse. On October 9 he writes again to [Peter] Taylor: 'The other night at a large party I suddenly felt an acute nausea as if I had been drinking heavily, then a rather comforting feeling of changing inside to ice, then I was being rolled about by six merry people on a low table, like a gentle practical joke. I had fainted. It may have been from accidentally drinking something like vodka and orange juice, or it may not. The doctors can't tell. [. . .] '" (*Robert Lowell: A Biography*, pp. 441–42).

300. Robert Lowell to Harriet Lowell

Milgate Park, Bearsted, Maidstone, Kent

October 9, 1974

Dearest Harriet:

I haven't written because nothing is harder for me than starting letters out of no where, unless it's speaking at dinner to a girl I've just been introduced to. "Do you really come from Wales?" or "What does your father do?" or "Do you have five children?"

I gather you are approaching your College Entrances, very tense and scary, even if you're somewhat unconcerned. I can't say between Harvard and Barnard, either could be much better for you. At Harvard you would not only be a little way from home, but you would be much more in a college world. It would be more of a new experience, new sights new sounds, more the [life] your life would be. Or would it. I think with the help of Bill Alfred I could get you in. There are so many quite good colleges, and Barnard ~~would~~ \might/ be best. It would be pleasant to be near Mother.

As she probably told you, I fainted briefly at a party ten days ago— probably from accidentally drinking on top of antabuse, but not necessarily. I'm going to a very big expert Friday, and dread having to stop smoking and taking restorative walks. I have two things to finish 1) a book of poems about half done, to come out in about two years, and 2) a book of essays and reviews written since 1943, and mostly done except for arranging and making small changes and notes. Shouldn't I make some remarkable discoveries and predate them 1945?

I'll be back in midJanuary, and see you then.

I love you very much—

Daddy

Daddy

301. *Robert Lowell to* Mrs. Robert Lowell[1]

Milgate Park, Bearsted, Maidstone, Kent
October 13, 1974

Dearest Lizzie:

I just had an examination by some very great heart-expert \(they all look like sons-in-law to me now)/, and was cleared of any heart-trouble, as earlier of lung-trouble. So now I am pushing crates and carrying buckets of coal upstairs.

Your description of Harriet is about what mine would be—I'd add a master of chaffing argument. Can she really get into Barnard with reasonably good grades? I don't know if Harvard would be better. We are upset by the riots, which tho they'll of course die down will remain smoldering in the air. I wonder if the negroes are pro Ulster Protestant. It's horrible: I think the busing in the \such an/ atmosphere is criminal.[2] We decided not to take our family to Cambridge—3 or 4 big difficulties—new schools for the children, the hell of finding a house for four or even six months, the rough feeling everywhere\, cost./

I'll come over alone, toward the end of January. Can I stop a couple of days with you and H?\, and disturb the studio?/

Doesn't something like a foot take forever at our age? I'm sorry for you. I had a bump then a bruise on my shin for a year [or] more. I think if I stared intently I'd [see] a vague yellow now.

I wonder how States Street[3] is doing for you? Are cautious investors the worst? I suppose it's just the opposite, but still they lose.

It's an indescribable consolation for me to be near to you so happily.

Love,[4]

---

1. Envelope stamped "DIVERTED TO SURFACE NO POSTAGE."
2. On September 12, 1974, the start of court-ordered busing to achieve racial integration in Boston's public schools was marred by violence in South Boston, where students were attacked and school buses were stoned. Riots continued into October; on October 8 the mayor of Boston requested the help of Federal Marshals to control the violence and protect the schoolchildren. The events were widely covered in the press in both the United States and the United Kingdom, but for an example of the kind of story appearing in the British papers that Lowell read, see Joyce Eggiton, "The battle of Boston," *Observer*, October 13, 1974.
3. State Street Trust Company.
4. Unsigned.

302. Elizabeth Hardwick to Robert Lowell

[15 West 67th Street, New York, N.Y.]

November 20, 1974[1]

Dear Cal: Are you well? We haven't heard for a good while and I some-
times wonder if all your pills are going in the same direction—not the
aptest way of imagining the dear, mysterious life-savers perhaps. But
I suppose we would have heard if you were in distress. It is impossible
to write letters, that I know well. I never have a minute any more and I
think of my past reasonably organized self as a lovely springtime long
gone. I am not so much disorganized as simply hopelessly overworked,
without Nicole or anyone, and the expense of life here is a horror I am
slowly, with panic, beginning to take in. I write a lot of small things,
go about lecturing a lot, have bigger matters on my mind in the way
of writing that I despair of ever reaching. But still I am hanging on,
cheerfully anxious.

Harriet is fine. I suppose she won't apply to Radcliffe; she feels her
grades and her scores aren't nearly good enough, apparently one needs
a lot of high school science to pass the required freshman science—
and a host of other \academic/ lacks. I don't know what will finally
come about for her, but she is marvelously real about it all and without
any sort of distress that I can see. She says that she does want to learn,
does want to work, doesn't have a ruling passion yet but expects it to
come—and that one can learn any place, which is the complete and
finest truth. I can't tell you how happy she seems in general, how calm
and gay and busy with her life. She is the most pleasing person to me
and I wish she were able to dip down in England to visit you more
often. She always has a marvelous time there and seems incredibly un-
cluttered in her feelings. Christmas is out this year because she does
have to take all the college boards just after New Year and the study
has been put off for the vacation. Do you quite realize that she will
have her 18th birthday on January 4? Maybe we can have some sort of
celebration all together when you get here. I can scarcely believe the
time has gone by.

Frank and Judy Parker are here for a few days in my studio. Frank
is on a very modest amount of drink, owing to Judy's insistence I guess

---

1. Crossed with Lowell's letter of October 13, 1974.

and his consent. It is nicer and he is well enough I think, doing a good deal of housework while Judy goes out to work—and \doing it/ with surprising and touching docility.

I cannot think of any news to pass on to you. Keep in all possible good health, whatever that may mean, and better spirits than health. Much love from both of us.

Elizabeth

303. *Elizabeth Hardwick to Robert Lowell*[1]

["Season's Greetings" Christmas Card: Pablo Picasso, *Françoise en Soleil* (1946), Museum of Modern Art]

[15 West 67th Street, New York, N.Y.]

[November 26, 1974]

Dearest Cal: My last letter to you must have seemed odd, but I hadn't heard since the telephone call about the fainting. The lovely, reassuring letter of yours, written October 13th, arrived today, November 26, coming by "surface" because of insufficient postage. The rats! Well, I had assumed you were well, but Harriet and I wondered indeed. Off to the Cottings for Thanksgiving, back the same night. I am happy to go and it is nice for Harriet but I always feel the Cottings are hanging on for our sake to the ritual . . . All is well and I look forward to seeing you. We will have a surprise 18th birthday for yours and mine own daughter . . . I very much anticipate your prose book since you write the form with such reckless, off-hand inspiration it puts me to despair and joy at the same time.

Tommy Thomas is coming over the weekend. I fear he is a little boring without Mary and talks about sex all the time. Wives put a stop to that! Mary and Jim are planning a Castine Christmas and I will go up perhaps for New Year. I love Christmas here with Harriet and the birds and flowers[2] and friends and her friends . . .

My foot healed in ten days. If it had been longer my head would

---

1. One of the twelve letters, postcards, and telegrams written by Hardwick that were included in the Lowell Estate's sale of papers to the HRC in 1982.

2. Harriet Lowell: "My mother had a very unusual [Christmas] tree. She had these flowers made out of crepe, in fuchsia and other bright colors, and birds, some of which flapped. She might have picked some of these decorations up in Brazil [in 1962]" (interview with the editor, July 5, 2016).

have cracked open. All the dearest greetings of all the old seasons to you.

Much love,
Lizzie

304. *Robert Lowell to* Elizabeth Hardwick

Milgate Park, Bearsted, Maidstone, Kent
December 13, 1974

Dearest Lizzie—

The fainting must have been drink and antabuse, or maybe the heat of the room, tho this seems odd, so very little and often experienced. Anyway my heart and lungs are completely cleared \by science./ Nothing is durable or easy-moving at our age. I have many small signs—the most noticeable—except for getting out of taxis—absentmindedness. I was always rather [a] parody of other people, now I am a parody of my old self. If I walk holding a letter to put in an envelope—both objects inevitably ~~end~~ reach in separate parts of the room.

You must be delighted with the reviews and choice-of-the-year of your book in England.[1] Strange your being reviewed with Patricia now a friend of ours—to my surprise I found her book heckling, emancipation treated with the ~~excessive~~ clarity and fervor of her Plymouth Brethren background.[2] But yours I didn't,—wonderful gothic portrait tales of women by a woman, a combination of Plutarch & ~~very~~ long book reviews. I read you through again after publication—they seem to have the passion of fiction, and as much unity as they should, 15 stories on some ~~one~~ part of the South. Of the

---

1. Claire Tomalin, "Anger and Accommodation," *Listener*, November 28, 1974; Rosemary Dinnage, "Men, Women, and Books: The Rule of Heroism," *Times Literary Supplement*, November 29, 1974; A. Alvarez, "Heroines and Victims," *Observer*, December 1, 1974; Margaret Drabble, "Women's Literature," *Guardian*, December 5, 1974; Philippa Toomey, "When Heroines Were Heroines and Not Just Decorations," *Times* (London), December 9, 1974; A. Alvarez and Mary McCarthy, "Books of the Year," *Observer*, December 15, 1974.
2. Patricia Beer, *Reader, I Married Him: A Study of the Women Characters of Jane Austen, Charlotte Brontë, Elizabeth Gaskell and George Eliot* (1974). See also her memoir *Mrs. Beer's House* (1968).

bad reviews, Ricks seemed knocked almost inarticulate with ingenuity and annoyance, Carey must have thought you were American.[1]

We are all going to be in Brookline, 33 Cypress St. The children even have schools. We will arrive toward the end of the month \January/. I'll try and get down soon ~~after~~ for Harriet's postponed birthday. I am calling you Christmas Eve, ghastly hour 3:30 A.M. here, 10:30 PM with you. I don't suppose anyone will be in, but it was the only vacancy I could get. Anyway, for now, love and Merry Christmas to you and Harriet. I am mailing my most original presents, checks.

I have a feeling that, like knowing one has entered the tennis singles tournament for the last time, I . . . Guess what I was going to write? It's less than my syntax might lead you to expect.

I gather that Harriet entering Columbia is set now, and assured. Maybe the best thing. I rather hope she will live at home. Perhaps my exaggerating fears from a distance for her safety.

Sad picture of Frank. He thinks all the time of drinking, I imagine. And if he does . . . [I] wrote him a letter long ago, and he seems to have tried innumerable times to answer. I have known him since we were 13—to think of him is to see my lifetime—joy and error.

Saw Mary and Jim rather quickly at a dinner at Gaia's. Mary has the same picture of Tommy.

Love for the coming day,
    Cal

305. Robert Lowell to Harriet Lowell

Milgate Park, Bearsted, Maidstone, Kent
[December 14, 1974]

Dearest Harriet—

Here is my long-considered Christmas present, one you can't refuse. Sorry not to send something English, but the difficulties of choosing, wrapping, clearing with customs is too much. Much love,
    Daddy

---

1. Christopher Ricks, "The Ruling Passion," *Sunday Times* (London), 15 December 1974; John Carey, "The Subjugation of Women," *New Statesman*, 29 November 1974.

306. *Robert Lowell to* Elizabeth Hardwick

Milgate Park, Bearsted, Maidstone, Kent

12, 14, 74

Dearest Lizzie—

I seem to act almost a hundred percent contra my humanist reactionary beliefs by sending you and Harriet this most abstract of acceptable presents, the easiest conveyer of value. We also have and like the detestable glow-coals on hand glowing for our breakfasts. Much love and Merry Christmas. Goodby I'll see you soon.

Love,
Cal

307. *Harriet Lowell to Robert Lowell*

[Telegram]

[New York, N.Y.]
[Received] 1974 Dec 21

MR ROBERT LOWELL MILGATE PARK
BEARSTEDMAIDSTONEKENT
NO LETTER SINCE OCTOBER. WORRIED. LOVE AND MERRY
CHRISTMAS TO ALL OF YOU IN KENT
        HARRIET

308. *Robert Lowell to Harriet Lowell*

[Telegram]

[Maidstone]
[Received] 1974 Dec 22

HARRIET LOWELL 15 WEST67ST
NEWYORKCITY
THANKS FOR CARING AM VERY WELL YOU ALL ARE IN MY HEART
HOPE TO PHONE 10 PM CHRISTMAS EVE LOVE
        DADDY

309. Elizabeth Hardwick to Robert Lowell[1]

[15 West 67th Street, New York, N.Y.]

January 2, 1975

Dearest Cal: A letter finally arrived and Harriet's check. Perhaps the postage has gone up and the stamped envelopes are going by ship rather than airmail. Anyway the mail has taken about three weeks. Harriet was pleased and we were both relieved to know you were all right and in touch. Christmas was exhausting and I have just returned from a few days at the New Year with Mary in Castine—an incredible two week undertaking of hers with house guests, parties for the whole town, presents for everyone, marvelous and endless food. I must say that this trip was utterly pleasing and beautiful for me. Castine was astonishing. This morning on the way to the airport, after a night of thick, white dry snow, the landscape was startling in its grandeur and strangeness, almost lunar somehow.[2] Without leaves a whole world comes out and you can see across the white fields, over to the bay, to the towns opposite. We had a picnic in the snow the day before, across the bay at Brooksville. My own house was boarded up, but looked very still there on the cold water. Philip Booth was in residence. It was a very beautiful, intense thing. Now I am back, with a terrible amount of trips to take, to universities . . . Bill Alfred was here for our Christmas Eve dinner. He is very well and has [a] flat in Manhattan, on the East side, as a substitute for Brooklyn.

I have only seen a few English reviews, but haven't unlimited curiosity this second time. I was more happily received here than I deserved; the book appears to be established, has sold well enough and I imagine will do perfectly all right in paper back. I haven't seen the C. Ricks review and don't wish to unless it turns up. I wonder why he reviewed my book, since it isn't the sort of thing I quite connect with

---

1. One of the twelve letters, postcards, and telegrams written by Hardwick that were included in the Lowell Estate's sale of papers to the HRC in 1982.

2. Hardwick: "A few years ago I spent the New Year season in Maine, on the sea. A heavy, thick snow fell during the night. The scene along the country roads was transformed, as by an unearthly, visionary stroke. [. . .] The land lay in a blind, lunar dream and all the forms of nature appeared fixed in a frozen, metallic perfection. The beauty, absolute as a frieze, made one gasp at the satanic glimpse of an unknown world. The dead, thrilling, moon-like architecture of the scene was like the region itself—unpredictable, gorgeous, never quite to be brought into scale, never entirely yours or anyone's" ("Accepting the Dare: Maine," *Vogue*, September 1976).

him. I don't know about the "books of the year list," but will ask you if I see you and you remember at that time.

Harriet isn't accepted at Barnard yet; the decisions aren't known until April. I expect she will be and certainly hope so since that was the only place she applied. It, and especially Columbia, are good; she will major in history and I feel quite happy about it all, except that she and Cathy will have their own place. Of course, Devie is up there now, and thousands upon thousands . . . But if she were still at home it would be just like staying on at Dalton. Yet they are all much changed, very grown up. She is working harder and reading a lot about World War I and other things. All will be well I think. And marvelous company, smoking, wine sipping on the weekends, and very anxious to see all of you. Quite interested in Sheridan. And eighteen years old when this reaches you.

I am exhausted from the celebrations in Castine and am going to bed on this January 1st.[1] I am so happy that you are feeling well and I expect to get all the diseases, including drinking, now that you haven't them. As we always said, Dilly[2] did Jack's drinking for him and now he's on his own.

Much love, always, and I am sorry for this dim letter. It is what is called an answer only.

Elizabeth

310. Elizabeth Hardwick to Robert Lowell[3]

[15 West 67th Street, New York, N.Y.]
January 4, 1974\5/

Dearest Cal: How stunned I am by the hospitality of your fifty dollars to me! I am touched that you wanted to send me a present and far from displeased that it should come in the form of cash. Thank you very much; and I will have something practical in the way of clothes for you when I see you. Too bad the handy Rosen's of Bucksport was closed on

---

1. Thus, although the letter is dated January 2, 1975.

2. Helen Keeler ("Dilly") Burke, John Thompson's first wife.

3. One of the twelve letters, postcards, and telegrams written by Hardwick that were included in the Lowell Estate's sale of papers to the HRC in 1982.

New Year's Day. Otherwise I might have replaced some of the more unfashionable, unEnglish, unmentionable items in your wardrobe. Also, this lovely, kind gift took three weeks and so I do think perhaps the postage has gone up on airmail or some such thing.

Today is Harriet's 18th, but all is unfestive here because she is, and quite happily I do honestly think, studying for her college board History achievement and, not happily, writing a paper in Spanish on *Don Quixote* which they have spent the semester reading in Spanish. She is also up at night, just now finished, with *Goodbye to All That*[1] for the World War I course. In spite of everything she is being, has been educated by the egregious Dalton. And she is in good spirits. It will still be Barnard or Boston University—the only two places she will consent to, since she didn't feel up to applying at Radcliffe. I am sure she could have gotten in Smith or Chicago and that sort, but she doesn't really like the idea.

In my last letter I didn't begin to do justice to Mary's house, the food, the incredibly detailed festivities, the miraculous landscape, the tree, the presents, the music, the guests, the expense, the pleasure. It was a great joy to me, even though I had Penelope Gilliatt in my pocket more or less since she somehow got into the invitation that originally went to Gavin Young, who was ill. I am friendly with Penelope and we had a good time—her clothes for the arctic occasion were teensy white patent sandals with very thin high heels, white stockings, a pastel cotton dress and lots of cologne, with fingers loaded with yellowish rings, all square, and lots of gold over the Miami Beach costumes. Extraordinary—but on purpose?

I will be very happy to see you when it is convenient for you to do so. Now, I must go to the market. Barbara E. and Alison Lurie are coming for dinner, to eat the scallops pulled out of Penobscot Bay by Billy Macomber.[2]

Much love,
Lizzie

---

1. Robert Graves, *Good-Bye to All That: An Autobiography* (1929).
2. Castine grocer.

311. Elizabeth Hardwick to Robert Lowell[1]

[15 West 67th Street, New York, N.Y.]
Monday [n.d. late April/early May 1975]

Dear Cal: Cathy and Harriet were just about at the door and I was glad you caught us because a visit can be exhausting. They are unperturbed about the cancellation and went out happily enough except that Harriet was concerned about you. I have reassured her and I am reassured by the "new" treatments[2] and what seemed your general heroic health when I saw you. Indeed I felt somewhat less healthy and can only hope to pull up to your own heights. I have been going about a bit and at last understand the hatred of readings, appearances and above all the tremendous weight on the soul occasioned by an interview, always conducted by someone who knows nothing about your nature and your work. I have come home to an essay on Simone Weil I promised to do for a magazine a colleague at Barnard is editing.[3] Of course I would rather give, if I had it, a thousand dollars than a page and actually I have neither.

This is just to wish you well. I am sorry there were so many people around when you were here. We haven't seen much of Darryl[4] since because he, in the visit with you, went to the top of the mountain. Next time you come we will go out to dinner so that I can really talk to you, although it is nice to have you here with Harriet, Devie, Barbara, your fan club.

Harriet is doing very well, I think, and when we hear from Barnard that all is agreeable for next year there will be general relief. This little

---

1. One of the twelve letters, postcards, and telegrams written by Hardwick that were included in the Lowell Estate's sale of papers to the HRC in 1982.

2. Kay Redfield Jamison: "In May 1975, during a trip to New York, Lowell suffered severe lithium toxicity and had to be hospitalized. During lunch with his editor, Robert Giroux, Lowell's head fell forward onto the table and he appeared heavily sedated. Robert Silvers, a friend and the editor of the *New York Review of Books*, described what happened some time later that evening: 'We'd all been to the opera, and at the restaurant afterwards Cal seemed in terrible shape—exhausted, excited, incoherent. He slumped at the table drinking glass after glass of orange juice.' [. . .] Lowell was treated for lithium intoxication and possible delirium at Mount Sinai Hospital; the experience left him and his friends shaken" (*Robert Lowell: Setting the River on Fire; A Study of Genius, Mania, and Character*, p. 188).

3. Hardwick, "Reflections on Simone Weil," *Signs: Journal of Woman and Culture in Society* 1, no. 1 (Autumn 1975); edited by Catharine R. Stimpson.

4. Pinckney.

note is just to send our love to you and our thoughts. We aren't worried so don't have our concern on your mind as an agitation. Keep in touch and may happy gods attend you.

Dearest love,
Lizzie

312. *Elizabeth Hardwick to Robert Lowell*[1]

The New York Review of Books, 250 West Fifty-Seventh Street,
New York City, New York 10019, PLaza 7-8070
June 4, 1975

Dear Cal: I believe this is something only you can fill out.[2] Another summer here—and indeed it must be another summer there. Harriet graduates in a few days and there will be a party afterward with some of us and her friends and their parents. It is all so strange in the \strange/ way of the universal and ordinary—her passage from the "five year olds" to the end. Saul Bellow will be there for his son, Adam; and so on and so on. I have a certain sadness I guess mixed with my great pleasure in Harriet. For a time the idea of an apartment around Columbia was horrifying to me; I saw a few and felt quite desperate. But I have seen a few more and my own spirits have lifted. I can see how much fun it will be, or can be, to have your own place. As for me, I am suddenly not quite so apprehensive about Smith; I'll be back here at a lot of the weekends and I am looking forward to the very convenient library and to a lot of writing. I will miss New York, but I expect to keep "in"—and there are holidays, all sorts of chances for coming down, and then it will be over December 15th. I went up to Maine last weekend; a wonderful blue sky and hot sun came out. My house is incredibly beautiful. It had been swept out and mopped and I had it all together in one day and then cooked lobster for the friend that went with me. Last summer was a nightmare because of the cost that kept mounting; I paid it, making myself broke, without a penny in the bank. But it's

---

1. One of the twelve letters, postcards, and telegrams written by Hardwick that were included in the Lowell Estate's sale of papers to the HRC in 1982.

2. Enclosure now missing, but possibly relating to Lowell's contribution to "A Special Supplement: The Meaning of Vietnam," *New York Review of Books*, June 12, 1975.

done and I am back saving a few nickels and dimes—and so the house became a joy again. I don't expect to go up for good until July at the earliest. I guess Mary will be there the 15th.

I have been reading some of Laforgue's prose, which is marvelous. Wonderful essay on Baudelaire, another, rather miffed and brilliant, about Corbière.[1] And *The Notebooks of Malte Brigge* again.[2] How romantic and moving it is, how much of its time and its author. . . . Well, the end of the page . . . I wish we had seen more of you, but the last visit was a good health pleasure—your good health. So keep your pills straight and all will be well. God is good, sometimes.

Love,
Lizzie

313. Robert Lowell to Harriet Lowell

[Telegram]

[Maidstone]
[Received June 6, 1975]

MISS HARRIET LOWELL 15 WEST67ST

NEWYORK

I HAVE ALMOST LIVED YOUR GRADUATION GRADUATED MYSELF

IM SO PROUD AND GLAD LOVE TO YOU AND CATHY

DAD

314. Elizabeth Hardwick to Robert Lowell

[Castine, Maine]
July 16, 1975

Dearest Cal: Looking out on the foggy bay, heavy sky with a sort of curtain of light behind it. The lawn has just been cut, the golf club

---

1. "Notes on Baudelaire" and "A Study of Corbière," *Selected Writings of Jules Laforgue*, ed. and trans. William Jay Smith (1956).

2. Rainer Maria Rilke, *Notebooks of Malte Laurids Brigge* (1910). Hardwick: "Rilke imagined that a tin lid had no other desire than to rest evenly and firmly upon its proper can" (*Sleepless Nights*, p. 121); Hardwick could have been reading a translation either by M. D. Herter Norton (W. W. Norton, 1949) or by John Linton (Hogarth Press, 1950).

rummage sale looms for the morning. It is beautiful here and my house is so pretty, warm, bright red and mustard colored inside, and so naturally warm from the high ground. I must say I love it with too much passion. Mary arrived in Bangor Friday, her maid arrived in Bangor Saturday, Jim arrives in two weeks (in Bangor). We've been marketing, dining, off to Ellsworth tomorrow. The old group thins and rearranges itself, often drastically. Without Mary I might have pulled out altogether, but since she is here the others are sufficient. Tommy had a back operation and so has not been much in "operation." The Booths are here and very agreeable they are.

Harriet came up for the 4th and perhaps will come up again in August. She's in New York where she and Cathy are looking after their dogs and cats while the Grads are in Europe. Cathy has a job at a cake stand in Grand Central Station, Harriet "applied" to every hamburger and ice cream seller, but no luck. She doesn't see England this summer. I think in August they will go biking somewhere here and then they must start at college about August 27th, with moving into their apartment a week before. Did I tell you that Mrs. Grad and I and the two girls have found a marvelously pretty, safe apartment for them. It belongs to a Dalton teacher who will be in England all year and it is quite beautiful, with plants, Mexican rugs, bright colors, books. What a joy and relief it was. My heart nearly stopped beating when we were looking around at the squalid, menacing things that turned up before.

I don't have too much to say as I face this second page. Letters cannot be occasional or intermittent, can they? Somehow it is the long, wide gap between lives that makes letters impossible rather than necessary. I'm sure one writes his best letters to the ones just around the corner or just here yesterday. By that I mean I understand both the inertias about your own letter-writing you spoke of—it is physical and also formal. All of this even though I think of you often.

Much love,
Lizzie

315. Elizabeth Hardwick to Robert Lowell[1]

[Castine, Maine]
August 7, 1975

Dearest Cal: Harriet spoke to me on the phone about having written you a letter, lost it, couldn't find a stamp and so on. I would find when she returned from Europe all sorts of letters home stuffed in her knapsack. Anyway, she wanted me to tell you that she has been working at the New York Review the last month—stuffing envelopes—and now for a few weeks she and Cathy will go camping on Martha's Vineyard—and then we'll all be back in New York by August 25th. So . . . How the time goes, racing or sometimes very slowly. I will be glad to get back to New York, even at the end of August, and yet it has been nice up here most of the time. But strangely altered, too. Somehow the tennis hasn't been going this summer with our group and the social life is more waiting to be asked to dinner or having to dinner. I have found it quite lonely a good deal of the time and that is something to think about, but I don't quite cherish it although one does fall into the rhythm of whatever the gods lay down on us. I'm afraid the evening schnapps are the most gratefully awaited visitor of the day. At least I have read hugely, rather as I used to do when I was young and lying about in Lexington. This afternoon the great blessing of the Penguin prose translation of Heine.[2] He grabs my heart.

Lots of little boats in the harbor. Clark Fitz-G. is marrying in a week or so[3] and likewise Margot Booth[4] and Mace Eaton was buried yesterday and Helen Austin is nearly blind and all[5]

---

1. One of the twelve letters, postcards, and telegrams written by Hardwick that were included in the Lowell Estate's sale of papers to the HRC in 1982.
2. Heinrich Heine, *Selected Verse*, with an introduction and prose translation by Peter Branscombe (1967).
3. Clark Fitz-Gerald's marriage to his second wife, Elizabeth.
4. Daughter of Philip and Margaret Booth.
5. The page ends here; second page of letter now missing.

316. *Robert Lowell to* Miss Elizabeth Hardwick

Milgate Park, Bearsted, Maidstone, Kent

August 23, 1975

Dearest Lizzie:

Glad to have all the Castine news. Do you mean more than you say about Sally Austin? Somewhere, (Home and Garden?) I saw a house like yours, only with no windows on one side and three floors on another. Harriet's working at the Review sounds like the inevitable footsteps of fate. I hope she'll meet people there, if any are young enough.

I've really done nothing but work, even more than usual, though only a moderate amount done. Isn't it said that if you let a bar tender drink all he wants, or a child eat a box of fudge a day—he'll tire. I never do. Tomorrow I am going to an Irish poetry festival partly run by Seamus Heaney.[1] A week and then back. Just because one loves writing doesn't mean one likes what goes with it. Had a sour letter from Jim Powers returning to Minn. because Irish schools are too hard for his daughters—also for economy, and Irish culture isn't worth the cost. Nothing breaks his irony and makes it seem a complaint.

It is hard writing to you so far away. I don't think I've seen anyone you know except Stanley at another festival. He is so much healthier than anyone, in touch with a thousand poets and publications, reforming our garden, playing tennis—it's hard to believe he was Auden's age. I too miss tennis. I can find no one good enough to play, who plays badly enough for me. Maybe Harriet could learn. I had a huge selected Heine, it must be still around. He is one of the greatest and funniest writers in his prose. I read Flannery's first novel.[2] The saint and grotesque don't jell quite well as I remembered at Yaddo. Still very much better than Updike's *Of the Farm*,[3] reams of fine conventional writing

1. Dennis O'Driscoll: "1975 [. . .] [Heaney] organizes and introduces poetry reading series at Kilkenny Arts week, hosting Robert Lowell, Norman MacCaig, Richard Murphy, Derek Mahon" (*Stepping Stones: Interviews with Seamus Heaney* [2008], p. xxvi; see also pp. 215–20). Lowell to Heaney: "Put us down for the Kilkenny last week in August festival" (April 29, 1975; see *The Letters of Robert Lowell*, p. 639).

2. Flannery O'Connor, *Wise Blood* (1952).

3. (1965).

strung around one wonderful Frostlike old woman. Now I'm reading Vanity Fair[1] and the Trial,[2] BBC television parts of War and Peace.[3] Prose is so entertaining after poetry, and so easy to read—simple language, plots[,] a style *simple enough* to draw you on for hundreds of pages. I think poetry is a sort of still-life meant not to run on with, but to gaze at. Hope your September in New York isn't murderously hot. We are thinking of living there—after two years of Brookline! All my love and to letterless Harriet

All my Love,
Cal

317. Elizabeth Hardwick to Robert Lowell

[15 West 67th Street, New York, N.Y.]
September 1, 1975

Dearest Cal: To write the date, September 1, brings back all the memories of school, fall, new shoes. I welcome it as I did years ago. Lovely, lovely to be back in New York as I have been for a week, but bright days and cool nights, a few marvelous movies, restaurants with every ill-bred course the price of a diamond. Now at the end of the week I am off to Smith, not entirely wishing to go and yet not miserable at the thought. I am only required to be there the first three days of the week and I will come back a lot. Actually I hope to return the first week, on September 11, for Gillian Walker's wedding to Al Maysles. Do you remember the film he did on you in Castine, with the bulldog direction of the English girl?[4] They, Gillian and "Alfie" as he is called, have been together for about five years. She is absolutely lovely, wonderful in a new way, a little fatter, messier, and astonishingly brilliant to talk to about her work, "family therapy." There are a lot of new ideas in this, striking new phrases for old afflictions. "Every report is a command." Beyond that Gillian herself is greatly gifted in this kind of speculation and sympathy and just to talk to her in an intellectual way about it all is

---

1. By William Makepeace Thackeray (1847–48).

2. Franz Kafka, *The Trial*, trans. Willa and Edwin Muir (1955).

3. Dir. John Davies (1972–73).

4. Albert Maysles and David Young were the cameramen for Carolyn McCullough's film *Robert Lowell* (1970).

most exciting. Bobby and Arthur[1] are doing the wedding out on Long Island and we can expect a kingly buffet since they have been doing recipes for the last year or so for *Vogue*. I hope to see Bill Alfred, the nicest anticipation always.

I am planning to "study" the collected Wallace Stevens because I don't really know his work well and all through the summer whenever anyone who can read poetry turned up in Castine the vehement insistence that he was better than Eliot or Yeats or almost anyone anywhere ever came into the conversation. Strange how the patterns go isn't it?

I did very little work in the summer; a lot of housekeeping and sunning instead. I didn't particularly enjoy Maine this year, but like Smith I did not "hate" it and my house is so beautiful and consoling, with its tides at the window, the moon on the bedspread. The thing is one changes in the most drastic way, as I realized. In order [to] take in the changes that come from the outside everything within the soul turns, steps aside, tilts now to the left, now to the right. Couples in their houses, with their gardens, their herbs and vegetables, their perfect cooking, their dinners for eight (that is four couples). The anarchic life of the city, the social breakdown of small town standards finally, may not be good in itself but when one is used to it the other is hard to shift back to. I haven't at all expressed what I mean because I love houses and dinners, but I had to break so many spells. Mary was beautiful and kind and interesting and I love her more and more and Jim is really a nice man, fun to be with, pleased with at least the Maine part of his life.

You see my Smith address enclosed but more importantly, Harriet's telephone number. She is fine, as dear as ever, and yet changed, grown up. They are set up in their apartment, classes are ready to begin. I know she adores being on her own and I hope she will like college. Her work is interesting with two of the best \Columbia/ history courses (France since 1848, Modern Ideologies) a philosophy course by the best woman at Barnard (Concepts of Death)[2] and a Spanish course. The titles of these courses are rather stylish, but the reading is classic and hard. The girls do a lot of partying, as they call it, and one doesn't inquire into the meaning. The vibrations of their liberation are overwhelming and I think even the shy, repressed Melissa was "liberated"

---

1. Robert Fizdale and Arthur Gold.

2. "The Concept of Death" taught by Mary Mothersill (*Barnard Bulletin*, February 28, 1974, p. 6).

in Paris this summer to the relief of everyone. I hope all is well with you. It will be wonderful to see you again after the New Year and Harriet told me to tell you how much she misses you and looks forward to your return.

Love always
    Lizzie

318. *Robert Lowell to* Miss Elizabeth Hardwick

Milgate Park, Bearsted, Maidstone, Kent
September 11, [1975]

Dearest Lizzie:

What lovely reverie and remembering letters from you! So much I ~~can~~ partly remember and imperfectly conjecture: Fitz-Gerald's marriage (we found him heavy, but surely fate stepped too heavily on him)[,] Gillian, lovely and right, but I think back with a September sadness on poor Bill,[1] though I'm sure this marriage will make him happy. He looks mostly like an old man now, slightly humped and bald-grizzled. His adoption of Don is an underworld task, like drawing water eternally in a sieve.

I wonder if you have my marked copy of the Collected Stevens—*my* selections built on Randall's. There are too many I like: much of Harmonium, Sailing after lunch, Aesthetique du Mal, half the Rock (his own elegies and the most felt of his poems).[2] He endlessly speculated on whether the actual or the imagined was the real thing—at his dying this question was more poignant. I can see how much you enjoy returning to New York; especially with that second Castine, the pastoral Smith, looming on you.

I am about to phone Harriet, and can hardly think she could be at the end of that new address and number. I envy her her classes—I could learn so much I think, as if I'd never been to college. You speak of changes, and I think you mean changing from one place to another—

1. Gillian Walker, a close friend of Alfred's, had also once been engaged to him (Elizabeth Hardwick, interview with the editor, 2002).

2. *Harmonium* (1923); "Sailing after Lunch," *Ideas of Order* (1935), *Esthétique du Mal* (1945); "The Rock," *Collected Poems* (1954).

but another is reaching the age when the whiplash of college is no longer held over you . . . and you descend to revising your own writing, and learning history from short book reviews. I gather from your use of the term "partying" you at least know what it means. But what can one do, children are so soon on their own as we are—independent in all ways except financially. I think one should worry over dangers, not morals, but what can one do?

I feel the worst of old maids ending on that last phrase—so far from Wallace Stevens . . . or just from his poems.

Love,[1]

319. Elizabeth Hardwick to Robert Lowell

[15 West 67th Street, New York, N.Y.]
September 19, 1975

Dearest Cal:

I see you are now addressing me as Elizabeth Hardwick. I go back and forth as a commuter. Lowell to all the old trades, elevators, Castine, Harriet's friends as her mother, some of mine—and then the Hardwick train of profession, women, students, readers. Neither seems quite to belong to me and alas they both have a deceptively rooted and solid sound for one so much a mutation in all stocks, all "roles" to use the unmentionable word.

About change I didn't mean change of place, but all change. I am struck by the drastic alterations that are possible, maybe inevitable; and by the ghastly discovery that alas one is never too old to change. I don't have anything quite definite in mind, and of courses the vices hold on like freckles. I was a little low this summer and now I am again feeling insanely cheerful. I adore going up to Smith\—2 days only—/, but I am not set up for my own work there and so I merely teach and read and see people. But, ah, the library and coming home through the tallest most comforting trees at midnight. Like you I am only reading every "journal" in the world, all the late issues. I am sure it is a waste, but what an easy delight for the tired mind. And for all my adoration I go on Monday and return on Wednesday.

---

1. Unsigned.

Harriet is very well . . . Aren't morals and dangers connected, or at least habits and dangers? But she seems very grown up and the gods are caring for her. I assume that because of her sweetness in spite of her souring descent from Zeus and Hera.

Bill did not go to Gillian's wedding. He felt it, I am sure.

I like Pasternak's short biography *Safe Conduct*, which I am teaching. It has a moving nostalgic tone, with the old names—Professor Cohen of Marburg[1] . . . and of course the account of Mayakovsky's death is lovely and right.[2]

Farewell for another letter. I'd write more but nothing churns up. It will be nice to see you again and be ever in good health and bright of soul.

Love, as ever
Lizzie

320. *Robert Lowell to* Mrs. Elizabeth Lowell

Milgate Park, Bearsted, Maidstone, Kent
October 1, 1975

Dearest Lizzie:

A few days ago we went to a party at Gaia's where just about everyone \like you/ had been through a summer depression. Gaia had reason because her son had had some dreadful crumbling disease of the knee in July. Now better. But even the indestructible John Gross, at work every morning at 7 for the TLS, had been depressed. I think I've been depressed, but confused with steady beaverlike revision and writing.

Change? But I don't think I change. I age. Last week my oldest[3] step-daughter, Ivana[,] the one who was burned[,] went off to boarding school. Sad and thrilling. It brought back my second form at St. Mark's. All those trees and old boys, old girls!

I keep trying to phone Harriet. She'll be a new version of herself

---

1. Hermann Cohen, whom Boris Pasternak studied with in Marburg and wrote about in the first half of *Safe Conduct: An Autobiography and Other Writings*, trans. Beatrice Scott (1958).

2. *Safe Conduct* (1958), p. 127; quoted in Hardwick to Lowell, June 20, 1976, below.

3. Thus, for "youngest."

by the end of the college year won't she? Just from Columbia, even without her brainy courses.

Things I suppose are waking up. This week Mary and Yevtushenko are arriving in London. I'm back to having a weekly lunch with Sidney. He tells me he's had a desperate year of heavy drinking and despondency. All over now, we think; but he does look thin and haggard and somehow different.

Thanks for the reverie of your wonderful letters.

Love,
 Cal

PS. I give you back the name Lowell. I thought you might take umbrage.

321. Elizabeth Hardwick to Robert Lowell

[15 West 67th Street, New York, N.Y.]
Sunday November 16, 1975

Dearest Cal: I am here at my typewriter writing letters when I should be merely writing. How happy I will be when the Smith session is over a few weeks from now. The dear old trees of Western Mass. will be heavy with snow then and all will be quiet and warm in the wooden mansions of Northampton, but I will be happy and warm in the rotten swarm of New York. It is the touring back and forth that I mind. The work, the people, the library—all are sweet. But then to go back to my apartment without a picture, an ornament, nothing but the faithful phone to break the sense of loneliness. It is ridiculous to speak of loneliness when I am only there one night a week, often. Still it has been very hard to get anything done of a slow and thoughtful nature.

I had a cocktail party for 45 people in honor of Stephen Spender and the visit to New York of Matthew and Maro Spender. It was the most unrewarding expenditure and meant to indemnify some of the many hosts and hostesses I am in arrears to. (Is that English?) Of course I have never been "entertained" and never will be by most of the guests, especially the most interesting ones. But it was Massachusetts that gave me that losing out feeling, the idea of being forgotten by dinner parties one doesn't want to go to. Otherwise all is the same, ever and ever. Harriet was here for the party and was very well in every way. She speaks perhaps of going to England for a week or so after Christmas. I don't think her mind is very fixed about it. It would be nice, rather like the cocktail party as an expense however. And nothing like in any other way. Of course you'll be en route in late January, but still and still visiting you on your home turf might be more of a connecting thread across the widening gap of experience and life. I am happy for you about your new poems. What a courageous dedication yours is. Wasn't the Nobel Prize to Montale nice and just?[1] I read over some of your translations along with the Italian. Why did you use "diffident" for "indifferente" in Dora Markus?[2] Otherwise they (your Montale) brought the drifting beauty of the works alive. Do you remember M. going up the Arno singing "In Questa Tomba Oscura" and along side, the "mosca?"[3] I remember all. Much love, dear old one.

Lizzie

[In November, Lowell was admitted to the Priory Hospital in Roehampton, London, for mania. He was transferred to Greenways Nursing Home in December and was released on January 4, 1976. From January 5, he received twenty-four-hour nursing care at home in Redcliffe Square.]

322. Elizabeth Hardwick to Robert Lowell

[15 West 67th Street, New York, N.Y.]
January 13, 1976

Dear Cal: I was happy to hear from you and unhappy to see that in some way we, or perhaps only I, were confused about Christmas and by somehow waiting for calls or signals that it would be convenient

---

1. "Montale, a Poet, Awarded Nobel Prize for Literature," *New York Times*, October 24, 1975.

2. Montale: "Non so come stremata tu resisti | in quel lago | d'indifferenza ch'è il tuo cuore" (Eugenio Montale, "Dora Markus," 22–24); Lowell: "I don't know how, so pressed, you've stood up | to that puddle of diffidence, your heart" ("Dora Marcus," I: 22–23, *Imitations*).

3. Nickname of Drusilla Tanzi, Montale's lover (later, his wife) when Hardwick and Lowell met them ca. 1950–1951 in Florence. "In Questa Tomba Oscura" by Ludwig van Beethoven, WoO 133 (1807). Hardwick: for Dr. Z, "there was still happiness to be found in reassuring the weeping nurse at the end of the day, in bringing home a *pâté* and cheese to his wife, in going down a dark canal on the arm of Simone and singing 'In questa tomba oscura'" (*Sleepless Nights*, p. 111).

Harriet missed coming over as she had wanted to do. I have spoken to her and she rejoices that all goes well and says, yes, she wants to come for spring vacation. I think she could leave here the 5th or 6th of March and return on the 13th. We will plan on it and indeed these months go quickly, or they do for me although some days go slowly enough when one is trying to work.

Harriet is fine. A new term starts in a week and everything here is very busy. Slush in the streets, lovely snow all weekend, grey rainy days and nice bright evenings in cabs slogging around the east side. Winter and the city; you know it all, of course. I am very pleased to be here without ever having to make my strange trips back and forth to Northampton, back to my one day at Barnard. But I am simply terrified of writing on this soi-disant novel. It goes about one trembling paragraph per day; confidence drips away painfully and one can't imagine it even being printed much less read. Yet I mean to persevere because I must, and why must? Having started anything in our poor economy of the arts is to be crushed by an investment of a sort, isn't it? I can't go on to something else while this is in front of me and strangely enough I do feel like writing just now and have fallen into a mood of reading books, thinking, idling about—all that puts one into the frame that makes writing possible and the life of literature beautiful and thrilling.

Let's see. All has fallen away and what steps into the old spaces is always so unexpected one cannot put it together as gossip, at least not quickly. I miss Mary very much and think of her a great deal. She has a gift for life I find myself trying to discover the shape of—that great Will and the blessing of not "lettings[1] things get to her." By the latter I suppose I mean that she does not linger too long over disappointments and she doesn't surrender her freedom over her feelings and actions. I look back on my own life of intense anxieties whose cause I have no memory of mostly. And yet one is given his own quivering self, at birth I suppose. I am much more able to block out a few things than I once was, but then again not very able. The odd thing is that I am rather happy in general, as much as one can believe is his due—not much. All of this has its roots, as you can imagine, in my very concrete situation at this very moment: trying to write my book before

---

1. Thus, for "letting."

taking up this letter and knowing I must go back to it after this letter. *Personally*—ah, if only there were just that, but personally I am having a very good time going about in my black dresses and high heels.

I am grateful for our talk and delighted that all goes fine with dear old St. Sebastian and his needle-arrows.[1] Parmigiano, isn't it?[2]

Much love,

    Lizzie

[In late January, Lowell was admitted to St. Andrew's Hospital (formerly the Northampton General Lunatic Asylum) in Northampton, England, for mania.]

323. Elizabeth Hardwick to Mary McCarthy

[15 West 67th Street, New York, N.Y.]

January 29, 1976

Dearest Mary: I understand from Ellie[3] that you are coming in February. Of course I am overjoyed at the thought of seeing you once again.

---

1. Lowell was receiving acupuncture as an alternative treatment for his mania. Hardwick to Mary McCarthy: "I have had several talks with Cal by phone. No doubt you know that he has given up lithium, of his own will, and is 'into' acupuncture. I have doubts, in my provinciality, about anything Asian, but I can't help but hope that some relief from the long, long lithium years might give Cal a period of at least physical lightness. It has always seemed improper to me that he should appear so old, walk so slowly, when lithium is not supposed to be a downer in that sense. Also he seemed to take pleasure in doing all these things on his own time so to speak and it might just be that he will have some sort of change. And, poor thing, he can always go back to the old routine and so I feel nothing but a groundless hope for him at the moment. In any case all of his case and the treatment is groundless. The new world, a sort of Lourdes, might just help" (Hardwick to Mary McCarthy, December 30, 1975). Seamus Heaney: "I went with him in January 1976 to two acupuncturists in Harley Street. He was at that time confined to a small private hospital [. . .] he carried me away in a taxi [. . .] [to visit] slightly quackish acupuncturists [. . .] He took off his shirt. He bowed a little and accepted the needles, one by one, in a delicate gleaming line, from the point of his shoulder to the back of his ear" ("Gulliver in Lilliput" [1987], quoted in Mariani, *Lost Puritan: A Life of Robert Lowell*, p. 436). Elizabeth Bishop: "I tried and tried to find a good Saint Sebastian to send you by Mary Morse (the friend). He's the Saint I want to get because once we went swimming in that Maine ice-water near Stonington [. . .] you inadvertently posed against a tree trunk, and looked just like Saint S for a moment!" (Bishop to Lowell, June 25, 1961—Sunday Morning, *Words in Air*, p. 365).
2. Thus, for Parmigianino, who has a drawing depicting St. Sebastian; but given "needle-arrows," perhaps Hardwick was thinking of one of Andrea Mantegna's three versions, particularly the 1490 Venice St. Sebastian.
3. Eleanor DuVivier.

I would love to have you stay with me—I am all alone amidst my Lowell *spoils* and *things*—that gets in both James[1] and Lawrence[2]—and it would be easy for me as well as thrilling. I don't have my studio and so I am asking you to stay here in my apartment. I really do hope you will want to. If it isn't the best for you at least allow me to give a smashing dinner.

The thought that you are reading all the books is too much.[3] I am giving up juries because I never have a winner, always somehow ending up intimidated. Actually I am on one right now, the PEN translation prize,[4] about which I know nothing and after begging off cannot get off.

Oh, dear, what news is there. Nothing seems very good somehow just now and even I have been sick with fevers for ten days. Tonight I am alright and so I suppose it is over. Dear old Cal is in the hospital again. Caroline has been utterly gracious about calling me, this time and the last time. I suppose now that we are all so deeply worried nothing really matters except Cal. Actually she said it wasn't very bad and he called here several times the week before and certainly was not totally deranged, whatever that is. I suppose it is back to the lithium. It is a lifeline, but somehow we are all depressed about it.

I am trying to write the "novel" after such a long time off. How hard everything is. I have only one wish and that is to write one more good thing. (I have the "more" in the wrong place and mean that I want to write something good.)

I believe you got a letter from Jane Kramer. She's rather nice I think and quite a good writer. I have only seen her once since the—how dreadful that the name of the great house won't come to me. Ah, senility. Not mansion, not inn, not—yes THE MANOR.[5] Dearest Mary,

---

1. Henry James: *The Spoils of Poynton* (1897), serialized as *The Old Thing* in the *Atlantic Monthly* (1896); cf. also: "Poor Miss Tina's sense of her failure had produced a rare alteration in her, but I had been too full of stratagems and spoils to think of that" (*The Aspern Papers* [1908]; alluding to *The Merchant of Venice*: "The man that hath no music in himself, | Nor is not moved with concord of sweet sounds, | Is fit for treasons, stratagems and spoils" [5.1.83-8]).
2. D. H. Lawrence: "Things" (1928 publication in *Bookman*; collected in *The Lovely Lady* [1933]).
3. McCarthy was a judge for the 1976 National Book Awards.
4. Awarded to Richard Howard in 1976 for his translation of E. M. Cioran's *A Short History of Decay* (1975).
5. In the summer of 1974, Jane Kramer and her husband Vincent Crapanzano rented a "derelict (literally falling down over our heads) abandoned old house, near the water, which for some reason couldn't be sold or restored and was referred to humorously in Castine as 'the Manor.' [. . .]

this is just a note of joy that you are coming. And how I wish Jim were coming with you. Maybe I'll dip over to Paris sometime before the summer. Of course I haven't a sou and have vowed to write every day until July . . . But . . . Much love. You can dictate a reply if you want to stay here and I am praying you will.

Lizzie

324. Elizabeth Hardwick to Robert Lowell

[15 West 67th Street, New York, N.Y.]
February 11, 1976

Dearest Cal: I wrote you a letter last week and forgot to put postage on it. So now I am back at it once more. I imagine you are back home in Kent and indeed I hope so. This has been such a difficult time for all of you—and yet I know it will be better. Isn't it partly getting the boring medicine straight, finding out what one can endure that is the best? I am sitting here thinking of all sorts of hopeful things that would be hypocrisy for anyone except you—things such as the conviction that there are so many good and sweet matters in your life.

Blizzards and snowstorms here and then suddenly days as warm as August. Harriet is very well, seems incredibly happy in her apartment life, works at her classes and got good grades the first term. I talk to her almost every day on the phone, but I don't see very much of her unless she needs to come to type a paper. Her routine up there is so demanding and full that she can't bear to break out of it. We are always very anxious to know about you. Very, very eager. You are so far away and yet you are always in our thoughts. Caroline was marvelously generous in calling me to reassure us. I am struggling along in my usual way. I have just been to Colorado for a few days, lecturing, and next week I go one day to N. Carolina. But how I loathe the speaking, the standing up talking away, and the dull, perfunctory dinners and cocktail parties. Occasionally one such affair works. I understand how you feel about the poetry readings finally. I am writing my novel, often discouraged, and nevertheless determined to persevere because of the

We celebrated the Nixon resignation together at the Manor, in front of a rented tv set on a crate in what had once been the living room" (email message to editor, February 1, 2016).

audacity in beginning at all. Life is fairly good, I suppose. I haven't any news at all. Would love just a word by cable from you. Much love,
Lizzie

325. *Elizabeth Hardwick to Robert Lowell*

[15 West 67th Street, New York, N.Y.]
February 15, 1976

Dearest Cal: How marvelous to talk to you on the phone and to know all is well. I have good news for you. Harriet does want to come over for the vacation in March. She will come on Saturday, March 6th and leave on Saturday, March 13th. I am delighted she wants to do it and feel it is very wise and good in every way. However, both H. and I are never averse to sudden changes and if it is not [convenient] now or should become inconvenient for you and Caroline you know you can let me call it off at [any] time. I will write in a few days about the exact times, the airlines and so on. Harriet definitely needs out a bit after all these months in the apartment up town, but most of all she wants to see all of you very much.

Jacob Epstein is in London, living in an apartment in the same house that Lizzie Spender lives in. I will have Barbara give him the Kent and the London numbers.

On Tuesday the bank will have a letter about your medical expenses from me and they will write you about it. I can imagine how terrifying it was for you, the expense of it all and I hope they can help. It always makes me feel sad to take money from you but I don't see how we could live otherwise or how I could keep this home for Harriet on my own, even though I work very hard all the time. You have been wonderfully generous and kind to both of us, especially to me, and I am grateful.

Will be back in touch soon. Thank you for calling me. I have thought and thought about you and we always want to know about you. There are a lot of "yous" and "knows" in this letter, but I am rushing it off.

Dearest love,
Lizzie

326. Elizabeth Hardwick to Robert Lowell

[15 West 67th Street, New York, N.Y.]
February 18, 1976

Dearest Cal: I sent off urgent letters to McLeans and to the New York Psychiatric Institute where you started the lithium with Dr. Platman[1] (?) not (Glassman) and I tried to make clear that it was urgent. I understand from a quite remote quarter that, in general, it takes time for these releases and so I hope they can start \in London/ whatever you are planning much sooner. As you see on the card, Harriet's plans are listed. The card about Jacob Epstein is to enable her to get in touch with him when all of you are in London.[2]

Let's see . . . lovely day here, clear and cold. I am expecting Mary McC. as a house guest next week. And of course I am overwhelmed with pleasure at the thought of the dear one here for breakfast and in and out during the day. Susan is struggling along, but with some hope as new treatments and prospects more favorable turn up.[3] This pitiful struggle of hers has been deeply involving to all of us. One of the sad aspects is that she lived in such a bohemian way and did her writing in a similar undomesticated fashion, up all night for days and then sleeping two days. Now she has very little energy for the time being and the only way she could write would be a few hours a day, and a bit here and there. I can easily see that way could be hard; it is for all of us since the real writing way is a kind of all or nothing.

Dearest Cal, I long to know this bad period is over for you, that you can settle into some life and medicine that is possible for you. You can't imagine how much we are thinking about you. I'm so pleased that Harriet wants to come over and I know it will be the greatest

---

1. Dr. Stanley R. Platman; see Hardwick to Lowell, June 5, 1970.

2. Enclosures now missing.

3. Hardwick: "This week has been a great sorrow. Susan Sontag went on Monday to the hospital for a lump that was, according to the best x-ray reader in New York, almost certain to be nothing. But it is not nothing. She is facing the terrible operation [. . .] She has in the last year become very close to Bob, Barbara and me and I must say that I love her very much. Her ideas are a good deal less chic and narrow than they used to be and the beautiful energy is very special. There is a sort of orphan quality about her and when this doom came crashing down on her it seemed that she really had only us and maybe Roger [Straus] to depend upon. In the long run, though, I think I would rather have my literary friends than anything, any family; they are what count, and I feel they know about love" (Hardwick to Mary McCarthy, October 21, 1975).

pleasure for all of you. Unless there is change, meet her British Airways, Friday night, the 5th of March.

Much love, Lizzie

327. *Elizabeth Hardwick to* ROBERT L[O]WELL

[Telegram]

[New York, N.Y.]
[Received March 1, 1976, Maidstone, Kent][1]

CELEBRATE THIS BIRTHDAY AND MOURN THE NEXT STOP HARRIET ARRIVES BRITISH AIRWAYS FLIGHT 590 AT 940PM ON FRIDAY[2] LOVE

LIZZIE

328. *Robert Lowell to* ELIZABETH HARDWICK

[Telegram]

[Maidstone, Kent]
[March 6, 1976]

ELIZABETH HARDWICK 15 WEST 67 STREET
NEW YORK CITY NY
HARRIET HAPPILY WITH US LOVE

CAL

329. *Robert Lowell to* Elizabeth Hardwick

[Telegram]

[Maidstone]
[March 9, 1976]

ELIZABETH HARDWICK 15 WEST67STREET
NEWYORKCITY
HARRIET ARRIVES SATURDAY BA FLIGHT 591 AT 8.50 PM TERMINAL THREE LOVE CAL

---

1. Lowell's fifty-ninth birthday.
2. March 5th.

330. Elizabeth Hardwick to Robert Lowell

[15 West 67th Street, New York, N.Y.]
Tuesday, April 20, 1976

Dearest Cal: I don't know why Blair sent you the Barnes review, as he told me he had, but of course he \(Blair)/ meant well. I am happy to rush this off to you.[1] The Barnes idiocy, so philistine, ignorant of America and the whole background of the plays, did make me despair of our enterprise in life, of writing, reading. Everyone around was appalled. It doesn't matter and indeed it was a nastiness telling off the "clever" people who don't know anything about the theatre.[2] And yet it does enrage and discourage. I left the house that morning and walked about furiously for hours.

All is well and it was absolutely marvelous to have the visit with you.[3] I will be coming to London for PEN in August I think—around the 20th—and I hope you will be in the country (England I mean) at that time.

Mary McC. has been here in New York this week, in very good form too, all discipline and propriety, always *married*, as all of us here in our various frayed conditions see with amazement \her life is/ like some sort of company with a president and a chairman of the board presiding. And yet what a strange heroine she is. I feel here, surrounded by Devie, Harriet, Barbara, Susan and assorted others, as if I appeared to her "brainwashed" and like Patty Hearst to be held accountable for joining the SLA.[4] She will be back in late May and we are going up to Castine for a few days—something I like to do just to get it all open. And then I don't want to feel obliged to spend every moment there either. As I told you—there are nothing except couples and that palls at times.

---

1. Martin Gottfried, "A Classic in 'The Old Glory,'" *New York Post* (April 19, 1976).

2. Clive Barnes: "Robert Lowell's trilogy 'The Old Glory' has become part of the younger glories of the American intellectual establishment. Seeing it reproduced by the American Place Theater [thus] as part of its Bicentennial celebrations, one idly wonders why. Mr. Lowell is a major American poet, but his sense of the theater is meager, and in these plays even his prosody is fundamentally prosaic. Looking at them one feels today slightly like a nervous witness at a dress show of the emperor's new clothes" ("The Stage: Lowell's 'The Old Glory,'" *New York Times*, April 19, 1976).

3. Ian Hamilton: "In April [1976], Lowell and Lady Caroline flew to New York for a performance of *The Old Glory* at the American Place Theatre" (*Robert Lowell: A Biography*, p. 454).

4. Symbionese Liberation Army.

Harriet seems to be looking for summer jobs and to be very well. We had an Easter dinner together. Nothing very interesting to say. Just to say how nice it was to see you and to wish you well.

With love,
Lizzie

331. *Robert Lowell to* Mrs. Elizabeth Hardwick Lowell

Milgate Park, Bearsted, Maidstone, Kent, Eng.
April 29, 1976

Dearest Lizzie:

My heartfelt thanks for your letter and the good review. I didn't [know] how the Barnes gloomed me, till I read the other. It was like a good piece of music criticism keeping the old performance in mind in toto.[1] The new production didn't come up to Jonathan's of course[2] and was often like the original coin restamped in plaster. However, I like the new man as Endecott much better than any I had seen.[3] Barnes is so glib and persuasive, that I hardly realized how much he misunderstood. He can't have read the plays. So many quotes mis-slanted and out of context and character.[4]

It's summer here, for the moment now. I've even done some weeding. I've vegetated here so long, I am hardly fit [for] the active life, the bustle of New York. I think we will try Brookline or Cambridge again. Mary is like James's description of being taken for an automobile tour

---

1. Martin Gottfried: "[*Benito*] *Cereno* is so beautifully composed, so intelligent, so tragically and ironically powerful that somehow, despite its several faults, it is nearly perfect [. . .] Austin Pendleton has staged the new production immaculately, as aware of the play's language as of its theater. He lets its references to racist and imperialist America speak for itself [. . .] Once again, Roscoe Lee Browne takes Babu from feline mockery to lionine explosion" ("A Classic in 'The Old Glory,'" *New York Post*, April 19, 1976).

2. Jonathan Miller directed two parts of *The Old Glory* (*My Kinsman, Major Molineux* and *Benito Cereno*) at the American Place Theatre in 1964.

3. Kenneth Harvey.

4. Clive Barnes: "In Mr. Lowell's writing empty wisps of poetry are flaking off the prose like rust. He can write things such as 'the iron of the Lord is more precious than gold.' He can coin phrases such as 'a raped Versailles' or 'You are dishonoring our nation, Perkins!' He has horrid fustian passages, such as, 'Only the unfortunate can understand misfortune,' or 'I have only one life, sir.' And the tone throughout all three plays seems faintly maudlin" ("The Stage: Lowell's 'The Old Glory,'" *New York Times*, April 19, 1976).

by Edith Wharton. We were taking her to the theater last fall, only I three times took her to the wrong theater—by the time we arrived at the right one our tickets had been sold. In retaliation, she took us and the Mostyn-Owens and a Dutchman to a very bad play, then a very slow, expensive dinner, where we searched endlessly for the meaning of the meaningless play. I don't see how her energy, money or courage hold out. But how can sloth ~~talk~~ \deflect/ to a torpedo?

Sorry that Harriet is probably not coming. She is welcome to rest with us indefinitely. I know of no jobs though but the New Review.

Isn't paying bills a torture\?/ I've been paying off medical bills all morning, and am confused. I should be paid for it.

It was lovely seeing you finally. We flew back the next day in the longest and slowest plane I've ever been in, then four days in the Hebrides—like Maine without trees, tourists and almost without people. I miss having you to talk to. I feel deeply all you had to put up with me for so many years.

Love,
Cal

332. Elizabeth Hardwick to Robert Lowell

[15 West 67th Street, New York, N.Y.]
May 30, 1976

Dearest Cal: The long Memorial Day weekend, an American notion for which there is surely an equivalent in every country with every country's war dead. Up to Castine last weekend to see if all was still standing after a winter in which Bangor, swimming in water on Main Street, made the national evening news. Everything was fine, strangely just as I left it last Labor Day, almost dustless, dry and quiet. I very much like going back and forth by air, renting a car and starting off on the long driveways of the Bangor International airport (where now there is a smallish Hilton hotel, usually quite without "guests"— conforming to the Maine emptiness), then on to Water Street, where the tides are threatening the bulkhead, but never quite winning. On my way in Bucksport, the rain starting, I hit a mid-afternoon shift change at the St. Regis Paper Mill. Down the long scaffolding came hundreds of men in work clothes, little caps, silently carrying lunch boxes and thermos bottles, all \the men/ pouring out, old and young, crippled, faces covered with an ash-colored dust. It was like the middle of the last century—the men and the mines. Behind the big barges with logs, the high factory whistle. Most extraordinary. Otherwise nothing much new there. The expense of such weekends is frightful, but if it were otherwise I would do it often rather than stay there. As it is I plan to teach two weeks at the Graduate Center at City University, stay here in N.Y. for the Democratic Convention,[1] go to Maine for about a month—mid July to Mid August. I'll be in London August 21st I think and hope it will find you near enough to have a meeting. All will be written to you when the time comes.

Harriet is well, has finished the year except for one Incomplete—a strange and popular burden the present day student takes on and as a consequence is years later writing papers in courses long since forgotten. Our girl doesn't come home very much but we speak on the telephone almost every day.

I hope you are feeling well and happy. Stephen Spender has just left and I bring him up since he seemed amazingly cheerful, no doubt due to the effervescence of some new "love" and his own tireless, ageless belief in this lucky charm. He is quite adorable I think. I told him I had received MacShane's *Raymond Chandler*[2] and looked up Spender, Stephen and Spender, Natasha in the index. "What did you think"— "Well, too many trips."—"That's just the trouble. Natasha loves to go abroad."

Goodbye, dearest one, and be in good health. No, no answer required. This is just an "on-going" record from the States.

Lizzie

---

1. From July 12 to July 15, 1976. Hardwick wrote about the 1976 presidential campaign in "Elections: Renewal or Just Replacement?" *Vogue*, July 1, 1976; and "The Carter Question II: Piety and Politics," *New York Review of Books*, August 5, 1976.
2. Frank MacShane, *The Life of Raymond Chandler* (1976); for an account of Raymond Chandler and Natasha Spender's romance, see Matthew Spender, *A House in St. John's Wood: In Search of My Parents* (2015), pp. 145–48, 155–61, 189–92, 208–11, 224–25, 319, 395.

333. *Robert Lowell to* Mrs. Elizabeth Hardwick Lowell

Milgate Park, Bearsted, Maidstone, Kent, Eng.

June 8, 1976

Dearest Lizzie:

I remember Ivor[1] once startling me by saying he sometimes didn't know whether he existed. That was in my Life Studies day, and I couldn't believe it. Now your nice letters bringing me back Maine almost from the blue . . . assure me I do exist.

Caroline has been ailing for almost three months, not back this time, but some obscure stomach trouble, difficulty in swallowing, difficulty in keeping food down. As hospitals and tests approached and receded, first London, then Zurich, she rapidly got better—is almost well now but not quite.

Elizabeth Bishop is about to visit here for two days—an informal visit, but not one to take lightly. The dog must be sent away because of her asthma but will that be enough? Half our chairs are tainted with dog hairs. Then so many things she can criticize, the disheveled garden, the carefree garden man, our care of Sheridan. Should he be sent away too? So many things down to my not writing meter, making errors in description. Of course no one is more wonderful, but so fussy and hazardous now. Her set subject in person and letters is scolding with affectionate fury over Frank Bidart (whom she half-depends on) a safe thing though grating.

Next week I am to hear sections of my Phèdre set by Benjamin Britten.[2] Do you remember our dinner with him and Pairs (?)[3] ages ago when I mortally wounded Bob Giroux by ordering another bottle of his expensive wine? The meeting otherwise went cordially, but I never heard again from Britten. This winter I learned he had had a very severe and incapacitating heart attack and had just now finished Phèdre (only her tirades)[,][4] his first work since partial recovery.[5]

---

1. I. A. Richards.

2. *Phaedra*, Op. 93, first performed at the Aldeburgh Festival on June 16, 1976.

3. Thus, for Peter Pears.

4. Cf. Lowell: "Your old-fashioned tirade—| loving, rapid, merciless—| breaks like the Atlantic Ocean on my head" ("Man and Wife" 26–28, *Life Studies*). OED: etymology "[mod. Fr. *tirade* (16th cent.) a draught, pull, shot; a long speech, declamation; passage of prose or verse, stanza, paragraph] . . . 2. spec. A passage or selection of verse, of varying length, treating of a single theme or idea" ("Tirade, n.," *Oxford English Dictionary* Vol. XI).

5. Donald Mitchell: "it was not until the very last years of his life that he [Britten] succumbed to

My students go in heavily for incompletes, it's the catch to assigning papers instead of exams. So Harriet is in vogue. We hope she'll come here, if New York gets too hot. Don't envy you City College in July. I suppose you feel awfully looked-at yet limited in motion at Castine. It all—the landscape—came back to me with Phil Booth's poems[1]—meditations like photos, but solidly something.

Look forward to August 21 and your London arrival.[2] You'll mail me your address. Our country number, if you will call, is 0622-38028 Maidstone. Why amn't I asked to the Penn Club? Dues? Tact? The Democratic Convention sounds like the heat of New York doubled. Won't you see it on television, as I did Chicago?[3]

Love,
Cal

334. Elizabeth Hardwick to Robert Lowell

[15 West 67th Street, New York, N.Y.]
June 20, 1976

Dearest Cal:

Quivering summer nights here in New York. And can you believe I am still going to things. Ballet with bewitching defected Russians;[4] *Threepenny Opera*, a perfect little work of art.[5] I can hear Philip Rahv's

---

a serious illness of the heart that had its origins in early childhood. [. . .] Among the works created against the odds in this final phase were [. . .] the dramatic cantata *Phaedra* (for Janet Baker)" ("Britten, [Edward] Benjamin, Baron Britten [1913–1976], composer" (*Oxford Dictionary of National Biography*. 28 Mar. 2016. http://www.oxforddnb.com/view/10.1093/ref:odnb/9780198614128 .001.0001/odnb-9780198614128-e-30853).

1. Philip Booth, *Available Light* (1976).

2. Hardwick was invited to speak at the P.E.N. International Congress, held August 23–28, 1976, in London.

3. The Democratic National Convention in Chicago, August 26–28, 1968. See "The Races" (*Notebook69-1*; -2; and *Notebook70*); and "Dream, the Republican Convention," "Flaw (Flying to Chicago)," and "After the Democratic Convention" (*History*). For a description of Lowell's experience in Chicago, see Lowell to Elizabeth Bishop, September 5, 1968, *Words in Air*, p. 650.

4. In the summer of 1976, Natalia Makarova and Mikhail Baryshnikov performed in *The Sleeping Beauty* for the American Ballet Theatre (production opened on June 15).

5. Bertolt Brecht, Kurt Weill, *Threepenny Opera*, dir. Richard Forman for the New York Shakespeare Festival revival (production opened on May 1, 1976).

unbelieving hiss: "culture monger!" But why monger for the excited audience?

In two months I will be in London. Will let you know where I'm to be and will call you to arrange a meeting before I step into the iron claws of the "agenda." I am only doing this for the ride, as we say here.

I am inspired by Pasternak's *Safe Conduct* and read it over and over again. For instance: "The beginning of April surprised Moscow in the white stupor of returning winter. On the seventh it began to thaw for the second time, and on the fourteenth when Mayakovsky shot himself, not everyone had yet become accustomed to the novelty of spring." "The seventh" is magically concrete and the whole passage uses nature in the most wonderfully dramatic way.[1]

Your *Selected* arrived and I read it over with a pounding of feelings of all sorts.[2] How unnerving it is to read work written by those close to us; the thickness of one's acquaintance with the brute stuff of the lives there on the page makes this kind of reading not like reading at all. It weaves in and out of the years, wrenching often, brilliant and glittering in the seeing and remembering. Sometimes the images are like knives, slicing through the block of experience. Of course I *mind* the lines *seeming* to have issued from me: especially the strange and utterly puzzling idea of Harriet being good and normal because of her good and normal parents.[3]

Ah, well, I noted that you attended the proper Abbey mummifying of Henry James.[4] I went to Colorado to speak this spring and grabbed a volume of the short novels and read right through: Washington Square, Daisy Miller, The Aspern Papers, The Pupil.[5] To do that

---

1. Boris Pasternak, *Safe Conduct: An Autobiography and Other Writings*, trans. Beatrice Scott (1958), p. 127. See Hardwick to Lowell, September 19, 1975, above.

2. *Selected Poems* (1976).

3. Lowell: "'She is normal and good because she had normal and good | parents'" ("In the Mail," 6–7, *The Dolphin*; see footnote 2 on page 293). See also Lowell to Harriet Lowell: "I love you for liking both your father and mother [. . .] that\'s/ why they are such extraordinarily normal, healthy and modest people" (April 2, 1972).

4. A floor stone commemorating Henry James was installed in the Poets' Corner in Westminster Abbey on June 17, 1976. "Among the 200 guests were C. P. Snow, the novelist, Dame Rebecca West, the writer and critic and James scholar, and Robert Lowell, the American poet" ("Henry James, at Last, Admitted to the Abbey," *New York Times*, June 18, 1976).

5. Probably in the edition *Short Novels of Henry James: Daisy Miller; Washington Square; The Aspern Papers; The Pupil; The Turn of the Screw*, introduction by E. Hudson Long (1962).

suddenly after a few years was a true literary experience—a sort of new, unexpected joyful exhilaration. The mystery of it, the mystery of him. Going back over some of your work had the same effect upon me of a trembling newness there to be taken in by the reader.

Saturday afternoon it is here and people streaming into Central Park. A steel band (Trinidad) playing in the street, the garbage truck grinding away. Dearest love and all of the joys of the season.

Lizzie

335. Robert Lowell to Elizabeth Hardwick

Milgate Park, Bearsted, Maidstone, Kent, Eng.

July 2, 1976

Dearest Lizzie:

You caught our James appearance. We went with Rolando,[1] who was disappointed that no one at all except literary people went—so different from the crowds of senators and members of parliament to receive [the] gold replica of the Magna Carta, also at Westminster, which we also went to. We seem to be on their list, this morning an invitation came to hear the ambassadoress[2] speak in the 900 year old Cathedral close, accompanied by soldiers and officials in dramatic many colored costumes—an advertisement for the disembarking tourist?

Just heard Stephen and Isherwood in a public conversation on the poets of the Thirties.[3] Stephen giggling, "Unfortunately, it seems that poets do have to be educated["] (on the limitations of their group not being proletarian). Isherwood matter of fact, no cant, his only cause homosexuality[,] this too his motive for going to Berlin.[4] Auden dominated the whole thing, the only name the audience could ask questions about—Poor Day Lewis, his wife,[5] there, only cited as a plagiarist. Others have distinction, but only Auden has a brilliant changing in-

---

1. Anzilotti.
2. Thus; Anne Armstrong, first female United States ambassador to the United Kingdom.
3. In conjunction with the exhibition "Young Writers of the Thirties" at the National Portrait Gallery, June 25–November 7, 1976.
4. See Isherwood, *Christopher and His Kind* (1976).
5. Jill Balcon.

tellectual outline—even his oddities: "Frogs won't do . . . Why go to plays, it's so unEnglish."

Thanks for Percival Lowell.[1] I hadn't realized his errors were so fruitful, I suppose that's the rule in science. In the family, we always doubted his Mars, but swore by the accuracy and orthodoxy of his Pluto . . . once to have been called Percival.[2]

I regret the Letters in Dolphin. The only way to make a narrative was to leave a few. I hesitated to send you a copy of the Selected Poems, but Giroux acted on his own, which was right because the bulk of them were written under your eyes. I'm glad some of it stood up for you. I read all in one day, trying to proofread—so much I hadn't taken in for ages—one doesn't really ~~attending~~ absorb what one is reading at readings. Autobiography predominates, almost forty years of it. And now more journey of the soul in my new book. I feel I, or someone, wrote everything beforehand. If I had read it at twenty would I have been surprised, would I have dared go on?

For a month, I think, the heatwave has been here, like an American city, like inland America—to the English the melting of the icecap.

Love, Cal

P.S. Greatly looking forward to your August.

---

1. Enclosure now missing, but Hardwick probably sent Lowell a clipping of "In Martian Orbit": "United States space scientists have scored a perfect interplanetary bull's-eye again with the punctual arrival of Viking 1 in the neighborhood of Mars [. . .] Percival Lowell [. . .] devoted much of his life to propagating the idea that the network of canals indicated a highly complex civilization. The canals which Schiaparelli and Lowell wrote about are now known to have been illusions; yet the actual Martian topography is in some ways even more remarkable than were the dreams of these pioneers" (*New York Times*, June 24, 1976).

2. Associated Press: "Pluto has been selected by scientists of Lowell Observatory here as the name for the recently discovered transneptunian body which they believe is the long-sought Planet X. [. . .] The announcement was made by Roger Lowell Putnam, trustee of the observatory and nephew of the late Dr. Percival Lowell, founder of the observatory, who predicted the existence of Planet X sixteen years ago. [. . .] Mr. Putnam added that Pluto lent itself easily to the monogram 'P.L.,' the initials of Percival Lowell, and 'would be a fitting memorial to him'" ("Pluto Picked as the Name for New Planet X Because He Was God of Dark, Distant Regions," *New York Times*, May 26, 1930).

336. Elizabeth Hardwick to Robert Lowell[1]

Castine, [Maine]

July 5, 1976

Dearest Cal: I am sitting on the deck outside, typing. The bi-centennial birthday (celebration for *us*, as they kept saying) has passed on. The "great ships" were extraordinarily beautiful and the fireworks all night from the Statue of Liberty were marvelous. I came up here but saw it all on TV. There is now a one hour non-stop jet to Bangor and so I have been week-ending like a stock broker. This afternoon, it is Monday, I go back to finish some work, then stay another week for the Democratic Convention and perhaps write about it if I can find any ideas.[2] Your George 3rd[3] was a lovely idea—perfectly inspired answer to the bicentennial laureate challenge. I enclose copy and also the clippings from Village Voice,[4] all excited and interesting indeed. Philip Booth was down this morning for renewal of date memory about the Castine Years, all in preparation for a Salmagundi Lowell issue.[5] Philip is well, but I wonder if he can do a portrait which I thought would be more valuable than the "encouragement to a young poet ("himself")["] theme.

Let's see—I always have a thousand things to share with you, but how the letter writing energy seems to diminish with the years. I suppose that if I had a period in a pension I could wake up and rush to it, but it is hard to find the communicating tranquility in one's own house with the chores standing there like hungry cats, waiting, calling out.

Harriet is studying typing, finishing term papers, swimming in the Columbia indoor pool and getting an apartment together on west 108th—apparently it is quite nice and even had a view from which the ships great and small, tall and short could be seen. She is thin, looks very nice and seems very happy. I hope I can entice her or impound her

---

1. One of the twelve letters, postcards, and telegrams written by Hardwick that were included in the Lowell Estate's sale of papers to the HRC in 1982.
2. "The Carter Question II: Piety and Politics," *New York Review of Books*, August 5, 1976.
3. "George III" first appeared in *Newsweek* as the voice of "The Great American Poet" in "Our America" ("nearly fifty American voices—speaking with Newsweek reporters across the nation"), on July 4, 1976.
4. Michael Feingold, "It's Older but Still Glorious" (review of The American Place Theatre's Bicentennial revival of *The Old Glory*), *Village Voice*, April 26, 1976.
5. Philip Booth, "Summers in Castine: Contact Prints: 1955–1965," *Salmagundi* 37 ("For Robert Lowell, on His 60th Birthday"), Spring 1977.

for a weekend at least here where she was as a baby and where she trod without I think it ever really gripping her soul somehow. She knows only the profound memories of New York, a New York girlhood. I am having I suppose a New York old age. I read in the paper that our city is now full of all the chic people from London, Paris and Rome. And to think one is already there himself. Columbus Avenue has become very interesting, a bit like old Third Avenue with shops and restaurants; and the Cafe des Artistes has been cleaned up and is such a success one must reserve days in advance. There is the 67th Street news . . . I am here sunning and typing before going off to Bangor and the Halls, David and Berenice, have just gone by, beachcombing for Americana and as heavily sentimental as ever. I was saying that I loved going and coming as if it were Long Island because I don't want to be here steadily any more . . . too lonely. She said, but don't you think it is just good for you to be here. I said, not particularly and they went off chagrined. I do love my house with a greedy intensity and the sea, the air, the people—thinning out somehow—are all dear to me, but still there is sometimes a sadness too.

I am sending off this letter to accompany things about you—all of them arriving on top of a \like/ packet sent by Bob Giroux probably. Anyway, I will be back in touch and you needn't write. I would like to see the Nolans when I come in August if they are friendly with me after I said no to the festschrift.

Much love
Lizzie

337 . *Robert Lowell to* Mrs. Elizabeth Hardwick Lowell

Milgate Park, Maidstone, Kent, Eng.
July 12, 1976

Dearest Lizzie:

Stephen called up to attach me to the Penn club meeting,[1] to put me on the same panel with you and Susan, I think. Was this your suggestion?

---

1. P.E.N. 41st International Congress, held August 23–28, 1976 in London, entitled "The Truth of Imagination." Spender was President of English P.E.N. from 1975–1977 (see John Sutherland, *Stephen Spender: The Authorized Biography* [2004], p. 485).

It will be a delight and honor. Our first official appearance on the same platform since Greensboro before Randall's death, and even then we were two separate days.[1]

Glad to get the review and poem. Reviews seem to be running better than my last books—the heavy joshing daily critic—having written *History*, I am now almost treated as if I already belonged to it, to its shadowy posthumous shadow-life. Is that what the pagan's world of shades meant? I did get the bicentennial poem to order wanting to get outside myself, as one might with translations. I got it done one drawn-out week-end. But I thought it never could be worked, first too short, then sprawling to two pages—portentously solemn with General Stark[2] contrast with my Tory Boston Winslows. I was glad to [be] lost in Newsweek's bad prose instead of dim verse. Did you read Mrs. Carter, unable to like people? Weren't they awful in general?[3]

Man is never happy. I have been chronically complaining about overconcentration on work, both because of what it does to one, how it distracts, and because I feel afraid of a certain stylistic callousness, plough-pushing if there's such archaic idiom. Now on the verge of mailing off my new book, 70 pages, longish typed ones, I feel in this ebb of the European heatwave, as if all the grass has been burned off the view. Pause and be wise;[4] but the machine goes on clanking in the head.[5]

I can see how Castine must be lonely for you, and exposed, perhaps, when you want to be invisible. In New York, you are seen when you intend to be, though screened from nature. The one hour Bangor

1. At the 21st Annual Writers Forum at the University of North Carolina at Greensboro (where Jarrell was on the faculty), March 17–19, 1964; Hardwick lectured on "Plot in Fiction" on March 17 and Lowell gave a "Poetry Reading and Commentary" on March 19 (*Corradi: The Fine Arts Magazine of the University at Greensboro* [March | Arts Forum 1964], p. 30).
2. Lowell's maternal ancestor John Stark (1728–1822), a major general in the Continental Army during the American Revolution; "the iconoclastic, mulish Dunbarton New Hampshire Starks" ("91 Revere Street," *Life Studies*, p. 16).
3. In *Newsweek*'s "Our America" (July 4, 1976), among the fifty American voices was "Jimmy Carter's Mother" (Lillian Carter), who said, "I never *have* had an intimate friend. I don't get intimate with anybody except my children."
4. Samuel Johnson: "Deign on the passing World to turn thine Eyes, | And pause awhile from Letters to be wise" ("The Vanity of Human Wishes," 158–59). See footnote 5 on page 56 (Lowell to Hardwick, June 14, 1970).
5. Lowell: "I hear the noise of my own voice" ("Epilogue" 5, *Day by Day*).

jet is an unexpected miracle of progress—I remember the last passenger train to Bangor. If the clock can't be put back, it can be put ahead.

I seem to be gassing to no purpose. What is exciting is your coming visit. I would be embarrassed to confess how much I count on it.

We have just gotten a house in Cambridge for fall term, the best we've ever had apparently, large enough for Harriet and Cathy. So glad to hear she is happy. First year college is a tricky time, so full of new chances, new duties and fears. I wrote a little while ago, but expect no answer, and trust we are together without exchange.

Have you read the mugging instructions issued to the Democratic delegates? Be careful you are not mistaken for one.

All my love,
Cal

338. *Robert Lowell to* Miss Elizabeth Hardwick Lowell

Milgate Park, Bearsted, Maidstone, Kent, Eng.
September 4, 1976

Dearest Lizzie:

I can't find the words or maybe the style to say how comforting and enjoyable your visit was. It was so strange seeing you and Caroline easily (?) together, that I almost feel I shouldn't refer to it. People with us seemed to take it as naturally as we did, one wondered if they were making an effort. I want to thank you for the strain you may have felt, but never revealed. I can never have too many compliments from you, and loved your liking what I said.

Also Susan. In my thickness, I think I wouldn't have known how sick she had been or have had doubts about her future wellbeing. She has always been a warm polite person to me and I felt she went further than that in London. (Sometimes I think I am the enemy of womankind, and sometimes coming in from the country, I feel I can't keep up a conversation, even with old friends like the Spenders. Two nights before our Murdoch-Spender dinner,[1] I ate alone with them. For half an hour I prayed that I wouldn't have to go. When I went, at first I couldn't talk, and never to Natasha, then it loosened, so much so

---

1. With Iris Murdoch and John Bayley.

Natasha suggested we go on shop-talking and she'd go home.) End of long parenthesis. You must have felt lonely arriving in a largely strange city, stuck in that Penta Hotel with such mobs of unknown, unmysterious clubmates. And to get back to Susan, how nice to hear her say, as she has more or less said in print that you are the best prose-writer in America,[1] and isn't it wonderful that she is someone younger not Mary's nannying age. Lord. Lord, I have been writing to Allen Tate and Jean Stafford (very sick) and wondering if I wasn't writing last letters.

I can't contain this paragraph. It fascinated me that your Billie Holiday was written as part of your novel.[2] I wouldn't have guessed, but now I think I see the cause of the more delicate, more poetic (?) prose. Don't tell me anything, but let me surmise that you are writing something close to autobiography, closer than plot will usually allow, that the style and selections will be artfully angled and chosen, so that the form might seem startlingly experimental even. Don't tell me either if, where and how I turn up. Shall I say you are welcome to anything about me in *Smiling through* you can use . . . even what you haven't shown me. What a ludicrous offer (what you have already)[3] [.] I do think you should use anything you can control. Caroline at this moment is piecing a bookreview of a leaking Irish house[4] into a piece of childhood autobiographical fiction.[5]

We fly on the 15th, 46 Sacramento St. Cambridge. I can see how poor Randall a little before his death, wondered how he could talk

---

1. Sontag: "It is this demand for an unremitting rhetoric, with every argument arriving triumphantly at a militant conclusion, which has prevented some feminists from properly appreciating that most remarkable of recent contributions to the feminist imagination of history, Elizabeth Hardwick's *Seduction and Betrayal*. A more specific reproach leveled against Hardwick's complex book is that it implicitly defends 'elitist' values (like talent, genius), which are incompatible with the egalitarian ethics of feminism. I hear an echo of this self-righteous view when Rich characterizes the feminist movement as 'passionately anti-hierarchal and anti-authoritarian'" (Adrienne Rich, reply by Susan Sontag, "Feminism and Fascism: An Exchange," *New York Review of Books*, March 20, 1975). Sontag would later say, "Her sentences are burned in my brain [. . .] I think she writes the most beautiful sentences, more beautiful sentences than any living American writer" (Hilton Als, "A Singular Woman," *New Yorker*, July 13, 1998).
2. Hardwick, "Billie Holiday," *New York Review of Books*, March 4, 1976.
3. Cf. Lowell: "I give you simply what you have already" ("The Vanity of Human Wishes," 384).
4. Blackwood, "A Big House in Ireland" (review of *Woodbrook* by David Thomson), *Listener*, December 12, 1974.
5. For *Great Granny Webster* (1977).

throu[gh] a class—the great teacher. I don't doubt now, though I am a very old number, replenished, I think in dour moments, by new reviews of old familiar books. How odd to talk about James's American[1] I last read first year Kenyon.

I think all the time about Harriet, with stiff, bearish affection. Could I meet David (?)[2] sometime in your apartment—not to approve but to acquaint myself. This is a moment, I suppose, before another unforeseeable moment. In my darkness, I am reassured. (over)[3]

No more really. I can't write these air-mail letters without running my last words into the fold. . . . I chose the sonnet you particularly detested because of the woodchuck lines at the bottom and didn't notice, I guess, the top.[4]

Caroline sends her love. Let me phone soon after I arrive.

Love,
    Cal

P.S. Will you ever see Sheridan? He came to breakfast helmeted in a huge pot, which has now burned the soup, so the whole long house asphyxiates. He's at a movie about a car without a driver, a masterpiece like the red balloon.[5]

[On September 15, 1976, Lowell was hospitalized at Greenways Nursing Home in London, for mania.]

---

1. (1877).
2. Grad.
3. The final part of the letter is typed on the verso of the aerogram.
4. "In the Mail" from *The Dolphin*, for inclusion in Lowell's *Selected Poems*; see footnote 2 on page 293.
5. Probably *Herbie Rides Again* (1974), dir. Robert Stevenson, sequel to *The Love Bug* (1968); *Le Ballon rouge* (1956), dir. Albert Lamorisse.

339. *Robert Lowell to Harriet Lowell*

[Telegram]

[London]
[n.d. October 1976][1]

HARRIET LOWELL C/O E LOWELL 15 WEST67ST
NEWYORKCITYUNITEDSTATES
I ALWAYS LOVE YOU WILL BE OUT THIS WEEKEND
 DAD

340. *Robert Lowell to Harriet Lowell*

[Cambridge, Mass.][2]
[December 13, 1976]

Darling Harriet:

I can't claim that infinite thought went into choosing this present for you, but it offers you almost infinite choices. All love to you and David for the oncoming year.

My love,
 Daddy

341. *Robert Lowell to* Mrs. Elizabeth Lowell

Milgate Park, Maidstone, Kent, England
January 11, 1977

Dear Lizzie:

To thankyou for so much kindness during my time in America—everything has been much quieter here. The great headache is how

---

1. In Hardwick's hand on verso: "Reply to cable Harriet sent Cal in hospital October? 1976." Lowell was discharged from Greenways on October 27, 1976.

2. Ian Hamilton: "In Cambridge the confusion was exacerbated: Blackwood was convinced that Lowell was still sick, and he was convinced that she needed help far more than he did. On November 25 Lowell called Blair Clark, as Clark records: 'Cal Lowell called, I having called him. He was at Frank Bidart's in Cambridge. He said, in effect, that he'd left the house and Caroline for a while to get some peace [. . .] .' Lowell stayed at Bidart's apartment for ten days. ([Bidart said that] 'he was just unbelievably grateful and relieved to be in an atmosphere that was not this terrific turmoil, anger, drama, tension')" (*Robert Lowell: A Biography*, p. 457).

and where to move from England before the new tax laws which cut unearned incomes to nothing, or so it seems. A rather undemocratic necessity. I wonder if we haven't all been unconscious secret capitalists for years. The real trouble of course is where to take or put the children. Nothing can be done until it is.

We spend our time writing. I am more than half way through the Eumenides working from translations. Terrible the Aeschylean translator's hackneyed grand rhetoric—it keeps smearing to my version. With luck I'll have the whole Oresteia ready to be acted late spring in New York.[1] The best translations I've see[n] are Yeats' Oedipus and Pound's Sophocles, an odd mixture of early Pound and Browning.[2] Most [of] the important poetry of the world, plays in particular, has never been done into English and perhaps never will now.

I must tell you later about our Christmas with the Mostyn-Owens—the Wests, seven children, seven hour train trips and seven hour dinners.

My socialist-anarchist earned income half-person will be at Harvard by the first of February with a room or rooms in Dunster House.

Aunt Sarah has told Jackie[3] she wants to see me, and I realize how much I've wanted this too. Jackie says she is so absent-minded she may forget.

How is Harriet's job-hunting? Natalya is doing more or less the same, but is now seriously trying to get into college and pass O-levels.[4] Genia lives in a world of rapidly changing holiday romance. Ivana is

---

1. Frank Bidart: "Lowell hoped his version of the *Oresteia* could be performed in one evening. *Agamemnon* and *Orestes* were written in the early 1960's; *The Furies* was added in the last year of his life, for a projected production of the entire trilogy at Lincoln Center. (*The Furies*, begun during December 1976, was finished by the end of the following January.) It wasn't produced. Lincoln Center decided to do *Agamemnon* alone, in the uncut translation of Edith Hamilton [. . .] When he returned from Harvard at the end of January 1977, with the manuscript of *The Furies*, he was ill—and eager to finish his new book of poems, *Day by Day*" ("A Note on the Text," *The Oresteia of Aeschylus*, trans. Robert Lowell [1978]).

2. W. B. Yeats, *Sophocles' King Oedipus: A Version for the Modern Stage* (1928); Sophokles, *Women of Trachis: A Version by Ezra Pound* (1957).

3. Jacqueline Winslow, Lowell's first cousin.

4. OED: "ordinary level *n. Educ.* (now *hist.*) the lowest of the three levels of examination in the General Certificate of Education in England [. . .] usually taken by pupils at the age of 16, and replaced in 1988 by the General Certificate of Secondary Education; abbreviation *O level*" ("O level, n.," March 2016. Oxford University Press. http://www.oed.com/view/Entry/261576 ?redirectedFrom=o+level, accessed March 28, 2016).

still a little girl doing charades, collecting dolls and wanting to become a professional actress. Sheridan is force ~~embodied~~ in person.

See you soon,
   love,
      Cal

PS. Tell Bob that reviewing Elizabeth is too much for many reasons[1]— and on top rushing Aeschylus to a deadline in March.

[Lowell flew to Boston on January 17, 1977. On February 1, he was admitted to Phillips House at Massachusetts General Hospital for cardiac failure. He was released on February 9.]

342. Robert Lowell to Harriet Lowell

[Cambridge, Massachusetts]
March 18, 1977

Dearest Harriet:

Here's an Easter present to save or spend on some bright wearable thing, perhaps a mark-down from your boutique. I had hoped to see you in New York soon, but will be with Caroline in Ireland during my vacation, March 30–April 10. Ireland? Caroline has found us two flats in a building on the outskirts of Dublin, looking like and almost as big as the Louvre—one for the teenagers and one for us.[2] She always says and writes that one of its advantages is you will come and visit. The other advantage is much lower taxes.

---

1. For *The New York Review of Books*. Bishop's *Geography III* was published in December 1976.
2. Ian Hamilton: "Lowell's sixtieth birthday coincided with news from Blackwood that Milgate had been sold, and that she had taken an apartment in a huge Georgian stately home at Castletown, near Dublin. The house was the headquarters of the Irish Georgian Society, and most parts of it were open to the public. Desmond Guinness, Lady Caroline's cousin and the Society's president, had suggested that she rent one of the house's small private apartments; for tax purposes, it was sensible for her (and perhaps for Lowell also) to establish residence in Ireland—and for Blackwood, certainly Castletown offered a convenient interim arrangement. According to friends, Lowell complained that the sale of Milgate had gone through without any consultation [. . .] To Blackwood, though, he wrote: 'What strikes me in this order is the teenager flat, the likeness to the Louvre (a vague feeling that we will live there as old royal Louvre pensioners, and the nearness of the Liffey) . . .'" (*Robert Lowell: A Biography*, pp. 460–61).

I am teaching Whitman. One of the critics' insoluble problems is whether he was a socialist . . . and believed in taxes. I think so often of you with happiness . . . your gentle (dazzling) beauty. Be seeing you early in May when I expect to spend a week in New York.

all my love,
Dad

343. *Elizabeth Hardwick to Mary McCarthy*

[15 West 67th Street, New York, N.Y.]

June 15, 1977

Dearest Mary: I have missed being in touch with you more than I can say. It has been for the last year or more so hard to find the time for anything like a real letter with so many non-real letters to be written. But I am setting forth on this before I take off for Berkeley, come back after being on the plane all night without sleep and take off for Russia the next day. I'm sorry you aren't going, but I will see \you/ in Maine sometime in mid-July. Then I'll have to come back before Labor Day because I will teach at Barnard on Monday and track up to the University of Connecticut on Tuesday at dawn to return at Thursday at midnight. And so even that, a few months away, haunts me.

I want to give you some idea of what has been happening here, give it as clearly as I can. Cal came to Cambridge in November, having been in the hospital and for some reason Caroline had fled to Cambridge in October. He was very well I heard and felt on the phone, very low and troubled, but things did not go well and he went to live across town with his friend,[1] but seeing C. all the time. Then she went back to England and he stayed on, waiting for the spring term and because she did not want him to come back with her. Soon after I had to be in Boston and spent three or four hours with him, where he was weeping and saying he would do anything he could to make the marriage work, and speaking of his deep love for Caroline. She did not give him the right to come for Christmas until a few days before and I had said he could come here and stay in the studio and have Christmas with us. \But he was allowed to go to England, as you know./

---

1. Frank Bidart.

He returned from England, very sad and troubled. Had congestive heart failure and was in the hospital for ten day[s]. I went up to see him, and talked to the doctors, but the water was finally drained from his lungs so that he could breathe and he took up his teaching for the second term, living very quietly in Dunster House. Caroline suddenly moved to Ireland, after the plan had been that they would move here, where he could teach, and since some move had to be made for her taxes. But he was still troubled and grieving and said he hoped she would consent to have him come for the Easter break. He was as "well" as Cal can be, most pleasing in being close to his feelings, serious about someone else, grieving for love (Caroline). At the last minute she said he could come to Ireland and I thought everything would work all right because he was very well, very sad over the long separation. He returned saying that she had said the marriage was over and he supposed it was for the best. Again, very grieved, quiet, troubled. Three weeks passed and he did not hear from her, although he wrote.

At this time, I said if you don't have any place to go you can come here. The term was almost ended and he only had to return once more for the papers, grades and so on. By the time he arrived here, Caroline had changed her mind and said she wanted him to return, that it could be mended. He said he didn't think it could. She insisted on coming to New York which she did. All this time, with Caroline and for the last few years—corroborated by people in England and in Boston during her stays—there had been drinking, depression, suicide attempts. Cal got a doctor for Caroline when he knew she was coming to New York, a doctor who had given a friend a treatment, lasting a few weeks, of pills that gradually help to lift depression, Caroline's life-long agony. They went to do the doctor, but before that, the night of her arrival, Cal called me from Lenox Hill Hospital where Caroline had been taken on a stretcher, having passed out in the hotel lobby. But she came to, and ran out of the hospital, and they went back to the hotel. (The *passing out* does not seem clear to me—maybe pills and alcohol, maybe suicide attempt, I don't know.) She went back to the doctor and Cal was told that she couldn't be left alone and he did not leave her alone, but she wouldn't take the pills, would drink ~~and~~ \at/ night, as she wasn't supposed to. He was terrified and would come back to the studio, which was really Blair Clark's because he had rented it [from] me—come back for an hour and rush back to see Caroline, out of fear and worry. I have never known him to take such care—it may not be much, knowing how careless he can be, but it was complete. She wanted him to come back to Ireland but he said he didn't think it would work and that he would come in September, before Harvard, as he plans to do. Cal was in tears, trembling, calling the doctor ~~the doctor~~ four or five times a day. He insisted that a doctor be found in Dublin and with great effort he and the doctor did that. The weeks went on and she stayed here in New York and finally Cal had to return to Boston for a final week. He was with Caroline the whole time and when he finally went to Boston she left for Ireland. Since then he has called, had his friends call, talks and thinks of nothing else, worries terribly. But she seems at least to be alive and not speaking of suicide at the moment, although he fears she can do it and it has been a horrible fear for several years.

I haven't been a part of this at all and Caroline has never mentioned my name to Cal. The fact is that I am not a part of it, there is no great renewed romance, but a kind of friendship, and listening to his grief. His intention is to stay here with me, staying mostly in the studio, but sharing the life here, the books, the records, his family setting (Boston), which is pretty much as he left it. He went up to Maine with me for part of the week I spent there opening up. It could be said we "are back together," but the phrase is not really meaningful—at least in the way it is commonly used. There is no thought of his getting a divorce, but there is a general peacefulness (except when there isn't) and a great preoccupation with Caroline, her future, the children.

For my own part, I was alone, not at all happy, but often having quite a good time, and adjusted to what pleasures I had, but quite lonely much of the time and worried about the future.[1] I am not at all as vulnerable to Cal as I used to be, but I care for him. He has learned something from love and from being as he said when he came back from England the last time, "unwanted."[2] The passion and the grief he

---

1. Blair Clark: "Last Monday I had dinner at the Café des Artistes with Eliz. She seemed ready, if not ecstatic, about resuming some sort of life that was close, if not exactly with, to Cal. In passing, she said it would mean the interruption of some aspect of her personal life that had not quite worked out but was there" ("The Lowells . . . notes for a never-to-be-written memoir," May 8, 1977, Blair Clark Papers, HRC).

2. Lowell: "'You know | you were an unwanted child?' | [. . .] Is the one unpardonable sin | our fear of not being wanted? | For this, will mother go on cleaning house | for eternity, making it

knew from Caroline and from his feeling for her have made him more like the rest of us. We are trying to work out a sort of survival for both of us, and both are sixty. He does not feel he is good for Caroline and that her thinking so right now is less real than her not thinking so most of the time in the last years. I think he would return immediately if he thought she could want it for more than a week.

We, together, are having a perfectly nice time, both quite independent and yet I guess dependent. I know that Cal can get sick again and will talk to the McLean doctor on the way up to Maine. Cal has been very much in touch with him, working out what could be most sensibly done if he \becomes/ "keyed up." I realize that is scarcely the way it happens. But that and our attempt to manage the heart problem—no salt, etc.—is about the case.

I put all of this down, leaving out much, hardly able to give the slightest picture of anything as I understand it. About Caroline—Cal thinks she's the greatest living writer—I do feel she has the greatest possibilities in Ireland and I hope so. I very much admire a new book—*Greatgranny Webster*, it is called—that is coming out.[1] I liked *Stepdaughter* too[.][2]

I hear what a hard and busy time you have had working, but also hear that both of you are well. I look forward to seeing you on Main Street very much. Forgive this letter and do not think it strange. I just felt a need to give the "narration." You don't need to answer because I will scarcely be in the house before Maine.

Dearest love always,
Lizzie

---

unlivable? | Is getting well ever an art, | or art a way to get well?" ("Unwanted," 48–56, 112–17, *Day by Day*).

1. (1977).
2. (1976).

344. Elizabeth Hardwick to Robert Craft

[Castine, Maine]
August 4, 1977

Dearest Robert: So the shifts, the caftans, the dressing gowns, the hair curlers cranked out of the driveway and are gone. I suppose these last items of severance are horrible for you, and indeed for Alfreda.[1] If you wanted to give someone a blessing, I suppose you'd wish that in all their connections the moment of the end would come for both at the same time. But, of course, it can't be; whoever utters the first good-bye is inevitably because of that "ahead." And so anger, resentment, the whole thing. I wish you both well, as the saying goes, and that all the friends on both sides insisting that each is "better off" turn out to be near the truth.

Catharine Huntington—I remember her face well from meetings here and there in Boston, although I cannot say that I know her or that she remembers me. Katherine Anne Porter's piece on Sacco and Vanzetti in a recent *Atlantic* was good[2]—and again marvelous photographs of the "girls rioting" as Allen Tate used to say.

Here. First of all my house is not as one-ly as I perhaps said. It is beautiful, I think, the old large barn as the main room and then a two-story wing was added. There are actually three bedrooms and two baths. It is just that there was no place for two to work. I work in the guest room and push things away when a guest comes—so far, mercifully, only two nights planned for the whole summer. Cal got a little boathouse on the beach, a sort of adorable shack, about three houses away and that is the only thing we needed in so far as housing for work is concerned. And some solitude during the day for both of us. I am working every day and have done a chapter, starting with fear to read it over just after this letter and make improvements that gleam out like flares, the need for the gleams I mean. But the summer has been very, very nice. A few drinks in the evening, dinner, music—and here one tends to get up soon after seven.

About my "situation"—the whole thing is astonishing and I have

---

1. Robert Craft: "Yes, I believe it has passed \I mean my marriage [to Rita Christiansen Craft]/, but I am grateful to you for even putting your mind on it" (Robert Craft to Elizabeth Hardwick, "Annotation of Elizabeth Hardwick's letter, dated August 4—" Elizabeth Hardwick Papers, HRC). "Alfreda" is a joke about Alfredo in Verdi's *La Traviata* (1853).
2. Katherine Anne Porter, "The Never-Ending Wrong," *Atlantic Monthly*, June 1977.

no idea exactly what the shape of it all will turn out to be. Cal is going to Ireland on the 1st of Sept. for two weeks, returning the 15th to teach at Harvard. *They* appear to be friendly from calls and letters and I think Caroline will make an effort again to mend her too hasty surgery on the marriage. Who knows? As for me, I spoke of the astonishment, by which I mean as clearly as I can say that I don't feel vulnerable, don't feel sent out on approval, as it were, don't talk or care about contracts and commitments, whatever those are. It is very odd—we are just going along, having a very agreeable time. I don't like being up in Maine alone for long periods and it has been marvelous to have Cal here. In New York everything is different; I am happy there in my old ways and if they return that is all right. I know this sounds strange, but as the thing has gone along day by day it seems real just as it is. Cal and I burst out laughing on July 28th— had it not been for the "gap" we would have been married that day for 28 years. I cannot say that such a record would have been a certain glory. So, don't worry, darling. It is not all up to *him*.

Mary McCarthy is here in her splendid mansion and that is a great pleasure. She is slim, looks very beautiful and is at every moment interesting—a triumph.

Storrs—the *winterreise*[1] falls down on my head like ice when I think of it. I get ideas about flying back and forth, renting a car at the airport each time—and think I remember that would cost two hundred per week. But it will all work out, the few months will pass and my course won't be good. I'll try to slide by the grease of *personality*.[2]

Am reading *Eugene O* in the odd Nabokov translation and dreaming of our night in the opera.[3] Will talk to you soon. I hope to see you in New York soon after Labor Day, on the weekends when I am there. Adored your letter, your card—all.

Dearest love,
Elizabeth

---

1. That is, her journey to and from New York to the University of Connecticut at Storrs, where Hardwick would be teaching for the fall semester; but see also Franz Schubert, *Winterreise* (D. 911, Op. 89, 1828).

2. Lowell: "A savage servility | slides by on grease" ("For the Union Dead," 67–68, *For the Union Dead*).

3. Aleksander Pushkin, *Eugene Onegin: A Novel in Verse*, vols. 1–4, trans. Vladimir Nabokov (1964). The Metropolitan Opera mounted a production of Tchaikovsky's opera of *Eugene Onegin* with a Russian libretto on October 15, 1977.

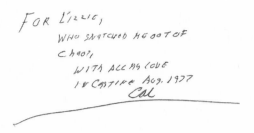

Inscription on front endpaper of *Day by Day*: "For Lizzie, | who snatched me out of | chaos, | with all my love | in Castine Aug. 1977 | Cal"[1]

⌒

[Associated Press, September 12, 1977, AM cycle. New York: Pulitzer Prize–winning poet Robert Lowell, 60, died here Monday of a heart attack while on a taxi ride from Kennedy Airport to Manhattan, said his former wife, Elizabeth Hardwick.

Miss Hardwick said Lowell's death was discovered by the taxi driver.

"He had been in Ireland for a week to see his son and was coming home from Dublin," Miss Hardwick said. "The driver said he got in the cab at the airport and died on the way, I suppose."

"The elevator man called me and I went down and we went to the hospital and they said he was dead. I think it was from a heart attack," she said. "The driver at first thought he was asleep. I guess he died sometime between when he got in the taxi and the time he got here."

Miss Hardwick, who was divorced from Lowell in 1973, said the poet was to spend a few days in New York before leaving for Massachusetts, where he was to teach at Harvard University this year.

The Boston-born Lowell received the Pulitzer Prize for poetry in 1947 and also had been awarded the poetry prize of the American Academy of Arts and Letters, the Guinness Poetry Award and the National Book Award.

Before winning the Pulitzer and Academy prizes Lowell had published "Land of Unlikeness" in 1944 and "Lord Weary's Castle" in 1946.

The son of Robert Traill Spence Lowell and the former Charlotte

1. First quoted in Jamison (2017), p. 365.

Winslow, Lowell grew up in Boston and attended Harvard University from 1935 to 1937. He was graduated summa cum laude from Kenyon College in 1940.

After graduation he served briefly as an editorial assistant with Sheed and Ward here. During World War II he was a conscientious objector.

In 1947 and 1948, he served as a consultant in poetry at the Library of Congress, and during the same period he had a Guggenheim fellowship.

His other works included "The Mills of the Kavanaughs," published in 1951; "Life Studies," which won the National Book Award in 1959; "Phaedra"; "Imitations," which won the 1962 Bollingen translation prize; "For the Union Dead," 1964; "The Old Glory," 1965; "Near the Ocean," 1967; "Notebook of a Year," 1969, and "History," "For Lizzie and Harriet" and "The Dolphin," all published in 1973.

Lowell's first marriage to Jean Stafford in 1940 ended in divorce eight years later and in 1949 he married Miss Hardwick, by whom he had a daughter, Harriet Winslow Lowell.

At the time of his death, Lowell was married to Caroline Blackwood, who lives in Ireland. He had a son by Miss Blackwood.][1]

⌒

345. Elizabeth Hardwick to Mary McCarthy

[15 West 67th Street, New York, N.Y.]
October 2, 1977

Dearest Mary: I feel as if I were a hundred years older than when I last talked to you here in my apartment, a day or two after great Cal died. We had the Boston funeral and the flowers from you and Jim were there in the beautiful church and lower Beacon Hill was on that morning just as it was around the time Cal was born. The family graveyard at Dunbarton lay under a mist of rain; great trees and a few autumn leaves on the ground and the old gravestones, beginning with General John Stark and ending with Dear Cal, since the place is small and be-

1. Associated Press. September 12, 1977, AM cycle. https://advance.lexis.com/api/document ?collection=news&id=urn:contentItem:3SJ4-DD60-0011-353T-00000-00&context=1516831.

longs to the New Hampshire Historical Society, having been endowed by Cal's grandfather. That was the end. But it was the beginning of a nightmare here for me. Caroline somehow moved in with me for 8 days and nights to prepare for the Memorial Service. I don't think any single night I slept for more than two hours. Her poor drunken theatricality hour after hour, day after day, night after night was unrelieved torture for me and I am sure for herself much more. Somehow she has put herself beyond help and sadly for her all help begins at the same spot—to stop drinking, at least for today, tomorrow, for a week, an evening.

Finally I had to go to work and when I went up to Storrs, Connecticut, to a lonely little furnished room I have there for my stay each week, only then could I burst into sobs and realize that Cal was truly gone forever. It is terrible. I remember that you said I was used to living alone and indeed that is true, but it has been much more painful than I thought it reasonable to show, much more lonely and sometimes frightening. Having the companionship of Cal this summer and some of the spring before was a wonderful break of lightness and brightness for me.

I understand you are to be at the London Memorial. I am sure it will be graceful and moving and I am glad you are to be present.

Dear Mary, I am still too tired to put much into this letter. But a lot I would like to talk to you about shouldn't go in a letter in any case. I do hope to come to Paris, perhaps in January, and I would always hope you were coming here if that were something that would please you, which I doubt it would just now. For the moment I will just send dearest love to you both.

    Lizzie

346. Elizabeth Hardwick to Elizabeth Bishop

[Castine, Maine]
August 16, 1978

Dear Elizabeth:

I am looking over the harbor imagining I see North Haven, but I probably don't reach that far in the blessed little bit of fog today. I never imagined I'[d] be longing for a bit of rain—all night and sun in the morning will do—but as the man who keeps mowing my grass-less, burnt-out lawn says, "I'm mowing out them fall dandelions the heat has brought on."

Frank read me your beautiful poem[1] over the phone and I wept when I went to sit outside and think about it. Oh, the magical details of North Haven and the way you bring them with such naturalness and feeling into a human landscape, to Cal. Your art is always able to do that—and the genuineness, the lack of strain, the truth of things. This poem moves me unbearably. I've just heard it read once and Frank will send me a copy soon I hope.

When Harriet came up with me [at] the end of May, Cal seemed to be about everywhere: his red shirt and socks were a painful discovery. The death is unacceptable and yet I know he has gone and it is very difficult to bring the two together ever.

I've been here since the beginning of July. Strange, I never loved Maine more, the place itself, my house, and the changing islands which you describe with such perfection. I have to go back on Labor Day and wish it were otherwise.

Much love to you,
Elizabeth (H.)

⌒

---

1. "North Haven (In Memoriam: Robert Lowell)," which was later published in the *New Yorker* (December 11, 1978).

347. Mary McCarthy to Elizabeth Hardwick

141 rue du Rennes, Paris 75006

June 4, 1979

Dearest Lizzie:

You'll have been puzzled—or hurt, or both—that I haven't written sooner about your book.[1] More than a month has gone by; I read it at once, of course, and ought to have sent a postcard immediately in the first freshet of my admiration. But a p.c. seemed too inexpressive for the occasion, and I had no time for a variety of reasons to write the letter that was in my mind. Well, on my return from the U.S., I had recklessly put an ad in the *Figaro* for a replacement for Maria; the result was 180 candidates presenting themselves by telephone. This halted all work on my page proofs,[2] already overdue at Harcourt, and every other activity. I interviewed throughout five days—twenty-five or thirty women perched nervously on the sofa—and finally chose one. You'll see her in Castine, a Spanish girl called Elvira, who is a mistress of the iron, if not much at the stove. After that, there were the proofs waiting and an acknowledgment page to do, and after *that*, a speech to write for the P.E.N. Club in London: I was an emergency substitute for Isaac Singer. Then the speech had to be delivered, and we went to London. On my return, there was fresh business for Harcourt to attend to and Elvira to break in. Carmen arrived, and I lent her *Sleepless Nights*, which she is very keen on, so much so that she was slow to return it. The weekend following the P.E.N. lecture I had to go to Los Angeles, where I procured another copy at the Beverly Hills Brentano's; I spent two days at the booksellers' convention, having a lunch given for me with reviewers and a reception at the downtown Hilton for 500 booksellers, followed by a dinner for HBJ personalities. Having left Paris on Sunday evening, I came back Wednesday evening in a dazed, virtually sleepless state with my memory almost blacked out and had to do the jacket copy for my book, which I'd been putting off owing to these other events. All that is now over, and it is a peaceful long weekend—Pentecost—and at last I can try to tell you what I think of *Sleepless Nights*.

It's a classic, Lizzie. That was my reaction when I closed it and

---

1. *Sleepless Nights* (1979).
2. For *Cannibals and Missionaries* (1979).

it grows stronger. You've done it, created a nearly perfect thing—I don't know why I say "nearly," maybe because of three printer's errors I marked. It's a true work of art, very moving, painfully so in places—the "mound of men" at the end *transfixed* me like the swords of the Seven Sorrows[1]—and yet utterly composed, in both senses, not the hair of a syllable out of place. What seem to me peripheral, random, almost fugitive reminiscences are held together by a magic centripetal force—the force of suffering, I suppose, refined to purity and acting like a magnet to pull all the little iron filings into its field. I'm dumbstruck. It had to be short, of course; compactness belongs to its essence. And what courage it took to be true to it; I don't mean the courage of autobiography—candor of revelation—but literary daring. You've made something new, unlike anything previous.

One thought that came to me was that I wish Philip could have seen it. He used to say "Lizzie is so *literary*." He meant it as half a compliment, in wonderment, shaking his head. You've proved him right, more than he knew; you've brought about a triumph of the "literary" over life's materials. And you could only do that by being incurably "bookish." You make my heavily plotted, semi-lifelike novel seem like a bone-crusher. And the faults I've occasionally found in your writing—of being pitched too high, too prone to dying falls of epigram—disappear here or turn into a virtue.

I wonder what Cal would think. He'd be put out somewhat in his vanity to find himself figuring mainly as an absence and absence that the reader doesn't miss. Even during the years when he was evidently on the scene, e.g. in Amsterdam. I like your idea of wondering whether you might not change his hair color to red[2]—very funny, and it demonstrates how little his thisness (*haecceitas*), rather than \mere/ thatness, matters.[3] When I read the first bits in the *New York Review*,

---

1. Hardwick: "Mother, the reading glasses and the assignation near the clammy faces, so gray, of the intense church ladies. And then a lifetime with its mound of men climbing on and off. The torment of personal relations. Nothing new there except in disguise, and in the escape on the wings of adjectives. Sweet to be pierced by daggers at the end of paragraphs" (*Sleepless Nights*, p. 151).

2. Hardwick: "How is the Mister this morning? Josette would say. The Mister? Shall I turn his devastated brown hair to red, which few have? Appalling disarray of trouser and jacket and feet stuffed into stretched socks. Kindly smile, showing short teeth like his mother's" (*Sleepless Nights*, p. 121).

3. Hannah Arendt, writing of Duns Scotus: "Contemplation of the *summum bonum*, of the 'highest thing,' ergo God, would be the ideal of the intellect, which is always grounded in intuition, the

I couldn't see how you were going to cope with the huge fact of Cal; it didn't occur to me that you could do it by simply leaving him out. That's a brilliant technical stroke but proves to be much more than that: he becomes a sort of black hole in \outer/ space, to be filled in ad lib, which is poetic justice: he's condemned by the *form* to non-existence—you couldn't do that in a conventional autobiography. In any case, he couldn't patronize your book by appearing to be generous about it, though I suppose he might try.

We'll talk about it more this summer; Jim has marked his calendar: "June 14; Lizzie arrives in Castine." He is enthusiastic about the book and is "selling" it by word of mouth. You've done wonders with Ida and with a wisp of Tommy Thomas that I think I recognize. But I can't place Alex or Louisa,[1] unless she owes something to Caroline and something to Natasha.[2] It's strange to read a book by someone one knows as well as we know each other and be puzzled by a few of the component parts. Even by internal evidence, it's clear, of course, that some alchemy has taken place. Yet there will be readers who insist on seeing it as "straight" autobiography, and I can hear myself patiently separating truth from fiction for someone like Ellie.[3] The fact that the effect, though subdued and controlled, is one of mounting pain, will worry some of your friends; it worried Carmen a little. To me, that is a \melancholy/ truth, evidently, but one of many in your nature, as though a secret part spoke suddenly for the whole. To me, the point is the artistic victory, which can't fail to exhilarate, i.e., to make one rejoice for you. Quite aside from the success the book is bound to have. (By the way, I haven't yet read the Diane Johnson review, expecting to quarrel with it since I don't like some of the things she has written.[4] But now I will, having said my own say to you. Carmen gently feared that the review contained misunderstandings of the text.)

Nothing else is new here. We are starting to do our income tax, due

---

grasping of a thing in its 'thisness,' *haecceitas*, which in this life is imperfect not only because here the highest remains unknown but also because intuition of thisness is imperfect: 'the intellect . . . has recourse to intellectual concepts, precisely because it is incapable of grasping the haecceity'" (*The Life of the Mind*, ed. Mary McCarthy [1978], p. 144).

1. Ida, Alex, and Louisa are characters in *Sleepless Nights*.
2. Caroline Blackwood and Natasha Spender.
3. DuVivier.
4. Diane Johnson, "Beyond the Evidence," *New York Review of Books*, June 14, 1979.

June 15. Jim is issuing invitations for my birthday June 21, which may be celebrated in Montmartre on a terrace belonging to Jon Randal of the *Washington Post*. I don't at all appreciate becoming sixty-seven—a fact which seems to have little to do with me until I look in the mirror.

With much love and large-eyed respect,[1]

P.S. For future editions, which the book will surely have: p. 5, second l. from bottom, "fossilized": p. 6, second paragraph, "diphtheria": p. 70, second paragraph "sulleness."

P.P.S. I've finished the Diane Johnson piece and find no fault in it.

---

1. Unsigned.

"WRITING A NOVEL"

BY ELIZABETH HARDWICK

It is June. This is what I have decided to do with my life just now. I will do this work and lead this life, the one I am leading today. Each morning the blue clock and the crocheted bedspread, the table with the Phone, the books and magazines, the *Times* at the door. It does not help to remember Rand Avenue in Lexington and old summer rockers still on the gray, dry planks of winter porches. A novel is always written on the day of its writing.

I begin, seeking distance, imagining or pretending to imagine thus:

"She often spent the entire day in blue, limpid boredom. The caressing sting of it was, for her, like the pleasure of lemon, or of cold salt water. This lovely boredom one saw in her eyes, in those pleasant, empty, withdrawn and peering eyes—orbs in a porcelain head. At such times she looked her best, very quiet, her face harmoniously fixed, as if for an important camera. Her skinny brown cat stared at her, hardly blinking. His yellowish-gray gaze was very like her own. They looked at each other, unseeing, into a mirror of eyes, before the cat fell asleep, his lids suddenly closing, tightly, quickly, strangely. 'That cat has been here with me for seven years and has never looked at television. They are indeed a different species,' she thought.

"Then she took a cigarette from the pocket of the smock she was wearing. She drew on it, as if it were opium; adding to the opium that was within her, the narcotic of her boredom, as we are told we carry our own heaven and hell within us. Immaculate drugs, hazy drifts of dreams, passivity pure and rich as cream.

"After a dreamy day, she went into her nights. Always she insisted they were full of agitation, restlessness, torment. She was forever like one watched over the whole night in the deepest sleep, who nevertheless awakened worn, with a tremor in her hands, declaring the pains, the unutterable, absorbing drama of sleeplessness. The tossing, the racing, the battles; the captures and escapes hidden behind her oily eyelids. No one was more skillful than she in the confessions of an insomniac, in those redundant yet stirring epics, which she intoned with the dignity of ritual, her hypnotic narration like that of some folk poet 'steeped in the oral tradition.' 'Finally, sleep came over me. . . . At last. . . . It was drawing near to four o'clock. The first color was in the sky. . . . Only to wake up suddenly, completely.'

"Unsavory egotism? No—mere hope of self-definition, the heroism of description, the martyrdom of documentation. The chart of life must be brought up to date every morning. 'Patient slept fitfully, complained of the stitches. Alarming persistence of the very symptoms for which the operation was performed. Perhaps it is only the classical aching of the stump.'"

An impasse. How can she, opiumstill, a dramatic star of ennui, with catlike eyes and abrupt disappearances, begin, continue? Her end is clearly too soon at hand. On the next page, verisimilitude would not be outraged to find her dead. Not smiling perhaps, as they say suicides smile, but reflective, sunk in last thoughts. Her still gaze would be downward, as if she, who knew nothing of literature, were thinking of poetry or philosophy.

Lasst uns lauten, knien, beten,
Und dem alten Gott vertaun!

Soon I abandon the languid girl. My mind is elsewhere. I have taken a journey in order to write my novel in peace. A steamy haze blurs the lines of the hills. A dirty, exhausting sky. Already the summer seems to be passing away. The boats will soon be gathered in, ferries roped to the dock.

A new scene: A short pear-shaped man came onto the stage for his lecture. He is the author of two peculiar novels, some shorter fiction of an in-between length difficult to publish, and a number of literary essays. All of his work is strikingly interesting and odd. His essays are gracefully and yet fiercely written, with the same teasing moil of metaphor found in his fiction; but of course their meaning is clearer and people are inclined to prefer them to his pure works of the imagination. His opinion is different: he feels his essays are works of the imagination but that somehow in the end they do not fully reward their hurting effort. They live and die in a day, a week at most. The orange, black, and yellow wings of opinion make a pleasant, whirring sound, dip down, soar up ward, and then disappear, their organic destiny achieved.

His mere name on the page can make you tremble if you are interested in him. Movement, agitation, somber explosion of thought and feeling—complicated learning and an aggressive, poetic style. He has no remarkable popular reputation. Only the most curious and the most alert care about him, but they care with some vehemence. He is enormously ambitious, resolute, assured, and seems not to know that he is rumpled, lumpy, looks far older than his forty-one years. His clothes are a scandal.

A pert-faced, slim wife, with very short hair, came into the hall with him. She sits down on the aisle in a row near the front, but not in the very first rows. The wife smiles a good deal and appears to be proud, but with moderation. Her smile disguises the frowning dilemma that never leaves her thoughts: the mathematical estimate of his talents, which are not precise in her mind, to be weighed against the score of his defects—acerbity, impatience—which are.

The author begins to speak of his obsession: the theoretical problems of contemporary fiction. In his life he is a man of reason, bound in his spontaneous actions and in his deliberated decisions to a loose, but genuine, reverence for cause and effect. There are times when he grows short-tempered because of the ignorance or bad character of many people. Then he angrily asserts the laws of cause and effect, and he accuses with a good deal of arrogance.

Fiction is another matter. He cannot, for us, for himself, accept a simple, linear motivation as a proper way to write novels, involve characters. He does not at all agree that if the gun is hanging on the wall in the first act it must go off before the curtain comes down. No, the ground has slipped away from causality. Muddy, gorgeously pol-luted tides of chaos, mutation, improvisation have rushed in to make a strewn, random beach out of what had not so long ago been a serene shore, bordering a house lot always suitable for building.

He accepts, embraces, adores the fragments of life. But he studies them with great sternness, with a clean, sharp rigidity, and in this way he puts together fictions that are new, difficult, obscure, and "really good."

As they are going home after the lecture, his wife says to him, "Is it actually OK to write stories about writing?" She has overheard this whispered remark during the question period. Fiction about fiction—Borges, etc. The skepticism thrills her, even as it brings on a little squeezing of her heart. He must not fail, and yet she feels perversity in him, nagging withholdings, a stingy reluctance to redeem his narra-tive promises. For instance, he has written a story about her mother, a woman he despises. Somehow it angers the wife that her own mother, the creator of brutal emotions in the heart of the author, the vigilant, dirty-fingered, blue-haired mother has come out like a beaded purse, pure design.

"Now, all writing is about writing, especially poetry," he answers thoughtfully, without rancor. After all it is *the* question. His wife, he knew, read a great deal, but never willingly. She reads as you keep the store for the good of the family: his work, those he has praised and learned from, those he disapproves of seriously.

One evening they went to hear a large, handsome English poet, first-rate for a long time, his career arching from the Georgian to the very moment of his appearance. In his scattered, fascinating remarks about his own work, the poet spoke in a hospitable manner of Frost and Ransom. Later, at the reception, a student tried to approach the poet. "I didn't know you particularly admired Frost. Wouldn't have thought it somehow," the young man said. "I don't," the poet said. "Not in the least. And Ransom only with reservation. Still if you name one, you must name two. One lone name out of a national tradi-tion, even a dreadfully short, patchy one, is no go. Arouses suspicion, doesn't sound genuine." The author's wife liked that. She has a feeling for paradox and for unfriendly appraisals.

The odd thing is that I have taken the two, husband and wife, from life, but they have come out false to their real meaning. The writer is not a fraud but a genius, a rare creature out of nowhere—actually from Shaker Heights around Cleveland, like Hart Crane. His seriousness, excellence, eccentricity stir my feelings. His wife is agreeable, sociable, but her "reality" and her lack of ostentation, her simplicity, her way of puncturing pretension are not the sly and cunning moral virtues I have made them appear. Those ideas of hers have nothing to do with literature, with the novel. Her husband rightly goes his own way.

But how is the man's genius to be made manifest—at breakfast, making love, engaging in his ruling passion which is writing? How is his art to become real in my novel? What is a writer's motif, his theme song, except stooped shoulders, the appalling desolation of trouser and jacket and old feet stuffed into stretched socks. And women writers, of course, interest me more since I am a woman. Remember what Sainte-Beuve said about George Sand: "A great heart, a large talent, and an enormous bottom."

An unhappy summer, and yet not a happy subject for literature. Very hard to put the vulgar and common sufferings on paper. I use "vulgar and common," in the sense of belonging to many, frequently, everlastingly occurring. The misery of personal relations. Nothing new there except in the telling, in the escape on the wings of adjectives. Pleasant to be pierced by the daggers at the end of paragraphs.

The phlox blooms in its faded purples; on the hillside, phallic pines. Foreigners under the arcades, in the basket shops. When you travel your great discovery is that you do not exist. I have for a long time had the idea of a sort of short-wave autobiography, one that fades in and out, local voices mixing with the mysterious static of the cadences of strangers. Truth should be heightened and falsity adorned, dressed up to look like sociable fact. Nevertheless, a memoir, a confession, is not as easy as it seems. It is not necessary for an autobiography to "have had a life"—that we accept now. Pasternak's line: *To live a life is not to cross a field.* The "not" perplexes me. Life is to be seen as climbing a mountain? That we can agree to because of the awful strain of the climb and at the top many of the same wild flowers as in the field below.

The murderous German girl with her alpenstock, her hiking boots, calls to the old architect, Higher, higher! He falls to his death and this is Ibsen's disgust with the giddiness of men. For himself, he adjusted his rimless spectacles and turned the corners of his mouth down when fervent young girls thought he was dumber than he was. The troubles in a memoir are both large and small. Those still living do not create the longest hesitations. I am sure no one makes an enemy without wishing to do so. The need is sometimes very pressing; the relief rather disappointing. No, the troubles are not with relatives, lovers, famous persons seen at a deforming angle. The troubles are all with yourself seen at an angle, yourself defamed and libeled.

Memoirs: felonious pages in which one accuses others of real faults and oneself only of charming infidelities, unusual follies, improvidence but no meanness, a restlessness as beguiling as the winds of Aeolus, excesses, vanities, and sensualities that are the envy of all. I have thought of calling my memoir *Living and Partly Living*. But I am not happy with "partly living." It comes down too hard on the aridity of modern life, on the dispirited common folk without tradition, on the dead gods and the banished God. It would not seem to fit the spirit and mood of the moment, a mood I partake of as a pigeon partakes of the crumbs that fall from fingers he cannot see.

Is it possible for a woman to write a memoir? Their productions often fail to be interesting because there isn't enough sex in them, not even enough longing for consummation. Can we seriously speak of the young lieutenant with his smooth hair, the hint of coquetry in the cruel charm of his glance? Women do not like to tell of bastards begotten, of pawings in the back seat, of a lifetime with its mound of men climbing on and off. That will not make a *heroine* of you, or even a *personage*. The question with us, in love, is to discover whether we have experienced conquest or surrender—or neither. Courage under ill-treatment is a woman's theme, life-theme, and is of some interest, but not if there is too much of either.

Maybe the shadows will suffice—the light and the shade. Think of yourself as if you were in Apollinaire's poem:

Here you are in Marseilles, surrounded by watermelons,
Here you are in Coblenz at the Hotel du Géant.
Here you are in Rome sitting under a Japanese medlar tree.
Here you are in Amsterdam. . . .

Dearest M: Here I am in Boston, on Marlborough Street, number 239. I am looking out on a snow storm. It fell like a great armistice, bringing all struggles to an end. People are walking about in wonderful costumes—old coats with fur collars, woolen caps, scarves, boots, leather hiking shoes that shine like copper. Under the yellow glow of the street lights you begin to imagine what it was like forty or fifty years ago. The stillness, the open whiteness—nostalgia and romance in the clear, quiet, white air. . . .

More or less settled in this handsome house. Flowered curtains made to measure, rugs cut for the stairs, bookshelves, wood for the fireplace. Climbing up and down the five floors gives you a sense of ownership—perhaps. It may be yours, but the house, the furniture, strain toward the universal and it will read soon like a stage direction: Setting—Bostonian. The law will be obeyed. Chests, tables, dishes, domestic habits fall into line.

Beautiful mantles of decorated marble—neo-Greek designs of fading blacks and palest greens. "Worth the price of the whole house"—the seller's flourish of opinion and true for once. But it is the whole house that occupies my thoughts. On the second floor, two parlors. Grand, yes, but 239 is certainly not without its pockets of deprivation, its corners of tackiness. Still it is a setting.

Here I am with my hibiscus blooming in the bay window. The other parlor looks out on the alley between Marlborough and Beacon. There an idiot man keeps a dog on a chain, day and night. Bachelor garbage, decay, bewilderment pile up around the man. I have the idea he once had a family, but they have gone away. I imagine that if his children were to visit he would say, "Come to see the dog on a chain. It is a present." In the interest of the dog I call the police. The man glances up at my window in perturbation, wondering what he has done wrong. Darwin wrote some place that the suffering of the lower animals throughout time was more than he could bear to think of.

Dearest love,
Elizabeth

Was that written for the archives? Who is speaking? Description and landscape are like layers of underclothes. Words and rhythms, a waterfall of clauses, blue and silver lights, amber eyes, the sea below like a burning lake. It has all fallen into obsolescence. The great power of words, the old tyrant, questioned; painted scenery is like taking a long train journey to an emergency. Who can remember the shape of a single face in fiction? The perfection of the pointed chin; eyes and ears as alert as those of a small, nervous dog. Sweeps of luxurious black hair, wavy brilliance—abundant, prickly forest of thick, amorous Levantine hair. Who can bring to mind the shape of the lithe-boned heroines, with fair glances, haughty eyes colored like semiprecious stones? Only one facial feature remains in memory: the sparse mustache on the lip of Princess Bolkónskaya in the early pages of *War and Peace*.

1962

Dearest M: Here I am in New York, on 67th Street in a high, steep place with long, dirty windows. In the late afternoon, in the gloom of the winter lights, I sometimes imagine it is Edinburgh in the Nineties. I have never been to Edinburgh, but I like cities of reasonable size, provincial capitals. Still it is definitely New York here, underfoot and overhead. The passage was not easy. Not unlike a great crossing of the ocean, or of the country itself, with all your things in wagons, over the mountains. I can say that the trestle table and the highboy were ill-prepared for the sudden exile, the change of government—as in a way this was for me. Well, fumed oak stands in the corner, bottles and ice bucket on top. Five of the Naval Academy plates are broken. The clocks have had their terminal stroke and will never again know life. The old bureaus stand fixed, humiliated, chipped.

Displaced things and old people, rigid, dragged with their tired veins and clogged arteries, with their bunions and broken arches, their sparse hair and wavering memories, over the Carpathian Mountains, out of the bayous—that is what it is here in the holy city. Aunt Lotte's portrait will never be unpacked again. She finds her resting place, in the tomb of her crate, in the basement, her requiem the humming of the Seventh Avenue subway. I play *Wozzeck* on my new KLH. Terrific reception in these old West Side rooms—at least for phonograph records.

Love, love,

Elizabeth

"Beginnings are always delightful; the threshold is the place to pause," Goethe said. But it is not true that it doesn't matter where you live, that you are, in Hartford or Dallas, merely the same. Everything has come to me and been taken from me because of moving from place to place. Youth and hope were left in Boston, but New York turned out to be the last thing I would have expected—sensible. Long dresses, arrogance, more chances for women to deceive the deceitful, confidences, long telephone conversations, credit cards. But, dear M, which part of the true story should I tell? Should I choose the events interesting today, or try, facing the shame of lost opinion, to remain true to what I felt and thought at the time? The girl with her brown hair cut in a Dutch bob?

1972

Dearest M: I have sold the big house in Maine and will make a new place there, beginning with the old barn on the water. "Existing barn," the architect's drawings say. But I fear the metamorphosis, the journey of species. The barn, or so I imagine of all barns, once existed for cows and hay. Then later it was— well, a place. (For what I do not like to say. Too much information spoils the effect on the page, like too many capitals within the line, or the odious exclamation point. Anyway, you have the information.)

Will the barn consent to become what I have decided to make of it? I don't know. Sometimes I am sure that I am building for a tire salesman from Bangor whose wife will not be kind to the sacred wounds of such a building—the claims, the cries of the original barn, the memories of the abandoned place. The claims and cries of Lightolier, Design Research, turkey carpets. As for the other, sluffed-off house, I mourn and regret much. The nights long ago with H. W. and her glorious 78 recording of Alice Raveau in Glück's *Orpheo*. I hear the music, see H. W. very tall, old, with her stirring maidenly beauty. The smell of the leaves outside dripping rain, the fire alive, the bowls of nasturtiums everywhere, the orange Moroccan cloth hanging over the mantle. What a loss. Perhaps my memories, being kind, betray me and bleach the darkness of the scenes, the agitation of the evenings. I am as aware as anyone of the appeal, the drama of the negative. Well, we go from one graven image to the next and, say what you will, each house is a shrine.

Meanwhile here in New York I just saw a horse and rider amidst the threatening taxi cabs. The man rides the horse indeed as if he were driving a cab, nervously, angrily, looking straight ahead, in his own lane, one way, held on the conveyor belt of traffic, needing only a horse horn of some kind to show that a man may in New York turn a horse into a Dodge.

When I first came here the house opposite was a stables. A handsome brick building painted a dusty mustard color, like an Italian villa. Sometimes the old structure seems to return, coming out of the afternoon haze, rising from the sea of cement. But what good would the return do itself, me? I will not look back. The horse and rider escaped to the park. Where the old stables stood there is a parking lot. A hundred beautiful chariots rest there in the afternoon sun. And at night sometimes the car of someone I know sits there all alone, waiting, long, long after midnight.

Much love, as always,
Elizabeth

Oh, M, when I think of the people I have buried. And what of the "dreadful cries of murdered men in forests." Tell me, dear M, why is it that we cannot keep the note of irony, the tinkle of carelessness at a distance? Sentences in which I have tried for a certain light tone—many of those have to do with events, upheavals, destructions that caused me to weep like a child. Some removals I have never gotten over and I am, like everyone else, an amputee. (Why do I put in "like everyone else"? I fear that if I say I am an amputee, and more so than anyone else, I will be embarrassing, over-reaching. Yet in my heart I do believe I am more damaged than most.)

O you could not know
That such swift fleeing
No soul foreseeing—
Not even I—would undo me so!

I hate the glossary, the concordance of truth that some have about my real life—have like an extra pair of spectacles. I mean that such fact is to me a hindrance to composition. Otherwise I love to be known by those I care for and consequently I am always on the phone, always writing letters, always waking up to address myself to B. and D. and E.—those whom I dare not ring up until the morning and yet must talk to throughout the night.

Now, my novel begins. No, now I begin my novel—and yet I cannot decide whether to call myself I or she.

(This is the opening of a novel in progress to be called The Cost of Living.*)*

"CAL WORKING, ETC."[1]

BY ELIZABETH HARDWICK

Cal's recuperative powers were almost as much of a jolt as his break-downs; this is, knowing him in the chains of illness you could, for a time, not imagine him otherwise. And when he was well, it seemed so miraculous that the old gifts of person and art were still there, as if they had been stored in some serene, safe box somewhere. Then it did not seem possible that the dread assault could return to hammer him into bits once more.

He "came to," sad, worried, always ashamed and fearful; and yet there he was, this unique soul for whom one felt great pity. His fate was like a strange, almost mythical two-engined machine, one running to doom and the other to salvation. Out of the hospital he returned to his days, which were regular, getting up early in the morning, going to his room or separate place for work. All day long he lay on the bed, propped up on an elbow. And this was his life, reading, studying and writing. The papers piled up on the floor, the books on the bed, the bottles of milk on the window sill, and the ashtray filled.

He looked like one of the great photographs of Whitman, taken by Thomas Eakins—Whitman in carpet slippers, a shawl, surrounded by a surf of papers almost up to his lap. Almost every day Cal worked

---

1. Excerpt from a letter and pages of notes addressed to Ian Hamilton, Lowell's biographer [n.d., 1981 or 1982].

the entire day and if we were alone he would go back after supper. Since he was in no sense an auto-didact, and not the sort of poet, if there are any, for whom beautiful things come drifting down in a snowfall of gift, the labor was merciless. The discipline, the dedication, the endless revision, the constant adding to his *store* by reading and studying—all of this had, in my view, much that was heroic about it.

Fortunately, Cal was "well" much more of his life than he was not; otherwise his large and difficult, for him, production would not exist.

The breakdowns had the aspect of a "brain fever," such as you read about in 19th century fiction. His brain was literally hot, whirling, but even at these times it was *his* brain that was fevered, askew and shaken out of shape. When I visited him in the hospital it was quite clear that few of the other afflicted were capable of this temperature, made or otherwise. We were always ordered rather grandly to bring the Vergil, the Dante, the Homer, the Elisabeth Schwarzkopf record. Of course he was not really "cool" enough to read or to listen, *that* being the problem. But he could make the patients listen to his scattered readings aloud. For the most part I got the impression that they didn't mind and looked on it in a sort of bemused daze, while of course mumbling the refrains of their own performance . . .

Then at last the books were brought back home, the socks, with their name-tapes as if for a summer camp, were gathered up. And there it was, with only the sadness, actually the unfairness of the fate, remaining.

Cal was very sociable, curious, fond of a large number of people—otherwise there would not be so much "testimony" about him. After literature, his passion was history, of which he knew a great deal. He liked music and liked to listen to it, but I never felt he could take it in the way he took in painting, for which his love was detailed, thoughtful and very strong. In Europe I often fell by the wayside, into the coffee bar, but he went on to each thing, each church, never seeming to have enough, to be tired.

Everything about him was out-sized: his learning, his patience with his work, his dedication, and the pattern of his troubled life. I think it is true, as he said, that he knew a lot of happiness in each of his decades, happiness that is when he was fortunately for such long creative and private periods "himself."

Ian: I put in the rather dull paragraph about painting and being sociable just in case at some point that could be helpful in moving from one thing to another. For the rest, I don't think of it as being all of a piece, but to be used perhaps broken up here and there to give some idea of what returning over and over to writing was like. I feel strongly about all of these points, especially about the amount of time well and the amount otherwise.

Strange, what I have written about the working habits, the coming out of the hospital is not new. It is what I wrote in the "notebook" I tore up, which did not seem to have a proper context for such reflections. It turns out that one has very few ideas finally and I have written more or less these same things to friends over the years in letters that also contained my distress over Cal's actions. [. . .]

ACKNOWLEDGMENTS

Gratitude first and foremost to the memory and the work of Elizabeth Hardwick and Robert Lowell, out of love and respect for which many hands have helped make this edition possible. Harriet Lowell and Sheridan Lowell supported its publication, alongside Evgenia Citkowitz and Ivana Lowell. Harriet Lowell and Evgenia Citkowitz gave generous and particular care to accuracy throughout, with spirit, candor, humor, and sensitivity.

For their generosity of time and knowledge with points of information or other matters large and small, my thanks to Bashir Abu-Manneh, Isabella Alimonti, Hilton Als, Alex Andriesse, Judith Aronson, Thomas Austenfeld, Steven Axelrod, Richard J. Bernstein, Bonnie Costello, Theo Cuffe, Christina Davis, Ronald Dworkin, Neal Earhart, Rachel Eisendrath, James Fenton, Jennifer Formichelli, Phillip Fry, Marilyn Gaull, Grey Gowrie, Neiti Gowrie, Jorie Graham, Eliza Griswold, Beth Gutierrez, Jeffrey Gutierrez, Robert Hass, Philip Horne, Madeline ter Horst-Mees, Michiel ter Horst, Fanny Howe, Janna Israel, Marina Klimova, Jerome Kohn, Jane Kramer, Sophie Lambrechtsen-ter Horst, Katy Lee, Jeremy Lever, Dale Loy, Frank Loy, Ben Mazer, Jim McCue, Anna Meister, Edward Mendelson, Warren Myers, Sophia Niehaus, Diederik Oostdijk, Katie Peterson, Paul Podolsky, Alice Quinn, Melissa Renn, Lloyd Schwartz, Robert Silvers, David Stang, Colm Tóibín, Thomas A. Traill, Thomas Travisano, Alyssa Valles,

Allison Vanouse, Margo Viscusi, Dianne Wiest, and Fiona Wilson. Thanks also to Frank Bidart for his help, his friendship, and his devotion to Lowell's work. Archie Burnett and the faculty, students, and staff of the Editorial Institute at Boston University helped provide the intellectual, textual, and bibliographic framework to address editorial questions raised by the letters. Kay Redfield Jamison lent her illuminating understanding of Lowell's illness and character. Christina Ellsberg, Emily Kramer, and Madeleine Walker read the letters with special scrutiny and insight.

For their support of the time needed to work on the correspondence, my gratitude to Christopher Baswell, Linda A. Bell, Leslie Cawley, Lisa Gordis, Mary Gordon, Ross Hamilton, LaShawn Keyser, Emma Murdock, Sarah Pasadino, Rio Santisteban-Edwards, Timea Szell, and other colleagues at Barnard; and to Danielle Barry-Alicea, Lowry Bass, Yasmin Begum, Cheyenne Gleason, Sasha Guseynalieva, Katy Lee, and Georgia Stiponias. I am deeply grateful to all of my family, and wish to thank for their specific help with this edition Andrew Hamilton, Claudia Hamilton, Emma Hamilton, John Hamilton, Julia Hamilton, Claar Hugenholtz-Wiarda, Elise Hugenholtz, Paul Hugenholtz, Lycke Kagenaar, Francis O'Neill, Belinda Rathbone, Eliza Rathbone, Arent van Wassenaer, Alexander van Wassenaer, Diederick van Wassenaer, Geertruid van Wassenaer, Louise van Wassenaer-Wiarda, Elise Wiarda, and Just Wiarda. Also, absent friends.

Thanks to the librarians and staff of the Barnard Library and its archives (with particular gratitude to Jennifer Green, Vani Natarajan, and Martha Tenney); the Butler Library, Columbia University; the Catherine Pelton Durrell '25 Archives and Special Collections at Vassar College (Dean M. Rogers and Ronald D. Patkus); the Cecil Beaton Studio Archive at Sotheby's (Emma Nichols); the Firestone Library, Princeton University; the Harry Ransom Humanities Research Center, University of Texas at Austin (Reid Echols and Richard B. Watson); the Houghton Library, Harvard University (Susan Halpert and Leslie A. Morris); the Manuscripts and Archives Division, New York Public Library (John Cordovez, Cara Dellatte, Nasima Hasnat, Thomas Lannon, Meredith Mann, Tal Nadan, Victor Ou, David Pedrero, Nikolas Swihart, Ted Teodoro, and Kyle Triplett); and the Mugar Memorial Library, Boston University (Brendan McDermott).

At Farrar, Straus and Giroux, my thanks to Scott Auerbach, Carolina

Baizan, Maureen Bishop, David Emcke, Victoria Fox, Robin Gold, Susan Goldfarb, Debra Helfand, Logan Hill, Spenser Lee, Jonathan D. Lippincott, Katie Liptak, Devon Mazzone, Pauline Post, Lauren Roberts, Jeff Seroy, Ian Van Wye, and Molly Walls—and especially to Jonathan Galassi, whose quickness of perception and deep sense of the past in the present guided the book through production with grace, wit, and precision.

The editors of the OED note in their definition of thanks that the feeling of gratitude and its expression pass so naturally into one another that it "is not easy to separate them." So it is with my gratitude during this editorial work for the exceptional understanding, accompaniment, and brightness of genius given by Catherine Barnett, James Fenton, Paul Keegan, Darryl Pinckney, Christopher Ricks, Claudia Rankine, John Ryle, Meg Tyler, and—most of all—Lucien Hamilton.

INDEX

Note: In subheadings, Robert Lowell is referred to as RL and Elizabeth Hardwick as EH.

Arendt, Hannah (1906–1975), political
philosopher: xxiv*n2*, xlvii, 130, 131, 183,
185, 186, 200, 207, 211–12, 234, 265,
267, 312, 380, 392, 456*n3*; death of, xlvi;
heart attack of, 390
Ariel (Plath), 210, 307, 309, 374
Armstrong, Anne (b. 1927), diplomat: 434
Arnold, Matthew (1822–1888), poet and
critic: ix, 27, 37*n1*, 44*n5*, 313
Arts Conference: 28
*As Consciousness Is Harnessed to Flesh:
Journals and Notebooks, 1964–1980*
(Sontag): 440*n1*
Ashbery, John (1927–2017), poet: 308,
314, 328
Asher, Elise (1912–2004), painter: 83*n2*,
276
Aspern Papers, The (James): xvi, 194
Atlantic, The: 449
Atlas, James (b. 1949), writer and
publisher: 129
Attlee, Clement (1883–1967): 19
Auden, W. H. (1907–1973), poet and
critic: 13*n3*, 248–49, 305, 323, 380, 412,
434–35
Austin, Helen Goodwin (1898–1986): 411
Austin, Sarah "Sally" Goodwin
(1935–1994), artist: 87, 207, 412

Bacon, Francis (1909–1992), painter:
64*n4*, 137
Bagehot, Walter (1826–1877), political
commentator and economist: 313
Balcon, Jill (1925–2009), actress: 434
Baldick, Robert (1927–1972), literary
scholar: *Dinner at Magny's*, 186
Barnard College: 160, 407; EH's teaching
position at, viii, xlii–xlvi, xlviii, 25, 29,
68, 71, 77, 151, 244, 420, 445; Harriet
as student at, xlvi–xlviii, 396, 397, 398,
405, 406, 407, 410, 414
Barnes, Clive (1927–2008), dance and
theater critic: 5, 427, 428
Barrett, Juliet Bigney (b. 1916), translator:
233
Barrett, William (1913–1992), philosopher:
233
Baryshnikov, Mikhail (b. 1948), dancer:
432*n4*

Bate, Walter Jackson (1918–1999), literary
scholar: 42
Baudelaire, Charles (1821–1867): 104,
181*n1*, 409
Baumann, Anny (1905–1983), physician:
59, 81*n2*, 141, 245, 328
Bayley, John (1925–2015), literary scholar:
44, 439*n1*
Beaton, Cecil (1904–1980), photographer:
204
Beauvoir, Simone de (1908–1986), writer:
xliv; *Le Deuxième Sexe*, 214
Beer, Patricia (1919–1999), poet: 401
Bell, Quentin (1910–1996), art historian:
293
Bell Jar, The (Plath): 194
Bellow, Adam (b. 1957), editor: 408
Bellow, Saul (1915–2005), novelist: 179,
408; *Herzog*, 74
Benito Cereno (Lowell): 129, 134, 205, 428*n1*
Bentley, Eric (b. 1916), writer and
translator: 24
Berg, Stephen (1934–2014), poet: 371*n1*
Berlin, Aline (1915–2014): 5, 27, 44, 168
Berlin, Isaiah (1909–1997), philosopher: 5,
19, 27, 47, 59, 168, 327
Bernard, Viola W. (1907–1998),
psychiatrist: 81*n2*, 219
Bernstein, Ann (b. 1927), writer: 100
Berrigan, Daniel (1921–2016), priest,
activist, and poet: 99
Berrigan, Philip (1923–2002), priest and
activist: 100
Berryman, John (1914–1972), poet: 137,
220; death of, xliii, 234, 238; *Delusions,
Etc. of John Berryman*, 270; "For John
Berryman" (Lowell), xlviii, 245, 247,
268, 270
Betts, Darby (1912–1998), minister: 75
Bicks, Patricia Hughes (1927–1996): 87
Bicks, Robert A. (1927–2002), lawyer: 87
Bidart, Frank (b. 1939), poet: xi, 114,
195, 237, 238, 261, 262, 286, 291, 328,
431; *The Dolphin* and, xxin2, xliii,
xliv, 154*n1*, 225–26, 238, 255–57, 259,
277–79, 282, 328*n2*; EH's letters
and, xvii–xviii; *Golden State*, 53, 226,
270–72; *History* dedicated to Kunitz
and, 299; letters to RL, 52–53, 277–79;

Cannibals and Missionaries (McCarthy): 455

Carey, John (b. 1934), literary scholar: 402

Carlisle, Henry (1926–2011), novelist and translator: 18n2, 74

Carlisle, Olga Andreyeva (b. 1930), translator: xxxix, 18, 42, 57, 63, 68, 72, 90, 99, 100, 192, 267

Carlyle, Jane Welsh (1801–1866): xliv, 205, 318

Carlyle, Thomas (1795–1881): 231

"CARPACCIO'S CREATURES: Separation" (Lowell): 289–90

Carrington, Dora (1893–1932), painter: 309, 311

Carruth, Hayden (1921–2008), poet and critic: 137

Carter, Elliott (1908–2012), composer: 266

Carter, Jimmy (b. 1924): xlvii

Carter, Lillian (1898–1983): 438

"Casabianca" (Bishop): 330n5

Cecil, David (1902–1986), literary scholar: 44

Cervantes, Miguel de (1547–1616): *Don Quixote*, 395, 406

Chandler, Raymond (1888–1959), writer, 430

Chiaromonte, Nicola (1905–1972), writer: 234, 266n3

Choate School: 283, 289, 292

Chubb, Thomas Caldecott (1899–1972), critic: 257n4

Churchill, Winston (1874–1965): 19

CIA, 185

"Cimetière marin, Le" (Valéry): 40

Citkowitz, Caroline: *see* Blackwood, Caroline

Citkowitz, Evgenia "Genia" (b. 1964), writer: xvii, xviii, xliii, 64n4, 66, 139, 173, 281, 291, 370, 443

Citkowitz, Israel (1909–1974), composer and pianist: 66, 70, 92, 101n2; Caroline's divorce from, xliv; Caroline's marriage to, 65n1; death of, xlv, 390; RL's poem about, 392

Citkowitz, Ivana: *see* Lowell, Ivana

Citkowitz, Natalya (1960–1978): xliii, 66, 173, 178, 291, 370, 443

City College of the City University of New York: 318, 430, 432

Clarissa (Richardson): xiv

Clark, Alfred Corning (1916–1961): 111

Clark, Blair (1917–2000), journalist: xl–xli, 9, 55, 61, 84n2, 91n2, 92n3, 117, 136, 139, 162, 234, 242, 294, 325, 442n2, 446, 447n1; *The Dolphin* and, xxin2; EH's letter to, 121–23; letter to RL, 124; RL's letters to, 111–12, 133–34, 220

Clark, Ian (born 1973): 325

Clark, Joanna Rostropowicz (b. 1943), critic: xlviii, 55n4, 234n1

Clark, Kenneth (1903–1983), art historian: 148n5

Cleaver, Eldridge (1935–1998), writer and activist: 197

Clemons, Walter (1930–1994), critic: 364n1

Coffin, Harriet: 79

Coffin, William Sloane (1924–2006), minister and activist: 91

Cohen, Hermann: 417

Cohen, Marshall (b. 1929), philosopher: 245

Coleridge, Samuel Taylor (1772–1834): 44, 78n3, 138, 313n2

Columbia University: 402, 405

Confessions (Rousseau): 266

Congress for Cultural Freedom: 185n2

Connolly, Cyril (1903–1974), critic: 129, 130

Conrad, Alfred H. (1924–1970), economist: 108, 117n1, 118, 120, 132, 157, 171, 187, 308n2

Conrad, Pablo (b. 1957), teacher and editor: 308

Corbière, Tristan (1845–1875): 409

Cori, Anne Fitz-Gerald Jones (1909–2006): 202, 341

Cori, Carl Ferdinand (1896–1984), biochemist: 202, 341, 346

Corso, Gregory (1930–2001), poet: 162

Cotting, Charles (1889–1985), investment banker and philanthropist: 133, 206, 289n1, 400

Cotting, Sarah Winslow (1893–1992): 54, 69, 72, 133, 289n1, 380, 400, 443

Cowley, Malcolm (1898–1989), writer: 347

Friend," 134n1; "From My Wife," 64n1, 92n2, 93n2, 94n3, 252, 260, 264n2; and gap in fall of 1970, xviii; "Green Sore," xxi–xxii, 153n1, 154, 160n7, 278n3; Harriet and, 356–58, 359n2, 360, 362, 366; "I despair of letters . . . ," 171n2, 172, 258n3; "In Harriet's Yearbook," 101n4; "In the Mail," xviiin2, 53n2, 115n3, 249n1, 262n1, 293n2, 358n1, 366n2, 368n1, 441n4; "Ivana," 235n1; "July–August," 255n4; "Knowing," xiii, 259n3; Kunitz on, 276; "Late Summer at Milgate," 258n3; "Letter," xxvii–xxviii, 86n3, 94n2, 98n2, 258n3; letters used in, xvi, xxin2; "Marriage?," 85, 243n1; Marriage sequence, 259n4, 264n1; Mermaid, xxvi, 256n5, 257n1; "The Messiah," 138n1, 249, 252, 264, 293n2; Modern Love as model for, xivn4; "Morning Away from You," 277; "Morning Blue," 256n1; "No Messiah," 137n7, 138n2; "Notes for an unwritten Letter," xxv–xxvii, 86n3, 94n2, 98, 107n2; "Old Snapshot and Carpaccio," 255, 260, 289n4; "Old Snapshot from Venice 1952," 128n1, 242n3, 255, 289n4; "On the End of the Phone," xxviiin3; "Overhanging Cloud," 158n1; "Oxford," 44–45n6, 188n1, 255; "Plane-Ticket," 278n1; "Plotted," 146–47n3, 172n6; "Pointing the Horns of the Dilemma," 131n2; publication of, xv, xx, xliii, xlv, 226, 250, 296, 311, 314, 328n2, 343, 350, 357–58; publication of complete draft of, xvi; Pulitzer Prize award for, xlv; "Records," 114n1, 256n4; reviews of, 356, 358–65, 371; revisions of, xv–xvi; Rich on, 371; Ricks and, 250; RL defends his use of EH's letters in, xxi, xxii, 261, 263–64, 361, 362, 363; RL regrets his use of EH's letters in, 435; sequences in, xxxvi; Sheridan's conception and birth in, 259n4, 272, 277–79, 282; "Sick," 264n1; Summer Between Terms, 256n2; "Voices," 64n1, 92n2, 93n2, 94n3, 252, 264n2, 272; "Walter Raleigh," 97n2; "With Caroline at the Air-Terminal," 278n2; "Wolverine," 257n2

Dombey and Son (Dickens): 209
Donne, John (1572–1631): xxvin3, 231
Donoghue, Denis (b. 1928), literary critic: 137
Don Quixote (Cervantes): 395, 406
"Dora Markus" (Montale): 419
Dorsch, T. S., editor: 104
Douglas, James (1867–1940), journalist: 252n1
Drabble, Margaret (b. 1939), novelist: 401n1
Dreiser, Theodore (1871–1945), writer: 70, 185
Driver, Clive (1936–1999), librarian: 22n2
Drummond de Andrade, Carlos (1902–1987), poet: 287
Dudley, Grace (1923–2016): 213, 214, 227–28
Duffy, Martha: 364n1
Dupee, Barbara "Andy": 86–88
Dupee, F. W. (1904–1979), literary critic: 86–88, 200, 345
Durocher, Leo (1905–1991): 83n6
du Sautoy, Peter (1912–1995), publisher: 73
DuVivier, David (1911–1994): 374, 380
DuVivier, Eleanor: 374, 380, 421, 457
Dvořák, Antonín (1841–1904): 160, 341n2
Dworkin, Ronald (1931–2013), philosopher: 45

Eakins, Thomas (1844–1916): 473
Eaton, Mace (1892–1975), boatbuilder: 411
Eberhart, Helen (d. 1993): 355
Eberhart, Richard (1904–2005), poet: 99
Edel, Leon (1907–1997), biographer: 306
L'Éducation sentimentale (Flaubert): 204
Edwards, P. W. (1923–2015), literary scholar: 3n2, 15, 16, 19
Eissler, K. R. (1908–1999), psychoanalyst: 210, 219
Eliot, George (1819–1880): 311
Eliot, T. S. (1888–1965), poet: xvi, xxiv, xxviin3, 21, 42, 103n1, 305, 314n3, 414; Four Quartets, 308
Eliot, Valerie (1926–2012), editor: 95
Ellsberg, Daniel (b. 1931), activist: 193
Ellsberg, Margaret "Peggy" Rizza, poet and literary scholar: 129
Ellsberg, Patricia Marx (b. 1938), activist: 193
Emerson, Ralph Waldo (1803–1882): 112, 113, 314n3

Gamelin, Maurice (1872–1958), general: 347

Gardner, Robert (1925–2014), anthropologist and filmmaker: 289

Garland, Patrick (1935–2013), director and writer: 322*n*2

Geography III (Bishop): 444*n*1

"George III" (Lowell): 436

Giambologna (1529–1608): 335

Gilliatt, Penelope (1932–1993), writer: 406

Gilman, Richard (1923–2006), drama critic: xl

Ginsberg, Allen (1926–1997), poet: 21, 104, 162*n*3

Giroux, Robert (1914–2008), publisher: 60, 109, 179, 182, 267*n*3, 407*n*2, 431, 435, 437; EH's letter to, on publication of *The Dolphin*, 357–58, 362*n*1, 365; letters and telegram to Monteith, 62, 73, 80–82; Monteith's letters and telegram to, 63, 77–78, 295–97; RL's letters to, 362–63, 365–66

Glück, Christoph Willibald (1714–1787): 339*n*1, 470

Goalie's Anxiety at the Penalty Kick, The (Handke): 81–82

Goethe, Johann Wolfgang von (1749–1832): 469

Gold, Arthur (1917–1990), pianist: 414

Golden State (Bidart): 53, 226, 270–72

Gomez, Nicole: 3, 23, 25, 26, 38*n*1, 43, 60, 61, 63–64, 188, 205, 379, 399

Good, John M.: 332

Goodbye to All That (Graves): 406

Goodell, Charles (1926–1987): 124–25, 126

Goodwin, Francis X. (1930–2008), naval commander: 72

Gordon, Caroline (1895–1981), writer: 137

Gordon, Mary (b. 1949), writer: 213

Gorky, Maro (b. 1943), painter: 418

Gotham Book Mart: 22

Gottfried, Martin (1933–2014), music and drama critic: 428*n*1

Gowrie, Grey (b. 1939), poet and politician: xl, 36, 40, 48, 85*n*1, 92, 199

Grad, Catharine A. (b. 1957), lawyer: 320, 325, 326, 329, 350, 352, 354, 365, 369–71, 391, 405, 410, 411, 439

Grad, David A. (1953–2007): 441

Grad, Frank P. (1924–2014), law professor: 326

Grad, Lisa (b. 1927), pianist: 350, 410

Graham, Frank (1893–1965), sportswriter: 83*n*6

Grass, Günter (1927–2015), novelist and poet: 352

Graves, Robert (1895–1985), poet: *Goodbye to All That*, 406

Gravity's Rainbow (Pynchon): xlv

Gray, Cleve (1918–2004), painter: 29

Gray, Francine du Plessix (1930–2019), writer: xli, 55, 68, 69, 72, 76, 79, 80, 90, 99, 100, 175, 192, 206

Great Granny Webster (Blackwood): 440, 448

Greenways Nursing Home: xxv, xl–xli, xlvi, xlvii, 78, 80–81, 89, 93, 96–98

Greer, Germaine (b. 1939), writer: 309

Gross, John (1935–2011) editor: 347, 417

Gross, Miriam (b. 1939), writer: 347

Guardian: 401*n*1

Guinness, Desmond (b. 1931), writer: 444*n*2

Haigh, Kenneth (1931–2018), actor: 160

Haile Selassie (1892–1975): 84

Hall, Bernice Dobkin (1915–1992) teacher: 100, 437

Hall, David (1916–2012), sound archivist: 100, 437

Hamilton, Ian (1938–2001), poet: xvi, xxix

Hamlet (Shakespeare): 146

Hampshire, Stuart (1914–2004), philosopher: 245, 246

Hampton, Christopher (b. 1946), playwright and dramatist: 323*n*1,

Handke, Peter (b. 1942), novelist: 81–82

Handman, Barbara "Bobbie" (1928–2013), arts activist: 69

Handman, Wynn (b. 1922), director: 389

Hardwick, Elizabeth (1916–2007), writer: apartment rental and, 12, 29; asks RL to return, and his response, 114–16, 118–19; Barnard College teaching position of, viii, xlii–xlvi, xlviii, 25, 29, 68, 71, 77, 151, 244, 420, 445; at Bellagio Center, Rockefeller Foundation, Italy, xlv, 367–69; Bicentennial celebrations and, xlvii, 436; Bishop's letters to, 364–65, 374–77; on Blackwood, 64–66,

Hardwick, Elizabeth (*continued*)
122, 198–99; breaks bone in foot, 395, 396, 398, 400–401; brother's death and, 390; car of, 12, 15; at Castine, xxv, xxx, xlii, xliii, 43, 47, 54, 63, 74, 76, 80, 81, 86–91, 98–101, 106, 151, 177, 192–93, 195, 200–203, 206–207, 210, 267, 292, 293, 380, 391–94, 404, 405, 429, 436–37; Castine barn renovated by, 288, 332, 333, 335, 336, 338, 342, 344–45, 353, 355, 367–68, 391, 393, 394, 408–409, 414, 449; Castine house sold by, xlv, 288, 332, 333, 335–46, 448–53, 355–57; cat of (Sumner), 4, 10, 23, 26, 178, 202, 203, 222, 301; on change, 416; Chicago trip planned, 228; Christmas tree of, 400n2; City University teaching position of, 430, 432; Cleveland Museum visited by, 227–28; cocktail party given by, 418–19; death of, xviii; *The Dolphin* as hurtful to, xix, 357–58, 366; *The Dolphin* as viewed by, vii, xix–xx, 265, 268, 273–74, 357–58, 366; falls in love with RL, 119n1; finances of, 41, 49–51, 60, 61, 71, 72, 99, 147–49, 159, 161, 171, 182–86, 198, 219, 287–88, 293, 311, 318, 351, 353, 355, 356; first sees *The Dolphin* upon publication, 357, 365–66; Harvard lecture of, 284; honorary degree awarded to, 390; inability to reread her letters to RL, xvi; income taxes and, 8, 49, 61, 147, 148, 152, 159, 171, 182–84, 198, 283, 287, 298n1, 307, 311, 313, 316, 317, 320–21, 324–26, 329, 333–34, 345, 347, 351, 354, 356; Italian trip and return, viii, xxxix, 3, 5; kidney infection of, 245, 247; letters to Bishop, xx, 366–67, 377–79, 454; letters to Harriet, 200–201, 203; letters to McCarthy, viii–ix, 63–66, 74–77, 91–93, 105–106, 124–26, 149–52, 175–77, 227–28, 266–69, 367–69, 379–81, 421–23, 445–48, 452–53; letters to RL (1970), 3–13, 16–18, 20–23, 24–26, 28–35, 37–38, 41–44, 49–55, 57–62, 66–72, 78–80, 82–84, 86–91, 94–95, 98–101, 103, 114–15, 117, 118, 141; letters to RL (1971–1972), 147–49, 159–62, 168–69, 171–72, 182–84, 192–95, 197–202,

206–208, 210–13, 217–20, 232–35, 239–41, 244–46, 265–66, 273–74, 282–84, 287–89, 292–95; letters to RL (1973), 306–308, 310–13, 316–21, 325–39, 341–42, 344–46, 349–51, 353–57; letters to RL (1974–1979), 387–96, 399–401, 404–11, 413–21, 423–30, 432–34, 436–37; letters to RL used in *The Dolphin*, vii, xiv, xx, xxii, 252–54, 261, 263–65, 357–58, 365–66, 371–72, 435; letter to Blackwood, 153–54; letter to Clark, 121–23; letter to Craft, 449–52; letter to Giroux about publication of *The Dolphin*, 357–58, 362n1, 365; as letter writer, xiii; Librium taken by, 141; literary correspondence as interest of, xiii–xiv, xv; in London, xli, 91–95, 433; on marriage to RL, 356; McCarthy's letters to, 226–27, 372–74, 455–58; on memoirs, 373n3; in Miami Beach, 292; in Nassau, 318, 319, 321; "notebook" of, 69, 218, 219, 223, 475; PEN and, xlii, xlvii, 193–94, 422, 427; plans to bring Harriet to London, 153–56, 161, 163, 168, 170, 171; plans to join RL in England, 29–32, 34–36, 38–40, 50, 51, 54, 58; political demonstration attended by, 175, 180; political engagement and views on current events, viii, xlii, 8, 17–18, 26, 28–29, 31–32, 44, 59–60, 84, 99–100, 105, 124–26, 171, 175–76, 193, 203, 211, 269, 292–93, 329–30, 393, 430; Princeton (Christian Gauss) lectures of, xliii, 151, 194, 207, 227, 228; Quebec trip of, xlii, 93; and reports from London about RL's disturbing behavior, xl, xli, 91n2, 92; Rich's letter to, 371–72; in Rio, 387–88; RL considers returning to, 127, 128, 130–32; RL moves back in with, xxx; RL on marriage with, 97, 116, 191; RL's Christmas visit to, xlii, 121–26, 128, 130, 139, 146, 151; RL's death and, xxviii–xxix, 451–54; RL's divorce agreement with, 298, 334, 340, 348, 353; RL's divorce from, xliv, 112, 121, 124, 197, 217, 282, 287, 294, 300, 307, 311, 353, 358, 362; RL's fear that she would destroy her letters to him, xvi–xvii; RL's gifts to, 232, 403, 405–406; RL's

letters saved by, xvi; RL's letters to (1970), 10, 13–16, 19–20, 27–28, 36–37, 40, 44–49, 55–57, 75, 96–98, 101–104, 107–109, 112–13, 116–19, 124, 128–29, 132–38; RL's letters to (1971–1972), 146–48, 152, 155–56, 162–63, 169–70, 179–82, 184–86, 189–90, 196–97, 204–205, 209–10, 213–19, 222–23, 229, 235–36, 242–44, 247, 263, 279–80, 289–90, 292; RL's letters to (1973), 305–306, 308–10, 313–15, 317–18, 320, 322–25, 330–31, 334–35, 340, 342–44, 346–49, 352–55, 358–59, 361, 364, 369–70; RL's letters to (1974–1979), 385–89, 393–94, 398, 401–403, 412–13, 415–18, 426, 428–29, 431–32, 434–35, 437–44; RL's manic depression and, x, xiii; RL's marriage to, 119n1, 290n1; RL's papers and, xv, xxxi, 6–7, 8, 12–13, 15, 18, 21–22, 25, 33–34, 41, 43, 49–51, 58, 59, 68, 184, 185, 190, 194–98, 201, 204, 280, 288, 292, 379; on RL's relationship with Blackwood, xli, 66–70, 76, 92, 94, 114–15, 198–200; RL's relationship with Blackwood discovered by, xviin2, xl, 64–65, 70, 73, 114–15; RL's return to, xxix, xxx, xlviii, xlix, 446–50, 453; RL's separation from, xiii; and RL's staying in England, xl, xli, 49, 52, 55, 57–58, 62, 64; on RL's writing, 66–67; Russia trip with RL, xxx, xlviii; Smith College teaching position of, 413, 414–16, 418; South Carolina trip of, 159, 161, 165, 168, 170; and telephone calls to England, 30, 87; on "transitional year" with RL, 331–32; two names used by, xxix, 416; University of Wisconsin trip planned, 228, 325
Hardwick, Elizabeth, writings of, xiii; "Accepting the Dare: Maine," xlvii, 404n2; Bay Poets parody, 99; "Cal working, etc.," 219n1, 473–75; essay on Compton-Burnett, 105; freelance work during summer of 1972, 293; "In Maine," xliii, 212, 375, 377–78; letters as device in, xiv; "notebook," 69, 218, 219, 223, 475; "Philip Rahv (1908–1973)," xlv, 385–86, 387; on presidential campaign, xlvii, 430n1,

436; "Reflections on Simone Weil," xlvi, 407; review of McCarthy's *Writing on the Wall*, 105n1; "Sad Brazil" (Hardwick), xlv, 387n3, 390; "Seduction and Betrayal," xlv, 233, 347; *Seduction and Betrayal: Women and Literature*, viii, xlv, 374, 390, 440n1; *Sleepless Nights*, see *Sleepless Nights*; "The Ties Women Cannot Shake and Have," xliii, 169n1, 183, 200, 204, 260n1, 328; "A Useful Critic," xl; Woolf article, 309, 310n2, 311; "Working Girls: The Brontës," xliv, 239, 280, 293n1; "Writing a Novel," xvn2, xvi, xlv, 339n1
Hardwick, Robert Carter (1918–1974): 390
Hardy, Thomas (1840–1928): xx, xlvi, 86, 164, 170, 251–52, 269, 337n2
Harmsworth, Desmond (1903–1990), painter and poet: 40
Harper's: 4n2
Harry Ransom Center (HRC): xxxi–xxxiii, 349n1
Harvard University: 7, 17, 36, 69, 79, 83, 95, 110, 113, 129, 133, 162, 223, 289, 366; Bishop at, 254, 261; EH's lecture at, 284; Harriet and, 397, 398; Houghton Library, see Houghton Library, Harvard; RL's papers at, see Houghton Library, Harvard; RL's salary at, 254, 261; RL's teaching position at, viii, xxx, xxxix, xlv, xlviii, 14, 195, 299n4, 450
Hatch, Francis W.: 99
Having Wonderful Time (Kober): 150n3
Hawthorne, Nathaniel: 103, 194; *The Scarlet Letter*, 180, 190
Hazlitt, William (1778–1830): 104
Heaney, Marie (b. 1940), writer: xlviii
Heaney, Seamus (1939–2013), poet: xlvi, xlviii, 412, 421n1
Hearst, Patricia (b. 1954): 427
Hecht, Anthony (1923–2004), poet: xlv
Heine, Heinrich (1797–1856), poet: 181n1, 411, 412
Hellman, Lillian (1905–1984), dramatist: 213
Hemans, Felicia Dorothea (1793–1835): 330n5
Hemingway, Ernest (1899–1961) novelist: 109, 193
Henry IV (Pirandello): 326

Newlove, Donald (b. 1928), writer: 193*n1*
New Republic, The: 363
Newsweek: 186, 359, 360, 364, 438
New Yorker, The: 59, 125, 321
New York Psychiatric Institute: 425
New York Review of Books, The: xxxix,
    xlii–xlviii, 4*n2*, 45, 50, 70*n3*, 126, 151,
    159–60, 175, 203, 207, 245*n1*, 293*n1*,
    314*n3*, 337, 372, 374, 407*n2*, 456; Harriet
    at, 411, 412; "In Maine" (Hardwick),
    xliii, 212; "Philip Rahv (1908–1973)"
    (Hardwick), xlv, 385–86, 387; and
    RL's telegram to Silvers, 166–67; "Sad
    Brazil" (Hardwick), xlv, 387*n3*, 390;
    "Seduction and Betrayal" (Hardwick),
    xlv, 233, 347; "A Useful Critic"
    (Hardwick), xl; "Working Girls: The
    Brontës" (Hardwick), xliv, 239, 280,
    293*n1*; "Writing a Novel" (Hardwick),
    xv*n2*, xvi, xlv, 339*n1*, 372–73, 461–71
New York Times, The: 55, 162, 174*nn2*, 3,
    364, 390
New York Times Book Review: xliv–xlvi
Nicolson, Nigel (1917–2004), writer and
    publisher: 380–81
Nietzsche, Friedrich (1844–1900): 309,
    440*n1*
"Night City (from a Plane)" (Bishop):
    286
Nixon, Richard M. (1913–1994): xliv, xlv,
    26, 28, 32, 44, 45*n4*, 84, 105, 125, 166*n1*,
    167, 176, 203, 240, 269, 293, 300*n1*, 331,
    347, 370, 380, 393
Nolan, Cynthia (1908–1976), writer: 148,
    437
Nolan, Sidney (1917–1992), painter: 45, 59,
    135, 148, 389, 418, 437
"North Haven (In Memoriam: Robert
    Lowell)" (Bishop): 454
Norwich, Anne Clifford (b. 1929): 215
Norwich, John Julius (1928–2018), writer:
    215*n1*
Notebook (Lowell), ix, xi, xiv, xxxvi,
    xxxix, xl, xlii, 21, 53, 59, 79, 102, 110,
    119*n2*, 132, 172, 173*n1*, 44–45*n6*, 199,
    199*n3*, 225, 246*n3*, 250, 251, 261–62,
    268, 285–86, 295, 299*n2*, 365; Bishop
    letter used in, 138–39; galleys for, 36,
    38; "Robespierre and Mozart as Stage,"
    230; sequences in, xxxvi; "Wall-
    Mirror," xl, 82, 85
Notebooks of Malte Laurids Brigge, The
    (Rilke): 409
Novikoff, Olga (1840–1925): 159*n2*

O'Brien, Edna (b. 1930), writer: 180*n5*
Observer: 401*n1*
O'Connor, Flannery (1925–1964), writer:
    xliii, 412
Of the Farm (Updike): 412
Old Glory, The (Lowell): xlvii, 389, 427,
    428*n2*, 436*n4*
"On Becoming a Person" (Shapiro): 377*n1*
Orcagna (c. 1308–1368): 335
Oresteia of Aeschylus, The (Lowell): 189, 443
Orpheo (Glück): 339*n1*, 470
Ortman, George Earl (1926–2015), artist: 91
Orwell, George (1903–1950), writer: 81*n1*
Orwell, Sonia (1918–1980), editor and
    writer: xli, 27, 67, 80–81, 91–93,
    151–52, 180, 185, 189, 214, 249
O'Sullivan, Benjamin C. (1915–1998),
    lawyer: 294, 331–32
Othello (Shakespeare): 164
Ottinger, Richard (b. 1929): 125
Ovid (43 BCE—17 CE): 20*n1*

Page-Turner, The (Shapiro): 377*n1*
Palgrave, Francis Turner (1824–1897): 80
Parker, Francis S. (1917–2005), painter:
    308*n7*, 319, 343, 399–400, 402
Parker, Judith (b. 1933): 399–400
Parker, Violet (1892–1990), mother of
    Francis S. Parker: 312
Partisan Review, 372
Pasternak, Boris (1890–1960), poet: xv*n2*,
    xlviii, 417, 433, 465
Pater, Walter (1839–1894): 313*n2*
Paterson (Williams): xxii
Paz, Marie-José Tramini (1934–2018),
    artist: 271
Paz, Octavio (1914–1998), poet: 254, 271
Pears, Peter (1910–1986), singer: 431
Pearson, Olivia: 297
Pendleton, Austin (b. 1940), director: 428*n1*
PEN International: xlii, xlvii, 193–94, 212,
    422, 427, 437–38, 455
Percy, Walker (1916–1990), writer: 159